D0869980

Flowering of the Cumberland

by HARRIETTE SIMPSON ARNOW

Introduction to the Bison Books Edition
by Margaret Ripley Wolfe

University of Nebraska Press
Lincoln

☉ The paper in this book meets the minimum requirements of American
National Standard for Information Sciences—Permanence of Paper for Printed
Library Materials, ANSI Z39.48-1984.

First Bison Books printing: 1996
Most recent printing indicated by the last digit below:
10　9　　8　　7　　6　　5　　4　　3　　2　　1

Library of Congress Cataloging-in-Publication Data
Arnow, Harriette Louisa Simpson, 1908–
Flowering of the Cumberland / by Harriette Simpson Arnow; introduction to the
Bison Books edition by Margaret Ripley Wolfe.
p.　cm.
Previously published: New York: Macmillan, 1963.
Includes bibliographical references and index.
ISBN 0-8032-5928-X (pa: alk. paper)
1. Frontier and pioneer life—Cumberland River Valley (Ky. and Tenn.)
2. Cumberland River Valley (Ky. and Tenn.)—History.　3. Cumberland River
Valley (Ky. and Tenn.)—Social life and customs.　I. Title.
F442.2.A69　1996
976.8'5—dc20
96-11178　CIP

Reprinted from the original 1963 edition by the Macmillan Company, New York.

Contents

v

Contents

Illustrations

1. Indian attack on a Cumberland valley station. Kendall: *Life of General A. Jackson,* 1843.)
2. Traveling family preparing a meal over a campfire.
3. Traveling backwoodsman and his family.
4. Young backwoodsman, his wife and pack animal.
5. A group waiting at a ferry.
6. Two pages from *The Royal Alphabet or Child's Best Instructor,* Boston, 1795.
7. Traveler and his pack horse climbing a hill against a brisk wind.
8. A backwoodsman and his dog.
9. Pioneers at work in the forest.
10. River scene showing flatboat and two keelboats. (Reproduced from *The Keelboat Age on Western Waters* by Leland D. Baldwin, with the permission of the University of Pittsburgh Press.)
11. Townspeople as they appeared in the eighteenth and early nineteenth century.
12. North Carolina paper currency of 1780.
13. A helmsman on a flatboat.
14. Group of travelers smoking and telling stories on a flatboat.

Illustrations 2, 3, 4, 5, 7, 8, 9, 11, 13, and 14 are sketches drawn from life in the wilderness by the early American artist, Joshua Shaw, and are reproduced here by courtesy of the Museum of Science and Industry, Chicago.

MAPS

Introduction to the Bison Books Edition

Margaret Ripley Wolfe

Harriette Simpson Arnow's life commenced 7 July 1908 in Wayne County, Kentucky, and ended 22 March 1986 near Ann Arbor, Michigan. During the almost eighty-year interregnum between these two milestones, she had married, borne two children, and established herself as a professional writer. Although Arnow passed most of her adulthood in Michigan, she spent her childhood and youth on the Cumberland Plateau. The author routinely revisited her native environment and its inhabitants in the stories that she spun and the past that she resurrected. Before she ever tried her hand at nonfiction, she already had three novels to her credit incorporating Appalachian scenes and themes: *Mountain Path* (1936), *Hunter's Horn* (1949), and *The Dollmaker* (1954). The publication of *Seedtime on the Cumberland* in 1960 and *Flowering of the Cumberland* three years later marked a departure from Arnow's usual literary métier. The author herself refused to call these works *history*. Nonetheless, first with *Seedtime on the Cumberland* and then with *Flowering of the Cumberland*, which Arnow labeled a "companion piece" rather than a sequel, she had tentatively ventured into the realm of the social historian (p. xvii).

Although Arnow was not a professional historian by training and never claimed to be one, the topics that she addressed and the data that she incorporated in both *Seedtime on the Cumberland* and *Flowering of the Cumberland* resemble those employed by respected social historians of the same era. Charles S. Grant, John Demos, and Kenneth A. Lockridge, whose published works on New England towns enjoyed considerable acclaim from the academic community during the 1960s and 1970s, readily come to mind.[1] Likewise, certain sections of *Flowering of the Cumberland* anticipate more sophisticated studies of childrearing and childbearing by such scholars as Philip Greven and Sally G. McMillen.[2] One can surmise that Harriette Simpson Arnow and the eminent David Hackett Fischer could have engaged in a lively discussion of the folkways to be found on the Trans-Allegheny frontier.[3]

More than thirty years old, Arnow's two volumes on the Cumberlands are not as outmoded as one might expect. They compare reasonably well with more up-to-date regional histories in the vein of Durwood Dunn's case study of Cades Cove, 1818–1937, an Appalachian community in the Great Smoky Mountains, and Jeanette Keith's account of the denizens of Tennessee's Upper Cumberland during the late nineteenth and early twentieth centuries.[4] Professional history, however, carries the responsibility of interpretation, and Arnow tends to present a compendium of facts. This aspect of her work, more than any other, suggests antiquarianism. Furthermore, her perspective is decidedly ethnocentric. In print, she wastes few words on Native Americans of either gender and deals parsimoniously with their enslaved African brothers and sisters.

Arnow's life-long interest in the southern highlands cannot be attributed to any longing on her part to return permanently to what she herself had left behind. She had chosen to abandon a fledgling teaching career and move north to become a writer. Still, she harbored no illusions about the hardships of life for many of her contemporaries on the Cumberland Plateau. From the 1920s to the 1950s, this region was anything but prosperous. Indeed, circumstances of these years provided the backdrop and the particulars for James Still's *River of Earth*.[5] It is a fictional account of the mining camps of Appalachia during the Great Depression and of a family literally starving to death that rivals John Steinbeck's better-known depression-era saga, *The Grapes of Wrath*, which garnered a Pulitzer Prize in 1940.

As attached to place as the people of the Cumberlands were, economic circumstances of the first half of the twentieth century forced them off ancestral lands and sent them north to the factory towns of the Midwest. Commencing in significant numbers during the 1920s, out-migration became a prominent feature of Appalachian life. Even with a relatively high birth rate clearly in evidence, the net population loss between 1940 and 1970 rose to more than three million; half of that occurred during the 1950s when, for the first time during a given decade, out-migration surpassed natural increase. The shifting Appalachian population of these years rivaled the displacement of the Irish, Italians, and other immigrants who had abandoned the rural villages of Europe and relocated in urban American during earlier eras.[6]

Arnow may have been an atypical Appalachian migrant. Certainly she was no Gertie Nevels, the principal character in Arnow's *The Dollmaker*, the story of a Kentucky family in Detroit during the closing years of World War

II. Nonetheless, Arnow went north in pursuit of a dream, and in that respect she was not so unlike thousands of her contemporaries.[7] Sociologists have produced statistical profiles that conjure up images of poverty-stricken and hopeless "hillbillies" abandoning the old homesteads, piling wives, kids, and a few possessions into their jalopies, and making the long trek northward only to settle into low-paying jobs and live in run-down sections of industrial cities. Although there is an element of truth to be found in such a stereotype, it fails to recognize that a great majority of these migrants achieved success by their own standards, did not feel inferior or displaced, adjusted to new-found circumstances, and provided their children with better opportunities.[8]

As tragic as the problems of the Cumberlands had become by the 1960s and as aware as Arnow was of them, she remained, from her vantage in Michigan, a caustic observer of the perennial human drama in the southern mountains. After reading an advance copy of Harry M. Caudill's *Night Comes to the Cumberlands: A Biography of a Depressed Area*, which was released in 1963, the same year as her own *Flowering of the Cumberland*, Arnow wrote to Caudill directly to praise his work; she also reviewed *Night Comes to the Cumberlands* for the *New York Times Book Review*.[9] "I find it hard not to gush," Arnow told Caudill. "So many years I have hoped something like this would be written, and not by one of those but-I-spent-a-month-there experts." Arnow also lauded Caudill's style in what for her were the most glowing terms. "I do rattle on," she admitted, "but few things have ever pleased me so much as your book. It is for me a slice of life seasoned somewhat with your clear plain writing—I think your style would have pleased Stendhal [Henri Beyle, 1783–1842]—remember what he said—but ungarnished by any sprig of parsley or spiced up to suit any man's palate." Somewhat self-effacingly, she added, "I am afraid I sound as if I thought myself an expert on the eastern Kentucky coalfields. I am not; but I have studied quite thoroughly three nearby counties."[10]

After rather detailed discussion of regional politics and peculiarities familiar to both Arnow and Caudill, Arnow ended her letter on a lighter note:

> I must get down to Kentucky and renew my laughter. I go down about twice a year; last fall there was this story of a fiercely fought nomination—it was decided to discredit the opposition by proving he was not a "good family man"; they hired a "Scarlet Woman," took the usual photographs in a hotel room, etc. The stubborn man took the case to court; testimony revealed the Scarlet Woman was also a Kentucky Colonel.[11]

The Kentucky native saw humor in the world around her and in her own life, observing on one occasion after Hollywood had its way with *The Dollmaker* that it seemed she was "being drug into fame on Jane Fonda's coattails." Fonda, of course, played the role of the fictional Gertie Nevels. Arnow could also be brutally frank. At the Appalachian Writers' Association meeting during June 1985, she loudly proclaimed to the founding editor of *Appalachian Heritage* that she intended to cancel her subscription because the publication had been moved from Alice Lloyd College at Pippa Passes, Kentucky, to Berea College on the edge of the Bluegrass. They "will make a sociological magazine out of it, just like the *Appalachian Journal* [published at Appalachian State University in Boone, North Carolina]." Such ire probably stemmed from the fact that she seemed to dislike everything about Berea, which she had attended as a young woman. When that institution many years later thought to confer an honorary degree on Arnow, a photograph of the recipient reportedly showed her "with a cigarette literally dangling from her mouth." She apparently had resented the college's rules governing the use of tobacco. She also remembered that when she had been enrolled there she "didn't find anyone at all at Berea who was interested in writing."[12]

"I have never written to please anyone," Arnow reflected toward the end of her life. "I try to get what's in my head onto paper, which isn't always easy because I don't always think in words. I think in images." She made it clear that such labels as "woman writer" or "Appalachian writer" had meant little to her. "Reviewers of all my books just called me a writer," she explained. "Of course, when I started writing there were no Southern Appalachians; there were just mountains. The term [Southern Appalachians] came into use during and after the Appalachian Redevelopment Act."[13] Despite Arnow's somewhat disingenuous, even erroneous, disclaimer, she was an Appalachian woman writer all the same.

Flowering of the Cumberland opens with an account of Sally Ridley Buchanan and the siege of Buchanan's Station on 30 September 1792, the last great battle between the newcomers and the Native Americans in Middle Tennessee. It concludes with Arnow's invocation of the name of the same brave and exceedingly pregnant woman who had carried bullets and whiskey on that fateful day. Whereas *Seedtime on the Cumberland* focuses on frontier men, its companion piece, *Flowering of the Cumberland*, is attentive to females and families. Arnow, in the latter, is concerned with the underpinnings of civilization. "The old Southwest," she observes, "was not won by armies, but crept westward forted farm by forted farm" (p. 419). Marriages, pregnancies, births, childrearing, and human vices garner Arnow's attention. Agriculture, industry, educational and religious institutions, and the professions are also part of the mix. Indeed, *Flowering of the Cumberland* is a potpourri. Shortly after the book's release, the *Saturday Review* called it "a tremendous grabbag of information, a welter of facts, figures, anecdotes, and opinions."[14]

Arnow's interest in women's roles and folkways and her inclusion of such topics in her writing suggests a certain prescience, for women's history would soon emerge as a legitimate specialty. Her comments about the role and status of females in American society, however, indicates a personal ambivalence. "It isn't necessarily harder for a woman to write than for a man in this country," she observed in 1983. "It depends on the woman and her circumstances. Certainly a married woman with children and a house to keep and cooking and most of the work to do has a harder time." She admitted, however, that she had once submitted a story to *Esquire* signed H. L. Simpson instead of Harriette Louisa Simpson because the magazine only accepted manuscripts from men. "When they wanted a photograph," she confessed, "I asked one of my brothers-in-law to let me have a little photograph of him, and I sent that in."[15] Still, Arnow seems to have yearned for a golden age when men were men and women were women and both sexes had their prescribed places. In 1958 she told Evelyn Stewart of the *Detroit Free Press* that she hated to "emerge from the Eighteenth Century" because "life was better for women way back then." According to Arnow, "women did not have to compete with men then," and they "had more power than now." Furthermore, she claimed that "men didn't hate women then, the way they do now." Instead, they were "yoke-mates, pulling together."[16]

"That the frontier created a spirit of equality among the sexes could not be farther from the truth," writes historian David Hackett Fischer.[17] As the advancing frontier and the presence of males of European descent in the back country undermined the status of Native-American women, it reinforced the subordination of white females. It also introduced the enslavement of their black counterparts.[18] Men expected women to perform the most grueling tasks associated with clearing forests, breaking ground, raising crops, and tending livestock, but that was about the extent of sharing and equality. "Travelers were startled to observe delicate females knock down beef cattle with a felling ax, and then roll down their sleeves, remove their bloody aprons, tidy their hair, and invite their visitors to tea."[19] For women, following their wandering husbands often also meant separation from parents, siblings, relatives, and friends. Isolation and loneliness exacerbated an already difficult existence for most frontier women.[20]

Whereas *Seedtime on the Cumberland* is "the story of how men, chiefly from the southern colonies, learned to live away from the sea and look to the woods if need be for most of their necessities," *Flowering of the Cumberland* deals with "the pioneer as a member of society engaged in those activities which . . . could not be performed by a lone man or family." (pp. xvii–xviii) Their chronologies are roughly the same, 1780 to 1803. With *Seedtime on the Cumberland* and *Flowering of the Cumberland*, Arnow produced "the two books," in the words of the *Christian Science Monitor*, that "form the basis for perhaps the most intimate picture we have of society in the trans-Allegheny phase of the Westward Movement."[21] "I think a mistake the young make is studying style over-much—say of such a writer as Faulkner," Arnow once opined. "Style alone does not make a writer, and I'm happy to say that I think there is less emphasis on style now than there was a few years ago." Once again invoking the name of one of her favorites, she observed, "I prefer reading the letters and journals of such a one as Stendhal, who wanted no style, who wanted his writing to be as clear and concise as a police report."[22] On this count, Harriette Simpson Arnow cannot be faulted. Following in the South's great oral tradition, she chose to be a simple storyteller in prose.

NOTES

1. Charles S. Grant, *Democracy in the Connecticut Frontier Town of Kent* (New York: Columbia University Press, 1961); Kenneth A. Lockridge, *A New England Town: The First Hundred Years, Dedham, Massachusetts, 1636–1736* (New York: W. W. Norton, 1970); and John Demos, *A Little Commonwealth: Family Life in Plymouth Colony* (New York: Oxford University Press, 1970).

2. Philip Greven, *The Protestant Temperament: Patterns of Child-Rearing, Religious Experience, and the Self in Early America* (New York: Alfred A. Knopf, 1977); and Sally G. McMillen, *Motherhood in the Old South: Pregnancy, Childbirth, and Infant Rearing* (Baton Rouge: Louisiana State University Press, 1990).

3. David Hackett Fischer, *Albion's Seed: Four British Folkways in America* (New York: Oxford University Press, 1989).

4. Durwood Dunn, *Cades Cove: The Life and Death of a Southern Appalachian Community, 1818–1937* (Knoxville: University of Tennessee Press, 1988); and Jeanette Keith, *Country People in the New South: Tennessee's Upper Cumberland*, Studies in Rural Culture, ed. Jack Temple Kirby (Chapel Hill: University of North Carolina Press, 1995).

5. James Still, *River of Earth* (New York: Viking Press, 1940; reprint, New York: Popular Library, 1968).

6. Margaret Ripley Wolfe, "Appalachians in Muncie: A Case Study of an American Exodus," *Locus: An Historical Journal of Regional Perspectives* 4 (spring 1992): 169–89.

7. Harriette Simpson Arnow, *Harriette Simpson Arnow, 1908–1986*, directed by Herb E. Smith, 36 min., Appalshop Production, 1988, videocassette. In her no-nonsense, crusty style, Arnow discusses her evolution as a writer and details the trials and tribulations of what she terms "the simple life," which she and her husband had tried for a relatively short time on a Big South Fork farm.

8. Wolfe, "Appalachians in Muncie," 169–89.

9. *New York Times Book Review*, 21 July 1963, 25.

10. Harriette Simpson Arnow to Harry M. Caudill, 5 March 1963, Harry M. and Anne Frye Caudill Collection, [unnumbered box labeled Publications—Correspondence, April 19, 1960–October 31, 1963], Margaret I. King Library, University of Kentucky, Lexington, Kentucky.

11. Ibid.

12. Harriette Simpson Arnow, "Harriette Simpson Arnow (1908–1986)," interview by Nancy Carol Joyner, *Interviewing Appalachia: The "Appalachian Journal" In-*

terviews, 1978–1992, ed. J. W. Williamson and Edwin T. Arnold (Knoxville: University of Tennessee Press, 1994), 67, 69–70.

13. Ibid., 71, 73.

14. *Saturday Review*, 23 November 1963, 42.

15. "Harriette Simpson Arnow (1908–1986)," 71.

16. Quoted in Wilton Eckley, *Harriette Arnow*, Twayne's United States Author Series (New York: Twayne Publishers, 1974), 124–25.

17. Fischer, *Albion's Seed*, 676.

18. Margaret Ripley Wolfe, *Daughters of Canaan: A Saga of Southern Women* (Lexington: University Press of Kentucky, 1995), 11–80.

19. Fischer, *Albion's Seed*, 676.

20. See Joan E. Cashin, *A Family Venture: Men and Women on the Southern Frontier* (New York: Oxford University Press, 1991).

21. *Christian Science Monitor*, 20 November 1963, 13.

22. Quoted in Eckley, *Harriette Arnow*, 123.

Introduction and Acknowledgments

Flowering of the Cumberland has in it even less of great events and famous men than had *Seedtime on the Cumberland*, published in 1960. The first was the story of how men, chiefly from the southern colonies, learned to live away from the sea and look to the woods if need be for most of their necessities from log house to lye. It told of how this long learning was then applied to exploring, hunting over, and at last settling the Valley of the Cumberland, or chiefly what is now Middle Tennessee. Attention was centered on the physical aspects of pioneering—food, clothing, shelter, and the struggle to hold the land against Indians and governments.

This work is not a sequel to that struggle. Rather, it is a companion piece, covering much the same years—1780–1803; or from the time of first settlement to the Louisiana Purchase that sent the frontier west of the Mississippi. Many characters met in *Seedtime* reappear here, but no longer are they solitary individuals or families preoccupied with supplying their immediate needs. *Flowering of the Cumberland* is concerned with the pioneer as a member of society engaged in those activities which, different from hunting or house building, could not be performed by a lone man or family. The first and most important of these was marriage, and the creation of another family with its consequent need of the offerings of any civilized society—language, education, agriculture, industry, and trade; activities that demanded intercourse with other people and often an exchange of goods and services.

During pioneer years none of these could be shaped to any pattern or hung on any frame of dates. All were more or less simultaneous. Education for the young never completely stopped, not even on the flotilla John Donelson led down the Tennessee. Still more trying for those of us who have some need of dividing and labeling, the pioneer period in the old Southwest was no age of specialization, either among individuals or their institutions.

Most life revolved about the home. The farm wife churning butter, singing as she churned, now and then taking time out to help the next-to-the-least-one with its letters, is an example of the multiple problems in labeling and grading. Her churning might represent the preparation of family food, or it might be one link in the trade and industrial pattern that sent butter down the Cumberland to New Orleans where it was re-shipped to the Sugar Islands. Her singing was an amusement to be put into the chapter by that name, while the teaching of her child belongs with education.

There are other problems of division. The singing woman we can imagine as the mistress of a pioneer household, far up a creek, shut off from the wider world. At first glance the pattern of life of our lone family would seem to be one the members had themselves made—log house, home-grown food, red cedar churn of local make, mother and children dressed in clothing of homemade cloth. Yet, the moment the woman begins to sing, or the child recites the alphabet, they become members of a society with an old, old culture, shaped largely in Europe.

So it was with most aspects of the pioneer's life as a member of society. First settlers on the Cumberland owed much to the generations behind them in America who had mastered the long learning needed to conquer the new environment. Yet, important as was this ability, it was the older learnings with their multiple rootings in Europe that made of the settling woodsman, his wife, and children civilized human beings, able to do their share of developing a society that would in time become an important part of the educational, political, and agricultural life of the nation.

Thus, where *Seedtime* emphasized the borderer's ability to conquer an environment unknown in the Old World, this work is concerned chiefly with his ability to transplant shoots of culture, rooted in the Old World. Seldom did the transplant grow exactly as had the parent plant, or one might better say ancestors, for by the time the Cumberland was settled, language, education, along with many other aspects of life, had been conditioned by plantings and transplantings on older borders to the east. Still, the shoots set on the Cumberland bloomed, and often well where, when one considers the hazards and hardships of the environment, the wonder is sometimes that they grew at all.

Just as most divisions as revealed in chapter headings are in a sense both arbitrary and artificial—for pioneering by its very nature had place for little fragmentation—so is it impossible to give exact boundaries of time and place to the research that went into the work. I have, for example, no memory of learning the rhymes for my toes, and feeling the sorrow of the little pig who cried and cried because he could not go; sad he was in a way as the pig fed on clover who when he died, "died all over." I have no memory of anybody's reading to me from the brown-backed *Mother Goose* in the house. The rhymes like many other things came handed down. I grew older, but when I read the *Mother Goose* I found the pigs a little different from my pigs. I wondered why.

It is a long road to the end of wonder, and some of us never reach it, but there is the joy of the trying. Much of my early listening, and hunting, and rummaging was only a part of living along, and could not be dignified by calling it research. Years ago when the actual note-taking with an eye to possible publication began, I looked into many sources not consulted for *Seedtime*, but in the main the same people and institutions that made *Seedtime* possible, helped in this.

Much of the research was done in the Tennessee State Library and Archives at Nashville, where Mrs. Gertrude Morton Parsley, Reference Librarian, State Library Division, was of untold help in many ways. A great deal of research was done before the retirement of Mr. Robert T. Quarles as President of the Tennessee Historical Society, and this work owes much to his interest and suggestions of materials to study. Ever a source of encouragement was Dr. Dan M. Robison, Tennessee State Librarian and Archivist during many of the years of my search, and now State Librarian and Archivist Emeritus. Dr. William T. Alderson who became State Librarian and Archivist at Dr. Robison's retirement was no stranger; he had as Editor of the Tennessee *Historical Quarterly* and

Chairman of the Tennessee Historical Commission already contributed much.

Dr. Josephine L. Harper, Manuscript Librarian, State Historical Society, The State of Wisconsin, answered many questions and furnished photostats of unpublished maps and manuscripts. Lois Mulkearn, Librarian, Darlington Memorial Library of the University of Pittsburgh, took the trouble to microfilm the whole of a very rare book. I am also grateful to members of the staff of the Joint University Library, Nashville, and the University of Kentucky Libraries. I am also indebted to the New York Public Library for use of materials in the Rare Book Room; and to the Ann Arbor Public Library for years of background reading. Much reading was also done in the Detroit Public Library, and I am particularly grateful to Chief James M. Babcock and staff of the Burton Historical Collection who furnished a very great many rare manuscripts, magazines, and books.

Many of the published works cited in this book were studied in some one of the libraries of the University of Michigan, and I am most grateful to Director Frederick H. Wagman for permission to use these materials. I am especially indebted to the rich sources of the Rare Book Room. Much reading was also done in the William L. Clements Library.

I am indebted to Mrs. A. S. Frye, Somerset, Kentucky, for many typescripts of Kentucky County Records and other hard-to-get material, much of it privately published and out of print. Many of the same families who contributed so much to *Seedtime* also helped this work along; they sang songs, told stories, or showed me tools, appliances, and utensils handed down from pioneer days. Particularly helpful were Mr. and Mrs. Henry Hail, Mr. and Mrs. Grover Foster, Mr. and Mrs. Hulon Dobbs, and Mrs. Mary Casada, all of Pulaski County, Kentucky; Mr. James Simpson, and Mr. and Mrs. John C. Burton of Wayne County.

I owe much to the staffs of various museums. Many visits were made to the Tennessee State Museum at Nashville. Others from which I learned much and whose attendants bore with my many questions were the Mountain Life Museum, Levi Jackson State Park, Kentucky; the Renfro Museum, Renfro Valley, Kentucky; the Purnell Museum at Snow Hill, Maryland; and the Military Museum at Kingston, Ontario. Also helpful in contributing to a better understanding of the past were the restorations visited; Williamsburg for the Virginia colonial, the Elizabethan Gardens and Museum at Roanoke, North Carolina, and the buildings and museum at Old Salem, Winston-Salem, North Carolina. A great debt is also owed the various organizations that have restored early homes and opened them to the public: of particular interest was the Blount Mansion at Knoxville, the well known Hermitage, the Sam Davis Home, the Tilman Dixon Home, the William Whitley Home in Kentucky; and Mr. Ed McMurtry gave us a half-day of his time in showing Cragfront before it was bought and restored by the State of Tennessee.

One of the dreariest of jobs is the reading of a disorganized manuscript with an eye to improvement. Many years ago when the work consisted only of fragments and snatches, Dr. Henry Lee Swint, Professor of History, Vanderbilt University, read it. Both works also owe a very great deal to the reading, comments, encouragement, and interest in general of Dr. Allan Nevins. I am most grateful, too, to R. L. De Wilton, Associate Editor, The Macmillan Company, who not only bore the heavy burden of editing both works, but did the extremely time-consuming job of selecting, organizing, and in the case of several maps overseeing the actual creation of all illustrative materials. Miss Susan Prink, copy editor of this and previous works, was of untold help not only in her painstaking search for mistakes, but in setting up the system of notation followed in both books.

None of these people, however, is in any way responsible for mistakes, or opinions. These are the sole property of the writer. Particularly grievous is the problem of which spelling, usually of a surname but sometimes of a given or even place name, to choose. Sources yield multiple spellings; even that of such a well known figure as John Sevier was sometimes written John Saviour.

The same individuals and institutions who contributed to *Seedtime* by the giving of permissions to quote publication or manuscripts, also contributed much, and to them I am grateful. I am indebted to William T. Alderson, Editor, *Tennessee Historical Quarterly*, in which portions of chapters V, IX, and XI appeared in December 1960 and June 1961.

My husband, Harold Arnow, edited, corrected, typed, examined as usual, and like the children, Tom and Marcella, bore with me on the long hunt.

H. S. A.

Explanation of
Bibliographical References

Unpublished Records

The county records of Tennessee are from the typescripts prepared under the supervision of Mrs. John Trotwood Moore. These are housed in the State Library Division of the Tennessee State Library and Archives, Nashville, and used by permission of Dr. William T. Alderson, State Librarian and Archivist. I have followed the original page numberings. The original early Sumner County Records are the property of the Archives Division, Tennessee State Library and Archives, Nashville; the others named are owned by their respective counties and housed in the county courthouses.

Early county court clerks had no standard method of labeling and enumerating records. Smith County, Tennessee, Court Record Books are quite typical; listed by letter—A, B, etc.,—one set of records was referred to as *Inventories and Appraisements*, with the first wills in another volume, while the minutes of the county courts were often labeled *Order Book*. I have, to avoid confusion, followed the system of Mrs. Moore; all volumes are listed by Roman numerals, thus A is now I. Standardized titles have been adopted, thus:

DC, I	*Davidson County Court Minutes, 1783–1790.*
DW, I	*Davidson County Wills and Inventories, 1784–1794.*
DW, II	*Ibid., 1794–1805.*
MW, I	*Montgomery County Wills and Inventories, 1797–1810.*
MW, II	*Ibid., 1810–1827.*
SC, I	*Sumner County Court Minutes, 1787–1791.*
Smith C, I	*Smith County Court Minutes, 1799–1804.*

Smith C, II   *Ibid., 1804–1811.*
Smith W, V   *Smith County Wills and Inventories, 1814–1816.*
SW, I   *Sumner County Wills and Inventories, 1789–1822.*

All the above county records are now a part of the Records of the State of Tennessee, but prior to 1790 Davidson and Sumner counties were parts of North Carolina; the same counties were parts of the Territory of the United States South of the River Ohio, 1790–1796; it was not until the creation of the State of Tennessee in 1796 that any county was officially a part of Tennessee.

The Kentucky counties studied were originally part of Virginia, and beginning in 1780 a part of Lincoln County, Virginia, with various changes through the years as new counties were created, but none of the three below was organized until after Kentucky became a state in 1792. Kentucky has made no copy of the original records; these are housed in the courthouses, and all references are to the manuscripts. I have taken the same liberty in volume numberings as with those of Tennessee, and have, in so far as possible, adopted standardized titles, thus:

CW, II   *Cumberland County Will Book* (inventories and sales are also included) *B, 1815–1825.*
PC, I   *Pulaski County, Court Minutes, 1799–1803.*
PD, I   *Pulaski County, Deed Book, 1799–1805.*
PD, II   *Ibid., 1805–1815.*
PD, III   *Ibid., 1815–1819.*
PD, IV   *Ibid., 1819–1821.*
PW, I   *Pulaski County, Wills and Inventories, 1801–1818.*
PW, II   *Ibid., 1818–1829.*
PW, III   *Ibid., 1829–1845.*
WC, I   *Wayne County Court Minutes, 1801–1824.*
WD, I   *Wayne County Deed Book, 1801–1821.*
WD, II   *Ibid., 1821–1823.*
WD, III   *Ibid., 1823–1827.*
WD, V   *Ibid., 1829–1831.*
WM, I   *Wayne County Mortgage Book, 1832–1837.*
WM, II   *Ibid., 1838–1842.*
WW, II   *Wayne County Wills and Inventories, 1827–1848.*

Published Records and Collections
ASP   American State Papers, Washington D. C., 1832–1861.
I   Illinois Historical Collections.
I, V   Clarence W. Alvord, ed., *Kaskaskia Records, 1778–1790,* Springfield, 1909.
I, VIII   James Alton James, ed., *George Rogers Clark Papers, 1771–1781,* Springfield, 1912.

I, XVI   (III British Series) Clarence W. Alvord and C. E. Carter, *Trade and Politics in the Illinois Country, 1767–1769*, Springfield, 1921.

Material from the three volumes above is reprinted by permission of the publishers and copyright holders, the Illinois State Historical Library, Springfield, Illinois.

M   Archives of Maryland, published by authority of the State of Maryland under the direction of the Maryland Historical Society, and edited by William Hand Browne.
M, VIII   *Proceedings of the Council of Maryland, 1687–1688*, Baltimore, 1890.
M, XXIII   *Ibid., 1696/97–1698*, Baltimore, 1903.
NCR   *The Records of North Carolina*, published under the supervision of the trustees of the Public Libraries by order of the General Assembly. The following were collected and edited by Walter Clark.
NCR, XII   *The State Records of North Carolina, 1777–1778*, Winston, 1895.
NCR, XIII   *Ibid., 1778–1779*, Winston, 1896.
NCR, XIV   *Ibid., 1779–1780*, Winston, 1896.
NCR, XVI   *Ibid., 1782–1783*, Goldsboro, 1899.
NCR, XVII   *Ibid., 1781–1785*, Goldsboro, 1899.
NCR, XVIII   *Ibid., 1786, with a supplement from 1779*, Goldsboro, 1900.
NCR, XIX   *Ibid., 1782–1783, with a supplement from 1771–1782*, Goldsboro, 1901.
NCR, XX   *Ibid., 1785–1788*, Goldsboro, 1902.
NCR, XXII   *Miscellaneous Records of the State of North Carolina*, Goldsboro, 1907.
NCR, XXIV   *Laws of the State of North Carolina, 1777–1788*, Goldsboro, 1905.
                The following volume was edited by S. B. Weeks.
NCR, XXV   *Ibid., 1789–1790 with supplement and omitted laws, 1669–1783*, Goldsboro, 1908.
TP   The Territorial Papers of the United States.
TP, IV   *The Territory South of the River Ohio, 1790–1796*, edited and compiled by Clarence Edwin Carter, Washington, D.C., 1936.
VS   *Virginia Calendar of State Papers and Other Manuscripts;* published under authority of the Library Committee, and edited by William P. Palmer.
VS, I   *Ibid., 1652–1781*, Richmond, 1875.
VS, III   *Ibid., 1782–1784*, Richmond, 1883.

Manuscripts

W   Manuscript originals in the possession of the State Historical Society of Wisconsin, Madison, Wisconsin.

My heavy use of this material, collected by Dr. Lyman C. Draper, takes two forms. Many published journals and other sources cited were taken from the Draper Manuscripts; heavier use was made of the microfilm edition of the manuscripts, issued by the State Historical Society of Wisconsin. In either case the original source is indicated by W, followed by series, volume number, and page when given.

Magazines

A   *American Historical Magazine and Tennessee Historical Society Quarterly,* pub., Tennessee Historical Society, Nashville, 1896–1904.

ETH   *The* East Tennessee *Historical Society's Publications,* 1929 –. Material used by permission of the publisher and copyright holder, the East Tennessee Historical Society, Knoxville, Tennessee.

FP   Publications of the Filson Club, 1–32, Louisville, Kentucky, 1884–1922.

FQ   *The Filson Club History Quarterly,* 1926 –. Material used by permission of the publisher and copyright owner, the Filson Club, Louisville, Kentucky.

RK   *Register* Kentucky *State Historical Society,* 1902 –. Material used by permission of the publisher and copyright holder, the Kentucky Historical Society, Frankfort, Kentucky.

THM   Tennessee *Historical Magazine,* Series I & II, 1915–1937. Material used by permission of the publisher and copyright holder, the Tennessee Historical Society, Nashville, Tennessee.

VM   Virginia *Magazine of History and Biography, 1893* –. Material used by permission of the publisher and copyright holder, the Virginia Historical Society, Richmond, Virginia.

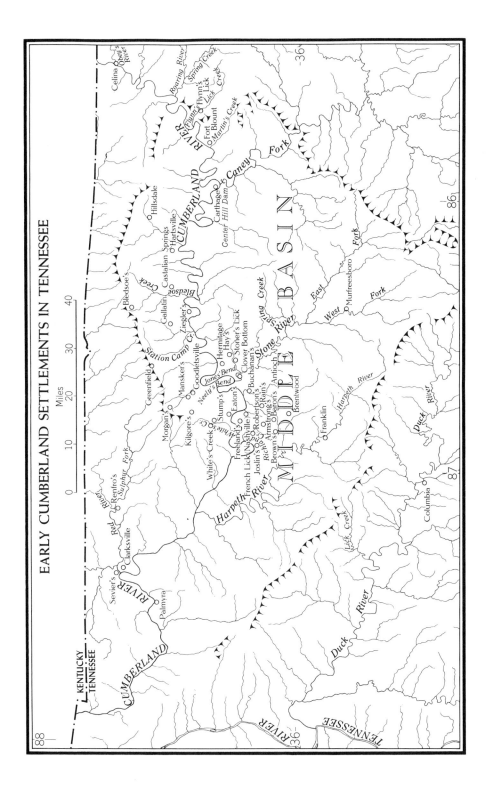

EARLY CUMBERLAND SETTLEMENTS IN TENNESSEE

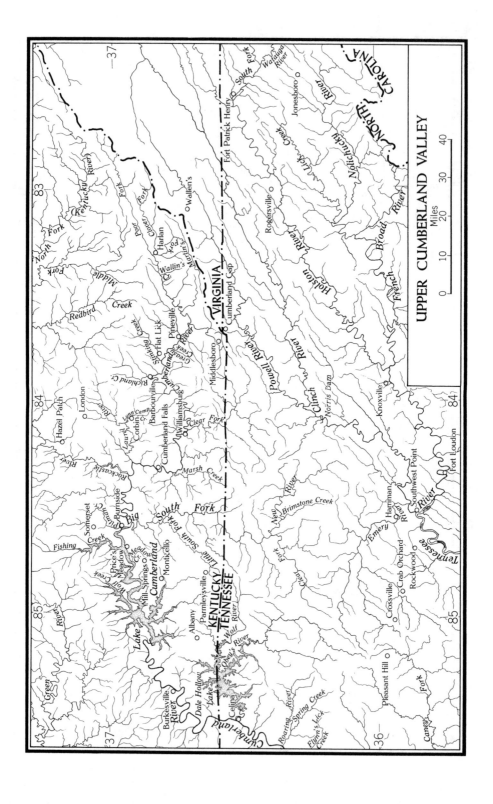

UPPER CUMBERLAND VALLEY

Miles
0   10   20   30   40

Flowering
of the Cumberland

Chapter One

The Siege
of Buchanan's

SUNDAY, SEPTEMBER 30, 1792, was a date so important in the history of what was to be Middle Tennessee that long ago the Tennessee Historical Commission set up a marker bearing the date and other information. The bronze plaque may be seen in Davidson County, Tennessee, near where the Elm Hill Road crosses Mill Creek, a tributary of Cumberland River, but now for much of its course running through suburban Nashville. Tennessee has many such markers, a large number commemorating, as does this one, the scene of a battle. Few, however, bear the name of a woman, and on this one not complete, only "Mrs. Buchanan."

There were many Mrs. Buchanans, but if any of the old ones or their children and grandchildren who heard the stories of pioneer days on the

Headpiece: Indian attack on a Cumberland valley station. (Kendall: *Life of General A. Jackson,* 1843.)

Cumberland could come alive to read the marker, they would know at once the woman referred to was Sarah Ridley Buchanan, more commonly known as Sally, wife of young John Buchanan. Judging from their many stories [1] of what happened that Sunday evening, some of the old-timers reading the plaque might wish for another name—Jemmy O'Connor; he, too, helped make history. Still, one should not quarrel overmuch at the lack of Jemmy's name on the marker. He seems to have been what one, looking into the past, might call a passer-by. There were many of these; some appear only as names defending a station, saving the life of a companion in an Indian battle, buying a horse, or as the subject of a story told by those who wrote of the old days to Dr. Lyman C. Draper. Such a one was Jemmy O'Connor.

Sally Ridley Buchanan, on the other hand, was wife to one of the leading men of the neighborhood, thirty-three-year-old Major John Buchanan,[2] and she was also very much a person in her own right. Many remembered her as a courageous, kind, and honorable woman, "much respected by all." Different from most women of the old Southwest who were as a rule smaller and frailer than is the average woman in today's United States, Sally weighed more than two hundred pounds. She was of a strength to match her size, for she could stand in a half-bushel measure, pick up, and shoulder a two and one-half bushel sack of corn, or 150 pounds.[3]

It is doubtful if Sally had done such things on this particular Sunday, for in the words of the day she was "in the family way" or, more aptly, "big with child." Her first-born was expected any time. The last days of pregnancy are not considered among most women a pleasant time, especially for a large woman in hot weather. True, in so far as is known no recording on "Mr. Fahrenheit's thermometer" had that day been taken down at Buchanan's Station, or anywhere else in the old West for the

---

[1] W, 30S, 526–527, and *ibid.*, 32S, 358–360, this last the account of Col. Robert Weakley, are among the best.

[2] Quoted by permission of Dr. William T. Alderson, Tennessee State Librarian and Archivist, from the Mss Book of Arithmetic by John Buchanan, 1781; owned by the Tennessee Historical Society, and housed in the Archives Division, Tennessee State Library and Archives, Nashville (cited hereafter as Buchanan, Arithmetic).

[3] W, 3XX (18), 5, the account of William Martin. See also George William Featherstonhaugh, *Excursion Through the Slave States from Washington on the Potomac to the frontier of Mexico with Sketches of popular manners and geological observances*, London, 1844 (cited hereafter as Featherstonhaugh, *Excursion*), I, 205. The author was particularly interested in Sally and described her, but it should be remembered his visit came forty years after the battle when Sally was dead, but he did talk with her father and stepmother.

matter of that,[4] but as travelers often complained of the heat, even in October, of Kentucky and Tennessee, the day we can be reasonably certain was hot. We know at least the weather was clear with a bright moon that night.

Worse than the weather for human comfort were the conditions under which Sally lived, for she, like all the rest of the around seven thousand [5] men, women, and children along the middle Cumberland, lived in a forted station. Stations varied in shape and size, but Buchanan's to which Sally more than a year ago had come as a bride was about average, the picketed walls enclosing around an acre with a blockhouse at each corner. This small space was shared with seven other families,[6] some like the Buchanans with slaves, and all living in what must have been rather small log houses as they were side by side in one straight row down the middle of the fort yard.

The forted life known to most who settled the old Southwest was described by many, but whether such a one as Reverend Doddridge [7] who spent his boyhood on the frontier of what is now West Virginia, or Colonel William Fleming [8] who endured the "hard winter" of 1779–1780 in various Kentucky stations, none had any good word to say for the forted life, save it was the only means of protection from the Indians. Families had on all borders been wiped out because they could not bear the crowding; almost always those on the Cumberland who tried to go it alone in a small weak station sooner or later moved to a bigger one or were ruined. It was only a few weeks now since the Indians had with

[4] Used by permission of the Henry E. Huntington Library and Art Gallery, San Marino, California, from *The Western Country in 1793 Reports on Kentucky and Virginia* by Harry Toulmin, ed. by Marion Tinling and Godfrey Davies, copyright Henry E. Huntington Library and Art Gallery, San Marino, 1948 (cited hereafter as Toulmin, *Western Country*), 75. Toulmin here states that at the time of his visit no temperature recordings had been taken in the West.

[5] TP, IV, 81. The total population as of September 19, 1791, was given as 7,042, of which 1,161 were slaves.

[6] W, 29S, 74–75, and *ibid.*, 30S, 227–233, give locations and descriptions of Buchanan's and others of the more important stations. W, 30S, 526, names several of the families living at Buchanan's.

[7] Samuel Kercheval, *A History of the Valley of Virginia*, Woodstock, Va., 1833; pagination, 1902 ed., Madison, Wisc. (cited hereafter as Kercheval, *Virginia*), quoting the Reverend Joseph Doddridge, "Notes on the settlement and Indian Wars of the Western parts of Virginia and Pennsylvania" (cited hereafter as Doddridge, "Notes"), 260.

[8] Newton D. Mereness, *Travels in the American Colonies*, New York, 1916 (cited hereafter as Mereness, *Travels*), "The Journal of Colonel William Fleming," ed. from the Draper Manuscripts of the Wisconsin Historical Society (cited hereafter as Fleming, "Journal"), 619–654.

bullets and fire destroyed Zeigler's Station, north of the Cumberland. A short time before that the whole Thompson family, save Alcey,[9] now an Indian captive, had been killed.

There is nothing to indicate that the pioneer valued security of any kind as highly as do we today, and to many a fort was somewhat like a prison. Neat, active, industrious Sally Buchanan [10] must at times have found the forted life a messy, nerve-racking business. Dusty and hot in summer with no cooling shade save that of the house walls, safety demanded that every great black locust, oak, or even any bush or little cedar big enough to hide an Indian be cut. Perpetually crowded with all kinds and conditions of people from newborn black babies or white babies to elderly widows as was Sally's mother-in-law, the acre of ground was filled for most of the daylight hours with noise of humankind and smoke from cooking fires. There was, too, all the gear and plunder demanded by the complex life of such farming families as the Buchanans—ash hoppers, shaving horses, barrels and troughs for the catching of rain water, piles of firewood, a still or so, "necessary house," smokehouse and loom house, with all tools, farming implements such as plows, along with saddles, bridles, and everything else an Indian could steal, lodged somehow, somewhere behind the fort walls. No activity was safe outside the picketing, so that the fort yard, cabins, blockhouses, and outhouses were often jammed with wool waiting to be washed, piles of flax straw ready for the break, or green hides soaking in a hollowed-log tanning vat.

Most weekdays of September, 1792, would have found Buchanan's no different from other stations in the neighborhood, filled with the whirr of spinning wheels, rattle and bang of looms, thump and glug of churn dashers, the hustle and bustle and smoke and steam of scrubbing days,[11] and washing days that meant boiling clothes in a great iron kettle set on its three legs over an outside fire. John Buchanan in time had a proper gristmill powered by a stream of water, but during the early years he, like the Hickmans [12] and most other frontier farmers, had the usual horse mill, kept for safety behind the fort picketing—and a cumbersome, creaking thing the wooden mill was, taking up room with the slowly walking

[9] ASP, *Indian Affairs*, I, 330. The name is sometimes spelled Elsey or Alcie; she was with Mrs. Peter Caffery and child when captured Feb. 25, 1792.

[10] W, 3XX (18), 5.

[11] *Ibid.*

[12] W, 30S, 464–472. Hickman's not only had a horse mill but also sheaves of wheat and the corncrib in the fort yard.

horses, not only trampling the earth into mud or dust, but now and then dropping manure; all in all making what Sally would call a "gome."

Some farmers with unusually fine horses kept their best stock inside the fort as did James Robertson,[13] but there is no mention of horsestock within Buchanan's Station. Still, there was on any forted farm no escaping the animals. Suckling calves were usually penned near the fort walls, and bawling now and then for their mothers gone to the cane-brakes. Penned also were the smelly, noisy fattening pigs, a fold of baaing sheep waiting to be shorn or lambs to be marked. There were chickens, ducks, and geese in and out, scratching, honking, crowing, cackling, hissing. Inside and out, sometimes sharing the family fire, were the dogs. Pioneering was impossible without dogs; the little feist was worth his weight in gunpowder when he warned of approaching Indians, while the great bear dogs, able to kill a man, and valued by many "to the worth of a horse," [14] were along with the gentle hounds a necessity for any successful hunt.

The dust, gnats, mosquitoes, flies, and horseflies of summer yielded in winter to seas of mud and more smoke from heating fires. Smell of horse or cow manure drying in the sun was replaced by the greasy odor of hog killing with its attendant lard rendering, soap making, and sausage stuffing. Many activities such as hog killing that required large quantities of wood and water almost had to take place near the spring branch or creek where both wood and water were more handily had. The killing and curing of meat was usually done by the farmer or his help, but much of the work then performed by women—the milking of the cows along with all matters pertaining to the dairy—had also to be done outside the fort walls. In times of extreme danger milkmaids like plow hands were guarded, but guarded or no there was for any farm wife and her help a deal of running in and out the fort.

Yet, no matter how often a woman must go to check on the family wash or lend a hand in the bringing in of the bleaching linen at the outset of a summer shower, the heavy fort gate had always to be firmly shut

[13] This was while he lived at Freeland's in 1781. See W, 6XX, 11.

[14] Used by permission of Gertrude Williams Miller and Martha Williams from *Early Travels in the Tennessee Country, 1540–1800;* ed. and compiled by their father Judge Samuel Cole Williams, copyright by the author, Johnson City, Tenn., 1928 (cited hereafter as Williams, *Travels*), 518–519, "Report of the Journey of the Brethren Abraham Steiner and Frederick D. De Schweinitz to the Cherokee and the Cumberland Settlements, 1799" (cited hereafter as Schweinitz, "Report").

as one went out. Back in 1787 in the same station in which Sally now lived, her husband's father, John Buchanan, Sr., had been killed and scalped as he sat with his wife by their fireside. A small band of Indians had been lying in wait, watching for the fort gate to be left open while the able-bodied men were at work in the fields.

Sally, one suspects, closed the gate without thinking each time she passed through and automatically reminded her help to do the same. Most of her life had been spent either in a picketed fort or within running distance of one. She had no memory of a world safe from Indians. Her father, Colonel Daniel Ridley, then living in a forted station of his own around two miles away, had, like many other settlers in Middle Tennessee, known many borders before settling on this one.

True, he had been born in Tidewater, Williamsburg, Virginia, in 1737, long after it was safe from Indians, but the year 1755 when he was only eighteen had found him deep in the "back parts." A survivor of the Battle of the Wilderness, he had, after the death of General Braddock, been one of the weary marchers from the Monongahela near Fort Duquesne back to the comparative safety of Fort Cumberland. All that was history now. Fort Duquesne had become Fort Pitt, and lately more and more people were calling the place Pittsburgh. The American colonel who had taken over the command on the death of General Braddock was now President Washington.

Colonel Ridley had also fought in the Revolution, though as a borderer he had known many battles and skirmishes undignified by the title of any war. Then, in the midst of the Revolution and while Sally was still a small child, he had taken a push still further west, settling in 1779 in what was then called the Holston Country, or the "back parts" of North Carolina, in time to be known as East Tennessee.

The ending of the Revolution had not brought peace and safety. Indian depredations had continued after the defeat of the Chickamauga in 1779, and in 1784 all the Holston Country had erupted into the bloody turmoil of a civil war when John Sevier and his followers attempted to form a state of their own—Franklin. Four years later, the State of Franklin collapsed; by late 1789 Sevier and all his followers had been pardoned.[15] Thus, by 1790 the more thickly settled parts of the Holston Country were at least more peaceful and safer than they had been. Strange, but it was at this time, after having survived eleven years of forted life, Colonel

[15] NCR, XXII, 728–729, Nov. 30, 1789. Sevier was the last to be pardoned.

Ridley took his family still further west into the most dangerous spot of all—the Cumberland settlements.[16]

No one knows exactly why any man or woman—and usually there was a woman—risked death to settle a far place. North Carolina had used land (she had no cash) to pay her officers and soldiers for their services in the Revolution, and the land was among the best on earth—what is now known as the Tennessee Bluegrass—but in 1792, close to ten years after many had received their unlocated warrants, few ex-soldiers had settled or even risked their scalps on the long and lonesome trip from North Carolina to the Cumberland settlements to look over the land and locate a boundary, 640 acres for a private, more for officers according to rank. Wealthy families such as the Bentons and Polks, able to buy much land and send lawyers to see about it, had not yet settled. Still, a high percentage of the forted stations now on the Cumberland had been built by ex-soldiers and officers of the Revolution on lands they had been granted.

Yet, none of the men out of the Revolution, no matter how great their sufferings during the rebellion or from Indians after settlement, had known the losses in blood, money, and time, or endured the hardships of the first settlers on the Cumberland. These had come away back in the winter of 1779–1780, or at about the time Sally's father had moved to the Holston Country.

Sally's husband, Major John Buchanan, had been among these first settlers. His family history was much like her own and that of many other settlers near them. Buchanans, natives of Scotland and among them several Johns, had been active for generations on the southern borders. Close to fifty years before or in 1745, a John Buchanan had been a member of the first county court of Augusta County, Virginia,[17] then a vast sweep of land to the Mississippi, unknown and unexplored, with even the very word *Kenta-ke* known to but few white men.

The Buchanans had continued on the borders, working as surveyors, and serving as justices of the peace or officers in the militia, often active on Indian campaigns, but basically farmers with a love of good land and always hunting better. Sally's husband, "a thick set man, five feet, six

---

[16] Featherstonhaugh, *Excursion*, I, 205.

[17] Joseph A. Waddell, *Annals of Augusta County, Virginia, with Reminiscences Illustrative of the Vicissitudes of Its Pioneer Settlers*, Richmond, 1886 (cited hereafter as Waddell, *Annals*), 25.

or eight inches tall," had been born in Harrisburg,[18] Pennsylvania, but his father, John, Sr., like so many Pennsylvania borderers, had migrated to North Carolina, settling in the neighborhood of Guilford Courthouse, now surrounded by the town of Greensboro. Not many miles west was the Yadkin Country from which Daniel Boone and many others went out on the long hunts that by the mid-sixties were taking them across the mountains and into *Kenta-ke*—now by 1792 the State of Kentucky.

The hunters had brought home with their peltry stories of the wondrously fine land there. They told, too, of another place to the south, the Middle Basin of the Cumberland, an old, old land, fertile, beautiful, rolling, farmed for centuries by a now-vanished race whose dead in stone-lined graves were found all around, then claimed by many tribes of modern Indians who used it only as a hunting ground. Living there was too dangerous, but all tribes had wanted to share in the fine hunting. Claimed, too, in time by the French who had come as hunters and briefly as traders to a town of the wandering Shawnee soon wiped out by the Cherokee and the Chickasaw. Won by the English in the French and Indian War, the French were remembered only in place names—the Old French Landing at the mouth of the Lick Branch and the French Lick, a short distance up the stream, both on the southern side of the river and now in the lowlands of Nashville.

Meantime, English settlement crept a bit closer. The King's proclamation of 1763 to the contrary, settlers, following the headwaters of the Tennessee, continued to push south and west, and in 1769 William Bean, not knowing exactly where he was, crossed the Virginia–North Carolina border, and built the first cabin in what came to be Tennessee. The land that was to be Kentucky and Tennessee grew somewhat safer after the Point Pleasant Campaign of 1774 that marked the end of Dunmore's War and the defeat of the Shawnee. Harrodsburg, Kentucky, was founded in that year. Also came the surveyors, locating boundaries for the land warrants Virginia had used to pay her soldiers in the French and Indian War. Some of these, including several hundred acres for George Rogers Clark, were located on the Middle Cumberland in the neighborhood of French Lick, for at this time most thought all the Cumberland was due west of Virginia instead of North Carolina. The only accurate map so far drawn, that of Thomas Hutchins, lay unpublished in London. The

[18] W, 31S, 332. See also *Peabody Reflector and Alumni News,* published and copyrighted by George Peabody College for Teachers, XI (Dec. 1938), 408–412, Thurman Sensing, "Buchanan's Station" (cited hereafter as Sensing, "Buchanan's").

boundary line between North Carolina and Virginia had not yet been carried past the headwaters of the Holston.

The following year, 1775, western settlement was given a further push when at the Treaty of Sycamore Shoals of the Watauga, Richard Henderson led his land company in treating with Attakullakulla and other Cherokee chiefs for a vast boundary of land that embraced most of the western two-thirds of Kentucky and the mid-section of what is now Tennessee or the Middle Cumberland Basin. The treaty was not yet finished before Boone, Michael Stoner, and other woodsmen were off on the Cumberland Gap trail to Kentucky where they founded Boonesboro.

The outbreak of the Revolution in which all Indians took the side of the British checked westward expansion, and in the bloody year of 1777 only three tiny stations held in Kentucky, one of these, Price's, was a few miles below the mouth of the Big South Fork, and about two hundred up the Cumberland from Buchanan's. Meantime, save for a few hunters, notably big Thomas Sharpe Spencer, the country of the Middle Cumberland was practically empty of white men.

The home governments of North Carolina and Virginia, hard pressed by the Revolution, could give the settlers on their western borders little help. The settlers had to take care of themselves. This they did. George Rogers Clark, aided by a few Virginians but chiefly Kentucky and Holston settlers, succeeded in retaking Vincennes, thus anchoring the Northwest Territory, and a short time later the Chickamauga, or the hostile faction of the Cherokee, gone south to Chickamauga Creek of the Tennessee, were defeated. Thus, by mid-1779 the picture of western settlement was brighter than it had been—at least, officially. There is, however, no complete explanation for the migrations of any people, and particularly those pushed forward neither by poverty nor by war. Most early settlers to the old West left plenty and comparative peace for nothing certain, not even life and bread. Yet, mid-1779 found many making plans for emigration, or already on the Kentucky Trace with families, pack horses, flocks, and herds.

The Buchanans—John, Sr., his wife and sons, Alexander, Samuel, and John—were among those who took the long, long horseback trek into Kentucky. Some say they went as early as 1778,[19] but whatever the date of their arrival, Kentucky seems never to have been their original

---

[19] Buchanan, Arithmetic.

destination. In any case, late 1779 found the younger Buchanans building a station on the southern side of the Cumberland River, above the French Lick, on the high ground "in the upper part" of what is now Nashville. On the other side of the Lick Branch, another station was soon being built, that of George Freeland, while north of the river about twelve miles away, near present day Goodlettsville, there was a finished station. This belonged to Kaspar Mansker who had by 1779 been hunting over the region for more than a dozen years.

The winter of 1779–1780 was one of the worst on record, but in spite of the bitter cold there was a constant trickle of settlers to the Cumberland Country. Amos Eaton [20] and family, John Rains, Haydon Wells, and Frederick Stump, to name only a few, came by pack horse driving flocks and herds before them. April 24, 1780, the well known flotilla, headed by John Donelson in his boat the *Adventure*, reached French Lick after a hazardous trip from Reedy Creek of the Holston on down the Tennessee and up the Ohio and the Cumberland.

Early summer of 1780 found several hundred people and more than a dozen stations in what was to be Middle Tennessee. The future looked bright; most, though not the Buchanans, had agreed to buy land from Richard Henderson's company, and so had signed the Cumberland Compact which also provided for government.

Then the Indians—Chickasaw, Cherokee, Chickamauga, and Creek—struck. The Cumberland settlements had by the winter of 1781 dwindled to three small stations—French Lick where the Buchanans had built, Freelands, and that of Amos Eaton on the northern side of the Cumberland, opposite the mouth of the Lick Branch or the Old French Landing. Many families such as the Donelsons and their in-laws fled to the comparative safety of Kentucky; others returned to North Carolina, and of the 131 first settlers who stayed, 63 were by the spring of 1784 dead. There is no record of how many of the living had by this date been wounded, but one cannot help but think of one-eyed Haydon Wells, scalpless David Hood, and twice-shot James Robertson.

A treaty was made with the Chickasaw in November of 1783, but

[20] Most names of the first settlers are represented in petitions, court records, and the Draper Manuscripts by multiple spellings; even now not all descendants of the same settler use the same spelling; there is still much uncertainty about Eaton; it appears in many sources as Heaton; many are now inclined to think it should be so spelled, though previous historians used Eaton for the most part; the controversy is now about 125 years old for in the early 1840's William Martin, son of Joseph Martin, one of the three who treated with the Chickasaw at the Treaty of Nashville, 1783, wrote, W, 3XX (14), 3, "the name was not Heaton but Eaton."

depredations from other tribes continued. Crops, outbuildings, cattle, sheep, and hogs were consistently destroyed, and by 1789 James Robertson estimated [21] the Indians had stolen from the Cumberland settlers five or six thousand head of horsestock. Men, such as the Buchanans, who risked death to put in a crop of corn or grow a little cotton seldom had the luck to harvest it; one year nobody raised anything but "cotton and a little garden stuff." Thus, most of those who survived knew hunger; the buffalo and deer, once so plentiful, had, even as early as 1780, almost completely disappeared from the neighborhood of French Lick. Such bear and smaller game as were left could be hunted only at the risk of a man's scalp.

Hunger, discomfort, loss, the constant threat of death or wounds or captured women and children were not the only troubles of John Buchanan and other first settlers. The North Carolina Assembly had, in spite of settlers already on the land, decreed the basin of the Middle Cumberland should be used to pay the soldiers of the North Carolina Line and others to whom the bankrupt North Carolina treasury owed money. True, the lawmakers did in 1784 give each original settler 640 acres of land. The trouble was that by this date most of the land was already surveyed for soldiers, surveyors, guards of the surveying party, and anybody else with money and time to get to the land office hundreds of miles away at Hillsboro on the other side of the mountains. Few of the first settlers could even show proof of ownership by having settled and cleared a boundary of land; the Indians had forced them all to live in forted stations.

Thus it was that in 1785 the Buchanans had come down to Mill Creek and started all over again, building, clearing, fencing; old French Lick Station where they, the Mulherrins, and several other families had worked and held off Indians for more than four years was in the boundary of land set aside by the lawmakers for Nashville.

John's brother Alexander was already dead from Indians at the time of moving, but first his father and then his brother Samuel had been killed after moving to the new station. John had also lost his first wife, Mary Kennedy, married in 1786; [22] she had died in childbirth, but the baby lived, so that Sally Ridley Buchanan was also a stepmother, a not uncommon situation on the Cumberland.

The story of death and loss among the Buchanans was no worse than

[21] NCR, XXII, 792.
[22] Buchanan, Arithmetic.

that of most other families who settled the Cumberland Country; widows, orphans, the wounded—twenty of these [23] were scalpless—captive children unheard of for years, families once prosperous now destitute with the last horse gone and the last cow found with an arrow in her ribs. The wonder is not that in 1792,[24] close to thirteen years after the beginnings of settlement, there were only seven thousand settlers in one of the most fertile regions on earth, but that there were any at all.

Historians, as well as the old ones who wrote their memories for Dr. Draper, give most of the credit for survival to one man, James Robertson,[25] at this time with the title of general; he was also a justice of the peace and sub-agent of Indian affairs. Titles of many varieties were no new thing to Robertson; [26] he had by 1792 been serving in civilian and military life for close to twenty-five years, and away back in 1769 had been a justice of the peace for Boutetourt County, Virginia. The following year he had emigrated to the Holston Country, and as he took an active part in both the civil and military life of this region, James Robertson is referred to by most historians as the Father of Tennessee. No other man was such a key figure in the formation of two parts of the state.

His exploratory journey into Middle Tennessee in early 1779 is usually considered the first step in the settlement of the Cumberland Country; all of the men with him, save one, were settled there by early 1780, many emigrating as did most of his family in the flotilla down the Tennessee, headed by John Donelson. All that was history now; big John Donelson was dead of Indians; Robertson had lost to them two young sons, a brother, and numerous nieces and nephews. No different from the other first settlers, Robertson had in 1784 to begin all over again. He now lived on his own land in a forted station down on Richland Creek, south of the Cumberland, down river and west of

---

[23] A, II, 26.

[24] James Gettys Ramsey, *The Annals of Tennessee to the end of the 18th century,* Philadelphia, 1860 (cited hereafter as Ramsey, *Tennessee*), 596–597, gives a summary of the Indian atrocities of 1792, and preceding years; unindexed, this, the most comprehensive history of early Tennessee, is so chronologically labeled and arranged as to be most helpful for any given year.

[25] Well represented in all source materials relative to early Tennessee; see in particular TP, IV (indexed), for his correspondence and A, V. See also A. W. Putnam, *History of Middle Tennessee or Life and Times of General James Robertson,* Nashville, 1859.

[26] TP, IV, 82, 141, 440, more or less explain the civil and military appointments held at this time by Robertson; his military titles are confusing; he was, *ibid.,* 82, Brigadier General of Mero District (Middle Tennessee), but at the same time, *ibid.,* 440, Lieutenant Colonel Commandant of the Davidson County Militia.

Buchanan's Station. Wounded the preceding June [27] along with his son Jonathan, he was again able to go about his duties that might include anything from pegging a scalped head, bargaining with Alexander McGillivray, chief of the Creeks, supervising a muster, corresponding with officialdom, or working in the cornfield side by side with his help. A big blue-eyed man, he was, in spite of little formal education, a master diplomat. He lived always the rope in the tug-of-war between two bitterly opposing camps—officialdom in far away Philadelphia determined on peace with the Indian at any price, and the eternally maimed, massacred, dispossessed settlers who wanted troops, ammunition, help against the Indians.

All this was an old story to Robertson; even the attempted recovery of stolen horses could bring down the wrath of officialdom. Still, he had managed to hold the settlement together; encouraging; feeding the hungry from his own often scanty stores; serving as the occasion demanded as Indian warrior or peacemaker, but most of all as a lonely horseman on dangerous roads, up to The Falls for salt and settlers, but chiefly off to North Carolina to beg help for the settlement. He is the one usually credited with having brought about a change of heart in the North Carolina Assembly—the pre-emptions for land originally given the settlers were suddenly, after years of refusal, changed to outright grants.[28]

Now by 1792 the first settlers, though much in the minority, were living for the most part in stations of their own. North of the river Amos Eaton had built a new station on Eaton's Lick Creek, about five miles down river from his first station. Frederick Stump, the middle-aged Pennsylvania German who had come with the Eaton party, had by now a flourishing settlement on White's Creek near the ford on the trace to Clarksville, like Nashville of 1792, little more than a name. Kaspar Mansker's first station had been burned by Indians, but he had long since rebuilt and again lived near present day Goodlettsville.[29]

Daniel Smith,[30] one of the most important men in the early history

---

[27] ASP, *Indian Affairs*, I, 330.

[28] Harriette Simpson Arnow, *Seedtime on the Cumberland*, New York, 1960 (cited hereafter as Arnow, *Seedtime*), gives, 328–339, a somewhat detailed discussion of early land laws and grants as they affected John Buchanan and other first settlers.

[29] W, 1s, 83. Arnow, *Seedtime*, 203–206, is an account of the settling, forts, homes, and early Indian troubles of the first settlers mentioned in this chapter.

[30] Daniel Smith (1748–1818) was active in Dunmore's War during the Point Pleasant Campaign, served in the Revolution, was a Justice of the Peace both in Virginia and in the Holston Country, mapped East Tennessee and much of Kentucky during the line survey of 1779–1780, published the first book on Tennessee, was represented in Carey's Atlas by his map of Tennessee; he would in time help write the Constitution of Tennessee, and serve in the U.S. Senate.

of Tennessee, also lived north of the Cumberland. He had during the hard winter of 1779–1780 been chief surveyor for Virginia in the extension of her southern boundary line from Steep Rock Creek of the Holston to the Mississippi. He had settled on Drake's Creek, and was now building a new home, stone. The first stone building in what was to be Tennessee, it still stands in its wide and rolling fields near the Cumberland. The Bledsoe brothers, Isaac and Anthony, who had with several others helped survey the line, had also settled. Isaac, not to be killed until 1793, now lived at his station near present day Castalian Springs, while Anthony, already shot from ambush, had built on Greenfield's Grant where his widow and family still lived.

Some of those who had fled in 1781 had returned to claim land. Chief among them, the Donelsons; the younger John and his wife Mary Purnell, for whom the trip down the Tennessee had been a bridal journey, were bringing up their family in a forted farm south of the Cumberland, but on the other side of Stone's River and several miles north and east of Buchanan's Station. John's mother, the widow, had settled north of the Cumberland, near the road from Nashville to Kaspar Mansker's Station. Her children, married well for the most part, were settling near by; daughter Jane had in 1786 married Colonel Robert Hayes, influential and wealthy ex-officer of the Revolution, who now lived not far away at Haysborough on lands he had been granted. Another Donelson son-in-law, pugnacious, slender, red-headed, and twenty-five years old, Andrew Jackson, was two years married to the youngest daughter Rachel, the former Mrs. Robards of Kentucky. He lived near his brother-in-law John Donelson, on the estate known as Hunter's Hill, some miles north of but in the general neighborhood of today's Hermitage. Less wealthy, less influential than most of his in-laws, Jackson was making money as a lawyer and land speculator, gaining a reputation as prosecuting attorney, and friendly with the right people. Among these, Judge John McNairy who had given him his first job, John Overton, and the Winchester brothers, James and George, ex-officers of the Revolution. George would soon be dead of Indians, but Cragfont, the great stone home James finished around 1803 on his plantation near Gallatin, is now owned by the State of Tennessee.

Major Tilman Dixon had already built his station east of Bledsoe's at Dixon Springs, where his substantial home of hewed logs is still standing, though enlarged with brick wings by later generations. Further east and with only the Cumberland between him and the Cherokee lands was the plantation of William Walton, opposite the mouth of the Caney Fork where Carthage would in time be. Near the western borders of settlement, or in the neighborhood of Clarksville, Valentine Sevier, brother of John, had a station with several others north of him on Red River. These were only a few of the better known settlers living in Mero District in 1792; in their world, so small when measured in numbers of settlers, each human being was important.

Nobody knows how any settler on the Cumberland spent the Sunday of September 30, 1792. Following the customs and laws of North Carolina, spinning wheels were stilled and plows stopped; ten years later a traveler observed the Tennesseans were not so religious as the Kentuckians, although "very strict observers of Sundays." [31] It all depends on what one considers religion. True, organized religion and professional religionists were less in evidence on the Cumberland during pioneer days than on any border studied. There was at this time, twelve years after settlement, only one permanently established minister in the whole region—this, the Reverend Thomas B. Craighead, of Nashville—and no building used exclusively as a place of worship.[32]

There was around any general-purpose farm such as that of John Buchanan with cows to milk, horses to feed, some work on any Sunday, and of course the usual cooking and other necessary housewifery. The chances are that no one sat in stiff churchly idleness observing the Sabbath; the children played, men and women read, wrote letters, cast up their accounts, and in general had a day of rest and amusement from their weekday work. Yet, we can be equally certain that no Sunday passed in any station without a good deal of Bible reading, hymn singing, children, each according to his age and ability, set a task of memorizing passages from the scriptures. The Buchanans,[33] like other first settlers studied, brought with them Bibles, books of sermons, hymnbooks, and various of the more popular theological works of the day. Religion was there, but it was not an institution separate from home life; few risked their scalps to go to church.

[31] André F. Michaux, *Travels to the Westward of the Allegany Mountains*, London, 1805, transl. of travels made in 1802 (cited hereafter as Michaux, *Travels* 1802), 304.

[32] Williams, *Travels*, Schweinitz, "Report," 510–517. This first hand account of organized religion in Middle Tennessee, made by two Moravian brethren after their stay of some weeks in the winter of 1799–1800, gives even at this late date no completed church building south of the river, and mentioned none north, though there appears to have been at least one log building in the Red River Country.

[33] DW, I, 69, 194, 166, are in order the inventories of John Buchanan, Sr., Jacob Castleman, and William Neely, all early killed by Indians, and all with Bibles and various religious works.

Scots with a background of covenanting ancestors, as were the Buchanans, had behind them a long history of religious controversy, and even on the Cumberland the controversy was not yet ended. Many Presbyterians would turn Baptist; others would decide upon the Methodist faith, while among the Presbyterians themselves there continued as in colonial days much dissension; the Reverend Craighead was in time accused [34] by one faction of general unorthodoxy and a leaning toward Pelagianism. Religion then was not taboo as a topic of conversation, and it is possible that on that Sunday there was some discussion or even a heated controversy on faith versus works or on the doctrine of original sin.

They may not have discussed religion, but they undoubtedly talked. Judging from their books and first newspapers, they, like the southern colonials behind them, were greatly interested in the wider world, events in Europe as well as America. The year 1792 was not an especially momentous one in history. There was, as always, war and unrest, poverty, and persecution in most of Europe. Britain was for the moment officially at peace, but the first stages of the Industrial Revolution and the grasping hands of the enclosure laws had already begun to undermine the home industries of cloth manufacturing, uproot the small farmer, and destroy village life. William Pitt was prime minister, and George III had recovered from his first attack of madness. Modern Germany had not yet come into being, but militaristic Prussia had managed to send an invading army within 140 miles of Paris, before it was stopped by France, already hard pressed and bloody from the first phases of her Revolution. The French Revolution, once cheered on by most Americans, was by now bringing doubt and disgust to many ordinary citizens, and in England frightening their rulers into repressive measures. Up at Mansker's Lick, Kaspar Mansker, who later hated the French because they had killed their king,[35] could not know the new French era of the old Revolution was eight days old or probably even that Louis XVI was in prison.

News, traveling slowly over even the more populous parts of the earth, was even slower and more uncertain in reaching the Cumberland Country. The one mail route into the west followed the old Hunter's Trail

[34] William Warren Sweet, *Religion on the American Frontier*, Vol. II, *The Presbyterians 1783–1840*, Copyright Harper and Brothers, New York, 1936 (cited hereafter as Sweet, *Religion, II*), 344–347, are the minutes of Craighead's trial in 1806.

[35] *Early Western Travels 1748–1846* ed. by Reuben Gold Thwaites, Cleveland, 1904 (cited hereafter as Thwaites, *Travels*), III, "André Michaux's Travels into Kentucky 1793–1796" (cited hereafter as Michaux, "Journal"), 94. This visiting Frenchman, father of André F., spent considerable time in Middle Tennessee.

from Ingle's Ferry across New River over the mountains through the Holston Country to Cumberland Gap; finished with this first 199 miles, there was still almost two hundred more before Danville was reached, all of it on horseback, for there was as yet no wagon road through Cumberland Gap. At Danville, mail for the Cumberland was brought every three weeks, that is, if the saddle bags were not lost at a ford, or the post-rider killed [36] on the Kentucky Trace with the mail turning up in a Chickamauga town as did that of Ross in 1793.

Someone may have quarreled about the lack of mail service and post roads, things promised by the Constitution—and it in force now for almost three years, or since reluctant North Carolina had at last ratified it on the second try. The United States, though still considered by many as a loosely held together collection of sovereign states and referred to by most travelers in the plural, was by 1792 a functioning, thriving nation, with the first census, not finished until the fall of 1791, listing close to four million inhabitants with only a partial listing of the slaves. The young country had accomplished much.

John Buchanan, pausing to open the fort gate as he came in from the barn, would have felt differently; the pickets in front of him were a reminder that the Federal government had done absolutely nothing for him or his neighbors. Worse, there were many in the more populous regions east of the mountains who not only were uninclined to build post roads for the Buchanans and their neighbors, but were also actively opposed to the acquisition of lands west of the Appalachians. This was an old story in New England and to a certain extent in Pennsylvania. The New Englander had never known the land hunger, the urge to move on to finer land so characteristic of the Southerner—not only the borderer, but the planter of Tidewater, wanting new lands for tobacco and corn and more land to bequeath to his children. A Revolution had increased the difference in outlook. New England, free now of British restrictions on trade and manufacturing, saw her future in mills and on the sea; George Rogers Clark had got no help from her in winning the Northwest Territory. She didn't want it.

Eyes, long used to measuring size in terms of the British Isles, saw even the original thirteen colonies as too big for their own good. Reverend Andrew Burnaby, after traveling only along the eastern seaboard from Virginia to Massachusetts, had doubted some years before the Revolution, "even supposing all the colonies of America to be united under one head,

[36] TP, IV, 263.

whether it would be possible to keep in due order and government so wide and extended an empire." [37] The Treaty of Paris in 1783 had found the United States with not only the settled portions of the thirteen colonies but also their back parts, a vast sweep of land extending northward to the wilderness of Lake Superior, south to Spanish Florida, and west to the Mississippi River. Too big. There is no record of how many agreed with Benjamin Franklin who at about this time declared that England had given the United States so much "waste land" on purpose so as to bring about her downfall. He advocated the selling off of a few states, one at a time.[38]

Most remote of the "waste lands" were the Cumberland settlements, an island almost two hundred miles from either central Kentucky or East Tennessee, and connected to these only by roads little better than bridle paths cut by the inhabitants themselves. The easiest, safest, cheapest route for farm produce to market was the Cumberland, but as long as Spain controlled the lower Mississippi, and John Jay "knuckled under" to her, this route was at best uncertain and for much of the time shut off completely. Most any talk in 1792 at Buchanan's and elsewhere on the Cumberland that began with crops and farming would like a great many other conversations have gone into national politics. Here, different from discussion of religion, there was little controversy. The Cumberlanders had, to begin with, voted overwhelmingly against the Constitution; as time passed national policies had for them gone from bad to worse, and there was quite general distaste for most measures and policies of the Federal government, particularly those pertaining to navigation of the Mississippi, import duties, the whiskey tax, and above all what appeared to be a "peace at any price" attitude toward the Indians.

Such steps as had been taken in most of these matters had been to the disadvantage of the settlers on Franklin's "waste lands." Picketed walls were still a prime necessity of life in spite of Indian treaties and much paper work on the part of various units of government. More than twelve years ago when John Buchanan and others had come to the Cumberland Country, the outcome of the Revolution was still in doubt, but certainty of any kind had never been a requisite of pioneering. None

[37] Reverend Andrew Burnaby, A. M., *Travels Through the Middle Settlements in North-America. In the Years 1759 and 1760*, New York, 1904, ed., reprinted from 3rd Ed., London, 1798 (cited hereafter as Burnaby, *Travels*), 102.

[38] Mathew Carey, ed., *The American Museum containing essays on agriculture—commerce—manufactures—politics—morals—and manners*, Philadelphia, Jan. 1787—Dec. 1792 (cited hereafter as Carey, *Museum*), I, 10–11.

was even certain, until the line was run, of what colony he would be a part. The boundary line surveyed, all settlers south of it automatically became a part of Washington County, North Carolina, that at its creation in 1777 had embraced all of what is now the State of Tennessee, though the Indians had legally owned much of this. The county seat was at Jonesboro, far up in the northeast corner, more than 250 miles from the Cumberland settlements, with no road, save Indian trails between. It was almost four years before the Cumberlanders had a county of their own, Davidson, with the seat of government at Nashville. Another, Sumner, had been organized before the region was given a superior court, presided over by Judge John McNairy, who brought with him a prosecutor of his own choosing, Andrew Jackson. The area served by the superior court was officially named Mero District, in honor of Estevan Miro, Spanish commandant of New Orleans. And a third county, Tennessee, was organized west of Sumner. However, most emigrants went to booming Kentucky or stopped in the Holston Country, now with close to thirty thousand inhabitants,[39] and spreading south and west with young Knoxville already a more noted place than the older Jonesboro.

North Carolina, bankrupt, and now that her soldiers were paid in land, receiving nothing but trouble from her territory on the other side of the mountains, ceded it in late 1789 to the Federal government. Not all the lawmakers were pleased with the gift, but it was accepted in April, 1790,[40] and organized into the Territory of the United States South of the River Ohio, or more commonly the Southwest Territory. William Blount,[41] scion of a blue-blooded, wealthy family with a long history of service in North Carolina, was appointed governor; Daniel Smith, secretary; and James Robertson, brigadier general of Mero District. John Sevier became brigadier general of Washington District, which until 1793 embraced all of what is now East Tennessee. Lesser appointments went

---

[39] TP, IV, 81, lists as of Sept. 19, 1791, the population of the four counties and the region "South of French Broad" that comprised Washington District as 28,649.

[40] *Ibid.*, IV, 3–8, "Act of Cession" as ratified by N.C. Assembly; *ibid.*, 9–13, Deed of Cession by N.C., Feb. 25, 1790; acceptance by Congress and President Washington, *ibid.*, 13–17.

[41] William Blount (1749–1800), not to be confused with his half-brother Willie, Governor of Tennessee, 1809–1815, had before this appointment served in the Revolution, four times in the State Legislature of North Carolina, in the Continental Congress, the Federal Convention, and the Constitutional Convention of North Carolina. He had also been interested in western land speculation. His correspondence during this period is contained in *The Blount Journal*, 1790–1796, ed. Tennessee Historical Commission, Nashville, 1955. See also William Henry Masterson, *William Blount*, Louisiana State University Press, Baton Rouge, 1954.

to lesser men; Andrew Jackson, for example, had in this September of 1792 been appointed judge advocate [42] to the Davidson County militia, the young man's first appointment that even hinted at the military life.

In spite of a good deal of correspondence, there was no improvement. The long lists of names, ninety-seven from the Cumberland Settlements alone between January, 1791, and October, 1792, forwarded by Governor Blount to the powers in Philadelphia,[43] seemed words on paper only to the Secretary of War, General Henry Knox, or even to the Secretary of State, Thomas Jefferson. Back on the Cumberland each name on the lists meant a man, woman, or child killed, maimed, burned alive, shot, scalped, or captured by the Indians.

The young country had to have peace and needed money. Such military resources as were available were kept in the Ohio woods as a protection for the Northwest Territory and Kentucky. In spite of all the letters Governor Blount wrote, he was never able to convince Federal officialdom that most of the settlers in the Southwestern Territory were not squatters lodged on Indian lands. True, mistreatment and cheating of Indians were old stories, but after the Treaty of Nashville in November of 1783, no Indian had the "color of claim" [44] to any land then occupied by the settlers of Middle Tennessee.

Governor Blount, caught between the determination of the Federal government for peace and the almost daily Indian raids on settlers, did little. Mostly he used a few friendly half-breed traders to the Creeks and Cherokees as spies. During the summer of 1792 the news sent in by John Boggs and The Breath from the lower Cherokee towns grew worse and worse. Blount heard at last from various sources that warriors from five of the lower Cherokee towns plus one hundred Creeks, the total amounting to six hundred warriors, had declared war on the United States and would most probably strike the Cumberland settlements.[45] The following day, September 11, Blount sent an express to Robertson commanding him to order out the militia.[46]

[42] TP, IV, 451.

[43] ASP, *Indian Affairs*, I, 329–331, 435, 453.

[44] TP, IV, 208–216, 226–234; Blount to the Secretary of War, Nov. 8, 1792; Jan. 14, 1793. Blount here goes into the history of the original claims and treaties of the various tribes; the Cherokee, according to Blount, never had legal right, but sold their "claim" to Henderson in 1775; there was not a Creek settlement within 200 miles.

[45] *Ibid.*, IV, 179–181. As early as Sept. 4th, Blount had heard that John Watts had returned from Pensacola (in Spain's Florida) with seven horse-loads of ammunition, guns and swords.

[46] *Ibid.*, IV, 182.

The order to Robertson to call out the militia was scarcely on the way before another express reached Blount with letters from The Glass and the Bloody Fellow, chiefs in the lower towns. There would be no war, they assured him; their braves were only going "peaceably to their Hunting." [47] Blount then on September 14th rushed another express to Robertson, ordering him to disband the militia. He believed none of the disquieting news that continued to pour in, not even when his own spies sent word that on the 15th and 17th of the month large bodies of well armed warriors had crossed to the northern bank of the Tennessee.[48]

Meanwhile, Robertson, his men encamped near Buchanan's, had received Blount's orders to disband the militia. He hesitated. His own spies, Richard Findelstone and John Deraque, had already warned him the chiefs were lying to Blount,[49] and that they and their warriors were now on the way. Robertson continued to keep his troops in and around Buchanan's twelve days after the warriors had reportedly crossed the Tennessee, twice the time needed to reach any spot in the Cumberland settlements. Advance guards sent out several miles south to search the woods had found no signs of Indians. Meantime, Blount's orders to disband the militia were growing old, and the militia men, taken from farm work, not to mention families who might need their protection, were restless. Robertson disbanded the men, Friday, the 29th,[50] and all went home, leaving at Buchanan's only the nineteen gunmen who ordinarily lived there.

Thus, there must have been a feeling of relief on that Sunday, growing by the hour as no warning word came, for Buchanan had the day before sent two scouts, Jonathan Gee and Clayton Powell, into the woods to look over the country. They had not returned, and their orders were that if they found no alarming signs, they were not to come in until Sunday evening.

Danger was so little expected that a number of the men permanently stationed at Buchanan's spent most of the day in Nashville. Jemmy O'Connor [51] went with them. The ways of the woods and of the Indians were new to him, and he seems not to have been long in the United States. In reading the stories of the old ones, one is struck by the many family relationships; early settlers had migrated in groups of kin and

[47] *Ibid.,* IV, 183.
[48] *Ibid.,* IV, 181, 183, 196.
[49] *Ibid.,* IV, 196.
[50] Sensing, "Buchanan's."
[51] W, 32S, 360.

in-laws; the intermarriages among the Ramseys, Eatons, Bledsoes, Mont-gomerys, and Shelbys made such a seeming newcomer as Hugh F. Bell, married to one of the Montgomery girls as was Isaac Bledsoe, kin and in-law at once of a large percentage of the population. James Robertson had not only his immediate family, but a brother Elijah and a sister Ann, also with families,[52] and in addition relatives of his wife Charlotte Reeves. Still others such as James Winchester, Robert Hays, and William Blount had served together in the Revolution. Colonel Ridley, for example, coming in 1790 from East Tennessee, would have known, at least by hearsay, most of the heads of families. Even young single men such as Joseph Bishop, who came out as a guard, knew somebody, in his case the Douglasses, before settling. Many, if not most of the settlers on the Cumberland, had the same general background, English and Scotch, Scotch–Irish, often a mixture, and usually with a family history of life in America for a generation or so.

Thus, a complete stranger in the small—when measured in terms of settlers—world of the Cumberland was a rarity. Yet, our hero Jemmy O'Connor was just such a one. He was, to begin with, Irish, his speech so unusual that many commented [53] upon it. True, travelers in the Revolutionary South now and then mentioned Irish, and, earlier, Virginia muster rolls gave Ireland as the homeland of several soldiers, but almost always the name given was Scotch. Many like the ancestors of James Robertson and Andrew Jackson had come from Ireland, but northern Ireland—Ulster, home of the Scotch–Irish, the most common nationality strain on the border.

Jemmy was not only strange to the people around him in background and speech, but like any newcomer from Ireland or Great Britain, he found most things about him, from fort pickets to water from a spring, strange. He could scarcely conceive of a country so vast that a river big as the Cumberland, different from rivers of the same bigness in his homeland, was untouched by tides from the sea. Horses he had of course seen, but never such a multitude, more horses than people, and it is doubtful if back home he had ever owned or even ridden one. Stranger still was the multitude of trees; Ireland seems never to have been so treeless as Scotland, but even so, trees were so scarce nobody thought of using wood for cooking and heating fires. Jemmy by now knew better

---

[52] James Robertson also brought with him his brothers Mark and John; both were killed; John when only a young boy.

[53] W, 32S, 360.

than any writer that "it is not easy for those who seldom saw a tree, to conceive how it is to be felled, cut up, and split into rails and posts." The ax like most of the other tools, save the spade, in common use about him—froe, maul, drawing knife, big hilling hoe,[54] foot adze—was strange to Jemmy.

In and out among the trees and all around were animals he had never known, particularly snakes and wolves that still lived within hearing of Buchanan's as did wildcats, screech owls, and a host of other birds, especially the red-billed, green-bodied parakeets, or "Cumberland parrots," that all through the summer flocked in the woods where they made an "unusual racket" in the higher trees.[55]

The names of numerous things new to him—rattlesnake, buckeye, mast, persimmon, 'possum, succotash, corn bread, fence rail, tobacco stick, ash hopper—were only the beginnings of his learning. The swing of the seasons would bring still more—Indian summer, tobacco stripping, corn gathering, flatboat, Natchez, New Orleans, cotton market, pirogue—but confusing as was the new vocabulary, it was nothing compared to the confusion of this Indian-infested part of the New World.

Jemmy may not yet have seen an Indian, but he had certainly heard of them. Most of the men then living at Buchanan's had for a good many years been fighting Indians when the need arose. Some like Sampson Williams, now sheriff of Davidson County, had come as first settlers, and even then, as borderers, Indians had not been new to them. At least one of the Buchanan guards, Clayton Powell, gone on this Sunday as a scout, had known a childhood, not uncommon on the Cumberland, as an Indian captive.[56]

Most names of people and places—Mrs. Caffery [57] and child now held captive, or the Sevier boys,[58] killed down on the Cumberland near the mouth of Red River—would only have added to Jemmy's confusion. He probably had nothing more than an idea of vastness, filled with everything but people. What was to be Middle Tennessee was a big place, with only

---

[54] Varieties of hoes were in common use all over Europe, but Toulmin, *Western Country*, 77, warned prospective English settlers to bring neither hoes nor axes as the "proper sort" was not made there.

[55] Williams, *Travels*, Schweinitz, "Report," 505. Schweinitz was only one of many travelers to describe these now-vanished birds.

[56] Sensing, "Buchanan's."

[57] ASP, *Indian Affairs*, I, 330; here spelled Cuffey, but seemingly Mrs. Cafery referred to by Blount, Jan. 9, 1794, TP, IV, 323. See also W, 32S, 363–364—Caffrey; more commonly Caffery, today.

[58] W, 32S, 208. This account, as do most others, states there were two, but ASP, *Indian Affairs*, I, 229, lists three.

twelve hundred men over sixteen years of age to hold its more than two hundred miles [59] of border against the Indians. Settlement stretched from present day Carthage on down past Clarksville to form a narrow sickle-shaped area of more than a thousand square miles, with most of the stations within a dozen miles, often less on the southern side, of the Cumberland. The Barrens—another word for Jemmy to learn—surrounded it on the north; in other directions stretched hilly forested land, cut by creeks bordered by canebrakes—another word for Jemmy. Most of even the settled portions was still forest land, canebrakes, and rocky cedar glade, much of the growth extensive and thick enough to hide a large war party even in winter. The river itself was a highway not only for the white settler but for the Indian as well. The friendly Chickasaw came often in hollowed-log canoes; back in the early spring the now-dead Sevier boys had mistaken a boatload of enemies for friends.

Jemmy doubtless listened bug-eyed to all the stories, though confused at times in place and person, but more than anything he would have marveled at the wondrous ways with guns of the men around him. He seemingly not only did not own a gun, but had never fired one, at least he was unfamiliar with the sound and feel of a firing blunderbuss.

Nashville, insignificant as it was as a town, still had at this early date several taverns, all, of course, open on Sunday. Any tavern keeper in getting a permit for an "Ordinary" had only to promise county court that he would not on the "Sabbath Day suffer any Person to Tipple or drink any more than is necessary." [60] Jemmy has come down in history as one who was "fond of a dram," [61] and some say he tippled more than was necessary, showing the effects of liquor when he came home to Buchanan's Sunday evening. If so, we cannot blame him for turning in his loneliness to, if not an old friend, at least an acquaintance. True, the whiskey then on the Cumberland, made usually in the early days of nothing but corn, was far different from the usquebaugh Jemmy had known in Ireland, there made chiefly of malted small grains; but all whiskeys are kin, and to Jemmy, even raw corn whiskey, single-distilled, would have seemed familiar in all the strangeness.

It may have been late with the moon rising, dew fallen, whip-poor-wills calling, and babies gone to sleep before Jemmy got back to Buchanan's.

[59] Blount, TP, IV, 231, used this figure when attempting to describe the place to the Secretary of War.

[60] A, V, 211.

[61] W, 32S, 360.

There was no hurry; there were still no returned scouts bringing word of Indians, and hence no immediate danger. John Buchanan may have been somewhat worried; he had told the men to come back on Sunday evening and they had not. On the other hand former Indian captives, as was Clayton Powell, made the most skilled scouts and woodsmen of all. Most men killed in the Cumberland settlements had been neither looking for nor fighting Indians, but working in their fields, traveling, surveying, or sitting at home as was John's father. Some say that Sally and John Buchanan sat up until near midnight watching and waiting for the return of the scouts; others make no mention at all of uneasiness on the part of anyone. Certainly, nobody worried much, for they all went to bed and slept soundly with, different from many of the stations, no guards.

Some slept more soundly than others, and continued to sleep when the cows stampeded home from the canebrake amid a jangling uproar of bells and bawls, for cows of all creatures save humans and a few birds love the sound of their voices when troubled, but not yet in pain. Hugh McRory, a seasoned Indian fighter, heard. He, from long experience, knew cows. Only one thing would make them run so. Indians. Such was the borderer's ability to spring from sound sleep to sudden battle, that by the time McRory had finished what must have been a shout like the trump of Armageddon, grabbing gun, bullets, powder horn, leaping out the cabin and to a blockhouse, men were rushing across the fort yard with him.

There never was such a battle in all the bloody annals of Tennessee. Right behind the cows, loped a screaming, howling flood of painted Indian warriors, no mob, but a determined, organized army of around four hundred of the flower of the Creek and the Chickamauga, led by the wiliest chiefs who ever lived—John Walker, George Fields, along with the Owl's son, White Man Killer, and John Watts, the Bloody Fellow who had less than three weeks before assured Governor Blount the Cherokee were not going to war. Remembered on the marker was another half-breed, Kai Iachchatalee, of Running Water Town on the Tennessee.

They had come to take the fort or die, and enough there were to encircle it with a ring of close fire, not ten feet from the walls. Each white man fought as he would have fought charging buffalo; powder dumped in unmeasured, handful of balls poured down her muzzle, prick her touchhole, prime heavily, and fire away. No time and no need at such close range for such niceties as patching and cleaning gun barrels. The bullets, no matter how wildly scattering, would find human flesh in the close-packed ring. The seventeen men were thinly scattered with most divided among the four blockhouses. Possibly no more than one man to hold each picketed wall, and from between the pickets bullets came singing and pinging, many against the walls of the cabins.

Here, the women could only put children under the beds, stay out of the way of doors and windows, and try to shut their minds to the uproar of yelling men and roaring guns while they went about their work of hushing babies, comforting frightened young children, and running bullets. They no doubt made many little throaty cries of, "Oh Lord, God save us, Lord ha mercy, Good God," and such like common to the people in time of stress. One distraught young mother, not fully awake one suspects, half crazed with fear, a newcomer she must have been, unfamiliar with green scalps and the ways of Indians, grabbed her baby, caught the toddler by the hand, and ran, carrying and dragging children toward the fort gate. She was determined, it was later said, to save the lives of her children by surrendering to the Indians, forgetting in her terror that to open the fort gate by so much as a crack would be the end of them all. She never got to the fort gate. Sally Buchanan ran out and brought her back, assuring the foolish one that four hundred Indians—though to the women it doubtless seemed that many thousand—could never take Buchanan's Station held by seventeen men.

The young mother got back to the cabins and Sally followed; pressing matters awaited her there. Crawled under a bed with the babies was a two-legged creature that had until now passed itself off as a man; it was this being whom the unkinder of the women called Jenny Glisten. Sally didn't call names, but she did get it to a porthole.

Prodigious tales, no two exactly the same in minor matters, were told of the siege of Buchanan's Station—the most Indians, the finest chiefs, the bravest warriors all come to one station at one time. There were the usual whoops, curses, roars of guns, bellowings of wounded cows, screams of horses, yells of the four hundred warriors, chiefs announcing their names, boasting, though little of what they said could be heard in the guns' roar, continuous, for led on by the seven chiefs, no warrior took cover.

John Buchanan after twelve years of the business was no man to let his ammunition run out. Most settlers kept in addition to a goodly store of bullets, several extra pounds of lead, but this battle like any defensive action in which heavily loaded smoothbore guns were used, took an enormous amount of both powder and ball. Men began to run low on bullets. They never ran out. It was then that Sally Buchanan "came amidst the raking fire of bullets singing through the picketing," a bottle of whiskey in one hand, bullets in her tucked-up apron. A handful of bullets, a drink of whiskey, and so she went her rounds, not once but many times. The tide would not turn. John Watts was carried away, a bullet through his thigh, but each time the warriors fell back, other chiefs would shame them into bravery.

We suspect Sally lingered an instant longer in one blockhouse than the others, that manned by her husband Major John, a hard-pressed spot filled with smoke, taste of burning sulphur, and such prodigious noise a woman, had she tried, could not have heard herself speak. It was, like the other three, held by only two or three men; Major John and another on the ground by the lower portholes, and a man on the ladder above; a hot corner, Indians pressing from two sides, outnumbering the defenders better than twenty to one.

All who spoke of the battle remembered Sally's courage, but even she, racing through the warm moonlight, may have shivered with fear as she slung sweat from her eyes. Major John's blockhouse was weaker than the others. The men who fought that night were a seasoned crew—save one. Major John had with him, trying to take the place of an Indian fighting man, that Jemmy O'Connor, fresh out of Ireland and with no more knowledge of guns than grubbing hoes. A gay child, but not an Indian fighter; he couldn't have killed a deer with a rifle at twenty paces; he couldn't have loaded a rifle so she wouldn't shoot wild. Still, all useless as he was, he had run out with the men, and got the loan of the major's old blunderbuss, but neither powder horn nor bullet pouch. No spot was safe, but Major John, taking pity, had put him on a ladder above the heads of the Indians where no straight-flying bullet could come his way.

Not an important place; each time he fired he had to run down the ladder to get powder and ball; he didn't even know the pioneer's trick of storing bullets in his mouth. Major Buchanan half scolded him once, declared he wasn't shooting his gun, that she only flashed fire. Nobody knew or could be certain, and certainly not Jemmy, unused to the sounds of guns in battle, and in all the roar of men and musketry he didn't know his own. There is the question, too, if the little sleep he had had was enough to defog his brain from Sunday's tippling.

Groggy or no, he stood on the ladder, pulled the trigger of the heavy blunderbuss, watched the blue flash from the firing pan, and doubtless from his high position yelled as loudly as the others. The yell and the drink of whiskey he got each time Mrs. Buchanan came by were good to put heart in a man. More and more from where he stood it was plain a man needed heart. The yells of the Indians as they pressed closer grew ever more triumphant; chunks of fire came flying over the walls; then Kia Iachchatalee ran forward, his hands filled with flaming brands to press against the pickets; a bullet found him, but he died giving his last breath to bring a flame from the smouldering logs.

Then, from an upper porthole of Major Buchanan's blockhouse there leaped out and down, a death-dealing sheet of flame and bullets, cannon-like and devastating. The blood-hungry scalp cries of a moment before changed into howls of fear and pain. The ring of faces by the walls swiftly became backs, receding, leaving wounded and dead.

Jemmy saw none of this, felt nothing, heard nothing; the overloaded blunderbuss, crammed almost full of bullets and powder from his loadings, had, when she did go off, knocked him from the ladder. He could only lie on the blockhouse floor, all breath and knowing knocked from him.

The tide had turned. The battle continued intermittently till daylight, but all heart was gone from the Indians. Mostly, they risked the defenders' fire to collect their dead and wounded. Monday morning came. The men of Buchanan's went cautiously out to find their world empty of Indians; they did find around the walls much blood along with Spanish swords, some richly mounted, and the usual hatchets, pipes, kettles, and "budgets of various Indian articles" carried by an army planning to stay. They found also a handkerchief known to have been worn by Jonathan Gee; neither he nor Clayton Powell was ever seen again, and it was not until years later that white men learned the manner of their entrapment and deaths.

No man at Buchanan's was scratched save Jemmy O'Connor. His wounds were bruises, some got from the fall, the worst from the gun-kick to his shoulder, for he couldn't use his arm for weeks. It was a great victory, but those who remembered it close to fifty years later gave most credit to Jemmy O'Connor, the old ones declaring that he, "blundering with his blunderbuss," had saved the day. All remembered, too, how Kia Iachchatalee had fanned the fire with his "dying breath," and how Sally Buchanan had carried bullets and whiskey.[62]

[62] The official report, ASP, *Indian Affairs*, I, 294, mentions neither Mrs. Buchanan nor Jemmy O'Connor; gives 15 gunmen and 3 to 400 indians; discovered by McRory. Daniel Smith, W, 4, 14, gave the number of Indians as 300. See also the account of Robert Weakley, then living on the Cumberland, *ibid.*, 32S, 358–361, and that in Ramsey, *Tennessee*, 566–567. Featherstonhaugh, *Excursion*, I, 206–208, gave the number of Indians as 900. The numerous other accounts such as W, 30S, 526–527, disagree in some matters, but tell basically the same story.

There was on that Monday morning rejoicing in all of Middle Tennessee, particularly on the part of those in Nashville who had spent the last half of the night in uneasy listenings to the uproar.[63] Had Buchanan's fallen, the victorious army would have destroyed everything south of the Cumberland, and maybe crossed over. One can only wonder what then would have been the fate of Middle Tennessee.

Even after the victory at Buchanan's nobody could be certain. Early morning found General Robertson in the saddle again, re-collecting his militia, sending out a reconnoitering party, and preparing to encamp again[64] on the Indian Trail south of Buchanan's. There was always the danger a defeated war party might strike again, or break up into small groups and steal horses or waylay travelers. Most of the surviving besiegers appear to have gone straight home. They had had enough. A few small parties remained; one band of seven fired upon a member of the scouting party, Hugh McRory,[65] but as at Buchanan's, he escaped unharmed.

The siege of Buchanan's was the last great Indian battle in Middle Tennessee, but for three more years lists of Cumberlanders, dead, wounded, or captured, continued to turn up in Philadelphia. Nobody there paid much attention, and even on the Cumberland life went on, not fragmentized and shaped much by any institution save one, the home with at least sleeping quarters behind picketed walls.

[63] W, 30S, 529.
[64] TP, IV, 196. Robertson was by October 3rd encamped with 300 men, four miles from Buchanan's.
[65] *Ibid.*

Chapter Two

The

Underpinning

SALLY BUCHANAN'S first-born came eleven days after the Siege of Buchanan's, and it was followed through the years by eight brothers and four sisters.[1] The Buchanan family was larger than most, but there was nothing unusual about the mother's activities during an Indian battle. There are from all borders many stories of female courage. Reverend Joseph Doddridge, remembering the preparations for an Indian attack on the western Virginia fort where he had lived as a boy, declared, "I do not know that I ever saw a merrier set of women in my life." [2] These women as they brought in a store of spring water, run bullets, and cut patching had shown no more fear than had Sally Buchanan.

The Cumberland settlements, never with any proper fort or paid soldiers,[3] knew Indian raids almost weekly for fifteen years, and there are

Headpiece: Traveling family preparing a meal over a campfire.

[1] Sensing, "Buchanan's."

[2] Kercheval, *Virginia*, Doddridge, "Notes," 232.

[3] Fort Blount on the northern side of the Cumberland across from the mouth of

thus a great many stories of brave women. Mrs. Bell loaded for her husband with the "shot pouch on her neck and two or three bullets in her mouth," [4] and dozens of women at one time or another "run a hundred bullets," as did Mrs. Hickman.[5]

The border moving south and west multiplied the stories. One of the most vivid memories of Admiral Farragut, not born until 1801, was that of his mother slamming the door, but unable to close it because the Indian on the other side had shoved the barrel of his rifle through, and so "she held a parley," with him at the door.[6] The Farragut home, even at that late date, though only a dozen miles or so south of Knoxville, was still close to Indian territory.

Dramatic as these acts were, they were only a small part in the long struggle of most women on the frontier to deal with all the complexities of life on a forted farm and at the same time bring up children as educated, civilized human beings. Around two-thirds of the wives of the original settlers were widowed before the ending of the Indian Wars in Middle Tennessee in 1795. Numerous others, settling later—Mesdames Anthony and Isaac Bledsoe, Edwin Hickman, Jacob Castleman, John Donelson, Sr., Henry Rutherford, William Ramsey, to name only a few, were also widowed.[7] Few seem either to have remarried or to have returned to kin and parents in the safer East. Leah Lucas, widowed in 1781, was not exceptional in staying, going in time to her husband's land, bringing up five children [8] and educating them as well.

Her lot was easy compared to that of Mrs. Jane Brown, whose hus-

---

Flinn's Creek, near present day Gainsboro, and mentioned by later travelers was not at this time permanently established. A group of militia was sometimes kept on the site, known as Big Lick or Big Salt Lick. See TP, IV, 311-313, Gov. Blount to James Robertson, Dec. 6, 1793; and *ibid.*, 411-414, Gov. Blount to James White, Dec. 14, 1795; still no permanent forts for Mero District.

[4] W, 30S, 255–256.

[5] *Ibid.*, 30S, 460.

[6] *Ibid.*, 6XX(60), 2.

[7] There is no complete list of all killed on the Cumberland; NCR, XXIV, 629-630, lists the first settlers men only killed up to early 1784. ASP, *Indian Affairs*, I, 329-331, 436, 453, 455, 456, 457, 458, lists most of those, including children, killed, wounded, or captured after Jan. 1, 1791. There are no lists from early 1784-1791; the Draper correspondents, letters in NCR, and now and then a chance remark in the county records yield many names; the inventories are there, but these do not usually mention the manner of death. Nor are the lists complete; NCR, for example, mentions none of the Renfroes.

[8] DW, II, 63-65. Widowed shortly after settling on the Cumberland, Leah Lucas was around fifteen years later sued by a grown son, because she had not as the law required given the court—the closest, Jonesborough 200 miles away—an inventory of her husband's property. The above is her letter of explanation with list of expenditures including those for education.

band, Colonel James Brown, as a soldier of the North Carolina line received a boundary of land on the Cumberland. In 1788 the Browns started down the Tennessee—the Colonel, Mrs. Brown, five sons, four daughters, and three sons-in-law. The Indians attacked and killed all except Mrs. Brown and the two younger sons and three daughters. Captured,[9] all were separated, and the widow lived for some months not knowing what members of her family had survived. Freed at last through the intercession of Alexander McGillivray, Jane Brown with three of her children—one had died—continued on to the family land on the Cumberland, where with the help of her son Joseph, survivor of around three years of Indian captivity, she made a home for her family, meanwhile writing letters to McGillivray, petitioning Governor Blount, questioning traders in regard to the whereabouts and possible release of one still-captive son.

The woman of the old Southwest had to learn to manage without a man, for even when the head of the house was alive he was often gone from home. James Robertson, for example, must have spent at least half of the first thirty years of his married life away from home on the many long trips made in connection with business and politics. Daniel Smith and the Bledsoes, like the rest of the party who in 1779–1780 surveyed the North Carolina–Virginia line, were gone from their families more than a year.[10]

Even a flatboat trip to New Orleans such as General James Winchester [11] made in 1789 with several of his neighbors could mean a six months' separation. Mrs. Thimote De Monbruen, living in Nashville during the siege of Buchanan's, had been much alone for her husband as hunter-trader had made, beginning in the early sixties, many long and dangerous trips from their home in the Illinois into the Cumberland Country. Still, she appears to have traveled with him more than most wives. She may have wished she could go with him when in early October of 1792 while the Cumberland Country was still filled with Indian alarms and talk of the doings at Buchanan's, he set off for Philadelphia, taking the most dangerous route of all, that by way of Knoxville.[12] There is nothing to indi-

---

[9] Ramsey, *Tennessee*, 516–517, 608–611. See also, TP, IV, 181, 222, and for one of her letters, John Walton Caughey, *McGillivray of the Creeks*, University of Oklahoma Press, 1938, 325.

[10] Lewis P. Summers, *History of Southwest Virginia*, Richmond, 1903 (cited hereafter as Summers, *Southwest Virginia*), 699–702, is Daniel Smith's brief account of the year's work; for a more detailed account of his activities see his "Journal," THM, I, 40–65.

[11] W, 3XX(18), 6.

[12] TP, IV, 197. Captain De Monbruen carried Blount's letter with its news of the attack on Buchanan's to General Knox.

cate she went. Most merchants in the old West had to make yearly business trips to Baltimore and Philadelphia,[13] and sometimes New Orleans. Gone they might be for months. Somebody had to stay home and run things, and usually this meant the wife.

Worse than business as a husband–thief, at least on the Cumberland, was politics. Home then was considered so important, the mistress of it, even when a Rachel Jackson with no children, did not leave it when the head of the house went to Philadelphia and stayed for months as a Congressman. At least there is no record that any of the wives of early U.S. Senators and Representatives—Daniel Smith, Andrew Jackson, John Sevier, or William Blount—went with their husbands. Matrimony was an institution sturdy enough to survive long separations, eased but little by such scanty correspondence as chance afforded.

Most in the old West took marriage on such a basis more or less for granted. They had behind them the traditions of British matrimony. The cursing, hungry wives of the seventeenth century sailors, hurling oaths at their betters, including Samuel Pepys, and weeping for their men, unpaid but forced into the service, knew that if alive, sooner or later their men would come home. Likewise, the sailor husband knew, hungry his wife and the children might go, but somehow, some way she'd hold the home together.

Generations later the Virginia or North Carolina borderer might roam a year or more, but if sooner or later he didn't come back, his wife could be certain he was dead, for always he did come back to the quarrelsome, scraggeldy-headed wife and the log house clamorous with children. All this was in sharp contrast to the French; the authorities of colonial Canada were often sorely troubled by the young Frenchmen who took to the life of *coureurs-de-bois*, leaving French wives and babies behind or young mothers unwed. Many were the laws passed and the threats, but nobody could make of the *coureur-de-bois* a good family man as was Kaspar Mansker,[14] one of the most widely ranging of Long Hunters.

Mrs. Mansker's life while Kaspar was gone hunting or scouting differed in degree though not in kind from that of thousands of other wives of the old South. There were no rules, but as a usual thing the more affluent the family the more time did the husband have to spend away

---

[13] Toulmin, *Western Country*, 125, found Lexington firms making two trips yearly to Philadelphia, but as they were usually partnerships each man went only once.

[14] William Martin, W, 3XX(40), 1, gave an account of Mansker, his wife, and home.

from home on business and politics. Life on even the larger plantations had demanded wives and mothers able to oversee if necessary the overseer, and at the same time manage the home, and bring civilization to the wilderness. Such wives hired and fired, built houses, bred the mares, distilled, reaped and planted, took care of the slaves with no one by to make the decisions.

The Southern wife, even those of Tidewater, had had a particularly hard time during the Revolution that in the Carolinas and Georgia partook of the nature of a domestic war, with husband taking one side and brothers and fathers the other.[15] Whatever happened and regardless of her politics, if any, it was the woman's job to keep her soldiering husband fed, clothed, sometimes horsed, and meanwhile hold the home together. Nancy Hart, of War Woman's Creek in Georgia who ordered the "Damned Tory carcasses" of the King's men she had captured hanged, and described as a "honey of a patriot but the devil of a wife," [16] was not unique. A band of soldiers in the Holston Country, having captured a Tory, took him to the home of Colonel Benjamin Cleveland to learn what disposition should be made of him. Colonel Cleveland was out, but Mrs. Cleveland, after asking the men what her husband would have done and learning he would have hanged the captive, ordered him hanged without "taking her pipe from her mouth." [17]

More typical of the revolutionary activities of Southern women was that of Mary Slocumb, a North Carolina planter's wife. Unable to sleep for thinking of her husband gone to war, she rose and saddled her mare; after a ride of forty miles lighted by moonlight and finally by dawn on "as fleet and easy a nag as ever traveled," she came at last to the battlefield where her husband had fought. She was just in the act of lifting a wounded man up to drink when up rode her husband, "as muddy as a ditcher and bloody as a butcher," to ask why she was "hugging the worst

---

[15] NCR reveals a good many domestic tragedies: *ibid.*, XVI, 514, 951, 955, 958, 963, 964–970, 968–969, are some of the many letters of Andrew Mclaine, prominent North Carolina Whig, to his son-in-law, George Hooper, Tory, fled to South Carolina; Hooper's wife, Kitty, remained with her family throughout the Revolution, but once it was ended her father felt "her mind should be easy it is necessary that she [Kitty] have you [her husband] with her." Mrs. McLean whose husband fought with the British, begs Gov. Alexander Martin, *ibid.*, XVI, 942–943, he be allowed to stay; *ibid.*, XXIV, 638,—the 1784 Bill of Divorcement granting Mary Dowd all property of her former husband, a Tory.

[16] Mrs. Elizabeth Fries (Lummies) Ellet, *Women of the American Revolution*, New York, 1840–1850 (cited hereafter as Ellet, *American Revolution*), II, 264–269.

[17] Lyman C. Draper, *King's Mountain and Its Heroes*, Madison, Wisconsin, 1881 (cited hereafter as Draper, *King's Mountain*), 448.

reprobate in the whole American army." It was a joke to make her laugh as she galloped home the next night, alone again, happy to know her husband was well, but worried now about the baby she had left with a servant woman.[18]

Mrs. William Moore [19] in 1780 rode from Washington County, Virginia, to Bickerstaff, North Carolina, to attend her wounded husband; Mrs. Duncan riding out to see if she could get "any intelligence of our army" and so help some soldiers [20] hidden in her home, had a shorter ride, but more dangerous one. Less dramatic but more dangerous still was the work of Andrew Jackson's mother during the Revolution. She, as did many women, took a long trip to get her captured sons—the older died—out of a Tory prison and home. This accomplished, she was off again to nurse more distant relatives, dying of "ship's fever" in the heat and flies of the prison ships, anchored off the South Carolina coast a hundred and forty miles away. Little is known of her trip—she may even have walked —save that she caught the disease and died.

Women among soldiers at war or in prison was an old story. Quite often the mistress of a well-to-do officer traveled with him by carriage and with servants, and many encampments in the Revolution found wives and sisters and daughters come to see about their men, bringing food, clothing, and news of home, with some wives sharing for a time camp life with their husbands. Many stories have been told of the wives of Marion's men, riding alone through the snake- and mosquito-infested swamps, carrying provisions and at the same time acting as spies and couriers.

The armies of the Southern states also had goodly numbers of what we today denominate "camp followers," a rather unfortunate term as all kinds of people followed an army, many men, often farmers temporarily turned sutlers, and selling whatever they happened to have— vegetables, meat, whiskey, or anything else a soldier might use and pay for. Respectable farm wives also brought all manner of things, from socks of their own knitting to butter, but many women suffering often from the raids of unruly soldiers on both sides, and their own men conscripted, sold services of various kinds to stave off starvation for themselves and children. Kept off the baggage wagons [21] and forced usually to walk, their lot was at times harder than that of the soldier. North Carolina had so

[18] Ellet, *American Revolution*, I, 347–377.
[19] Summers, *Southwest Virginia*, 341.
[20] Draper, *King's Mountain*, 515.
[21] NCR, XII, 462, 493.

many that in 1777 we find the command: ". . . every encumbrance Proves very prejudicial to the service, Especially those women who are pregnant or have children, are a clog upon every movement; the Commander-in-Chief therefore recommends it to the officers to use every Reasonable method in their power to get rid of all such as are not absolutely Necessary." [22]

A good many were necessary. They nursed the sick, cooked, washed, and mended, but the only pay, even for laundry, women following the Virginia line had was diet.[23] This was scanty as that of the Virginia soldiers who were by this date, 1780, not only so naked they could not be put into service, but hungry most of the time.[24] Many of these women who shared all the dangers and hardships of the men were undoubtedly, to use the word of the day, "whores," [25] but unpaid ones.

Today, looking back with eyes that have known Guinevere groveling at the feet of King Arthur and Kipling's "rag and a bone and a hank of hair," we are inclined to lump all camp-following females, whether food-carrying wife or hungry whore, as immoral, scarcely deserving the title of human being. The Southerner, like generations of British behind him and the borderers ahead, or any society with high regard for human rights, was much inclined to see a woman as another human being, differing in many respects from a man, but still an individual, members of the sex varying quite as widely among themselves as did members of the male sex.

There was thus no great debate on Woman's Place, for her place like everything else in life "all depended." Shortly after 1700 John Lawson, first historian of North Carolina, remarked that the girls of that colony

[22] *Ibid.*, XII, 480.

[23] VS, III, 231.

[24] NCR, XVI, Preface, iii. "—nothing can be more wretched and distressing than the condition of the troops, starving—without tents—. Those of the Virginia Line literally naked—300 without arms—"; General Nathanael Greene on the state of the Southern army in 1780 shortly after he had taken command.

[25] The word prostitute when used as a noun during pioneer days usually signified one who prostituted religion, belief, or honesty for popular favor or mercenary ends. Whore was in common use, even for children. The most common text in the teaching of spelling and other aspects of English was that by Thomas Dilworth, School Master, Wapping School. In his *A New Guide to the English Tongue in Five Parts*, 1740 (pagination, Boston ed., 1773), Part II, "Table of words same in sound but different in spelling," is "Hoar, a frost; whore, a lewd woman." See also "Mother Goose's Melody or Sonnets for the Cradle," London, 1791, a reprint, copyrighted by Jacques Barchilon and Henry Petit as a section of *The Authentic Mother Goose*, Denver, 1960, 64, whore is made to rime with door.

were "educated equally with their brothers" [26] and not bred up to the spinning wheel alone, but taught the management of the dairy and other matters.

Girls so bred were not noted for their meekness. Mrs. Lootons, of Baltimore County, Maryland, was not by 1692 the only woman to have waved her "arms abroad," meanwhile scolding and quarreling at "a parcel of strange Indians." [27] The women of Maryland seem to have been unusually obstreperous. In 1698 in one small neighborhood, "said Mason's wife took a drawn sword in her hand and swore she would be the death of them that touched her husband," and a neighbor, "Hanna Clark wished she had the Governor's heart's blood cold in her hand," and for Colonel Low, "she wished she had a spit to roast him." Faring still worse were the governor's men, who in trying to serve a warrant on John Wilson for the impressment of a horse, were met by his wife who "came with a case knife and swore she would cut his hand off if he did not loose the horse." They showed her "His Excellency's Warrant," but Mrs. Wilson merely remarked that the governor could "kiss her arse." [28]

The women of colonial Virginia were not much better. Anne Brown, for example, went into a 1751 court in Augusta County, Virginia, where she "abused William Wilson, gentleman, one of the justices for this county, by calling him a rogue, and that on his coming off the bench she would give it to him with the devil." [29] Sarah Harrison,[30] beautiful and wealthy lady of Tidewater, daughter of Benjamin Harrison, two times during her marriage ceremony said, "no obey"; on the third try the harassed Church of England clergyman married her with the "no obey." Other southern belles jilted their lovers, sometimes made them wait for years, ran away with the overseer, and some never married. Others were stubbornly faithful. Catherine Cole, of Augusta County, bore a bastard child; she was brought before the court, and on "refusing to pay her fine or give security for the same according to law" (this meant naming the father), the court ordered twenty lashes on her "bare back." [31]

[26] John Lawson, *The history of Carolina; containing an exact description of the inlets, havens, corn, fruits, and other vegetables of that country together with the present state thereof. And a journal of a thousand miles, traveled thro several Nations of Indians. Giving a particular account of their customs, manners, etc.*, London, 1709 (pagination, 1903 ed., Charlotte, N.C., cited hereafter as Lawson, *Carolina*), 47–48.

[27] M, VIII, 348.

[28] *Ibid.*, XXIII, 466.

[29] Waddell, *Annals*, 43.

[30] Mary Newton Stanard, *Colonial Virginia*, Philadelphia, 1917 (cited hereafter as Stanard, *Virginia*), 169–170.

[31] Waddell, *Annals*, 48.

Catherine Cole refusing to talk and Mrs. Wilson talking too much were by colonial days mere sprigs and blossoms of British culture older than the colonies, much of it unconsciously absorbed by children before they were weaned. Theirs was the heritage of all the females in *Mother Goose*. The old woman who took her ". . . calf by the tail, And threw it over the wall," was like the old woman who lived in a shoe, managing her household as she wished—self-reliant females entirely different from those of Grimm. *Mother Goose* women did all manner of things from going to market and falling asleep on the King's highway, through selling hot codlings, to climbing an apple tree and staying there till Saturday. Jenny jilted Robin; even a maid with only her face for a fortune could be quite pert, and the old woman of Surrey, forever in a hurry, called her husband a fool.

There was by the time the Cumberland was settled quite a body of English fiction, much of it found often in inventories of early settlers, that portrayed women as individuals, their roles as various and sometimes lustier than those of *Mother Goose*. Moll Flanders, "born in Newgate, twelve years a whore, five times a wife, twelve years a thief, eight years a transported felon," was still much more a human in her own right than any female of present day literary art in which women, when anything more than symbols of evil, are almost invariably shown as existing only in relation to men, and that relationship often a purely physical one.

The works of Tobias Smollett were owned by several early settlers on the Cumberland.[32] Dr. Smollett, more so than even most eighteenth century novelists, went furthest in portraying a woman as a human being, an individual, not only in relation to men, but also to the world around her. In *Roderick Random* he reformed a whore, in *Ferdinand Count Fathom* he had a hero born of a camp follower, and in most instances the wife was referred to as "the yoke fellow." His women held all kinds of jobs from keeping shop to managing a dairy by mail as did Tabitha Bramble. Smollett was concerned with social decay; but different from most modern writers also concerned with social decay, his writings are a portrayal, not in themselves a reflection, and are quite free of totalitarian attitudes toward women.

The Cumberland pioneers did not need fiction to learn of strong-minded women. Most on the Cumberland were descended from generations of Scotch and English women, unafraid to bring upon themselves the wrath of churchmen or kings. Scotch women long since dead signed the

[32] DW, I, 255, 268; *ibid*, II, 105–106.

covenants in defiance of the law as had their husbands, sons, and brothers. We do not know, but little John Buchanan, listening like other children in the chimney corner of winter evenings to stories of other days, may have heard much of the doings of the clan Buchanan, and how James Buchanan went down with the English prison ship near the Mulehead of Darness; [33] and he may have heard, too, the old tale of Scotch woman Margaret Wilson.

The good men under devout King Charles II during the "killing time" of 1685 did not want to stain their hands with woman's blood, and so when eighteen-year-old Margaret and an older woman refused to recant their Presbyterian faith, they "chained them to posts within the flood mark." There was time to think as the tide roared in. Margaret was so young the devout ones wanted to give her another chance. They cut her loose, half drowned as she was, revived her enough to question, but to their questions came only her unregenerate cry, "I am one of Christ's children," and so they tied her up again to wait for the next tide.[34]

Margaret Wilson was Presbyterian, a faith closely akin to that of the Puritans, and oddly enough it was the Puritan, liberal in some matters, who dealt most harshly with women. Colonies in America had ever in varying degrees reflected the religious, political, and social patterns—if upheavals can be called patterns—of Europe, particularly those of the British Isles.

One of the things the old South rejected was that facet of British culture, flowering to its fullest in New England, that saw woman as little more than "female for race." The Puritans had also found women particularly susceptible to witchcraft, for most any New England intellectual could prove through a quoting of the Bible the existence of witches. The less intellectual Southerner was less certain, and it was a Southerner, visiting Salem, who dared put human life above reason and intellect by helping his condemned wife escape from a Massachusetts jail. New England fathers, sons, and brothers of the condemned witches accepted the dictates of the judges and saw their womenfolk hanged.

The Puritan's outlook on life was somewhat like that of many of us

[33] Waddell, *Annals*, 5. This partial list of the men who went down with Buchanan of Argrennock has many names familiar on all southern borders—Wilson, Clark, Miller, Young, Campbell, Reid, Cameron, Anderson, Ramsey, Craig, Finley.

[34] Charles Augustus Hanna, *The Scotch-Irish, or the Scot in North Britain, North Ireland and North America*, New York, 1902 (cited hereafter as Hanna, *Scotch-Irish*), I, 461–462, gives one of the many versions of this story, differing in some points from that of Sir Walter Scott in *Tales of a Grandfather*, IV, 11 (Boston, 1861 ed.).

today in that it was based, not on human experience, but on an intellectual pattern demanding unquestioning belief in many matters. The pattern under which the Puritan lived was so all embracing it shaped much of his life from birth to death, with Blue Laws and churchly rule interfering with even his home life. Sin and any joy of living were almost synonymous, and the Puritan, like men of the Middle Ages, was inclined to see woman as forever the temptress in the Garden of Eden—Milton's picture of Eve.

Tidewater also had Blue Laws and in Virginia indentured servant girls who got pregnant might be sent to the whipping post. Still, from Tidewater came no multitude of stories such as that of the English sea captain, given thirty-nine lashes, because after a long separation he kissed his wife when greeting her on a Sunday in Boston harbor.[35] William Byrd, of Westover, a good Church and King man, observing the Sabbath even when in the backwoods, was critical of the New Englander whose wife, fallen sick on a Sunday, could get no help because her devout husband would not break the law by traveling. Byrd felt this was carrying religion too far.

Byrd, different from a New Englander, had no fear of a plain-speaking woman. Once in looking at a swift mountain stream, which the men of the party had named Matrimony Creek because of its noise, he compared it to women, "who make themselves plainest heard it was likewise clear and unsullied." [36] This was not a radical belief; years later in London the learned Dr. Samuel Johnson, another good Church and King man, would in one of his many discussions on women and matrimony declare that even a pretty woman should be able to add something to the conversation. In his *Lives of the Poets,* a work found in inventories on the Cumberland,[37] Johnson had deplored Milton's failure to educate his daughters and his attitude toward females in general.

The South in its attitudes was closer to Dr. Johnson than to Milton. William Byrd was not the only wealthy planter to give his daughters the advantages of English travel and such education, usually private, as the London of that day afforded. Years later, Thomas Jefferson in his many letters to his daughter abroad evinced the same concern, while Theodosia Burr, under her father's urging, continued her studies in Latin long

---

[35] Burnaby, *Travels,* 104–106.
[36] *The Writings of Colonel William Byrd, Esquire of Westover in Virginia,* ed. by John Spencer Bassett, New York, 1901 (cited hereafter as Byrd, *Writings*), 155.
[37] DW, I, 255; *ibid.,* II, 132.

after she was the wife of the governor of South Carolina. All this was much in keeping with the general thought of the day, particularly that of England where formal education for even men of the upper classes was not a how-to process, but the study of books that had for a thousand years formed "the intellectual character of England." [38] The average Southern gentleman did not "use" his education to earn his livelihood, so that the cry in the United States that women need no higher education because "they will never use it, but only marry" would have shocked any Southern colonial with pretensions to aristocracy.

The Quakers with their democratic ideals that embraced women as well as Negroes and Indians were another influence unknown in New England, but felt in varying degrees in the more tolerant South, especially North Carolina, where marriage laws made special provisions for the Quaker ceremony. Reverend Dr. Burnaby even commented of Philadelphia, where Quaker influence was strongest, that the women were "Much more agreeable and accomplished than the men." [39] This same pre-Revolutionary traveler, different from many, found the women of the South ". . . rather handsome, but on the whole not to be compared with our fair country women in England. They have but few advantages, and consequently are seldom accomplished; this makes them reserved and unequal to any interesting or refined conversation." [40] In contrast, the Philadelphia women were "exceedingly handsome and polite—naturally sprightly and fond of pleasure." New England women he apparently got to know little, for he found them appearing with "more stiffness and reserve" than in the other colonies.

Most travelers after the Revolution were even more critical of American females; Thomas Ashe, tourist of 1806, praised only the women of New Orleans and described Kentucky women as "florid beauties," lacking in grace and charm, too far from centers of culture to have any accomplishments, though he did find the "rude beauties" of Pittsburgh better educated than the men.[41]

There was for the American traveler of those days no escaping women; he stopped often in establishments supervised by landladies, and even when there was a landlord, the landlady was much in evidence. Women rode

---

[38] John Gibson Lockhart, *Peter's Letters to His Kinsfolk,* Edinburgh, 1819 (cited hereafter as Lockhart, *Letters*), 200.

[39] Burnaby, *Travels*, 97.

[40] *Ibid.*, 57–58.

[41] Thomas Ashe, *Travels in America performed in the year, 1806,* London, 1809 (cited hereafter as Ashe, *Travels*), 313, 171, 20.

out in their carriages, drove wagons, traveled in the public stage coaches of the day, and were met with in most parties of travelers. Still, woman's world in the United States would never be so wide as in old England. One has only to go a-wandering with Pepys in mid-seventeenth century England to feel the wideness of woman's world; he visited the "seller of ribands and gloves, a pretty wench," did much business with Mrs. Russell who dealt in ship chandlery ware, went often to "my little milliner's," spent still more time with "Mrs. Mitchell, my bookseller," now and then saw Mrs. Johnson, "My Lord's semptress" (seamstress), and his wife bought a mask from Madame Charett. He visited Captain Beech on his ship, *Leopard*, and Mrs. Beech was there, "a very well bred and knowing woman." Pepys, like most Englishmen of his day and class, admired "knowing women"; he spent a good deal of time in instructing his wife in geography and music; she, in turn when his eyes grew bad, read to him, and though he once referred to the "poor wretch" as a fool, he insisted his brother and his father treat her with respect.

Pepys may have become enamoured with more females than the average man, and spent more time than most in seduction and attempts at seduction, but all in all his loves represented only a small percentage of the women with whom he was surrounded. At home there were maids and a "cook-mayd," and usually a gentlewoman in attendance on his wife. Now and then he gave a stag dinner at home, but most of his entertaining was for mixed company and quite often females alone—relatives and the wives of friends. Past the home, he met in the course of his business not only female shopkeepers of all kinds, but barmaids, landladies, actresses, and female porters such as the woman who carried his groceries home. None of these or all of them together could compare with any one of the great ladies on whom Pepys "glutted" his eyes, especially My Lady Castlemaine, mistress of the King. Towering over them all was Queen Elizabeth, of whom in the time of Pepys there were still handed-down stories to hear in the taverns.

Most of the women Pepys knew had, in common with Queen Elizabeth, lives of their own, not entirely circumscribed by sex. The pattern weakened quickly in the United States, and as early as 1793, a traveler commented that though the wives of planters attended to dairying and household manufacture, one rarely saw a woman shopkeeper.[42] The predominantly agricultural South, with relatively little business, still had for many years a good many women keeping shops of various kinds, widows

[42] Toulmin, *Western Country*, 39–40.

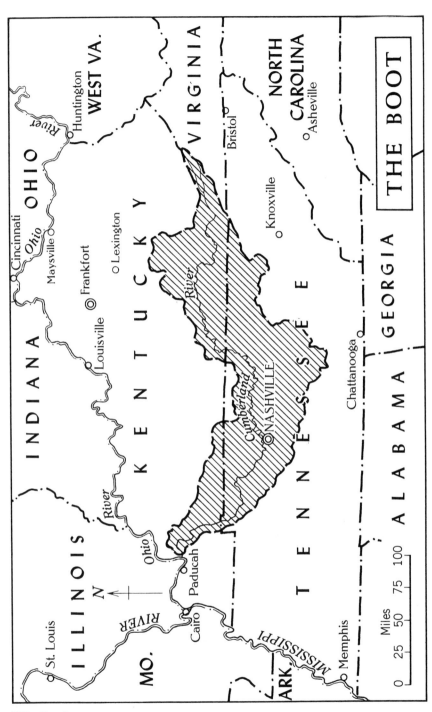

"The Boot"

owning taverns as did "Granny" White, of later years south of Nashville, and other widows carrying on the businesses of their late husbands.

There is nothing to indicate that men of that day objected to spending a good deal of time in the company of women. At the outbreak of the American Revolution, many American men were in their attitudes toward women still closer to the world of Pepys than that of today's businessmen or even Kipling's career men, men's men in a man's world. Few important men of today would doubtless play the role of a John Jay, writing three different letters to the same French firm so that his niece, Miss Kitty Livingston, might be assured of at least one imported silk chemise and other needed articles in spite of the precarious ocean voyages caused by the Revolution.[43] North Carolina fathers would interrupt letters dealing with grave problems to request sprigged muslin, gloves, chip hats, cloth in the "black mode" [44] for daughters and wives and their friends.

John Sevier, noted for his prowess as an Indian warrior, rather enjoyed, that is judging from the many notations in his journal, buying "dress patterns" for the females of his family, taking his whole family, including help, to house raising and corn shuckings, and, like Boswell in Edinburgh, drinking tea with this lady or that one. Sevier, like many men of the old West—George Rogers Clark or Andrew Jackson—did love a ball with dancing. Jackson was famous for his politeness to the ladies, and though he was ever a poor manager of women, never able to bring happiness to his perpetually harassed and troubled Rachel, or bend his niece, Emily Donelson Donelson, to his will in the matter of "the Eaton affair," he seemed to enjoy having women about him. Some one or several of Rachel's nieces or great-nieces were usually visiting the Hermitage,[45] and in later years they were in and out of the White House.

The Southerner in general appears to have been much less inclined to make a temple of sex than was the Puritan, who was as much aware of the physical side of sex as we are today; he made of it a temple of the devil, and though we no longer admit the devil we make of it a temple still. It seems unquestionable that the average pioneer, like other men of that day, was more highly sexed than is today's average male; the bed session appears to have filled only a part of his sex needs.

The young boy, free of any shadow of doubt concerning his maleness

[43] Ellet, *American Revolution*, II, 137, gives the letters; he varied the monotony by changing the colors of the several articles requested.

[44] NCR, XVI, 954–955; and *ibid.*, 951 "wine for Kitty."

[45] *Correspondence of Aaron Burr and his daughter Theodosia*, ed. by Mark Van Doren, New York, 1929, 213, gives an engaging picture of General Jackson's "two lovely nieces," visiting the Jackson home at the same time as Burr.

and unconditioned by the world around him to fear and hate women, could grow up, loving women, both in and out of bed, of all ages, sizes, and occupations as did Pepys, and in general looked more to women for companionship than does the man of today.

Yet, for all their love of females, the early settlers of the old Southwest were rather hardheaded when it came to the taking of a wife. I never found a Cinderella story on the Cumberland. Most wife hunters apparently agreed with Mr. Bradford, editor of the *Gazette*, who advised caution in marriage as a "wife was a man's best or worst fortune." The average marriage in those days was broken only by death and, like any long-term investment, was the subject of much advice. Captain John Donelson, brother-in-law of Jackson, warned his son, Stockly, attending Transylvania College in Lexington, "Let nothing divert you from your time and attention to your studies as you will have many inducements from time to time and perhaps every now and then meet with a black-eyed filly that may addle your brains and stop further proceedings as to business or education, as it is a critical time in your life." [46] Captain John wanted no such creature for a daughter-in-law for he seems to have been a great admirer of sensible, strong-willed women; writing of his son John's bride, Eliza Butler, who had kept the bridegroom dangling for many years, "She brings Jack no fourtion, but hur good sense is a fourtion and [she] no doubt will make a good wife." [47]

Jackson, an ailing President, off in the White House, and with no Rachel to manage the Hermitage, now going to ruin, advised his ward Hutchings, ". . . seek a wife, one who will aid you. . . . Look at the economy of the mother [Jackson had boarded with his future mother-in-law for some months] and if you find it in her you will find it in the daughter . . . recollect the industry of your dead aunt [Rachel], and with what economy she watched over what I made, and how we waded thro the vast expense of the mass of company we had—her care and industry—saved me from ruin. . . . Think of this before you attempt to select a wife." [48]

---

[46] Used by permission of G. Bowdoin Craighill, Executor of the Estate of Mrs. Pauline Wilcox Burke, from *Emily Donelson of Tennessee* by Pauline Wilcox Burke, Copyright 1941, by Garrett and Massie, Richmond, Va. (cited hereafter as Burke, *Emily Donelson*), I 135; Captain John Donelson to his son Stockly, January 14, 1825.

[47] *Ibid.*, I, 99; Captain John Donelson to General John Coffee, his son-in-law, Nov. 10, 1823.

[48] Quoted by permission of the publisher, Carnegie Institution of Washington, from *Correspondence of Andrew Jackson*, ed. and compiled by John Spencer Bassett, copyright Carnegie Institution of Washington, Washington, D.C., 1926 (cited hereafter as Bassett, *Jackson Correspondence*), V, 60.

There was less of moonlight and roses in Andrew Jackson than even the intellectual Dr. Johnson who once declared a man might be happy with any one of ten thousand women, but constantly urged the marriage state upon men; "marriage is the best state for men in general—every man is a worse man in proportion as he is unfit for the married state. No money is better spent than what is laid out for domestick happiness. . . . Marriage, Sir, is much more necessary to a man than to a woman. I had often wondered why young women should marry as they have so much more freedom."

Much of the same sentiments were later expressed in American publications; the American *Museum* declaring in 1790, "You cannot express your contempt of a man more pointedly than by calling him an old bachelor." [49] Years later, Dr. William Montgomery, president of the Philosophical Society of Columbia, in the summer of 1803 addressing the Nashville Society of that name, apologized for being a bachelor. Matrimony was considered so important in any man's life that the bachelor state was at this time frowned upon in both East and West, quite as much as is that of spinsterhood today. The job of hunting a mate and rearing a family was a man's job; the wife might be the "yoke fellow," but he was the lead ox.

In spite of a world forever praising the joys of matrimony, many men on the Cumberland—George Winchester; John Rice, a wealthy merchant; Obediah Terrell and Edmund Jennings, Long Hunters and scouts; and Alexander Donelson, brother of Captain John, never married. They no doubt felt as did William Gale, writing from North Carolina in 1703, that "Marriage att ye best is butt a happy or unhappy chance." [50]

Judging from the age at which many men married—John, son of Captain John Donelson was thirty-six, and John Coffee was getting close to forty—they approached matrimony with considerable caution. Others, however, like young John Buchanan, left a widower with a small child, almost had to remarry. The feeling was that no matter how many servants a man had, no one could take the place of a wife not only in general management, but in the overseeing of the educational, cultural, social, and sometimes spiritual needs of growing children. The American *Museum* of 1790 in "Reflections on Second Marriage of Men," advised the widower hunting a wife to "search for one whom you cannot but

[49] Carey, *Museum*, I, 56–57; VIII, 186–187.
[50] NCR, XXII, 732. Newly settled in North Carolina, young Gale, writing to his father in England, hoped for a wife with "2 or 300 pounds."

rationally esteem, for her good sense, sincerity, benevolence, and skill in domestic matters." [51] The reader was further advised not to expect too much from a young wife, and that in order to "enable her to support the fatigue of her household," [52] he should provide her with some relief and amusement.

Choice of a life mate could be unorthodox; the best known example is that of Joseph Martin who for his third wife took a half-breed Cherokee girl, daughter of the beloved Nancy Ward.[53] Back in Virginia the parents of Elizabeth White Mansker had apparently felt that Kaspar was no fit mate for their daughter, for she ran away with him.[54]

Such matches, however, were rather rare. There was little mixing and mingling; tenant's daughter didn't often marry landowner's son; the bound girl did not marry her widowed master; nor was there at this time much marriage between families of Germanic descent and the rest of the population. Ramsey married Montgomery, Bledsoe married Shelby, and the Donelson girls, daughters of a large landowner with an ancestral background of several generations of well-to-do English colonials, married for the most part men of similar backgrounds; Jackson was something of an exception, but he like a great many other noted men "married well." Henry Clay, like Aaron Burr, married wealth and social position; Lincoln, "man of the people" with little formal education, married the extremely well educated daughter of a wealthy, socially prominent family as did Thomas Hart Benton.

The Southerner of that day had no more scientific knowledge concerning heredity than had anyone else. A few may have believed as did James Boswell that the mother was to her children as the earth to plants, merely a source of nourishment. Most Southerners would undoubtedly have taken Dr. Johnson's side; they had learned from experience that scrub mares seldom if ever dropped first-rate foals. The few descended of English nobility as was Governor Blount may have felt as did Sir Henry Sidney, Lord Deputy of Ireland under Queen Elizabeth, writing to his son, Sir Philip: ". . . Remember, my son, the noble blood you are descended of by your mother's side; and think that only by virtuous life and good action you may be an ornament to that illustrious family;

---

[51] Carey, *Museum*, VII, 437–439.

[52] *Ibid.*, VII, 437.

[53] Williams, *Travels*, Schweinitz, "Report," 490, described the Martin home in 1799; "hewn logs, well chinked and covered on the inside with clay—woven chairs, a table of walnut wood—clean and in order."

[54] W, 3XX(40), 1–2.

otherwise—you may be counted a 'spot on your kin,' one of the greatest curses that can happen to man." We do not know how the average Cumberlander felt, but the many expressions still heard, such as "laziness runs in her breed," "he got his sense from his mama's side," "but his mother comes of good stock," would indicate he believed heredity was important in women as in mares. Also, still heard at times are numbers of the old proverbs having to do with blood and birth: "You can't make a silk purse out of a sow's ear." "Blood will tell." "What's bred in the bone can't be beat out of the flesh."

There were no rules. In general the great importance of the home on the frontier and in the South made the mistress of it a much more important person than is the average woman of today. A man's plantation seat was in a sense himself, the thing that marked to a large degree his place in the community, and this place could never quite be measured in terms of size or splendor. Captain John Donelson and his wife Mary Purnell lived out their days in a log house—comfortable and large, but still logs.

The Tennessee *Gazette*, like other papers of the day, now and then had editorials directed chiefly toward women; discussion of styles, advice on reading, discussion of the influence of the female character in society,[55] and a bit of advice on deportment, such as "do not be guilty of prudery, discard hypocrisy," [56] but never did the editor attempt to tell the female her duties, or set up standards for her conduct as a wife.

The idea seems to have been that just as good men made good citizens, so did good women make good wives. The many complaints of today's soldiers who, on returning from tours of duty in Germany or the Orient, feel that American women do not try so hard to please them as the women they have met would have fallen strangely on the ears of either a Samuel Pepys or an Andrew Jackson later. A wife living only to please would have been quite useless to both. Men can now trust banks, but Pepys could trust only his wife and his father for the hiding of his gold, and Jackson had often to leave the running of the plantation and sometimes the stores to Rachel.

John Coffee, trying to hire an overseer by mail through a friend,[57] stipulated his young wife should be pleased with the man, as she would

[55] Tenn. *Gazette*, April 13, 1803.
[56] *Ibid.*, Dec. 2, 1801.
[57] James Parton, *Life of Andrew Jackson*, New York, 1861 (cited hereafter as Parton, *Jackson*), I, 369–370; John Coffee to his father-in-law, John Donelson. This was during the War of 1812, just before Coffee left on the campaign with Jackson.

have to oversee the overseer while her husband was gone to war. It was not for John Coffee, certain of his own worth, to worry that his wife might learn to manage without him. It was to his advantage that she learn; years later after his death, for he was much older than she, her abilities at growing fine cotton were praised by Jackson,[58] whose own plantation was, without Rachel, going to ruin.

The more religious would have objected to the woman living only to please her husband on the grounds that human beings should strive only to please God. Women living chiefly to please men were more commonly found in the whore-house than the marriage bed. Marriage laws varied from colony to colony and later in the different states, but in the early years nobody considered marriage as a jaunt in a pleasure boat, to be ended when the pleasure dwindled. In North Carolina, it was primarily "a lay contract"[59] between male and female; each party or more often the parents of the parties, agreeing on what lands and other hereditaments each should bring to the union. Marriage was also, as in the other colonies, an unwritten contract between the man and society in that he was to support any children born of the union. It could also be a religious vow, though North Carolina, different from Virginia, had never required it; not only could the ceremony be performed by the minister of any religion, but the ceremony of the Quakers who used no ministers was also recognized, or a couple could go to a justice of the peace.

In colonial Virginia where by law all marriages were required to be performed by a minister of the Church of England after the reading on three different Sundays of an announcement of the intended wedding—publishing the banns as this was known—marriage was primarily a religious vow, but always among people of means accompanied by written property agreements. These quite often permitted the eldest son instead of the wife or a number of children to heir the home place.

Primogeniture, as this was known and made illegal in Virginia in 1785, had never been too popular in North Carolina. In 1784 it was done away with through a change in the marriage law of 1777 as it pertained to dower rights of the widow. Not only was she to get a share of the husband's property, but unless such a division worked a hardship on the children, she was to have one-third, and in any case at least a child's part. More important to her, the portion assigned had to include the home; no

[58] Bassett, *Jackson Correspondence*, V, 373.
[59] Byrd, *Writings*, 63.

longer could the widow be given as her share land without a dwelling or even uncleared land beyond the mountains.[60] The North Carolina marriage laws were incorporated into the body of Tennessee law and remained in force for many years.[61]

Most early marriages on the Cumberland were performed with scant ceremony. The North Carolinian had never much cared for any kind of ritual, while many Protestant faiths, particularly the Presbyterians, were as opposed to rings and other "trumpery" as were the Puritans. The practice of marriage by a minister instead of a justice of the peace became more common, but marriage continued to take place in the home for many years, even among the wealthy.[62] The elaborate church wedding, "beautifully executed with a double-ring ceremony," accounts of which may be found in any country weekly of the South, was not a common feature of Southern life until later.

The first marriages in Middle Tennessee are said to have been performed by Robertson; the couple commonly stood in the fort yard,[63] their altar the cabin door behind them, and exchanged their marriage vows. Much searching brought to light, even in the later, more affluent years, neither wedding veil nor wedding gown. The ceremony was in itself not important; in their eyes words of any kind could not make or unmake a marriage. There is some question if in the remote settlements up the river in Kentucky, for more than twenty years many miles from a county seat, there was any ceremony save man and woman standing up and announcing in the presence of witnesses that henceforth they were man and wife, and at least one prominent Cumberlander married the mother of his several children.

Regardless of how simple the ceremony, somebody must give a wedding dinner; it might be no more than a feast of bread made of pounded meal and what meat happened to be handy, as tradition relates of the Ruddle wedding performed in one of the most Indian-troubled years of all, 1782. More settled times brought more food, and after the first lean years there was an abundance—turkeys and hams by the dozen,[64]

[60] NCR, XXIV, 575.

[61] John Haywood, *A Revisal of all the Public Acts of the State of North Carolina and of the State of Tennessee now in force in the State of Tennessee*, Nashville, 1809 (cited hereafter as Haywood, *Laws*), 65–66, 106.

[62] Burke, *Emily Donelson*, I, 26, 36, 62, 116, gives accounts of the weddings of the Donelson girls and their kin—leading citizens of Middle Tennessee—and all took place in the home.

[63] W, 32S, 320–321, is an account of several such marriages.

[64] Judge Joseph Conn Guild, 1802–1883, *Old Times in Tennessee with historical,*

and, of course, plenty of whiskey for the middle-class farmer, wine for the fashionably wealthy. Such marriages with plenty of liquor, laughter, dancing, and with neither prayer nor preacher, endured better than ninety-nine times out of a hundred.

Marriage was considered a permanent institution, the most important one on the Southern frontier, and a framework for life. Pleasurable it might not be, and the happy widow is part of the folklore of most countries, but the marriage was not lightly to be cast aside. There was divorce, and at least two people prominent in Tennessee history, Rachel Jackson and Sam Houston, became entangled in it, but divorce was on the whole rather rare. Marriage laws, to begin with, provided few excuses for divorce, the most common being that of "the case of one whose husband or wife shall be continually remaining beyond the seas seven years together." [65] Bigamy was explicitly signified as "marrying again, the former wife or husband being alive." [66]

Still, a few did go through the lengthy, time-consuming, not to say embarrassing process of getting a divorce. The first step had to be a public announcement, usually an advertisement in the most convenient newspaper, much like that of Thomas Simpson in the Tennessee *Gazette*, August 5, 1801. "My wife, Sarah, hath eloped from her bed and board without any just cause," Mr. Simpson began, and went on to make it clear he would "pay no debts of her contracting." The actual divorce had to come from the legislature, and since legislative bodies were slow, the process might take years. A bill for divorcement, no different from other bills, had to follow the usual steps through both houses.

Mr. Simpson, one notices, does not say Sarah eloped with another man. The Simpsons, no different from many other families, showed a deplorable sameness in their choice of given names; we, thus, cannot be certain this was the same Thomas Simpson who signed the Watauga Petition in 1776; if so, his Sarah, miffed, probably only left him to go live for a while with a married son, and he retaliated; or this Thomas may have been a son of the other Thomas, and his young wife left him to stay a while with her parents.

It is doubtful that, considering the smallness of the population, the

---

personal, and political scraps and sketches, Nashville, 1878 (cited hereafter as Guild, *Old Times*), 35, described the wedding dinner Col. Archie Overton, of Carthage, gave for his niece, and another wedding as "rousing," *ibid.,* 352.

[65] John Haywood, *The Duty and Authority of Justices of the Peace in the State of Tennessee,* Nashville, 1809 (cited hereafter as Haywood, *Justices*), 10.

[66] *Ibid.,* 49.

several men announcing the elopement of a wife were taking the first step toward divorce. Certain it is that now and then there was a happy ending as in 1804 Benjamin Gainer called the attention of the reader to the fact that ". . . Rebecca hath come home," all differences were settled, and his previous announcement of non-responsibility for her debts had been rescinded.[67]

It is entirely probable that some of those runaway wives had what would be considered today in most states just cause for divorce—infidelity. The makers of marriage laws in early America had behind them the traditions of Europe, and behind Europe, the old, old story of man's inability to get both children and complete sexual satisfaction and pleasure from the one woman, a problem only complicated by the life of such a wise man as Solomon. Much has been written of the extramarital relations of men of the old South, but there is no proof the Southerner was any more lax than other men. The absence of large towns made it hard for him to hide his activities. Secrecy in the small world of Middle Tennessee or in the Cumberland settlements up river was impossible.

Any "single woman with child" could by law be brought before an especial court formed of only two justices of the peace. I found no record of a woman being whipped in the Cumberland Country as in Virginia, but many were the fines meted out for bearing a bastard and for being pregnant out of wedlock.[68] However, the old saying, still heard at times in the hills, "It takes two to make a baby," was, judging from the court records, then a widespread belief. Some of the females fined for second and third offenses may not have known the father of the child; some were undoubtedly tight-lipped Hester Prynnes, but many did name the father. Fines were given for the "begetting of a bastard," [69] but punishment of the father was only the beginning. Law, religion for those who had it, tradition, and social custom—all demanded the father support his offspring. We thus find in early records citizens giving as much as 250 pounds bond for fathering a bastard,[70] a high figure, as Leah Lucas estimated during the period 1780–1795 the "victualing and clothing" one child for fifteen and a half years at only $544.[71] The court in setting such heavy bond was only making certain the child and its mother would

[67] Tennessee *Gazette*, Nov. 28, 1804.
[68] DC, I, 23–27, contains many such cases; fines varied.
[69] *Ibid*.
[70] DC, I, 27.
[71] DW, II, 63–65.

not become public charges. Suffering even more was the man of small means unable to pay anything for the maintenance of his child; in Smith County [72] a father was ordered to pay the mother of his bastard or stay in the custody of the sheriff, a not too satisfactory arrangement as a man in custody could earn no money. In South Carolina the court, at least according to a visiting Englishman, ordered a delinquent father bound out until his earnings should pay the debt of twelve years' maintenance of his "natural wife," and the child she had had by him.[73]

Some men had mistresses, an old custom followed by kings as well as Scotch and English traders to the Indians, while others, usually single men or men long gone from home as was George Morgan, English trader in the Illinois, bought slaves for mistresses. Parting was not always easy as Morgan discovered; he had before returning to his wife in Philadelphia wanted to sell his Angelica, but as she was "averse to going," he left her in charge of a friend who was to sell her for the price, a high one in 1769, of two hundred pounds, but as Morgan explained he had spent a great deal on her.[74]

It seems to have been rare, but now and then a stranger settling in a new community might take a new wife, leaving the old one to wonder. The only instance found of this was that of a Cumberland County, Kentucky, settler who, after living with the second wife for many years, revealed in a conscience-stricken affidavit that his first or "true wife" had been living all the while in Charlotte County, Virginia, "but," he added, troubled it would seem for both women, "in justice to an injured woman which has been occasioned by my own imprudence, I make these statements." [75]

Young men of those days were in some circles more or less expected to "sow their wild oats," and even the older of the more respected members of society were sometimes hauled into court on charges of fornication; in many such as that in which a man of unquestioned veracity swore he saw the defendant and "said Sarah in bed together," [76] the accused was acquitted and seemingly suffered no loss of reputation. Still, even the young boy had to learn to be careful; Tennessee law provided, as did that of North Carolina, a term of five years imprisonment for

---

[72] Smith C, I, 56.
[73] William Faux, *Memorable Days in America; Being a Journal of a Tour to the United States*, London, 1823 (cited hereafter as Faux, *Travels, 1818–91*), 87.
[74] I, XVI, 603.
[75] PD, III, 31, June 25, 1816.
[76] DC, I, 57.

"any male above fourteen who takes any female below sixteen from the protection or against the will of father, mother, or guardians" or ". . . without their consent he deflowers her or contracts marriage." [77] The young lady could lose her dower rights, but was not sent to prison.

There was, on the other hand, in much of the United States a good deal more tolerance of and sympathy for female missteps than today. The American *Museum* wrote of Miss Polly Baker of Connecticut who made such a fine speech in defense of her right to "bear a fifth bastard child," she not only convinced her judges she should have no fine, but one of them took her to wife.[78] Editors and contributors often expressed sympathy for the fallen woman, the betrayed girl, the neglected wife,[79] and saw the man who deserted a wife and children as a low creature, scarcely deserving the title of human being.

Also censored, though less severely, was the coquette, "in no danger of any fatal indiscretion," protected as she was by "the coldness of her temperament." [80] Once she was chided:

> "God molded thy face
> But the devil thy heart;
> What a pity that Satan
> Should spoil the best part."

In sharp contrast were the kind words for "a woman of the town found dead," and the "virgin honor which he has murdered." [81]

No sympathy whatever was shown for male weakness; strong men pitied others less strong than they, never themselves. There thus was, outside the Puritan fold, little feeling that the world should be made safe for weak men. As in the days of Pepys, temptation was an expected part of life, and the hatred and consequent attempts to do away with all forms of temptation from "lewd women" to gambling and alcoholic beverages, so much a part of our thinking today, was not much in evidence during pioneer days, not only on the Cumberland but, save for New England and adjacent areas, in the rest of the United States.

Nobody felt any part of the world and its people could ever be perfect. Life on the Cumberland as elsewhere seems to have been seasoned

---

[77] Haywood, *Laws*, 66.
[78] Carey, *Museum*, I, 243–245.
[79] *Ibid.*, II, 221; VIII, 218.
[80] *Ibid.*, XI, 280.
[81] *Ibid.*, X, appendix 20, 282, and *ibid.*, VIII, 5, in order.

with a good bit of philosophy. Happiness and heaven were not considered the inalienable rights of man. Judge John Overton quoted Pope, "What is, is right," and Captain John Donelson wrote of his daughter Emily, young, beautiful, well-to-do, and newly married to her childhood sweetheart, "She is now commencing her trouble and it will only end with her life." [82] Trouble and sin were old as man. Even Reverend Francis Asbury, riding back and forth across the Appalachians, bedeviled by whiskey topers and carelessly shooting young bucks, thought it would be "well if some or many do not eventually lose their souls." [83]

No community was ever free of "whore-makers, fathers of bastards, cheats, idle vagabonds, night walkers, and eavesdroppers." [84] The law was there to deal with these; there was on the whole in all matters much less "trial in the court of public opinion" than today; in fact the process was frowned upon, and a man's sex life was considered pretty much his own affair—as long as he "deflowered no maiden" and supported his children born out of wedlock. The law made it possible for such children to have their names changed so that they might inherit their father's property.

Southern wives have been portrayed as suffering mightily because of the infidelities of their husbands, particularly when they found mistresses among the family slaves. This is debatable; in the first place the wife never seems to have concerned herself overmuch with learning things she did not want to know, and Southern mores demanded at least the semblance of secrecy; the mistress was not to be flaunted, and who was there to dare to tell the wife? It is doubtful, too, if the average pioneer wife, bearing a child every two or three years, suckling it until pregnant with another, busy in mind and body from before breakfast until bedtime—teaching the next to the least one its letters, doctoring sick help, rushing off to give a hand at a birthing or at least be in attendance, writing letters, sewing, overseeing the dairy, the loomhouse, the kitchen, making room for constant visitors, here, there, and everywhere all day long, had much time or mind left for pondering. Most visitors to the South commented on how hard was the lot of the mistress of a large

[82] Burke, *Emily Donelson*, I, 32, and *ibid.*, I, 142; Overton to A. Jackson after his duel with Dickinson.

[83] Quoted by permission of the publisher, Abingdon Press, from *The Journal and Letters of Francis Asbury*, ed. by Elmer T. Clark, copyright Abingdon Press, Nashville, 1958 (cited hereafter as Asbury, *Journal*), II, 125–126 (March 25, 1797).

[84] Haywood, *Justices*, 176; such was the thinking of the day that eavesdroppers were in the same class—could be bound over to court by one justice—as were "whoremakers."

plantation. The more help, the larger the farm, the busier she was as a rule. Her husband could never be the whole of her life.

No matter what the wife heard or even saw, she was not "to besmirch her own honor," for "What is sauce for the goose is sauce for the gander" did not hold in all matters. Just as it was expected a man should support his children in or out of wedlock, it was also expected the wife should be faithful. It was just one of those things brought from Britain. Dr. Johnson had explained the reason for complete faithfulness on the part of the wife as a matter of property rights; unfaithful wives made it impossible for men to be certain their children heired their property and titles, but the big reason seems to have been the difference in attitude toward self; the woman could not keep her self-respect. There were, of course, some unfaithful wives, but such was the thinking of the day that a man who let himself "be cuccolded," no different from the man who paid a high price for a scrub horse, was an object of derision instead of pity—he deserved no better than he got.

Marriage on such a basis was not always easy or even pleasant, but the resulting home was the foundation upon which all life in the old Southwest rested. In speaking of "the Southern home," one is inclined to think of a building, white-columned, gracious, a thing of verandas set in a wide lawn, or for the ordinary man a good log house with a chimney at either end, unless of course a family was very poor, and then the dwelling might be nothing better than a one-room log cabin, badly made and illy chinked. Most of the wives of first and early settlers on the Cumberland had seen times when a little cabin with just husband and children in it would have been a paradise. Rachel Jackson had known months on a flatboat, the smoky, cold discomfort of an open-faced camp, flight, followed by cramped quarters in another station, and the strangeness of moving from a good frame house to a little log one when Jackson used most of his resources to pay his debts.

Many remembered Rachel. There is no mention of her having complained at the long trip down the Tennessee or any of her other temporary homes. Her complaints and sorrows poured out much later. "What a vacuum is in my soul that you are gone," she once exclaimed to the absent Jackson; or again, "How long, oh Lord, will I remain so unhappy?" she asked, wanting to know the expected time of his return. Once in answering she compared his just-received letter to sunshine, melting the snow of her heart.[85]

[85] Bassett, *Jackson Correspondence*, I, 283, 459, 499.

Jackson tried as best he could, delegating friends, ". . . I must now beg of you to try to amuse Mrs. Jackson and prevent her from fretting; the situation in which I left her [bathed in tears] fills me with woe." [86]

Rachel wanted what many pioneer women never had—a husband always home. Yet, she neither begged to follow nor neglected her work through sorrow.

[86] *Ibid.,* I, 39.

Chapter Three

The Most Important Crop

THE NEWLY WED young couple usually moved at once into their own home, for the Southerner, like the Englishman behind him, insisted on one home for each family, no matter how poor. The new home might be one in a row of little cabins enclosed by fort pickets, and only a few steps from that of a parent as was the first home of Major Buchanan and Sally Ridley, but it gave what all wanted—at least some privacy. The custom of married children living with the parents, or several families of brothers and sisters sharing the same dwelling as was common among the peasantry on the Continent was not a British heritage. Sometimes the youngest child heired the home place and lived with or near the old

Headpiece: Traveling backwoodsman and his family.

people, but those old enough to break up housekeeping became ap-
pendages of the young instead of the other way around.

Much has been written of Southern family life and the closeness of
family ties. Still very much a part of the scene are the great reunions
all up and down the Cumberland where the kinfolk flock from far
places to meet again for one day, bringing their children and spouses to
see the old people or the family burying ground. Such activities also
bespeak a people who never let family ties interfere with their settling
elsewhere, often taking mates with backgrounds different from their
own.

More than one historian and traveler commented that pioneering
weakened the family as a unit and tended to strengthen the individual.
This was undoubtedly true in many cases. Andrew Jackson, Daniel Smith,
John Coffee, after the death of his mother, and many other men lived
completely cut off from whatever family ties they may have had on
the other side of the mountains. Some families such as the Bledsoes did
come in groups of kin and in-laws, but on the whole, family ties were
seldom as strong as they had been in Virginia, and certainly much less
strong than in northern Scotland where the clan ruled. No family relationship in Scotland or America was as clannish as in many sections of
Europe where the peasant stayed with the land until almost every one
in a village was kin, but the young ones still feared to marry strangers
from the next village.

It is doubtful if at any time in the South family ties and loyalties were
ever as close as in some ethnic groups in the United States today in which
the immigrant, failing to find a completely un-Americanized wife, goes
back to his original country, usually the home village, to get one, sometimes taking a distant cousin. Intermarriage was frowned upon, but
relatives, sometimes first cousins, did marry. More common was the
marrying of two or more members of one family into another; Daniel
Smith's son and daughter each married a Donelson.

Still, the hard core of all life in the rural South and later the Cumberland was the single family—father, mother, children. Around this unit
all kinds and conditions of people revolved, not as members of a class,
each segregated with others of his own kind, but as part of or an ap-
pendage to a family, each feeling in varying degrees the influence of
the others. The great plantation with many slave families, teachers and
pupils, skilled workmen, visitors, maiden aunt, helpless grandsire, the
whole complicated with a mill, stills, blacksmith shop, and often a store,

had in colonial Virginia and the Carolinas been more in the nature of a small town.

The pattern was repeated on the Cumberland with, in the early years, yet more complications—guards, visiting Indians, captive Indian children, orphaned white children, and around all these the customary ebb and flow of life—visiting preacher, surveyor, relatives, traveling tinker, peddler, horse trader, or in a home like that of Elmore Douglass or Frederick Stump, neighbors gathered to hear a preacher. Many homes of even well-to-do farmers, convenient to a main road, also took in travelers. Early schools were sometimes held in a home, and, as in any rural region, home was hospital, undertaking establishment, and usually, as times became more settled, there was nearby a family graveyard.

Most important events in life took place in some kind of home and one of these was birth. The lying-in establishment, though common at this date in Europe, was unknown in the South. The young couple expected babies as a matter of course, generally hoped for them, and usually had one within a year or so. The Southern pioneer had few taboos, no theories in regard to birth, nor could he have; babies came on flatboats, in lean-tos, in caves, and sometimes in movers' camps. The early Puritan intellectual had known the human gestation period was exactly nine months, and hence any woman who bore a perfectly formed baby 260 days after wedlock, or the night of "Tarrying" was a harlot and a hussy, deserving of stripes at the cart-tail.

The nonintellectual Southerner was inclined to trust his womenfolk more than rules. He never, for example, or at least I found no mention of it in the South, felt it necessary to make certain he was getting a proper female by spending a premarital night with her, or "Tarrying," [1] as it was known in Massachusetts. The Southerners appear to have been on the whole much more sophisticated and wiser in an actual working knowledge of sex with its ramifications of begetting and birth than are most people, even today. Most had had from babyhood two excellent teachers—the Bible proclaiming the joys of sex as well as its pitfalls, and the farm animals, surrounding them. Women, they might reason, were somewhat like mares; two covered by the same stallion two days apart could drop foals on the same day or a week apart, yet each foal be perfectly formed. Nor did the male as physician or family adviser seek to tell the girl expecting her first how it was to bear a child, or that it was a "natural

[1] Burnaby, *Travels*, 141–142. If after Tarrying the two did not wish to marry they separated, never to meet again, unless a pregnancy occurred; in that case they must.

process" painful only if the mother were afraid. If he quoted any authority it was usually the Old Testament—"in pain thou shalt bring forth children," and pain was expected. There were no learned men around to tell the woman "in a family way"[2] her craving for a certain food, be it ordinary buttermilk or something not to be had on any frontier such as apple butter, only represented a subconscious attempt to get attention. Many believed that if the mother did not get the food she wanted, her unborn child would want it the whole of its life. There were numerous superstitions and sayings concerning pregnancy, many of which survive; in general everything added up to the belief that a happy, satisfied mother made for strong and happy children.

Birth was in all the civilized world quite dangerous for the mother, though possibly less so in many rural regions than in some of the dirty, overcrowded lying-in establishments of Europe. Still, some like John Buchanan's first wife died of it, and the whole cycle of pregnancy, childbirth, suckling, and child rearing was taken less matter-of-factly than today.

Most physicians delivered babies when called upon, and the celebrated Dr. Benjamin Rush of Philadelphia urged women to use "men midwives,"[3] but for many years most babies continued to be helped into the world by women.[4] Few of these were what one might call professionals. Usually older women, their skills learned from mothers, and with families of their own, they could bring nothing to a birthing save a clean apron, their skillful hands, and a few herbs. Yet, the pioneer had great faith in them as demonstrated by Major George Blackmore; only a neighbor instead of kin, he risked his life from lurking Indians and ruined a good horse into the bargain, to go for the "granny woman" when Mary Bledsoe Shelby, daughter of Anthony, was having her first baby.[5]

[2] "In the family way" can still be heard, and was in common use as Jackson to John Donelson, June 7, 1829, Bassett, *Jackson Correspondence,* IV, 41–42: "Emily is in the family way." The word *craving* though now and then still heard in the back hills to designate the overpowering desire of a pregnant woman for some particular food, seems to have been less commonly used. Though grown up near a small town in the hills, I had never heard the word so used until one hot August afternoon I came home from school, and invited by my landlady to have some watermelon freshly brought from the spring-branch cave, I eagerly accepted saying that in the heat I had been craving cool watermelon all afternoon. I was young and single; she stared at me a moment, shook her head, then she and the children burst into whoops of laughter.

[3] Dr. Benjamin Rush, *Medical Enquiries and Observations,* Philadelphia, 1794 (cited hereafter as Rush, *Observations, 1794*), 62.

[4] Toulmin, *Western Country,* 67.

[5] Guild, *Old Times,* 393.

Early marriage records when available did not give ages of the bride and groom, but everything indicates the average age of the mother marriage, especially for men, was frowned upon. An English visitor to bearing her first child was a good bit higher than today. The United States was still close to England in social outlook where very early Kentucky in 1793 commented that few women remain unmarried when "arriving at mature age. Early marriages are so common that few are single at one and twenty." [6] Today, with many of both sexes marrying before they have finished high school, we are inclined to think of eighteen as a "mature age," for the marriage of girls.

Childbed was attended by the husband, and when possible not only his father-in-law, but his father as well, for the old-time midwives wanted, and quite often needed, men at such times. There were, of course, always a number of women gathered, so that any birthing was a less dehumanized process than today, amid strangers in the cold sterility of the assembly-line procedures of the average hospital. It would appear that the pioneer mother was better prepared for birth than is the average modern young mother. Rarely was the mother unable to suckle her child, and I found no case of mental illness in a young mother or any violence to child or self to indicate it. The girl had learned from the world around her—the mare dying with her foal half born, scream of woman in childbirth, too clearly heard in the close confinement of the fort—that birth could be cruel and was prepared for it. The treatment immediately after birth may have helped; the baby was, of course, cared for by someone else, often a slave, but mother and child were never separated for long periods of time. Nobody saw anything strange in this; some may have thought of cows, cross, contrary, often giving no milk at all if calves were taken away too soon after birth, and everybody knew if a ewe got separated from her newborn lamb she might never claim it at all.

Another help was the custom of giving the mother plenty of bed rest, though this was not for Mrs. Peyton with her first or Mrs. James Robertson with Felix. Each woman, one on a flatboat on the Tennessee, the other, Mrs. Robertson in a fort, lived through an Indian attack with very young babies. Even today in much of the South, the custom of keeping the mother in bed for at least ten days, and usually two weeks, is still followed; a short time compared to that of seventeenth century England, where even the unmarried mother had enjoyed a three months' lying-in

---

[6] Toulmin, *Western Country*, 66.

with a nurse [7] for a month—provided, of course, the baby's father could pay the bill.

Grown up with all manner of young things from the puny peacocks to the tough bull calf, the young human couple had learned before marriage a great deal about the needs of growing animals, enough that they were not apt to believe in rules. Some foals were stronger and bigger than others at birth, some fed unusually often, and there was a runt in most litters of pigs. The newborn human animal was treated much like any other newborn animal. He had, of course, to be cleaned, often with lard, dressed usually in simple clothing much like that used today, for swaddling clothes had been outmoded for generations, and elaborate garments for young babies had not yet become fashionable. Source materials of the early years made no mention of christening parties, though in the Southern Colonies, Church of England communicants had often, though not always, held them.

Proper nurseries with cradles had been a part of life in the colonial South, but Cornelius Ruddle [8] was the only first settler found who had even a small bed, for his trundle bed was referred to as a "chile's bed." A small trundle bed more commonly held the next-to-the-least one, or two, or three, than the suckling infant. It was not until close to 1800, and then among only the well-to-do, that "cradles with clothes" became more common.[9] The Robertsons were among the wealthier of the first settlers, but Felix was in bed with his parents when the Indians attacked. The snake tales of Judge Guild have the baby in bed with the mother, and such seems to have been the rule for most families. William Faux, traveling in South Carolina in 1818, stopped in the home of a well-born, quite well-to-do, but newly settled young family where father, mother, and children occupied one bed, and he the other, while a slave slept on the floor "in readiness to hush the children." [10]

Snuggled down into the feathers against his mother was the one safe and sensible place for the baby. The puncheon floors of the first homes

[7] This is part of the picture given by Moll Flanders; the establishment offered three grades of services; the more expensive, the fancier the bed linens and the greater the attention, but each had a nurse for the designated time.

[8] Cornelius Ruddle, DW, I, 54, July 2, 1787, was a first settler early killed by Indians.

[9] Thomas McCain in 1789, DW, I, 107, was only one of several men listed as having had a cradle, but such was its position in the inventory that it like the others appears to have been an agricultural tool, though different from several—no scythe was listed with it; but it is not until the late nineties that such entries as "cradle with furniture" and "cradle with clothes" are found; see *ibid.*, II, 189, 232, 243, 272.

[10] Faux, *Travels, 1818–1819*, 83.

were cold and drafty in winter, and in summer there were snakes. Francis Baily, stopping in the home of quite a well-to-do farmer, saw a snake crawling up between the floor boards,[11] and the snake tale, like many cures for snake bite, was ever a part of pioneer folklore.

Another reason the baby slept with his parents was that he and his mother wanted it that way. Most Southerners liked the high-spirited things—children, wives, and horses. Anything that tended to break the spirit in either a child or a foxhound pup was not good. Regardless of baby's age or the condition of the household, the least one was king. The first thing most any pioneer baby on the Cumberland learned, even before he could open his eyes, was that he was a mighty creature; when he cried the world about him sprang into action. Quickly he learned his power to shape his world, and that it was not for him to shape himself to fit this world. Different from the newborn baby of today, the pioneer baby's first lessons in life were not those of adjustment. It was only the children of slave women who had to cry and wait.

He was essentially his own boss, himself determining when and where he should sleep, and his food, like that of practically all babies in the English colonies, was his mother's milk. In the young United States [12] the custom of putting the baby out to nurse was but little followed, save in the case of twins or the mother's death. Dr. Rush even declared that the refusal of mothers to suckle their young was a symptom of moral decay and marked the beginning of a country's dissolution. He cited as proof the Roman Empire that declined when mothers ceased to breast feed their babies, and instead turned them over to wet nurses.[13] It was much later that the wealthier and more fashionable mothers in the South used slave women for suckling their young as well as tending. Many years past the pioneer period Emily Donelson suckled her baby while in the White House.[14]

The average baby continued to be breast fed until his mother became

[11] Francis Baily, *Journal of a Tour in Unsettled Parts of North America in 1796 and 1797*, London, 1856 (cited hereafter as Baily, *Tour 1796–1797*), 421.

[12] Materials used by permission of the copyright owners, the President and Fellows of Harvard College, from *This Was America*, by Oscar Handlin, Harvard University Press, Cambridge, 1949 (cited hereafter as Handlin, *America*), 141, a transl. quoting, Giovanni Antonio Grassi, "The Jesuit Scholar" (cited hereafter as Grassi, "Observations," 1819).

[13] Rush, *Observations, 1794*, 63.

[14] Burke, *Emily Donelson*, II, 69; Emily Donelson to A. J. Donelson, July 20, 1834. Earlier, Theodosia Burr, 1783–1813, wife of the Governor of South Carolina, Joseph Alston, suckled her son.

pregnant again, and he might be two or even three years old when weaned. Most families studied had children spaced much like the young Robertsons, seldom less than two years apart, and often three. The mother with four children under four years of age, a not uncommon circumstance today when procreation is apparently hastened by artificial feeding, was not a part of pioneer life. The baby could enjoy his mother and the mother the baby with no other crowding on his heels before he was two years old or so.

He would during this time feed when and wherever he wanted to—in bed at any hour of the night, at the family table while the mother ate, when she took a quiet pipe of tobacco and talked to a visiting preacher, or in the middle of church service imbibing mother's milk and Watt's hymns at the same time. He went wherever his mother went; if her destination happened to be an all night ball in New Orleans, the baby went along; "and young mothers, finishing a waltz, go off to suckle their babies, which the freedom of their costume makes possible with slight effort." [15]

Taboos, however, were already on the way. In 1812 a Jesuit priest, living in Washington, commented that mothers in "suckling their offspring themselves would be even more worthy of praise if they would do it more modestly." [16] It was only among the more unsophisticated in the back hills, that the custom of suckling the baby in church lingered until well into the present century. Still the baby continued boss on the Cumberland for many years. Andrew Jackson, in his old age, worried and quarreled about his delicate daughter-in-law who when ill insisted on suckling her "Hercules of a child" each night to put him to sleep.[17] Jackson saw him as a big thing, five months old, able and willing to swallow a "large spoonful of pap at once," but to the mother he was a little baby in need of her milk and he continued to need it until he was around eighteen months old.[18] Andrew Jackson could do many things, but he could not wean a baby.

[15] Handlin, *America*, 136, "A Bourbon Who Refused to Forget," a transl. portion of De Montlezun's *Voyage fait dans les années 1816 et 1817, de New-Yorck à la Nouvelle-Orléans et de l'Orénoque au Mississippi* (cited hereafter as De Montlezun, "Travels 1816–1817").

[16] Handlin, *America*, Grassi, "Observations, 1819," 141.

[17] Bassett, *Jackson Correspondence*, V, 287. This was the son of Jackson's adopted son, taken when three days old from his mother Mrs. Severn (Elizabeth Rucker) Donelson because he was one of twins. Rachel, his aunt, somehow brought him through babyhood; legally adopted, named Andrew Jackson Jackson, he is not to be confused with Andrew Jackson Donelson, Jackson's secretary.

[18] *Ibid.*, 364.

The pioneer baby sucking his mother's breasts got a great many things along with milk. Possibly, the most important was a self-esteem that amounted at times to cockiness, for the average wife on the Cumberland was a much more self-assured human being, more certain of her own worth and her place in the world, than is the average woman of today. Mothers, like brood mares, were treated with kindness and sympathy, and it was on the whole a happy time for mothers and children. Puritanism was by that date so weakened that even the citizens of Boston were playing cards; nor, during pioneer years, did any religion on the Cumberland dwell overmuch on the hard, cold intellectualism of Calvinism that destined even the dead baby to eternal hell-fire and damnation.

The overweening consciousness of sex and consequent prudery [19] that were beginning to appear in Philadelphia before 1800 had not yet come to the South; a woman was still a human being, able to talk with men outside the family circle without being exposed to "loss of reputation." Nor was there any hint of today's version of the medieval evil eye—the emphasis, seen everywhere from literary art to baby books, on woman's capacity for evil both on her child and her husband. Nor did anyone preach to the mother that her children were her job alone. Whatever the baby got from his mother it was not guilt or fear or shame at breaking rules.

There were no more rules for the psychological, social, and emotional shaping of babies than for making whiskey. The pioneering couple could afford few orthodoxies of any description. There was a proper way to load a rifle and a blunderbuss, but Jemmy O'Connor had to load the best he could. A farmer who knew that the distilling of whiskey required a copper still, malted barley, and yeast had no more business on the frontier than the woman who would have felt unmarried and guilt stricken without a religious marriage ceremony, or worse, have felt inconsolable at the death of an unbaptized baby, not because it died, but because it died unbaptized.

The person who knew exactly how to raise a baby was nowhere in the world. The manipulation of human beings as a science had not yet evolved. There was, throughout this period, little attempt to manipulate

---

[19] Handlin, *America*, "The Bitter Thoughts of President Moreau," a transl. portion from Elie Moreau, *Voyage aux Etats-Unis de l'Amérique, 1793–1798* (cited hereafter as Moreau, "Travels, 1793–1798," found, 101, the Philadelphia women much changed from the "sprightly" females met by the Rev. Burnaby before the Revolution; Moreau not only observed that their prudery betrayed rather an "excess of knowledge than of ignorance," but found them "not altogether pure" in manners. Close to forty years later Isidore Lowenstern, *ibid.*, 182, found the Philadelphia ladies still unusually beautiful but "Amiability and enjoyment of company expose her to loss of reputation."

children; over and over Messers Watts [20] and Dilworth appealed to their reason, conscience, and self-respect.

The many superstitions now so commonly held, such as, it is bad for baby's psychological development to suckle past a definite period, sleep with its mother, or get overmuch attention, and in general the very great emphasis now placed on the environment of the young child—after it leaves the hospital—were all unknown. The pioneer could not by his very nature believe environment made the man. His big job in life was to change the environment, shape it to his will. The mother who knew that sleeping with and suckling her son until he was two years would ruin him for life would have been a nervous wreck, torn between fear of snakes and guilt at breaking rules.

She could, no matter how crowded and unlovely and rough the forted life might be, comfort herself with sayings and proverbs: "blood will tell" —"the mistress lends dignity to the cottage"—"a woman who won't keep a log cabin clean has no place in a mansion." Mrs. James Robertson, the Bledsoes, Buchanans, and most others knew not only crowded, temporary quarters, but had often to move during the first Indian-troubled years.

Lack of worry over the future personality and mental health of the growing pioneer baby was more than balanced by concern for, first, his physical and, later, his moral and intellectual life. He was scarcely born before the many gathered to help with the borning were in an argument over the kinds and quantities of teas to give him; one holding for walink; still another, white oak; [21] and always somebody to insist the toddy should be stronger. More teas were needed to break out the hives, cure the thrush, more commonly called "thrash," get him through teething; and as settlement progressed and domesticated herbs such as catnip became common, the variety of teas increased as did the choice in patent medicines and physicians.

---

[20] Isaac Watts (1674–1748) is so well known for his hymns and Psalms set to music we forget his numerous theological writings and poetry. Dr. Johnson included him in his *Lives of the English Poets*—and schoolmaster Dilworth took liberal quotations both from his prose and poetry, particularly *Divine and Moral Songs for Children*, 1720 (cited hereafter as Watts, *Children's Songs*); best known of these is possibly
> "Hush, my dear, lie still and slumber
> Holy angels guard thy bed
> Heavenly blessings without number
> Gently falling on thy head."

[21] Many of these teas—walink (walking leaf) catnip, watermelon seed, rattleroot were some of the most common—are still used in the hills for babies, but I never encountered an infusion of white oak bark, though it is often mentioned in early source materials.

Not all homes were so fortunate as to have a household of children; Andrew Jackson and Kaspar Mansker never had any; Joseph Bishop, only one surviving to adulthood; and Daniel Smith, two. Many widows, Leah Lucas for instance, never remarried, though widowed early with five children. The average home on the Cumberland in 1795 probably had fewer children than the four or five Michaux [22] judged was in the average Kentucky home of 1802. Statistics are lacking, but certainly the pioneers, no different from other families of that day, saw many of their children die while still young. The Moravian elder Frederick De Schweinitz, visiting a Sumner County German family in 1799, commented on the number of small graves in the family graveyard.[23] It is doubtful, however, if many of these were of young babies. Though childbirth was a much greater hazard to the mother than today, being born may have been less. The danger to the young baby from over-anaesthetization, blindness from too much oxygen, birth injury, diarrhea, and other infections, all too common in many of today's hospital nurseries, was almost nonexistent.

Possibly somewhat indicative of infant mortality and birth rates in general during pioneer days were the studies made by Dr. John C. Campbell of birth and mortality rates in the Southern Appalachians. Much of the survey was made in rural regions during the second decade of this century, and though living conditions approximated to some extent those of the pioneers, they were in many ways much less conducive to long life. Poverty caused by eroded lands and small farms made for housing and food not so good as that enjoyed by the average pioneer. Typhoid, diphtheria, and tuberculosis—rare during pioneer years—were prevalent. Yet, in common with pioneer days, physicians were scarce, hospitals, even when not a great many miles away, inaccessible because of very poor roads; and birth, in the rural regions, was largely in the hands of midwives.

Dr. Campbell found the infant death rate in relation to living births lower in the Southern Appalachians than in the United States as a whole,[24] and life expectancy greater. Hill babies were at this time born in the home and, like the pioneer baby, breast fed; seldom weaned before eighteen months, many were a good deal older. The dangerous days for both hill and pioneer babies seem to have come past weaning, but even during young childhood the death rate was probably lower than in mid-nine-

[22] Michaux, *Travels 1802*, 241–242.
[23] Williams, *Travels*, Schweinitz, "Report," 510–511.
[24] John C. Campbell, *The Southern Highlander and His Homestead*, Russell Sage Foundation, Philadelphia, 1921, 209.

teenth century. "Calomel doctors"[25] who gave this drug in large amounts even to very young children came past the pioneer period, though early physicians were much inclined to remedies such as arsenic and purges that killed far more than they cured. Faced with a young child stricken with dysentery, one of the most dreaded diseases of childhood, the physician would at times order a purgative that hastened death.[26]

Compared to the New England child, the Southern baby was reared with great tenderness. Practically all early travelers in colonial Virginia had praised the mothers; "as good wives and mothers as any in the world,"[27] the Reverend Burnaby had observed; and after the Revolution the praise continued; "almost as tenderly as the English,"[28] one wrote, and another found the children in Virginia treated "with unparalleled tenderness. Their every fancy is satisfied."[29] In England, at least in some circles, interest in and care of young children—boys, of course, were sent away to school when by today's standards they were still quite young—was the mark of a lady. "High people, Sir," the celebrated Dr. Johnson said, "are the best. . . . Trades women (I mean the wives of tradesmen) . . . who are worth ten to fifteen thousand pounds are the worst creatures upon earth . . . ladies of quality, you'll find them better mothers—the higher in rank, they are the better instructed and the more virtuous."

Cumberland mothers of the early years, though yet without the benefit of Dr. Johnson's opinions, must have indeed been eternally watchful of their young. Mrs. Peyton's baby, thrown overboard with the bedding in the uproar of an Indian alarm, was the only accidental death found of a child. There were of course no play-pens or baby beds with slatted sides, and no mention of any mechanical means such as the harness or the baby carriage with straps. All such services were performed by human arms. Rearing a baby in the pioneer household, beset with innumerable dangers from rolling off a high bed to toddling into the open fire, was almost a full-time job for somebody, though of course in the larger households everybody helped, including older sons.

[25] Guild, *Old Times*, 41.
[26] Dr. Rush was the most advanced physician of the day, respected even in Europe and quoted by such men as Aaron Burr; he often emphasized the importance of cleanliness, fresh air, light exercise, and rest, yet even he, *Observations, 1794*, 136, advocated mild purges for dysenteries in children.
[27] Burnaby, *Travels*, 26; he could not refrain from adding "not quite so much tenderness and sensibility as the English ladies."
[28] Jedidiah Morse, *The American Geography*, Elizabethtown, New Jersey, 1789 (cited hereafter as Morse, *Geography*), 390.
[29] Handlin, *America*, Moreau, "Travels, 1793–1798," 91.

One of the most dreaded jobs was that of weaning the baby; this meant he would cry, and nobody wanted to hear a baby cry, but upon finding himself suddenly deprived of a thing he had been led to think was his personal property for the whole of his life, he put up a loud and spirited fight. The battle of the weaning was a thing to be remembered by his mother for the rest of her life though he was one among many. Years past the pioneer period a young Cumberland mother wrote her husband of their eighteen-month-old, a sturdy, nimble-footed child, able to climb the parlor table, "I have at length weaned Mary; it would have amused you to see how she would fight it, she would get tired of crying and stop and give me a slap and then spit in my face. I can't think where she learnt it from. She can say, pa, ma, and many words quite plain." [30]

The father, grandson of Daniel Smith, must have been proud of his daughter, high-spirited enough to fight for what she wanted. A child so reared, king or queen of all creation, was so filled with self-assurance that even the frustrating experience of weaning, followed in less than a year by a baby on which all attention at once centered, did not humble it; nothing the future could bring, bereavement, poverty, or war, or all together could quite break such a spirit. Nobody wanted to break it, not even in a girl child, for men of the Old South admired "spirited women."

Parents wanted both sons and daughters, and most fathers [31] undoubtedly hoped their first-born would be males, but there seems to have been on the whole little glorification of mere maleness; manliness did not, as demonstrated by Jenny Glisten under the bed during an Indian attack, automatically follow. The ability to take responsibility, to put others ahead of self as demonstrated over and over by such men as James Robertson and Daniel Smith [32] was more truly a mark of manhood than mere maleness as evidenced by a man's abilities in bed. This seems to have been taken pretty much for granted; more teaching was directed toward the acquisition of manhood than in giving pride in the accident of male birth. A baby was a baby and the awareness of sex with which we now surround our children at birth with pink or blue was then unknown.

[30] Burke, *Emily Donelson*, I, 273; E. Donelson to her husband Andrew Jackson Donelson. Jan. 31, 1831.

[31] *Ibid.*, I, 64, Captain John Donelson writing to John Coffee, "Rachel [Capt. John's daughter] has got a daughter and Mr. Eastin crying about it, but it has black hair and eyes which nerely cures the misfortune," Aug. 26, 1817.

[32] General Daniel Smith is so well known for his political activities, his prowess as woodsman is apt to be forgotten; during the hard winter while encamped on the Cumberland just below the mouth of Fishing Creek in what is now Pulaski County, Ky., supplies ran low, but he left camp so less food might be required, and hunted buffalo on foot; see THM, I, 40-65.

The men who would undergo untold hardships in the "Starving War" of 1812 were at the end of the Indian Wars in Middle Tennessee, 1795, little lads still in dresses and with their hair in curls or a braid. There was no rush to get the boy into trousers. Judging from tradition and family life in the hills, small boys not infrequently played with dolls. Willingness to protect the weak and watch over children were, at least for those Cumberlanders who elected Bailey Peyton to Congress because he carried a stranger woman's baby on horseback many miles through the woods, more truly a mark of manhood than the fighting of duels. I found no evidence among the pioneers or the South in general of any attempts to inculcate aggressiveness. Boys were not urged to fisticuffs and Dr. Watts, by that date long familiar to their grandfathers, was quoted:

> Let dogs delight to bark and bite
> For God hath made them so
> Let bears and lions growl and fight
> For 'tis their nature to
>
> But children, you should never let
> Such angry passions rise
> Your little hands were never made
> To tear each other's eyes.[33]

The insistence now on the close cropping of the male infant's hair almost before he can sit in a barber chair would doubtless have puzzled any pioneer. He could have pointed out that a haircut never made a man. Samson even lost his strength when he had his hair cut; most Indian scouts and fighters had longish hair, not so long as Andrew Jackson's on his first trip to Congress when he wore his hair in a circle of eelskin; on the other hand, there was Colonel Anthony Bledsoe, one of the bravest of men—his hair was very short for he commonly wore a wig. There were no rules, and when rules did come to the army, many on the Cumberland were mightily disgusted that a proven general should be commanded to cut his queue.[34]

[33] Watts, *Children's Songs*, 15 (pagination, Charleston, 1824 ed.).
[34] ASP, I, *Military Affairs*, 173–174. Major General Andrew Jackson, Bassett, *Jackson Correspondence*, I, 67, wrote Thomas Jefferson on the subject of General Thomas Butler's queue, "Should it be decided that the hair is a part of the uniform and subject to the order of the commander in chief it may also be extended to the nose ear eye and so forth, they are all equally the gifts of nature . . ." The order was "too near to the Despotism of a Sarrow." (Prince Suvarov, a strict Russian general.)

They likewise had no rules concerning the work of the young male. Boys commonly helped their fathers or the help in the field and around the farm, doing many things that young boys did for generations—going to mill, watering the horses, hunting the forever straying horses and other farm animals. Most of those, however, who left us memories of life on the frontier spent much time helping their mothers. Dr. Daniel Drake, whose family settled in northern Kentucky in 1788, was in a home short of girls. He churned, scrubbed—after he had made the hickory brushes and brooms with which the work was done—carded wool and spun it, spent much time caring for the younger children, helped in the cooking, and "had often to leave the field to help my mother." [35]

Dr. Drake did more about the house than most boys, but his work was not unusual for any farm home. There was behind the pioneers of Scotch and English origin no tradition of judging the importance of work by the sex of those who performed it, or even much of "man's work and woman's work." We now for some reason always picture the spinning wheel or loom of pioneer days as powered by a woman, yet the cloth industries, one of the most important to the Scot whether of Scotland or Northern Ireland, had been carried on in the home by both sexes. Andrew Jackson's maternal grandfather was, for example, a spinner; old Joe Robertson who settled on the Cumberland was a weaver; Hugh Rogan, with the surveying party in the hard winter, had been apprenticed to a weaver; and in Kentucky of 1793 much spinning and weaving was still in the hands of men.[36]

The revulsion most men of today feel against doing such work as mending their clothing, cooking, and other jobs, even shopping for food or anything now considered woman's work was unknown in the early years. Men liked independence, and men without servants yet dependent upon women to "cook and wash for them" as were the German settlers of New Bern, could never have been Long Hunters, surveyors, or soldiers. John Smith, father of the noted minister, was none of these things, only another small farmer with a large family in need of more and better land. He thus in the early nineties removed from East Tennessee to a fertile valley, Stockton's, on a tributary of the Cumberland in what is now McCreary County, Kentucky. Leaving wife and younger children be-

[35] Quoted by permission of the publishers, Abelard-Schuman, Ltd., from *Pioneer Life in Kentucky, 1785–1852* by Dr. Daniel Drake, ed. from the original manuscript (a series of letters to Drake's children) by E. F. Horine, copyright Abelard-Schuman, Ltd., New York, 1948 (cited hereafter as Drake, *Letters*), 96–109.

[36] Toulmin, *Western Country*, 97.

hind, he came ahead with the two older boys to raise a cabin and put in a crop of corn. He probably felt no less a man for doing all the work of a woman in the servantless home, making deerskin trousers for his sons, and doing the most womanly work of all—milking the cows.[37]

Women, on the other hand, engaged in and even managed many activities no longer in the hands of women. The press of today speaks, for example, only of dairying, but the American *Museum* directed all articles on dairying to women alone—"The person who by milking her cows. . . ."[38] It is doubtful if Mrs. James Robertson, for example, milked her own cows; she had plenty of help, but she like the other farm wives managed the dairy just as women had in the British Isles for generations. The *Museum* directed many other articles on agriculture to the general reader, rather than to men alone. This was, of course, the expected thing in a day when many farms were owned and operated by women. In a discussion of silk production, Mrs. Sabin, listed as having 23,000 worms, may have been a widow, but Miss Sherman had 12,000 and Miss Barney, 8,000.[39]

There were many jobs—blacksmithing and other heavy work—I never met a pioneer woman doing; nor did even the wife of the small Kentucky or Tennessee farmer work in the fields, a situation so different from France that Michaux must needs comment on it. In spite of numerous tales of female heroism I never found an Annie Oakley or a huntress, but women managed all manner of businesses and industries from tanneries[40] to hatters' establishments.[41] Most were, no doubt, widows, carrying on. In general it seems safe to say that the place of the pioneer wife was much like that of the pioneer husband—she did, or tried to do, whatever the immediate circumstances demanded. Field work, for example, could be done by half grown sons or semiskilled slave labor; most woman's work whether making butter, sewing, or teaching the young their letters required not a little knowledge and skill.

Usually she was, through training and education, quite well equipped for management. Women who gave proof of illiteracy by signing with a mark were rare on the Cumberland; true, they had less time for reading and usually, though not always, less education than their menfolk, but as

---

[37] John Augustus Williams, *Life of Elder John Smith* (pagination from 2nd ed., Cincinnati, 1904 (cited hereafter as Williams, *Smith*), 24–34.

[38] Carey, *Museum*, XII, 179–183, "Remarks on the management of a dairy."

[39] *Ibid.*, VIII, 244.

[40] VS, I, 608. Mrs. Parks, supplying the Virginia Line with leather, wrote in 1781 of the cords of bark, etc. needed to carry on her business.

[41] Nashville *Clarion*, Nov. 12, 1811; Ann M'Connel announces she will carry on the hatting business of her late husband.

colonials they had ever taken a lively interest and sometimes a hand in events, both political and military, that went on around them. The rage many now express against "women working" was, of course, unknown. In the first place everybody looked upon the work that went on around the home as one of the hardest and most important jobs on earth. The young man or widower was urged to get good mothers for his children and not to trust domestic concerns to "a young and giddy girl." [42] Servants were much more common, of course, than now, so that even what we would today denominate the middle-class home usually had at least a cook, and many of the activities carried on by women after marriage— inn-keeping, dairying, a small shop or school—were in a sense an extension of home life as were the cloth industries.

Still, no matter how important mother's role, father was head of the house, not only by law, but often we find him making the more important decisions. It was Daniel Drake's father who decided that young Daniel should get an education better than that to be had in their local community. There is no record Daniel's mother objected, for source materials of the South do not yield a picture of father as a domineering tyrant that so often comes from New England. In the South, life continued primarily agricultural for many years, and the interests of the male and female in the matter of work did not follow entirely separate paths. Even among the better element of the non-farming population, father was expected to take an interest in his home life with no neglecting of his children.

There were no women's sections in the *Museum*, nor later, the *Gazette*. The great many items concerning food, marriage, the education of girls, methods of curing meat and preserving fruit, suggestions as to how young ladies should spend their Sundays, complaints that women did not dress warmly enough, were along with such things as cures for colds and influenzas all directed to the general reader. [43] Discussions concerning matrimony were written, not by women for women, but by men for men. Home and what went on there came under the heading of manly affairs. Readers of the *Museum* not only were unashamed of their interest in women and home life, but criticized the Russians and Dutch for paying so little attention to their wives. [44]

[42] Carey, *Museum*, VII, 437.

[43] *Ibid.*, each issue carried much material that would now be found only on "The Woman's Page," but see in particular, *ibid.*, III, 25 (1788), "An Address to the Young Ladies of Philadelphia Academy"; *ibid.*, III, 50–51, "Letter on Marriage"; *ibid.*, V, 375, "On Marriage"; *ibid.*, VII, 307, "Female Heroism"; *ibid.*, VIII, 219, "The Good Husband"; *ibid.*, XI, 197, "Education of Girls."

[44] *Ibid.*, I, 61 (1787).

Society of that day demanded that the man take in the home and matrimony as much interest and responsibility as the woman is expected to take today. There thus fell on the average man, not only the whole burden of his own life, but also that of the most important thing he had—not his job—but his wife and children.

It was not, however, a work he usually did alone; mother was a great deal more than a gourd vine in need of support for her fruit; she was the yoke-fellow and trusted usually above anyone else in the world. Early wills on the Cumberland well demonstrate this. Most North Carolinians and later Cumberlanders appear to have felt as did the basically conservative, but humanistic Dr. Johnson that "self and she ought to be of a side. . . . It cannot but occur that women have natural and equitable claims as well as man, and these claims are not to be . . . lightly superseded or infringed."

Not all in the United States would have agreed with Dr. Johnson. Dr. Thomas Walker, for example, was a Virginia gentleman of the old school. Dying in 1794, he left his wife Elizabeth only the family carriage and the use of one slave until her death. She, as a second wife, had in the marriage articles agreed to "disavow any right of dowry" in Walker's estate. Thus, Dr. Walker left no property to any female, for all his money and goods were divided between sons and sons-in-law, who in turn could dispose of it as they wished.[45]

This is in sharp contrast to early wills on the Cumberland; unmarried men often left much property to female relatives; John Rice [46] giving a great deal of land to his three sisters, and young Mark Robertson, to nieces.[47] Some men, such as John Coffee,[48] making a will before going off to war, left everything to childless brides; others stipulated a child's portion in case the wife should be pregnant.

The wills of most men dying with many children and a good bit of property were as a rule like that of Anthony Bledsoe; [49] daughters shared equally with sons, and the mother was made executrix and given the home place. Some wills stipulated the home place should be the property of the wife only until she remarried; to others no strings were attached. A few men directed what should be done with the property on the death of the

[45] Francis Marion Rust, ed. *Doctor Walker's Diary*, Barbourville, Ky., 1950, quoting Albemarle County, Virginia Will Book, III, 232.

[46] DW, I, 249; different from most, Rice drew up a will in 1784, eight years before he was killed.

[47] *Ibid.*, 53–54.

[48] Parton, *Jackson*, I, 369–370.

[49] SW, I, 19–20.

wife, and others left commands in regard to children. Tilman Dixon, for example, stipulated his daughter Eliza was "to be kept in Lexington until her education is finished." [50] Women of all kinds also made wills.[51]

The doing away with entails and primogeniture in the United States had been so emphasized, we tend to forget that by no means all fathers of families, South as well as North, had much believed in the system in the first place. In cases in which the head of the house was killed by Indians and left no will, the court almost always made the wife executrix. Home, unless there were grievous debts or mother died, went on for the child; even when debts left the widow destitute, the court usually gave food enough to make it possible for mother and children to live together as a family. The child not only got his first lessons in democracy from the home life around him, but there was in spite of Indians, death, multiple movings, a certain stability in life.

There were exceptions of course. The saddest found was that of a widow in Pulaski County, Kentucky. Her son had already been taken from her by her father; not through legal adoption, but through binding which amounted to much the same thing, save the young one would not automatically heir the property of the man to whom he was bound, though there was no law against property being bequeathed him. The grandfather at his death cut the daughter off with a dollar and requested the court to bind the child to an uncle.[52] The grandfather, since the court had already given him custody of the child, was acting within his legal rights. Any dying father could direct that the children be bound out, or if there were sufficient funds he could order them taken from the mother's custody and placed in the hands of a guardian. I never on the Cumberland found such a guardianship; guardians were to begin with rather rare, save those appointed by the court for children with neither parent. Sometimes the mother of a family with a guardian remarried or died, and the children when older spent all or part of their time in the guardian's home as did the wards of Andrew Jackson.

In the two guardianships studied, the mother lived with her children, and the guardians merely gave an accounting to the court as they were by law required to do. The "Account of William Smith, guardian for the

[50] Smith W, V, 211

[51] Marget Mitchell, DW, I, 77; Selah Puckett, MW, I, 208; Hannah Preston, PW, I, 22.

[52] PW, I, 26. Son Jeremiah, along with his nephew also got all the property including "my plantation in Prince Edward County, Va.—my plantation whereon I now live with all horses, stock, etc."

estate of Jonathan Smith, deceased," [53] though coming past the pioneer period, 1816–1825, sheds much light on family activities and expenditures in Pulaski County, Kentucky, in the early years. The family was not by Pulaski County standards wealthy, as the division of property among the older children required only the consumption of two gallons of whiskey. Much of the income of the remaining children came from the farm and the hiring out of the slaves.

The lists of expenditures show all the joys and sorrows of the growing Joseph, Lucinda, Peggy, and Anne. Anne, for example, came down with the white swelling and the doctor bill for this alone was $20. In the bills for tuition, we know that all the children were sent to school. We can imagine the happiness of Lucinda with her new saddle and bridle that cost $36.50, though nice things were not too rare in their lives— Morocco slippers, combs, fancy shawls, materials for dresses. The most expensive item was Lucinda's Leghorn bonnet that with trimmings cost $15.50, more than a month's wages for an unskilled worker in that time and place, or in terms of whiskey at the Pulaski County price, better than seventy gallons.

In spite of Indians and sudden death from diseases no physician of the day could cure, a good many children of first and early settlers were fortunate enough to grow up with both parents. One of the best of fathers was Captain John Donelson, son of Flotilla or Colonel John. Captain John who had lost his first child, born in an open-faced camp in the cold spring of 1780, never ceased to worry over his children. His youngest, Emily, married to a cousin, Andrew Jackson Donelson, ward of Andrew Jackson, went off to Washington with her Uncle Jackson. Captain John was by no means overwhelmed by the great honor done his daughter; rather, he feared Emily's life in the "grandest circles in the City" would "spile" her, and once wrote to the young lady, "Home that sweet name Home, I think you will find it is calculated to give more Happiness than a splendid room in a President's House." And to another daughter, married to General John Coffee and moved to Alabama, he wrote, "Things are strangely altered—when you were all about us scratching, crying and balling, it was the only time if we had known it that we were happy. Anxious care will always hant the parent mind."

He was sometimes sharp with his sons as, "You put me in mind of a man with a high fever, water, water, water, and I think you have none for your cry is money, money, money." Still, he sent money and more money

[53] PW, II, 109–324.

to the boy in college, urging him: ". . . be sober, be virtuous, and be modest," yet, reminding him, "Cannot you have more patience, you are not the first person who has been in debt." [54] His own children were not enough, and he once advised Jackson, then President and as usual having trouble with somebody—this time his ward Hutchings who had, among other misdeeds, threatened to "blow out John Coffee's damned brains . . ." because Coffee had insisted he return to school, ". . . now, I give my friendly advice never to let him into a school house again; for if he is forced, he I think will run away and perhaps be his ruin." [55]

Captain John believed in reason, but more than anything he seems to have believed in kindness. It is doubtful if he would have agreed with the Jesuit priest who some years before had complained: "The . . . fathers . . . especially in the South, yield sadly and foolishly to their children whom they seem unable to contradict and whose capricious wishes they do not restrain." [56] Captain John expected the young to learn to restrain themselves. Young Hutchings in time did; he married one of the Coffee girls, settled down, and became a good husband, son-in-law, and prosperous planter.

In spite of the disinclination of parents to follow the rule beloved by the Puritans—"Spare the rod and spoil the child"—and in its place put the old saying, "You can't spoil a baby," the spoiled babies often grew up and showed an ability to take responsibility at an early age. Twelve-year-old boys manned portholes and when even younger took long trips alone to mill; young girls milked cows and sometimes managed households when mother—usually Ma or Mama—was sick or dead; at times both sexes had to perform when scarcely in their teens an adult's work in house or field.

Tennessee early earned her name of Volunteer State; the spoiled young males made mighty warriors, though poor soldiers, for nothing in the home life of the South or the old West was aimed at producing a man who would be no more than a cog in a well greased military machine. The world changed: Andrew Jackson, different from Sevier, wanted and needed at times a meek and obedient soldiery, and was, while attempting

[54] Burke, *Emily Donelson*, I, 135, 199, 35, 135–136, following order of quotations.

[55] *Ibid.*, I, 190–194, gives excerpts from the letters exchanged in 1829 between Jackson, Coffee, William Donelson, young Hutchings, and John Donelson, concerning the refusal of "my little ward Hutchings" to attend another school after having been discharged from one for "attempting to knock down one of the profesors with a chair," as William Donelson explained to Andrew Jackson Donelson then in Washington as Jackson's secretary.

[56] Handlin, *America*, Grassi, "Observations, 1819," 142.

to hold troops in the War of 1812, mightily disgusted with soldiers who wanted either to fight or to go home.

Methods of warfare were not the only things to change before Captain John's death. The increasing importance of trade during and after Cromwell followed soon by the beginnings of the speed-up in the use of machinery that we now call the Industrial Revolution had while Captain John Donelson was still young begun to change the pattern of home life in England. Years before Captain John was married, Dr. Johnson was complaining that English tradesmen neglected their families.

The home, never a strong institution in trade-loving New England as in the agricultural South, was weakened still more by father's preoccupation with trade. Industry, beginning with cloth making, took more and more manufacturing activities away from the family fireside and separated the parents. Such physical changes cannot, of course, explain fully why it was in America, first among the populous centers of the North and East, that concepts of women and home life tended more and more to follow the ideals of the peasantry on the Continent, rather than of the better classes in England. Marriage as in early New England became a patriarchal dictatorship; mother ceased to be a yoke-fellow, becoming instead only another subject moving in a separate and less important orbit, but always fixed around the head of the house, and he in turn orbiting around his occupation, usually business.

As early as 1797 a visiting Frenchman found the average Philadelphia wife much like the United States wife of today: "She becomes a woman who exists only for her husband and the care of her household. She is little more than a nursemaid; often, indeed the first and only servant—it is commonly believed that failure to find a husband is a reflection of some fault which repells lovers." [57]

Fifty years later the Viennese pianist Henri Herz found the home life of the average Philadelphia businessman, for whom trade had become a "veritable ministry," a great deal like that held up by modern writers of love-lorn columns as the ideal for wives of today's businessmen. "Mr. G's" whole life was devoted to business and business associates.[58] He had neither time nor inclination for the sharing of books, poetry, music, conversation, cards, and plays with his wife as had the very successful business-and-career man Samuel Pepys, close to two hundred years before.

[57] *Ibid.*, Moreau, "Travels, 1793–1798," 100.
[58] *Ibid.*, "Obligato by Herz," selections transl. from *Mes Voyages en Amérique*, by Henri Herz (pub. 1866; travels made in 1846; cited hereafter as Herz, "Travels, 1846"), 193–195.

Pepys has, alas, in some circles become almost a symbol of the unfaithful husband; too few remark the vast amount of interest he took in his home life—everything from food to furnishings and remodelings. He spent considerably more time instructing his bound boy and helping his brother with Latin, not to mention the hours spent with his wife, even shopping with her, than "Mr. G" gave his wife and children combined. Most of even "Mr. G's" evenings were spent with business associates.

As the American home became more and more a mere building housing people and less an institution, complaints of its custodian multiplied. An 1819 visitor, Adlard Welby, Esq., to the larger cities along the Seaboard and what is now the Midwest, found the education of the average woman had been totally "neglected" and as a result she was "a completely insipid" being, neither "sedate" as were the English nor filled with "lively wit" and "fascinating manners" as were the French. And of the women in the German colony of Harmony, Indiana, he wrote, ". . . to use the phrase of a polite man, [they] are the least handsome I ever beheld." [59]

Mrs. Trollope, who no more than Welby visited Tennessee, but concerned herself chiefly with the West as represented by Cincinnati and environs in the 1820's, was horrified to find housewives little more than unpaid servants, segregated from their husband's lives, with no amusements upon which society did not frown, save religion, and without even the dignity of pocket money. Few reminders of older attitudes toward home and family life remained, though in Cincinnati husbands still went to market, and carried home the heavier articles such as hams.

American complaints and ridicule of the female intellectual—"bluestocking"—came considerably later and are well known. Less so are the worries of the few who continued to see the wife and mother as something more than a housekeeper for a man who was often "half brute, half baby." [60] "Large numbers of our married women," a minister declared in the 1850's, "degenerate into housekeeping drudges or drones with scarce a thought save cooking and dusting." He deplored the life of the housewife who had often to "walk the round of her duties alone with none to help or cheer her," and advocated that before marriage she be educated

[59] Thwaites, *Travels*, XI, a reprint of *A Visit to North America and The English Settlements in the Illinois*, by Adlard Welby, Esq., London, 1821 (cited hereafter as Welby, *Travels*), in order, 337, 266. Welby as a well brought up Englishman was particularly horrified by the education of many American women at this date—they were sent to a form of domestic science class; he did not feel that "a practice in tarts, cheese-cakes, bons bons, &c" exactly prepared a girl to undertake "the important concerns of a wife and mother."

[60] William Henry Milburn, *The Rifle, Ax, and Saddle-bags*, Cincinnati, 1857, 165.

and have the "hallowed influence and choicest inspiration of the sages and the poets."

Moses Fisk down near Nashville had long before held much the same beliefs, and by that date his Fisk Female Academy was recognized throughout the South as a place where education for girls was not confused with training in the "domestic arts," for home in the South continued for generations important as an institution. The young continued to be shaped by its influence, and home as in many primarily agricultural societies was usually the center of the individual's world.

Still, it was never so important again as during the early years of settlement when it was not only the only institution but the center of most activities. The chapters following this are neatly labeled this and that, but all the activities discussed are chiefly a product, tangible or intangible, of home life. Yet, in the end home's most important contribution was the young ones.

Chapter Four

The Makeup
of Society

IT WAS NOVEMBER, 1795. Sally Buchanan's first-born was getting on toward three years old, and Felix Robertson, born shortly before instead of after an Indian attack, was close to fifteen. The special census of the Territory of the United States South of the River Ohio, taken as a first step toward statehood, had shown 2,832 white boys under sixteen in the three counties of what was soon to be Middle Tennessee, and about the same number of girls, the children under sixteen outnumbering every-body above by one-eighth or more.[1]

Most of these young ones had from the time of birth or at least since

Headpiece: Young backwoodsman, his wife and pack animal.

[1] TP, IV, 404–405. In this census as in others of this period, males were divided into those below and those above sixteen; females were not.

moving to the Cumberland known little sleep save that behind fort walls, but the year before, Felix's father, James Robertson,[2] had directed a successful attack against Nickojack Town on the Tennessee, and up in the Ohio woods Mad Anthony Wayne had won the bloody battle of Fallen Timbers. The Indians were defeated and along the Cumberland the fort pickets were coming down.

Peace would bring more settlers to Middle Tennessee within the next five years than in all of the first fifteen. Children, moving to their parents' lands away from the varied and often crowded life of the fort, might find loneliness, though everything indicates the Cumberlander, like the Southern colonial, rather enjoyed living apart with plenty of elbow-room, and what with help and visitors, the average farm was far from lonely.

Felix still lived with his parents at Traveler's Rest on Richland Creek, and though the four families who had lived in the fort during the Indian-troubled times would go elsewhere, Felix, in addition to his younger sister Lavinia and others of the family, still had plenty of companionship. Nearby, if not exactly next door, were the eight young Masons, the oldest a few years older than he; the Shutes lived in the same general neighborhood, and closer to Nashville, a whole houseful of young cousins was coming on. These were the children of John Cockrill and Felix's paternal aunt, Ann, the widow Johnston. The three little girls—Mary, Elizabeth, and Charity—for whom their stepfather had risked his life in the bitter times of 1781 to get bear meat, had now grown to womanhood. Their mother and stepfather had a new family—John, Nancy, Starling, James, Mark Robertson, Susannah, and Sarah—a lucky family,[3] no one had died or even lost a scalp to the Indians. Mark Robertson Cockrill, destined to see the havoc of The War but to make a great name in agriculture, was now seven years old, named for his Uncle Mark Robertson who, dying of Indian wounds and without issue, the year before Mark was born, had left much land to his three nieces, the Johnston girls,[4] and the mother out of gratitude had named the next baby for him.

Such luck as a whole family and no child dead was unusual among the first and early settlers. Valentine Sevier out at Clarksville had lost

[2] Robertson was severely reprimanded by Blount; see TP, IV, 356–359; he had had Major Ore, commander of a few troops, to lead his troops and the Cumberland militia, hoping to make the campaign official so that the men would be paid.

[3] Louis D. Wallace, *Makers of Millions*, Tennessee Dept. of Agriculture, Nashville, 1951 (cited hereafter as Wallace, *Millions*), Book II, 21.

[4] DW, I, 53–54.

four sons, and the Bledsoe wives had each lost a husband and two sons, plus brothers, sons-in-law, nieces, and nephews. In other families both parents had been killed to leave orphans like the Mayfields, the Stewarts, and little William Hall who grew up to be a general after losing most of his family at Hall's Station back in 1787 when he was six years old. The luckier of the orphans lived with relatives or were cared for by guardians; others, propertyless, like the little LeFever girls, were bound out as servants or apprentices.

There were ups and downs in life; a child had to learn to take them, but there was, now and then, a happy ending. The widow Brown had finally got back her youngest son, almost five years an Indian captive, and Miss Alcie Thompson had been ransomed for eight hundred pounds of deerskin; home again, she had married Edmund Collinsworth,[5] and in 1798 she would bear a daughter, Susan, who would be wife to Mark Robertson Cockrill. Tilman Dixon's sons and daughters [6] were filling the big low house at Dixon Springs; Captain John Donelson and Mary Purnell were getting a houseful—Tabitha, Alexander, John, Lemuel, Rachel, Mary, and William with others to come,[7] and over in East Tennessee David Crockett was ten years old. There were Douglasses, Smiths, Browns, Edmonsons, Castlemans, Weakleys, Budds, Clarks, with many who had come as children now grown and getting married.

There was by now a goodly scattering of log houses above the broad river and creek bottoms in what are now Cumberland, Wayne, and Pulaski counties of Kentucky—Richardsons, Pitmans, Campbells, Smalls, McFarlands, Dodsons, and other families—chiefly English and Scotch-Irish. A few had settled still further east near the Kentucky Trace; such a one was John Tye, soldier out of the Revolution, who built a double log house on Big Poplar Creek in what is now Whitley County.

The close to six thousand children scattered over a wide territory, in what was to be Middle Tennessee in 1795, with from a third [8] to a half that number up the river in Kentucky, represented various backgrounds and economic conditions. But practically all lived in log houses, often went barefoot in summer when they were small, had no memory of learning to ride, any more than they had memory of learning the names of

[5] Wallace, *Millions*, 13, 15.

[6] Smith W, V, 211, Dixon's will gives the names of the children.

[7] Burke, *Emily Donelson*, II, end papers, "A part of the Donelson Family Chart."

[8] This figure is an estimate based on the number of men listed when each county was created. Pulaski and Cumberland were not organized until 1799, followed by Wayne, 1800.

dozens of plants both wild and tame, or of the first bucket of water carried from the spring.

School accounts,[9] wills, guardians' accounts, binding agreements, and family Bibles yield hundreds of names of children, but the faces of these children have not come down to us. A biographer [10] of Andrew Jackson wrote that Felix Robertson was often mistaken for Jackson, "the same long slender head—and bristling hair." One can in looking at the portraits of Mark Robertson Cockrill and his Uncle James see a family resemblance, and a resemblance still, though faint, between the longer, thinner face of Andrew Jackson and that of James Robertson. Felix was somewhere in between, blue-eyed, sandy-haired, fair-skinned, as were many children of mixed Scotch and English.

There were no rules, no pioneer face; some of the Scotch were like John Buchanan, Sr., tall and spare, blue-eyed, black-headed. Some were chunky, ruddy-cheeked, bright-haired on the order of Hugh Rogan. A few would be large like James Robertson, the elder John Donelson, and Hugh F. Bell, six feet, two inches and of "a heavy build with dark hazel eyes." [11] The long mingling of Scot, English, Welsh, and French behind many, made for a great variety of bodily characteristics, and in even one home, the row of heads on the wall bench could be all colors from tow on the baby to black on the grown son. Eyes were often blue, but could be black and sparkling like those so prized in the Donelson women; they might be gray as were those of Edmund Jennings, but many showed the mingling—blue-gray, brown, green-flecked.

As a group the children of the pioneers were probably smaller, livelier, thinner-faced than are the children of today; soft roundness there may have been in some past babyhood, but I see them as big-toothed little girls with thin cheeks and big eyes; boys, shy and scrawny, growing sometimes into scrawny, thin-fleshed men, and all, if the old portraits of their elders be anything to judge by, with more of nose and chin and mouth and eye than the average American has today, their faces less flat and more animated, for chance accounts indicate the pioneer child was gigglesome, restless, forever singing or shouting or racing about when not studying or working. No traveler during the early years mentioned a hungry child or one mistreated on the Cumberland. Brother Schweinitz remembered the pretty children of Germanic descent on White's Creek, who, when visit-

[9] DW, I, 247, the inventory of Joseph Sitgreaves, an early teacher, lists the amount each parent owed.
[10] Parton, *Jackson*, I, 47–48.
[11] W, 30S, 273.

ing preachers came and Frederick Kapp played his flute, were given front seats in the room that served as meeting house.

It is doubtful if any settler on the Cumberland started at the sound of a language different from his own, for just as the river was a part of the network of rivers and trails that tied the world together, so was the average Cumberland settlement a knot of strands drawn from practically every national, religious, economic, and social group known in the colonies, with a few like Hugh Rogan from Scotland or Samuel Cole Mountflorence of France come directly from the Old World.

The Cumberland settlements, especially those in the Middle Basin, had an even greater diversity of settlers and visitors than had the Virginia and Carolina borders—half-breeds such as Findlestone, and the friendly Chickasaw constantly in and out to visit or trade or bring their guns for mending to Mr. Snyder at Clarksville. Spanish traders up from Natchez or New Orleans; others from St. Louis and the Illinois; *coureurs de bois* with boatloads of goods brought on the long, long trip by way of Vincennes or Kaskaskia; wealthy travelers from the eastern cities come to see about lands they had bought sight unseen. There were, too, as on any border, wanderers, staying only long enough to get in debt to some merchant such as De Monbruen,[12] or run up a board bill with a tavern keeper.

This mingling of peoples and goods that characterized the settlements in Middle Tennessee from earliest years was made possible partly by the Cumberland that, different from either the Tennessee or the Ohio, offered no serious obstacle in high water to navigation for close to four hundred miles. It came about, too, because the settlements in Middle Tennessee were not only the American frontier in relation to the wilderness and Indian tribes, but they were the border in regard to French and Spanish holdings. Geographically, English holdings were remote in Canada, but to anyone on a navigable stream in the Mississippi Valley, Canada, especially the Indian war party equipped with British ammunition, was close.

Yet, for all her colorful visitors and wanderers, the backbone of the Cumberland settlements were the families with children, and most of these Scotch-Irish and English. Many such as the children of James Winchester, no doubt already hearing in 1795 family talk of the great stone

[12] DW, I, 75–76, is a listing of 98 debtors from whom De Monbruen's agent was trying to collect; practically all inventories of men who had been in business left numerous debtors; some familiar, but many never found elsewhere; see in particular, *ibid.*, I, 255–259, John Rice, merchant; and Edwin Hickman, store and tavern keeper, *ibid.*, I, 223–230.

home that would some day rise on the hill above the millpond, were wealthier than others. A few spoke French, several German; though most had a Southern background, a good many families were from elsewhere, particularly Pennsylvania as were Frederick Stump and the Masons. One of the most flourishing communities up river was that at Albany, Kentucky, established by Simon Barber [13] and his family from Albany, New York. Matthew Lyon, settling soon at Eddyville down river in Kentucky, was from Vermont.

Yet, no matter how diverse their origins, language, or economic conditions, these children and their parents had much more in common than have the members of most any community today. Only a small percentage of the families living on the Cumberland in 1795 were those of first settlers, but all had in some degree the bond of remembered danger, had known the forted life, and suffered loss, if not of a relative, at least of crops and livestock. All, too, had in a sense the same occupation—John Smith, son of a small farmer in Stockton's Valley, and George Smith, son of Daniel, wealthy and widely known, were both part of a world in the building.

All shared the same environment. It was not so much that practically all lived in log houses—there was a vast difference between a great log house with tongue-and-grooved floors and good chimneys such as merchant Anthony Foster had on Budd's Creek, and the first, poor home of a not-too-well-off, newly settled family. Rather, it was the shared world of earth and sky and weather. A drouth in August, a flood in June, an untimely frost in April were tragedies to all, for all were in varying degrees concerned with the land and growing things.

This does not mean that all were land-owning farmers. The percentage of the community owning land cannot be exactly determined for any given time during pioneer days. Thomas Perkins Abernethy [14] estimated that in 1787 only one out of every eight white adults in Tennessee owned land. This figure on first thought seems low, but then one remembers the size rolls of colonial Virginia around thirty years before; less than half of the soldiers in this predominantly agricultural region gave their

[13] Samuel R. Brown, *The Western Gazetteer or Emigrant's Directory*, Auburn, N.Y., 1817 (cited hereafter as Brown, *Gazetteer*), 327–328, was greatly impressed by Simon Barber who, coming from New York around 1786, had by 1816, sixty-six descendants.

[14] Material used by permission of the publisher, The University of North Carolina Press, from *From Frontier to Plantation in Tennessee; A Study in Frontier Democracy* by Thomas Perkins Abernethy, copyright The University of North Carolina Press, Chapel Hill, 1932 (cited hereafter as Abernethy, *Frontier to Plantation*), 209.

occupation as farmer or planter;[15] possibly half of these were tenants so that one arrives at a figure between one-fourth and one-fifth. True, tax lists especially from the world of small farmers up river[16] give a much higher proportion of landowners, but as in any tax list one never knows how many men in the community are not represented. Not all men who had to pay only poll tax took the trouble to enter their names on the tax rolls.

Still, everybody with a family had at least a garden and a cow or so. A 1793 visitor to Lexington, Kentucky, a thriving place by that date with more industry than all of Middle Tennessee, observed there were no public markets for everybody had a garden.[17] The average garden of those days of children early taught to work and of cheap land was considerably more than a turnip patch, a few radishes, and a lettuce bed. The garden furnished in addition to summer vegetables a goodly store of potatoes, onions, dried beans, pumpkins, and cabbage for winter food, and sometimes corn and pumpkins for the family cow. The cow did not require a fenced field; open grazing was disappearing from the more fertile lands in Sumner and Davidson counties by 1800, but in outlying regions, especially up river, stock of all kinds continued on the open range in some localities until after World War II.

The Cumberlanders, more so than most people, spent a great deal of time outdoors. Parton, biographer of Jackson, commented in wonder on their habits, for even when not outside, most families, no matter what the weather, closed their doors only at night. True, life for most demanded they spend most of their time outside. Even the merchant, unconcerned with farming, though most merchants, judging from their inventories, did have farms, took business trips that could mean weeks of living on horseback, and in the early years, camping out. Lawyers such as Jackson traveled from one end of the state to the other, and though his horses were undoubtedly better than those of Davy Crockett, a flooded creek or a sudden violent thunderstorm wetted each, for such was life; no amount of money could entirely shield any human being from the discomforts of the weather.

[15] VM, I, 378–390; II, 37–60.
[16] In the first tax list of Cumberland County, for example, 193 of the 348 men over 21 owned land, none with less than 100 acres. Material used by permission of the copyright owner, Judge J. W. Wells, from *History of Cumberland County* by Judge J. W. Wells, Louisville, 1947 (cited hereafter as Wells, *Cumberland County*), 32–39, "First Tax List of Cumberland County (Ky.) May 1, 1799."
[17] Toulmin, *Western Country*, 128.

Judging from the remarks of the old, they enjoyed the woods and the river and the roads in all weathers. Few places on earth have ever held so much of beauty and of wonder as did the varied lands of hills, never too high for a boy's climbing, caves, sinkholes, creeks, waterfalls, glades, meadows, and stretches of heavily timbered land along the Cumberland. The trip to county court, the ride to mill, or even the walk to school was through a constantly changing world that held something of interest and often of value—chestnuts, an unusually fine arrowhead washed into the gullied road, a swan on the river—for rich and poor alike. There were hundreds of different plants, many more beautiful than most in any garden—Virginia cowslips by the river, the wonder of a freshly opened passionflower half hidden in the bushes, witch hazel flowering in November, and on hills and ridges high enough for sandstone, azaleas, laurel, ivy, now and then in a rich cove, wahoo; and all over the little things, seen less maybe by the sharp-eyed boy hunting squirrels than the old woman gathering ratbane—tiny bluets sometimes in February, earlier than arbutus, and later the fragile wild columbine growing on limestone bluffs below pawpaw thickets where now and then one might glimpse the rich red brown of a wild ginger flower.

This world when the Indian Wars were ended opened more widely; the walk to school for both girls and boys, rich and poor, sounds today to many a great hardship; long it often was and through all weathers, sub-zero cold to burning heat, hail, sleet, thunderstorms, fog; the Cumberland had them all. Yet much of it was down paths and along little roads where a child could linger to watch and often try to catch the crawfish in the spring branch, or turn aside to hunt grapes or pawpaws, or simply stand and wonder by an opened stone-lined grave.

All shared this world and its weather. Even those in the largest town, Nashville, were for many years practically in the country. Rural slums were not yet around, and though many were wealthy, the day-to-day life for most of the children was much alike. Donelson went to school with Castleman, and even food was much the same, and whether cooked by Mama or a slave, tasted faintly of wood smoke and embers. Cook stoves in even such a great place as the last Hermitage were but little used. Everybody had outdoor toilets, were warmed by open fires, and got their water from rainbarrels and a spring. Long past the pioneer period, most of even the wealthier plantations, many with brick homes, offered as an added inducement when put up for sale, a "never failing spring."

There were neither "oldsters" nor "teen-agers." Statistics had not yet come into being; retirement was unheard of for a farmer as long as he was able to oversee things, and the old lived scattered among the young. There was no unemployment; all travelers mentioned the demand for workers and the high wages in the old West. They remained high for many years.[18] Even as late as 1818 when there were thousands of unemployed in New York, and the Quakers in Philadelphia [19] were organizing soup kitchens, there was no suffering in the West.

Long before the ending of the Indian Wars, the Cumberland knew plenty of food. No woman need ever go to bed wondering how many children within the radius of a few miles were sleepless with hunger. Poverty is of course relative. Political supporters of Davy Crockett and Abraham Lincoln, for example, made much of their poverty, yet the land, livestock, and stores of food of their families would have seemed great riches to the always hungry poor of much of the Continent or a New England cotton mill employee or a spade-wielding Irishman. Michaux, traveling through the rough lands of western Pennsylvania, was impressed, for in spite of poor housing and bad roads, he did not in this region of still-fertile hillside land find "a single family without milk, butter, smoked or salted meat—the poorest man has always one or two horses." [20] This seems always to have been true in any newly settled, well timbered region—until the land washed away, the population increased, and the timber disappeared.

In economic opportunity as represented by cheap land, cheap building and fencing materials, and for the laborer high wages and cheap food, Middle Tennessee during pioneer years and for some time after was, for the lucky and the strong, a greater economic paradise than anything known since, and almost as good as colonial Virginia had been when most travelers commented on the lack of poverty.

All these fine statements hold true only if one forgets the large number of children along with their parents in the Cumberland Country who left neither name nor face—the slaves. These during pioneer years formed the only group on the Cumberland that could be defined as a class apart

[18] Michaux, *Travels 1802*, commented often on the high wages, particularly in Ky.. 153, 246, but found them higher still in the Cumberland settlements, *ibid.*, 246.
[19] Faux, *Travels, 1818–1819*, 124, 160, told of 1,500 families unemployed in New York, and in Pennsylvania such was the excess of laborers that many worked all winter for nothing but their keep; but in the West he saw—Ohio and Indiana—he found no want of the "common necessaries." See also Welby, *Travels*, 299, 302.
[20] Michaux, *Travels 1802*, 35, 59.

with little hope of advancement. Slavery was an accepted part of life in most of the United States; [21] some of the early Baptists and Methodists, but most especially the Quakers, were opposed to it. Opposition was not a regional matter. There was for much of the time before 1850 more abolition sentiment in East Tennessee alone, not to mention the rest of the South, than in all of New England. The first abolitionist paper in the United States was Elihu Embree's *The Emancipator*, published in 1820 at Jonesborough, Tennessee. Yet, as late as 1835 an abolitionist [22] was mobbed in Boston, Massachusetts. Possibly the greatest feeling against slavery came, not from religionists, but from the belief, rather widespread during and for a time after the Revolution, that any human being had certain rights just because he was a human being. Religionists of later years used the Bible in their arguments for slavery, and such abolitionists as John G. Fee, the Bible-quoting educator connected with the founding of Berea College in Kentucky, felt it necessary to cut all references to slaveholding from their Bibles.

This belief in human rights, though held by many in the old West, was not peculiar to the frontier, nor was it reserved for the Negro. The members of St. Andrew's Society in New York were undoubtedly playing politics, but they were also manifesting something of the spirit of the times when at Tammany Hall, in August of 1790, they entertained the visiting mestizo, Alexander McGillivray, chief of the Creeks, by singing to the tune of "Nottingham Ale": [23]

> "The time is at hand, nay, already appears,
>> When the empire of reason shall govern the world
> And error though sanctioned by thousands of years
>> With contempt, as it ought, from our bosoms be hurled.
> That in feature or colour no difference can be
>> In the eye of that mind which called forth mankind
> To make them one family happy and free."

All this had no effect whatever on McGillivray, several of whose braves were present two years later at the siege of Buchanan's Station,

---

[21] Pennsylvania with its high percentage of Quakers, not only had no slavery but was a center of the antislavery movement; practically all issues of Mr. Carey's *Museum* carried articles urging the freedom of slaves. *Ibid.*, I, Volume I, is typical; see especially, 128, 238; and "Quakers Petition against Slavery," *ibid.*, 388–389.

[22] Hanna, *The Scotch-Irish*, I, 99; this was William Lloyd Garrison.

[23] Carey, *Museum*, VIII, Appendix, 9.

and in general the Cumberland pioneer gave the Indian better treatment than he got from him.[24]

The early Cumberland Country seems to have been a world remarkably free from hatred of all kinds. Few are the expressions of hatred for any Indian, and the man who hated all Indians was almost non-existent. There were likewise no expressions of hatred for the Negro. One finds instead, pity, sometimes love, and often understanding. Slave or no, the black man was to most still an individual. Not all slaves on arrival in the Colonies had been of the same mental and physical endowments, and by the time the Cumberland was settled they varied even more widely as individuals. Many had, in addition to goodly mixtures of white blood, not a little Indian, the mingling taking place for the most part in Georgia and South Carolina where Indians had been used as slaves, though with little success.

The slave in the eyes of many is forever seen as but a darker version of the man-with-the-hoe, the hard-driven field hand of the deep South. He was in late years sometimes this, but he or she was also often the most skilled person in a given craft to be found in the community. Agriculture as practiced in Virginia and North Carolina had been unable to utilize large numbers of unskilled laborers. It was only in the West Indies and the rice and indigo fields of the deeper South that sheer brawn and endurance counted for more than skill. Virginia slaves had to be able to train and shoe horses; cultivate, cure, and strip tobacco; and do a dozen and one other skilled and semiskilled jobs connected with the plantation. Slave women not only cooked, but wove, spun, and performed many of the crafts and skills of the white housewife.

The numerous taboos against mingling with all persons of any known amount of Negro blood that in time appeared in the southern states in the form of laws were unknown during colonial and pioneer years.

---

[24] During the pioneer period many attempts were made in several Cherokee towns of East Tennessee to establish missions and schools among the Indians: see Williams, *Travels*, Martin Schneider, "Account of a journey made to the Cherokee in 1783 with the hope of establishing a mission," 250–265. The Moravian brethren who visited the Cumberland settlements in the winter of 1799–1800, had on this trip spent much time among the Cherokee in East Tennessee; they, no different from Schneider, also a Moravian, found the white settlers most helpful; Schweinitz, "Reports," 468, concluded: "We can truthfully say that everywhere and by everybody we have been treated with the greatest friendship as Moravians, and this was always because we have undertaken this journey for the sake of the Indians." Moses Fisk, who later founded a girls' school near Nashville, also visited the Cherokee in 1799, seemingly under the auspices of Dartmouth and the Society for Propagating Christian Knowledge, but nothing came of his visit.

There was, it is true, little intermarriage, for most white blood that mixed with Negro came through white males whose wives were also white.

There were no laws against the education of Negroes and none of the fear so characteristic today of the deeper South. The word Negro was used only for a person whose blood was entirely, or almost so, of that race, and in place of Negro they often used "person of color." Others were designated as mulattoes or "persons of mixed blood"; the use of the word slave was avoided; people spoke instead of the help, the blacks, or the black family.[25]

The North Carolina colonial planters had seldom objected to certain of their slaves living in town and carrying on trades and businesses as long as the slave turned over most of his earnings to his master. North Carolina, the State, was less lenient, and in 1785 passed detailed laws to "restrain and regulate the conduct of slaves . . . and others." [26] These laws stipulated among many other matters that free Negroes must wear badges, and revived an old colonial law forbidding slaves to own homes and business establishments in town.

The laws of 1785 were in force in Tennessee as long as it belonged to North Carolina, but they seem not to have been enforced. Two early places of business in Nashville—Bob Renfroe's tavern and Caesar's cakes and beer stand—were owned by Negroes. Barbershops and other small businesses, owned and operated by Negroes and patronized by whites, continued common in much of the South for many years, particularly in New Orleans.[27]

Slavery was a well established institution throughout the New World long before the old West was settled. The first slave known to have been taken across the mountains was the mulatto boy with Christopher Gist on his exploration of Kentucky in 1750; and as many Negroes had the same ability in woodscraft as did white hunters and explorers, they were brought by many such groups. Jamie, the mulatto boy who cared for James Smith, crippled by a cane stub in his foot in 1766, is the first record of a slave living on the Cumberland. Another came with James Robertson on his exploratory journey in 1779, and they continued to come with most emigrating families. John Donelson's *Adventure* alone carried thirty, and

[25] The word *hand* was used almost exclusively for field help, as Major W. B. Lewis to Jackson, Bassett, *Jackson Correspondence*, V, 65, "I told him if an overseer would be constantly with his hands, very little whipping would be required."
[26] NCR, XXIV, 725–30.
[27] Ashe, *Travels*, 310.

on the trip down the Tennessee a slave from the Jennings boat was killed, and still another died of frostbite.

During the early hardest years black man and white prayed, fought, traveled, worked side by side in the fields, and sometimes, as when Freeland's was attacked in 1781, shared the same room. Negroes often helped defend stations. They were particularly remembered in the defense of Renfroe's Station on Red River, destroyed by the Indians in the summer of 1780;[28] Robert survived to keep a tavern in Nashville but others were killed. Many also wrote of how "a Negro Cuff" and "Abraham an intelligent old mulatto" fought at Greenfield's.[29] Black man fighting with white was not new. Many Southern Negroes had fought in the Revolution,[30] and long before that had helped defend the South Carolina border against Indians.

Slaves continued to be brought to the Cumberland as elsewhere to the settling West in ever increasing numbers. The 1791 census gave only slightly more than 1,100 slaves or somewhat less than one-sixth of a total population of around 7,000; four years later the proportion was close to one-fourth, almost 2,500 slaves to a total of 11,924; by 1801 when the census was completed the proportion had risen above a fourth, or 8,074 slaves to a total of 31,669.[31]

The pattern of ownership in Middle Tennessee during pioneer years was different from that of the deep South later or the great Tidewater plantations of colonial days. Middle Tennessee was and continued to be basically a land of well-to-do working farmers, rather than plantation owners with overseers. The plantation with fifty to a hundred slaves was not too uncommon in the richer districts of Middle Tennessee by around 1840, but the average pioneering farmer had no overseer and seldom more than a dozen slaves including children. Most of those who owned slaves or about half the householders had only one or two adults with children uncounted. Slaves, though less numerous, were more widely distributed during pioneer years than later. Michaux found most Middle Tennessee farmers owning slaves,[32] as had Francis Baily five years earlier.

Slaves, cheap as they were in the very early years, were no particular mark of affluence, and were owned by men so unfortunate in business

[28] W, 30S, 247.

[29] *Ibid.*, 31S, 385, 390.

[30] Draper, *King's Mountain*, 267.

[31] TP, IV, 81, 404, lists the earlier census figures; Tenn. *Gazette*, Nov. 11, 1801, gives the last.

[32] Michaux, *Travels 1802*, 256.

as Michael Stoner, ferryman up in Wayne County, Kentucky. Slave-holding was in this region of smaller areas of fertile soil much less common. Two districts of Wayne County had in 1801 only 121 slaves to 344 white men above twenty-one.[33] In District Number Two of adjoining Cumberland County,[34] only one-tenth of the 350 white adult males owned slaves with a total of 87. This ratio of scarcely one slave to four white men was in sharp contrast to Sumner County where in 1800 there were a third more taxable blacks, that is above fourteen years of age, than grown white males.

Treatment of slaves varied from family to family, but as a rule the slave of the middle-class farmer[35] enjoyed better living conditions and less dehumanization than did the field hand of the cotton country of a later date. However, the welfare of the slave depended almost entirely on his master and chance; on many of the larger plantations the slave had better medical care, more regular and less strenuous hours than he could ever have known under a debt-ridden farmer or a tenant on poor land, but in general the overseer system with the actual owner scarcely knowing his field hands and interested only in cash profits made for a hard life. The only restraining factor for some of the more vicious owners and overseers was the cost of the slave. Food on the Cumberland was undoubtedly better and more abundant than either in the East or later in the deeper South where pork and meal for the slaves had to be imported, much of it from Middle Tennessee.

The strong hatred of slavery later manifested in the North and by visitors such as Mrs. Trollope was not during pioneer years in evidence. Most travelers to the Cumberland mention slavery no more than any other ordinary aspect of life. Francis Baily remarked that the whole drudgery of farm life in both the house and the field was committed to the slave, but he in no way showed himself opposed to slavery. Michaux the younger, though considering himself a man of republican principles, saw slavery as a very good thing indeed, and was the first instance

[33] RK, XXVII, No. 79, 34, 37—author's count made from the tax lists as handed in by Edward Cullon, and Micah Taul, clerk.

[34] Wells, *Cumberland County*, 39.

[35] Toulmin, *Western Country*, 57, commented of slavery in Virginia, after deploring the evils of the system, "—though I am of the opinion that a large proportion of the slaves—are better off than the poor of England." Welby, though in general one of the harshest critics of the United States, commented of slavery in South Carolina of 1818, *Travels*, 289, "—not once during the journey did I witness an instance of cruel treatment, nor could I discover anything to excite commiseration; doubtless there may be instances of cruelty, but I am inclined to think such are of rare occurrence." He also, *ibid.*, 229, found the slaves well clothed, fed, and taken care of.

I found on the Cumberland of the attitude toward slavery later a feature of the Cotton Kingdom; that is, the consideration of the slave or "hand" as a unit of production,[36] capable of showing a given profit each year, with future prosperity bound up in the acquisition of more slaves.

Families such as the Neelys, Buchanans, Gowens, and others who owned as a rule less than a dozen slaves and many of these children, practiced a pattern of agriculture that was a way of life. They could not measure their slaves in terms of money earned any more than they could or would attempt to measure the earnings of their wives and children. A very great deal of slave labor, like a very large percentage of their own time and money, simply went into making life a bit richer and more comfortable. The skilled black woman in the kitchen could have added a good deal to the family income by being turned into a field hand or weaver of cloth to be sold, and make of the wife a cook to wrestle with heavy ironware over a hot fire. They did not see life that way; even the small establishment usually had a separate kitchen, and in the household with only three or four slaves almost always one of these served as cook and house servant.

Many slaves had been freed in all sections of the South before the Revolution, and as early as 1792 an antislavery pamphlet was published in Lexington. The Tennessee Constitution of 1796 [37] gave suffrage rights to the around four hundred freed male slaves then in the state, and sentiment continued such that in 1798 Henry Clay found it politically feasible to favor abolition.

However, such was the temper and the needs of the times, sympathy for the Negro, like that for the Indian, did not thrive. Clay soon found it even more politically feasible to forget abolition. More settlers increased the pressure to send the Indian west of the Mississippi; the more land in the South cleared for cotton, the greater demand for slaves. The price rose sharply after importation was stopped, at least officially, in 1808, and in New England moral indignation rose in proportion as profits from slavery and the slave trade dwindled. Yet abolition followed no set pattern, and directions for the freeing of some or all of the family slaves can be found among the court minutes of any county on the Cumberland.[38]

---

[36] Michaux, *Travels 1802*, 294–295.

[37] Haywood, Laws, 1–13, gives the first Constitution of the State of Tennessee.

[38] DW, II, 32 (1795), Nelly is set free; PW, II, 74, "free Lucy and free Jack"; PW, III, 420, David Roper not only freed Hector and Lucy but gave them all his goods; Smith W, V, 210, the freeing of several; in other cases the owner, as in

There was always a good deal of sympathy for the Negro whether slave or free. One of the most popular poems of the day was "The Negro's Complaint"; printed in the American *Museum* in 1791, it appeared ten years later in the Tennessee *Gazette:*

> Fleecy locks and black complexion
> Cannot forfeit Nature's claim
> Skins may differ but affection
> Dwells in white and black the same.[39]

Another published the same year and by popular request was the long narrative poem, "The Sorrows of Yamba," [40] in which the whole woeful lot of the slave and the dark pattern of slavery were blamed on the eagerness of English ships' captains for the lucrative trade.

No early visitor to the Cumberland mentions cruelty to slaves, and one might almost wax lyrical over the many examples of kindness to and concern for not only slaves, but the free "person of color." The Tennessee *Gazette* through April of 1802, for example, gave much space to the plight of a seventeen-year-old mulatto girl stolen from her mother down in Robertson County. It was feared she had been taken south to be sold as many Negroes both slave and free were; she was described and readers were urged to be on the lookout for her. Earlier still, we find the justices of Davidson County Court breaking the binding agreement of a mulatto who had bound himself for a year at too low a figure.[41] More than twenty years later the justices of Smith County gave a great deal of time to Rebecca Budman. Rebecca was free; everyone knew she had settled in the community as a free woman, but she had no papers. In her case it was particularly important; she had children and children born to a free woman were free. The Court at last legally established her freedom,[42] so that no unscrupulous trader might come through and carry her children off into slavery.

Once a slave it was almost impossible to free oneself, for slaves were not permitted to testify in court. The law was all on the side of the owner; even if the slave died under the lash, bringing charges against the

---

the will of James Simpson, PW, III, 203, stipulated the slaves should be kept together on the farm; or PW, I, 56, have the privilege of choosing a master.

[39] Tennessee *Gazette*, Oct. 7, 1801.
[40] *Ibid.*, Oct. 28, 1801.
[41] DC, I, 78.
[42] Smith W, V, 241.

murderer, trying him, and getting a conviction were under the existing law almost impossible. True, "killing a slave was the same as killing a free man," but, the "but" was a big one, "provided the slave was not in an act of defiance or dying under moderate correction." [43] The murderer could always say there had been an act of defiance, and who was there to contradict?

One could point out that throughout this period the whipping of whites was common. I never on the Cumberland found a white woman whipped, but Dr. Doddridge wrote of the beating given a bound girl in Philadelphia after the Revolution. She had helped herself to the family sugar; this was theft, and under prevailing law the amount stolen was of no consequence; even a small amount could mean the death penalty. The 1792 order of a Sumner County Court that Nathaniel Holley be taken to the public whipping post [44] "and there receive 39 lashes on his bare back well laid on" was not unusual in its day, when the whipping to death of a common soldier or sailor in most armed forces of the world was a punishment taken pretty much as a matter of course.

The tender concern Andrew Jackson in the White House took in little Hannah, crippled by blows from the black cook, makes a touching contrast, for Jackson felt that little Negroes should be beaten with "a small switch only." [45] Still, one cannot help but remember announcements in the Tennessee *Gazette* of more than thirty years before in which the attention of the reader is called to Andrew Jackson's mulatto who "could pass for a free man." He had run away, wearing a drab greatcoat, dark mixed body coat, both a ruffled and a plain shirt of cotton homespun with the usual overalls.[46] A reward of $50 was offered for his capture which seemingly took place soon, as the ad was not long continued. Another Jackson slave ran away southward, but Jackson soon captured him.

The man nameless, able to read and write and so forge a pass and be accepted as a freed slave or even a white man, was only one of a great many, their flight recorded in the same fashion; "Robert Cartwright's Negro man"—"likely Phyllis, cut much with the whip"—Jason, a cake baker—Judge McNairy's Negro fellow who "plays well upon the violin" [47]— a mulatto boy who spoke French—Cato a cooper—the slave Andrew belonging to E. Evans.

[43] Haywood, *Laws*, 245.
[44] SC, I, 52.
[45] Bassett, *Jackson Correspondence*, V, 24.
[46] Tennessee *Gazette*, Oct. 3, 1804.
[47] *Ibid.*, March 11, 1801.

Their chances of escape were slight. Thievery was one of the most hated crimes of the day and any slave who ran away was a thief in that he stole not only himself but the very clothing he wore. He could be punished for both thefts. The slave was often hunted with dog and gun, as a wild animal was hunted, not necessarily by the gentlemanly owner, but by someone who wanted the reward, for most owners offered a reward as did Jackson.

Judging from the announcements of runaways, the educated, literate slave, often a mulatto, skilled in some craft, was more inclined to run away than the field hand, though it is possible the percentage of skilled, literate slaves was extremely high on the Cumberland. Those capable of nothing save unskilled field work were more commonly sold to southern planters. Slaves ran away for various reasons, and some owners had more trouble than others. No matter what his situation the slave was still a human being. People like Captain John Donelson and John Coffee who lived in peace with the neighbors appear to have had no trouble with slaves. Not so the fiery Jackson to whom at first the life of a slaveholder was rather new. He is said to have had one mulatto girl when he rode into Tennessee, but most of his first slaves came as a part of Rachel's dowry.[48]

Jackson also found his trade in slaves particularly wearisome, and almost always each boatload made less profit than he had expected. The slaves Jackson took in exchange for goods from his various stores had, like everything else—cotton or pipe staves—to be sold, and the slave, different from pipe staves, would almost always, particularly in the deeper South, bring cash instead of more goods; also, different from the staves, the slave on his way to market had to be fed and clothed. This irritated Jackson.

He reckoned the average cost of slave transportation from Nashville to New Orleans should be no more than $15 per head,[49] this usually for women and children. A strong male slave could on the trip down to market earn $50 for his master as boatman or handy man.[50]

Jackson was particularly incensed when the master of a boatload of

---

[48] DW, I, 199, Rachel Jackson in the division of the Donelson property—not all divided at this time—got George and Moll.

[49] Bassett, *Jackson Correspondence*, I, 217.

[50] John M. Gray, *The Life of Joseph Bishop*, Nashville, 1858 (cited hereafter as Gray, *Bishop*), 145–183. Bishop came out to the Cumberland settlements in 1791 when he was 21 years old; primarily a hunter and Indian scout, he, when the country became more settled, turned to other means of earning a living; one was buying two slaves on credit and taking them to Natchez; he and his Negro man were each to get $50., the whole of course to go to Bishop.

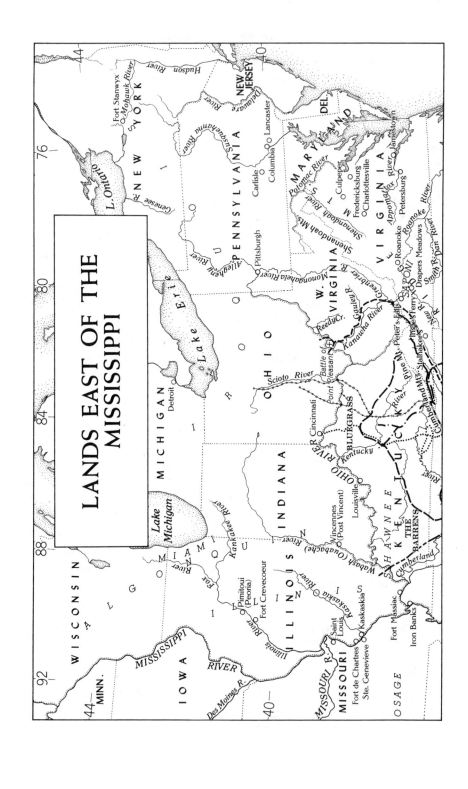

LANDS EAST OF THE MISSISSIPPI

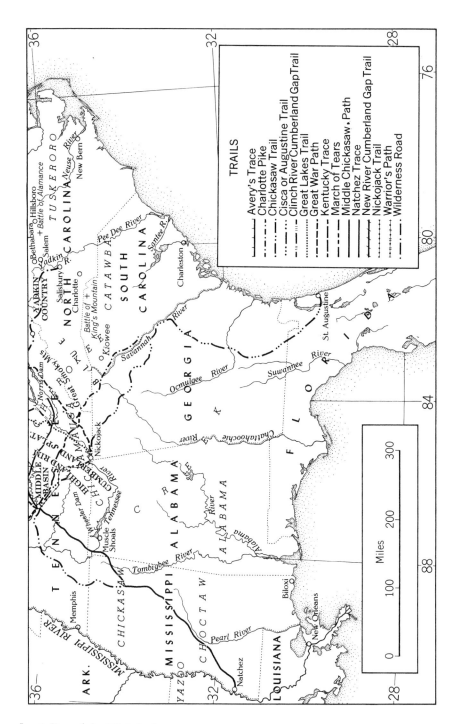

Lands East of the Mississippi

TRAILS

Avery's Trace
Charlotte Pike
Chickasaw Trail
Cisca or Augustine Trail
Clinch River Cumberland Gap Trail
Great Lakes Trail
Great War Path
Kentucky Trace
March of Tears
Middle Chickasaw · Path
Natchez Trace
New River Cumberland Gap Trail
Nickojack Trail
Warrior's Path
Wilderness Road

"25 grown negroes and 2 suckling children" stopped on the way and spent $60 on clothing, so running up the cost, the whole averaged $44.66⅔ per head to sell. Jackson felt the man, if he bought anything, should have bought cloth only, and let the "13 wenches" in the party make the clothing as they rode down to be sold.[51] Most disappointing was the mother, Lucy, sent down with two young children and a suckling baby; the two little ones sold quickly enough, but the woman, a weakly thing to begin with, and worse, with a baby given to fits, had to be kept three months in Natchez, and then she brought with the baby only $325, a low price for Natchez in 1809. Still, Jackson held her up as a model of cheapness, for Lucy, sickly as she was, and with a little baby, saved Jackson money, paying the whole of her three-month board bill by doing laundry.[52]

The earliest court minutes on the Cumberland attest to the importance of the slave as a commodity.[53] John Turnbull, trader to the Chickasaw, dealt much in slaves as did any other trader, for almost always the sale of a slave meant cash. The end of the Indian Wars and consequent rapid settlement increased the demand, and hence the traffic. The slave, like the horse, was a popular medium of currency for the larger transactions, as, for example, John Nelson[54] was in 1799 mainly interested in disposing of a 1,100 acre plantation near the Big Harpeth; he would take cash or "likely Negroes." The casual commerce in slaves was of course not confined to the Cumberland, for at this date they were still being imported by New England sea captains.

John Coffee, for example, quite a well-born man and soon with good connections on the Cumberland, came out in 1797 with a coffle of slaves for which he had paid $1,800 in Virginia. These he sold in Middle Tennessee for $2,646.[55] This profit when reckoned in land, choice at this time worth only from three to five dollars an acre, and most selling for considerably less, represented more than a first settler got for building a fort and holding it four years against the Indians.

[51] Bassett, *Jackson Correspondence*, I, 218–219.

[52] *Ibid.*, I, 196, 217.

[53] DW, I, 13, 14, 56, 86–88, are only a few examples of sales, some to Turnbull, of slaves; these do not include inventories in which slaves were sold or divided among the heirs.

[54] *Rights of Man or the Nashville Intelligencer*, Aug. 28, 1799. One often finds the same kind of exchange in early court records as, DW, I, 56, a 1785 debt of "900 pounds or nine likely Negroes."

[55] Facts used by permission of Dr. William T. Alderson, Tennessee State Librarian and Archivist from the Robert Dyas Collection of John Coffee, Donelson Family and Jackson papers, owned by the Tennessee Historical Society and housed in the Archives Division of the Tennessee State Library and Archives, Nashville (cited hereafter as Coffee Papers, these are unnumbered but dated), Coffee Papers, 1797.

The slave was not only at the mercy of his owner but all the adversities of the owner's world. In cases of financial disaster the slaves as the most valuable and easily disposable assets were almost always the first things to be sold. Death, even of the well-to-do, brought division of property and sometimes of slave families; other times, as in the case of the Jackson slaves, death of the mistress and absence of the owner brought sufferings hitherto unknown. Slaves belonging to orphaned minor children were not, save in case of debt, customarily sold, but often rented, usually on a yearly basis, and many were the ads announcing slaves for hire,[56] while others asked for them.[57]

The famous jockey Monkey Simon belonged to minor heirs and was hired on a yearly basis. Many were skilled and earned much for their masters; in Pulaski County, Kentucky, when women in the New England cotton mills were working for a dollar a week without keep, and newly transported Irish workmen were with pick and shovel earning without keep around forty cents a day, we find one of the Smith Negroes earning $104.50 plus keep for eight months' work,[58] and none made as little as $50 yearly, the standard wage with keep for an unskilled laborer.

Differing only from the slave in that his servitude had an end was the bound or indentured servant, in the early colonial period the most common form of cheap labor. He is not to be confused with the free laborer—overseer or farm hand—contracted for on a yearly basis or a season or until a given job, chimneys or brick wall of the new home, was finished; payment would come when the work was done. The bound servant was paying a debt he already owed; and if he or she ran away before the end of servitude, it was considered a theft, and quite frequently a reward was offered as in the case of a runaway slave. All through colonial days and during the first decades of the United States the debt most commonly paid in such fashion was that incurred for transportation from Europe to America. People too poor to pay their own passages or thrifty souls like the Germans, willing to sell each child for several years, made a much cheaper source of labor than did the slave,[59] for many could be bought for

[56] Tennessee *Gazette*, Dec. 2, 1801: "Thomas Johnson, guardian of Henry Hart will hire out Negroes."

[57] Typical was Montgomery Bell, ironmaster, wanting to hire, "good negro fellows," for Cumberland Furnace, Tennessee *Gazette*, Feb. 22, 1804. Others asked for a "smart active Negro man," *ibid.*, Jan. 4, 1801.

[58] PW, II, 35.

[59] Handlin, *America*, "Peter Kalm, Scientist from Sweden," a selection transl. from Kalm's *En Resa til Norra America 1753–61*, 29–30, discusses kinds of servants used during the late colonial period; the Germans seem to have been the only ones who, after paying their own fares, let their children out to the highest bidders.

five years for as low as five pounds each. In contrast a maidservant in Pennsylvania working on a yearly basis earned between eight and ten pounds in one year with everything furnished save clothing.

Indentured servants were of many varieties and a good many of the Scotch-Irish had come to the South as bound servants during colonial days. The bound servant, a stranger in a strange land, unfamiliar with his work and sometimes the language, had a hard lot. Years later Mrs. Trollope felt the adult Irish laborer, working long hours in unhealthful conditions for less than subsistence wages, was worse off than the slave. Many of these, like later laborers imported from other countries, lived for many years under a form of binding. In their cases some American industrial firm had recruited them, put up passage money, and then taken it from their wages, thus earning a triple profit—the passage itself, the labor at low wages, and the constantly accumulating interest.

The South was not primarily interested in cheapness; as more and more slaves became skilled in all manner of occupations from blacksmithing to caring for horses, the bound servant grew much less common, though as late as 1793 Harry Toulmin, visiting Englishman, met a Virginia planter who yearly sent for "persons from North Britain who were indebted to him for five years, but all got plantations of their own."[60] This seems to have been the usual story of the Scotch-Irish bound servant in the early years. He in time became a land-owning member of the community.

Fewer still were brought to the old West. Toulmin found none [61] in Kentucky in 1793 and there were few on the Cumberland. Ann Harkness, "late of Ireland" and bound to finish her term of servitude in the establishment of the merchant John Rice, was the only indentured person found; [62] Jemmy O'Connor may have been a bound servant, sold as many were to the highest bidder by some ship's captain and resold to someone going west. The unskilled male immigrant might with fair readiness fit

---

[60] Toulmin, *Western Country*, 42. The author remarked, "There are no families in Virginia who continue merely hired laborers from one generation to another."

[61] *Ibid.*, 65.

[62] DW, I, 106. Ann had been sold to Rice by her former master, John Thompson of Baltimore, for "16 pounds current money," and was to serve five years. There may have been a few others; the announcement, Tennessee *Gazette*, Aug. 3, 1803, "Ran away, Philip Kuhner, 25 years old—speaks broken English—took with him a German grammar and a red pocket book," would indicate a bound servant rather than a bound boy learning a trade; these were free at 21. The 1801 census, *ibid.*, Nov. 11, 1801, lists 34 "other persons" in Mero District; this included free Negroes, Indians, and bound servants, if any.

into the less demanding farm life of New England, and as manufacturing increased, the United States became a haven for the unskilled, the illiterate, and the destitute. The frontier could use neither diggers of ditches nor spindle changers unfamiliar with guns and trees.

Most of the paid, white help in the early years, the men who served as guards, cattle drovers, boatmen, or handy men in general, came, as did the men for whom they worked, from Virginia and North Carolina, and were strange neither to the ways of the frontier nor to all the members of the community. There were a few exceptions but most mentioned as guards—Hugh F. Bell, Edwin Hickman, the Castlemans—were highly respected and responsible men. They had relatives, and, though working for wages, cannot be lumped together as a class of unskilled laborers apart from the farming community. Most aspired to and often succeeded in becoming landowners, as did Joseph Bishop.

The unskilled white laborer, his services contracted for on a yearly basis, never got less than fifty dollars a year plus board and lodging. Working by the day, the pioneer laborer got fifty cents and often more. He did not have to worry about unemployment; the demand ever exceeded the supply. In 1800 his day's work would buy around seventeen pounds of good pork,[63] slightly more of beef, two bushels or more of corn that when ground and the toll paid would yield close to a hundred pounds of meal. He could afford a fair log house,[64] far better than the tar-paper shanties that came in time to the hills, or those of the slums that later came even to the county seat towns. Clothing was a different story —that is if he wanted to buy cloth; a yard of the cheapest cost almost a day's wages. Still, one should not reckon without his wife; it was taken for granted as in England and Scotland that all wives worked—not in the fields,[65] but over the more profitable loom and spinning wheel. Children,

[63] All travelers to the western frontiers commented in wonder on the high wages and cheap living; see in particular Michaux, *Travels 1802*, 153, 246, 255. The Accounting of Leah Lucas, DW, II, 63–64, gives a good idea of the cheapness of living during the first fifteen years of settlement; Tennessee *Gazette*, Nov. 13, 1802, and *ibid.*, May 30, 1804, "Prices Current at Natchez" give an indication of the cost of basic commodities, cheaper in Tennessee.

[64] Coffee Papers, 1803, gave only $247.95 labor costs for a large store with many pigeonholes and shelves, windows, a stairway, fireplaces, etc., while an office building in Nashville, *ibid.*, 1809, cost $189.85 including window glass, hall, etc. If a man could content himself with logs, few nails, and do much of the work himself, he had only a reasonable expense; he could exchange work with his neighbors, though I never on the Cumberland found an account of a "house raising" save a schoolhouse in Stockton's Valley, see Williams, *Smith*, 27–29.

[65] Michaux, *Travels 1802*, 241.

too, were economic assets in a world where everybody had a garden and a cow—ten or twelve dollars with young calf; nor did the work of children prevent their attending school or studying at home.

The working man of 1800 earning only fifty cents daily could buy more food than can the factory worker of today only if he used home-grown produce. A pound of coffee like a pound of sugar took a day's wages—silks, satins, and imported calicoes were beyond his reach; [66] nor could he usually afford a horse; the shoeing of one cost eight days' wages. On foot and in homespun he might go, but he could have food and shelter, and though unable to afford sugar and coffee he could buy all he needed of cheap maple sugar and whiskey—a month's supply of the latter, two gallons, could be had up river for little more than a day's wages.[67] His daily wages would also buy a larger chunk of farming land than will the daily wage of the factory worker today.

Long before the Indian Wars were ended the Cumberland settlements were, no different from other frontier communities, attracting all manner of skilled workmen from carpenters through hatters, boot and shoemakers to millwrights.[68] There were enough that by 1800 Nashville had a flourishing Mechanics Society, meeting on the third Saturday of each month; by 1803 the group had a Mechanics Hall [69] where the members celebrated the Fourth of July and other events.

The hall and the celebrations, some quite elaborate,[70] were made possible because the members of the society were as skilled workmen earning more in terms of what money would buy than at any time before or since. All early travelers commented on the high wages and the great need for skilled workers in the West.[71] Only one of these men, Michaux, came into Tennessee, but he found wages there even higher than in Kentucky.[72]

[66] John Coffee Papers, 1801–1804 (Coffee kept a store at Haysborough for some years), give a good idea of the cost of most imported articles of the day; see in particular, "Account of Thomas Butler, per Lady, Haysborough, 1804."

[67] PW, II, 87, 225, though past the pioneer period gives whiskey prices at the farm of between 25 and 30¢ a gallon.

[68] Court records indicate skilled craftsmen through binding agreements and work contracts; see DW, I, 9, "Articles of Binding" for John Pierce, aged 13 years to John Gallapsy, carpenter in Davidson County, 1785; *ibid.*, I, 78, young Sinclar Pruitt to a hatter in 1787; MW, I, 30, Patrick Murphy to a merchant, 1799. DC, I, 123, example of a work contract.

[69] Tennessee *Gazette*, Feb. 11, 1801.

[70] *Ibid.*, July 13, 1803.

[71] Toulmin, *Western Country*, 65, found carpenters in Kentucky earning a dollar a day and provisions, and declared that all "mechanics and husbandmen" were certain of finding employment.

[72] Michaux, *Travels 1802*, 246.

Board at Talbot's Tavern, one of the best, was only $104 a year; John Coffee [73] planned to pay a blacksmith $300 yearly with keep. Skilled joiners, such as those who came from Baltimore in 1802 to do the woodwork and fit the roof beams in General Winchester's home, earned even more. They need never fear unemployment; practically all *Gazettes* carried advertisements asking for all manner of skilled workmen from "sober and industrious well diggers" to silversmith apprentices.[74]

Yet, in spite of the need for craftsmen and their high wages, the story on the Cumberland was much like that of the rest of the United States. The Mechanics Society passed into oblivion. The Industrial Revolution, already a hungry, lustily growing force in New England, tended to make of the skilled workman either a businessman or a factory hand. Much of the skilled work in the South was done by Negroes, but the explanation that this was the reason craftsmen seldom went there or stayed if they did go does not seem valid when one considers the West as described by Faux and Welby. Even Ohio where there were no slaves was in constant need of craftsmen. The South at most seems to have had only a slight intensification of the feeling widespread even then in the United States that craftsmanship was of little importance; today we make a fine distinction between the craftsman and the artist; in many societies of Europe they had been one.

All during pioneer years the landless tenant appears to have been a greater political force with more social position than even the well-to-do master silversmith with journeymen and in need of apprentices. However, one should not think of the early tenants as having much if anything in common with the sharecropper of later years. They were not destitute; most brought at least horses and cattle, and above all they were on the high end of the seesaw of supply and demand. Large landowners offered what would seem today outrageously favorable terms on fine land. In 1793 Kentucky Bluegrass farmers were offering good land, cleared and fenced with barns and dwellings for a rental of only ten bushels of corn

[73] The Coffee Papers with their many work contracts and lists of expenditures are among the best sources for wage rates 1797–1810, the period in which he was chiefly businessman; particularly revealing is his "Estimates for working the Salines" drawn up in 1803; lowest paid were handy boys, $50 a year with keep; blacksmiths, $300; and kettle attenders, $2.66 daily.

[74] Tennessee *Gazette*, March 17, 1802; silversmith apprentice, *ibid.*, June 24, 1801. The most persistent sufferers from a lack of skilled labor appear to have been the editors and owners of the newspapers. Beginning with John McLaughlin, asking in his *Rights of Man or Nashville Intelligencer*, March 11, 1799, the ads continue through the years; Benjamin Bradford owner of the *Gazette* was almost perpetually in need of either a journeyman printer or an apprentice boy; see *ibid.*, May 23, 1804.

an acre;[75] ten years later Michaux found the rental eight or ten bushels an acre, but as much Kentucky Bluegrass had by that date been farmed for more than fifteen years, usually with no manure or rotation of crops, the old average of from sixty to eighty bushels an acre had declined. Meantime, Frederick Stump was able to rent his fertile lands, fenced and with homes and outbuildings,[76] along White's Creek north of Nashville for fifteen bushels of corn an acre. Should the tenant clear and fence the land, he got at least four years use of it rent free for his labor.[77]

There was, in contrast to the attitude toward the skilled craftsman, no feeling whatever against businessmen or tradesmen. Most of the well known men on the Cumberland were at one time or another in some form of industry or business or both. Everybody from Blount downward was in the land business, and a very great many kept store. The seventy-five men of Middle Tennessee who in 1805 petitioned for Colonel Butler's queue each gave his title or occupation; twelve listed merchant,[78] and this figure does not include such men as Andrew Jackson who though he had long kept a store, preferred to be known by his military title. Many of these merchants such as Anthony Foster were community leaders, for no man, not even General James Winchester, felt it beneath his dignity to keep a store; even Daniel Smith sold peach brandy of his own making.[79] It was a day of many-sided men; many such as James Winchester, Jackson, and Daniel Smith held both political and military titles, and were, as in the case of Jackson, also professional men, but the professions, no more than business, formed at this time a group apart.

The closest thing to a separate community in the early years was that of the Germans on White's Creek, but even here sermons had to be preached in English as well as German. Most were substantial farmers, taking an active hand in the business and industrial life of the Cumberland, and with a history of settlement in the German communities of North Carolina and Pennsylvania.[80] Germans never came to Middle Tennessee in sufficient numbers to form a community large enough to live

---

[75] Toulmin, *Western Country*, 76–77.

[76] Williams, *Travels*, Schweinitz, "Report," 508–509.

[77] PD, I, 39; in this Pulaski County rental agreement, the tenant got the use of the land free for seven years, but he had to set out a peach orchard.

[78] ASP, I, *Military Affairs*, 174.

[79] Michaux, *Travels 1802*, 254.

[80] The Moravian missionaries, Williams, *Travels*, Schweinitz, "Report," 508, 509, 510, often met on the way or in the neighborhood of White's Creek families they had known or heard of in North Carolina or Pennsylvania; no mention is made of any newly settled from the Old World.

more or less within the cultural pattern, including language, of the Old Country as they lived in Pennsylvania, Ohio, and elsewhere. The folkways and language of Stump and the German settlers about him disappeared almost without a trace.[81]

All in all the British heritage of the agricultural South smothered out all others. I used to think of the superstitious, unsophisticated farmer of the deep South as the carrier of a rabbit's foot, and when I went as a teacher into the back hills I smiled at the curious custom of taking turpentine pills, but rather liked the way they played the fiddle—one to draw the bow and another to beat the strings. Kentucky folklore I was certain I was learning. Years later I read more Pepys, and not only found him declaring that a dulcimer "played on with sticks knocking of the strings is very pretty," but on the last day of 1664 Pepys blessed God for the good plight of his health though he was uncertain whether it "be my hare's foote" or "taking every morning of a pill of turpentine."

The Southern Negro learned the language of his new country, accepted the religion about him, and learned to eat the food offered, more quickly than any comparable group of non-English speaking whites brought in later years for the same purpose as the Negro—cheap labor. Learning was hastened by the fact that all—slave, skilled worker, bound girl—were, for at least part of the time, an adjunct to somebody's home life.

There was thus not in the Cumberland settlements any group of have-nots or ethnic islands with interests common to themselves and at variance with the rest of the population. Nor was religion a divisive factor. The lack of church buildings even inclined casual travelers sometimes to conclude there was no religion at all, and one early minister, John Harvey, advised, "the inhabitants are so Godless that they must first be roused by threatening preaching." Martin Armstrong, military man, merchant, surveyor, and planter, complained that among his neighbors on the Cumberland, "deism and irreligion ruled beyond all bounds; that the Saviour of the world not only meant nothing to them but that, also, at gatherings the whole story is gone over satirically and mocked in the coarsest manner." [82] Yet, in spite of the fact that Asbury more than a year later spoke of "calmly sinning Nashville," and Michaux two years later found the Tennesseans

[81] Stump's descendants by no means disappeared; see for the history of this community with Stump's second marriage at 93 and his failure in 1819, Ed Huddleston, *Big Wheels and Little Wagons*, Nashville, 1959.
[82] Williams, *Travels*, Schweinitz, "Report," 509, 513.

"not so religious" as the Kentuckians, organized religion was getting from behind fort walls and into church buildings.

Organized religion was never the whole of it. Judging from the results, many felt as did Andrew Jackson, writing in 1835 to Ellen Hanson who had begged Jackson to reassure her grandmother. The old lady thought Jackson was "at heart a Roman," and feared the establishment of an Inquisition in which Jackson would "go hand in hand with the blood thirsty priests." "Charity is the real basis of all true religion," Jackson wrote, "and charity says judge the tree by its fruit—let it always be remembered that no established religion can exist under our glorious constitution." [83]

This feeling colored much of the thought on the Cumberland; though overwhelmingly Protestant and suspicious of any religion with a long background of Church and State as one, Tennessee was anti-Know Nothing and the bloody riots that Louisville and other cities knew were never known on the Cumberland. The Ku Klux Klan was outlawed in short order, and in general the Cumberlander continued to believe that men should be governed by laws, not public opinion. True, there were hot theological battles that split families and even church groups at times, but religion did not as a rule get into politics. Such troubling questions as birth control, public funds for religious schools, or what books a public library should and should not possess, could not of course vex the pioneer. Most believed in individual responsibility; if a book were bad, the individual could refrain from the reading of it; nobody believed that the function of society was to protect the individual from either strong drink or lewd women. Even today the banned book and the picketed movie are less commonly found in Nashville than in larger, but less sophisticated New York, Detroit, and Chicago.

Middle Tennessee, thus, looks around 1800 like a dream of democracy come true—no hatred, religious or otherwise, nobody hungry, nobody wanting a job without a job, cheap land and high wages that made for a fluid society, few symptoms of social decay, or taking Michaux's word, the Cumberlander lived "happy and in plenty." [84] This story was repeated by later travelers. Nobody ever quarreled at conditions in Middle Tennessee. Featherstonhaugh, widely traveled Englishman, wrote in 1834, "No

[83] Bassett, *Jackson Correspondence*, V, 330, 333.

[84] Michaux, *Travels 1802*, 256. The German Moravian visitors were more critical, complaining, Williams, *Travels*, Schweinitz, "Report," 517, "Many of the people cannot boast of great activity, they are rather proud of being able to say, 'We do not need to work so hard here as in other places.' This is their greatest happiness."

traveller who comes into this country as I have done can feel anything but respect for what he sees around him in this place."[85]

The region, up river as well as down, was undoubtedly for some years after the end of Indian troubles about the closest thing to paradise the world has ever known. The populace not only shared a common, unsegregated environment, but there was a surprising amount of agreement in politics, especially at the national level. Even after the common need for protection against the Indians was ended, all continued to want freedom of navigation on the Mississippi, no standing army, as few taxes as possible, low tariffs, post offices, post roads, and of course westward expansion.

They were in the early years further drawn together by the common bond of mistrust of the Federal government. Sumner County did not even bother to vote, but both Davidson and Tennessee counties were in 1795 overwhelmingly opposed to becoming part of a state. It was more populous East Tennessee that carried the day. Middle Tennessee primarily agricultural, her only highway for goods the Mississippi, more keenly felt the ever widening split between the Northeast Seaboard and the South. The War had in a sense already begun, or, more properly, it remained unfinished from Cromwell's day. New England had been one horse, Virginia and the rest of the South with different ideals, entirely different religious viewpoints, different occupations were very much another. The Constitution had put them, and now their daughter Tennessee, in the same field with New England, but it could not make them drink from the same trough. The New England Puritan industrialist pulled the Cumberland settlements together almost as much as had the Indians and John Jay while Secretary of State.

Yet, regardless of how much the Cumberlanders all had in common in attitudes, aspirations, and beliefs, their world, no different from any other community no matter how deep in the backwoods, was not without social distinctions. Middle Tennessee was never one big happy family. One looks in vain through source materials for much indication of any belief in the equality of man. There continued to be, no different from most rural communities, little discernible segregation—not that the pioneer used the word or even thought much about such matters. Pride was a common heritage, and the situation in Virginia where "even the peasant felt good as the large land owners" was equally true of the Cumberland, not that anybody ran around declaring, "I'm just as good as you are."

He took it more or less for granted. True, some men uncertain of their

[85] Featherstonhaugh, *Excursion*, I, 198.

positions and on the way up, as was Andrew Jackson to some extent, insisted on all the earmarks of the Southern gentleman from sword to frame house which Jackson could at first ill afford, but as Parton observed, ". . . he was a *convert*, not an heir; and a convert is apt to be over zealous." [86] Andrew Jackson was always very much aware of his position; he would not fight a duel with Mr. Swann whom he considered no gentleman.[87] Equality to Judge Jackson extended to the law and not much further.

Yet, Jackson the convert had in time a great many followers, though he seemed for much of his life to be spending more time and trouble in making enemies than winning friends and influencing people. Life for him was not a popularity contest. In fact he seemed rather to scorn the common kind, for in his eyes, once a man "yealds his Judgt to popular whim he maybe compared to a ship without its rudder in a gale; he is sure to be dashed against a rock." [88] Jackson would probably nod his head to Mr. Abernethy's summing up, "Jackson never really championed the cause of the people; he only invited them to champion his." [89]

There is nothing to indicate Jackson was in this unique. James Robertson, never a part of the inner circle that Jackson entered when he married, and so losing power when Tennessee became a state, spent most of his life in working for the common good, and also in fighting the will of the majority. The majority overruled his opinion on time and place for the Treaty of Nashville; he could never please everybody in the matter of Indian warfare, but he did manage to preserve the settlements and at the same time keep down a full-scale Indian war—and lived to see his efforts unappreciated.

Part of Robertson's failure to win position in the young state of Tennessee undoubtedly arose because different from the Blounts, Polks, Rutherfords, and most others prominent in Tennessee history, he had not been born into the pattern. Most of the leaders in Tennessee were either descended from or allied through marriage with families important in colonial history long before the Revolution. This meant that all the early leaders and those to come, the men who put Jackson in the White House and kept Jackson men there for a generation, were well-to-do with large

---

[86] Parton, *Jackson*, I, 265.
[87] *Ibid.*, I, 265–285.
[88] *Ibid.*, I, 237–238.
[89] Abernethy, *Frontier to Plantation*, 249.

holdings of land.[90] Still, wealth alone could never put a man on top. Frederick Stump was at the end of the pioneer period one of the wealthiest men in Middle Tennessee, yet he no more than any early settler of Germanic origin was important in the political picture of Tennessee.

It was a Scotch-Irish, Scot, and English world. I found nothing to indicate actual hatred, but certainly the "bacon, potato, and bonny clabber people," as William Faux dubbed the Germans, were not admired in the South; their thrift in the eyes of many seemed stinginess, and most Scots and Englishmen abhorred the hard treatment they gave their wives, on whom, as the Scotch trader James Adair observed, fell the weight of the oar as among the Indians. Toulmin urged prospective settlers not to consider Pennsylvania; he had found "the most fertile spots too much encumbered with Germans for a man to hope for rational society proportionate to the population." He found the Shenandoah Valley "perhaps the least objectionable on this head, but here the Germans are increasing." [91]

It was, thus, wise, if one hoped for entry into the inner circle, not to have been born of German parentage, but qualifications outside of wealth and long-established connections are somewhat nebulous. Leadership did not demand blue blood or even kinship with the first families of Virginia. Many had behind them generations of prosperous, quite prominent colonial ancestors, but few indeed were descended of English nobility as was William Blount. How much Cavalier blood, or even that of first families of Virginia, survived the Revolution and found its way into the West is a question.

The Kentucky Bluegrass that in time became a center of aristocracy did not in its first decades show much promise in that direction. Toulmin in 1793 did praise Kentucky, ". . . I may say that I have met with no people in America more regular or more thriving," but he added, "I compare not the body of the people with my own circle of selected friends in England, but with Americans in general." [92] Michaux, who had little but praise for Middle Tennessee, found in Kentucky liquor and gaming carried to excess, camp meetings, and "incredible confusion over land."

The man in the white pillared mansion of later years was more apt to be on the order of a Henry Clay or an Andrew Jackson, descended of

[90] *Ibid.*, chapters III, IV, V, IX, XII, discuss the early attempts at democracy, first in North Carolina and then in both sections of Tennessee; and explodes, at least for this reader, the myth of "pioneer democracy."

[91] Faux, *Travels, 1818–1819*, 154; Toulmin, *Western Country*, 132.

[92] Toulmin, *Western Country*, 135.

Scotch-Irish forebears who had in the main been small farmers, weavers of cloth, and herders of sheep.

Owners of blue blood, not ambitious for land, money, and power, were apt to get lost in the shuffle. There was, for example, a young Virginia couple—the Joshua Frys who removed to the neighborhood of Danville, Kentucky, in 1787. Peachey the wife was the youngest daughter of Dr. Thomas Walker, guardian of Thomas Jefferson; her husband Joshua was a grandson of Joshua Fry, and thus between them there was much of the oldest and bluest blood of the South. The children of the couple married into the first families of Kentucky—Speeds, Bullitts, Breckenridges—were often wealthy, and through the generations produced many good citizens, including Adlai Stevenson; but the Joshua Frys cut no figure in the social and political life of pioneer Kentucky, nor did they leave an ancestral mansion. They turned their home into an academy, and students who could not pay were boarded free.[93] This was in the old tradition of the Virginia aristocracy—work for the common good without pay—but it was not the way to wealth and fame in the old West.

There is little to indicate the leaders of the old West were, aside from James Robertson who early lost power, much concerned with the common good. Rather it seems to have been luck that the needs and aspirations of the many middle-class farmers who were the backbone of Middle Tennessee coincided with those of the leaders. The actual first settlers who built stations and held the land against the Indians had to a certain extent been overlooked back in 1784 when Davidson County was organized. The most important jobs, even at the county level, often went to newcomers from North Carolina or to the Donelsons who had been gone through the worst years.

Six years later the appointment of William Blount as governor of the territory followed the pattern long since begun. Blount did not live in the Territory; he came of a wealthy family, influential in North Carolina long before the Revolution, and Blount himself had held many offices both military and political before becoming governor. Blount, in one sense, kept to the pattern; under him men who had been important at the local level continued in power, but he did enlarge it to such an extent that the pattern touched almost every thread of the material. Counties,

[93] Lewis Collins, *Historical Sketches of Kentucky*, revised by his son, Richard H. Collins, Covington, Kentucky, 1882 (cited hereafter as Collins, *Kentucky 1882*), II, 625. See also FP, 13, J. Stoddard Johnston, *First Explorations of Kentucky*, Louisville, 1898, "Sketch of Dr. Thomas Walker," 23–24.

for example, usually had from six to ten justices of the peace; Davidson County when it embraced all of Middle Tennessee had had eight, though the first court sat with only four.[94]

Blount appointed eighteen justices for Davidson County alone, and a proportionate number for other counties. In addition there were officers for the muster and various other appointments to make a total of fifty-eight Davidson County officials [95] for a population that must have been less than the 639 free white males shown in the census a year later. Still others were always being appointed by the court itself—men to oversee the laying out of a road, or collect and store taxes, no small job when taxes were paid in provender. Additional were the jurors, both grand and petit, so that a very high percentage of the voters were in some way engaged in county government.

Most of the jobs were important, especially that of justice of the peace. Sitting as a body they could not only function as a court at the county level, but they could levy special taxes, invoke the poor tax, order a road laid out or worked, determine if a man were incapable of work and hence free from taxation, or "ascertain by inquisition if a person were a lunatic or idiot, and in need of a guardian." [96] Enough there were that no man need be a stranger to his justice of the peace, and in the small population the jurors in any trial knew the accused, the witnesses, and the defendants.

True, the custom of giving one man several titles and appointments continued to some extent, but less so than in 1783–1784. Blount saw to it that first settlers were well represented; we find in the court or militia officers such well known names as James Mulherrin, Samuel Barton, Thomas Molloy, Edwin Hickman, John Blackmore, the Robertsons, of course, James and his brother Elijah, and along with these, good substantial men who though not first settlers had been there many years such as Robert Weakley who would in time go to Congress. Appointments for Sumner County at the same time yield even more of the first and early settlers; Kaspar Mansker was made a lieutenant colonel.

The pattern of spreading responsibility was continued through the years. No new counties had been created under the Territorial Government, but after Tennessee became a state in 1796, the counties in Middle

---

[94] Arnow, *Seedtime*, 315–317, gives a summary of the first Davidson County Court.

[95] TP, IV, 438–442, contains the appointments of Dec. 15th for the three counties on the Cumberland.

[96] Haywood, *Laws*, 236, 242.

Tennessee doubled and tripled—Montgomery, Robertson,[97] Smith, Williamson, Stewart, Dickson, and Rutherford. Once again we find large numbers of appointments in proportion to the population, and among these such substantial citizens as the Douglasses and the Edmonsons along with first settlers—Edward Swanson who had come on the exploratory journey with Robertson back in 1779, and Haydon Wells.

Everybody must have been quite well satisfied. The same large landowners who had been running things first under North Carolina, and then under the Territorial Government—Daniel Smith, James Robertson, and Andrew Jackson, just now getting near the top—were chosen by popular vote to attend a Constitutional Convention in Knoxville; members of the Convention in turn chose from among themselves a group to do the actual drafting of the Constitution.[98] The resulting Constitution, adopted in 1796, was in use until 1835. The document in many ways promised no more democracy than had the colonial government of North Carolina. The whole pattern of justices of the peace appointed for life by the state lawmakers, property taxes based on acreage instead of valuation, poll taxes, and road workings was retained. True, the suffrage base was broadened, but few offices were made elective. Still, on the surface everybody was happy, and with even freed slaves allowed to vote, and with neither property nor religious qualifications, Jefferson could hail their Constitution as the most democratic in the land. There was no outcry against undemocratic taxes, and at this date the average citizen of Middle Tennessee seems to have cared little whether or no he voted in Federal elections.

Save for Robertson who in 1796 lost his appointment as Brigadier General of Mero District, the group of which Andrew Jackson was by now very much a part grew more powerful. Yet, there was at least during the early decades a certain kind of democracy by which we set great store today—the mixing and the mingling. The great leaders, soon to be shaping the destinies of the Nation, were not shut away from the common kind in neighborhoods of "executive-homes." They lived on roads traveled by

[97] When the State of Tennessee was formed, the County of Tennessee disappeared, parts going into Robertson and Montgomery; see Ramsey, *Tennessee*, 664.

[98] Abernethy, *Frontier to Plantation*. Chapters III and V, 33–43, 64–90, are accounts and discussions of the attempts made in North Carolina and State of Franklin toward more liberal laws in regard to taxes, etc., Each failed. The framers of the Constitution of the State of Franklin drew up a particularly liberal document for its day with much recourse to popular suffrage; the North Carolina Constitution was adopted instead.

rich as well as poor. Jackson might be very much aware of his role of gentleman, but "Put down in your book," an old neighbor declared, "that the General was the Prince of hospitality; not because he entertained a great many people; but because a poor, belated peddler was as welcome as the President of the United States." [99]

It was probably Rachel, the heiress rather than the convert, who made the hospitality possible. It was Rachel who down at New Orleans in the early spring of 1815 could not, in the midst of the pomp and festivities honoring the conquering hero, her husband, forget the "nearly one thousand" who had lately died.[100] All who wrote of Rachel spoke of her charity, not the giving of food and money, but of herself; she visited the sick and comforted the bereaved. This was true, of course, of many other women in similar circumstances. Charity was not delegated; each woman did her own good deeds, and with help, neighbors, and in later years a church, to which all kinds of people came, the human relationships of women as well as men were far broader than those of the average person today.

Rachel's actions, like those of many on the Cumberland for many years, were colored by memories. She had known hunger as a young girl riding on a flatboat up the Cumberland, the coldness of a half-face camp, the kindness of Kaspar Mansker, and over and over had seen it demonstrated that courage, generosity, and all the other manly virtues could belong to penniless hunters or even slaves. First settlers, lucky enough to survive, continued to live among the wealthy; Edmund Jennings keeping a ferry was pretty much of a man.

Yet, remembered as he was by many of the old, Edmund Jennings was not made a justice of the peace, nor was he invited to the grand balls. One also seldom finds a Germanic name in lists of appointments, military or otherwise; nor were the Donelsons and Winchesters inclined to marry into the German families, nor did Joseph Bishop, mighty hunter and warrior though he was, mingle socially with Andrew Jackson. The Southerner was adept at building invisible walls.

He could build these walls and never resort to rudeness; rather as an Englishman observed of the South Carolinians of 1818, "It is a pleasing feature of this people that all are outwardly social, bordering on something like equality. This feature, though delusive, strikes and is highly

[99] Parton, *Jackson*, I, 308.
[100] *Ibid.*, 265.

interesting to strangers." [101] He found a familiarity of the rich with the poor, and both classes pretending to be no respecter of persons.

The invisible walls were always there. The children living in 1795 would see them grow higher and higher. The settler, for example, on hill land in 1795 growing crops almost as fine as those in Sumner County, would each year see his fields produce less. As his land wore out, good land in Middle Tennessee or the Kentucky Bluegrass grew more expensive; unable to buy it, he or his children would go into the constantly opening West or become sharecroppers. Slaves grew more expensive; the great landowner like Jackson with only a few during pioneer years could keep his and in time have a hundred and afford an overseer. Roads in the outlying regions that had in the early years been no worse than those in the fertile lands got little attention. There was no road open in all weathers in the southern section of Pulaski County, Kentucky, for example, until 1936· and that paid for by Federal funds as was the first bridge over the Cumberland in this section coming still later. In Kentucky all things went to the Bluegrass from penitentiary to state-supported institutions of higher learning.

Tennessee was in this respect much more democratic, though East Tennessee had many advantages, including more and better land, lacking in East Kentucky. Tennessee also suffered less from the thing in Kentucky that impoverished thousands—land troubles. Bad titles, dishonest men with money enough for lawyers, poor surveying, ignorance of the constantly changing land laws had by 1800 brought poverty to thousands of Kentucky's first settlers. The stories of Daniel Boone, landless in Illinois, George Rogers Clark, landless, dispirited, and turned to drink, living out his days in a little cabin near Louisville where he had failed to get land, are well known.

If one could on the morning of October 10, 1801 [102] have gone up the Cumberland to the site of Price's Station built in 1775 and talked to Michael Stoner, he might have disputed, at least with his glance for he was a silent man, some of the fine things said here about prosperity. He was by 1801 fifty-three years old; [103] thirty-five years before with James Harrod he had first seen Middle Tennessee, and not long after had laid

[101] Faux, *Travels, 1818–1819*, 85, 116–117.

[102] WD, I, 204–208, contains the depositions, including that of Stoner, given on this date in connection with the disputed title to land Stoner got from his father-in-law Andrew Tribble.

[103] RKs, XXIV, 189. Bess L. Hawthorne, "Reverend Andrew Tribble, Pioneer."

claim to the fine land in time known as Clover Bottom, a claim good enough to be recognized by Henderson.

Stoner had been one of the first settlers in Kentucky, helping Boone clear the road to Boonesboro. He was the man who rode back alone to meet Henderson. He had ridden through and into many things—tall cane that could hide Indians, ivy-beech bottoms, and at long last Boonesboro and great sweeps of fine land, but mostly he rode into seven bloody years of warfare, wounds, hunger, pain, hard work of clearing land and building fence, all set about with death and disaster from Indians.[104] He also rode into debts and the loss of all the land got in both Tennessee and Kentucky by right of settlement. His father-in-law Andrew Tribble bought a boundary down near Price's Station, and now on this October morning Stoner was preparing to fight another losing battle.

The settler with little money for lawyers, clerk's fees, or the travel costs of witnesses never had a chance. Losses to Stoner, as to thousands, came slowly after long delays, trials, depositions where men went into the woods and hunted "a wind-topped walnut"—"three hickories"—or a waterfall "on the contrary side of the creek." Kentucky had followed the system of Virginia in fixing the boundaries of land, using for the most part natural features, and thus warrants were located in the new and nameless land chiefly by water courses, known only to a few. Filson's map coming in 1784 was worse than none at all.

Suffering equally with such men as Boone, Simon Kenton, and Stoner were the soldiers of the Virginia Line. Led on to fight by promises of land they could never hope to get, they, like Stoner, learned the hard way that promises meant nothing. There was in the boundary set aside for the soldiers a little good land with timber for fuel and building, free of Indian title, but as the land speculator was in a much better position to spot out this land than the soldier, he got it by buying the unlocated warrants of men with no hope of settling, and hiring surveyors who were ever more eager to run large boundaries of good land than small holdings of poor land—and so got it.

The soldiers who never even tried to settle their lands were usually the

---

[104] Practically all historians of the old West at least mentioned Stoner, as did many of Mr. Draper's correspondents; see in particular W, 11CC, 146–147; *ibid.*, 17CC, 191–209; and *ibid.*, 12CC, 43–56; this last, 43, tells of Stoner wounded at the siege of Boonesboro; he fainted from loss of blood after he had refused to let anyone risk his life to come to him, for he was outside the fort walls; his wounds were "only flesh wounds," one in the hip and another in the arm.

luckier ones. A man might move out to what he thought was his land, clear fields, build fence, house, barns, as did Stoner, then lose it all on a bad title. The owner after buying it once frequently "had to buy it two or three times more or lose his home and labor." [105] There was for many years no statute of limitations on land titles, and just as today a man's past loyalty can be investigated and reinvestigated so could a Kentucky land title. There was also land trouble in Tennessee, but little compared with Kentucky, where most travelers used such descriptive phrases as "worst mess" and "incredible confusion."

The children living in 1795 would see these things build the walls of poverty higher. Higher still would grow the walls of mistrust and suspicion and at last hatred between North and South. Some would live to know the full bitterness. There were other changes they would see, such as the growing wall between black man and white man, for they were the children of transition. It was not just the beginnings of a new state in a young nation or the moving west of the frontier. It was not even the Industrial Revolution that would bring railroads and steamboats, while the old ones among them remembered buffalo.

These children were in a sense the first native-born citizens of the United States in that section. Their fathers though they had fought as Revolutionary soldiers had been born and bred as British colonials. Attitudes would change; even the facts of life. The children, for example, would more quickly than the old ones learn to reckon in the new dollar and cents and take more quickly to the words, if not new, at least unfamiliar, creeping into the language—Congressman, Democracy, U.S. Senator. Post office, they would say, giggling at the old ones who said "mailhouse," for the language even as they learned it would change like the river, reflecting in its flow the weather and the makeup of a world often many miles away.

[105] Michaux, *Travels 1802*, 197, 199–201. See for a thorough discussion of the land problems and conditions on Virginia's frontiers, Thomas Perkins Abernethy, *Three Virginia Frontiers*, Louisiana State University Press, Baton Rouge, 1940. Part III, 39–96, pertains to the last Virginia frontier—Kentucky.

Chapter Five

The Sounds
of Humankind

THE PIONEER baby might from time to time be weighed on the family steelyards, and he might not be. He would by the time he could talk have heard all manner of human sounds from scalp cry to the calling of the hogs, but one thing he would never hear as they weighed him or on any other occasion of his life was the word *normal*. The normal human being had not yet evolved.

No first settler, risking death and loss of all his goods when he could have lived comfortably in a safe place, would today be considered normal. Could the average citizen of today see and hear Andrew Jackson, partly intoxicated with liquor but more so by his own wrath, eyes blazing, spittle drooling, black oaths flying as he chased a man with a fence rail, or charged down the center of a long food- and drink-laden banquet table,[1] he would probably call the police. John Rains, painted and dressed like an Indian, slipping through the woods with Abraham Castleman, got

Headpiece: A group waiting at a ferry.

[1] Parton, *Jackson*, I, 341–342.

up in the same way, would to many be a more heart-chilling sight than an Indian on the warpath. Fresh scalps, the dried blood yet dark red instead of black, might today frighten even our TV-hardened children, but young Abraham Mason, after looking up from his book in a school down on Richland Creek to see white men riding by with prisoners and scalps, "upon long canes, carrying them like colors," [2] went back to his lessons with a lighter, warmer heart. The night before he had, with others of the community, sat up with the neighbors, killed and scalped by Indians. And now the dead were revenged.

He and others accepted the scalps Edmund Jennings wore at his belt just as they accepted Edmund. It was right and proper a man should make his will before fighting a duel or going into battle as did he. Edmund directed that if he died at Nickojack, his cows should be driven into Daniel Smith's range, and there killed and left for the wolves; the wolves would come quickly to the dead cattle, but would soon turn from them to the general's stock and so destroy, Edmund hoped, the rich man's cattle. [3]

Colonel Daniel Ridley, living down near Buchanan's, was a stern, strict man [4] who, like most of those around him, had never learned the art of keeping shut for: "What he felt he professed and what he professed he felt. It was his fashion to avoid all circumlocution and to speak plainly; he flattered no man, feared no man, and courted no man; when he spoke he was believed; when he promised his word was never forfeited." [5] And if Colonel Ridley wanted to keep his coffin ready made and waiting along with burying clothes, that was his business, though many commented on Daniel Ridley's coffin.

It was somewhat unusual to make such preparations for death. The pioneers as a group had a great love of life and a flair for living; life was too fine a thing to ruin with overmuch quarreling at death or anything else they could not change. All the original settlers had, before the end of the first year, seen not only men, women, and children mutilated and dead, but others dying slowly of painful, hopeless wounds, for at this date and for many years to come, any man shot in the abdomen knew he must die. Colonel John Donelson, shot in the woods with only two companions and these chance strangers, pushed his intestines back in, got a leech for he was near a creek, put it into the wound, and even

---

[2] A, III, 88–89.
[3] W, 32S, 513–520.
[4] Featherstonhaugh, *Excursion*, I, 210–211.
[5] W, 6XX, 211–217.

ate and walked about,[6] knowing no doubt that it was all a waste of time, but like other men of his day, living, doing what he could until he died, never waiting.

The Indian Wars were scarcely ended before the dueling began. The actual pioneers had needed no duels, but others went out at dawn to the chosen place, knowing they would die and having made their wills accordingly.[7] Men usually tried to keep such matters from their women-folks, and as a result, some wives like Rachel Jackson lived in eternal dread of "dueling business." [8] Rachel in time sought the consolation that many in later years found on the Cumberland, that of religion, the exercise of which around 1801 was filled with sights and sounds that would terrify any of today's believers in normalcy—grown men seized with uncontrollable fits of head-jerkings meanwhile barking like dogs; daintily dressed young women rolling head over heels unchecked by briar patch or mud puddle. Others, long hair loosed of its pins and flying in every direction, jerked their heads backward and forward with seemingly inhuman rapidity meanwhile laughing uncontrollably. Staid matrons and stiff-legged farmers danced with the spryness of acrobats, while, still others, their eyes red-rimmed and gaunt from weeping and lack of sleep, told in voices hoarse from much crying of visions and dreams. There is no record of anybody having been alarmed by the many symptoms of mass hysteria.[9] Rather, many watched with jokes and scoffing laughter.

No one with years behind him in a forted station would have been shocked by anything seen in a camp meeting. Most settlers of the old West had by that date long since learned it took all kinds and conditions of people to make a world, though the "strong and silent man" was not much in evidence. Strong many of the men were, but silent they were not. Travelers of later years wrote of the "morose habits of the sad Americans" [10] found in Philadelphia and other eastern centers, but no visitors ever accused the Cumberlanders of cold reserve. Rather, the average pioneer of the old West was obstreperous as the man of Merrie

[6] *Ibid.*, 32S, 310–311; this account by his daughter-in-law, Mary Purnell, gives the date of death as April or May, 1786, at the age of 60. See also *ibid.*, 30S, 504–509.

[7] DW, II, 178, the will of Dr. Francis Sappington on the eve of a duel; the inventory followed, see *ibid.*, II, 189.

[8] Bassett, *Jackson Correspondence*, I, 87.

[9] There is a large body of literature on The Great Revival. Works by observers or participants include: L. Garrett, *Recollections of the West*, Nashville, 1834; *Sketches of the Life of John M. Saffitt*, New London, 1821; Richard McNemar, *The Kentucky Revival*, Cincinnati, 1808; Sweet, *Religion* (indexed), also contains many accounts (particularly Vol. II) by firsthand observers.

[10] Handlin, *America*, De Montlezun, "Travels 1816–1817," 134.

England a hundred years before, cursing, crying, laughing, singing, whistling, forever making sound.

In spite of death and loss and constant danger one of the sounds most often heard was laughter. They loved practical jokes, and one of the more common was to pretend there were Indians about, or even at the risk of being shot pretend to be one.[11] Joseph Bishop, in spite of a hard life and constant danger, ever had time and mind for a practical joke—overloaded muskets put into the hands of the unsuspecting or torturing a lazy hunter with heavy sweatings under pretense of believing him when he said he was too sick to hunt.[12] The capacity for laughter was not confined to the young and feckless. Long after the pioneer period, Mrs. Daniel Smith, then a great-grandmother, was described as a spry old lady, never one to let a joke pass.[13]

True, their ideas of humor were often different from our own, but still we can almost hear the chuckle of a Tory at King's Mountain, taking time out from the debacle of screaming horses and men killed even as they lifted white handkerchiefs in token of surrender, to write in his journal, "My dear friends, I bid you farewell for I am started to the warm country." [14] When three-hundred-pound Colonel Benjamin Cleveland of East Tennessee asked a neighbor, "What news from Hell this morning?" the others, listening, guffawed at the answer, "Why, soap grease is getting scarce down there and I have been sent to look for you." The storyteller remembered how Cleveland laughed with the others, but a few paragraphs later he wrote, "Cleveland, with tears coursing down his cheeks, adjusted the rope, regretting the necessity for hanging the trembling culprit." [15]

Colonel Cleveland was not exceptional; most other frontiersmen such as he not only shouted in battle, laughed, cursed, but they also wept often and freely. Not many were so versatile as young Joseph Sevier who all in the instant could feel grief and a rage that made him want to shoot down men carrying a white flag when at the Battle of King's Mountain he thought the Tories had killed his father, and "cried, with tears running down his cheeks, 'The damned rascals have killed my father, and I'll keep loading and shooting till I kill every son of a bitch of the lot.' " [16]

[11] W, 30S, 252–253, is an account of an elaborate practical joke of pretended Indians at French Lick Station in 1787.
[12] Gray, *Bishop*, 45–46, 49–51, and 140—a rough practical joke on a preacher.
[13] Burke, *Emily Donelson*, I, 273, quoting Emily Donelson, Jan. 31, 1831.
[14] ETH, XIV, 105, "A King's Mountain Diary," ed. by Mary H. McCown.
[15] Draper, *King's Mountain*, 445.
[16] *Ibid.*, 282.

The father himself wept when his comrades came to rescue him from his political foes. "Old Joe Young," a noted Indian fighter up in Kentucky, always cried when he talked of his wife carried away by Indians;[17] and even Andrew Jackson cried when he couldn't get supplies for his sick men. Joseph Bishop, a fearless hunter, shed tears for many things—dead Doublehead,[18] a reunion with his father, and from pain; George Rogers Clark wept when his men mutinied;[19] and Captain Jacob Hartsell wrote of his East Tennessee company in the War of 1812, ". . . the most of the men was melted into tears under the sermont."

Later, Cumberlanders searched out excuses for crying. One of these was the great criminal lawyer Felix Grundy,[20] who could so work upon juries as to set whole courtrooms weeping, and in all the years of his practice only one of his 165 defendants was executed. Men of Middle Tennessee would ride sixty miles to weep as they listened to him plead. Sermons, even after the days of the great revivals, made strong men weep.

They also cursed. It is doubtful if many on the Cumberland could compare with Colley Cibber, of whom Dr. Johnson had observed in 1775, "and he had but half to furnish; for one half of what he said was oaths." Some pioneers in letters and conversations sound much like characters out of eighteenth century English fiction, but as it so often happens, there is that invisible wall—the meanings of words, and in this case, cursing. Many words now considered profane and "dirty," though, as others have observed, it is not the tongue but the mind that makes an obscene word, the Cumberlander found unobjectionable, and much of what we today think of as profanity, he would have considered no profanity at all.

Three pages taken at random from Smollett's *Roderick Random*, a work stocked by merchant John Deadrick, yielded: "Hell and damnation . . . spies you bitch . . . send them all to hell . . . Lord have mercy . . . I'll be hanged . . . God forbid . . . Heaven be praised . . . Ods bobs . . . For Christ's sake . . . have mercy upon us . . . you dog . . . Zounds . . . Damn me . . . Gad so . . . dog of a doctor . . .

[17] W, 12CC, 58.

[18] Gray, *Bishop*, 149; this was a hunting dog of that name and not the Indian chief.

[19] Mann Butler, *A History of the Commonwealth of Kentucky*, Louisville, 1834, 152.

[20] Felix Grundy (1777–1840) was a famous criminal lawyer, friend of Jackson, U.S. Senator, and Attorney General under Van Buren; Guild, *Old Times*, 478; see also Joseph Howard Parks, *Felix Grundy, Champion of Democracy*, University, Louisiana, 1940.

The Devil go with him . . . by gad . . . this rogue of a vicar." The speakers were two farmers, an exciseman, and a curate. At no time were they cursing, for when a character, such as the sergeant with the burned leg, cursed, Smollett, not wishing to offend, merely described.

There were on the Cumberland as elsewhere laws against profane cursing; that is by God, Christ, and the Holy Evangels of Almighty God; but the body of laws aimed at uplifting the morals of the citizenry was not taken too seriously,[21] and the borderer was little inclined to let any power save his own conscience regulate the use of his tongue.

Certainly neither laws nor social censure gave them any horror of a damn. It was used as adjective, noun, verb, and adverb, appearing in letters: "he would be damned if he did not burn you and your agency" [22] —"damn the rascal, he will not even convey me land"—"I would take a gun and blow his damned brains out." Conversation was likewise peppered: "You damned infernal scoundrel . . . I'm damned if I don't run that red hot andiron down your throat" [23]—"I'm damned if I can't whip the man." Even under such polite circumstances as an affair of honor, the mortally wounded man might forget himself enough to shriek of his opponent, "Great God, have I missed the damned scoundrel." [24]

The religious such as Martin Armstrong and Captain Edmonson who settled near Haysborough heeded the Third Commandment, but sometimes even they got carried away in the heat of battle and cursed without knowing,[25] for oaths were common as in Shakespeare's time. In a world where woman was the yoke-fellow of man, she was considered a creature of sufficient moral strength her soul would in no wise be spotted by the sound of oaths. Jackson, gallant as he was, had one of his most noted outbursts [26] in the presence of Rachel when a teamster bumped the carriage in which he and she were riding. The taboos we now know against

---

[21] Fines were given in county courts, but most of these such as the ten shillings John Rains had to pay, DC, I, 31, were for swearing in the presence of the court; see *ibid.*, I, 37–swearing and drunkenness, *ibid.*, I, 51, in presence of court, and *ibid.*, I, 77. The laws against profane swearing were much more strictly enforced in East Tennessee, and still more so up river in Pulaski County; for example, a grand jury of 1799, PC, I, 4, returned a "presentment" against Wiatt Adkins for profane swearing on hearsay—"by name (by God) on this day at Henry Francis's by information of Robt. Anderson, George All Corn."

[22] Parton, *Jackson*, I, 355–356, quoting letter of Christopher Stump, son of Frederick.

[23] *Ibid.*, I, 368.

[24] Burke, *Emily Donelson*, I, 33.

[25] Draper, *King's Mountain*, 407–408. The name Edmonson is variously spelled, Edmiston, Edmonsan.

[26] Parton, *Jackson*, I, 340.

the use of such expressions as "Oh Lord," "Dear God," "My God," "Lord have Mercy," and "Almighty God" did not, save among the Quakers, then exist. No different from many of the religious, Rachel Jackson, though in prayerful way, used many in her letters, and as late as after The War, Judge Guild in addressing mixed audiences used such now-taboo expressions as "Oh, Lord."

Mr. Carey's American *Museum* was a staid publication, in sympathy with many Quaker beliefs, and with articles by ministers of all faiths, yet such expressions as "God knows" and "Gracious God" were common.[27] The Draper manuscripts contain a fair amount of what we today consider profanity; the story was told of a man almost struck by lightning. He looked up at the heavens and cried, "God, damn you, try it again." According to the story, the "Deity" did.[28] James Robertson, for example, back in 1774 when writing of his struggle to keep a company of men gathered for Dunmore's War, remarked he had had to use both "good words and bad"; he did not repeat his "bad words"; a short time later we find him writing with sympathy of two lost, half-naked hunters, "poor sons of bitches," [29] found by his company, which would indicate that Robertson who was ever a gentleman had ideas of "bad words" different from ours of today.

"I am in the middle of hell and see no alternative but to kill or be killed" [30] was but a simple statement of trouble. Such expressions as "hell fire," "what in the hell," "what the devil," "the devil only knows," "between the devil and the deep blue sea" were common as those alluding to the higher regions and their occupants. When a loving but long-suffering relative of "my little ward Hutchings" wrote, "And I did give him as genteel a cursing as ever the youth received," [31] we can be certain the words were stronger than a few damns affixed to members of the Trinity.

As a child I used to hear talk of the wondrous cursers of old; the teamsters and the steamboatmen, but more than anything, the oil men. The talk whetted my curiosity, for I could only wonder what it was

[27] Carey, *Museum*, III, 388–389; *ibid.*, IX, 313; and *ibid.*, X, Appendix 20.

[28] W, 5S, 56; many swore by God as *ibid.*, 32S, 369, and others by Christ as did Hugh Rogan.

[29] Reuben Gold Thwaites and Louise Phelps Kellogg, *Documentary History of Dunmore's War*, 1774, Compiled from the Draper Manuscripts in the Library of the Wisconsin Historical Society, pub. Wisconsin Historical Society, Madison, 1905 (cited hereafter as Thwaites-Kellogg, *Dunmore's War*), 94, 140.

[30] Parton, *Jackson*, I, 395.

[31] Burke, *Emily Donelson*, I, 192. Billey Donelson to John Coffee; a patient man, though he took "a very good one" (cursing) from the young one he "did refrain from giving him a thumping."

they said; through all our generations cursing under the house roof had been bad manners, and by the time of my childhood the shadow of Calvinism had so darkened all life up river—that is, for the saved—that even *darn* was a sinful word. Yet, even then the saved did not try to deny the unsaved their oaths—so long as they were not sounded within the hearing of women and children.

I had a few times the somewhat stolen opportunity of listening; once to an old driller; he had without benefit of modern technology put holes into the earth for oil from Trebizond to Torrent and could, it was said, curse in seven languages and four religions. I could understand little of what he said, but there was a beauty and a rhythm about the flow of words—and something else—I could not then quite understand; more it was than simple sorrow or anger. He reminded me of Dr. Mc-Conaghauh, one of my teachers—I was then spending most of my time away from home in a Presbyterian school—reciting to us in Latin a passage from the Bible. But what? Job in his hopeless, helpless sorrow? Not exactly; in the roll and the thud—for never think cursing was but a string of epithets—he was Paul, Paul demanding charity. In any case as I listened, the devil was not there at all, rather the tongues of men and of angels.

There was another, able it was said to curse two hours and never repeat himself; but him I never heard. I could only wonder. Profanity was on the whole something of an art, requiring imagination, good wind, a fair knowledge of the Bible, and other matters, but, above all, a feeling for words and a sense of rhythm, a form of soul's easing now lost for the most part. The old South and hence the West were still a part of the then rather unselfconscious and highly articulate world of the British Isles, a world that expressed itself in many ways—the London mob might throw mud on the man who walked the streets too finely dressed and into the bargain cover him with curses, while their betters at times indulged themselves in writings of various kinds, some of which are today considered both profane and obscene.

The latter part of the eighteenth century has been labeled the golden age of letters; pioneer source materials indicate that at least in the old West it might better be considered the golden age of sound. Most sang a great deal, casual singing as they went about their work or rocked their babies. The teamster talked to his team, cursing, cajoling, or sometimes he sang them a song as the boatman sang to himself and the river. Many of the sounds they made in calling or managing farm animals grow yearly more lost and forgotten. The calling of the chickens, like plowing with a team, demanded words—sounds only they would now be to most of us—and the words varied from neighborhood to neighborhood. We, for example, said *sooee-sooee* to drive the hogs away and called with a loud and ringing *pigooee-pig-pig-pig*, but I knew a family who called with a *sooee*, and no two families called their dogs in the same way, though most, even foxhounds, would come to the sound of the dinner conch shell.

Different from boys on the older borders,[32] the lads of Middle Tennessee had no need to learn the call of a turkey or bleat of a doe; deer and turkey were gone from the farm lands there before 1800, but even up river where they continued to be hunted for generations, it was probably more fun to learn to caw so convincingly that one small boy well hidden in the roasting-ear patch could keep the family running most of the day to chase the crows away.

Still, for all the sounds they made, no longer much heard today, the most common sound of humankind was that of talk. Debating societies waited for the most part until the Indian wars were finished, but in the meantime there was the fort yard, the mill, blacksmith shop, tavern, livery stable, and all the knots of men who ever gathered during court week, at elections, and the muster. Even travelers meeting, instead of going their separate ways, stopped to talk, sometimes all night, as did Joseph Bishop.[33]

Everything indicates the Cumberlanders were a talkative people; too much so, the editor of the *Gazette* no doubt thought, when he warned, "Whether in Congress or a kitchen the person who talks too much is little regarded." [34] This did not hinder such a one as Mrs. Daniel Smith from sitting up all night to talk with a visiting great-niece.[35]

It is hard to imagine in the great silence of today when appliances and machines have largely taken the place of human beings and animals, how rich and varied were the opportunities for and topics of conversation in most any home with all life revolving about it; nor was there away from home any keeping still. A woman can today buy a week's supply of groceries in a self-service store and never say a word; a trip to Laneer's Store in 1787 with tallow, linen cloth, and a few deerskins to be exchanged

[32] Kercheval, *Virginia*, Doddridge, "Notes," 284.
[33] Gray, *Bishop*, 138.
[34] Tennessee *Gazette*, March 28, 1804.
[35] Burke, *Emily Donelson*, I, 273.

for fishhooks, scissors, and rum would have required a deal of conversation just to judge the quality of the cloth and the skins, weigh and reckon the worth of the tallow, then translate the whole into goods. There was along with this always conversation.

In a world where nothing was standardized, nothing could be taken for granted, everything in process of rapid change, work done by human beings and animals instead of machines, and the whole accomplished by many-sided men and women who shared continuously in the lives of others—everything from helping bring a baby to taking a flatboat down river with the baby's father—there was a constant need of conversation. Nothing—birth, death, the laying out of the dead, the pegging of the scalped head or sawing off the mangled leg—was hidden behind institutional walls. The complexities of their lives as farmers—manufacturers gave still more needs for conversation.

A hogshead of tobacco going down river required in the course of its life many conversations, from the discussion of when and where to burn the tobacco bed to the dickering with cooper, teamster, boatman, and all the others needed in the process of growing, harvesting, and selling; the whole topped off by the yarns of men returned from New Orleans or Natchez. Everything had need of conversation; today we drink water and seldom discuss it unless the chlorine be unusually strong; then, water was never just water; there was hard, soft, sulphur, rain, but best of all that from a fine spring to keep the butter cold and fill the mash barrels. The spring, like the weather, the river, the growing crops, the rotting flax, was a living, changing thing.

Men sit in silence today on trains or planes and read the news. There was on the Cumberland, even in Middle Tennessee, for close to twenty years, no regular source of news. Most came by word of mouth, and even that brought by letters and newspapers was spread orally. The mail carrier galloped into the Nashville square and blew his horn as a preliminary to telling important news.[36] Word traveled out from him as well as other sources in ever-widening, overlapping circles. Church meant long sermons, and often the song because of a scarcity of hymnbooks

---

[36] Guild, *Old Times*, 92–96. See also for Mr. Swaney, carrier on the Natchez Trace in the early 1800's, Miss Jane H. Thomas, *Old Days in Nashville, Tennessee*, Nashville 1899 (cited hereafter as Thomas, *Nashville*), 52. The postmen would tell no news until they reached the post office, but there was no mail service into Middle Tennessee until April 1, 1796, and this fortnightly, TP, IV, 396–397; John Gordon was the first postmaster.

was "lined out." School was sometimes a "blab" school, and much of formal education consisted of memory work to be recited aloud.

Conversations, news, trials, orations, sermons were by no means the full measure of their talk. The pioneer was not many generations removed from a bookless, newspaperless world where most of the living culture of the race had been carried in head, tongue, and hands. There was behind them all a wealth of ballad, tale, proverb, song, and rhyme, a store that during pioneer years was being constantly enriched. The pioneer boy, his father making history, heard not only of the dim times in Scotland and Northern Ireland, but of the immediate past—men under Clark wading breast-high water, the wild times on the trip to and from King's Mountain, and the still wilder days in the Lost State of Franklin. All these were but the beginnings of the many tales.

In the average outlying farm home, particularly those up river where every article had been either made on the spot or brought on some formidable journey—over mountains or up the river—most anything could become the ancestor of a story; the exciting trip to Nashville or even Philadelphia for the silk in the new bonnet, the meanness or untimely death of the black ram that made possible the gray linsey of the new petticoat. The best corner cupboard had a history that would take hours for the telling, all the way through from the finding of the cherry tree to the life story of the journeyman carpenter who lived with the family while he made it, and left behind him not only a good cupboard but more stories.

These stories could have been true ones of his own life or the lives of people he had known, but some were apt to be witch, ghost, and fairy tales. Others like Mother Goose were the old things handed down—Bluebeard to the harrowing tale of the "Meanest Man on Earth."

Our father told a rousing tale of Jack the Giant Killer, lusty with roars and squeaks, and the squawks of the stolen hen, differing no doubt in some points, but basically the same story Daniel Drake heard as a child in the 1780's.[37] Another favorite was a version of the old, old tale of the man-who-tried-to-do-the-work-of-his-wife-and-found-it-not-so-easy-as-he-had-thought. Many countries have folk tales built around this theme, such as that of the peasant who tied the cow on the roof and got pulled up the chimney. In our story, the wife was at church and the "know-it-all" husband tried to get dinner; in trying to cut up the hen

[37] Drake, *Letters,* 158.

he cut his thumb, and showed his Carolina origin by doctoring himself with turpentine. This, he spilled on the chicken, and from there went into multiple disasters, including blood in the dishwater and bandages in the dumplings, and this like most stories was seasoned by laughter.

Grimmer and usually from another source were the numerous tales of the weak-woman-who-triumphed, as had the long gone grandmother who kept an Indian out of the house with feathers. Most of these were based on fact, as all frontiers had stories of how women had without rifles saved their families. In one account she let a band of Indians through the door one at a time, while behind her a faithful slave killed them, silently with an ax; in another the cabin roof was set on fire by besieging Indians; there was no water; no man could be spared from the portholes; the woman put out the fire. In some of ours, never found in print, weak women with husbands gone from home defended themselves from visiting villains in various ways—one beguiled a man into sharpening "the very ax" she later used to split his head, and another, "utterly helpless," poured sizzling melted lead into the ear of an intruder drowsing by the hearth.

Possibly the most exciting were the ghost tales, and among the most numerous, for every community had its "hainted house," or cave or road. These, too, were often funny, as were stories of preachers, the humor a heritage from pioneer days, for the sanctimonious attitude with which we now approach religions, government, death, or even third and fourth marriages was unknown to the pioneer.

Saddest of all was the story, only one of many, built around the theme of the "steadfast man." He was one of the "poor mistreated Tories" who had his choice of staying in Virginia and being hanged or leaving his young wife. His wife, a practical woman, pointed out that in either case the children would be deprived of a father. He chose the leaving, and managed to get through Kentucky of 1777 into Canada, but once there the British never quite trusted him, and shipped him off to India. There, he served as a soldier for many years, always faithful to his wife. He in true Enoch Arden fashion did, in time, get back to Virginia. There, it was hunt for his wife, and how we children did cry when he stood by a window in Wayne County, Kentucky, and looked in on his wife, snug and safe and happy, while he stood out in the cold gray rain—forgotten. She'd thought him dead, but wanting a father for his children, now grown and gone away, had married another man, and now around her were more children.

Even the language of our stories, if phonetic spellings be anything to judge by, was somewhat like that of the pioneers. Still, it must be remembered that not all pioneers at any time spoke exactly alike, and in the early years the differences were most pronounced. True, English was almost universally spoken, but there were in the eighteenth century in the British Isles a great many varieties of the English language. Differences in speech patterns were accepted parts of life; dictionaries were just coming into use, and even Dr. Samuel Johnson, author of the most comprehensive one, clung to many provincial pronunciations. Somewhat to the worriment of Boswell and the merriment of Garrick, he insisted on pronouncing *punch, poonsh,* for Johnson held the inhabitants of his childhood home, Lichfield, spoke the "purest English"; *there* rhymed with *fear* instead of *fair,* and *once* was *woonse.*

These different patterns traveled to the colonies. As a rule Tidewater used the broad *a*'d accent of English ships' captains, with the various dialects more common on the frontier. During colonial days, there seems to have been in America little demand for complete orthodoxy in either pronunciation or word usage. What a man said was still more important than the sounds he made in the saying of it.

Things changed quickly after the Revolution, and as early as 1795 a visitor to Philadelphia commented: "Despite their pride, the Americans have a vague feeling that they are somehow inferior to the Britons. Their tastes, customs, and, most of all, their habits, make true Englishmen of them. . . . The inhabitants of the Eastern States scorn the Southerners, the Virginians, Carolinians, and Georgians." [38] The long struggle of the East to emulate England in matters intellectual, that is, in the purely obvious, was well under way.

Philadelphia, New York, and New England had become the standard-bearers of American culture. A later traveler in the East noted, "The English language here is not corrupted by a variety of dialects as in England." [39] The visitor was, of course, no Englishman, for the English were much slower than the Americans to accept a pattern of orthodoxy that would make the words *difference* and *corruption* synonymous when used in connection with language. The South, and the West even more so, were ever to suffer in the comparing. The New England judges had, to begin with, little of the other England that influenced the South most, less of the Scot and Scotch-Irish, and nothing at all of the sublime British

[38] Handlin, *America*, Moreau, "Travels, 1793–1798," 93.
[39] *Ibid.*, Grassi, "Observations, 1819," 140.

self-esteem and assurance that could make an Andrew Jackson as equally unafraid as a Dr. Johnson of mispronouncing a word.

Eternally scorned by the Eastern intellectual, the language of the old West was as truly a child of British culture as anything heard in New England. It was, to begin with, heavily seasoned by the Scot, but the Scot of Northern Ireland, far from being ashamed of his speech, boasted that he spoke an older, purer English than did the Englishman of London.[40] This "older, purer English" may in the days of Queen Elizabeth have sounded much as does "Irish dialect" today.

The language that went from Scotland to Northern Ireland stayed two or three generations, came at length to Western Virginia or North Carolina, spent another generation or so mixing with Scots–English or English or both, eventually reaching the Cumberland, was not the same language that had gone to Ireland two hundred years before, nor did all Scotch–Irish speak alike any more than did all Scots or Englishmen.

The Virginia size rolls of the French and Indian War reveal more than any other single source the diversity of backgrounds: some men were fairly specific listing Yorkshire, where *reasons* were *raisins;* others Tipperary; but most gave the country only—England, Scotland, Ireland, Germany, Holland, with a few from other colonies, notably Pennsylvania.[41]

Englishmen visiting the western borders of Virginia and the Carolinas during the Revolution made no comment on the accents of the populace. They spoke instead of the Scots, Irish, English "peasant," and English gentleman, each speaking what anyone familiar with the British Isles would have expected him to speak. Nor did early travelers in Middle Tennessee, familiar with many varieties of English, find anything peculiar about the language of the first settlers. Francis Baily, an educated young Englishman, had no trouble in understanding or making himself understood.

This speech of the man from Yorkshire or Lancashire would in time appear crude and rude, especially to Americans. Dr. Drake, old and looking back from an age that said "epistle" instead of letter, wrote of the speech of his boyhood in Kentucky of the 1780's; "all was rudely vernacular, and I knew not then the meaning of that word; we spoke a dialect of old English in queer pronunciation and abominable grammar."[42]

[40] Hanna, *Scotch-Irish,* I, 170–172.
[41] VM, I, 378–390; II, 37.
[42] Drake, *Letters,* 126.

Mrs. Trollope, visiting the United States at about the same time Drake was remembering his childhood, was horrified by the language she found among the country people in the neighborhood of Cincinnati. She might have been less horrified had she taken the trouble to spend awhile in rural regions of England, for as Professor Abernethy [43] points out many expressions used by the frontiersmen and still heard in the rural South were known in Yorkshire and Wessex. He gave as examples, *dang* for damn, *wrassle* for wrestle, *afore* for before, *chaw* for chew, *agen* for against, and many others all of which are still fairly common in the hills.

Even today anyone planning to go on a "Kentucky folklore" hunting expedition would do well to read Smollett, giving particular attention to his conversations, in which one finds such common hill expressions as *heerd* for heard, *pore, this here, yuse, the Lord knows, none of your jaw, karcasses,* and dozens of other expressions and pronunciations, old when the Cumberland was settled. Milton wrote *afeard* and the horror we now have for the use of *like* when *as* can possibly be made to serve was unknown to either Milton or Shakespeare—"featured like him; like him with friends possessed," the old ones memorized, and wrote, "There never was seen the like of him."

Judging from phonetic spellings, the language most commonly heard on the Cumberland had more in common with the dialects of seventeenth and eighteenth century England and Scotland than with any group in America today, save possibly a few older people in out-of-the-way places in the South. There may have been early settlers on the Cumberland who spoke in the manner of George Washington, saying "daunce" for dance; if so, they left no record in phonetic spelling, possibly they were too well educated. The Cumberlander was more inclined to "daance," the *a* long, and the word closer to two syllables than one, for as a group they were much addicted to long *a*'s and extra syllables.

A few, writing of happenings during pioneer years, speak of Mansker's German accent or the Irish brogue of Jemmy O'Connor, but no one commented on the speech of the Donelsons, and though there was, of course, much less homogeneity than today, we can be reasonably certain the accent and word usage of the Donelsons were fairly typical. Though among the wealthier and more influential of the early settlers, the family had as a group less formal education than many middle-class farmers studied.

Rachel spelled almost entirely by ear. She wrote *git* for get; *aney,*

[43] Abernethy, *Frontier to Plantation,* 145.

any; *tanderness,* tenderness; *elligent,* elegant; *cillibration,* celebration; *etarnaly,* eternally; and she may have made a slow and soft three-syllable word of stranger as she spelled it *strainger;*[44] danger spelled also with an extra *i* may have been spoken in the same fashion. Rachel's older brother, John or Captain John, though his spelling was more orthodox, had the same general speech pattern, writing *spile* for spoil; *hant,* haunt; and *sayed* for said. Both he and his sister spelled many words as did Smollett in dialogue: welcome, *weelcome;* bosom, *boosom;* and copy, *coopy.*[45]

Rachel's nephew, John Hutchings, in business with his Uncle Jackson,[46] appears to have had even less formal education than the older generation; in his writing, reached was *retched;* very, *vary;* waiting, *weighten;* both, *boath;* show, *shew;* raised, *raisted;* violent, *vialint;* and in general Hutchings showed the same tendency to soften hard *ing* sounds, give the *ed* the sound of *t,* and add syllables and vowels.[47] Among isolated hill people seeing is often a soft but two-syllabled *sean,* being becomes *bean*—not pronounced like the vegetable or the English been; some also still say *sheare* for share as did James Robertson. Hutchings, for all the softness of his sounds, never softened his meanings any more than did his uncle John Donelson, who never left the reader wondering what he had meant to say. They lived in a world that praised Colonel Ridley for his lack of circumlocution.

James Robertson, basically Scotch-Irish, spoke much as did the Donelsons, showing the same liberal use of vowels: any—*aney;* many—*maney;* unjust—*unjest;* their or there—*thar;* certainly—*sartainly;* whether—*wheather;* was—*ware;* yellow—*yalow;* near—*nigh to;* and parcel—*persel.*[48] The pioneer Cumberland was in general a place where most had "years" on their heads, not short and sharp as today's earth's orbit to the east, but finely rolling so that the listener knew there was a *y* and plenty of *r;* not too

---

[44] Bassett, *Jackson Correspondence,* I, 283, 459, 476, 498; *ibid.,* VI, 450–451.

[45] Burke, *Emily Donelson,* I, 35, 135, 136, 196, 198–199.

[46] Jackson, even before he had a well educated secretary, grew quite careful of his spelling; some idea of his pronunciation may be gathered from early letters; see Bassett, *Jackson Correspondence,* I, 5, 17, 22, 24, 27.

[47] The letters of John Hutchings, father of "my little ward" and in business with Jackson in the early 1800's, are wonderful examples of a man's writing as he spoke and speaking as he thought; see *ibid.,* I, 86, 140, 141, 142, 145, 146.

[48] Robertson is well represented in most source materials of early Tennessee but many of his published letters were either written by someone else or heavily edited; for what appears to be unchanged letters see, Thwaites-Kellogg, *Dunmore's War,* 94–95, 99, 103–106, 142, 174; Bassett, *Jackson Correspondence,* I, 69–70, 319; TP, IV, 36, 359.

many years ago there were still such "yearres" in the hills. Children chant-
ing "Cock Robin" had no trouble rhyming lark with clerk and many so
spelled the word; a canebrake was a canebrack, but a horse was a "hoss,"
and even a man could "nuss a baby," nurse meaning to hold a child on
one's lap, not to suckle it.

Many said *git* and *whar, et rosin-yearres* (ate roasting ears), [49] and like
the Andrew Jacksons talked of *yestardayes* and *charectores*, though few
spelled with such reliance on the ear as did James Hartsell, captain in the
War of 1812: "On the same night I dremp I met my mother and went into
my hourse with hur whar I saw my wife making of cornbread and saw
the tabel set with plates, copes [cups], knives, and other articales. . . . I
toock a walk round—the hole loines—I could not git one yeare of corne
and I fetched a verey large load of cane—some horses lay thar, and as I
passed throw the horses nickered for my cane tell my hart aked for
them." [50]

Many used *fotch* instead of fetch and similar pronunciations as indicated by a well-to-do woman who when unexpected company dropped
in on scrubbing day remarked, "You have cotched me with my britches
down." [51] This pronunciation can in remote regions among the unsophisticated be heard at times as can a good many of Captain Hartsell's; a few
older folk in out-of-the-way places still say *pint* for point and *whar* for
where, and, no different from early court clerks who spelled as they spoke,
they have *sassers* instead of saucers, *cags* for kegs, and *rebands* for ribbons.[52] Most on the Southern borders were in the early years as unselfconscious of their speech as of displaying their emotions—or their spelling.
The speech pattern indicated by the Donelsons, Robertson, and numerous
phonetic spellers was not the only one, but it appears to have been the
most common up the river as well as down.

None of the phonetic spellers mentioned was of Irish origin, but certainly many localities would have been seasoned with a few Irish. Costello,
Murphy, Kennedy, Casada (Cassidy), and other Irish names were found

---

[49] A, V, 99–100, "Journal of John Lipscomb"; see also *ibid.*, V, 41–47, "Letters of
Davy Crockett."
[50] ETH, XI, 93–112, "The J. Hartsell Memora: The Journal of a Tennessee
Captain in the War of 1812," ed. by Mary Hardin McCown.
[51] W, 3XX (18), 5. This was a quote by William Martin who like most of the
Draper Correspondents and those in NCR and TP—Daniel Smith, the Bledsoes,
Blount—spelled too well to give any indication of how they spoke.
[52] Early county court clerks seldom did their work, but farmed it out, often for
no pay, to apprentice clerks, sometimes young boys, good penmen but poor spellers;
see PW, I, 1; PW, III, 626; DW, II, 33.

in muster rolls of the French and Indian War. Many of the Scots who had lived in Northern Ireland had undoubtedly fallen somewhat into an Irish way of speaking, though the two groups as a rule mingled but little. As late as 1910 the "mountaineers" of Western Virginia were portrayed as speaking in the customary Irish dialect of fiction, featuring such expressions as, "Faith, and it's th devil." [53] Even today the listener is struck by the similarities between the speech of some hill communities and some Irish-Americans of Cincinnati and Detroit; pronunciations, diction, certain expressions, and at times a curious lilting overflow of expression, all seem to have something in common.

There are questions, their answers not even partially revealed in writing, of syllabication and stress. They undoubtedly stressed the syllables of many words differently than do we today. We smile, for example, at the hill boy who says "git-tarr," giving his instrument plenty of *g*, *t*, and *r*, but with more *git* than *tar*. There was no one by to smile at Samuel Pepys who must have pronounced the word in much the same fashion, as he sometimes spelled it guittar.

There was, however, in spite of much similarity in pronunciation, soon a great deal of difference in diction between the language of the English colonies and the British Isles. The New World demanded names for all new things—Indian tribes to buffalo and humming bird. Sometimes the white man used the Indian name, but he more commonly thought up one of his own. Many of these names, though used by early historians and mentioned often in inventories, never found their way into any dictionary. One of their most widely used herbs for example was Seneca snakeroot, described by many writers and stocked by early physicians and still used in the hills; yet Webster listed a senega, so far unfound in any source material relative to the South, but fortunately rescued by Mitford M. Mathews and put in his *Dictionary of Americanisms*. Others, such as walink mentioned by Doddridge, are found in no dictionary, though Webster does give walking leaf.

New situations also called for new words. Indian warfare alone produced a whole new vocabulary; [54] scalped, skelped, green scalps, war whoop, Indian scout. The Draper correspondents and others used expressions such as "the men treed" or "I took tree," always meaning not to

[53] *America*, V. 251, Littell McClung, "Mountain Life in the Virginias."
[54] Thwaites-Kellogg, *Dunmore's War*, and Summers, *Southwest Virginia*, are especially good for the vocabulary of Indian warfare.

climb, but to get behind a tree.[55] Indian warfare passed, but the verb "treed" survived in the South; the many animals, such as raccoons and opossums, unknown in Europe that the Southerner hunted often took to trees and were treed, almost always by a dog. Dogs trained for such hunting are still referred to as tree dogs, and advertisements for tree dogs can be found in almost any county paper of the Middle South, but they seem as yet to have found their way into no dictionary.

Guns, particularly rifles, were more commonly owned and used on the Southern borders than in New England, and hence many expressions arising from them and their use, such as "hold your fire"—"flash in the pan"—"keep your powder dry"—"the biggest bullet doesn't always make the most noise," were more common in the Middle South and can still be heard in the hills.

The almost unique situation in regard to land produced a vocabulary strange to most visiting Englishmen—squatter, land office, entry taker. The land itself, though without any natural features unknown in Europe, gave rise to a vocabulary peculiarly American, and many were the English visitors who explained and commented upon such terms as river bottom, dividing ridge, sidling pass, sinkhole, and bluff.[56] Even when the old term was kept, it often knew a change of meaning, as in the case of creek, in England a narrow arm of the sea touched by the tides, but to us of the South, pronounced the same as the creak of a rusty hinge, it was bigger than a branch and smaller than a river. We had many sizes of branch—spring branches were little, but creek branches were big. We on the Cumberland, though the mouth of our river was a thousand miles from the sea, also had tides until the water was dammed; there were little tides and big tides, spring tides, and Christmas tides—these last to the old people did not mean tides that came at Christmas but a fall tide early enough so the little steamboats could get up from Nashville with candy and other good things for Christmas—but only when the Cumberland rolled over Burnside did we have a flood tide.

The Constitution and resulting government brought a whole new vocabulary, most of which quickly found its way into dictionaries, but

---

[55] W, 1S, 59; *ibid.*, 32S, 324, 491.

[56] Thwaites, *Travels,* V, John Bradbury, "Travels in The Interior of America in the years 1809, 1810, and 1811 including A Description of Upper Louisiana, together with The States of Ohio, Kentucky, Indiana, and Tennessee, with the Illinois and Western Territories," reprinted from the 2nd ed., London, 1819 (cited hereafter as Bradbury, *Travels, 1811*), 69.

the language of local government in the South, largely patterned on the English system, never got much attention. A county, for example, usually had a stray-pen and a stray-master appointed by the court, but these never got into dictionaries.

Travelers, once they had crossed the Appalachians, found more strange words. There were, for instance, on the Virginia size rolls several watermen, who, as in the days of Pepys, transported passengers or light cargo in small boats. These disappeared on navigable streams flowing into the Mississippi, and in their place came flatboatmen, keelboatmen, and at last steamboatmen; each form of navigation had a language all its own, though it might vary somewhat from river to river.[57] I never found a perve any place except on the Big South Fork, but practically all travelers wrote of the craft as well as the planters and sawyers on the Mississippi.

Amusements, too, were different; barbecue to Bradbury had meant a way of cooking meat, but in Kentucky and Tennessee he found it was a kind of social gathering, but different from a bee. Hunting had numerous vocabularies, especially the peculiarly American brand of fox hunting that grew up in the rough lands of the South where men could not as in England follow the hunt on horseback. And so they listened; the sounds the hounds made thus became as important as the sight of them had once been, and hounds were valued not only for their speed but for their mouths; there are still soft mouthed, pretty mouthed, bugle mouthed hounds advertised, but like much of the language of fox hunting, unfound in dictionaries.

Colorful as amusements and other activities were, they yielded when compared to the fields, homes, and kitchens of the South few new words. The Southern colonists, though closest to England in religion, local government, and social life, depended upon crops strange to the Old World. It was in the language of corn, cotton, and tobacco that travelers explained most terms. They were particularly impressed by the culture of corn,[58] "the grain that was neither sowed nor reaped"; planting, replanting, laying-by, fodder pulling, topping, and corn-gathering were all new words to them as was the language of tobacco.[59] Most were never accepted by Webster, nor would he list such early agricultural tools as corn knife and

---

[57] Byrd Douglas, *Steamboatin' on the Cumberland*, Nashville, 1961, 379–387, gives both the signals of bells and gongs and the terminology of steamboating on the Cumberland.

[58] John F. D. Smyth, *A Tour in the United States of America*, London, 1784 (cited hereafter as Smyth, *Tour*), I, 294–299.

[59] *Ibid.*, II, 129, 134.

cane hoe. Equally neglected by most standard dictionaries though many were recognized by Mathews were the numerous terms such as glut, ground log, stake and rider,[60] associated with rail fence; many are not only found in common speech, but also appeared in inventories and numerous renting and fence-building contracts.

Farm animals were almost wholly neglected; we have not only lost the sounds by which we managed them, the common names of their multiple diseases, but it grows increasingly hard to find an old-timer able to explain the earmarkings recorded in all early county records—under-keil, overbit, half penny, and dozens of others.

The log house, like corn, was not unknown in New England, but of much later date; the many words and terms used in connection with the building and occupation of log houses were neglected. A corner man to John Coffee, reckoning the cost of his Nashville land office,[61] was an entirely different person from that given by Webster.

Many expressions such as "second table" [62] used in connection with food and eating have all but disappeared. In out-of-the-way regions two women can still go to the local store, each ask for a "mess of steak," and one will receive two pounds, the other four, for *mess* meant enough to give the household one meal. Meanings varied; Clark's soldiers [63] thought of a "mess of corn" as three pints, or enough when boiled and pounded to feed six men, the number who customarily cooked in the same kettle. Many foods—succotash, cushaw, pomegranate—when mentioned at all by Webster or H. L. Mencken are given a meaning different from that of the pioneer and much of the present day South. Succotash, for example, was not corn and lima beans—in the first place we said butter beans—but anyway, succotash was corn and green beans seasoned with bacon. A pomegranate to us up river was a little sweet-smelling, orange-mottled melon, brought into the kitchen for its pleasant smell. Nobody now remembers, but artichokes were to us, as to Peter Kalm visiting in 1748, roots. Even steak and gravy differed; plural the two dishes were, as they had been for generations, breakfast stand-bys of my childhood; the steak fried and served on a platter, the cream-colored gravy, made much as was cream

---

[60] Mitford M. Mathews, *A Dictionary of Americanisms on Historical Principles,* The University of Chicago Press, 2nd ed., Chicago, 1956, not only describes a stake and rider fence but as in the case of ash hopper and many other appliances known to the pioneer has illustrations.

[61] Coffee Papers, 1809.

[62] Gray, *Bishop,* 49.

[63] I, VIII, 477.

gravy with fried chicken, served in a bowl. We had both sallet and salad as well as souse-meat. We also "set the table" [64] as in Asbury's day, and had "case knives," though this appears to have undergone a change in meaning. A case knife to us meant a table knife, but Mrs. Wilson, when in 1698 she wished for one to cut off the officer's ears, was probably thinking of a cased knife, a sharp-bladed, sheathed instrument, long known in hunting and warfare, but on the American border referred to as a long, sheathed, or sheath knife.

Save for the words and expressions demanded by his new environment with all its ramifications, the Southern pioneer used few of what we today consider Americanisms. The epithet given on a nationality, racial, or religious background that so fascinated Mencken seems to have been as little known to the pioneer as to Pepys who, mingling with all manner of men, saw none as part of a group entirely apart from the rest of humankind; good or bad, each was an individual. I found only one instance and that during the Revolution by a Tory who referred to his Southern enemies as *crackers*.[65] Epithets the pioneer hurled, at times fighting duels for the privilege, but no matter how abusive, they were given on an individual basis. The bad manners of abusing a group for the misdeeds of one was not a part of their upbringing. I never found an Indian, even Dragging Canoe, one of the most hated, called by anything save his name. Neither was the slang that later so horrified Mrs. Trollope much in evidence.[66] Ordinary language always seemed enough. They never, for example, appeared to feel the need for cuteness; one finds drawers and shifts but nothing like "undies." They skirted nothing; people "made water" as they had for generations, a function that had nothing to do with one's toilet. Death beds and starvation had not yet yielded to terminal illnesses and insufficient nutrition.

Different as were the diction and pronunciation of the language of the average pioneer, there was a difference between their language and ours of today, much deeper than mere sound. Any speech, spoken or written, in addition to whatever meaning it conveys, reflects to some degree the temper of the times as well as the individual who uses it. There seems to have been in the United States during pioneer years little fear and uncertainty in society as a whole; the "tyranny of public opinion" was less strong in the early days, and there was much less tendency for men in all

---

[64] Asbury, *Journal*, 239.
[65] Draper, *King's Mountain*, 593.
[66] Bassett, *Jackson Correspondence*, I, 181, yields "rotten in the State of Denmark" but one cannot be certain whether Jackson was using slang or quoting Shakespeare.

walks of life to throw up smoke screens of words. Men were not afraid of holding wrong opinions and speech as a result tended to be forthright and plain.

Speech was, with no radio or TV and much less time spent in school, a more personal thing, learned from language heard in the home, for English of some variety was the mother, rather than the adopted tongue, for most. The average person was much more at home with it, more inclined to the use of similes and metaphors, while the terror of colloquialisms, even among the educated, was less widespread.

Nor was there during pioneer years much evidence of an attempt by any group to create a private language. The learned like Dr. Johnson discussed poetry in words comprehensible to the layman of good sense and some education, for poetry was not held to be a subject for only the initiate. This was true of most other fields. Language was considered primarily a means of communication. Even silver-tongued orators, often more noted for their silver tongues than the sense they made, and soon to be very much a part of the American scene, were not a feature of pioneer life.

Words were not apt to be chosen for their beauty or seemliness. Most, like Smollett's characters, lived in a world that held bellies, bottoms, guts, and not infrequently "arses." People puked and belched, and in general said what they had to say in the clearest possible way.

Many years ago when teaching one-room schools in shut-away hill regions, I found remnants of a forthright manner of speech older than the Cumberland settlements. I became quite well acquainted with a moral and modest old woman, of whom her grandchildren—sophisticated by going away to "public works"—complained. She was so "dirty-mouthed," they disliked to take their little ones to see her. The great-grandmother had been but little out of her back-hill community, and her speech was inherited; she unabashedly used such expressions as, "He rattled on like a bell-clapper up a goose's ass." She had a strict code of her own, would never have condoned a detailed description of the sex act as it figures in much literary art; or a close-up of the birth of a child on TV, and disliked the pictures of "bare-assed" girls in bathing suits. Yet, she quarreled at the young women "too proud" to suckle their young in church.

Rarely, even then in that remote place, was unselfconscious expression found in the young. I do remember a small girl, my youngest pupil, and oldest child of one of the more shut-away families up a creek on a road scarcely navigable by a mule-drawn sled. Not yet of school age, she came in good weather, as her mother explained, mostly "to larn" the ways of school. The child on the morning of her first full day came up to the desk, her shy and troubled, but clear, whisper of, "Teacher, can I go shit?" shrilling over the whole of the small room.

None of the children giggled; instead an older girl laid a book in the door for her, as was the custom on leaving the room. They did not use the word in school, but they had not yet reached the stage of civilization where it brings either giggles or blushes. The child soon learned from the others the more acceptable expression was "to be excused." The expression "go to the toilet," or almost as bad, "go to the bathroom" was of course not used. Years later a hill grandmother described to me with a mixture of amusement and disgust how one of her visiting grandchildren, raised in Cincinnati, had in the middle of the woods asked to "go to the bathroom." Not many years ago some back-hill mothers who would have blushed at the word *bull,* saying *cow-brute* instead, used the four letter words of Shakespeare in discussing the bodily functions of their babies or the farm animals.

The little girl mentioned knew no world save that of her home with a younger brother and a baby. She talked much of this world, and as an older child tending her baby brother at times was now and then troubled by all the vicissitudes of baby care. One morning her woes overflowed in the middle of school; we listened while she told of how the baby, a lusty, well-toothed infant of around a year, able to climb the picket fence and sit alone on the family mule, had bit the "titty" the night before, so sharp her mother slapped him before she'd thought, and so hard she'd left a red mark on his face; her Mama had cried, and they'd all cried to think anybody would slap a little baby "that away." He bit her again in the night, so hard she'd screamed out, and now they didn't know what to do; it would kill him to wean him now, his second summer not over, but if he kept on biting the "titty that-away" her Mama was afraid she'd quit giving her milk down, dry up, and have no milk.

The children listened in composed sympathy. At last an older boy, one of a large family, gave it as his opinion that they were all pretty foolish. Lots of babies bit; it was his back teeth beginning to cut, he said, and dog days; he'd get over it and she wouldn't dry up; and so they discussed it, matter-of-factly, a little remnant of some old world where a woman's teats, like a cow's, were in a sense, if not communal, at least family property, for through them and them alone for the back-hill baby lay the way to life.

This community represented merely one pattern of speech, an old one, but not entirely that of Middle Tennessee during pioneer days; polite folks would have said "necessary house," and it is doubtful if many in Middle Tennessee used the four letter words of the child, but many words used freely by the pioneer were taboo in the hill community. The older children were inclined to giggle at rump, and to them ham was part of a hog and not of the human anatomy. The early Cumberlanders, like many in the South, but different from the New Englander, not only used such words but never tripped around the word "bull" and female dogs were, of course, bitches.

Tom Johnson, Kentucky's first poet, though he did not give detailed descriptions of what we now refer to as "the sex act," for such would have been considered bad taste, did use a great many words more frowned upon today than the delineation of scenes that would during pioneer years have been dwelt upon only around the tavern or the blacksmith shop. The Kentucky *Miscellany* containing Johnson's poetry had a wide circulation in the old West, though so quickly did the world change that by 1834 an Ohio critic had his decency outraged when his Kentucky landlady gave him a copy of the verses.[67]

Published in 1789 and later advertised in the Tennessee *Gazette*, the volume undoubtedly found its way into the hands of many on the Cumberland, and as the pioneer, like generations behind him and a few after, was fond of learning things by heart, especially if they rhymed, more than one may have recited some such doggerel as that concerning the wedding night of the aged Parson Douglass who after various struggles, "with full intent—love's engine bent; try'd again—but all in vain;" was at last forced to cry, "it will not do; Faith, Betty, you'll not get your due." Others of Johnson's poems were concerned with a lady "who suffered a Loud Escape at Craig's Meeting," "The Author's Hatred of Kentucky in General," and for the "Low Wits" the story of William Pettit's mare.[68]

Lord Henry Hamilton, passing through Kentucky in 1779, complained that he was "accosted in coarse terms by women," [69] but I found no mention among travelers on the Cumberland of coarse or abusive language. True, much of their conversation would by today's standards be con-

[67] John Wilson Townsend, *Kentucky in American Letters, 1784–1912,* Cedar Rapids, Iowa, 1913, I, 20.
[68] Quoted by permission of the editor and publisher, John Wilson Townsend, from *O Rare Tom Johnson,* Lexington 1949, a facsimile of an 1821 edition of Johnson's poetry, first published as *The Kentucky Miscellany,* Lexington, 1789, 7, 17, 21, 27.
[69] John D. Barnhart, *Henry Hamilton and George Rogers Clark in the American Revolution,* copyright R. E. Banta, The Banta Press, Crawfordsville, Indiana, 1951, 196.

sidered coarse, but they were ever a polite people, at times too polite. Andrew Jackson, torn between honest forthrightness and fashionable politeness, for his instincts ever warred with his adopted principles, once found it necessary to postscript a polite but insulting letter to a newly made enemy with, ". . . and these expressions I wish to be taken in the worst possible sense of the word." [70] As a rule this was not necessary; if any man, including Jackson, thought another was a "coward and a poltroon," the thing to do was to say so, or better, publish it in the newspaper. Hypocrisy was frowned upon. Governor Blount, on hearing of the death of a former Continental Army General, remarked, "Thus, the world is rid of one man who can well be spared." Young Hutchings writing to Jackson of the "pleasing nuse" of Dickinson's horse's defeat wished he "might of had the pleasur of seeing them in their aggony." [71]

It was all part of the pattern of being unafraid to let others know what one thought. First settlers tended toward such ungentle adjectives as ill-turned, chunky, spare, wicked, boney, crazy, nasty, mean, ugly, stingy, and these used with harsh little nouns—fool, coward, rascal, glutton, drunkard, whore, horse-thief, hypocrite, devil, fornicator, and many others now considered "coarse." A Kentucky farmer of 1802 was not being consciously crude when he wrote in his diary, "Becca Bell, who often fell, is now big with child to a wicked trifling school master . . . who says he'll be damned to hell if he ever marries her." [72]

In ordinary conversation they were ever specific. Such a modern sentence as "Farmers produce cereals and industrialists produce consumer goods," could never have been written by any early settler. Produce when used at all was usually a court term—a man produced evidence or a witness. Farmers grew, raised, or made crops and the crop was specified—eighty bushel corn or chaffy oats. He raised hogs, horsestock, cattle, and also children, and always he was specific; different from the modern TV star who speaks of his horse while riding a mare or a gelding, he said, "John Leeper rode a large bay horse; Big Harpe rode a bay mare." [73] The listener could relax and enjoy a longish account of the chase, knowing that no matter what, Big Harpe was good as caught; a mare was often speedy as a horse, sometimes speedier, but almost never did she have the bottom.

[70] Bassett, *Jackson Correspondence*, I, 35; this to the man who only nine years before had given him a start in life—Judge McNairy.

[71] *Ibid.*, I, 141.

[72] Sweet, *Religion*, II, 89, quoting John Lyle's Diary, here concerned with the doings in a camp meeting in Kentucky.

[73] W, 5S, 70.

Early farmers had mares, horses, geldings, colts, fillies, just as they had bulls, cows, calves, steers, work-steers, fat-steers, heifers, boars, barrows, sows, gilts, pigs, rams, ewes, lambs, and wethers; these were often described —"brindle calf—sawed-horn heifer—muley cow—sorrel mare with a white patch on the off shoulder." The farm family did not at first have even chickens, but "dunge-hill fowels" and game chickens.[74]

Reminders of this exact turn of mind lingered longest in the hills where men would seldom say "tree," but name and often describe, "wind-shook white oak, dead chestnut, shag-bark hickory," and like the correspondents of Mr. Draper one hundred and fifty years ago, never did they speak of soil and seldom of land or ground alone—but of "rocky cedar ledge, sandy pine ridge, damp beech bottom." Even now when the hill man talks of his foxhounds, cur dogs, feists, tree dogs, family dogs, and hog dogs, one remembers Macbeth's "hounds and greyhounds, mongrels, spaniels, shoughs, water-rugs, and demi-wolves."

"Rifle-gun" in the mouth of a hill man is now often good for a laugh, though the one amused seems to forget that the use of the word "rifle" as a noun is rather new, and "rifle-gun" is but a shortening of the correct name as listed by court clerks—"rifled barreled gun," for there were many guns and in inventories each was designated. The same is true of the expression, "play-party," now and then heard; party was to the pioneer as to any Britisher of that day a group of people; Draper correspondents wrote of war parties, scouting parties, and parties of travelers; to take the word party and make of it a social occasion would have struck such a one as John Sevier strange—he attended teas, dances, dinings, balls, house-raisings, and met with friends to play cards or billiards, but he did not attend parties.

Most in the old Southwest lived almost as much as did Shakespeare in a world of verbs and nouns. Farming families and their help warped and hoed and chopped; they stripped, drew, tapped, gouged, wove, spun, burred, tanned, turned, filled, wound, hewed, brewed, stilled, topped, pulled, leached, laid, swingled, run, sheared, picked, suckered, bolted, scalded, and performed dozens of other operations. Each verb had a noun to match—loom, tobacco, cotton, tobacco, staves, sugar trees, bread trays, cloth, thread, wool, leather, bowls, shuttle, bobbin, logs, methiglen, whiskey, corn, fodder, ashes, fence, flax, bullets, sheep, cotton, tobacco, logs, and hogs.

Many words and expressions we now use in connection with the pio-

[74] See in particular MW, I, 3, 17, 27–28, 117, and DW, II, 5.

neer he would have found more redundant than the hill man's "rifle-gun." He never wore, for example, long trousers or knee breeches; during pioneer years all trousers were long and all breeches short, so adjectives were never applied. One looks, too, in vain through inventories for flintlocks and muzzle-loaders; there was at this date no other kind of gun.

They did use many descriptive phrases, particularly in the naming of creeks, but they were almost always the matter-of-fact names given by a people who never beat their brains in thinking up names to catch the fancy of some future passer-by. A creek that sank out of sight as many did in limestone country was a sinking creek, and hence a good name; in Wayne County, Kentucky, for example, there is Big Sinking, Little Sinking, and Cedar Sinking, all of the Big South Fork; there was, of course, too, a Little South Fork; across the Cumberland in an adjoining county there were Sinking Creek of Fishing Creek and Sinking Creek of Buck Creek, and on down the river were other Sinking Creeks. A creek with plenty of fish was good for fishing and hence, Fishing Creek, and so does one find Otter Creek, Turkey Creek, Buck Creek, Wild Goose Shoals, and others remembering animals or some part of their anatomy such as Turkey Neck Bend. Water falling was Falling Water and hence the name; a creek with rocks was rocky and naturally it was Rocky Creek, just as a Creek with rich land along it was called Richland Creek; there were at least two of these but only one Marrowbone Creek, for land could be rich as a marrowbone. Cane figures prominently in many names—Caney Fork, Cane Ridge, Cane Creek, though cedar and other plants are well represented. They continued also until all nameless creeks were exhausted to name them as had the Long Hunters for members of whatever party found them first. South of the Cumberland in Middle Tennessee, this usually meant surveyors.

Church bodies almost never tried to think up holy names, believing that God gave a holiness not to be added to by man in a name. If all the Cumberland should be dammed and taken over by the Federal government with all the creeks stilled, their names forgotten, the river and its tributaries would live in the musty pages of the old minutes of the Baptist churches—Big Sinking, Sinking Creek, Fishing Creek, Clear Fork, Goose Creek, Casey's Fork, Howard's Bottom, and after each the words Baptist Church.[75]

[75] Wells, *Cumberland County*, "Religion," 59–81, is a particularly good discussion of the many early churches in this section of the Cumberland Country—Mud Camp, Bear Creek, Flat Rock, Rock House were names typical of churches on the upper Cumberland.

Their language, like any language, was constantly welcoming new words. The 1797 visitor to Natchez might come back to Nashville riding an "apalousa" as did Francis Baily, and refer to the local jail as a "callibouse." [76]

In spite of voluminous correspondence, they used, on the whole, fewer words to say a given thing than do we today, and were sparing of relatives and adverbs. In these matters they were not much different from their age. The critic writing that so-and-so, "the author of such-and-such is now currently engaged in producing a great literary work that . . ." was employed neither by Mr. Carey, editor of the American *Museum*, nor by Mr. Bradford, of the Tennessee *Gazette*. Dilworth's *English Tongue*, their most popular English text, gave much space to the art of elision.

The modern psychological-social-political-economic jargon coloring even our daily newspapers was, of course, no part of life. A termination was an end, and if he had a motivation he didn't know it; he ate, wore, drank, used, but was not given to consumption—the name of a disease. Antisocial, underweight, togetherness, adjustment, abnormal, controversial, subversive, loyalty, free enterprise, communistic, outgoing, and allied words used to describe an intangible state with a good or bad connotation were not in the pioneer vocabulary. True, he used many of these, but never with the single meaning—men adjusted machinery or their plans. Nor was he much inclined to take a word of many meanings and give it only one as we today use such words as prostitute, deviate, professor, undertaker, pregnant, vulgar, stout, installment, along with still more—left, right, red, amusement, business, remark— in the process of being given one or so new meanings at the expense of all the old.

Shift is such an emasculated word. Once it was truly wonderful. Thomas Walker, a cleanly man, often shaved and shifted while exploring Kentucky in 1750. Shift was also a woman's undergarment, and many farmers now and then had to make shift to get in a crop with little help, but nobody wanted a shifty-eyed woman or a shiftless man; on the other hand a good shifty wife able to turn last year's silk, and make petticoats for little girls out of her old short gown was a good woman to have around.

Turn, too, is almost dead. It is not so much that we no longer take turns to mill—we do not go to mill—but turn, meaning disposition, is sel-

[76] Baily, *Tour 1796–1797*, 289, 311–312.

dom heard, nor do we do one another good turns, nor get turns from bad news, lightning and such.

One often becomes aware of the crippling only when reading an eighteenth century conversation or an old advertisement, such as that in an 1802 *Gazette*: "Wanted a teacher to undertake the tuition of small children," and we remember that tuition once meant care of as well as the sum paid for tutoring. Sevier, always buying dress patterns for his daughters, reminds us the word pattern once meant, and is still so used in the hills, the amount of material needed to make a given thing. We now and then hear of some whose appetite was whetted, but seldom is any person "gone a whet."

One can still in the hills hear of little piddling things, and of children who piddle on the way home from school; children's hair is towseled instead of tangled, and people still pester [77] each other as in the days of Andrew Jackson. Yet, even by my childhood the wonderful word *bait*, when used in connection with food, was a noun only and considered a crude word; to eat a great bait or even a bait meant the person had taken more food than he should have, but Pepys could say "we baited" and mean his party of travelers had stopped, rested, and partaken of a meal. In reading the North Carolina records we are reminded that vermin once meant any predatory animal such as wolf, panther, and wild cat instead of worms and fleas.[78] We never collect debts any more by "shuffling" the money out of the debtor,[79] and almost never do we meet people who are tolerable or wear clothing of a "tolerable good blue," [80] and now we only talk and talk and never "harp away." [81]

I can now find waiters only in the old Twelve Song—"five of the small bell waiters"—or some one like Judge Guild [82] who remembered the waiter—attendant—at his wedding, but many years ago a few older preachers in the hills referred to those who sat with them near the pulpit as waiters. They also called me, then young and single—mistress.

We now use the adjective *distant* mostly as a measure of space; one can in the hills still hear the word as John Donelson used it of his daughter Emily, a distant person, one not overly friendly or eager to please. Also,

[77] Bassett, *Jackson Correspondence*, I, 18.
[78] NCR, XXIV, 133.
[79] DC, I, 32.
[80] Nashville *Clarion*, March 31, 1812.
[81] Gray, *Bishop*, 162.
[82] Guild, *Old Times*, 351.

now and then, an older person in the South will say another is "breaking fast,"[83] meaning to show signs of advancing age.

Most such expressions are now labeled crude or colloquial; we seldom jar and jaw with each other as in John Lawson's day. We do not carry our cars to town as Sevier carried his carriage or Boswell carried Johnson or a childhod neighbor carried his mule. We never light from cars or even planes as did Pepys from his carriage and early farmers from horseback.

Seldom now, save here and there in the hills, does a traveler reach his destination "in the evening by sundown"[84] as did Jackson, or, like Captain Hartsell's men, at "two o'clock in the evening."[85] The word afternoon was seldom used, nor were they much inclined to say "early in the morning" or even give a specific hour. Old school contracts call for the assembling of pupils, "an hour by sun"; others came at sunrise, the sensible procedure where life for many revolved about the sun. The day was further divided by the chores and such expressions as milking time and dinner time—noon—can still be heard. The year as in most farming communities was divided by the farm work swinging through the seasons; practically all farmers had corn-gathering time but lambing time like kraut-making time was not universal.

Time, too, was often measured by flowers, especially among the story-tellers: "It was dog-wood blooming time" or "the pretty-by-nights were open but it was too early for whip-poor-wills or dew." "It was way late, the morning glories were shut." The morning glories disappeared, bind-weed came instead; love vine became dodder, and so it was with many of our old flower names—farewell-to-summer, old maid, bridal wreath, candle sticks, snow-on-the-mountain, and others are now become ageratum, zinnias, and such.

Most completely lost because they are no longer needed are the names of the various objects and activities that went with their vanished way of life. Some such as dresser, office, and closet remain though with changed meanings. Most of us would be puzzled by talk of tare and tret, barm and wort, the cast of the hand in sowing wheat, webs and cuts, tuns, firkins, keeler's, the glebe, courts of oyer and terminer, half-joes, wallowers, teeter poles, and battling sticks.[86]

We can only wonder on what beautiful private words they had, or

---

[83] Burke, *Emily Donelson*, I, 195, 198, quoting Captain John Donelson.

[84] Bassett, *Jackson Correspondence*, I, 257.

[85] ETH, XII, 124. Hartsell, "Journal."

[86] In general *Oxford Unabridged* is the best source for pioneer words and expressions, unconnected with things peculiarly American.

what one might call family slang, handed down. Gome, for example, did not mean a sticky mass to us, but any kind of mess in need of cleaning up from the state of politics to milk spilled on the table. We preferred as a rule more specific terms; bolox, a verb, was better used when one tried to do a thing such as making a dress, and boloxed the business—did a poor job; both cattywampus and antigodling meant careless construction, usually applied to a house not set four square with the world or a crookedly hung gate.

So accustomed were the early settlers to think in terms of living things, the neuter gender was much less commonly used than today. A good many objects were masculine, but more commonly feminine—boat, gun, river, weather, or even of the mill it could be said, "She runs fine." There were, of course, no faceless, sexless siblings. Rather, men were much inclined to give, if not gender, at least life to all the world around them. The editor warned farmers their "ground must be in good heart" before planting seed; boats could go down river, "the waters answering"; [87] debts were often desperate; mud was not only black but fat as well; [88] and even a petticoat might be middling old or middling new.

Speech was rich in simile, metaphor, and proverb, most old when the Cumberland was settled. The young one knew what another meant when he threatened to "jump down your throat and gallop every chitterling out of you."

Many of their similes were drawn from the world around them—tough as hickory, of tried grit, felt like a sheep-killing dog,[89] mad as a hornet, stubborn as a mule; others from their reading, "A Xanthippe of a landlady," "A Cassius looking fellow"; and a very great many—whey faced, butter fingered, tallow complected—had long been used in Scotland and England. Old, too, were the many Biblical allusions; true, compared to today, only a small percentage of the early settlers belonged to any church, but the Bible was widely studied and read and influenced language more than any other work. Biblical characters and situations wandered in and out of speech: "a veritable tower of Babel, a doubting Thomas of a man, a widow's barrel for talk, stubborn as Balaam's ass, strong as Sampson." Many, no doubt, were spoken with lifted brows: "He's not one to be crucified." "What does she think she is, a lily of the field?" "A Delilah, that one," or "There's not been the like of her since Jezebel died." The splen-

[87] *Southwestern Monthly*, II, 75, "The Journal of John Carr."
[88] Thwaites-Kellogg, *Dunmore's War*, 326.
[89] Guild, *Old Times*, 73, 71, 88.

dor of the Queen of Sheba, the wisdom of Solomon, the hairiness of Esau, the patience of Job were along with the characteristics of dozens of others often referred to as was The Last Judgment and Peter at the Pearly Gate.

Their proverbs, like their language, showed an attitude toward life: "What's bred in the bone can't be beat out of the flesh." "You can't make a silk purse out of a sow's ear." "Blood's thicker than water." "An idle mind is the devil's workshop." "An ox can work," or the younger variant, "Even a mule can pull." Still, no proverb was the last word; there were for many, rebuttals. A wife, weary of a forever-moving husband might chide, "A rolling stone gathers no moss," but the itchy-footed husband could retort, "A setten goose has got no feathers on her belly."

A few of the sayings and proverbs survive, though yearly grow less common. "You're measuring my corn in your basket" is now and then heard. People still "go to pot," and families "run to seed."

Setting geese are gone from most farmyards, and gone, too, for many, is the sky. The old ones looked up at the sky dozens of times a day, nor was it entirely forgotten in the clockless home at night, for how else could a man or woman know on awakening if it be time to get up without at least an attempt to see the stars, not always visible in the Cumberland's foggy valleys. But fog or no, there revolved around the sky the weather lore of many generations. There were rhymes to tell the next day's weather by the sunrise or the sunset, and any child knew the look of the new moon with the old moon in her arms, a dry moon, a wet moon, and the meaning of a falling star, and the time it was in October when the handle of the Big Dipper stood straight up in the sky. The pioneer boy, like the children behind him in Scotland, knew to look for a shred of rainbow near the sinking sun when his father decided they'd best round up the sheep; bad weather was coming for he had seen a sun dog.

Yet change even then was on the way. An English traveler, stopping at a North Carolina backwoods inn during the Revolution, asked for "meat and drink" for his horse. The ostler, surprised, thought he had not heard aright; the traveler repeated his request. The ostler hurried away, returning soon with water and a chunk of bacon on a stick which he tendered the horse. Meat to the Englishman meant any victualing for man or horse;[90] had he meant animal flesh he would have specified, and the Cumberlander usually did. Still, the old pattern of specific words for specific thoughts was breaking up.

There were over most of the English-speaking world changes in atti-

[90] Smyth, *Tour*, I, 77–78.

tudes and circumstances that would affect the language. As early as 1795, a visiting Frenchman observed that Philadelphia women had "certain ridiculous scruples about being unwilling to hear certain words pronounced. And the extent to which that scruple is observed discloses rather an excess of knowledge than of ignorance." [91]

Victorianism, though the Queen for whom it would be named was not yet born, was well on the way. The extent of its influence can possibly best be understood by thinking of some one of Hogarth's sketches—the forthright honesty of *The Harlot Lodged in Bridewell* is good enough—then remembering the Cincinnati milkmaid Mrs. Trollope found in the 1820's. The milkmaid was a figure painted on a signpost, and she, like any milkmaid, was in a somewhat shortish gown that left her ankles bare; these obscenities were by popular demand covered with a ruffle of dresstail.

Prudery, hypocrisy, timidity were not the only currents blowing across the land. Not long after Mrs. Trollope, De Tocqueville came and studied and complained that American writers hardly "ever appear to dwell upon a single thought," and warned "without clear phraseology there can be no good language." At about the same time and close to forty years after Baily who had found no fault at all, another visiting Englishman, Featherstonhaugh, did complain of the language, especially of the deeper South. He was more hopeful of Middle Tennessee but critical still: "The dialects of Lancashire and Yorkshire are . . . the ancient language of these districts . . . the people have been furnished with one of the finest languages in Christendom, yet, although accustomed to it, I frequently am left ignorant of what they mean to say." [92]

The self-conscious use of slang, the racial or religious epithet, the growing fear and uncertainty that along with ignorance of the concrete would in time make of obscurity a mark of literary worth were when Featherstonhaugh visited in 1834 all much in evidence. Yet on the Cumberland and for many years to come, now and then a writer would threaten, "I will splatter his brains all over the face of the earth, by God." [93] and we, up river, continued to gape instead of yawn.

Most important of all, *Huckleberry Finn* was written. There is in its seeming simplicity much of the early settler, his language, and his attitude toward a world in which a man had often to make his own decisions. There is in it no Perfect Answer.

[91] Handlin, *America*, Moreau, "Travels, 1793–1798," 101.
[92] Featherstonhaugh, *Excursion*, I, 198.
[93] Gray, *Bishop*, 175.

In time the children came who never saw the sky or knew a little "nubbin of a man," nor could they understand if he should say, "Don't kick before you're spurred." The horses on TV never kick and are never spurred, and if there should be a nubbin among the hybrid corn the corn-picking combine can never mention the matter. But all that was far away; the young of 1795 had beyond the Cumberland Country with its varied weather, soils, rocks, river, earth, sky,[94] plants, animals, and people, a wide, wide world of books, and custom demanded that at a very early age they must begin to prepare themselves for looking into these.

[94] Parton, *Jackson*, I, 41–44, quoting McSkimin's *History of Carrickfergus*, gives much of the moon and the sky and the weather lore of Northern Ireland when Andrew Jackson's father was a boy there; certain it is that some of this came to the Cumberland during pioneer days, for many of the terms like "dog in the sky" or "sun dog" are still used up river.

Was a Cherry Tree, pleafing to View.

Was an Eagle, and foar'd to the Sky.

Was a Drummer, and beat a Tattoo

A fine Lady, with head near as high.

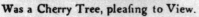

Chapter Six

Intellectual Background
and Education

SOMETIMES WHEN studying early will books in the back of the long reading room of the Tennessee State Library at Nashville, the pioneers would vanish, and in their stead came half remembered things, rummagings as it were among the odds and ends my head has at random gathered. Who wrote Ossian's poems? And I would sit fishing for the name Macpherson; often I forgot the will book for a memory—the joy of a first reading of *The Vicar of Wakefield*. More often still, I think, there would come the

Headpiece: Two pages from *The Royal Alphabet or Child's Best Instructor*, Boston, 1793.

ghost of a big and ugly man, a Tory so opposed to the American Revolution he wrote in London a tract pointing out the virtues of England's side—Dr. Samuel Johnson.

He came, for instance, with John Rice, an early Nashville merchant, in business many years before his death in January, 1792, near the mouth of Red River.[1] Rice was a wealthy bachelor with many small luxuries such as "framed pictures." He also owned several thousand acres of land; Memphis stands on land owned, though not then clear of Indian title, by John Rice. He made a will some years before he died,[2] and in it left land to be sold, the proceeds to go "for schooling" the poor of Cumberland.

He seems at first glance to have nothing whatever in common with Dr. Johnson, eight years dead in London. Even the terms describing the occupations of Rice—land speculator, storekeeper—were unknown to Johnson and his world of literary men. Then, in scanning Rice's inventory one finds along with *Tom Jones* and other books Dodsley's *Collection of Poems*, and one remembers Johnson was a friend of Robert Dodsley. We cannot be certain that Dodsley's *Collection* owned by John Rice was the same as that published in London in 1748; it may have been an American edition pirated in whole or part, or only one volume of the original three.

Yet, whatever the edition, it was a link between John Rice, dead at the mouth of Red River, and the rich intellectual life of the British Isles of the eighteenth century. James Boswell in giving us Dr. Johnson gave us much of the life of his day. The man Johnson and such great ones as Hume, Goldsmith, Chesterfield, Adam Smith, Whitefield—names found often in early Cumberland inventories—could not be separated. All were in turn part of a world much wider than that of their own time and place. Johnson and his circle read and discussed Rousseau and Voltaire, and all men of their day with any pretensions to education were conversant with the language and literature of ancient Greece and Rome. They had almost as much respect for the literature of the past as we of today have for the technology of the present and the future.

Such was the influence of this world that no settlement in the old West, no matter how remote, could quite escape it. James Smith,[3] the first traveler to leave a record of his stay in the wilds of what was to be Middle Tennessee, had for company in 1766 a mulatto boy, a Psalm Book, and Watts' *Upon Prayer;* previously, while a captive at Fort Duquesne he had

[1] ASP, *Indian Affairs*, I, 330, January 7, 1792.
[2] DW, I, 255, 268.
[3] Arnow, *Seedtime*, 134–138, is an account of Smith and the verses he wrote.

studied the Bible. The Long Hunters usually carried with them at least a few books. The story that "Lulbegrud" Creek in Kentucky got its name because a party of hunters encamped there was reading *Gulliver's Travels* is well known.

Most of those who left accounts of childhoods on the border speak of the books owned by their families—works ranging from the Bible and Watts' *Poems for Children*,[4] through the usual Dilworth texts to *Lord Chesterfield's Advice*, a work widely owned on the Cumberland, though not too well thought of by Dr. Johnson. Early, one finds Johnson's *Lives of the Poets*, now and then his "Big Dictionary," or bound copies of the *Rambler*. Johnson's works, however, are less commonly found than those of Smollett, Whitefield, Shakespeare, Voltaire, and several other men.

Books came to Middle Tennessee by flatboat and horseback through the hard cold of the winter of 1779–1780. Practically all inventories beginning with that of Nicholas Gentry, killed owning a Bible and a spelling book, to wealthy John Deadrick more than a dozen years later, whose eight volume Hume's *History of England* sold for $18, list books. True, many pioneer families such as those of John Buchanan, Sr., and Jacob Castleman had chiefly works of a religious nature. The books of William Neely, killed in the summer of 1780, are fairly typical of the pioneer with a religious bent. He had the usual Bibles, the hymns of Isaac Watts, and several works on theology, including two of the most popular in the British Isles—Crook's *Confession of Faith* and William Law's *Serious Call to a Devout and Holy Life*,[5] read by Dr. Johnson when a student at Oxford.

A small library, compared to that of such a one as Richard Henderson [6] who spent much of 1779–1780 on the Cumberland. He brought west with him Dr. Johnson's *Dictionary* in two volumes, Blackstone's *Commentaries*, the *Laws of Virginia*, Smollett's *Letters*, and a thirty-five volume edition of Voltaire. All of these were soon appearing in Cumberland inventories. Mr. Gubbins, for example, admitted to the Davidson County bar in 1785 and killed the year following, had both Blackstone and Montesquieu.[7] Unfortunately the pamphlets, magazines, and newspapers left by Gubbins

---

[4] Drake, *Letters*, 112, 161–162, 167–168, is one of the most detailed accounts of the books in an ordinary farm home on the frontier.

[5] DW, I, 166; John Buchanan, Sr., *ibid.*, I, 69; Jacob Castleman, *ibid.*, I, 194.

[6] THM, II, opposite 155, a facsimile of Henderson's letter with book list, March 15, 1784. Richard Henderson is considered to have been the author of the Cumberland Compact, a governmental document of land-buying agreement, drawn up in 1780 and signed by most of the first settlers.

[7] DW, I, 59.

were not listed by title so that we cannot know what periodicals he read.

Thomas Molloy was living in the Cumberland settlements at least by 1783 as in that year he held office under the Cumberland Compact, but we cannot be certain his largish library that included Pope and Blackstone was owned at this time, for his death came almost ten years later.[8] Many inventories list only "some books" [9] as in the case of David Lucas, killed in 1781, or "fifty books," [10] the only thing we know of Dr. Mark Sappington's library.

Inventories are not available for the libraries of many of the most bookish men in the region. Daniel Smith, who in the hard winter compared his Kentucky landlady to Xanthippe, undoubtedly had one of the best libraries in Middle Tennessee, but his many leather bound volumes, representative of the best, not only in English but with translations—even the works of the French scientists, Lavoisier [11] and Fourier—were never inventoried, though some are still owned by descendants. The books owned by the Robertsons, Bledsoes, Stumps, Winchesters, and many other first and early settlers were also not listed. We only know of Samuel Newell, officer at King's Mountain, and in time a settler up river, that he had "a pretty good library and was a great reader." [12] Rhodes Garth, a teacher who came in 1799 to Wayne County, had at his death twenty years later, several hundred volumes including histories, law books, novels, and works in Latin and French; and thanks be to the court clerk who took the time to list the titles.[13]

It is doubtful if Rhodes Garth brought with him all those books; before this date books and educational materials were being sold by most general merchants, in such unlikely establishments as De Monbruen's tavern, and soon in small places like Russellville and Eddyville.

The books General James Winchester [14] stocked in his store near present day Gallatin are good examples of what could be had in a country

[8] *Ibid.*, II, 319–321.

[9] *Ibid.*, I, 46.

[10] *Ibid.*, II, 274.

[11] Michaux, *Travels 1802*, 253–254.

[12] RKs, XXVIII, no. 79, "Memoirs of Micah Taul" (cited hereafter as Taul, "Memoirs"), 15. Taul when two years old was brought by his family to Kentucky in 1785, and at the age of sixteen was appointed county clerk of newly formed Wayne County.

[13] WW, II, 513–517.

[14] Items reprinted by permission of Dr. William T. Alderson, Tennessee State Librarian and Archivist, from the Mss bill of Jan. 7, 1797, owned by the Tennessee Historical Society, and housed in the Archives Division, Tennessee State Library and Archives, Nashville. (Cited hereafter as Winchester, List.)

store of Middle Tennessee of 1797, and also give an indication of the wealth of reading material for sale in one store in Philadelphia,[15] for the several hundred volumes costing 264 pounds, 9 shillings, 4 pence were all from the one Philadelphia merchant.

There were works by Hume, Locke, Lord Chesterfield, Bolingbroke, Gibbon, with a goodly representation of translations; Rousseau, Cervantes, and Voltaire, including his *Philosophical Dictionary*. Theology was also heavily stocked, Fisher's *Catechism*, Clark's *Confessions*, and Whitefield's *Sermons*. Watts was by this date having to share place with Wesley for there were twelve Methodist hymnbooks. The ever popular Thomas Paine was represented by forty-two volumes; listed also were fair quantities of most of the better known textbooks of the day from primers to John Love's *Geodaesia*, or the *Art of Surveying and the Measuring of Land Made Easy*.

The books owned by Nashville merchant John Deadrick,[16] each represented by the one copy only, appear to have been personal possessions rather than goods for sale as were those of General Winchester. John Deadrick was a wealthy bachelor who loved to live well—$100 gold watch, soft flannel or nankeen drawers against his skin, and silk stockings on his shins, for he had eight pair. Like many of the more prominent Cumberlanders he was not interested in theology, preferring the skepticism of David Hume, represented in his library by both his famous history and his essays; there were the ever popular Smollett and a six volume set of Shakespeare, along with samplings from numerous other authors—a four volume set of *The Rambler*, a translation of *Gil Blas* in four volumes, *The Fool of Quality* in five, Moore's *Travels*, *The Sentimental Magazine*, William Guthrie's *Grammar of Geography*, a good bit of poetry that included Thomson's *The Seasons*, and that most popular of hoaxes, Ossian's *Poems*. The more important men then on the Cumberland or coming soon—the Reverend Thomas B. Craighead, Dr. James White, Judge John Overton, Moses Fisk, former teacher at Dartmouth, Judge John McNairy, Eusabius Bushnell—all would have had at least as many books as John Deadrick and most more.

The first newspapers in the old West, the Kentucky *Gazette* in 1789,

[15] Philadelphia as a center of the intellectual life of the period is well known; announcements of books "newly published"—usually pirated editions of the better known English works and translations—were to be found in almost all issues of Carey's *Museum*. Vol. VII (1790) is fairly typical; works by Anburey, Gibbon, Blackstone, Goldsmith, Adam Smith, and Priestley were advertised along with several translations; Voltaire was the most popular.

[16] DW, II, 105–106, 132.

the Knoxville *Gazette*, 1791, followed by the first paper in Nashville in 1799 all carried announcements of books for sale.[17] Books, different from most personal possessions, circulated; the "big dictionary" owned by Eusabius Bushnell was at the time of his death in 1789 in the hands of the Reverend Craighead,[18] and many were the *Gazette* ads asking that books, belonging usually to someone lately dead, be returned;[19] few lenders were so meek as Thomas Adams of Pulaski County, Kentucky, who on his deathbed reconciled himself to the loss of his *Writings of Josephus*[20] —and bequeathed it to the borrower, James Gilmore.

Middle Tennessee inventories[21] before 1800 reveal in their entirety works by practically all of the better known authors from Homer to William Robertson, through joke and song books, *Family Physicians*, with in time works by American authors. There were many dictionaries, including French, Latin, and German and now and then a work in the original, all these over and above the textbooks, stocked in many stores or listed in inventories such as that of merchant Lardner Clark, trustee of Davidson Academy.

Books, numerous as they were, usually represented a sizable outlay. Deadrick's five volume set of Shakespeare, for example, sold for $5, ten days work for an unskilled laborer, two hundred pounds of beef at the price then current, a medium-grade cow or a goodly-sized fattened hog.[22] Lack of money, however, did not prevent a family from owning books; the Buchanan Arithmetic is an example of a homemade text and quite often one finds in an inventory such as that of John Jenkins in Montgomery County of 1798, "stitched books," that always sold quite cheaply, sometimes for only a few cents.[23]

[17] One of the most persistent advertisers of books was the printer; Tennessee *Gazette*, Jan. 7, 1801, Dec. 25, 1802, for example carried the usual popular works, *Rights of Man, Age of Reason, Spirit of Locke*, More's *Utopia*, but a few offerings such as the Tennessee *Almanac* and *A Wonderful Miracle*, "Just Publishedf, 6¼¢," Jan. 1, 1803, were of local imprint. Others such as *The Kentucky Miscellany*, Feb. 13, 1805, were from Kentucky. He also advertised periodicals as, *ibid.*, Aug. 5, 1801, the *Cabanet* and the *National Magazine*.

[18] DW, I, 120.

[19] Typical, Tennessee *Gazette*, June 8, 1803, "Books for A. Polly's library must be returned."

[20] PW, I, 46.

[21] DW, II, 28, 31, 189, 231—not only a Morse here but a Gordon's *History of the American Revolution*—272, 303. Particularly interesting are those of the Feas family, MW, I, 26–27; and that of merchant Lardner Clark, DW, II, 264; many of the works listed are textbooks, but he also had a wide selection that included *Gulliver's Travels*, volumes by Erasmus, Dryden, Morse, and Hume, and works in French and Dutch.

[22] MW, I, 26-27, Morse's *Geography*, sold for $5.

[23] *Ibid.*, I, 69.

It seems safe to say the average Cumberlander spent more time with and money on books than does the average citizen of the United States today; and certain it is the books furnished sturdier intellectual fare. Taken as a whole they also represented a much less narrow intellectual pattern than could be found in a community of comparable size today. The Cumberland Country with less than thirty thousand people in 1797 was still big enough for the skepticism of Voltaire and Hume, the piety of White-field, the urbane and worldly-wise Lord Chesterfield, pious John Wesley, and that non-believer in organized religion—Thomas Paine. Theology, history, literature, philosophy, letters, government, and economics were all to be found in General Winchester's list, and that only one bill of goods to one country storekeeper.

It was through books and to a certain extent through people that this wide, wide world of the late eighteenth century was brought to the pioneer child on the Cumberland. Early the average young one would have been exposed to at least a few of the many and varied political, social, and cultural influences of the day. We now tend more and more to read or permit the young to study only those things with which we feel they should agree. The Cumberlander, shaped usually by a South that was in turn shaped largely by Church and King England, had no such tradition. The thoughts expressed in the books owned by Cumberland settlers were no more diverse than those found in many libraries of the colonial South.[24]

The intellectual as well as the political and cultural climates of the South and most of Pennsylvania were more varied, more humanitarian than those of New England. It was not by chance that Virginia produced a Jefferson and Massachusetts a John Adams. The Revolution in time brought religious freedom under the law, but tolerance never came to many sections; a traveler of 1818 declaring of the East,[25] "There is more intolerance here than in England." Toulmin, more inclined to praise than most visitors, found in 1793 no Episcopal minister in Kentucky, largely because of the "fanaticism and bigotry" of the other sects.[26]

I never found in source materials of the Cumberland any attempt to teach the young democracy, but there seems to have been for many years an easy tolerance, not always met in the rest of the United States. No traveler complained of religious or political bigotry, and there is no record that those whose religion was that of the minority, De Monbruen

---

[24] Stanard, *Virginia*, Chap. XI, 295–307, gives a résumé of colonial libraries.
[25] Faux, *Travels, 1818–1819*, 103.
[26] Toulmin, *Western Country*, 70.

the Catholic or the Church of England Bledsoes, ever in any way suffered because of their religion. Though ever in a minority in Middle Tennessee, the Episcopalians from earliest years had a good deal of influence, and, different from our world up river, Good Friday was to the whole populace a day considerably more than that for planting beans.

Friction there was from earliest years over a multitude of vexing matters—to join or not to join the State of Franklin,[27] choice of a muster master, or the site of a seat for a new county—but men seem never to have been guided in their loves or hatreds by religious or nationality backgrounds. Andrew Jackson was, for example, first-generation-born Scotch-Irish, but the names [28] of the seventy-six men who would in 1806 have the daily paper put into mourning because of his killing of Dickinson sound like a gathering of the clans. Most of the devout Presbyterians were at this time opposed both to Jackson and to dueling on general principles. East Tennesseans were strongly Scots Presbyterian. Yet, their most beloved and popular leader was John Sevier, descendant of Huguenots; the Blounts and Butlers were also prominent and popular and they were communicants of the Church of England with English backgrounds.

The pioneers as children never had lessons on getting along with other people, yet they, most especially those on the Cumberland, more so than any other people before or since in America, had to develop to a high degree the ability to get along with other people. All of the first settlers who survived knew fifteen years of the forted life, usually with several families jammed into one small space as at Buchanan's. This was achieved not through any attempt to make each like the other, for no place had such a diversity of human beings, but through an awareness that men were different.

There was no hero worship; feeling for Washington, the Father of their Country, was at best lukewarm,[29] and though they were rather fond

---

[27] Middle Tennessee never joined, but there must have been much discussion. "Politics in this part of the country run high," Anthony Bledsoe wrote to Gov. Caswell March 26, 1787, "you hear in almost every collection of people frequent declarations for North Carolina and others in the like manner for the State of Franklin. I have seen it in much warmth." See NCR, XX, 654.

[28] Parton, *Jackson*, I, 303, gives the names.

[29] *Ibid.*, I, 209–211, gives the details of the struggles of the House—Jackson was at this time a member—to agree on a proper reply to President Washington's Farewell Address. Jackson voted with William B. Giles of Va. who was willing to compliment the President, but not his administration. "I hope we shall adhere to the truth," said he. "I think that nothing so much as a want of wisdom and firmness has brought us to the situation in which we now stand. —I wish him [Washington] to retire. I wish that this was the moment of his retirement. I think that the government of the United States can go on very well without him. . . ."

of Jefferson many like Jackson disagreed with him often. They were given to the blind following of theories no more than to the blind following of men. Infallibility in the eyes of most who believed in God belonged solely to God; and for the majority who did not so believe, infallibility either in men or in systems of government did not exist. They, thus as a group, put much less faith in patterns of thought, either religious or political, than do we today, and hence did not teach them to the young. Yet, read of them they did.

The men of Middle Tennessee rejected not only the Constitution of the United States, but voted not to become a part of the nation. They were not in their thinking unique for that day. Many others had voted against the Constitution, and still others believed as did Joseph Lathrop writing in Mr. Carey's *Museum* [30] of 1789 ". . . good people make for good rulers. . . . Whether we shall be safe and happy now depends much more on our own conduct than the form of government we have adopted or on any other that can be devised."

There was also a good deal of criticism of matters more or less taken for granted today. Mr. Carey was especially concerned about the lack of religious freedom and the growing practice of taking oaths for any and all occasions, "worse than in England," he maintained.[31] "A moral obligation is not capable of addition or diminution—To take the oath is an implicit acknowledgement of innocence; to refuse it is an implicit confession that the person has aided and abetted the enemy. This is rank despotism."

Most popular writer on the Cumberland, appearing in many inventories, stocked in stores, and reprinted in the *Gazette*, was Thomas Paine. He believed in the supremacy of the individual over his political or religious institutions, and was free with his criticisms particularly of England where, "They were beginning to consider government as a profitable monopoly and the people as hereditary property." [32]

These thoughts from books and periodicals, whether read by the young themselves or heard discussed by their elders, were of course only a few of many influences shaping the lives of children all up and down the Cumberland. Felix Robertson in his middle teens, reading the Bible, singing hymns, struggling with Cicero, seeing all around him Tidewater's love of living—good clothing, fine wines, carriages, his father's fine horses—the

[30] Carey, *Museum*, VI, 443–444.
[31] *Ibid.*, V, 157–158.
[32] Tennessee *Gazette*, Dec. 18, 1802, quoting from the *Rights of Man*.

Scots Presbyterian's distaste for symbolism of all kinds, was like other children influenced by many traditions, beliefs, and attitudes. Yet, practically all, like the books of John Rice, John Deadrick, and most of those stocked by General Winchester, had one thing in common. They were transplanted shoots of British culture, be they got from Paine, Watts, Chesterfield, Dilworth, Hume, or Whitefield. Even the classical authors studied—Sallust or Cicero—were the same as those known to generations of British schoolboys.

Many facets of middle and late eighteenth century thought—skepticism, man's determination to use his reason, the continuing fight for freedom of the individual conscience—might be thought of as outgrowths of the Reformation, still a vital force in Scotland and England; felt, too, in varying degrees in most of the rest of Europe. The children of the old Southwest stood somewhere near the crest of a great wave that made men think of themselves as individuals, each with his own conscience and the right to believe or not to believe, the right to criticize his church if he had one, or his government, both its form and its leaders. Faith was in the individual. This thinking would be reflected over and over in the education of the young, in sermons and in religious talk in the home; even in the hymns, the one who stood on Jordan's stormy banks, considered the old-time religion, or was a poor wayfarer, was not the mass, but I.

And all the songs, theology, even the money with which they reckoned for many years after the Revolution had come from Britain. The first and early settlers on the Cumberland were much closer in spirit and outlook on life to the England of their day [33] than to New England. There is in the early years, in spite of many having served in the Revolution, no indication of the hatred of England that came with the War of 1812. Certain it is that many who as Whigs fought the Revolution thought of themselves, not as men fighting for a nation separate from Britain, but as Britons fighting only for rights they felt a Briton should have.

Life in Tennessee, especially on the Cumberland, was little changed after the Revolution. Men were no longer British subjects, and no longer in their toasts and songs would they proclaim health to King George, but

---

[33] Possibly more so than any other one man, James Boswell gives an awareness of the varied intellectual, and to some extent social and political, currents of late eighteenth century Britain with not a little of the rest of Europe. The Yale Edition of *The Private Papers of James Boswell*, ed. by Frederick A. Pottle, McGraw-Hill, 1950–1961, containing as they do much material not hitherto made available as well as helpful notes gives us much of this world, often almost worshiping the literature of the Greeks and Romans, but standing on the edge of the Industrial Revolution and not knowing it.

local government, law, business, education, including textbooks, money, language, none was for many years different from what they had known as English colonials. Save for the manuscript textbooks, cook, and "doctoring books" that had been a feature of life in the colonial South, there was among the books of the first Cumberlanders almost nothing written by or for Americans; the most notable exception was the *Laws of Virginia.* Intellectually, the average settler on the Cumberland continued to be an Englishman long after he was a citizen of the United States.

Merchant Deadrick, dying in 1798, had been on the Cumberland many years, was a friend of Jackson who by that date had served as Congressman; he had taken quite an active part in community affairs yet his library gives no indication whatever that he was an American.

Even the first newspapers [34] gave more space to foreign news than to doings in the United States. Any single issue might carry items concerning happenings in Rome, Paris, Madrid, St. Petersburg, Toulon. This, too, was part of an old pattern. The Southern colonials, close to Spanish holdings, given much to travel to the Sugar Islands or back-home "England," using goods from the four corners of the world, and as colonials supplying tobacco, rice, indigo, and woods-products, ever feeling in their pockets a war that closed a port, were aware of the wider world. They seem to have had, too, an intellectual curiosity never completely satisfied with books.

It is not entirely fair to say that because there were no reading materials concerning America, the young did not learn a great deal about their country. Any border by its very existence attracted the already well traveled and the venturesome. This was particularly true of the Cumberland settlements. The average settler there, up the river as well as down, had by the time of his coming seen more sights, been to more distant places, experienced more of humankind different from himself, than has the average American citizen of today. Once settled on the Cumberland, one did not stop traveling. Long before there was a newspaper, merchants traveling to Philadelphia brought home news. Others such as General James Winchester who went down with goods in 1789 knew firsthand the situation in Natchez and New Orleans.[35]

Few settlements have had such a large proportion of men who were not only widely traveled, but well enough educated to absorb much of what they encountered. General Daniel Smith was almost a walking

[34] Nashville *Intelligencer or Rights of Man,* March 11, July 17, Aug. 5, 1799.
[35] W, 3XX (18), 6.

geography. Educated, it was said, in Baltimore, he had made maps of East Tennessee, Kentucky, and Tennessee for Mr. Carey, but none of his maps could compare with the maps that must have been in his head of the land between all the places he had known—Philadelphia, New Bern, Point Pleasant, The Falls, Vincennes, Cumberland Gap, and Fort Jefferson.

Dr. James White,[36] Indian agent, lawyer, physician, educated in part by the Jesuits in France, not only knew from travel much of the American colonies, but made on business and politics many trips to New Orleans. Timothe De Monbruen, though he did not permanently settle until the mid-nineties, had been visiting the region since the mid-sixties. Born in Canada of French nobility, American by choice, he had traveled up and down and all around the Mississippi Valley, knew Detroit, Montreal, Mackinac, Kaskaskia, where he had served the cause of George Rogers Clark, Vincennes, Natchez, New Orleans, and of course, Philadelphia. He had floated down rivers, been attacked by Indians, hunted buffalo, held both political and military office, and would in time keep a tavern and visit with the Dukes of Bourbon when in 1797 they came to Nashville. He appears to have been a well educated man, fluent in both French and English.

His education and experiences were nothing to compare with those of Samuel Cole Mountflorence, a licensed lawyer, who spent several years on the Cumberland, leaving around 1792. Mountflorence, born in France, had been eight years at the University of Paris studying mathematics, and two more studying philosophy. He was by 1778 teaching "Greek, Latin, and French, with arithmetic, the principles of mathematics and Book Keeping" in New Bern, North Carolina,[37] and served for a time during the Revolution as an officer in the Quartermaster Corps of the North Carolina Line. One could continue with a long list of men in the small world of the Cumberland such as Samuel Newell up river who represented the combination of wide experience and travel with if not as much formal education as Mountflorence, at least a good deal, coupled with a love of books.

Such men as James Robertson, James White, General Winchester, and Andrew Jackson traveled chiefly on business, but more travel may have been done by young men like Joseph Bishop; into the Illinois, down the Mississippi, a trip back East, all taken chiefly just to see the world. We

---

[36] THM, I, 282–291.
[37] NCR, XIII, 335–336, Mountflorence to Gov. Caswell, Dec. 23, 1778; see also TP, IV, 441, and NCR, XVI, 527.

read of James Rogers who with four others "made a ramble to the Columbia River and was gone three years." [38] No date was given but it was undoubtedly pre-Lewis and Clark. Visitors remark the journeys and the wanderings; some were found not knowing where they were going; others, whole families, hunted grazing for their cattle. A traveler to the Cumberland Country in 1799 commented, "Thus, the spirit of wandering is in the people; ever they are seeking a paradise and finding it nowhere." [39]

Much of the wandering was caused by the same thing that sent them into books—curiosity. As a people, the pioneers appear to have had more curiosity than we have today. This same curiosity concerning the face of their country in time caused them to read about their country, for the first work by an American for Americans found in early inventories is usually Jedidiah Morse's *Geography*. True, it was published in 1789, and did not often appear until the mid-nineties, but it was a beginning for the average well read farmer as was Mr. Edmiston.[40] William Gordon's *History of the American Revolution* [41] also began to appear in the late nineties, but it was of British origin, first published in London in 1788. *Poor Richard's Almanac*, already with a long and popular life in much of colonial America and the United States as well as England and Europe, was noteworthy on the Cumberland by its absence. Franklin with his "A penny saved is a penny earned" had never appealed to the Southerner.

General James Winchester's list of books for sale, though overwhelmingly European in origin, does show in its choice of texts for the young, the beginnings of Americanization. There were twelve *Constitutions of the United States*, Morse's *Geography*, and though outnumbered by the older English texts, Noah Webster was on the way, and represented by six dozen spelling books. There was also one Gallatin, *On Finance*.

The change in inventories of family bookshelves through the years shows possibly more than any other single source the change in attitude toward America and her leaders, though soon the national leaders were on the Cumberland. Jumping back to early 1779 when James Robertson made his exploratory journey, we pick up Edward Swanson, then scarcely more than a boy. He returned the next year to settle on the Cumberland, and, one of the lucky ones, his inventory is not listed until more than sixty years later.[42] The world had changed; Jackson had served his terms and

---

[38] W, 32S, 299.

[39] Williams, *Travels*, Schweinitz, "Report," 507.

[40] Thwaites, *Travels*, III, Michaux, "Journal," 85, commented on how well read farmer Edmiston (the name is variously spelled) with whom he stopped, was.

[41] DW, II, 231, 303.

[42] William Henry McRaven, *Life and Times of Edward Swanson*, copyright

Jackson men were still in the White House, Sam Houston was in Texas, Davy Crockett was dead, and steamboats plied the Cumberland.

Edward Swanson's library included many of the works found in early inventories—the Bible, of course, the ever popular Josephus, *History of the Jews,* and several titles, among them a five volume edition of *The Life of Buonaparte* to indicate the old interest in European affairs was not dead. Yet, most of the books were by and for Americans: a *Life of Jackson, History of the United States,* the *Works* of Benjamin Franklin, *History of the American War, Life of Washington, Life of Marion.* The times Swanson had known as a young man were now history, and most men who had fought under Marion as had Frederick Stump were dead.

Middle Tennessee, and particularly Nashville, had by the time of Swanson's death in 1843, long since become an intellectual center for all of the South west of the Appalachians. Books continued to be widely stocked and advertised and by 1811 there was at least one store selling nothing but books.[43] There was, too, at this time a subscription library,[44] managed by D. S. Deadrick who had from time to time to remind his subscribers dues must be paid or else they could get no more books. The following year, 1813, John Carter [45] established a book bindery; Benjamin J. Bradford the printer who had been turning out many titles—almanacs to military instructors—since starting the *Gazette* in 1800,[46] may have done his own binding.

There were other changes in the intellectual life of the Cumberland; many paralleled the intellectual history of the United States. Among those, the attitude toward education. Illiteracy was, by the time of Swanson's death, on the increase. Education, even among the upper classes, was becoming more and more a how-to process, and among the lower the feeling was growing that if a man could make money without it, he didn't need it at all. There are no statistics, but judging from source materials of all kinds, from the comments [47] of travelers to the few who could not sign their names, literacy in the United States among the white population was higher at the beginning of the Revolution than it has ever been since.

William Henry McRaven, Nashville, 1937; his inventory, *ibid.,* 185, quoting from Williamson County, Tenn., WB, 1842–1847, 111, Nov. 1843.

[43] Nashville *Clarion,* May 28, 1811—John Inston's bookstore.

[44] *Ibid.,* Sept. 1, 1812.

[45] *Ibid.,* March 30, 1813.

[46] See Chapters X, "Industry," and XI, "The Professions."

[47] Handlin, *America,* Moreau, "Travels, 1793–1798," 102; *ibid.,* Grassi, "Observations, 1819," 143–144, though scornful of the intellectual level of that part of the United States he visited—chiefly the eastern seaboard—he did find periodicals and books in most homes. Toulmin, *Western Country,* 69, found in Kentucky of 1793, practically all literate and many with grammar school educations.

Yet, in 1802 Michaux found "education an object of solicitude"[48] in every Tennessee home. This was but a manifestation of a tradition, old in the British Isles before the Cumberland was settled. Possibly the most all-pervading single factor pushing men and women of little means toward literacy was God. The average Protestant looked upon the reading of the Bible as a duty, less to God than to himself. The early settlers lived at a time of intellectual ferment—new forms of government, new religious sects taking shape; seldom was there blind following of any creed. Children dropped the sect or sects of their parents for a new one or none, and parents might change from Presbyterian to Baptist or Methodist—the most rapidly growing sects. The Great Revival in a sense marked the end of religion based on theology rather than emotion, but theological arguments among kin and neighbors continued to my childhood, not based on opinion but "chapter and verse." In the early years society was determined that each individual, even the bound boy or girl, should be able to read the Bible.[49]

There was, too, for many another need of literacy, pressing as God. A man or woman who would transact any form of business had to be able to read, write, and cipher in an age of unstandardized currency and innumerable written agreements. Joseph Bishop, learned in hunting and woodscraft, had but little formal education, and was forced to the expense of a lawsuit because he signed a paper he did not understand; it made him responsible for a debt he did not owe.[50] Business morals in the United States were not high; a man or woman unable to read was fair prey for the land shark or even the man whose written agreement did not jibe with his verbal promise.

However, little learning was needed to read a contract or figure wages, nor was much education required merely to recognize the words in the King James Version of the Bible. More influential for many than God was Tidewater; the borderer almost always rejected Tidewater religion; he might say "git" and "whar," but still if he lived south of the Ohio River the chances were he and the more influential of his neighbors looked to the aristocratic families of Tidewater for social and educational patterns. Tidewater in turn looked to the upper classes of England.

Older in England than the tradition of literacy were the universities of Cambridge and Oxford. The aim of these institutions was not to turn

[48] Michaux, *Travels 1802*, 244.
[49] DC, I, 83, 96—indigent orphans; the boy was to be taught to read and write and cipher to the rule of three; the girl to learn to read the Bible.
[50] Gray, *Bishop*, 207–208.

out lawyers, physicians, army officers, or even ministers, but men, culti-vated to the fullest extent of their intellects. This was achieved through rigorous training in the Greek and Latin authors, a training that began in the early years of what we now denominate grammar school. The boy planning to attend Oxford had a very different elementary education from the boy planning for medicine or an apprenticeship.

Eighteenth century Scotland had if possible even less illiteracy than England. She was noted, too, for her many men of learning such as David Hume and Adam Smith. Her great universities—Edinburgh was particularly noted for medicine—turned out so many young professional men in proportion to population they must often go to England or even the colonies to find work. Higher education was a great deal cheaper than in England, and the universities educated "in proportion to the size and wealth of the two countries, twenty times a larger number than in England."

The young Scotchman with a university training was prepared to take "a keen and active management in the affairs of ordinary life" [51] but he was not so "thoroughly accomplished" in classical learning. Greek and Latin were of course taught in Scotland, far more than in the United States today, but never to the same extent as in England.

The English system of higher education, though admired by many in America, was never completely transplanted. Rather, the whole American system was in the end a good deal more like that of Scotland. This was especially true of Princeton, described by a traveler as intended "for the education of dissenters, erected upon the plan of those in Scotland." [52] The most important early educators in Tennessee were Presbyterian ministers, graduates of Princeton, and at least one pioneer boy on the Cumberland had, after attending a local academy, graduated from Prince-ton by 1805. [53]

The young in the old West could never hope to get the early ground-work in classics that would fit them for Cambridge or Oxford, but all things—God, worldly wealth, tradition, and social custom demanded they learn to read. And learn the young did, though it meant stepping

[51] Lockhart, *Letters*, 199–201, gives a brief summary of the difference in content, method, and aims between education in Scotland and England of 1819.

[52] Burnaby, *Travels*, 103.

[53] Tennessee *Gazette*, March 20, 1805, gave an account of death by dueling of young Micajah Green Lewis, son of William T. Lewis, and brother-in-law of Governor Claiborne of Louisiana Territory; young Green, killed in New Orleans, had, before attending Princeton, graduated from Mr. Martin's seminary near Nashville.

out of their world of "hosses" and "yalow dawgs" into another dominated by England. The majority of the pupils were Scotch–Irish Americans, but the language of Dilworth, Watts, and the Bible was purely English.

The first step, almost always done by the mother, was the teaching of the alphabet. The child first learned to recite it, next to recognize each letter. He was then ready for the first page of Dilworth or most any other text, save the *New England Primer*,[54] suitably illustrated by New England standards for children with a woodcut of John Rogers burning at the stake while his wife and children looked on. The work was little used in the South. The theology "in Adam's fall we sinned all" was offensive to Methodist and Church of England communicant alike. Regardless of what text was used, the child began, not with words, but first with syllables only—*ab—ac* . . . *az;* next followed *e* coupled in its turn with all the consonants, and on through the vowels, each coupled with all the consonants until *uz* was reached. In the process the child had learned the sound and spelling of all the syllables beginning with vowels and a good many two letter words. He had formed the beginnings of his reading vocabulary.

However, there were no rules. Not all the first settling families with young children had textbooks, though most had books. A mother could, and often did, use the Bible, their most commonly owned book, as the first text. She could cut a pen from a goose quill, make ink of poke berries or oak galls,[55] and with an account book or sheets of paper, make a speller or an arithmetic. Lack of teaching materials was never accepted as an excuse for illiteracy; a smooth board and charcoal from the fireplace were tools enough for the learning of the alphabet, ciphering, and the rudiments of spelling and penmanship.

Judging from inventories and the numerous references to books, few of the Cumberland pioneers had such meager tools for learning, and the first forts had teachers. Zachariah White,[56] the first found, was killed early in 1781, but James Mulherrin,[57] another first settler, con-

---

[54] The only mention found of a book that might have been some edition of the *New England Primer* was in Drake, *Letters*, 195, and the only identification here is his mention of John Rogers at the stake; Drake however lived in a neighborhood entirely Baptist.

[55] Thwaites, *Travels, III*, Michaux, "Journal," 83.

[56] W, 32S, 314. Another very early teacher was George Hamilton on the other side of the Cumberland at Bledsoe's Station, *ibid.*, 6XX (99), 5.

[57] The only mention of James Mulherrin as teacher was found in Buchanan, Arithmetic, and judging from the number of entries in which he was remembered as surveyor, D Deed Book I, he gave most of his time, after 1784, to this work.

tinued to teach part time for several years as he taught at least one son of John and Sally Ridley Buchanan, not born until 1792. Another early teacher was Joseph Sitgreaves, who was also licensed to practice law in the lower courts, and was in 1790 appointed Clerk of the Court of Equity of Mero District.[58] He had at his death in 1792 a large school of all ages and sizes—young Budds, Castlemans, Clarks,[59] Donelsons, and children of other families well known during pioneer years.

The first schools such as that Zachariah White kept at French Lick Station in the spring of 1781 were unpatterned institutions, taught on an individual rather than a class basis, each child reciting in the order of his arrival, "some going by daylight to say first." Though not supported by taxation, they were open to all, and not so expensive—around fifteen shillings ($2.50) a quarter[60]—but the average family could send each child for at least a few terms. There were of course in the fort schools neither grades nor adopted texts. Pupils brought whatever texts they had; sometimes homemade spellers and arithmetics.

John Smith[61] learned to read from *Pilgrim's Progress*. Jonathan Ramsey[62] began with the Bible but was soon at work in Dilworth's *Grammar*, the most popular text[63] among the early settlers of the old West. This work, like most popular English publications, went through many and divers editions in the American colonies and the young United States; sometimes the whole text, other times only the grammar, and quite often merely the first part or speller. The work as originally published was most comprehensive. Beginning with the alphabet, followed by two letter syllables, it continued into three letter combinations and syllables. Finished with "zuz" the pupil was ready to begin the study of actual words in addition to those learned by chance combinations in his tables.

[58] TP, IV, 442.

[59] DW, I, 247.

[60] Leah Lucas, *ibid.*, II, 63–65, had paid this amount; the dollar was usually reckoned at six shillings, or as Mrs. Lucas wrote the amount, 2.3s. Prices varied; in later years A. Jackson paid $5 a quarter for the education of his wards.

[61] Williams, *Smith*, 17.

[62] W, 5S, 73–75.

[63] Thomas Dilworth undoubtedly had more influence on the educational life of first the colonial South and later the old West than any other man. All early settlers, both in Kentucky and Tennessee who left accounts of their educations used Dilworth: see Williams, *Smith*, 17; Taul, "Memoirs," RK, XXVII, 2, 8; Drake, *Letters*, 146, 164; Ramsey, W, 5S, 73–75. Dilworth is found in most early book lists; see A, V, 212, list of books Daniel Smith was getting for an academy and DW, II, 264, list of Lardner Clark's Nashville Academy books. General Winchester in 1797 stocked Dilworth—6 doz. of his spellers alone. Up river the work continued to be used for generations; see, CW, II, 187, 321, inventories of 1821, 1826.

He first took up the *ab* family—*dab, nab, tab;* his study, not a mere recognition but the learning to spell and pronounce each. Next, he studied families of four letter words—*dump, lump, bump;* or members of *eam*— *ream, seam, beam,* quite often as in the case of *stump* or *stream* going past four letter words. He was now ready for the reading of easy material, and could read and memorize many passages from the Bible and the poetry of Watts and others.

Syllable by syllable he waded into the longer words, studied abbreviations, punctuation, and pronunciation; this last done chiefly through a long table of words, the same in sound but different in spelling: "aunt— uncle's wife; ant—a pismire." During most of the time after mastering words of one syllable he studied grammar, begun by learning first the parts of speech: "A noun substantive is the name of any Being or Thing perceivable either by the senses or understanding." Soon he was mastering declensions and conjugations including that of the preterpluperfect tense. Finished with declensions, he was ready for diagramming and parsing along with the study of syntax, rhetoric, transposition, analogy, and ellipsis.

Dilworth's text was old when the Cumberland was settled; Ashe's *Grammar,* Entick's *Dictionary,* various primers, and in time Webster's *Spelling Book* were also used. Yet, Dilworth's influence continued for generations; his method of stressing phonetics and rules was copied by Webster as was the subject matter of his reading lessons, for Dilworth, like the McGuffeys a hundred years later, tried to give the student a sense of right and wrong. Dilworth used many quotations, particularly from the Bible and the works of Isaac Watts. Regardless of what next was used in the teaching of English,[64] the aim was also to teach good morals, for whether in Charles Town or Boston, the emphasis in education was on inculcating knowledge and building strong individual charac-

---

[64] Winchester's List included 1 doz. Ashe's *Grammar,* 6 Sheridan's *Dictionary,* but only 1 doz. of the dictionary most commonly mentioned by the first settlers, that of John Entick, 1703-1773, Englishman; it was used by Jonathan Ramsey and continued for several years to be listed in inventories as, DW, II, 189 (James Dean, 1802). The texts named were by no means the only ones in use, for early the old West published many of her own textbooks. Frank L. McVey, *The Gates Open Slowly; A History of Education in Kentucky,* Lexington, 1949 (cited hereafter as McVey, *Education*), 65, gives a list of books copied from a 1798 Kentucky *Gazette* containing at least one text printed in Kentucky—Samuel Wilson, *The Kentucky English Grammar,* Lexington, 1798. The Tennessee *Gazette,* Jan. 7, 1801, carried one of several similar announcements of a *Primer upon an Entirely New Plan,* "just published," and its cheapness, 6½¢, would indicate it had been published by Mr. Bradford.

ter rather than the acquisition of attitudes, pleasing personality traits, and ability in group adjustment.

Judging from those educated on the frontier who left accounts of their lives, no attempt was made to indoctrinate the young. No single pattern was held up as perfect; though forced to read the Bible, religion was not urged upon them, or, in the words of Dr. Drake, they were taught "morality rather than superstition." Patriotism was not looked upon as a separate facet of life; most disliked any form of symbolism, and there was as yet no strongly nationalistic spirit. Still rooted in the culture of the British Isles, where there had never been "an English way of life," or "a Scotch way," there was as yet no "American way" to be held up as an ideal. The bare-footed little boy on a rough log bench in a poor schoolhouse up the creek had in one sense a good deal in common with the wealthy young lord at Oxford; each was part of a system trying to cultivate the intellect, rather than shape a human being to give unquestioning obedience to a given pattern.

The most important subjects were reading and spelling, grammar and penmanship, but arithmetic was less neglected and more rigorous than today. Most children who started to school knowing their letters and able to spell a few words also knew the digits and could count and cipher to some extent. The young one on the farm had to learn arithmetic, for there was always something to count and reckon: eggs for the three-year-old, and on through the years; the length of a rail measured by the two-and-one-half-foot ax handle, turns of the reel, skeins for the web, ounces of madder for the dye pot, while a trip to the store called for a fair knowledge of arithmetic. First, the country cloth, beeswax, feathers, bacon, ginseng, tallow or whatever else was brought had to be weighed or measured, then reckoned in terms of money, and the never-seen money in turn translated into sugar, curtain calico, door latch, or guard bit. The average pioneer had to be able to estimate cost and size of farm buildings, area of fields and panels of fence needed, rocks for chimneys, capacity of a still or a corncrib, tonnage of a flatboat, and above all the interest on the many notes he held or others held on him.

Well calculated to prepare him for a lifetime's wrestling with all this and more was another Dilworth text, *The Young Bookkeeper's Assistant,* an eleventh edition of which was published in Philadelphia in 1781. This also was a comprehensive volume, suitable for all arithmetical learnings from primer to college preparatory. Young boys and girls after learning the digits learned what was a whole number and what a vulgar fraction, a decimal, and a duodecimal. They memorized numerous tables beginning: "three barleycorns, one inch; two and a quarter inches, one nail; four nails, a quarter yard." The student went on through Flemish ells, English ells, fathoms, perches, poles, furlongs, miles, and leagues; likewise did he learn firkins, gallons, barrels, and hogsheads, along with stones, burdens, and other units of weight.

Past addition, subtraction, multiplication, and division, pupils—usually referred to as scholars—were soon able to solve problems involving single and compound interest, discount, loss and gain, barter, square and cube root, proportion and inverse proportion. At last came the rule of three in which ". . . the fourth number sought bears the same proportions to the first as the second does to the third number." [65] Past this, bound boys and students not preparing for academy admission were not required to go. Meantime, they had solved many problems concerning cheese mongers, linen drapers, wheels turning between London and York, and the cost of curing the coachman's broken knee, for even the Philadelphia edition of 1781 was, like most other texts, completely English in application.

We see an early awareness that the educational needs of the American pioneer were not identical with those of the Englishman in the John Buchanan Arithmetic, written in 1781. Many of the problems and tables are, it is true, so much like those in Dilworth the book might be called the Buchanan edition, but the buckskin cover and cotton plant were not the only difference. More space in proportion to the whole is given to one of the pioneer's most pressing needs—ability to measure and compute land areas. Much emphasis is placed on the units of measurement commonly used by the surveyor such as poles, links, and chains along with directions for the finding of acreage through the breaking down of irregular plots into triangles and rectangles. Likewise, the Donelson Arithmetic,[66] written around 1785, tried to meet the special needs of the settler in the Mississippi Valley with problems concerning the cost and profit on goods shipped from Philadelphia to Middle Tennessee.

In spite of numerous references to early schools and teachers, few, if any, children of first settlers got anything like the whole of their formal educations at school. Classroom work was often interrupted by Indians,

[65] Thomas Dilworth, *The School Master's Assistant* (pagination from the 11th ed., Boston, 1781), 120. This work usually referred to as Dilworth's *Arithmetic*, or *Teacher's Assistant*, though not as popular as the author's *English Tongue* was widely used. G. Winchester stocked one dozen; see also, A, V, 212 and RK, XXVII, 2.

[66] Albert C. Holt, The Economic and Social Beginnings of Tennessee. A Dissertation submitted to George Peabody College, 1923, in fulfillment for a Ph.D., 144.

lack of teachers, and constantly moving families, while practically all children, regardless of the status of the family, were taught the alphabet at home. General Jonathan Ramsey, for example, who came as a young boy to Eaton's Station in 1781, expressed himself well with few lapses in grammar or spelling. He had learned his letters "and spelling from a mutilated copy of Dykes old spelling book" well enough to read the Bible.

He soon got a Dilworth's *Grammar* and studied this; sometime during his early teens he went three months to Thomas Mosby who kept a school in what was later Robertson County. This was the whole of his formal education. He wanted something all his own to read, and in 1795 while going down the Cumberland, bought at Russellville the second volume of the three volume work, *The Fool of Quality*, written by Henry Brooke of Ireland. Ramsey did not realize his volume was only part of the whole until he started to read it. He next bought a dictionary, the most commonly mentioned in early days, Entick's, and with the help of this read the book. He then bought the other volumes, and so began his library, "on a little board shelf resting upon a couple of wooden pins inserted in the logs." A few years later he made a trade with Matthew Lyon, printer, politician, boatbuilder, and storekeeper at Eddyville, whereby Mr. Lyon got a horse and Jonathan got books and pamphlets.[67]

Not all the first schools had separate buildings, though Zachariah White is described as teaching in a schoolhouse in 1781. Tradition relates that James Robertson's widowed sister taught her small daughters and the Robertson children on the flatboat that carried them to Middle Tennessee in the winter of 1779–1780. School, like church and court, was often held in a home, and George Hamilton who taught at Bledsoe's Station seems to have had no separate building. However, by 1799 when grammar or "English schools" were "to be found everywhere,"[68] most communities, up the river as well as in Middle Tennessee, had some form of school building, put up and paid for by donations of time and materials from the parents.

The less prosperous neighborhood would have had a building rough as that in Stockton's Valley, built in 1796 of "round green logs thrown up in a day," with wooden shutters by the glassless windows. The benches were rougher than those ordinarily found in other public places, for they were but the split halves of small logs with short legs pegged into bored

[67] W, 5S, 73–75.
[68] Williams, *Travels*, Schweinitz, "Report," 517.

holes. They of course had no backs; but, on these, their feet swinging sometimes out of reach of the floor, the scholars sat to do most of their work, slates when needed for ciphering, diagramming, or the beginnings of penmanship, laid on knees.[69] Practically all other work—spelling, reading, reciting of tables, the study of poetry, and most of grammar—was oral; Dilworth, like later texts, gave much space and many directions for proper reading aloud.

The most important exception, and sometimes the only one, to oral recitation and work on the slate [70] was the practice and study of penmanship or how to write "a joining hand," for usually the young child learned to shape each single letter as he learned the alphabet. Paper was expensive, thus limiting the practice of penmanship to the more advanced students. A rough board on two pegs in the wall, with a section of log above it sawed out to admit light, served as the writing desk in the Stockton Valley School. Here, the students stood to practice over and over, for in those days of many letters, numerous written agreements, and even homemade books, it was important to be "a good scribe." Some used homemade ink, but ink powder, easily transported and fairly cheap, was always quite plentiful in Middle Tennessee; lawyer Gubbins had papers of it when killed in 1786.

Elementary schools varied widely. A charter pupil of the one described remembered an early teacher as a drunken, uncouth Irishman, little more than a wanderer upon the frontier. His students in Stockton's Valley were, however, enough to drive a man to drink; when he told a future minister to make a problem in arithmetic the boy complied by asking, "Master, how many grains of corn will it take to make one square foot of mush?" A few days later while the teacher was in a drunken sleep, a pupil put a shovelful of hot coals into the pocket of his linsey coat and the coat was burned up. Thus ended school for the season and the "articles of agreement" were thrown into the fire.[71]

Schools like everything else were custom made, and hence the patron signed articles of agreement with the teacher. An agreement entered into in Montgomery County, Kentucky, November 8, 1800, is probably fairly representative of the better class of grammar school. The year for

[69] Williams, *Smith*, 27–29.

[70] DW, I, 47, 63, 255–259, for inventories of early merchants; even up river one could by 1800, PW, I, 3–5, buy from such a merchant as John James inkstands. Most of the accounts in the Coffee Papers contain numerous writing and educational materials; see in particular Account of Thomas Butler, 1804.

[71] Williams, *Smith*, 29.

Lullebegrud Reading School was to begin the first of January, and to continue five days a week for 224 days; holidays were to consist of one court day each month, five days for Easter, Whitsuntide, and Christmas, with ten days for harvest. The teacher was to have "special regard" to the "Morals and Behaviour of the Pupils" and teach them in the "arts" of "spelling, reading, writing, etc."; for all this he was to receive forty shillings per pupil per year, but only one-fourth of his pay was to be in cash, the rest was to be in produce taken at a fixed rate so that the eighteen-shilling hundredweight of pork might be worth twelve or twenty when actually received.

Most space was given to the nineteen rules: pupils were to "appear at the Schoolhouse each Morning if possible, by half an hour by sun; with hands and faces cleanly washed and Hair neatly combed." The boys were to keep the fires going and the girls to do the sweeping, but none of them was to dirty or tear books and clothing, nor was there to be teasing, laughing, "hunching, whispering, or making mouths to provoke others," nor were they at any time to quarrel, swear, curse, lie, use obscene language, or give one another the lie, and fighting would "deme the severest kind of punishment—the rod"; the "laugh block" and imprisonment were to be used for lesser offenses. The boys were free to run, jump, or play Prison-base from half past eleven until one in the winter and "so in proportion as the Days lengthen," but not to climb or wrestle or do anything "so as to endanger clothing or limbs." The girls were to exercise innocent diversions to themselves, nor were any of them at playtime or coming to and from school "unnecessarily to be Halloing, Shouting, Noising or making fearful outcries." If they had the itch they were not to come at all.[72]

This may or may not have been a blab school. Dr. Daniel Drake attended one in Kentucky and regretted the idea was discontinued. I am less certain. Years ago while teaching a one-room school, the pupils and myself in discussing our past decided to try the old ways from time to time. Our trouble was that too many stopped to see how the others were sounding; had we continued for several days until the novelty wore off we might have overcome the difficulty. It was a fine way for the learning of number combinations until a child got started wrong on a multiplication table; I then had to let him run on in his ignorance, or risk stopping all with curiosity while I got him back on the right track.

[72] McVey, *Education*, 30–31.

This particular group of children in the Kentucky hills were, however, accustomed to learning "by heart."

Most county histories have stories of the early schools: the custom brought from rural Scotland of barring out the teacher; the fights when someone passing by called out "school butter"; and all the other fun, bombshell acorns thrown into the fireplace behind the teacher's back; fights between overgrown boys and the teachers, but always the good teachers who took their children squirrel hunting or helped gather chestnuts, or would unbend enough to play the fox in a great game of fox and hounds that kept the scholars out till dark.

Such schools and such stories formed only a part of the educational picture. Good teachers at all levels were scarce,[73] but judging from the writing abilities of such as Felix Robertson, Christopher Stump,[74] William Hall, Lavinia Robertson Craighead, and other children of early settlers who received all their education on the Cumberland, the grammar or English School accomplished much.

History and geography were little stressed. The very early schools had as their only text William Guthrie's *Grammar of Geography*, but by the mid-nineties Morse's *Geography* was being taught. True, the earlier part was taken up with general information such as the Signs of the Zodiac, but much space was also given to describing the political and natural geography of the young United States, not as a curiosity seen through the eyes of a traveler as were most works on America at that date, but as an attempt to teach young Americans about their country. This work was published a few years later than the well known spelling book of Noah Webster, but Webster's work had much competition from similar texts, notably Dilworth's, nor did Webster, borrowing as he did from older English texts, supply a need peculiarly American as did Morse.

[73] The Tennessee *Gazette* carried many ads for teachers; typical is that of Dec. 2, 9, 1801, "Wanted an English teacher who will undertake the tuition of small children." The Nashville *Clarion*, Nov. 30, 1810, "Wanted a man who can come well recommended for his literary acquirements and moral deportment to take charge of Harpeth Academy"; *ibid.*, April 14, 1812, "Wanted a Latin teacher"; *ibid.*, Feb. 16, 1813, "Wanted a school master who understands English language."

[74] Parton, *Jackson*, I, 355–56, contains a letter of Christopher Stump. Felix Robertson is not only well represented in Draper Manuscripts, but in the Nashville *Journal of Medicine and Surgery*, VIII. His sister Lavinia also wrote for Mr. Draper as did many other children of first settlers such as Mrs. Thomas Eaton, daughter of William Stewart who was killed near his station on Mill Creek, see W, 1S, 87–88. Though most of the pioneers noted in later life such as Daniel Drake had considerably more education than that afforded on the frontier, many who wrote well such as Micah Taul and Elder John Smith, the noted minister, had no formal education save that to be had locally.

The English School was by the mid-nineties fairly standardized in the wealthier and more populous sections of Middle Tennessee. General James Winchester, serving what are now parts of Sumner and Smith counties, stocked in one order a gross of primers, many reams of paper, blotting paper, slates, slate pencils, and for the older children, there were in addition to histories, geographies, grammars, dictionaries, and the ever popular *Schoolmaster's Assistant,* school Bibles, and *Constitutions of the United States.* Nor was his store the only one stocking books. Children no longer attended school mainly to learn the three R's; by that date one of the primary functions of the grammar school was to prepare students for some one of the several academies that eventually prepared the young ones for college subjects and for the study of a lifetime profession.

There was during and immediately after the Revolution considerable popular belief that the state should at least bear part of the financial burden of education at the higher level. In North Carolina this took the form of setting aside public lands, or even the erection of schoolhouses.[75] The first and only such school chartered in the Cumberland settlements under North Carolina law was Davidson Academy, established in 1785 through a bill presented by William Polk, grandfather of the President.[76] The school was functioning at least by 1789,[77] and possibly for a few years before, as its first teacher, the Reverend Thomas B. Craighead, settled in 1785, and in that year is said to have started keeping a school for boys that in time became Davidson Academy. This school as a chartered school had a grant[78] of 240 acres from North Carolina and a ferry at the foot of Broad Street in Nashville. The land was later divided into lots and sold with the proceeds going to the school as did the monies from the operation of the ferry.

One of the first things the State of Tennessee did was to set aside a good deal of land for public education, but not as much as that stipulated by Congress in 1806. Unfortunately, public education profited but little; as in Kentucky some of the land fell into the hands of land

[75] NCR, XXIV, 605, An act for the promotion of learning in the District of Hillsborough. *Ibid.,* XXIV, 607, "An act to amend an act for establishing a school house at New Bern."

[76] NCR, XVII, 316, 319.

[77] A, V, 211–212, is a contract of 1789 whereby John Boyd promised to pay Lardner Clark, a trustee, 30 lbs. yearly for the rent of the Academy ferry.

[78] Tennessee *Gazette,* July 20, 1803, carried the announcement by Daniel Smith, a trustee, of the sale of the Academy lots. See also *ibid.,* May 30, 1804, one of several notices of meetings of the Academy trustees.

speculators, or was sold on credit and the debts never collected.[79] The early interest in state or federally supported education waned in both states, and it was not until the 1850's, while future President Johnson was governor, that a bill was passed levying a tax for public education in Tennessee.

This did not mean of course there were no schools. Education—among those able to pay—flourished. There were by 1800 several schools serving Middle Tennessee and one school in Wayne County, Kentucky, that gave some secondary education. One of the most popular schools in Middle Tennessee was that kept by George Martin, so large the closing exercises for the third quarter of 1801 had to be held on two successive days in October in order that the more than fifty speeches, farces, and dialogues of the younger pupils and public examinations of the older could all be heard. This school, known as the Valladolid School, and near the plantation of Colonel Joel Lewis, accepted pupils of all degrees of learning from primer to college preparatory.[80]

Another early and popular school was Sumner Academy taught by S. P. Black; [81] while south of the river the pupils of Federal Academy [82] in February of 1800 marched in the funeral procession paying tribute to the memory of Washington, and impressive they no doubt looked, for "seminarists" as well as their teachers customarily wore, as did lawyers and judges, black gowns. Nashville could by 1802 boast of a college, though the institution had only seven or eight pupils and one teacher,[83] but eleven years later the Nashville newspapers in October gave much space to the public examinations of the students of Cumberland College as the institution was known. It had grown so three days were required for the examinations, with students examined class by class, and happy the examiners were to report the junior class had excelled in Xenophon, the comedies of Terence, along with Virgil, Simpson's *Algebra*, and Euclid's *Elements*. The sophomores had also done well in English grammar, Sallust, Homer, the Greek Testament, Logic, and Arithmetic.[84]

[79] Abernethy, *Frontier to Plantation*, Chap. IV, "The Great Land Grab," 44–63; *ibid*., XI, "The Public Domain," 182–193; *ibid*., XVI, "Land Legislation and Education," *ibid*., 250–261, tell the sad story of public lands and public education in Tennessee. Kentucky's story, worse, has never been so thoroughly told.

[80] Tennessee *Gazette*, October 7, 23, 1801.

[81] *Ibid*., May 13, 1801, an announcement of the public examinations, farces and orations to be held May 26. *Ibid*., June 10, 1801, contains a lengthy account of the examinations conducted by James Winchester, E. Douglass, and B. Rawlings.

[82] *Ibid*., Feb. 18, 1801, referred to this school as "The late Federal Academy."

[83] Michaux, *Travels 1802*, 246.

[84] Nashville *Clarion*, March 30, 1813.

The classics would never be stressed as in England, but they were important. In one short list of books sent from Philadelphia to Daniel Smith in 1793 [85] there were Cicero, Ovid, and most of the Greek and Latin authors studied for generations in Europe. The study of these, aided by lexicons and preceded by work in Greek and Latin grammars, formed the backbone of the academy curriculum and later that of the college on the Cumberland. Mathematics consisted of Dilworth's *Assistant*, algebra, geometry, with now and then in accounts of school examinations, logarithms mentioned as a separate subject. Astronomy, quite widely taught, was the only science found. Dilworth's *English Tongue* continued to be used, for English grammar and rhetoric were stressed throughout the educational period.

There were no courses in English literature; even Shakespeare though often found in inventories of family libraries was not on school lists. Many if not most of the better educated men of the day felt that, compared to Homer and others of the old, nothing had been produced in England worthy of study by the young. The novel was little regarded, and though all the better known novels, many in translation, could be found in private libraries or for sale, the teaching of any in school would have been considered a waste of time. The editor of the *Gazette* once complained that young ladies were wasting time on "too many novels." [86]

The chances are the average pupil learned his lessons well, for at the end of each quarter he must in public examination give evidence of his progress. However, secondary school was selective; cost, distance from the seat of learning, the farm family's needs for young workers, all tended to limit attendance to those more or less interested in serious study. It is possible, too, that the intelligence of the average American was considerably higher than now. It was not until long after the Revolution that illiteracy, hastened in the South by impoverished land and in the North by large bodies of immigrants with no tradition of literacy, began its rapid climb.

There was always within reach of the pioneer child some means of getting the elements of reading and writing and arithmetic, and though the first academies were primarily day schools, pupils in outlying districts could board in some home near the school. The best known example of pupils boarding away from home in order to attend school is that of the two young Bledsoe boys, cousins, who in 1794 were ambushed by Indians

[85] A, V, 212. See also DW, II, 264; list of Academy texts with Lardner Clark.
[86] Tennessee *Gazette*, July 27, 1803.

while on their way to school from the home of General Daniel Smith.[87]

The academy designed especially for boarding pupils became common after the Indian Wars were finished in 1795. Farmer's Hall, thirteen miles north of Nashville on Mansker's Creek, appears to have been fairly typical of the small academy, not too expensive for the sons of middle class farmers. Here, tuition, including Latin and Greek, was only four dollars a quarter, and board with "washing and mending" forty dollars a year, though in this school as in others of that day the student must find his "own bed, etc." [88] Farmer's Hall was only one of many academies; some like Harpeth Academy,[89] near Franklin, were noted for generations, and others such as that of James Davis [90] where both Latin and surveying were to be taught with board for boys under fifteen for $15 yearly, though twice that for older boys, seem never to have got past the planning stage.

The Tennessee *Gazette* in early 1800 gave much news of the union of the Kentucky Academy and Transylvania Seminary at Lexington. The newly formed college offered law, chemistry, medicine, and surgery along with the customary humanities. Board with Mr. Welch was "15 lbs per year" but nothing was furnished save food; each student was responsible for his bedding, laundry, wood, and candles. This school was soon attracting young men from the Cumberland, including the grandsons of John Donelson II (Flotilla John) and Daniel Smith. Meanwhile, grammar schools multiplied; Robert Searcy, for example, announced in 1813 the opening of his grammar school attached to Cumberland College.[91]

Girls attended the day grammar schools along with the boys, and were among Zachariah White's pupils when the Indians attacked in 1781. However, coeducation stopped when the academy level was reached; the only exception in all of the United States of that day was Blount College, chartered at Knoxville in 1794, and ancestor of today's University of Tennessee.

Coeducation beyond the very early years was not in the British tradition, though girls' boarding schools had long been known in England. An English woman with a fair knowledge of music, able to speak French, reading Greek and Latin, and even capable of demonstrating a theorem in Euclid was no great rarity, and eighteenth century England had several

[87] W, 30S, 241.
[88] Nashville *Clarion*, March 30, 1813.
[89] *Ibid.*, March 8, 1811.
[90] *Ibid.*, April 30, 1812.
[91] *Ibid.*, March 30, 1813.

female authors. Most of this learning, however, could be had only by those with parents wealthy enough to afford tutors.

The American colonists had, as a rule, seen simple literacy as sufficient education for a female; this was especially true in intellectual New England. Save among the Quakers, the Moravians, and the wealthier of the Southern planters, female education was never taken very seriously. The United States was not destined to produce either a Jane Austen or a Madame Curie.

There were during pioneer years few girls' schools in the whole of the United States; there was one in Philadelphia and another, also in Pennsylvania, at Bethlehem.[92] The Cumberland settlements, compared to the older parts of the country, were rather quick to establish schools for girls. Best known of all girls' schools in the South was that founded in 1806 by Moses Fisk at Hilham, but his, like other girls' schools, came past the pioneer period.

One of the earliest was begun by Mrs. Eleanor Clopton,[93] March 15, 1804, in the former dwelling of Mr. James Saunders in Nashville. She offered to teach young ladies almost, one might say, whatever they needed or wanted to know. She would teach reading and writing, and English grammar "if they chuse" or the tables in arithmetic, also "embroidery and all other useful needlework . . . as far as their capabilities will allow," and of course the fashionable art of that day—wax work. Another early institution was Mrs. Tarpley's Female Seminary where, ". . . young ladies will be taught Reading, Writing, Arithmetic, English grammer, Sample work, needle work, Embroidery, Drawing, Painting, and Fillagree." [94] Board and tuition were $75 for the school year. There was by 1811 also a school on the West Harpeth in Williamson County where girls were in addition to the usual subjects taught "geography with the use of the globes and maps." Tuition here was $100 yearly.

In 1810 Mr. and Mrs. Green [95] announced they would teach young ladies so as to enable them to read "the best authors with pleasure and profit; to think with method, to speak with propriety, and to compose with ease and accuracy." Mrs. Barbour [96] offered much more, but one wonders how successful was her school, going as it did against the pre-

[92] Morse, *Geography*, 322, 328. Girls from Middle Tennessee may have attended these schools at an early date; in 1799 one of the Butler girls of East Tennessee went to Bethlehem, Williams, *Travels*, Schweinitz, "Report," 467.
[93] Tennessee *Gazette*, Feb. 22, 1804.
[94] Nashville *Clarion*, Nov. 23, 1810.
[95] *Ibid.*, Oct. 12, 1810.
[96] *Ibid.*, Feb. 9, 1813.

vailing American attitude toward female education. In her school young ladies were to be taught most of the usual academic subjects including natural history, "the use of the globes," principles of taste and criticism, and civil history; also included were moral philosophy, material philosophy, and first principles of chemistry. "Needle work," Mrs. Barbour announced firmly, "will form no part of my plan of instruction."

Mrs. Barbour's school like most schools for girls was expensive when compared to education for boys. Board was $80 yearly; tuition, $40; music, $18 per quarter extra and French, $3. Her curriculum that included chemistry but omitted needlework was probably a shade too radical for most believers in female education, but certainly Mr. Fisk's school, in time the most highly regarded in the South, produced young ladies not only versed in the social graces, but at least some who also took great interest in political affairs and had not a little skill in writing.[97]

There were in addition to all these, various specialized schools. Forerunners of today's adult education programs, these were often taught by itinerants, and usually their lives were short. Most popular of all was the dancing school. Andrew Jackson as a young man attended dancing school; Sevier [98] sent his sons and daughters to dancing school; and Micah Taul lived [99] for a time in a Kentucky home where dancing was the only formal education the children had. In Nashville of 1801 Charles V. Lorumier taught dancing every other Friday at the home of Thomas Talbot from ten in the morning until two, and from three till sundown.[100]

Singing schools also became quite common. These were often attended by a whole family, though later ones were usually held in connection with the neighborhood church with most emphasis on the hymn. There were also writing schools, while the art of eloquence which was soon to be in most of the young United States "after gold their highest ideal" was cultivated not only in reading and declaiming while in school, but in the debating society, flourishing in even remote Stockton's Valley by 1797.[101]

As the proper school with a paid teacher grew more important for

[97] The heroine of Burke, *Emily Donelson*, was educated by Mr. Fisk as were most of her friends and cousins with whom she corresponded; most not only expressed themselves well, but like Mary Coffee took a good deal of interest in Washington's political as well as social life.

[98] THM, V, VI, "Journal of Governor John Sevier 1790–1815," ed. by John H. DeWitt (cited hereafter as Sevier, "Journal"). *Ibid.*, V, 243, "Children went to dancing school"; *ibid.*, "A dance at Mr. Gordon's," are typical of many items through the years.

[99] RKs, XXVII, 12.

[100] Tennessee *Gazette*, Dec. 2, 1801, and *ibid.*, July 27, 1803.

[101] Williams, *Smith*, 38.

those who could afford it, the main educational stay of the less fortunate, used in Europe for centuries, was falling into disuse. This was the teaching of the crafts and trades through apprenticeship or binding out of the young to serve a master craftsman—joiner, printer, or goldsmith—until he was twenty-one. The apprentice was then a journeyman and free to work for wages. He could in time become a master craftsman with a shop and apprentices of his own, in Europe a member of his Guild and respected citizen of his community.

This system had been used to some extent in the colonies, particularly New England, but between British restrictions on manufacturing and the thriftiness of the average New Englander it was never very popular. The Revolution that was in New England twin of the Industrial Revolution changed the whole industrial picture. Businessmen and industrialists found it cheaper to import skilled workmen when needed, and use child labor at low wages, for little training was demanded by the factory. There were, of course, indentured servants, many of them children, but their five to seven years' labor was work only to pay a debt, not a training period.

The South with little industry and young slaves who could be taught the various skills needed had had little place for apprenticeship. Most of the binding agreements on the Cumberland were made by the court for orphans such as the little LeFever girls. However, in the early years we do find, both up the river and down, a few apprenticeships in which the father bound out his son, usually at twelve years of age,[102] to learn hat-making as was Sinclair Pruitt in 1787, or to be taught in "the trade and majesty of a merchant" as was little Patrick Murphy. He was only six years old at his binding in 1799 to Hugh McClure, merchant in Clarks-ville; he was to be taught to read and write and "as far in Arithmetic as the rule of Practice," and to have "Meat, Drink, Apparel, Washing and Lodging." Free when twenty-one, he was to get one full suit of "good cloathes which shall be new," and one hundred dollars or a horse and saddle.[103]

Girls when bound out, sometimes to a good farm wife to learn the "domestick arts," or now and then to learn a trade as was Margaret Murphy, to be taught the art of seamstress,[104] were free at eighteen, but almost always got less than boys. Nancy, the orphan of Abraham Paul,[105] bound when little more than two years old, was an exception. She was to

[102] DW, I, 78.
[103] MW, I, 30–31.
[104] *Ibid.,* I, 120.
[105] *Ibid.,* I, 278.

"learn the whole art of spinning and weaving," and the making of plain
cloth; different from most girls she was not only to be taught to read and
write, but to "cypher to the rule of three," and was to get "a good horse
worth fifty dollars," with saddle and bridle and a "good feather bed and
furniture compleat."

Indentures such as these grew fewer in proportion to the population,
in spite of an ever growing demand for apprentices. Beginning with a boot
and shoemaker in the first newspaper of 1799, all manner of craftsmen
begged for apprentices, from the silversmith of 1801 to the wagon-maker
of 1812.[106] Once got, bound boys, if the ads for their return be anything
to judge by, were much inclined to run away, and, as in the case of runaway slaves, rewards were often offered for their capture.[107] Many were
undoubtedly strangers brought by settling craftsmen, for the records yield
few binding agreements. It was a life not many parents in the old West
wanted for their sons, most of whom aspired to farming and the professions, and on any farm the work of the young was needed at home. As
early as 1802 Michaux commented [108] on the small number of children
apprenticed in Kentucky, and mentioned none on the Cumberland.

The professions, especially law, continued to be learned in the office of
an individual or firm for many years after law was being offered at Transylvania. However, the relationship was entirely different; it was not a
mutual exchange of labor for learning with the labor in excess, but the
young lawyer paid tuition, the sum depending on the lawyer who taught
him.

The Cumberland Country was soon famous for its many good institutions of learning, its professional men, especially lawyers, and its early interest in science as evidenced by the writings of Haywood, or the bringing
to the community of such learned men as Dr. Gerard Troost. Yet, none
of these achievements should be thought of as entirely the product of
an educational system. Most children of pioneer days and for generations
to come were much more a product of their homes than are children
today. Time spent in school was relatively short; Organization Child was
far away, and school itself was an expression of the heritage of the citizens, rather than a pattern imposed by professional educators. The pioneer
teacher was part of the pattern but he did not shape it.

Believe in formal education though the Cumberlander did, he would
never be described as an intellectual. True, Michaux the younger [108]

---

[106] *Rights of Man or Nashville Intelligencer*, July 17, 1799; Tennessee *Gazette*,
June 24, 1801; Nashville *Clarion*, March 31, 1812.

[107] Tennessee *Gazette*, July 14, 1802, a $50. reward for two bound boys.

[108] Michaux, *Travels 1802*, 152.

found them "well-informed" as had his father,[109] six years earlier, but Michaux comments more on their manners, "engaging though using little ceremony"; he also found the populace happy as did earlier travelers; phrases such as "law abiding," "filled with curiosity" were also used; even Aaron Burr, man-of-the-world with not a little sophistication and education, wrote his daughter he was "astonished at the number of sensible, well-informed, and well behaved people" he had met in Middle Tennessee on an 1805 visit to Andrew Jackson. Yet, the word most commonly used by travelers was "happy," or phrases indicative of happiness such as "live in comfort."

Save for politeness, few of these qualities could be taught; good manners were insisted upon from the cradle, and most schools, following the customs of England and Scotland, began, as did that attended by Dr. Drake, with the pupils rising and bowing to the teacher.[110] Even here the purely intellectual knowledge of when to bow and curtsy and the skill to do so with grace could not in themselves guarantee engaging manners or make of hospitality an art.

And so it was with most things. There was no belief that any book or school could teach the young exactly how to behave at any given crisis in life. The world around the pioneer child after 1795 changed more rapidly than has any other world before or since; he had to face the change of his own world from frontier outpost, besieged by Indians, to center of politics, education, agriculture, and business in less than a generation; all this complicated by the shift in agriculture, the Industrial Revolution, and changes in attitudes toward many matters. Born to consider himself part of the Western frontier, he would with no moving become in time a Southerner, yet many would yield as had their parents to the pull of the further West. Still, there was no cry among the old for "education for a changing civilization." Some even felt that man was not made to adjust to any and all changes.

Life promised a rich variety. The pioneer boy might be a professional man, farmer, less often a skilled worker, and though the old many-handedness was on the way out, seldom would the child born during pioneer days follow the one calling only. Yet, regardless of how he earned his livelihood, almost never would he be in a position where laws or other men or both could tell him exactly what to do. He had also in his multiple transactions as a farmer to learn something of the ways of

---

[109] Thwaites, *Travels*, III, Michaux, "Journal," 85; see also Williams, *Travels*, 285, and *ibid.*, 360, for comments of earlier visitors.

[110] Drake, *Letters*, 149.

men. He lived in a society not prone to pity grown men, nor did men wish to be pitied. Most believed that people deserved the kind of government they would stand for—weak men, strong governments—and that a poor judge of women or horseflesh deserved no better than he got. The pioneer boy learned this world of mankind, not found in books, chiefly through association with adults of all kinds.

Boys such as Sylvanus Castleman and Felix Robertson would, for example, have known Kaspar Mansker, the old Indian fighter and Long Hunter. Felix was old enough to have remembered 1791, the year the men had got up a "Memorial from the Civil and Military Officers of Mero District to George Washington." [111] His father's name was there as a general, and with it the names of other men who had for eleven years held a goodly territory of land for the United States—among them Josiah Ramsey, John Rains, and Kaspar Mansker as Lieutenant Colonel.

That, though, was 1791. When, in 1794, officers were being chosen for the Nickojack Campaign, Kaspar stood for election as Colonel. Most of the men with whom he had fought were dead, and Kaspar, to begin with, was an uninfluential hunter of Germanic descent. Kaspar failed of election and when the vote was finished said, "Well, I reckon if Colonel Mansker can't go, Kaspar can. He can kill as many Indians as the Colonel can." [112] And so Kaspar who had held military title for many years, and knew more about the business at hand than any man over him, went as a plain enlisted man. The old ones admired a man more than a military title, and, remembering, wrote of it to Mr. Draper forty years later when the names of the officers were forgotten.

Many of the old ones also wrote with admiration of James Robertson, but there is no record of what he said when two years later he, too, lost titles, earned as was Kaspar's with blood, money, and hard work. Still, Robertson as did Kaspar went on to serve when and where he could. Turned down by Jackson for a military appointment in the War of 1812 on the ground he was too old, Robertson, then around sixty, accepted the much more hazardous job of agent to the restless Chickasaw. There, in the Chickasaw Country, he died attended only by his wife. [113] Jackson after many misadventures, such as rushing off down river without making certain of supplies for his men—a thing neither Robertson nor Sevier would ever have done—went on to glory.

[111] TP, IV, 73.
[112] W, 29S, 67.
[113] *Ibid.*, 31S, 51, the account of Felix Robertson.

Young Felix accepted this world as had his father, and lived in it as a man, able and willing to take the consequences of his actions. He became a physician, and was never active in politics, for he was not a staunch Jackson man. He was in his early twenties when Jackson killed Dickinson, and among the ninety-nine outraged citizens who drew up a petition,[114] and presented it to Mr. Eastin, editor of the *Impartial Review* and in-law of Jackson. Mr. Eastin was willing to grant their request—put the paper in mourning—provided those who wanted it done would let their names be published; twenty-six withdrew their names; young Felix, along with Judge McNairy, Timothe De Monbruen, and other leading citizens, did not.

Felix's cousin, Mark Robertson Cockrill, would live to taste the bitterness of The War, but when seventy-five years old could still stand up and tell the Union Army, "I have loaned the Confederates $25,000 in gold—I voted for separation every time; I do not think that the two sections can ever be brought together—I have been very much aggravated. . . ."[115]

Up river little John Smith, ten years old in 1795, riding off alone to mill more than a hundred miles away, was also learning what it was to be a man. Years later when on a trip to Missouri to preach, he was told to obey the law and take the Union Oath of Missouri, upholding abolition. John Smith who had never owned a slave declared, "Were I to take this oath I would no longer preach by the authority of Jesus Christ, but by that of an unbelieving legislature." [116] He refused, preached, and was arrested, jailed, and indicted.

John Smith's feeling against oaths was possibly an echo of his early education in a day then gone, when many felt about oaths as had Matthew Carey; yet no book or system of education had taught him how to behave in Missouri.

The young, grown up on the border as had John Smith, had seen more of life at sixteen years of age than any American of today can know in a lifetime. There was in a forted station no escaping life, the good and the bad. This life did not always produce either a Felix Robertson or an Admiral Farragut. Some it may have brutalized, a debatable question, and many it may have inclined toward violence, a still more debatable point. Numerous writers have characterized the whole of the old South—and it must be remembered that all of it west of the headwaters of the Tennessee

114 Parton, *Jackson*, I, 303.
115 Wallace, *Millions*, Book II "Mark Robertson Cockrill," 60–61, quoting "Annals of the Army of the Cumberland . . . Including its Police Records. . . ."
116 Williams, *Smith*, 462.

was well seasoned by the descendants of Cumberland settlers—as violent. Yet, compared to the British Isles, the South was on the whole less violent. Much of the history of Britain was bloodied because the average Englishman or Scotchman preferred the risking of violence to his person to the acceptance of a violent hand laid on his mind and conscience. In general the British through their long and bloody history had been inclined to rise up and break any institution—Church or King—when it grew stronger than the individual or his home.

Not all violence on the Cumberland as in England was directed at ends so noble. The cocksure baby grew at times into a cocksure man with no fear of violence and not always good. Court records yield numerous accounts of trials of crimes and misdemeanors common to a hot-blooded, high-handed, self-willed, proud, passionate, but withal shrewd and often wise people—manslaughter, adultery, fornication, assault and battery. Few of these activities were premeditated; yet they were for the most part committed by men who when they felt the need could exercise a high degree of self-control; even hot-blooded Jackson had much of crafty caution, a man who seldom let either shrewdness or rage get the better of wisdom, or in the words of Parton, "no man knew better than he when to get into a passion and when not."

This was an important learning for those who would spend their lives among people and animals, especially horses, and though horsemanship and knowledge of horses were more or less taken for granted, the learning of these things, unconscious though it may have been, was a part of education.

Chapter Seven

The Horse

HORSES WERE more universally owned than household goods or farming tools, for a man—or a woman—had to be neither farmer nor householder to need a horse; even the bound boy got one at the end of his servitude and sometimes the bound girl. Thus, the horse, more so than any other one thing—land, Indians, feather beds, or guns—entered into the lives of all the Cumberland settlers. Most incidents of history from Robertson's exploratory journey from which he returned with his Spanish brood mares to Andrew Jackson's killing of Dickinson because of a quarrel that began with horses gave a leading role to horsestock.

The "strawberry roan"—"bay yearling colt"—"gray horse"—"roan mare"—"dark chestnut gelding 15½ hands high"—"beautiful golden chestnut filly with both hind legs white halfway to the hock"—"bright sorrel mare"—"black horse"—"brown horse"—"Eagle mare"—"flea bitten mare" run forever through inventories, advertisements, court minutes, and Indian battles. Nor were they, like other animals, always nameless—Humming

Headpiece: Traveler and his pack horse climbing a hill against a brisk wind.

Bird, Rosseta, Atlas, Maria, Bagdad, Whynot, and dozens of others trotted, paced, cantered and galloped, stood at stud, or were sold.

These were quite different from those nameless, perpetually hungry, scrawny, cheap, and generally ill-treated beasts of burden, the pack and draft horses that brought all things to the frontier from whiskey to Asbury's Bibles, not to mention settling families and their goods. The Cumberland was from earliest years an important highway, but a long and arduous one, and even when the river was used the horse was the link between riverbank and final destination. Pack horses were so much a part of life we read of them as we do the weather, only an incidental thing, part of a more important story, as when William Overall was killed in January, 1793, at the Dripping Spring and his flesh cut from his bones, he had with him nine pack horses loaded with goods.[1] Reverend Asbury who, like Jackson, never got along too well with his horses complained often of his pack animals that would neither lead nor drive. Other travelers mentioned them only when they ran away, "with the pack swinging and knocking against every tree, like a dog with a kettle to his tail." [2]

The pack horse had, generations before the Cumberland was settled, replaced the Indian burden-bearer as a carrier of goods to the Southern Indians and the bringer of deer and beaver skins to seaports. English explorers, different from the *coureurs de bois* who, when they could not use canoes went on foot, had crossed the Appalachians on horseback with pack horses as did Dr. Thomas Walker in 1750; a few years later had come the Long Hunters on horseback and sometimes each man with more than a dozen pack horses.

The horse figured one way or another in many stories of Indian warfare on the Cumberland, as in the early fall of 1790 at the stockaded farm of Edwin Hickman on Sulphur Creek, a mile north of the Cumberland and about ten miles west of Nashville. "When at the moment a rumbling noise was heard, they looked and saw a party of horsemen making toward them at full speed; the men leaning upon the horses' necks with rifles in hand." After the one quick glance, men grabbed guns and leaped to portholes, while women rushed for the extra guns, looked to their priming, caught up powder horns and bullet bags. The Indians had for some weeks been constantly on the prowl, "killing the cattle, destroying the corn and potatoes," and now it looked like a full-scale invasion.

Instants later women were building up the cooking fires, boys running

---

[1] ASP, Indian Affairs, I, 436.
[2] Baily, *Tour 1796–1797*, 356.

to open the fort gate, and men putting away rifles. The "war party" was a group of white men led by Elijah Robertson, brother of James, riding back from a fruitless chase after Indians. Long in the woods, both men and horses were hungry. Help went flying about; some to the eight-hundred-bushel corncrib to get feed for the horses, others hitched a team to the horse mill to grind meal for bread.[3]

We do not know the food they had when they at last sat down in the Hickman home—plenty we can be certain for the Hickmans were tavern keepers as well as farmers.[4] Everything about the scene was part of a story old when the Cumberland was settled. Food, home grown and tasting faintly of wood smoke, rifles leaned against a wall, tired men smelling of horse sweat and leather, eating, but not until their horses were fed. So had it been along the borders when a group of men returned from a foray in the French and Indian War, and so had men and horses been fed in Sevier's household and Robertson's.

The thing that made these scenes possible was the horse. All border warfare, including King's Mountain, depended upon the horse; in warfare as in early travel, a man might be worse, but never better than his horse. The food both men and horses ate at Hickman's had been cultivated by the horse, the bread ground by horsepower, while horses had dragged the logs for the buildings and fort walls. This dependence on the horse for practically all power was also a part of the life in East Tennessee that had in turn inherited the horse from Virginia and North Carolina. Horses were found in all the colonies, but in no other two save Pennsylvania did they serve so many purposes. Northward, particularly in New England, oxen were more commonly used,[5] while on the rice and indigo plantations of the deeper South, even the very heavy work such as ditching was done by slaves with hoes.

The place of the horse in Middle Tennessee might be thought of as the seed of some hybrid plant with a long ancestry of cross-pollination in many regions, chiefly Virginia where by 1730 most planters "would walk two miles to hunt a horse in order to ride one." Virginia horses were by the time of the Revolution earning praise from that most critical of visitors—the English Tory. New England horses might be "goose-rumped

[3] W, 30S, 457–471. Major Edwin Hickman was born in Albemarle County, Va., 1750; settled on Cumberland in 1785; killed 1791, *ibid.*, 30S, 507.

[4] DW, I, 223–229, gives separate lists of those indebted to Hickman for "foriages" and goods.

[5] ASP, Finance, I, with its summaries of taxable property in each state sheds much light on patterns of agriculture. New Hampshire of 1796 had, for example, 20,000 oxen to 11,000 horses, 442.

and cathamed," able only to "shuffle along at an unaccountable wriggling gait," that left the rider "more fatigued in riding two miles than in a whole day's fox chase," but the Virginia horse, either the stud of English blood or the "beautiful Chickasaw," was admired.[6]

The Virginians had tried constantly to improve the breed; even Patrick Henry, never wealthy enough to afford the English Thoroughbred, wanted his mares with "fine delicate heads, long necks, small ears, deep shoulders and chests, large arms, well legged, upright pasterns, clear of long hair, loins round and very wide, haunches to be as straight as possible," and if they had "small stars or blazes," so much the better.[7]

Middle Tennessee enlarged and enriched the pattern of horse usage. The good limestone land produced ideal food for the horse in which bone, wind, and muscle counted for more than fat. Many of the settlers were great breeders and horse lovers, but it is doubtful if any early settler had as much good horsestock as had Robertson. In removing to the Cumberland the settler drew closer to two sources of supply—the Illinois noted for its fine Spanish stock, and the Chickasaw, famous for their horses which were also a mingling of Spanish strains.[8]

The Colberts who lived for generations in the Chickasaw Country and in time kept the tavern and ferry where the Natchez Trace crossed the Tennessee were especially noted horse breeders. George alone had in 1799 five hundred head, but planned to sell none until he had a thousand.[9] Some of these were no doubt fine animals, but many may have been little Apalousas, scrubby and tough, but cheap enough a flatboatman might save himself a walk home by buying one in Natchez for fifty dollars or less. These like much of the cheaper horsestock in the South were the descendants of Spanish strays that by the late eighteenth century had so multiplied great herds roamed the plains west of the Mississippi. As early as 1797 Francis Baily bought two of a man who made a business of going west, lassoing Apalousas, and bringing them to Natchez to sell.[10]

Judging from prices, most horsestock on the Cumberland was considerably better than the wild horses of the West, and the owner tried to

[6] Smyth, *Tour*, I, 193.
[7] I, VII, 77, Patrick Henry to George Rogers Clark, Dec. 12, 1778.
[8] James Adair, a Scotch trader who spent close to forty years among the southern Indians, chiefly the Chickasaw, had in his *History of the American Indian*, London, 1775, much praise for the Chickasaw horsestock, giving the origin as Spain by way of New Mexico, 205. Pagination here follows the edition published with notes and index and copyrighted by Judge Samuel Cole Williams, Kingsport, Tenn., 1930.
[9] Williams, *Travels*, Schweinitz, "Report," 457.
[10] Baily, *Tour 1796–1797*, 311–312. See also Michaux, *Travels 1802*, 234–235.

furnish the comfort and protection of a stable. The first outbuildings mentioned were stables, and lacking stables, horses were kept in fort yards as were Robertson's in 1781. Oats, usually intended for horse feed, are more commonly found than wheat before 1790, and as early as 1784 oats are mentioned in connection with the death of Jacob Castleman, Sr.; he was killed while cutting them.[11]

All the items of horse furniture from silver spurs and bridle tips to wagon gears and saddle bags are constantly encountered in inventories [12] and store accounts. Numerous industries depended upon the horse; in addition to the blacksmith who looked chiefly to the horse's feet for his livelihood, there was the saddler, carriage and wagon maker, lady's or gentleman's habit-maker, the wheelwright, and the long list of workers and businessmen who made possible gold carriage lace, coachmen's hats, ladies' riding whips, and the multitude of other things needed for proper traveling with a horse.

Many of the first settlers who never lived to see coachmen in top hats around Nashville were killed hunting horses or food for them. Cows, hogs, and sheep were usually expected to get their food from canebrakes, barrens, and woods. All suffered much from Indians, for the Indian even when he failed to take a station as in the case of Freeland's, destroyed everything he could in the way of crops and domesticated animals. The horse was never harmed; instead, he was stolen; over and over parties of Indians slipped in and stole horses. Governor Blount writing in November of 1792 declared that not one "less than five hundred" had been stolen since the first day of January,[13] and by that date the total taken since settlement was in the thousands. There was only one thing Indians could do with so many horses—sell them. The stolen stock was, often with the help and connivance of white men, usually taken a discreet distance—Georgia, New Orleans, or some town in Spanish Florida—and there sold, but Major David Wilson [14] of Sumner County, Tennessee, insinuated to Governor Blount in 1793 that some of the horses stolen by Indians out of

[11] W, 32S, 325.

[12] Found in most farm inventories. But see in particular John Buchanan, Sr., DW, I, 69; William Neely, *ibid.*, I, 166; William Gowens, *ibid.*, I, 175–176; Samuel Buchanan, *ibid.*, I, 296–297; Joseph Conrad, MW, I, 3; and Charles Fease, *ibid.*, I, 28–29. The store accounts of the Coffee Papers are good sources for prices of horse furniture of 1802–1805.

[13] TP, IV, 210.

[14] *Ibid.* Major Wilson, settling around 1785, represented Sumner County in the North Carolina Legislature, and was later sent to the Tennessee Legislature, see W, 31S, 336.

Middle Tennessee, were finding their way into the hands of white dealers in the Holston Country.

The average man or family was helpless without a horse, and most owners tried to forestall theft by keeping the horses in stables, the fort yard, or a field. This made horse fare a very great problem, especially so when for the first five seasons Indians destroyed most of the corn. In late winter and early spring men and boys risked their lives to go out and cut brush or the branches of trees on which the buds were beginning to swell, and a soldier at Freeland's Station in 1783 was killed when carrying a load of cane on his shoulder to his horse in the fort, for the rustling cane covered the sight and sound of the approaching Indian.[15]

Even the man with only one horse was hard put to feed him in such fashion; the farmer like Robertson with many, who between the fall of 1788 and July of 1789 [16] lost thirty head to the Indians, could only turn his horsestock on the open range, and the foolish horse, different from the cow, would let himself be taken by anyone, white or Indian.

Many of the horses had originally belonged to Indians, particularly Chickasaw, and some Indian horses on the Cumberland had not been bought but "taken." John Rains and the "Fool Warrior," Abraham Castleman, were adept at recovering stolen horses, and a contemporary went so far as to say they had been on at least one "horse-stealing expedition" that yielded several head. They got most on one occasion when, disguised as Indians, they slipped into the forbidden territory south of Duck River, and were thus able to get close enough to a party of breakfasting Creeks to shoot with some accuracy. The surprised party ran away, leaving dead men, horses, and plunder. It is doubtful if Rains and Castleman considered it stealing, rather a balancing of the few they got against the many taken by the Indians.

We read with pity of Daniel Boone's brother killed by an Indian who stole his horse, then jangled the bell when Boone came looking for the animal. We can only pity the Indians John Rains killed in the same fashion; a "horse belled and hobbled was used as a trap, the men treed themselves," and waited.[17] They didn't have to wait long, for Indians often lay in the woods listening for the bells that horses on the open range wore.

It is possible that Middle Tennessee ought to give at least some thanks to the Indian for the rapid development of permanent pasture and stables,

[15] W, 6XX(70), 4–5.
[16] NCR, XXII, 790–791; Robertson to Daniel Smith, July 7, 1789.
[17] W, 31S, 333; see also for such forays, Ramsey, *Tennessee*, 475–478.

for Tidewater had gone for more than a hundred years with almost no permanent pasture and few stables, and North Carolinians as late as 1737 were denominated by one historian [18] as the "worst horse masters" in the world. Their horses were never shod and seldom housed. True, the sandy lands of Tidewater were unsuited to grass and clovers and hence made poor pasture, but when we consider what the Tennessee farmer had to wrestle with, it is doubly surprising to find references to stabling, fodder, hay, and pasturage as early as July of 1784,[19] and from that date on such items are frequent. Isaac Mayfield, who came early enough to get a preemption, but without money enough to hire guards, was by 1792 [20] able to offer a tenant an acre and a half of horse pasture. Francis Baily, coming five years later, found horse pasture at several plantations; even Mr. Jocelyn on the then frontier south of Nashville had several acres of meadow.[21]

Pasture, however, considering the price of most other home products and labor was expensive; in 1788, for example, it cost two pounds to keep three horses three months and twenty days, or less than a year's keep for one horse, and a small horse, part of the same inventory, brought only eight pounds, two shillings.[22] Fifteen years later ten weeks' horse pasture cost John Coffee $15,[23] or more cash than a farm hand might earn with keep in the same length of time. Even the mare visiting the stud horse was sometimes charged three shillings or fifty cents a week.

The desire for permanent pasture and hay, most of both going to horses in the early years, is reflected in the many references to grass and clover seed, but good hay was long a luxury; as late as 1812 [24] it was selling for slightly more than fifty cents a hundred pounds, or, pound for pound, a shade more than corn.

The first census for Middle Tennessee did not enumerate horses, but up the river in Kentucky where they were taxed at one-twelfth of a dollar

---

[18] *The Natural History of North-Carolina with an Account of the Trade, Manners, and Customs of the Christian and Indian Inhabitants,* by John Brickell, M.D., Dublin, 1737; pagination follows ed. of J. Bryan Grimes, reprinted and copyrighted by the Trustees of the Public Libraries of North Carolina, Raleigh, 1911 (cited hereafter as Brickell, *North Carolina*), 53–55.

[19] A, V, 211, a 1784 Davidson County rental agreement in which the farmer promises both stable and pasture.

[20] *Ibid.,* V, 205–206.

[21] Baily, *Tour 1796–1797,* 409.

[22] DW, I, 107. This was in connection with the settlement of the Thomas McCain estate.

[23] Coffee Papers, 1809. See also *ibid.,* 1808—$10. for 30 days horse pasture.

[24] *Ibid.,* 1812. See also for comparative prices of ten years earlier, the James Dean sale, DW, II, 242–244. Prices varied with the locality.

per head, they were counted. The tax lists of Wayne County in 1801 give 344 white males above twenty-one and 749 horses and mules [25] or slightly more than an average of two for each grown man. Pulaski County in 1799 had 886 horses for 383 men.[26] In Middle Tennessee the proportion of horses to men would have been greater; James Robertson probably had more than a hundred most of the time, depending on how bad the Indians were. Most families, as seen in inventories, were at least as well off as Jacob Castleman [27] who had two mares with colts and two saddles.

The horse, more so than any other animal, varied in price from nothing for a "blind gelding, age unknown," to the $8,000 John Harding [28] paid around 1812 for the purebred Arabian, Bagdad. It is doubtful, however, if many horses during pioneer years brought much more than the "1,000 hard dollars" Abner Green of Natchez District paid in August of 1789 to James Robertson for his "high blooded horse Whynot." [29] In general, horses like other domesticated animals were during the very early years cheaper than later—the scarcity of food, danger of Indians, and inabilities to get fence laid explain this. Samuel Buchanan's [30] horses averaged only a little more than $30, but ten years later Joseph Conrad's best brought $90,[31] a rather high price; a good horse with furniture was reckoned at $100, the price paid by Michaux in 1795.

Regardless of how cheaply the horse was got, the upkeep was almost beyond the pocketbook of the man unable to raise feed. If a vacationer of today had to spend as much on oil and gas and garaging for his car when not traveling as he spends for himself on food and motels, the chances are he wouldn't have a car. The traveler through the Cumberland Country sometimes had to spend more on his horse than on himself. True, the first tavern rates of Davidson County [32] allowed the keeper to charge only a shilling for keeping a horse, "one natural day or twenty-four hours," the same as his master paid for the whole or part of a bed, but a gallon of corn was two shillings and fodder was eight pence extra.

[25] RKs, XXVII, No. 79, 33–37.
[26] Alma Owens Tibbals, *A History of Pulaski County, Kentucky*, copyright Grace Owens Moore, Louisville, Kentucky, 1952.
[27] DW, I, 194.
[28] Louis D. Wallace, ed., *The Horse and Its Heritage in Tennessee*, Tennessee Department of Agriculture, Nashville, 3rd ed., 1951 (cited hereafter as Wallace, *Horse*), 18.
[29] DW, I, 111.
[30] *Ibid.*, I, 296–297.
[31] MW, I, 3.
[32] DC, I, 26.

As prices for the traveler rose so did those for the horse; the Sumner County traveler of 1789 had to pay three shillings for his own dinner and three more for a horse feed of corn; twenty-four hours pasturage cost two shillings, stablage with hay or fodder cost the same with oats three pence per quart, but one night's lodging for the traveler had gone up to six shillings [33] or one dollar. These were legal rates; travelers did complain of high prices in Nashville, but they complained more of those in the homes and inns between Nashville and Knoxville; as late as 1799 travelers near the Plateau had to pay a dollar a bushel for corn; [34] others bought wild dried grass for hay. The traveler with a hungry horse couldn't be choosy.

The passing years bringing more taverns and floods of corn and oats didn't improve things; when Talbot's Tavern in 1811 announced it had reduced its yearly board to $104, horse keep remained the same—$104.[35] A year later one could at the Chealybate and Sulphur Springs, a health resort four miles east of Clover Bottom, keep a child or servant for $1.50 a week, but horse keep was $2.[36] In the fall of 1810 William Roper who kept a tavern on the Nashville Square in front of the courthouse charged a man $2.50 for one week's board, but for a man with a horse it was a dollar a day.[37]

We can be certain, however, that the horse in the good inn was well taken care of, for nothing angered a traveler so much as poor horse accommodations; even the patient Moravian missionaries complained [38] when a makeshift innkeeper attempted to feed their horses in a field with other animals. They did as other travelers; no matter how tired or hungry, they stayed with the horses and saw to it they got their feed. There was, of course, no such foolishness in a great place like the De Monbruen tavern, and innkeepers took care to advertise good ostlers.[39]

Horse keep, either for the farm animal or for a good saddle horse, meant a great deal more than food. Saddles, even secondhand ones at sales,[40] sold usually for between $12 and $15 or a month's wages, while at

[33] SC, I, 12.

[34] Williams, *Travels*, Schweinitz, "Report," 502, 506.

[35] Nashville *Clarion*, Feb. 15, 1811.

[36] *Ibid.*, July 13, 1812.

[37] *Ibid.*, Nov. 30, 1810.

[38] Williams, *Travels*, Schweinitz, "Report," 500.

[39] Nashville *Clarion*, Aug. 11, 1812.

[40] Saddles for both men and women appeared in most inventories, but see in particular, DW, I, 107, 166, 175, and MW, I, 17.

Haysborough in 1803 "ladies' ready-made" saddles cost $28. The average farmer could manage more cheaply by collecting leather, trees, and irons, and taking the whole to a saddler, but even so it was still expensive. The saddle was only the beginning of the horse furniture; there must be a saddlecloth and bridle. Bridles could be had at sales for as low as $2, but if one wanted a really good one, the "polished guard bit" alone cost $2.50 at the store of Coffee and Harney in 1803; the bit, with leather, bridle tips, and any desired trimming, plus labor, could easily run the cost of the bridle to $10. Spurs, riding habits, and such items as "ladies' switch whips" that cost $3 were by around 1800 all part of the horse furnishings for the middle-class farmer and his lady.[41]

Joseph Conrad [42] was a well-to-do farmer with only a few slaves, and not by the standards of Middle Tennessee a wealthy man; yet as he rode about on his $90 horse with a good saddle and saddlebags, dressed in boots and silver spurs, not to mention his greatcoat and good hat, the whole outfit represented more than a $200 outlay, a year's wages for a semiskilled workman.

All this was but a drop in the bucket to the cost of buying and keeping a carriage. Several years later John Coffee, then living in Alabama,[43] estimated the value of his with harness at $300, and as he liked good horseflesh, usually paying around $150 for the animals he rode and $180 for a team of work horses, his team of matched carriage horses would have cost better than $300, but considering the roads of the day, he could scarcely have managed with only one team.

There were other matters such as the coachman's livery and whip, and of course the cost of the coachman. In spite of their cost and the roughness of the roads, carriages were by 1797 not too uncommon; in that year Francis Baily met "within three or four miles of Nashville, two coaches, fitted up in all the style of Philadelphia or New York besides other carriages," [44] and all these in the more thinly populated section south of Nashville, where the furthest limit of southern settlement was less than ten miles from the Cumberland. Buggies or "carriages for pleasure" as they were listed in ferry rate-tables were not a part of pioneer life, and

[41] Coffee Papers, 1802–1804. See also PW, I, 3, the 1800 inventory of the John James store in Pulaski County where at this date travel by horseback was almost the only mode of travel and every respectable family needed at least one pair of saddlebags; one "with hangings" sold for one pound, four shillings, and another for 19 shillings.

[42] MW, I, 3.

[43] Coffee Papers, 1828.

[44] Baily, *Tour 1796–1797*, 408.

the average farm family after the Indian Wars were ended, traveled often by wagon, but even these usually cost from sixty to eighty dollars, second-hand at sales.[45] All of these conveyances, fashionable coach or homemade sled were in the early years pulled by some kind of horsestock. The mule and to some extent the ox in time took over much of the drudgery of the Southern farm, and in New England oxen were often used for heavy work, but for generations throughout the United States the mainstay of travel and transport was the horse.

They pulled the heavy Conestoga wagons from Philadelphia to Pittsburgh, the roads so rough that six horses for one wagon were common; they struggled through mud and over rocks, across creeks, and up and down steep hills on roads so poor that after spring thaws they were impassable. Philadelphia was, for example, the cultural, political, and business metropolis of the young United States, yet such was the condition of the roads leading to it, a traveler of 1796 had to wait in Baltimore a week before the road to Philadelphia was navigable by the public coach.[46] Once started, the passengers had often to lighten the load by walking, or even help get the vehicle out of a mud hole; the road from Philadelphia to New York was even worse with yet more time spent in walking. Worse still for much of the way, were the roads into the Cumberland Country, yet somehow the horses got there with wagons, sleds, carriages, coaches, carts loaded with goods and people.

Ordinary draft and pack horses were comparatively cheap and hence expendable. Visitors from Europe complained often of the rough treatment given them and of drivers who made "free use of the whip." [47] These, the horses of commerce and industry, led very different lives from the expensive, carefully matched teams of carriage horses and the fine horseflesh of racing, riding, and hunting that in time were the pride of every fashionable family in Middle Tennessee, or even the well-cared-for draft and work animals of the average farmer. The scraggeldy, unkempt beast, fetlock deep in the mud of the Natchez Trace, head hanging, saddle-sore and fly-bitten, unshod likely as not, would not be recognized as a

---

[45] Wagons and carts were common, though some of the owners were killed before they got them assembled as was Cornelius Ruddle, DW, I, 54; *ibid.*, II, 274, 303, and MW, I, 27; John Coffee in his 1803 "Estimates for working the Salines," planned to pay $100 for each of fifteen wagons.

[46] Baily, *Tour 1796–1797*, 107.

[47] David Thomas, *Travels through the Western Country in the Summer of 1816*, Auburn, N.Y. 1819, 77. Thomas covered much the same territory as many other travelers, but he gave a more detailed account of means of conveyance than did others, though he was not in Tennessee.

piece of horseflesh by a modern child familiar only with the strange animals on TV—sleek, fat, and shiny-rumped at the end of the long ride as at the beginning. Even the good saddle horse was at the end of a trip from Knoxville to Nashville a sorry looking sight. Uncurried on the road, scantily fed, going sometimes for whole days without water while on the dry rocky Plateau, neck galled from the bell collar—for usually he suffered the indignity of a bell at night and was hobbled into the bargain— he often reached his destination streaked with mud and dried sweat lather, Spanish needles in his tail, and on his ribby sides reminders of the creeks he had swum, for any long trip took flesh from the mount.

Still, he was usually good for some years while the mare, able to drop a foal yearly, was a steady source of income. Yet, no matter how cheaply got or how useful, the upkeep of any piece of horseflesh, not including food and furniture, was a constant drain on the owner's purse. The average family on the Cumberland in the early years probably spent a higher percentage of the family income on horseshoes than the family today spends on both gas and tires. Blacksmith bills, though not always for shoes, represented a considerable item in the expense listed by most men whose accounts have been studied. As late as 1799 it still cost $4 [48] or better than a week's wages to shoe a horse, half for the work, half for the iron which cost a shilling a pound, or a month's wages if translated into the pay of a woman worker in a New England cotton mill. The price is higher still when one remembers that a horse might in the course of its lifetime wear out several sets of shoes, though the old shoe had some salvage value.

Shoes, food, furniture, and ferriages—a shilling for a man on a horse or a pack horse, eight pence for a horse with neither man nor pack [49]— were the major expenses of horse keep; but a man or woman who wanted to make a good appearance must pay considerable for the horse's toilet by buying or hiring a groom, or engaging the less elegant stable boy. Even the farmer who did it himself must buy brushes and currycombs and put in a good deal of time. There is no way of measuring the time and money spent on horse remedies; Sevier and John Coffee were always jotting them down. There were on the frontier no veterinarians [50] and horses had more ailments, accidents, and weaknesses than humans.

[48] Williams, *Travels*, Schweinitz, "Report," 514.

[49] DC, I, 26. Ferry rates, established as were those for taverns, by county courts, varied from ferry to ferry, but there is the question if the ferryman always kept to the legal fee.

[50] Michaux, *Travels 1802*, 233, nor did I in the early years find a bill for a veterinarian, or farrier, as he was still called at times.

In spite of high upkeep the horse continued to flourish and multiply, and by 1786 and possibly sooner, Kentucky traders were coming to the Cumberland for horses.[51] Soon, horse drovers, taking herds back East, were common on the lonely roads across the Plateau. The Cumberland farmer, however, was seldom satisfied with numbers alone, but worked constantly to improve the breed, and as in Virginia, the studhorse, with his Negro groom sleeping with him in the stable,[52] early became an important but expensive part of the wealthier plantations. The studhorse was a valuable animal, an especial object of taxation,[53] carefully tended, fattened, and rested against the strenuous work of breeding.

James Robertson on one of his many trips to North Carolina may have left a few mares to be serviced by Young Northumberland by imported Northumberland at stud near Knoxville in 1792.[54] The word "imported" really meant "from England," for the importation of English Thoroughbreds by Virginians after beginning around 1730 had continued, interrupted only by the Revolution. In spite of two wars, breeders continued to favor the English breeds over the Arabian so that in time the English Thoroughbred became a must for every fashionable planter of Middle Tennessee.[55]

Lacking a thoroughbred, the Cumberland pioneer farmer would still pay good money for a stud with one imported ancestor some generations removed. Such a one was Spotted Medley, "got by Gimrack, got by Imported Medley, a beautiful dapple gray, rising six years, full 15 hands high," that during the season of 1799 stood at stud on Flowery Spring Plantation eight miles from Clarksville. Spotted Medley cost three dollars the leap or twelve dollars to insure the mare with foal.[56] Tippoosaid, at stud the same time, cost only five dollars and a bushel of corn on credit or four dollars cash for the season.[57] Two years later Zisca was cheaper still, only $1.50 the leap, or four dollars the season,[58] but in general as breeding stock improved prices rose. Gray Medley, owned by Richard

---

[51] FQ, I, 172–173, James Wilkinson to Nathaniel Massie, Dec. 19, 1786.

[52] Thomas Anburey, *Travels through the interior parts of America*, London, 1789 (cited hereafter as Anburey, *Travels*), II, 359–360, described in some detail the care of the studhorse Shakespeare, "a dappled gray, 15½ hands high," owned by Col. Randolph of Tuckahoe.

[53] Method and rates of taxation varied; in Kentucky studhorse taxes were by the head; a back-hill farmer with a sway-backed plug paid no more than the Bluegrass breeder with a $5,000 English Thoroughbred; Tennessee rates were based on stud fees.

[54] Wallace, *Horse*, 20.

[55] *Ibid.*, 15.

[56] Nashville *Intelligencer*, March 11, 1799.

[57] Tennessee *Gazette*, Feb. 25, 1800.

[58] Tennessee *Gazette*, March 17, 1802.

Cross and also only partly of imported ancestry, cost four dollars the leap and sixteen to insure a mare with foal; his powers of fatherhood appear to have been more highly prized than his breeding, for he was advertised [59] as having got 125 mares with foal. By 1803 Robert Weakly who had early built a forted station south of Nashville near that of Robertson on Richland Creek was asking ten dollars the leap, but only sixteen to insure a mare with foal from Phoenix who had been "got by Venetian whose pedigree will be found in the British Racing Calendar, and foaled by the imported mare Zenobia." [60]

This Phoenix was cheap compared to another Phoenix who eight years later stood at stud during the usual season of March 30 to July 31 near Palmyra. A "dark chestnut, 15 hands, 3 inches high, bred by the Duke of Bedford, foaled in 1798," he cost forty dollars to guarantee a foal. All who brought him a guest, even for one leap only, had to pay an extra fifty cents to his groom [61] at the stable door. Soon, those wanting the services of a thoroughbred had to pay the groom a dollar as well as board for both mare and groom,[62] for the mares, of course, must also have grooms.

Newspapers of the passing years reflect the ever increasing cost of bettering horsestock. March was usually marked by extra editions of first the *Gazette*, and later the *Clarion* given up entirely to advertisements of the pedigrees and powers of fatherhood of the more important stallions. Front pages were illustrated with large woodcuts of Atlas, Wonder, Diomede, Collector, Truxton (owned by A. Jackson), Young Diomede, Royalist and numerous others, their names printed in the boldest, blackest type the editor owned. Following the description of pedigree, size, appearance, age, and price, there was always a long list of names of the most noted horsemen of Middle Tennessee who attested that all information,

[59] *Ibid.*, April 8, 1801.

[60] *Ibid.*, March 16, 1803.

[61] The groom, often a Negro, was contracted for on a yearly basis; a typical contract is one found in Coffee Papers, 1807: "An agreement between Sampson Sawyers and John Tracy who agrees to serve as a groom for his stud horse Masimus during the approaching season commencing 17th of March and ending the last day of July. —Said John Tracy must abstain from excessive use of ardent spirits so as not to prevent him from discharging his duties in every respect." Tracy was to get $12 per month, one half in cash, and keep of course.

[62] Mares for Flying Childress, Tennessee *Gazette*, April 13, 1803, would be kept for only 3 shillings a week with good pasture and "plenty of grain," but as more and more monied men entered the field, extra charges climbed; see in particular the Nashville *Clarion*, Feb. 22, 1811, *ibid.*, March 8, 1811 and *ibid.*, March 23, 1811 for offerings of the coming season.

particularly the pedigree, was true; among those who both advertised and attested was often Andrew Jackson.[63]

Hand in hand with the interest in the English Thoroughbred of course went that of racing. One of the most famous of early Tennessee's racers was Haynie's Maria,[64] the mare that no horse of Andrew Jackson could ever beat. Pioneer racing did not on the Cumberland wait either for the thoroughbred or the race track. Races between men on horseback are old as the history of the horse, and the first ones on the Cumberland as in Virginia were much like those described by James Adair, extemporaneous affairs down roads with no or only chance spectators.

Quarter racing grew out of this, which meant usually no more than two horsemen, racing one-quarter mile down a road, a form of racing that demanded not only speed but a tremendous acceleration at once. The slow starter never had a chance; a horse trained for quarter racing was no steed for the poor horseman mindful of either dignity or bones.[65]

Even by the time of the Revolution, quarter racing was in Virginia considered a plebeian pastime, and racing on an oval track came quickly to the Cumberland. Horse Hollow, for example, is today a remote place up on the Big South Fork in Wayne County, but the pretty oval of flat land among low hills was by tradition a racecourse used before 1790. The earliest Tennessee *Gazettes* give many announcements of races to be run. One of the most important events of early years was the three-day meet at Columbia. Here, the races of one, two, three, and four mile heats were run "agreeable to the New Market rules," and in 1803 a chief contender was to be the "aged horse" Childress carrying 140 pounds.[66] More famous soon were the meets of the Nashville Jockey Club at Clover Bottom on land once known as "Buchanan's old Fields," [67] but owned in time by Andrew Jackson.

[63] Nashville *Clarion*, March 29, 1811, in which A. Jackson attests to Royalist is typical. Jackson was by this date spending a good deal on horses; one racing horse care bill that covered a period of around two months was $320, Bassett, *Jackson Correspondence*, I, 245.

[64] Guild, *Old Times*, 247–252, gives a colorful account of Haynie's Maria and her great jockey Monkey Simon, for whom a yearly mule race at the Iroquois Meet was named. See also, Wallace, *Horse*, 17–18.

[65] Guild, *Old Times*, 84–88, is the story of how Guild and Bailie Peyton, fledgling lawyers, trained a judge's horse for quarter racing, and is possibly more typical of the methods and attitudes of the pioneer farmer with a good horse and a love of fun, than are the Jackson activities; his were a serious and expensive business—one early racer cost $1000—done in the hope at first of beating Maria; Jackson merely paid the bills, and did not as a rule even select his own animals.

[66] Tennessee *Gazette*, July 13, 1803.

[67] *Ibid.*, March 27, 1805.

The breeders, studhorses, races, and horse farms of Tennessee soon became famous in most parts of the world that loved good horseflesh. The Belle Meade Farm of William Giles Harding, now in the suburbs of Nashville, was outstanding in the United States as were many others. During the twenty-six years, 1834–1859, almost twelve hundred races were won by horses with Tennessee sires; [68] less than seven hundred by horses with sires from all the other states, but the great history of the Thoroughbred in Tennessee is not within the scope of this work. Royalist, bred by the Prince of Wales, and the earliest known name in current pedigrees, was not imported by Joseph Coleman until 1807.[69]

Love of horses on the Cumberland had many developments of which English Thoroughbreds and racing formed only a part. Horse racing was never, even in Middle Tennessee, a universal pastime. Robertson, "father of Tennessee," though he never owned an English Thoroughbred, might also be considered the father of horse breeding in Middle Tennessee, but I found nothing to indicate he was ever interested in racing. He may have felt as did a writer [70] of 1811 who insisted horse racing was a cruel sport that "ruins that noble and vigorous animal and runs him down."

It was out of such love of horseflesh and horseback riding not as a spectator sport, but as a pleasant necessity or enjoyable pastime that three other pure-blooded types, all native to Tennessee, were developed—the American Saddler, Standardbred, and the Tennessee Walking Horse.[71] All came long after Robertson, who would have loved such horses, was dead. Just as dear to the hearts of all as a fine five-gaited saddle horse that could take prizes at the fair was a good horseman or horsewoman.

Years later, surrounded by all the ruin and sorrow of The War, old men's eyes could still brighten in remembering a trip home from a "rousing wedding," of fifty years and more ago at "old Jimmy Dry's on the river. It was so cold they had to gallop from house to house and stop to warm, in order to keep from freezing—and Miss Sally Van Horn led the way. She had a fine well-trained pony, and during the ride her hair came down; she dropped her reins, took off her bonnet, held the strings in her mouth, and with both hands twisted up her hair, replaced her bonnet, and tying the strings, she gathered up her bridle reins without even

[68] Wallace, *Horse*, 18–19.
[69] *Ibid.*, 17.
[70] Nashville *Clarion*, Nov. 12, 1811, quoting *The Boston Chronicle*.
[71] Wallace, *Horse*, 53–79, is a brief and concise history of the development of these breeds and has pictures of the great ones, including Midnight Sun, champion Walking Horse of the world, in 1945, 1946, and Ace's Japanette, along with farms and breeders.

slackening the speed of her horse. The women were all in that day skillful riders." [72]

Miss Sally Van Horn galloping along with her hands in her hair and her bonnet in her teeth represents a little of all the life that revolved around the horse and can never be put into hard cold facts and eludes cold words on paper, needing instead the storyteller's tongue.[73] We never, I am sure, in all our generations had a thoroughbred, but many were the horse stories from Granma's groaning mare to the fine horsestock that starved along with the men when they went north in the War of 1812. Just as the importance of the mill could never quite be measured in the amount of meal ground, so were the livery stable and the blacksmith shop immeasurable in terms of pure business.

Horse swapping was another thing that cannot be reckoned or even discussed in any words I know. Neither business, nor profession, amusing as a rule only to the spectators, it somehow got a hold on certain men—and women, too, at times—that endured through ridicule and poverty unto death. John Lipscomb, crossing the Indian-infested territory between Middle and East Tennessee, had in 1784 time and mind for horse swapping, and so did men swap through the years—while fording or ferrying a river or sitting up with the dead.

It is doubtful if the Cumberland farm wife could know a worse trial than an inveterate horse-swapper for a husband, particularly if his judgement of horseflesh were none too good. All errands of his life were lengthened by the long circumlocution, followed by the equally long dickering, before any horse swap could be finished—and if the newly acquired animal died before he got home, the owner had no recourse, for in the buying or swapping of a horse no warranty was expected or given save in the case of the thoroughbred, and even the many men attesting to the expensive studhorse swore only to his known past performance and to his pedigree.

We suspect that John Faulkner warning all persons not to buy the note for $51 he had promised to pay Micajah Barrow as there was a fraud in the horse for which the note was given [74] got little sympathy for his pains and had to pay the note, for "an opinion has generally prevailed in this

[72] Guild, *Old Times*, 352.

[73] Countless stories, both written and oral, revolved around the horse; the combination of horse and preacher was unbeatable. See Wallace, *Horse*, 16, for the story of the Rev. Mr. Cryer, owner of half a race horse; he was willing for the sake of his congregation to give up the sin of racing, but unable to figure out how to keep his half in the stable while the other owner's half ran.

[74] Tennessee *Gazette*, Oct. 26, 1803.

part of the country that cheating in the sale of horses is no cheating at all." [75]

It was one thing to cheat a man of his back teeth in a horse swap but very much another to steal a sway-back, ancient mare, blind in one eye, and bell-less on the open range. Hatred of the horse thief was universal, but of all crimes horse stealing must have been to the criminal on the Cumberland the most tempting. Pasture continued so scarce for many years that horses of average value often fed on the open range, and horse stealing like murder was during pioneer years almost always blamed on the Indian.

Most any horse was easily stolen; he could be ridden out of the country and sold hundreds of miles away before the owner discovered his loss. The farmer finding a horse, even in his own cornfield, had to do as prescribed [76] by law—in some way advertise the fact. During the first years on the Cumberland this meant telling the neighbors or in some way spreading word. As soon as there was a county seat, strayed animals could during court days and Saturdays be displayed in the stray pen. Governor William Blount in 1790 appointed [77] a stray-master for each county, and the finder then had to tell him. The Nashville newspapers, beginning in 1799, simplified matters; the finder had only to advertise, charging the owner for advertising as well as keep. Judging from the many announcements of strays—all colors, conditions, shapes, sizes, and ages—finders were mightily careful. Typical is the announcement of Samuel Thornton that a yellow bay horse, "14½ hands high, brand C on left shoulder and buttocks," [78] had come to his plantation. Losers also often advertised, sometimes for rather unglamorous beasts as in the case of a "flea bitten horse—paces and trots—carries his tail as if nicked—rather thin in flesh." [79]

Early *Gazettes* also carried, low on the page, small notices—Henry Bieler, for horse stealing, sentence of death; to be executed the 29th. Samuel Carmon, larceny, sentence of death; to be executed the 29th.[80] Andrew Jackson was then, in 1801, judge, and he of all men understood he was not God, able to encompass infinite justice with infinite mercy, and so he ever stuck by justice.

Leniency was at times shown in East Tennessee. The culprit first had

[75] Nashville *Clarion*, June 11, 1811.

[76] Haywood, *Laws*, 257, "An act to prevent abuses in taking up strays." This Tennessee law of 1799 was based upon North Carolina law.

[77] TP, IV, 441.

[78] Tennessee *Gazette*, June 22, 1803.

[79] *Ibid.*, Feb. 3, 1802.

[80] *Ibid.*, Dec. 2, 1801.

his ears nailed to a board; while in this position he was sometimes branded, H on one cheek, T on the other; he was then freed from the board by having his ears cut off, kinder treatment than that given some suspected Tories who were forced to cut off their own ears with dull case knives. Here and there in both print and memories are the old stories of strangers who always wore large wigs; sooner or later someone got curious; the wig was lifted, and lo, the man was earless. This meant he was the lowest of all creatures—a horse thief.

It was a strange thing, but I remember no story of a mule thief or even of a mule, though in time many mules were more valuable than many horses. Mules in time took over much of the work now done by farm machinery and trucks, for the Cumberland Country horsemen were, like most of the others in the South, never interested in importing or developing any breed of the big-footed, hairy-ankled draft horses, soon familiar in Pennsylvania and other states both north and west. Instead the Southerner turned to mules. The breeding of mules was an old, old practice, but had been little followed in the colonies; as early as 1700 John Lawson was pointing out the advantages of the mule to the North Carolinians, and thirty years later Byrd, in the backwoods of Virginia, wished for mules. Nobody was interested. Here and there in accounts of Revolutionary warfare mention is made of a mule having been killed, bought, or stolen, for a few had been bred, chiefly in Connecticut.[81]

Mules became more fashionable when, after the Revolution, the King of Spain presented George Washington a jack and jennet, but breeding progressed slowly. There were a few on the Cumberland; Luke Anderson[82] rode a mule to the Battle of Nickojack in 1794, and a few were undoubtedly brought up from Spanish Florida where they were common. Victor Collot as early as 1796 commented[83] on a Louisiana cane mill powered by five mules, but no early visitor to the Cumberland mentioned mules, nor did I find them in early inventories or advertisements. The earliest announcement found for jacks at stud was not until 1812—that of Samson and Nimrod near Nashville.[84] This does not mean none was around, but does indicate rarity.

[81] ASP, Finance, I, 455 —79 stud jacks and almost 600 mules.

[82] W, 1S, 93.

[83] George Henri Victor Collot, *A Journey in North America* (1796), tr. from the French by J. Christian Bay, copyright, O Lange Firenze, New York, 1924 (cited hereafter as Collot, *Journey 1796*), II, 196. Collot did not visit the Cumberland, but his account of travel, commerce, and industry in the Mississippi Valley helps form a basis of comparison.

[84] Nashville *Clarion*, May 6, 1812.

Soon, however, Middle Tennessee was famous for mules as well as horses, and continued to be until World War II when the already familiar shift to mechanization of the farm was speeded up. In 1890 the Jack Stock Breeding Association, organized two years before in Missouri, met at the fashionable Maxwell House in Nashville. Many were the exciting tales told by members who had scoured the mountains and lowlands of Spain and France in search of better jack stock. Fabulous prices were paid for the King of Inca, Jumbo Giant, Longfellow, Benjamin Franklin, and Napoleon—all giant imported jacks, some 16½ hands high. These and like jacks found mates among Black Ann, Black Girl, Belle of Tennessee, Bonnie Kate, and other fine jennets, most 16 hands high.[85]

The male offspring of such a union, the jack, would be shipped to some farm in a neighboring state and there live out his life in loneliness, never again to find a mate among his own kind, but see only mares, proud beauties that quite often scorned his services. In time there were, in some Tennessee counties, more mules than horses [86] and the mule instead of the horse became the dependence of the "one-horse farmer," for no animal could live on so little and work for so long as the mule. His future development was planted in Middle Tennessee during pioneer years by men like James Robertson with his many fine mares, for good mules could never be dropped by poor mares. Yet the mule, important as he came to be, was as lacking in glamour as the family cow and most other domesticated animals save the horse.

[85] The pictures of these and their life stories may be found in *The Jack Stock Stud Book*.

[86] Louis D. Wallace, Ed., *Farming and Progress, the 37th Biennial Report of the Tennessee Department of Agriculture*, Nashville, 1948 (cited hereafter as Wallace, *37th Report*), 314–315, gives the overall story in statistics of mules in 95 Tennessee counties; see also *ibid.*, 442–443. Concentration was heaviest in West Tennessee, Fayette County of 1935 had almost four times as many mules as horses, and in Henderson, *ibid.*, 490–491, the ratio was seven to one.

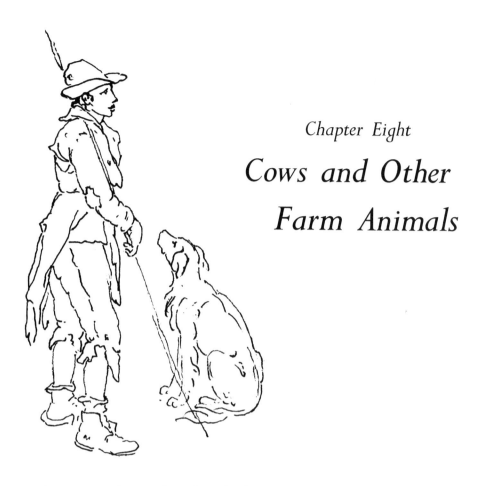

Chapter Eight

Cows and Other
Farm Animals

ANY FORTED farm such as that of Edwin Hickman was a world of animal sounds—squealing, gobbling, nickering, bawling, bleating, grunting, howling, barking, neighing, meowing (cats were scarce but I found mention of a cat hole even in a temporary camp), whining, cackling, crowing, potracking, and baaing of their many horses, cattle, hogs, sheep, and fowls, sometimes penned and often congregating near the fort walls.

It is true that king of these animals was the horse; none other could compare with him for first place in value, glamour, beauty, and usefulness. The Cumberlander with no family—midwife, young single lawyer, or traveling trader—usually neither needed nor wanted anything but horse-stock. Even the cow and her progeny seem at first glance to have been during pioneer years taken pretty much for granted as was the pack horse. Nameless and of no definable breed, cattle are mentioned by travelers and in stories of the old ones as only incidental to more important matters.

A backwoodsman and his dog.

All farming families brought cattle. The Cumberland with its cane, wild grasses, and clovers was a cow's paradise as it had been for the deer and the buffalo. They fed on the open range and multiplied; all sizes, conditions, and ages—black cattle descended from the black cattle of Scotland, the white such as Dr. Thomas Walker had, spotted, pied, red, brown, yellow, the pied red cow, barren white-faced cow, red yearling heifer, dun bull for $1.25, muley cow, horned cow, sawed horn cow, the bred heifer, and the fat steer.[1]

Only a small percentage of the early cows knew the semicivilized life of "the good old milk cow," prized for her milk and butter. Most cattle went into beef, so plentiful that all through pioneer years it was cheaper than pork, and in time much Tennessee beef was shipped south, but the Cumberland Country was only a part of the bigger story of cattle on the frontier. Forerunners of the plow and fenced field, cattle on the open range had, at the settlement of the Cumberland, long been a part of Southern frontier life, and it is doubtful if any pioneer farmer had the thousand head and more owned by some North and South Carolina planters eighty years before.

Small herds of from fifty to a hundred head, wintering in a canebrake, were a common part of frontier life in the very early years. Daniel Smith as he went down the Cumberland in March of 1780 saw a herd in what would now be Cumberland County, Kentucky; the Donelsons wintered their cattle in a canebrake on the Clinch; Robertson's cattle after getting to Middle Tennessee spent the rest of the winter near Kaspar Mansker's; and up in Kentucky grazing was by this date so scarce on Dick's River that William Sloan drove his cattle over to Salt River to winter on the cane.[2]

In my opinion cane as a cattle food was vastly over-rated. During our first year in the Cumberland National Forest we wintered a few head in the canebrakes on the Big South Fork, and thither must we go to hunt them. The cane was much smaller than the thirty-foot plants found by Michaux; still, it was almost impossible to walk through, hot and filled with snakes in summer; slow, bitter walking in winter when there was something unreasonable about the green cane leaves above ice and snow. Judging from the numbers of cane hoes early farmers had, and the quick-

---

[1] Practically all families with farming tools had cattle, but for variety and good descriptions see in particular: DW, I, 175–176, William Gowens; *ibid.*, I, 283, William Overall; MW, I, 27–28, Charles Fease; *ibid.*, I, 118, Robert Edmonson.

[2] W, 29S, 121.

ness with which the plant disappeared,[3] the average farmer liked it as little as did we.

Cane was prized by farmers whose herds on the open range constituted their most important source of livelihood, but the Indian Wars were scarcely ended before cattle in a canebrake disappeared from most of Middle Tennessee. As early as the winter of 1799 several families with around sixty head of cattle stopped on Flinn's Creek south of the Cumberland. In spite of many children, "without roof or lodging" in that cold and sunless place they planned to winter so their more than sixty head of cattle might find grazing. At the same time other families were emigrating from the more thickly settled parts of Middle Tennessee to the Caney Fork Country so their cattle could winter in the canebrake.[4]

Middle Tennessee was not yet twenty years old, but plantations dotted the road between Fort Blount and Nashville. The open range in what are now Smith, Sumner, and Davidson counties was already gone. True, cattle grazing in the rougher wooded lands and remnants of canebrakes would be a part of farm life in the more remote and unsettled regions on the Plateau and up river for the next one hundred and fifty years, but in the main cattlemen would seek the wider world west of the Mississippi. There, in Texas and elsewhere the pattern of cowboys watching range-bred herds, established in the Southern colonies long before the Revolution, would flourish, while disappearing from the more fertile lands of the Middle South.

The pioneer milk cow curling her tongue around tender cane leaves, returning at twilight to her calf penned by the fort walls, or as in the case of Buchanan's, rushing home at odd hours and so giving news of lurking Indians, was a different story. Never with the glamour that surrounded the horse and in time the cow-tenders of the West, she was possibly for many the best beloved and sometimes the most highly prized of all the farm animals. The horse conjures up visions of deeds of derring-do—men charging into battle or betting their all on the outcome of a race. The pioneer cow, scrawny, pretty by no known standard, brings visions of women and children, and churns warming on hearthstones. It was unthinkable that any young married couple, no matter how poor, should start life without at least one cow, and usually the girl had one or more as a part of

---

[3] Thwaites, *Travels*, III, Michaux, "Journal," did not mention cane in Middle Tennessee until reaching Fort Blount. Later travelers seldom commented upon cane at all. Hogs more than hoes seem to have accounted for its quick disappearance.

[4] Williams, *Travels*, Schweinitz, "Report," 505.

her dowry. The first settlers on the Cumberland were for the most part of British descent, and dairy products had long formed a large and important part of their diet. Even single men, soldiering, hunting, or trading as was Charles Morgan in the Illinois, complained if they had no milk and butter, and the per capita consumption was undoubtedly higher than now.

The old ones writing of childhoods on the borders almost always remembered the family cow, though few with as much fondness as did Dr. Daniel Drake on whose boyhood farm the cow was so gently tended she seemed almost a member of the family. Boys did not learn to milk, but at milking time there had to be a boy or so to help get the calf away from the cow, and when the country grew safe from Indians children hunted the often straying ones. As game grew scarcer the emigrating family—as in the case of John Smith's, moving from East Tennessee to Stockton's Valley—usually had no fresh food save milk from the cows they drove. Travelers first in the old South and later in the West often praised the good milk and butter.

Springhouses were common in Middle Tennessee before the Indian Wars were ended,[5] and nothing could be quite so pleasant on a hot summer day as a good stone springhouse, so built that cold spring water flowed over the floor. Set in deep shade, often of a sycamore, and best on the side of a hill so that the spring could flow from deep underground and be cold, the springhouse was in summer a storehouse of good things—butter, cheese, buttermilk, fresh milk, sweet cream, watermelons, muskmelons, and all food that was best kept chilled. Smelling faintly in summer of peppermint that almost always grew near by, it had something no refrigerator can ever have, and a good one even in the coldest weather kept the milk from freezing. Peculiarly American, developed largely on the Piedmont where the happy combination of limestone lands with many underground streams made them possible and extreme summer heat unknown in England made them a necessity, springhouses were replanted on each succeeding frontier until the Mississippi was reached, and the world of springs bubbling from the sides of hills ended along with the building materials. Strange to most travelers from Europe, many were the comments upon them, but they continued to be the joy of some up-river farm wives until the 1940's when REA put electricity in even remote valleys. Early, the springhouse was not enough for many, and by 1811 advertisements [6] for plantations mention dairies, for the pioneer milk cow, scrawny

[5] W, 31S, 390, is typical; an ambush by an Indian, "hiding behind the spring house."
[6] Nashville, *Clarion*, March 1, 1811.

as she was, planted an industry on the Cumberland that would in time bring fame to Middle Tennessee.

The wives of first settlers crowded into forts could at best have nothing more than temporary log springhouses shared with neighbors, but most inventories listed churn with "staff" or dasher, as we up river and many others said. The Jacob Castlemans might be taken as a fair example of a pioneer family, trying to fill some of its needs through the trading or selling of butter.[7] The father, killed in 1784, had less livestock than most—eight cows, eight calves, six heifers, two sheep, a lamb, and two saddle mares.

He is remembered primarily as a brave man, and one of the many who got nothing for his services in Kentucky. His wife, Eve, might also be remembered as one of Middle Tennessee's first dairy women. It was not that Mrs. Castleman had more cows and calves than anyone else, but they did comprise the largest proportion of the total assets of the family in any inventory studied, and in the cows, heifers, and calves, the three coolers, three pails, two churns, and one milk piggin we see the work and plans of Mrs. Castleman.[8]

Busy she was; the activity that went on about the "milk vessels" was endless—scrubbing, airing, sunning, scalding, for the wild yeast the housewife encouraged in her pot of emptins ruined fresh milk, clabbering it before the cream rose, and as most containers were of wood, the job of perfect cleanliness was not easy. The pioneer housewife overcame many hazards to make good milk and butter. In hot weather, even when the milk was properly cooled and skimmed, there was still the danger the cream would sour too fast, and the butter come white and puffy. Puffy butter was of course not fit to eat, and the buttermilk from too rapidly soured cream was wheyey, fit only for the chickens. On the other hand if the cream was left too long in a cold springhouse, it would sour too slowly and be too cold for churning. In winter even the best of housewives could fall behind in her churnings, so that around the hearth in most farm homes in cold weather was the clabbering cream, slowly warming under the watchful eye of the wife; if it got too hot it was ruined, but if it never warmed at all the butter would come slowly amidst a great frothing of milk; once come, it wouldn't gather and the churning would take forever.

---

[7] Tennessee *Gazette*, Nov. 20, 1802; *ibid.*, May 30, 1804, listed bacon at only $7. per CWT, but butter was 25c a pound.

[8] DW, I, 194.

Not all churns were described and the barrel type turned with a
crank that can now be seen in The Hermitage may have been there, but
all descriptions found were of churns "with staff," and whenever wood
was mentioned it was cedar. Even to my childhood the red cedar churn,
powered by the hand and the dasher, was quite commonly used in families making butter chiefly for home use.

I knew no other, though ours had copper instead of wooden bands,
and around it, many were the anxious ponderings, the debates, and the
wonderings that went on between my mother and one or other of the
grandmothers. Summer and the sound of gathering butter come too soon,
for housewives such as my mother cooked and worked by sound [9] as well
as by sight and taste; when the jelly "smoked its pipes," and sounded just
so, it was done; my mother could be in another room and hear the chicken
frying, know it was getting too hot, and rush in just in time; so did she
and my grandmothers hear the churn, and sad was the sound when the
butter sounded puffy, but somehow it never was.

More anxious still was the debate in winter when the butter wouldn't
come or gather if it did come, and the milk sounded cold; could they or
could they not risk a little hot water; sometimes they did at the risk of ruining the buttermilk, but fresh buttermilk was never much good; it ought to
be two or three days old, fairly thickish with little dots of butter, firm, but
bright yellow only in summer. Once the butter was gathered there followed the washing, the slight working, the setting aside until next day
when it was worked again, salt added, but not too much. It was then
molded, and I never did know the flower in the butter mold, or "moles,"
as pioneer apprentice clerks often spelled it.

A dull siege of churning when I alone thought the milk sounded cold,
but nobody agreed and hence no hot water to hasten matters was often
brightened by Granma's stories of the old days when the antics of the
milk in the churn were blamed on witches. Such a story at such a time
was logical for always the witches of England, Scotland, and the South—
less feared than those of New England—had shown a fondness for med-

---

[9] The pioneers, like generations of country people before and many since, used
their senses more than people now do in a ready-measured world. I used to hear
stories of the women who need never go into the loomhouse; sounds of the looms and
spinning wheels told them all they needed to know; just as they and their menfolks,
even when abed in a tight log house knew the direction of the wind from the sound.
There are still a few men who never need rulers; they know to a fraction the width
of their thumbs, exactly how to place their hands to make a foot, can walk by a
horse and know its height, and with fair exactitude judge the acreage of a field.

dling in the dairy, and did all manner of things from keeping cows from giving down their milk to making bright yellow butter in winter.

It is doubtful if the smallish, thin-flanked pioneer milk cows on the Cumberland were much troubled by witches; they were too busy eluding Indians, nor should we think of them in terms of breeds. It was not until around 1795 that the first purebred dairy cows were brought to America, and these Holsteins to Pennsylvania. The Jersey cow on which the great butter-producing herds of Middle Tennessee were in time built was not a part of pioneer life.

The first milk cows on the Cumberland were, like those in the colonies, no more than general purpose animals selected for their milk-giving qualities, or because as heifers they looked as if they might give milk. The very early laws in the South aimed at producing better horsestock were not applied to cattle, and there was no systematic breeding of dairy cows; a heifer calf might be saved from a high-producing mother, but in a range-bred calf nobody knew the bull. Dairying, as in any frontier community where such corn and fodder as there was had usually to go to horsestock, was pretty much a seasonal matter; calves were dropped in the spring, and the cows gave milk enough for both calf and piggen to make milking worth while for some months. In most years the Cumberland had dry late summers and pasture was not too good. The calf might or might not be weaned, for hunting the cows with no calves to bring them home was a dangerous job, and a cow that had calved in the woods cost Samuel Barton, hunting her, a gunshot wound from Indians.

The pioneer cow, judged by today's standards, was no dairy animal at all, possibly averaging no more than three gallons a day under the best of conditions; a pure guess, but it was some years since old Five Pints [10] of Maryland had received the name in gratitude for the large amount of milk she gave at each milking—five pints.

North Carolina cows were by the time of the Revolution averaging two or three quarts at a milking, though dairying as practiced on the Western borders of that colony was a purely seasonal matter, and more like the pattern in the rougher lands up river where even the milk cow was expected to get most of her feed from the woods. In spring the herd of milk cows was driven into some good grazing area that might as in the

---

[10] Used by permission of the copyright owner and publisher the Carnegie Institution of Washington from *History of Agriculture in the Southern United States to 1860* by Lewis Cecil Gray, Washington, 1933 (cited hereafter as Gray, *Agriculture*), I, 205.

case of Daniel Boone's family be several miles from home. Pens were built for the calves, and sometimes larger ones to hold the cows at night.[11] If close enough for daily trips, the farm wife and her help carried on their dairying with home as a base, but often a group spent summer at the cow pens making butter and cheese enough to last for some months. The calves, the only thing to bring the cows in from the woods, were never weaned, but returned to the cows when the milk flow slackened.

Such cows could not be expected to give as much as Tabitha Bramble's Aldernay of 1750 that with good English pasture gave four gallons daily after her calf was sold, and this amount, though milk of fiction, is probably closer the yield of the cows of the dairy-minded plantation owners of early Middle Tennessee than that of old Five Pints.

Milk, beef, and butter with a little cheese and, of course, clabber were the prime products of cattle on the Cumberland, but like cattle elsewhere in the United States they also furnished hides for leather and steers for work oxen. Leather in the early days was scarce and none of the first settlers studied owned "work-steers," nor did I find mention of ox shoes, ox yokes, chance accounts of oxen being shot in the Indian Wars, or travelers who met ox carts as they met horse-drawn wagons. All in all, oxen seem to have been little used until close to 1800, and then, compared to steers that often sold for as little as $4, they were expensive; each of the two pair found bringing more than $40.[12] As horses became more expensive, oxen grew more common even in Middle Tennessee, and though never rivaling horses and mules as a source of power, they for a time had a definite place in the scheme of things, particularly industry. Montgomery Bell and other iron manufacturers [13] used them in hauling ore, and up river [14] they continued to be used for a few jobs almost until the present.

Following the cattle about the barnyard, rooting in the canebrakes,

[11] William Bartram, *Travels through North and South Carolina, Georgia, East and West Florida, the Cherokee Country*, Philadelphia, 1791, 310, gives a good description of a North Carolina cow pen of 1776, and dairying on a frontier unhampered by Indians.

[12] MW, II, 40; also Coffee Papers, 1804; though the year before in 1803 Coffee had in his "Estimates for Working the Salines" planned to use horses for even the heavy work of hauling salt.

[13] Dr. Gerard Troost, *Fifth Geological Report of the State of Tennessee*, Nashville 1840 (cited hereafter as Troost, *Fifth Report*), 35–36, gives a summary of the mules, oxen, slaves, and corn needed to do the work of one iron furnace.

[14] Wallace, *37th Report*, does not list oxen, never at anytime numerous as compared to horses, after the 1890 census. I once rode in an ox cart, but this in Lee County, Ky., where they were used chiefly to move heavy oil well drilling machinery and supplies.

wandering through the muddy streets of young Nashville to nose among the piles of smoking horse manure for corn was the barrow, the sow with her squealing litter, the gilt, and less commonly the boar. Hogs were ever plentiful but considering the high price of pork as compared to beef, and how much less often hogs are mentioned than horses and cattle in chance accounts of Indian warfare, the hog never became really abundant until around 1790. One might better say pork did not become plentiful, for the hogs offered for sale went at pitifully low prices.[15] William Neely's twenty head of hogs sold for only $15, though many of these may have been small pigs, but as late as 1787 a sow and six pigs brought only three pounds, and at about the same time Frederick Stump, ever a canny trader, paid $146, six shillings for four cows with calves, a yearling steer, and a bull. True, everything depended upon the quality of the animals; a second-rate cow with a scrub calf might not bring half the price of a fine sow, but this ratio of low hogs and high cows was fairly consistent all through the first ten years or so. The main reason for cheap hogs was scarcity of corn for fattening; hogs would grow and breed on the open range in Middle Tennessee; they could keep alive on cane shoots, but compared to the Highland Rim there was little mast and they wouldn't fatten.

As corn became more plentiful, hogs increased in price; in 1794 William Gowen's ten barrows brought thirty pounds, eleven shillings, as compared to only three pounds, five shillings for a cow and calf.[16] In 1799 a white barrow belonging to Robert Edmonson sold for $6;[17] pork was at that time selling for around three cents a pound after salting; and thus we can be certain that such an animal was, like the Gowen hogs, a pen-fattened porker of good quality weighing between five and six hundred pounds.

As the years passed, bringing plenty of corn and cheaper salt, pork grew more abundant, and became an important export—pork from Kentucky and Tennessee fed the field hands in the deeper South. It is doubtful if in the early years any farmer ever got rich selling pork at $7.50 per 196 pound barrel, and beef at $6.[18] The barrel itself never cost less than 75

---

[15] DW, I, 166, 230.

[16] *Ibid.*, I, 175–176.

[17] MW, I, 117–118. See also Bassett, *Jackson Correspondence*, V, 422, though many years past the pioneer period, it indicates good-sized hog stock in Tennessee as Jackson wanted breeding animals from a neighbor whose stock averaged 400 pounds.

[18] This was the Natchez price as listed in the Tennessee *Gazette*, May 30, 1804. Prices fluctuated; see *ibid.*, Nov. 13, 1802, and the Coffee Papers, 1799–1804. The

cents and more commonly a dollar; down river freight was sometimes 2½ cents to New Orleans, and the cost of salting could run to 75 cents. I found no salt pork shipped during pioneer years, though John Coffee now and then carried bacon as part of a cargo, for it often sold for 18 cents a pound.

Locally, pork was another story. The pig in some form—on foot, bacon, lard, or salted—became one of the most common forms of legal tender for smallish amounts. Prospective breeders without cash for the high stud fee for Atlas were invited to bring pork,[19] and in 1812 Benjamin Bradford, owner and publisher of the Nashville *Clarion*, suggested somewhat wistfully that "A few hundredweight of pork would be taken from those indebted to the editor."

The big fat hog munching corn in a rail pen was only part of the story of hogs on the Cumberland. Judging from the low price brought by some hogs, many may have been much like certain Southern hogs of three hundred years ago as described by a startled Englishman. "The real American hog," he wrote, "is what is termed the wood hog; they are long in the leg, narrow in the back, short in the body, flat in the sides, with a long snout, very rough in their hair, in make more like the fish called a perch than anything I can describe. . . . They will go to a distance from a fence, take a run, and leap through the rails three or four feet from the ground, turning themselves sidewise. These hogs suffer such hardship as no other animal could endure."[20]

Less than thirty years ago there were still ownerless "razor-backs" in remote bends of the Cumberland above Smith Shoals, but trying to catch one, even with two good hog dogs was a dangerous job. They were probably descendants of animals strayed from neighboring farms, though the first known Englishman, Gabriel Arthur, to visit the Cherokee had in 1674 gone wild hog hunting with them. These early hogs were possibly descended from those brought by De Soto. Whatever his antecedents a wild hog was a fearsome thing; stories revolving around them were bloodcurdling, and childhood trips to the local bank were enlivened by the boar's skull on the door; most fascinating of course were the tusks, several

---

Revolution had given the meat-packing industry in America quite a setback; in 1791 only 66,000 barrels of salt beef and pork were shipped from the whole United States. The Cumberlander could scarcely compete with Ireland, even on the eastern seaboard; Ireland could sell a barrel of pork in Philadelphia for $8.; see Carey, *Museum*, IX, 122.

[19] Nashville *Clarion*, March 22, 1811.
[20] Gray, *Agriculture*, I, 206, quoting Parkinson's "Tour."

inches long. Years later in the back hills I knew a man who was split "clean to the bone from hip socket to ankle joint," by the tusk of a razorback, but different from those in the stories, he got well. Wild hogs in Middle Tennessee were not too common, though I did in Montgomery County records meet a "clan," [21] but past the pioneer period.

Tennessee was by 1803 on the way to becoming corn and hog capital as well as center of horse breeding and dairying. The War wrecked many things,[22] while the rapid settlement of the present corn belt with the introduction of farm machinery, further changed the agricultural pattern; but after The War, Tennessee brought the Jersey to her present day perfection, developed the first butter-testing apparatus in the country, discovered hog cholera serum,[23] developed a corn that would consistently yield two ears to the stalk, became famous as a center of both jack and mule breeding, and had long been noted for sheep and wool.

The seeds of all these achievements were planted, one might say, as Robertson, Stump, Jennings, Amos Eaton, the Buchanans, and others came through the woods with their herds, droves, and clans. Sheep were also destined to bring glory to Middle Tennessee; in 1835 Mark Robertson Cockrill owned sheep that won the grand prize in Kentucky in competition with those of Henry Clay, considered the best in the United States. In 1851 the grand prize in London for the best wool in the world went to sheep owned also by Mark Robertson Cockrill,[24] then farming in Davidson County, Tennessee.

Yet for all this, sheep were the one seed of Tennessee's agricultural future that, though planted, did not flourish in the early years. The Cumberland like the Piedmont was, in the matter of natural grazing, good sheep country; but if the hog stands for hardihood and self-sufficiency, the sheep occupies the opposite end of the scale; wolves, panthers, bears, wildcats, eagles, not to mention the family dog, were all enemies of sheep. Unlike a pig, a sheep could be bitten in the nose and die of snakebite; in regions where there was mountain ivy he would in winter, when snow covered the fern and dried grass, eat it and die; like the cow the sheep had to be salted, but, unlike the cow, he needed shelter from the

[21] MW, I, 432.

[22] Wallace, *37th Report*, 452–453, showed some increase of sheep in Sumner County between 1816 and 1870; but other animals declined; horsestock by one-third in Davidson, *ibid.*, 396.

[23] Wallace, *Millions*, "The Story of Dr. Marion Dorset," III, 1–79.

[24] *Ibid.*, "Mark Robertson Cockrill," II, 1–65.

cold rains so much a part of fall and winter all up and down the Cumberland; yet, unlike the cow, horse, and hog, he could not survive penned up over long periods, but needed enough wide fields to give a change from time to time.

Sheep in the earliest days were less commonly owned than any other farm animal save mules and work-steers. Those found in inventories were most probably survivors of larger flocks that had started to the Cumberland. Badly needed as was wool and scarce as sheep were, nobody seemed much interested in taking the risk of trying to keep them alive. Six belonging to Nicholas Gentry sold in 1781 for only four shillings,[25] though his cow brought only six shillings, two pounds less than his bullet molds. William Neely's widow had fourteen pounds of wool in 1791, but only one sheep and it sold for only a dollar.[26] The Jacob Castlemans had only two sheep and a lamb, and most of the early farm families studied had none.

There were by the mid-nineties small flocks of from ten to twenty head,[27] and the growing demand is reflected in the better price of around three dollars each. Wool remained scarce and expensive in all the United States, bringing 33⅓ cents at Philadelphia in 1790,[28] and was by 1804 selling for 20 cents on the Cumberland, that is when it could be bought at all.[29] Most wool in the early years was used at home in cloth or stockings or gloves or sold already made into such articles. However, the wool sold at John Blackamore's sale in 1804 had little in common with that later produced by Mark Robertson Cockrill's flock. The prize wool was from purebred Merinos of imported ancestry. Broadcloth made of American Merino was to the men's clothing industry what vicuña was in 1958, and President James Monroe was inaugurated wearing clothes of American Merino.[30] As early as 1812 a farmer could buy near Nashville purebred Merino rams and ewes with certificates from "men of character in North Carolina," attesting to their breeding for only $400,[31] a suspiciously low price as a good ram often sold for $2,500.

---

[25] DW, I, 7; see also Jacob Castleman, *ibid.*, I, 194, one sheep one dollar; and William Ramsey, *ibid.*, I, 176, 2 sheep, 20 shillings, same price as a grubbing hoe.

[26] *Ibid.*, I, 231–232. See also *ibid.*, II, 348—John Blackamore's 20 lbs of wool, $20.

[27] MW, I, 28, 117, 433.

[28] Carey, *Museum*, II, 189.

[29] I never found wool mentioned in store accounts or freight shipments, and Michaux, *Travels 1802*, 263, commented on the scarcity of sheep.

[30] Wallace, *Millions*, II, 12.

[31] Nashville *Clarion*, July 28, 1812.

There were in time on the Cumberland sheep farms, as well as horse farms and dairy farms. Most farmers had a preference; some like Robertson specialized in good saddle horses, others of later days like Giles Harding and General W. H. Jackson of Belle Meade were noted for the English Thoroughbred. On the opposite end of animal husbandry were the families who practiced herding as their main form of agriculture, but all farmers' inventories studied listed several kinds of livestock.[32] The Edmonsons had fair amounts of just about all animals save mules and work-steers.

All farm animals, except the few horses that could be kept in the fort yards, were in the first years on the open range; and in the sparsely settled districts they continued to be, almost until the present. The problem of finding was partially solved by the bell; men, boys, girls, and women hunting horses, cows, sheep, and hogs were ever a part of life on the Cumberland as elsewhere in the South; even planters like Andrew Jackson who kept everything under fence had constantly to wrestle with the problem of strong animals and weak fence. However, such farmers as he in later days never had to use bells; in pioneer days the bell was a must. John Porter, killed before he could claim and settle his land, had nine bells for his eight horses and twenty head of cattle; William Neely had four, and even young David Gowens, killed in 1781, had along with "two cows each with calf" and two heifers, one bell.

Bells were of all grades and sizes. There were little ones for the sheep,[33] big fancy ones for the horses that often sold for more than $2, but seldom for as much as the $4.50 brought by one of Joseph Conrad's bells with a collar, or earlier a bell belonging to Thomas McCain, bringing one pound, eleven shillings. Like everything else, bells served as currency; a historian tells of a "clear toned bell" that with a rifle was swapped for 640 acres of land.[34]

Digging in my garden one day down on Indian Creek, I found a small bell, little more than a sheet of copper, roughly rolled into a cone, the edges lapped but not welded, and the clapper an irregular chunk of rusted iron; it had plainly been manufactured on some farm forge. Such bells

---

[32] DW, I, 16, 54, 45, 166, 176, 176, 194, 183, are in order the inventories of Harrod, Ruddle, Porter, Neely, Ramsey, Gowens, Castleman, and Overall. All were first or very early settlers; all had farming tools; all were killed before 1795, most before 1790, but each had a different combination of livestock.

[33] MW, I, 433, 2 bells, 37½¢.

[34] Parton, *Jackson*, I, 138, quoting Putnam.

graced the bellwether, for sheep with their close-herding instinct needed fewer bells than did horses or cattle. One can in the early wills and deeds of Middle Tennessee see the advance of fenced fields, for even as early as 1790 bells in proportion to animals were fewer, and by 1795 good farmers such as the Edmonsons must have kept most of their animals behind fence for they had few bells. Hogs were an exception; the prize sow that could bear twelve to a litter and suckle them all may have worn a bell, but I never heard of a hog bell.

Once the owner found his animal in woods or canebrake, he must be able to identify the beast, for it was only the stallion, the "good bay mare," or "the gelding that both trots and canters" that could be proven in court by name and description. Less outstanding horsestock was branded, an old custom going past Western civilization and early used in the New World; by 1700 traders to the Indian nations were branding both pack horses and Indian burden bearers. Branding irons were commonly owned by first settlers.[35] Even without an iron, the Cumberland pioneer farmer, forever having to make-do, could still brand, and at least one mare was "branded on the off cushion with a pot hook." Brands on the Cumberland were, as a whole, somewhat fancier than those used later in Texas and the West—there were diamonds, fleurs de lis, squares and circles,[36] almost always accompanied by initials, and in the case of cattle, earmarkings also.[37]

A few cattle were found with brands as their only means of identification; "All the above cattle are branded with a large T on the off cushion." Most, however, like sheep and hogs had earmarkings. Earmarking like branding was used in Virginia and the Southern colonies before 1650.[38] Everybody who kept farm animals must, as soon as a county was established, record his brand and earmarkings with the county clerk.

Mark Robertson's stock mark as recorded in Davidson County in 1784 was a swallow fork and an underkeil in each ear. Obediah Terrell recorded a "crop and an underkeil in the right ear and a cut downward in each side of the point of the left," and, not taking any chances, also the brand *OT*. Isaac Bledsoe, in addition to a branded diamond containing his initials, had a crop and a slit in the right ear, with an underkeil in the left. The cattle

[35] DW, I, 166, 230, 252, 283.

[36] DC, I, 19.

[37] All early counties on Cumberland have numerous stock-mark records; see in particular, DC, I, 8, 15-21, 41—this last the stock mark of John Rains.

[38] Gray, *Agriculture*, I, 140.

and hogs belonging to John Rains traveling toward the Cumberland in the winter of 1779–1780 had a crop, a slit, and an underkeil in each ear, while Benjamin Drake who came with the Stumps and the Eatons used a crop and an underkeil in the left ear, an underkeil in the right, and also a brand—*BD*.

There were underkeils, overkeils, crops, holes, squares, swallow forks, overbits, underbits, under slopes, smooth crops, and the half penny— known as the "rogue's mark"[39] because it was easily changed to either an underbit or an overbit. Marking was done usually with shears; an expert[40] could fold the ear and with one clip come up with whatever was desired, a half penny or an underbit, neatly as a woman cutting quilt pieces, but, lacking shears, a man could use his pocketknife.

The combinations of marks were seemingly endless, but by 1788 they were getting so scarce that Thomas Hardiman bought the mark of Obediance Gower. The same mark was used on the family stock until sons and daughters got old enough to have their own; and as soon as the young-one was old enough to "make his mark," he had to think up some combination not yet recorded and not easily changed.

There was one animal that needed no marking, could never be stolen by the Indians, never had a bell, could somehow live through the leanest of seasons, and was almost never lost or strayed. This was the family dog. In and out through all the early history of the Cumberland and on down until today was the dog, hated by sheepmen, but a must for the pioneer. Time and again settlers were saved from the Indians as were Freelands by the warning bark of watch dogs; others such as McFadden, who "would have been killed except for three or four large dogs who kept the Indians at bay,"[41] were saved by fighting dogs; while others were kept from starvation by hunting dogs; twelve to fifteen of these "powerful dogs" were owned by many families, some when well trained were valued to the "worth of a horse."

[39] I am indebted to several old-timers, notably my mother, for a description of each mark with a drawing; most names were indicative of their shape—a half penny half a circle, etc., but several I have been unable to find. WC, I, 25, for example yields an "under half fox;" the "swallow folk," *ibid.*, I, 26, in left crop is possibly an example of phonetic spelling, for even today in this section *fork* in the mouths of many sounds somewhat like *folk;* but overkick is also confusing.

[40] There was no stock enclosure law in the community of the Big South Fork to which we moved in 1939, and sheep known as "Piney Wood yoes" continued to range in the Cumberland National Forest until around 1950, and were the only animals with ear markings; unrecorded, yet in that sparsely settled section each owner knew those of his neighbors.

[41] W, 30S, 243.

Even more indispensable to the average farmer was the general-purpose farm dog; the first fences were often makeshift brush-affairs, and it was the dog that saved the crop, keeping out the wandering hogs and cattle, a greater menace than the wild things. The average family needed several dogs for few were so versatile as Daniel Drake's old Lion,[42] but many general-purpose dogs could go on the hunt for big game, catch chickens for cooking, guard the children from rattlesnakes and copperheads, help round up the hogs and cattle, or turn the squirrels if his master wanted to pay a part of his taxes in "squirrel scalps."

Yet for all his mighty services he was so little appreciated that the earliest one officially recognized by name was Tennessee Lead in 1852, and he a hound, but a mighty one since he was foundation sire of the present day Walker. The dogs that helped save French Lick Station are immortalized in a painting in the State Capitol Building, but by 1812 civilization was so far advanced Editor Bradford of the *Clarion* was complaining, "We cannot too earnestly call the attention of the citizens of Tennessee to the erroneous habits of the country in rearing too many dogs, every man, woman, or child in many cases having one or more." The Cumberlander continued to love his dogs, and one of the longest trials in the history of Grundy County, far south on the Plateau, was the damage suit for the hearing of Sharp, the slow-track hound, ruined, or so it was alleged, by the defendant's noisy puppies.[43]

Sharing the work of the watchdog were sometimes a flock of forever "potracking" guineas, better than a butler and a watchdog combined at announcing company, but as late as 1794 guineas were still so scarce that one brought $4,[44] the price of a fair-sized steer or two or three good-sized, but unfattened, hogs.

Beloved as the guinea was, she had not the regal air that made a peacock in the barnyard, supplying fly-shoos for the table, a must for any respectable family past the pioneer stage, and the two of these together could not rival the goose. At John Law's sale in 1794 eight geese brought six pounds,[45] eight shillings, as compared to four pounds, sixteen shillings

---

[42] Drake, *Letters*, 51–52.

[43] Guild, *Old Times*, 452–8. The first trial lasted only a week, but as the plaintiff was awarded a damage—$2.50—too low for acceptance for the hearing of a slow-track hound, his lawyers managed to get new trials, not once but for several years.

[44] DW, II, 9.

[45] *Ibid.*, I, 308; *Ibid.*, II, 229, and MW, I, 433.

for four two-year-old heifers, an unheard-of high price, but feathers were selling at a dollar a pound, hard money. Geese for many years brought more than a dollar each, and feathers were long quoted at fifty cents a pound or more.[46] The goose was undoubtedly queen of the poultry yard, even though she had sometimes to wear sticks about her neck to keep her from slipping through the fence; fat roast goose was ever a highly prized dish, and to hasten the fattening the goose sometimes had her feet pegged to a board and this made fine, rich liver. Farmers up river continued for many years to raise geese, yearly sending droves to market, and the owner must pay the goose's fee, as for other animals, at tollgates and ferries.

Chickens were somewhat scarce in the first years, and were less commonly owned than geese. William Gowens [47] had in 1792 more "fowles" than any found up to that date—thirty, as had Angoles Geter somewhat later. Chickens were kept for meat as well as eggs, for the high-producing hen laying eggs during most of the year was not around in pioneer days. I found no first settlers with gamecocks, but they were occasionally mentioned. Ducks were never too popular; William Gowens' [48] eighteen brought only one pound, four shillings.

The multitude of foxes, skunks, weasels, wildcats, and other small predators, not to mention hawks, made the lives of pioneer fowls hazardous. I found no mention of a henhouse or poultry yard among the first settlers; most fowls were guests in barns and stables; lacking these, they had to roost in trees, though the hen, huddled with her brood on the ground, might have a length of hollow log, one end stopped with a rived board or even rock, and when she had taken her chickens in for the night the other end was then covered. Up river around Price's Meadow the Stoners and other families would have tied some articles of clothing, lately worn, around the trunk of the tree where the chickens roosted; [49] no animal, or so the hunters said, would cross the cloth that smelled of man. In Middle Tennessee such makeshift ways were not for long; two turkeys selling at a farmer's auction in 1804 for four dollars [50] stop one with a jerk. It was such a little while ago that wild turkeys were all around.

---

[46] *Impartial Review*, Jan. 17, 1807.
[47] DW, I, 176, 252.
[48] *Ibid.*, I, 176. See also *ibid.*, II, 229.
[49] W, 12CC, 58, the account of Andrew Tribble.
[50] DW, II, 244.

Chapter Nine

The Farmer
and His Crops

LITERATURE IS filled with such phrases as "the simple farmer" and "the rustic farm lad," but any boy who would farm on the pioneer Cumberland somehow had to learn a vast amount of not mere skills—these he could often buy—but wisdom. He had to learn many of the unteachable things known to the Long-Hunter farmers of earlier generations—rich ground when he saw it in timber, a proper tree for barrel staves, a creek unsafe for fording, a poor piece of horseflesh, the poison in wilted cherry leaves, rock that when burned would fall readily into lime, rock that would stand the heat of a chimney for generations.

Headpiece: Pioneers at work in the forest.

He had also to know the needs and the habits of domesticated animals, for he would at one time or another raise most everything from horses to peacocks. His crops were equally various. The Cumberland Country was in climate a meeting place of North and South. Daniel Smith [1] writing in 1795 of crops that throve there listed wheat, barley, oats, rye, buckwheat, corn, pease, flax, beans, and potatoes—all familiar from New England to Virginia. He also thought rice and indigo—stand-bys of the more southerly sections of Tidewater—would do well, as would cotton, hemp, and tobacco, these three also requiring long growing seasons. I never found anything indicative of rice culture, but indigo must have been at least attempted for I found one listing of the seed.[2]

Though no one farmer found grew all the other crops, several were by 1795 raising a great variety, especially corn, wheat, oats, rye, tobacco, hemp, cotton, and flax. Add to all these the pasture that most soon had, a field of hay, a large vegetable garden, and one has a combination to keep the farmer, his family, and help busy throughout the year.

It was also in the United States as a whole a time of experimentation. Publications of the day carried numerous articles on the production of silk worms, the establishment of vineyards for some hoped to rival France in wine, and others tried to grow better hemp than Russia. The world was primarily agricultural; this was particularly so in the United States. Philadelphia was the largest city, yet Mr. Carey's *Museum*, like other publications of the day, had numerous articles in every issue on some phase of agriculture as did the Tennessee papers of a later date. As early as 1777 the North Carolina Assembly had taken a first step toward what we now call soil conservation by passing an act forbidding the woods to be burned, because such a practice was "prejudicial to the soil." [3] Much of this was a heritage from England where the upper classes and the nobility, though they would never even have to oversee the dreary details, leaving all in the hands of competent stewards and gardeners, took much pride in well-kept estates, fine fruit—some from private greenhouses—and better breeds of domesticated animals.

Early agriculture on the Cumberland, especially in the matter of small

[1] Daniel Smith, *A short description of the State of Tennessee, lately called the Territory of the United States south of the river Ohio*, Philadelphia, 1796 (cited hereafter as Smith, *Description*), 12, 24.

[2] DW, II, 272. See also Estwick Evans, "*A Pedestrious Tour of 4,000 miles*, Concord, 1819 (cited hereafter as Evans, *Tour*), gives in some detail, 197–198, an account of indigo culture in Tennessee, but as he never actually saw it, his account is somewhat suspect.

[3] NCR, XXIV, 134.

grains and dairying, owed much to England, but there were numerous other influences, and the pattern varied from settler to settler. Stump, the Pennsylvania German, and some of his German neighbors on White's Creek would have been more inclined to see farming as a way of earning money instead of a good way of life as did many of their neighbors. English tourists to America often criticized the Pennsylvania farmers for paying "more attention to barns than dwelling houses." [4] The Southern planter was apt to go to the opposite extreme—a beautiful home, with slave quarters and other needed buildings near by, but most farm animals save the best horsestock wandering in the woods.

The Cumberlander heired most patterns of agriculture in the United States of his day, not forgetting that of the Indian who not only grew fine corn, but made a garden of his cornfield, growing there beans, peas, pumpkins, melons and tobacco. Many families on the Cumberland grew only a small field of corn in this fashion, had a garden and a cow, but these one could scarcely call farmers. In that day of no machinery, many workmen of all kinds were needed, but almost always the workingman, even the slave, produced some of his own food. Other families practiced, at least for a few years, the grazing of cattle on the range as their sole means of livelihood, and up river there continued for generations families in the rougher lands who cultivated little land, but kept great droves of hogs and herds of cattle on the open range; such ways of life were not by Middle Tennessee standards farming.

Society as a whole may be more complex today, a debatable question, but certainly the lives of individual Cumberland farmers—and in thinking of farmers one should remember that many were widows—were a great deal more complex. The actual growing and raising of the many varieties of livestock and crops were only the beginnings of the average farmer's activities. The farm, throughout the United States of that day, was also the center of much manufacturing; the New Englander preferred to sell his apples in the form of hard cider and his milk as cheese. The Southern planter had been among the few to sell his most important crops—rice, tobacco, and indigo—in a more or less raw state, but all these, particularly indigo, had required a good deal of preparation before going to market; and on even the larger plantations most of the food, save flour, was grown and prepared at home.

The average Cumberland farmer seldom manufactured as much as the

[4] Anburey, *Travels*, II, 279. The old saying, "A big barn may make a big house, but a big house can never make a big barn," was not popular in the south.

New England farmer, but considerably more than the Tidewater planter; he almost always in the early years made cloth, sold his surplus milk as butter, much of his corn as fat hogs and whiskey, and often his hogs as lard and cured meat. Most of a family's staples—meat, dairy products, vegetables, meal, and flour—were produced and usually processed at home. As a rule the more affluent the plantation was, the more apt it was to have its own mill, distillery, dairy, and slaughterhouse. Yet the Cumberlander sold most of his cotton and tobacco in an unmanufactured form, and much of his livestock on the hoof.

Farming was for most, not a job, but a way of life, and though forever at the mercy of the seasons and the markets, the farmer was essentially his own boss. He had constantly throughout his life to be making troublesome decisions on what to plant and what to sell and what to buy. In spite of the great deal of advice on farming in current books and periodicals, nothing could tell the farmer how much the corn he planted in April would bring in December, or as long as Spain controlled the lower Mississippi, if it could be got to market at all. Success in farming required in any couple not a little skill in planning and management. The ability to plow a straight furrow from sunup to sundown didn't insure a fine farmer, and the woman who neglected the churning for scrubbing the pewter was bad as the woman who couldn't take time out from farm management to teach her children the alphabet.

Complicated as it was, farming as a full-time occupation and life pattern was one of the last things to take shape on the pioneer Cumberland, in spite of the fact that most of the first settlers who built stations were farmers. First things had to come first. Settlers could in more fortunate locations live in tents or sod houses, and put the farming first, but not the men on the Cumberland, constantly harassed by Indians. The first settlers were often reduced to a mere subsistence farming as in 1781 when they raised nothing but "cotton and a little garden stuff." It was the fall of 1783 before there was corn enough to make the building of a water-powered mill worth while.

James Robertson, for example, was well-to-do with plenty of horse-stock and help, and able to afford a forted station, big enough to shelter four other families. Yet, a penciled sketch of his station as it was in 1787 shows only two fields of around fifteen acres each, fenced and in cultivation.[5] This was eight years after his first attempt to have a corn crop in 1779. Few families could in the early years give more than a fraction of

[5] W, 1S, 60.

their manpower to farming. Even after a station was fortified with some land cleared and fenced, it was in many families as with the Browns south of Nashville where "Father and the older men made corn and I chased Indians." [6] Quite often there had to be almost as many guards as field hands.

A greater hindrance to the establishment of a farm in many cases was the forced moving of most first settlers in 1784 after Davidson County was created. This meant that most of the survivors such as the Buchanans had to move and leave cleared fields and forted stations to others given title to the land. Robertson's forted farm on Richland Creek thus seems quite an accomplishment when one realizes it represented only two years' work instead of seven. It is then not surprising to learn that it was 1789 before Middle Tennessee farmers as a group produced enough surplus farm produce to send a small convoy of flatboats down the Mississippi.[7]

Another thing limiting the size of early crops was the need for fence. Regardless of what the farmer grew, it had to be behind fence. The reasoning then on the Cumberland, no different from that in the rest of the United States,[8] was that the world belonged to animals, and in Tennessee it was to be made safe for them. We read with some sympathy of John Mulherrin who in 1786 had threatened he "would shoot said hogs if they were not kept from his door." [9] Said hogs had been shot, and John Mulherrin, haled into court, was in trouble. A Tennessee law of 1797, for example, fined saltpeter makers the very large sum of $100 if their works were found unenclosed and hence tempting horsestock and cattle to fall into the pits or poison themselves.

Statistics are lacking, but judging from sources the ratio of farm animals to people was unusually high on the Cumberland, and each wander-

[6] *Ibid.*, 6XX, 51.

[7] *Ibid.*, 3XX (18), 6–7. This, the account by William Martin of a trip he, General Winchester and others made down to New Orleans with produce in the winter of 1789–1790 is the earliest found of a trip by flatboat made primarily for the taking of farm produce; there was always from earliest years a good bit of travel between the Cumberland settlements and New Orleans and Natchez.

[8] Philadelphia seems to have been the only city in the United States where in the early years domesticated animals were banned from the streets. Hogs in many places were welcomed as scavengers; Mrs. Trollope as late as the 1820's complained of the hogs in Cincinnati. North Carolina, though never barring all animals, barred more than most, though her laws varied from town to town; in the town of Hillsborough, for example, "swine, geese, and goats" were forbidden, but other animals could wander at will in 1784, NCR, XXIV, 623. Very early colonial laws, such as a Virginia law of 1640, making it unlawful for hogs to run loose at night, and decreeing keepers by day, Gray, *Agriculture*, I, 145–147, were modeled on English laws, and soon fell into disuse.

[9] DC, I, 15.

ing animal was an enemy of the growing crops. The first aim of any new settled farmer was somehow, someway to get up fence—that is, after he had fenced himself off from the Indians with fort pickets. William Neely and others who put in the first corn south of the river built the never-very-satisfactory brush fence, and brush fences are sometimes mentioned in the early years.[10] However, the pioneer never used brush fence if he could do better; it was no protection against hogs, and it was with such poor fencing the family dogs were worth their weight, if not in gold, at least in feathers; nor would brush fence satisfy the law.

Calves might be kept in pole pens no bigger than the poles were long, and some settlers made temporary pens by weaving grapevines from tree to tree as did the Indians, but the most important early fence on the Cumberland was the zigzag rail fence. Contracts for the making of rail fence, references to rails, and rail splitting are so numerous that one might be inclined to think this was the only kind of fence, and it is only by chance references that we can know there were paling and rock fences. The rail fence was commonly eight to twelve rails high,[11] with the rails ten or twelve feet long. A good man could in a day split one hundred and earn about fifty cents; a man such as Thomas Sharpe Spencer who could "tote a ten-rail cut"[12] might do even better, especially when he used the best of big straight-grained timber—chestnut and oak were preferred.

The man mauling rails went about it in the first steps much as did the board maker. The log length was bolted with a maul on gluts and wedges, but from there on instead of changing to mallet and froe, the rail mauler continued with gluts and wedges, and above all the maul, for in making a rail the aim was to get a stout piece of squarish timber, a job that took both muscle and skill. Most Cumberland farmers were old hands at making or teaching the making of rails, for the rail fence was an old story in the Southern colonies, though little used from Pennsylvania northward. As late as the Revolution, New Englanders would remark of a staggering drunk that he was "building Virginia fences."[13]

More common in New England and Pennsylvania was the post and rail fence, symbolic of the New England way of life as contrasted to

[10] W, 30S, 332 is typical, "David Hood crept off to a brush fence."

[11] PD, I, 39, "nine rails high with a ground log." Coffee Papers, 1803, "eight racks high with a large ground log." A farmer in order to prosecute another on the grounds his horsestock or cattle had torn down fences and damaged crops must have a fence at least 5 feet high; see Haywood, *Justices*, 326.

[12] W, 30S, 245.

[13] Anburey, *Travels*, II, 324.

that of Virginia, for the post and rail fence [14] took a deal more work to put up and quite an assortment of tools—post-hole diggers, saws, augers, broad axes, and additionally all the tools needed for the rail fence; and once, after much labor, on a rocky New England hillside, the fence could not be taken down and moved as could the rail fence. It was a simple job to take the rails down and put them up again, build higher or lower, reinforce with ground logs against hogs, or set stakes and put on riders to keep the smarter of the cattle and horsestock from pushing the fence down, one rail at a time. Another beauty of the rail fence was its peculiar adaption to rough and rocky ground; it could be laid even on steep hillsides, so rocky post holes for gateposts had to be blasted.

One great fault of the rail fence was that it was not chicken-, rabbit-, or even pig-proof; thus, in fencing gardens, yards, graveyards and such the Cumberlanders commonly used a paling fence though it meant making and setting posts. The builder of paling fence proceeded as for a post and rail fence, but with only three rails to the panel, while the bottom rail, set touching the ground, had for its full length a groove down the side that would lay uppermost; the second rail was set in holes bored midway of the post, and the third rail set near the top. Pickets or palings, rived usually of white oak or cedar as were shakes or shingling boards for a roof but narrower, were inserted with the ends in the groove of the bottom rail; they were then forced to one side of the second rail and back again to the opposite side of the top one. "Such a fence," wrote William Byrd after viewing one of 1728 in North Carolina, "doth surprising well." [15] Fencing could be woven of hickory bark or withes and palings, or of most anything save wire, a thing nobody in the United States of that day had. Rock fence, as the dry stonewall was known and now common in Middle Tennessee, did not come into its own until after the Indian menace had ceased.

Any settling family, laborer or farmer, usually tried first to fence and plant a garden, but corn, first, last, and always, was the most important crop for the pioneer farmer. Corn was the first seed planted on the Cumberland, unless one wants to argue which it was that Dr. Thomas Walker's companions planted first in 1750—corn or peach seed.

How many grew or tried to grow corn on the Cumberland in 1779 is a question. Some was grown up river at Price's and Pittman's stations;

---

[14] Michaux, *Travels 1802*, 31, described those near Philadelphia that had five rails.
[15] Byrd, *Writings*, 84, described here as "wreathing of the pales."

Kaspar Mansker, north of Nashville, certainly harvested some, as nobody mentioned scarcity of food in his household, but there is no record of any harvest from that planted in the neighborhood of French Lick by members of James Robertson's party.

Much has been written of the hard drudgery of clearing land and planting corn; a job that never stopped completely from the time James Town was settled until the present, for new-ground fields can still be seen on the Cumberland Plateau and up the river.[16] Some men cleared land one way and some another; the pioneer farmer harassed by Indians and with a thousand jobs to do sometimes only cut out the underbrush, deadened the trees, and without benefit of a plow "dug in" the seed with hoe and mattock.

William Neely and others who stayed behind in the spring of 1779 to plant corn while Robertson went to the Illinois planted in this fashion, for they had come by foot and boat and hence without horses. It may have been done, but I never found a record of any human being, white or black, having pulled a plow in the old Southwest, as was often done by the peasantry on the Continent. Instead, most male hands got calluses from long straight hoe handles, for the hoe used by the Cumberlander was in principle little different from that of the Indian and other primitive peoples who stirred the earth—a blade set at right angles to a long handle.

There were by the time the Cumberland was settled many varieties of hoe—but most of those used by the white man had metal blades, heavier and thicker than the blades of modern hoes, each blade set in the back with a round opening, much like that on today's grubbing hoe, and known as an eye. The handle, almost always of hickory, was straight and varied in length to suit the user. The grubbing hoe, meant for a bowed back swinging out every ounce of power, had a short handle on the order of a foot adze.

The most common hoes on the Cumberland were hilling and weeding, these much alike in shape—heavy, broad-bladed, with the hilling hoe bigger than the other. There was a special narrow-bladed hoe for cane, and more rarely onion hoes, and the little "sang-hoe," small enough

[16] There was until heavy emigration began with World War II in certain sections of the hills what one might almost call a definite crop rotation that permitted the land to go back to brush or pine; sooner or later, sometimes by the next generation it would be cleared again and put in corn. The old Cotton Kingdom knew no rotation; worn out fields were let grow up, usually in pine; in the last decade many have been cleared and fenced for beef cattle pasture.

to carry through the woods in a capacious apron pocket.[17] Regardless of how much or how little he plowed, the farmer throughout the history of the Cumberland used hoes. The most important crops—corn, cotton, tobacco, as well as potatoes and vegetables—were row crops, and many, like tobacco, are, on the small farm, still cultivated partly by hand.

Hoes, like horses, cows, guns, and carpentry tools run through the inventories of practically all men whose other effects show them to have been farmers. Lawyer Gubbins, like poor John Bond, had neither hoe nor bell, but Nicholas Gentry, a would-be-farmer, killed before he could settle his land, had two small hoes and an old mattock, while John Buchanan, Sr.,[18] another farmer, had two mattocks and three weeding hoes, for a man needed no more hoes than he had field hands.

Simple in design as were all hoes, they could be made by a blacksmith, and judging from the old ones, rusted and without handles, that can still be found in ancient log barns, most were. Requiring little iron, hoes sold quite cheaply,[19] usually for around $1.50, though like everything else, hoes were unstandardized. John Sevier [20] paid his blacksmith $3 for one grubbing hoe in 1797.

Weeding and cane hoes had to be kept sharp, and for this, the user often carried a whetstone. Armed only with an ax, a grubbing hoe, a hoe, and his own two hands, a farmer could put in a crop of corn with the usual beans, peas, pumpkins, cymlings, and watermelons in the hills, but the first crop of corn at French Lick when the men came down without horses, was one of the very few put in in such fashion; all Middle Tennessee farmers studied had horses and plows.

We do not know the kind of corn either Robertson or Mansker planted. They may have had more than one kind, for when the white man came to America the Indians were growing several varieties. Among these were dent corn—called "she-corn," a smooth, flinty variety good for hominy—and both sweet corn and popcorn.[21] At the settlement of the Cumberland, the white man had progressed little if any in the growing of corn over the Indian; some tribes, notably the Cherokee, were great corn growers.

Corn in size and yield varied from the scrawny stuff of a thin-soiled

---

[17] Good examples of all hoes mentioned here may be seen in the Mountain Life Museum of Levi Jackson State Park near London, Ky.

[18] DW, I, 7, Gentry's inventory; *ibid.*, I, 69, Buchanan's.

[19] MW, I, 27; for earlier prices and varieties see DW, I, 7, 16, 69, 296–297, 311.

[20] THM, Sevier, "Journal," V, 194.

[21] Gray, *Agriculture*, I, 67, 173.

New England farm to the stout twelve-foot stalks common in Middle Tennessee that on new ground made without selected seed up to one hundred bushels an acre with an average yield of fifty to sixty.[22] The ears, higher from the ground than a tall man, were borne on strong stalks with broad blades good for fodder. Yet, for all its bigness and toughness, corn had many enemies at planting time. The old rhyme, "One for the squirrel, one for the crow, three to come up, and two to grow," would not have been chanted by the Cumberland child dropping corn, for as late as 1802, crows had not yet come to the Cumberland,[23] but the words do illustrate the precarious life of sprouting corn. Replanting was ever a part of corn culture.

This was done at the first cultivation, and the dreary work of hoeing row upon row of corn in land too stumpy for a plow was an old part of life in America when the Cumberland was settled. It was, at least for the Cleveland boys of East Tennessee, not so much the labor as the dullness, and so when their father set them the task of hoeing up to a certain large stump, they dug up the stump and replaced it a good distance closer to the beginning of their rows, though this meant more and harder work than the hoeing of the corn.

The pioneer farmer had fewer weeds to contend with than has the farmer now; but forty per cent [24] of all weeds in the United States today are native, and a large proportion of these was found on the Cumberland. Spanish needles and bull-nettles were two of the most hated, but worse than any weed was the cane with its underground runners always shooting up and spreading and, of course, the forever-sprouting stumps. A lusty stump would continue to send up sprouts after the corn was laid by; bad for the corn, but worse, it meant another battle the next year.

The first cultivation—or "chopping out," as some called it—with the replanting was followed, usually, by two more. It was then time to lay the corn by; in late June if planted early, later for late-planted. Depending on the season and the time of planting, the farmer went into his field around mid-August to "pull fodder," which meant stripping the blades, while the ear, now fully grown and out of the milk, was left on the stalk.[25]

---

[22] Smith, *Description*, 12.

[23] Michaux, *Travels 1802*, 293; he here also describes "Indian corn" in Middle Tennessee.

[24] W. C. Muenscher, *Weeds*, copyright The Macmillan Company, New York, 1952, 21.

[25] The Draper Manuscripts contain, usually in connection with Indian attacks, many references to corn culture as W, 1S, 60, "Robertson hoeing corn"; *ibid.*, 32S, 206, "James Sevier pulling corn." Sevier's "Journal," THM, V, has many references to

The blades were tied into bundles and saved for fodder, the only winter forage from his fields the pioneer farmer had. Cured, the bundles of blades were usually stacked into piles, and covered with the corn tops that were cut next, while the ears were left on the now-bare stalks until November or even later when "corn gathering" began. The fodder shock came later, and there are even now a few families in the rough hill country, where little hay is grown, who strip and tie and top and gather corn much as did the first farmers on the Cumberland.

Corn gathering meant taking shuck and all. Corn shucks, especially in the early years, were a valuable addition to the animal food supply; a hungry cow would take them along with her nubbins and be glad. Shucks were also used in mud-mats by the door, the shuck tick that usually went between the first feather bed and the bed cords, horse-collars, and now and then a doll.

Iron plow points of several varieties were an ordinary part of pioneer farming in all the old West; iron plow points were left behind by the Indians at ransacked Ruddles Station in Kentucky, and on the Cumberland figure in practically all farm inventories, though some settlers such as David Lucas and John Porter were killed before they had a chance to get the points, usually the only part of the pioneer plow made of metal, onto the wooden frames. John Buchanan, Sr., and James Harrod,[26] first settlers, had not only the usual forms of plows, but also shares with coulters. Requiring little iron, plows sold rather cheaply. Samuel Buchanan's [27] barshare brought in 1787, $6.00, 7 shillings, as compared to a weeding hoe for $1.00, 4 shillings, 6 pence, while Richard Shaffer's barshare with two axes and a hoe brought three pounds.[28] A plow, complete with singletree, sold a few years later for only five dollars.[29]

In general, the farmer on the Cumberland made greater use of the plow than did the tobacco growers of Virginia or the rice and indigo planters of South Carolina who depended upon slaves with hoes for even the heavy work of ditching rice fields, but the Cumberlander, raising many row crops—corn, tobacco, cotton—still depended upon human labor and the hoe more than did the Pennsylvania farmer, growing a greater proportion of small grains.

---

corn crops through the years: May 5, 1795, "began planting new ground," *ibid.*, 176; "began laying by" (a different field), June 11, *ibid.;* "began fodder pulling," Aug. 17, *ibid.*, 178.

[26] DW, I, 16.
[27] *Ibid.*, I, 296.
[28] *Ibid.*, I, 311.
[29] MW, I, 27.

Early settlers on the Cumberland such as the Neelys, Buchanans, Stumps, Robertsons, and Edmonsons were not large slaveholders, but neither were they "one horse" farmers concerned chiefly with subsistence farming. All of the families named owned a few slaves, but all were working farmers, eager for large stump-free fields. And once a field was cleared with the timber snaked off, the plowing of it, even with a good team and a stout plow, took about as much physical exertion as digging in the corn. The plow had to be jerked away from big stumps and lifted over roots, and, worse, the point was always catching under roots too tough to yield. Usually it took two hands, a man to manage the plow and a boy to ride one horse, or even lead the team, though leading is hardly the word for many were the "yea-backs" needed.

The most man-killing labor of all was that with the heavy, short-handled mattock or grubbing hoe, and judging from the number of these found in inventories a very great deal of grubbing was done. Small stumps and roots that would break a hoe handle or a plow point had to yield to the grubbing hoe—provided there was a strong back and good arms to swing it. Year in and year out they grubbed, smoothing fields for garden stuff, and wheat, rye, barley, oats, flax, and pasture. Some, such as John Sevier, could afford to hire extra help to do it, but the cost was sometimes greater than the original price of the land, Sevier in 1797 paying Joel Hancocke $4.50 for grubbing an acre and a half.[30]

Still, the picture of the pioneer farmer forever struggling with stumpy fields should not be used for all Middle Tennessee farmers. There were stretches of land such as Clover Bottom that had no timber, only wild clovers and grasses; canebrakes, though the cane caused as much work as stumps, had in rich river and creek bottoms smothered out other growths, while most of the forested lands tended to be "park-like." All in all the first farmers on the Cumberland had less clearing to do than had the settlers in such places as Ohio or, later, West Tennessee. Still, grubbing, stump burning, cutting trees went on continuously in any spare time snatched from fighting Indians, building, fortifying, cultivating, and harvesting existing crops.

More men were killed while trying to farm than while following any other occupation; surveying was extremely dangerous but surveyors usually went in groups. Typical of many stories is that of Samuel Buchanan who came across country in the fall of 1779. He took part in

[30] THM, V, 240. He spent at various times much more than this for grubbing, but the acreage is not given.

the bloody battles in the neighborhood of French Lick, did the dangerous work of clearing land, hunting, farming, and fence laying that claimed the lives of so many of his kin and neighbors before 1784. He then, with the rest of his family, went down to Mill Creek and began all over again. On May 8, 1786, "The Indians came upon him, ploughing in the field, and fired upon him. He ran, and was pursued by twelve Indians, taking, in their pursuit, the form of a half moon. When he came to the bluff of the creek, below the field, he jumped down a steep bank into the creek, where he was overtaken, killed and scalped." [31]

It was not until the Indian wars were over that the cornfields could really widen, and then they boomed. Tennessee farmers were, by 1850, not only growing corn enough to keep their three million hogs,[32] but were sending corn south, much of it in the form of meal and whiskey. Even from earliest years some farmers sold corn; as time passed often for less than fifteen cents a bushel, though the price showed a wide variation. There were always some men such as John Coffee [33] and John Sevier who seldom raised enough to feed their help and stock, and these traded with local farmers for corn, as did the larger of the distillers. Tavern keepers like De Monbruen with twenty-four horse stalls all filled to overflowing on Saturdays and during court week, bought corn as did the early iron manufacturers with many oxen and much horsestock to feed.

Still, corn, though at the bottom of all life, was never a great cash crop.[34] The average farmer needed a good bit to feed his workstock, distill whiskey for his own use, fatten the meat he needed, and of course for the family bread. Whatever surplus he had, he preferred to sell in the form of fat hogs or pork and lard, or, more profitable still, whiskey.

The most important cash crop of pioneer Middle Tennessee was cotton; for close to forty years after settlement this region was the Cotton Kingdom of the United States. Small amounts of cotton had been grown in the Southern colonies and northward even during the seventeenth century, and by 1730 the crop was well enough known that

[31] NCR, XVII, 609, and Ramsey, *Tennessee*, 478.

[32] Louis D. Wallace, *40th Biennial Report, Tennessee Department of Agriculture, A Century of Tennessee Agriculture*, 1954, 310–311, in a summing up of Tennessee agriculture in 1850 shows the state first in hogs, fifth in corn and cotton, seventh in oats, and ninth in dairy cattle.

[33] Coffee Papers, 1809 –320 bushels corn, $40.

[34] Not all corn was sold by the barrel or bushel, but could in any state of growth be sold by the field; Mr. Mountflorence, for example, bought an 8-acre field, DW, I, 155.

William Byrd mentioned land that looked as if it would grow cotton.[35] Here and there it continued to be grown, even in the Illinois,[36] but it was not until the outbreak of the Revolution and the consequent cutting off of cloth from England, that cotton began to be grown to any extent. Cotton clothing had, before the Revolution, become fairly common in the South, but the fine calicoes and muslins had been made of Egyptian or India cotton, woven in and imported from France and England.

Cotton was in the United States a common enough crop by 1780 that first settlers to the Cumberland brought the seed, for all historians of Middle Tennessee mention the Indian attack on the cotton gatherers at Clover Bottom in the fall of 1780. It continued to be grown, as cotton had many of the same advantages as had corn for the farmer in new-ground soil. It throve in rich soil with a high nitrogen content, and growing in rows as it did, could be cultivated by hand, and, hence, did not require an even seed bed as did flax and wheat. Equally advantageous was its ability to conserve at least part of its crop until late autumn; a man's station might be destroyed and his fence torn down with the corn crop ruined by hungry hogs and cattle, but the owner, or more likely his survivors, could slip back and pick a few pounds of cotton, enough to make several yards of cloth. A group in 1787 went back to the abandoned Hall place[37] to pick that of the dead Mr. Hall, and many families in the bloody year of 1781 grew no corn at all, but only a "little cotton and garden stuff."[38]

All this talk of cotton and of early Middle Tennessee as the Cotton Kingdom should not give the impression large quantities were grown in the first years. Judging from inventories, a great many families did grow cotton, but always in small amounts. The 231 pounds of cotton "in ye seed,"[39] Cornelius Ruddle had when killed in 1787 may have been his entire crop, but it was more than many of his neighbors, larger farmers, had. Even so, this amount, insignificant by today's standards, still meant a yield of about fifty pounds of fiber when ginned on the family gin. This, carded and spun, and the Ruddles had along with their gin both cards and wheel, would make enough thread for around 150 yards of some heavy cloth such as bed ticking, more of calico.

[35] Byrd, *Writings*, 84, 208.
[36] Mereness, *Travels*, "Minutes from the Journal of Mr. Hamburgh's Travels in the Michigan and Illinois Country, 1763," 364.
[37] W, 32S, 277.
[38] *Ibid.*, 6XX (50), 17.
[39] DW, I, 54.

There was, in spite of Indians, enough cotton being grown that farmers early sold their fiber instead of the cloth, and by 1786 Nashville was well enough known as a center of cotton production that James Wilkinson of Kentucky sent his partner to trade for cotton or "elegant high blooded mares." [40] Cotton acreage gradually increased, but compared to that in corn, continued small. It took more hands to pick it than to grow it, and more hands [41] still to separate it from its sticky, grayish seed, so hard-hulled that ashes were often mixed with them at planting time to soften and hence facilitate germination.

Some years before the Revolution the basic idea of the cotton gin had been developed. Two boys, one to feed the cotton between the wooden rollers, the other to turn the crank or work a foot treadle, could seed better than fifty pounds a day.[42] The wooden gin continued to be used up river almost until the present; one of my mother's neighbors did away with hers only a few years back, and on it had for many years seeded cotton grown in her garden, but the wooden gin, even the improved variety with grooved rollers, was not only slow, but it tore [43] and shortened the fibers and dirtied them with crushed seed.

Sometime, somewhere, maybe on the Cumberland, somebody, weary of the clumsy wooden rollers, thought up the idea of using steel rowlers on the turning wooden cylinder. These were common enough that Jacob Castleman, killed in 1784, had "steel rowlers for a cotton gin." [44] Eli Whitney on his trip south may or may not, at Mrs. Nathanael Greene's where he stopped, have seen a gin with steel teeth; whatever the truth, some version of such a machine was in use at least twelve years before his patent in 1796.

In any case, such was the doubt that Mr. Whitney had invented the gin that it was hard to convince the cotton growers on the Cumberland they should pay 25 cents for the right to use each gin saw when in 1803 the State of Tennessee bought the patent rights.[45] Regardless of how much, if any, actual inventing Eli Whitney did, the cotton gin, bringing

[40] FQ, I, 172.

[41] Families up river, growing only very small amounts of cotton for quilt batting, continued to seed by hand and use cotton cards until World War II. One story goes that at night each member of the family had his or her shoe stuffed with cotton, and was not allowed to go to bed until this amount was seeded.

[42] Gins were common in Virginia during the Revolution: see Smyth, *Tour*, II, 68–71, also Anburey, *Travels*, II, 425.

[43] All viewers of the early cotton gins, including Collot in Louisiana, *Journey, 1796*, II, 167–168, complained of how the gins harmed the fiber.

[44] DW, I, 194.

[45] Tennessee *Gazette*, Aug. 27, 1804, carried a long discussion of the law passed Oct. 22, 1803, but not yet put into effect.

quicker and more efficient methods of ginning, brought an increase in acreage and a consequent decrease in price. As late as 1789, fifty pounds of cleaned cotton brought twenty pounds,[46] but only a year later, William Gowens' cotton sold for only four shillings the pound,[47] or less than half the price of the other. Ten years later cotton was selling for as low as 12½ cents a pound,[48] and there were by this date, 1800, several large gins driven by horsepower. These machines could, depending on the number of saws used, seed from two to three thousand pounds of cotton a day,[49] though they also tore and dirtied the fiber.[50]

Cotton had by 1799, only four years after the last Indian invasion, moved from a small crop planted with the hope of getting a little cash, into the realm of big business, and was giving employment to ginners, balers—by 1804 little Jonathan Robertson who had come as a child in 1779 had a cotton gin and press on his plantation [51] as had Andrew Jackson—waggoners, boatmen, boatbuilders, growers of hemp, rope makers, and weavers of coarse hempen cloth for cotton-bale covering. Hand in hand with these was the cotton broker, who would, for a fee, take all problems of transportation, sales, insurance, and commission off the farmer's shoulders; others bought the cotton outright on the plantation.

André Michaux, visiting Nashville in 1802, saw the whole future of Middle Tennessee, then known as West Tennessee, as built upon cotton. He estimated that the average family, "a man or a woman with two or three children," could, along with the corn needed, grow and harvest four acres of cotton at a profit of $212. He felt that through cotton "a poor family" might in five or six years be able to buy "one or two negroes," and annually increase their number.[52] He also pointed out the cheapness of the land, but forgot to mention the time needed for clearing and fencing. It is possible, too, that his estimated average yield of better than 350 pounds to the acre was too high, though Daniel Smith gave 800 pounds to the acre as a maximum, a prodigious amount of cotton fiber, and more than twice the average yield of later years.

He also neglected to mention the cost of ginning. The small farmer

[46] DW, I, 107.

[47] *Ibid.*, I, 175.

[48] Coffee Papers, 1801, "25 pounds of cotton, $3.12."

[49] Williams, *Travels*, Schweinitz, "Report," 516–517.

[50] Bradbury, *Travels, 1811*, gave, 265, a detailed description of a gin, but complained much of its destructive powers. There is a good example of an early gin in the museum at Old Salem, Winston-Salem, N.C.

[51] Tennessee *Gazette*, Aug. 8, 1804.

[52] Michaux, *Travels 1802*, 248–249; 294–298.

was by 1800 taking his cotton to the bigger plantations for ginning; the toll for this was twenty per cent.[53] The average farmer thus had to produce close to 440 pounds an acre in order to have 350 from the gin; baling with rope and hempen covering cost usually about two cents per pound.[54] Even if the small grower did it himself by putting the mouth of a hempen sack between two floor boards and pressing down with his feet, he still had the cost of time, sack, and rope. There was also the hauling, easily done by the small farmer—provided he had time, horsepower, and a cart or wagon.

Michaux was, in giving "18 pence" as the average price per pound, quoting from a good season in New Orleans. John Coffee, in 1801, paid twelve cents a pound for cotton at Haysborough, and in 1803 a load of slightly more than 25,000 pounds brought only $15.05 per hundredweight in New Orleans.[55] Out of this in addition to the costs already mentioned, must come freight, commission, insurance, and inspection—ten cents per bale at the point of embarkation.[56] The cotton market fluctuated widely in later years; for a short while after the War of 1812 prices soared as much cotton was needed to supply the dearth in England caused by the war, but in 1819 cotton along with everything else crashed.

Andrew Jackson's defeat and dispersal of the Southern Indians, followed in 1818 by the purchase of the old Chickasaw land in West Tennessee, opened for settlement two regions much better suited to cotton culture than was Middle Tennessee. Cotton prices tumbled and cotton for Middle Tennessee declined in importance as a cash crop.

The weather on the Cumberland was another hazard; cotton requires a long growing season; Jackson wanted his in the ground between the 15th and 25th of April,[57] but every few years a late frost in early May killed the young plants. Other years an early fall frost caught many cotton bolls unripened. A rainy fall was also bad; picking the bedraggled

---

[53] Williams, *Travels*, Schweinitz, "Report," 416–517.

[54] Tennessee *Gazette*, March 27, 1805—"15.00 for loose cotton—$17.00 if baled."

[55] Coffee Papers, 1801, 1803.

[56] Haywood, *Laws*, 301, "An act to prevent the exportation of unmerchantable commodities"—all produce by this 1801 law from cotton to tar had to be inspected and labeled; inspection points were established at Nashville, Clarksville, Port Royal, Palmyra, etc.

[57] Bassett, *Jackson Correspondence*, I, 65. Jackson as a merchant in the early 1800's took cotton in his stores and sold it in New Orleans; the letters of his partners, Hutchings at this time, reveal the fluctuations of the markets; *ibid.*, I, 112–113, 141–142, 146, tell the story of Hutchings waiting for cotton to rise above 24¢ in New Orleans, instead, he had to sell at 20¢.

plants along the muddy rows was a disheartening job, but no more so than the tedious work of drying the cotton on scaffolds, for damp cotton could not be ginned.

Cotton continued to be an important cash crop for some years, though few planters appeared to have depended on it so heavily to keep a plantation going as did Jackson while President. Jackson, however, should not be classed among the working farmers who seldom owned more than a dozen slaves and many of these children. He, like many large landowners, was not basically a farmer. True, he owned more land and slaves than did any of the little group of settlers whose inventories have so often been mentioned, but a study of his correspondence after Rachel's death indicates that he could not either in cash or produce make enough to feed and clothe his slaves and take care of the many other needs of his plantation.

Farming was for Andrew Jackson, as for the cotton planter who settled in West Tennessee and the deeper South, a capitalistic enterprise in which he invested, not himself, but only money. He had, beginning in 1795, an overseer, and managed very well—as long as Rachel lived to manage for him. The frantic, yet always hopeful, letters to his adopted son during his second term as President, though coming past this period, demonstrate too well the problems of the absentee owner of the Cumberland, trying to keep a plantation going almost entirely on money from the cotton crop.

The letters tell a tale of mismanagement and bad judgement, coupled with low cotton prices, a drouth one year and an early frost another, that would have sent Jackson to the poorhouse had he not had friends. He tried different overseers, but the down-hill road of The Hermitage could not be checked. It was a story of weeds in the lawn and the garden, poor fences, not enough food for the slaves, no corn and fodder for the stock, oxen too thin and poor for work, hog stock run out, not enough work stock, sweet potatoes in late and ruined by frost, never enough pasture so that animals must graze in the hayfield, and thus there was no hay. Neighbors wrote Jackson of Negroes sick and several dead; one suspects from brutality and ill-treatment in general from the overseer. There was no Rachel around to oversee the overseer, and after her death the slaves were sometimes well clothed, but other times they had to work through the frosty falls without shoes.

Grazing in a harvested cornfield instead of pasture, Jackson's blooded colts were stunted for lack of feed; his ninety-two sheep bore only fifty-nine lambs, and there were no fowls at all, no seed wheat, and at last even the best of his horsestock had to be put up for sale. Jackson at last wrote in despair, "We cannot depend upon cotton for support." [58]

It was only under certain very favorable and unusual conditions that a man with nothing but money and unskilled help could succeed in agriculture. These conditions were found in the cotton and sugar cane country of the deeper South where farming was less a way of life than a business. The Mississippi cotton planter with virgin soil, a perfect climate, a closer market, could stay away from home half the year, buy corn and salt pork for the slaves, cord and hempen cloth for his cotton bales, most domesticated animals, much of his food including wines and whiskey, and still make money. The Cumberland farmer, further from market, paying more freight both on what he bought and on what he sold, wrestling often with a poor season, could not.

The counties in Middle Tennessee gradually lost their importance as producers of cotton; instead they furnished the things the cotton planters could not or would not grow for themselves—horses and mules, meal and corn, pork and more pork, and though much less than Kentucky, some hempen rope and bagging. No one of the counties in the rich Bluegrass land north of the Cumberland was by 1850 up to twentieth place in cotton production.[59]

In contrast to Michaux's enthusiasm for cotton culture in Middle Tennessee were the brief remarks on agriculture in the same region by Brother Schweinitz, the Moravian missionary, who, after a visit in 1799–1800, wrote: [60] "Agriculture consists mainly in the raising of corn. Some cotton and tobacco are grown, but not much wheat; partly because good mills are rare; partly because so much of it is consumed by worms." He was critical of much he found—the Cumberland cattle, the lack of vegetables, and the mistreatment of the sugar maple trees through the tapping of them in December. He did mention in an offhand sort of way that Mrs. Frederick Stump had raised 450 pounds of cotton to the acre, but his talk of fruit and other things indicates that he and the farmers he met in Middle Tennessee saw cotton as only one crop among many, not "the crop" it came to be in West Tennessee and the deeper South.

The effects of all farmers studied give this same picture of farming

[58] *Ibid.*, V, 59, 61–65, 233, 248, 289–290, 301, 303–304, 307, 308–309, 337, 373, 385, 394, 397, 426–427; chiefly the letters of the neighbors, telling the sorry state of The Hermitage.

[59] Wallace, *40th Report*, 318.

[60] Williams, *Travels*, Schweinitz, "Report," 516.

that was a way of life never at the mercy of one cash crop. In some of the very early inventories there was no crop; plow points without plows and wheels without wagons indicate the owner was killed before he could do more than fence and clear land. More typical of early Middle Tennessee agriculture as a whole than Jackson's troubles were such men as John Buchanan, Sr., William Ramsey, William Overall, Robert Edmondson, and Philip Conrad. All had several varieties of livestock along with varying amounts of corn, cotton, flax, the small grains, and often hemp and tobacco, though few showed such a variety as William Gowens,[61] killed in 1790; he in addition to the usual grain, livestock, and fowls, including ducks, had both flax and hemp.

As the years pass farm inventories become increasingly more varied. Fairly typical of the possessions of the middle-class farmer with a few slaves, a farm wagon, but neither overseer, carriage, brick nor stone mansion are the possessions of James Dean,[62] dying in 1802. Plainly he and his family thought well of their home, for they had most of the things substantial farmers had by 1802—plenty of bedding with extra linen, including four tablecloths. There were not only walnut and cherry chests and beds, but a good cupboard, chest of drawers, and what was still rather rare, a cradle for the baby, and many other small things that the forever-being-burned-out, Indian-chased first settlers could not always have—more books than usual, baskets, all tools including warping frames for the manufacture of cloth, fat gourds, enough teaspoons, twenty-five, to go around at least part way when company came. There were also goodly quantities of pewter, iron, brass, woodenware, and crockery. The base of all this life lay partly in the many appliances for home manufacture of cloth, but largely in the barn; along with many farm animals and geese, turkeys, ducks, and hens were corn, hay, rye, oats, and wheat.

John Blackamore,[63] Davidson County farmer of 1803, had all manner of things from a thirty-five dollar "writing desk" to a hundred bushels of corn. Different from Mr. Dean, he had barley and was more interested in small grains than most farmers, for he had the still rather rare wheat fan, as well as scythe and cradle. Showing even greater variety were the effects of Dr. Mark B. Sappington[64] who in addition to the more common crops had hay, barley, grass seed, rye, spelts, potatoes, peas, and black-eyed peas.

[61] DW, I, 175–176.
[62] *Ibid.*, II, 242–244.
[63] *Ibid.*, II, 348.
[64] *Ibid.*, II, 290–293, 348.

The never-entirely-the-same yet always farming-that-was-a-way-of-life persisted. The Shutes, for example, built a station around 1790 three miles west of Nashville near Robertson's Traveler's Rest; it was to their fort that Mrs. Mason and ten children went at night while the father was gone to mill. Mr. Shute [65] had by 1811 twelve or fourteen head of horse-stock, thirty head of cattle, sixty or seventy hogs, fifteen sheep, along with several feather beds and the usual house and kitchen furniture. In spite of the stock he had had to feed, his barn in February still held three hundred bushels of oats, two hundred barrels of corn, and thirty bushels of wheat, with plenty of bacon and lard in the smokehouse. His help, in addition to his family, had consisted of three Negro men, a woman, and a girl. This number was about average for Middle Tennessee at this date, for the region was, like Virginia, made up largely of middle-class farm families, the head of the house unashamed of working in the fields at times with his help, the wife mistress of all the home arts and crafts from butter making to spinning. Families such as the Shutes, instead of the rather rare planter with an overseer, a hundred slaves, carriage, and coachman, made the backbone of Middle Tennessee agriculture.

The *Clarion* in a summing up of crops for 1810 mentioned most of the crops grown by the pioneer,[66] including turnips, widely grown as a fall crop for they could be stored for winter use by both humans and animals, or if a man didn't have time to harvest them the hogs could do so. One crop not found on the list, but important to the first settler was flax. Flax hackles and flax wheels are found in most of the early family inventories; both Cornelius Ruddle and Jacob Castleman left small quantities of flax, and this crop is quite often mentioned in accounts of Indian warfare as: ". . . the Indians were seen advancing, each with a torch of combustible faggots of wheat straw, flax straw, and dry cane." [67]

The first settlers used linen cloth as had their ancestors, for linen cloth was already an old, old story when its manufacture became an important home industry in the British Isles. It is doubtful if much flax got planted in the first year of settlement on any border, for flax, sown broadcast as it was, needed a plowed seed bed with enough loose dirt to cover the seed with a rake or harrow. True, none of the inventories of first settlers listing flax listed a harrow, but makeshift ones could be made with lengths of brush. Land for flax also needed to be free enough

[65] Nashville *Clarion*, Feb. 8, 1811.

[66] *Ibid.*, Nov. 9, 1810.

[67] W, 30S, 459. One reason given for the rapid burning of Zeiglar's home was the large quantity of dry flax straw stored there, *ibid.*, 6XX, 88.

of stumps and cane roots that sprouts could not smother out the young plants, for, different from row crops, they could not get help from hoe cultivation.

A flax field was, so the old ones told, a pretty thing in flower, all blue and even as a carpet, and usually it was allowed to go to seed, for the seed were used for linseed oil. The plant was pulled and dried until the seed could be threshed out. There was then little but the stalk left. These were soaked in a pool of water, usually one especially made below the springhouse, and left until the coarse outer bark had rotted enough to come off easily. The length of the stay depended on the weather; warm, a few days; colder, much longer. It was a tricky business; if the flax were left too long, overmuch rotting would not only weaken the outer bark but also the inner fiber; the resulting thread would be hard to spin, and weave into rotten cloth, hard to bleach. If left too short a time in the water, the outer bark would not rot enough to come free, and the "shoves" or bits of bark would stick to the fiber.

Rotted for the proper length of time, the flax stalks were taken out of the water and dried, quickly so that the rotting might be checked at once. In damp weather the flax was spread on scaffolds above low fires, kept usually in pits. Dried, it was time for the break, a contraption made entirely of wood, three cross pieces below, two above, the upper hinged so they could be lifted, the whole in the shape of an elongated triangle and set on a three-legged frame.[68] The top of the frame or break was lifted, and the end of a handful of flax straw put across the three lower, and the top was dropped over it, crushing, but not breaking the stems down between the three cross pieces. This was the "break"; a handful broken, then followed the "shake" to be rid of the loose "shoves"; so it went, "break and shake," through the length of handful after handful; then followed the banging and heating with the long limber, wooden swingling or scutching knife, which like the cross pieces of the break were dull, designed to break rotten bark but not inner fiber. Flax breaking required not a little skill, for "If you didn't get all the shoves out, it was terrible stuff to wear." [69]

Once the flax was broken and swingled, the work of the women began, with the hatchel or hackle,[70] a simple tool made by setting iron teeth

[68] Good examples of the flax break as well as hackles and little spinning wheels may be seen in the Mountain Life Museum, Levi Jackson State Park, Ky.

[69] I am indebted for most of this account to Mr. and Mrs. Grover Foster, Antioch, Ky.

[70] DW, I, 46, the inventory of Samuel Vernor, an early settler who also had a loom

into a paddle-shaped board with a hole in the end so that it could be kept on a wall peg. Hackling was to flax what carding was to wool and cotton, and prepared the fibers for spinning by further cleaning and separating. The very coarse were sometimes woven on the 400-sleigh into coarse tow cloth, but woven or not, tow was a handy thing to have for cleaning gun barrels, or, lacking hemp or old hempen rope, flax tow could be mixed with pitch to make oakum. Fine fibers were spun into fine thread to be used in the 1200-sleigh when woven into cloth for baby's best dress or the Sunday ruffled shirt. There were no rules; the fineness of the linen cloth depended on the time and skill of the workers and the needs of the family.

Wool and cotton were usually dyed as thread, but unbleached flax took dye rather poorly, and as many linen articles were customarily white, a very large proportion of flax thread was woven in its natural color, and then bleached. In this case the warping of the loom came next after the reel, and warping was no job for a nervous woman. The average web was a yard wide and forty yards long; bed ticking, for example, was, like the better grades of linsey, usually woven on the coarse 600-sleigh, but double-sleighed, that is, with two threads between cane splints. Thus, for a web of twelve hundred threads, each forty yards long, about twenty-five miles of thread was needed, a pretty mess if allowed to tangle and still more complicated if warping for some striped cloth such as ticking. Warp was made more manageable by sizing with a gooey mixture made by cooking meal for a long time in a large quantity of water—an ancestor of today's cornstarch.

Once sized, it was time for the warping frame, and on the Cumberland in the first years there must have been much borrowing of warping frames. Compared to looms and sleighs they were scarce, but once again as in the case of any other item, there are all the lucky families who never had to sell their household goods, and some of these undoubtedly had warping frames. At long last the sleigh was threaded, and the loom ready waiting with the warp. Now, there was nothing to do but fill the spools that went into the bobbin, a job for a nimble-fingered child; several families had extra spools, though few had as many as the sixteen owned by the Thomas Browns.[71] They were a must for checked cloth, and a great timesaver even on plain.

---

as had Nicholas Gentry, *ibid.*, I, 7, a first settler killed before he could settle his land. Tools and appliances for the making of thread and cloth are well represented among the first settlers; see in particular; James Harrod, *ibid.*, I, 16; William Gowens, *ibid.*, I, 175–176; William Neely, *ibid.*, I, 230.

[71] *Ibid.*, I, 207.

The James Dean family had in 1802 "home made linen cloth" and in 1804 Mrs. Thomas Butler paid much of her bill at John Coffee's store with "country cloth," [72] but by this date cotton cloth was more commonly made at home than linen. Michaux found the cottons made in Middle Tennessee finer than any he had seen, but said nothing at all of linen, and long before this date merchants were stocking Irish linen. A good bit of flax continued to be grown in Middle Tennessee for several years past the pioneer period, but chiefly for seed to make linseed oil.

Up in Kentucky as in East Tennessee where the climate was not favorable for cotton, families who made their own cloth continued to grow flax until after The War, and a very few until the present century. My mother used to tell of how when a teacher she visited in a home where, in doing honor to the company, the very unsophisticated family removed the tablecloth of hand spun and woven linen, and in its place put the family treasure—a length of the horrible, ill-smelling oil cloth of that day, probably little better than that sold in John Coffee's store of a hundred years before.

As flax declined in importance, hemp increased. Different from flax, hemp had no history of widespread cultivation in the American colonies. England had long offered bounties for its production, but most farmers in a position to grow it, for hemp required a very fertile soil and a long season, felt as did William Byrd—the hard and long labor of producing hemp fiber made the crop a non-profitable one. England in order to supply her rapidly expanding navy with rope had to depend largely on Russia, producer of a very high grade, snow-rotted.

The Revolution cut off hempen rope, and the growth of the plant became more widespread, for with a scarcity of imported cloth and all cloth expensive, even the hempen variety increased in use. As early as 1780 hemp was being grown in Kentucky for cloth.[73] Yielding sometimes as much as fourteen hundred pounds of fiber to the acre, the Indian-harassed pioneer could grow a small patch, less than a quarter of an acre, and from it get fiber enough to make needed rope or cords, coarse clothing, towels, even tablecloths and feather ticks for a whole family. The poor white man often wore hempen clothing during pioneer years, while the field hands of the deeper South knew little else for work clothes.

[72] Coffee Papers, 1801–1804.
[73] FQ, II, 95–128, "Reverend John D. Shane's Interview with Pioneer William Clinkenbeard," ed. from W, 11CC, 54–66 (cited hereafter as Clinkenbeard, "Interview"), 108, 119.

Still, such was the demand, hemp fiber sold on the Cumberland for eleven cents a pound in 1790,[74] low compared to cotton, but almost twice the price of flax fiber. As early as 1801 Nashville merchants were asking for hemp along with other produce;[75] ten years later hemp had grown so plentiful that John Coffee sold the dew-rotted fiber for only five cents a pound, and the better quality water-rotted for five and a half;[76] up river twenty-seven pounds brought only three shillings, less than two cents a pound in 1801.[77] Even hempen rope that took a deal of work, though little equipment, to make, was by 1802 selling in Nashville for only nine cents the pound.[78]

Yet, such was the yield on rich soil, it was a profitable crop, and Middle Tennessee papers encouraged the growth of it through articles on its culture. The cultivation of hemp was further encouraged by the widespread publication of the articles written by John Quincy Adams, who while Minister to Russia, 1809–1814, made quite a study of its needs.

Hemp had to have a soil sufficiently rich to support a stand of plants thick enough there could be no branching out, but with a tall growth, sometimes fourteen feet, with stems only one-fourth to three-eighths of an inch in diameter. The farmer was told to plow very deep in the fall and again at the time of sowing, between the first and twentieth of May, then he was to pass a heavy, strong-toothed harrow over the field. Next, "with majestic sweeps of the arm," [79] he broadcast the seed, a bushel, sometimes five pecks to the acre, an even distribution no small art, as was that of any small grain before the advent of seeders. Hemp, like the small grains, was covered with a second harrowing and grew with no cultivation.

In the heat of early August, the tall stuff had to be pulled as was flax, for the hemp hook with which a man could cut half an acre a day had not yet come into use. The pulled hemp was left on the ground, but turned often so that it might cure evenly. Dried, it was put into shocks, not greatly different in appearance—though taller, thinner—from the corn shocks that came later.

Properly shocked hemp might stand for some time with no damage, but the farmer could begin the rotting any time after curing. Some hemp was

[74] DW, I, 283, John Haggard; see also *ibid.*, I, 348, John Blackamore.
[75] Tennessee *Gazette*, Aug. 5, 1801.
[76] Coffee Papers, 1811, 1812.
[77] PW, I, 1, the inventory of Willam Womsley.
[78] Tennessee *Gazette*, Nov. 13, 1802.
[79] Nashville *Clarion*, Nov. 9, 1810; this a reprint from the Russellville *Mirror*.

merely spread thinly on the ground and the rains and wet snows of late autumn and winter allowed to do the work, but this, known as dew-rotted, sold for less. Water-rotted hemp brought more because the fibers were whiter and stronger, almost as good as those of the Russian snow-rotted. In cool weather the rotting time for hemp on the ground took from a month to six weeks, but water rotting, in fairly warm weather required only a few days; the hemp, of course, poisoned the water, killed all the fish below it, if in a branch, and in all cases gave off a "disagreeable odor." [80]

Once rotted, the hemp was treated much like flax, but during pioneer years there was, after drying, no standard way of getting the fiber free of the bark. The hemp break, a larger and heavier version of the flax break, was not in common use until around 1810.[81] Most beat it on a log or stump as had long been done by English convicts. In Kentucky various methods were tried, even mills,[82] but none was successful, and in time all farmers used the heavy and cumbersome, back-breaking break.

The fiber was hackled much as was flax; if wanted for cloth fine fiber was separated from the coarser, but in any case it was made into hanks, ready for spinning or the rope walk.

Practically all crops mentioned, save some of the vegetables and tobacco, were harvested at maturity so that seed for the next season was never a problem. Hemp was a troublesome exception; it was not only harvested before maturity, but it is one of those plants which, like the cedar, has dioecious flowers. Hemp for seed was planted and cultivated in rows, much as was corn, and, in contrast to that grown for fiber, was encouraged to branch out as much as possible by means of wide rows, with still more room given when, after the pollination of the female was completed, the male plants were cut out. The work is reflected in the high price—25 cents [83] a quart—of hemp seed as late as 1793, and an acre cost at

[80] FQ, II, Clinkenbeard, "Interview," 108.

[81] The *Clarion* article of Nov. 9, 1810, speaks of a labor-saving device "now in use" that would break 240 pounds a day. The Mountain Life Museum has good examples of the hemp break.

[82] The culture and preparation of hemp were during the pioneer period in a state of experimentation; the American *Museum* carried numerous articles on cleaning and culture, and in Kentucky mills were tried for some stages of the work; Michaux, *Travels 1802*, 152, mentioned machines capable of cleaning 8,000 pounds a day. See also FP, 28, Mary Verhoeff, *Kentucky River Navigation*, copyright The Filson Club, Louisville, 1917 (cited hereafter as Verhoeff, *Kentucky River*), 91, quotes an ad from a 1793 Kentucky *Gazette* for a hemp mill, charging a toll of one-eight, but these early devices seem to have been supplanted by the break and the hackle.

[83] DW, I, 283.

this rate eight dollars for even a thin sowing, but twenty years later the price of seed had dropped to one dollar a bushel.[84]

Hemp, in spite of the year-round work entailed in the growing of it, became in time an important crop all up and down the Cumberland, though the center of hemp culture was to be in the Kentucky Bluegrass, main source of supply as the ever-expanding cotton fields of the deeper South called for more and more hempen rope and bale covering to get the cotton to market.

Tobacco required even more time, trouble, and greater skill, for the stuff could be ruined at almost any stage of cultivation. During pioneer years, and for generations to come, a tobacco grower had the crop on his mind for around eleven months in the year, and sometimes twelve. Yet, of all crops, it is the one best loved by many of the upper Cumberland today, and among its many growers are men—and women, too—whose ancestors loved it in Virginia or the Carolinas close to three hundred years ago. Men have loved it and grown it through good times and bad, not even turning against it when, during the 1930's, farmers in Wayne and Pulaski counties of Kentucky, with no roads and forced after long hauling to sell in Lexington, found themselves at the end of the season in debt for transportation costs and warehouse fees. Much the same thing had, two hundred years before, happened to Virginia growers, shipping to London. Still, they grew tobacco.

Basically, tobacco culture has changed surprisingly little in three hundred years; men still talk of tobacco beds, suckering, topping, curing, cutting, and hanging as in the days of Thomas Glover who in 1671 wrote quite a detailed description.[85] The first step was to find a good little patch of ground, preferably on the southern side of a hill, and the canny farmer, ever aware of the uncertainties of life, would choose three or four. He would then on each spot build a big brush pile, and on some still dry November or December day, burn the brush as completely as possible, for any bits of charcoal or unburned wood had to be raked off.

Ashes were left and worked into the ground with a spade or mattock; that is, if there were not too many, for he didn't burn primarily for the ashes but to kill all weed seeds; burning could be done away with entirely if a spot of new ground could be found with deep, rich leaf-mold and free of weeds and undergrowth. The powderlike seeds were in the early years sown during the Twelve Days of Christmas, and covered with more

[84] Coffee Papers, 1812.
[85] Gray, *Agriculture*, I, 215–216.

brush, over which cloth was thrown for protection. Some farmers sowed cabbage for early setting in the tobacco bed. If all went well and the plants survived hard cold, heavy rains, and deep damp snows, they were in Virginia set around the first of May.

The aim in tobacco culture was exactly opposite that of hemp; instead of long thin stalks the grower wanted big thin leaves, and so he, in a spell of rainy weather, set the plants singly in hills four feet or so apart in the row, with rows about the same distance apart. Thus, tobacco, requiring rich ground as it did and demanding hoe cultivation, was a favorite of farmers with rich new ground and the time and wherewithal for building a barn for curing. If the plant survived the dry spell that always seemed to come immediately after it was set, the farmer cared for it with "diligent weedings," resetting as needed.

A tobacco field in flower is a pretty sight, but one no pioneer farmer wanted to own; it marked him as a lazy man, for tobacco was supposed to be topped when flower buds appeared. At tobacco-topping time all hands, big and little, black and white, went forth to pinch the beginning flowers; but tobacco was a determined sort of creature; she would make seed, and so sent forth suckers at each leaf joint; then they had it nip and tuck between the farmer and the obstinate plant. Suckering could be done by small hands, but was a nasty job, what with the green tobacco juice, the great green tobacco worms, and the green-tobacco smell in the hot sun.

Yet, it went on, "the plucking away, once a week, till the plant comes to perfection, which it doth in August; Then in dry weather, when there is little Breeze of Wind, they cut down what is ripe." And so it still is, with tobacco-cutting time usually in August, and though not used in the seventeenth century, the tobacco stick with plants hung by their slit stems had come into use by the time of the Revolution.[86] The green gold stuff was hung in an especially made tobacco barn, an airy place with room enough so the plants would not touch, and here it cured, slowly, a change more than a mere drying. Rainy days in fall, unfit for other work, made good tobacco-stripping weather; the stripped leaves were tied into hands, and these packed into hogsheads for shipment.

It is only within the last generation that farmers have moved up the date of sowing their beds, though tobacco-bed canvas has long since replaced the brush covering. Spraying with arsenic of lead and other chemicals is also a modern invention, and still more modern is weed-killer

[86] Smyth, *Tour*, II, 134.

instead of fire as the first step in making a bed. Gone, too, is the belief that topping is of prime importance; more strength on both sides went into the sucker fight than could ever go into flower or even seed. The biggest change was in the variety. The big-leafed, thin-stemmed White Burley now commonly grown on the Cumberland above Nashville was then unknown; most common in the early years was a variety of Oronko known as Kite's Foot,[87] a large plant with a broad thinnish leaf, seemingly much like the dark flue-cured tobaccos of today. Tobacco, almost as much as corn, has entered into the speech of the people in many localities; one hears talk of tobacco-stripping weather, tobacco-setting time, cutting time, and biggest time of all, "warehouse-opening-time."

Laws for the establishment of tobacco inspectors and inspection points were an old part of life in Virginia and North Carolina. The first inspection point on the Cumberland was established at Nashville [88] in 1785, but there was little tobacco to inspect during the very early years. Still, as in North Carolina and Virginia what little there was served often as currency, as in 1785 Hannah Porter, appointed administratrix of the estate of her husband John, gave bond of a "thousand weight" of tobacco.

The Revolution had increased the demand for cotton and hemp along with goods formerly imported, but tobacco, chief export of the Southern colonies, could not get to market. True, in 1778 Congress made an arrangement to exchange it for French cannon,[89] but the North Carolina farmers who furnished the tobacco were paid in warrants, later almost worthless. In 1782–83 North Carolina tobacco was bringing in hard money only one pound per hundredweight, not a bad price for a farmer near the market, but in the old Southwest, tobacco was not only further from market, but lower in price, and twenty years later was bringing only two dollars the hundred.[90]

Still, cheap as it was, tobacco was one of the earliest cash crops of the pioneer, and as early as 1786 we find in what was to be Wayne County a debt to be paid in 9,000 "weight of tobacco." [91] Tobacco in smallish amounts, one hogshead or a thousand pounds, was fairly common among Middle Tennessee farmers by 1790,[92] though in importance it could not

[87] *Ibid.*, II, 129. Smyth described (with some detail) tobacco culture as practiced in Virginia and wrote that turkeys were used to keep the plant free of worms. See also Gray, *Agriculture*, I, 218.

[88] NCR, XVII, 352.

[89] *Ibid.*, XIX, 710–711.

[90] DW, II, 9—"1,000 wt. tobacco, $20.00." See also Michaux, *Travels 1802*, 226.

[91] WD, I, 22.

[92] DW, I, 244, 252.

compare with corn or cotton. John Coffee, beginning in the late nineties, made several shipments to New Orleans, but always in small quantities of a thousand pounds or so. It is, however, impossible to judge the amount of tobacco grown by the number of times it appears in court minutes or cargoes. Much tobacco during this period and for many years to come was manufactured at home into cigars or sticks of twist before being sold. Beginning with the James Laneer stock in 1787, with 200 sticks of twist,[93] most stores studied carried tobacco in this form, the stand-by of the tobacco-chewing or pipe-smoking small farmer, workingman, and his wife. The elite used "best James River Tobacco," and smoked "Spanish and American Segars." [94]

Tobacco, in proportion to total income, figured more prominently in the lives of the farmers up river; as much could be grown on a small amount of fertile soil as a small farmer and such help as he had could handle; and tobacco, no different from other crops, never minded a hillside.

One of the earliest warehouses in the region was established around 1800 on the Cumberland in Pulaski County, Kentucky. Known as Stigall's Warehouse it was by 1818 old, and of it the Pulaski County inspectors for that year wrote: ". . . found the old warhouse in situation for reception of tobacco . . . about 22 feet in weadth and 80 feet in length, but no situation for securing the tobacco. The scales was not hung so we could not tri them—the prise [for forcing in the head of the hogshead] was not found, we cannot say about it. The wates we did tri by Wm. Buster's steelyards and found them about as formerly, about 1377, which we are of opinion if they all wey together they would be the 1380 wate. The room we was given last year for bookkeeping is not fit for the purpose, it wants shutters to doors and windars." They recommended that the floors "be raised so as to [keep] the tobacco from receiving damage from the dampness of the earth"; "the scale fixt for wate of hogs-heads, and the prise well fixed for the convenience of coopering the tobacco." [95]

Crude as these warehouses were, they sent much tobacco down the river; Stigall's reported the inspection of 217 hogsheads, while nearby Montgomery Warehouse for the same year reported 294, and as each

[93] *Ibid.*, I, 63.

[94] Tennessee *Gazette*, Jan. 14, 1801; Bustard and Fasin also offered, "English and East India dry goods, Hardware and cutlery, Japanned and tin ware, Stationary and Saddlery, cotton and wool cards, Queen's glass and China, Loaf Sugar and Coffee, Young Hyson, Hyson Skin, and Bohea Tea, Pepper, All spice & ginger, copperas, alum, Brimstone and Indigo."

[95] PD, IV, 262.

hogshead held a net of at least a thousand pounds, this was no small amount of tobacco; the largest single consignment found from this district was 104,030 pounds shipped by Caldwell Stewart to Amsterdam.

The small grains, though difficult for any pioneer farmer and much less suited to the region than tobacco and corn, were also grown at an early date. Any crop, wheat or flax, sown broadcast and uncultivated did poorly in a stumpy new-ground field, and the same fertile virgin soil that would grow one hundred bushels of corn to the acre would make wheat and oats that were little more than rank grass with no grain at all. As a rule farmers did as suggested by Daniel Smith: reduced the land two or three years with corn before attempting wheat.

The aim of the newly settled farmer was usually only to harvest enough wheat to supply the family's needs. In spite of the difficulties of cultivation, wheat fields and wheat sheaves are incidentally mentioned in accounts of Indian warfare before 1790,[96] and by 1795 wheat and flour were commonly found in inventories.[97] More and better mills and the introduction of kiln drying encouraged wheat production, and wheat became in time an important cash crop as did oats to a lesser extent. Wheat, compared to corn, was always expensive,[98] sometimes selling for more than 75 cents a bushel and seldom less than 50 cents, but in 1802 flour was at Natchez bringing only $3 to $4 per 196-pound barrel, a very bad year; two years later it was double the price, though meal was bringing only $2 a barrel.[99]

Many small farmers grew a little patch of wheat as a minor crop sown in late August between the rows of still-standing but stripped corn, "brushed in" chiefly with the hope it would yield enough grain to supply flour for biscuit, pie crusts, and gravy. Small crops such as these were harvested with a sickle in June, flailed on a flat rock with hand flails, winnowed by tossing on a sheet, and then carried to the nearest mill as was corn.[100]

It is doubtful, however, if such farmers as the Neelys, Buchanans, and

[96] W, 30S, 465; *ibid.*, 31S, 389.

[97] DW, II, 31, 229, 272, 348.

[98] MW, I, 89. "Account of the Expenditure of a Family, Oct. 31, 1806–Oct. 31, 1807," gives retail price in Middle Tennessee of the most common foods: wheat, 75¢ a bushel; beef, $2.50 per CWT; pork, 3 and 4¢ per pound; 50 lbs. butter, $6.25; bacon, $12.50 per CWT.

[99] Tennessee *Gazette*, Nov. 20, 1802; *ibid.*, May 30, 1804.

[100] Richmond Kelly, *The Kelly Clan*, Portland, Oregon, 1901 (cited hereafter as Kelly, *Clan*), 70. The Kellys were not in one sense pioneers, not settling in Pulaski County, Kentucky, until 1807, but in most ways, save Indian warfare, their lives were like those of earlier settlers.

Edmonsons grew wheat in this fashion; Thomas McCain,[101] killed in 1789, had a wheat cradle and they continued common, though some like Thomas Brown, killed at almost the same time, used reap hooks. But soon wheat fans, advertisements [102] of bolting cloths, and great stone mills such as those at Cragfont, mentioned by travelers in 1799, indicated that wheat growing had moved out of the reap-hook-flail stage onto the threshing or "treading floor" [103] with oxen or horses walking round and round, help standing by with shovels, and quick handed they had to be to catch the dung.

Oats, either used as summer grazing for the hogs or harvested and fed to the horsestock, were early an important crop; even the Halls, not first settlers, were growing oats by 1787. Always in demand by horse owners, oats are never in the early newspapers described as dull, and down at Natchez in 1804 were bringing 31½ cents a bushel. Barley and rye were also grown,[104] usually in small quantities, some to be used at home in bread, chiefly by such Scots as clung to the old ways; for it was not until after the end of the eighteenth century that wheat was grown in Northern Ireland—bean and oat cake and rye bread were the stand-bys of that short-summered region, and were also commonly eaten in Northern Scotland. The whiskey distiller liked at least a little barley and rye, either in the malt or in the mash, or both, though generations before the settlement of the Cumberland farmers had learned to make whiskey of nothing but corn.

All good farmers tried to have at least a little permanent pasture as soon as possible and some grew hay, but during pioneer years there was never enough of either, and it was only when a man died or bad luck overtook his horsestock that much pasture [105] was rented or hay sold. None was found until around 1795. Potatoes were much the same story; everybody grew potatoes in small quantities and they are often mentioned in accounts of Indian warfare, but it was after 1790 before I found an inventory containing sweet potatoes,[106] and their price—83 cents a bushel

---

[101] DW, I, 107.

[102] *Ibid.*, II, 348.

[103] It is doubtful if there were many, if any, treading floors in Middle Tennessee before 1800; the flail was widely used, even in Pennsylvania, in the 1790's; Carey, *Museum*, had many articles on the threshing of grain, and diagrams of better treading floors; *ibid.*, VII (1790), 64–65, described the ideal treading floor as 60 to 100 feet in diameter and 12 to 24 feet wide; oxen were in that section more commonly used than horses, but horses were, by tradition, used in our section.

[104] DW, II, 252, 274, 290, 348.

[105] *Ibid.*, II, 244, 348.

[106] *Ibid.*, II, 292.

—would indicate great scarcity, though ten years later Irish potatoes were quoted as selling at Natchez at only 25 cents the bushel.

Even less commonly found than potatoes were fruit and fruit products. Judging from the several accounts of men and boys killed while gathering strawberries, mulberries, and other wild fruits, cultivated fruit of any kind was scarce in the early years. The Stumps at their settling in 1780 planted apple and peach seed Robertson had sent back from the Illinois,[107] and more fortunate than other first-settling families the Stumps did not in 1784 have to move and leave their orchard. A nursery of seedling fruit trees is now and then mentioned in accounts of Indian warfare,[108] but apples were found in no inventory, and no young fruit trees for sale until 1806. These, belonging to James McCorkle of Montgomery County,[109] brought only seventeen cents each and were probably ungrafted, for many farmers of that day did their own grafting. Orchards were in time common on every farm, though few were so large as that tried by Andrew Jackson who in 1801 bought five hundred apple and five hundred peach trees.[110]

Apples, slow maturing as they were and not well suited to the climate of Middle Tennessee, were scarce for many years, and scarcer still in the deeper South. John Coffee's repeated efforts to plant an orchard in Alabama at a later date are well preserved in his notes;[111] among the varieties of apples are many of which I heard much as a child—limber twigs and horse apples—along with others now but little known. Peaches were a different story, and though some farmers were already suffering from the peach borer, there were enough that by 1802 Daniel Smith could make and sell peach brandy.[112] Peaches, long grown by the Indians, were often among the first things planted, as up in Pulaski County we find a tenant leasing uncleared land, agreeing to set a peach orchard of three hundred trees "20 feet apart each way." [113]

In spite of a widespread interest in grape culture with an especial concern for wine grapes, the grape did not in Middle Tennessee thrive. Imported plants brought by way of Philadelphia cost five dollars each, but

[107] Williams, *Travels*, Schweinitz, "Report," 512.

[108] W, 31S, 388–389.

[109] MW, I, 301.

[110] Bassett, *Jackson Correspondence*, I, 101.

[111] Coffee Papers, 1820, "This day planted an orchard." He tried plums, cherries, quince, pears, etc., and through the years continued to try, but few throve in Alabama.

[112] Michaux, *Travels 1802*, 254.

[113] PD, I, 39.

the efforts of J. J. DuFours, lately of Switzerland, to raise $10,000 to establish a grape nursery in Middle Tennessee were unsuccessful, though he promised cheaper and better plants.[114] Most farms advertised had, at least by 1810, quite a variety of fruit in addition to peaches and apples. Dr. Mark B. Sappington's plantation, sold on his death in 1801, had along with a "never failing spring," meadow land and crop lands, an apple and peach orchard, and an acre in Chickasaw plums, these last no doubt intended for brandy.[115] Willie Barrow's plantation, for sale in February of 1803, had a cotton gin of "54 saws" with a good press, a copper still, fields sown to wheat and rye, apple trees, and a peach orchard.[116] The passing years brought a greater variety of everything; in 1812 a 657-acre plantation near Franklin on a branch of the Harpeth had in addition to the usual crops and buildings small fields of red clover, white clover, and bluegrass, fruit trees of many varieties, and a garden of gooseberries, currants, raspberries, and strawberries.[117] Another offered an "elegant garden of raspberries, figs, grapes, and Chickasaw plums," while that of J. Bruff on Mill Creek had an even greater variety that included currants and gooseberries.[118]

As in many other aspects of life, the Cumberlander in his farming operations was never guided entirely by prime necessity. Few had the formal garden that in time became fashionable and brought a taste of Tidewater. Yet even the poor farm in the back hills had a bed of tansy by the doorstep, catnip, horehound, horse-radish, and sage in out-of-the-way corners, with mint in the spring branch and hop vines for the yeast by the kitchen windows. The yard that had to graze colts could have iris, yucca, honeysuckle that in time went all over, burning-bushes, and cabbage roses with a rambler on the smokehouse.

The English had ever loved their herbs and flowers, and in many pioneer gardens one would have found at least a few—lavender, rosemary, and thyme; digitalis and chives—their growth often disappointingly slow or not at all in the hotter summers and colder winters of inland Tennessee. Still, they tried as their ancestors had tried in Tidewater; one can see in the Elizabethan Gardens at Roanoke, at Williamsburg, the Blount Mansion, and at the historic shrines of Middle Tennessee the herbs and flowering shrubs best known to the Southern pioneer.

[114] Tennessee *Gazette*, Aug. 19, 1801.
[115] *Ibid.*, Sept. 16, 1801.
[116] *Ibid.*, Feb. 16, 1803.
[117] Nashville *Clarion*, April 17, 1812.
[118] *Ibid.*, May 12, 1812.

The vegetable garden also contained such things as popcorn, peanuts—known then as ground peas—and groundnuts, artichokes they were called by us. None of these was needed any more than was a peacock, but the useless pomegranates and pretty little gourds were as highly prized as the ugly but useful wormseed, left in an out-of-the-way corner by the paling fence where the children wouldn't find it and pull it up.

Not all crops harvested by the Cumberlanders grew behind fence; as on all other forested borders, the woods held many riches, but Middle Tennessee farmers on the whole used the woods crops less than most pioneer farmers. In the rougher regions up river where every farmer had his "clan of wild hogs," a late frost killing the mast was as great a tragedy, sometimes more so, than the "June tide" that took the crops in river or creek bottom.

There were also the many products of the woods gathered in the days of William Byrd and still gathered by a few families in the hills. Most important to the up-river family was ginseng,[119] and a few of the very old remember the pleasurable occupation of walking through the woods with a "sang" hoe, and the joy of finding an extra fine root. They would, along with "sang," gather other things, sometimes to be dried and saved with the surplus sold as were Seneca snakeroot, May apple, yellow root, and sassafras. There was puccoon (bloodroot) for drug and dye, ratbane for cough syrup, pokeroot to steep in whiskey for rheumatism, crow's foot for sallet greens, wild ginger for headache, and so on through several dozen, with many gathered just for a taste of strange food as were white blackberries and pawpaws.

The variety of soils and formations up river made rich hunting. Any farmer and his wife looked with favor on a thin-soiled, rocky limestone ledge, set about with maple trees; there was always the chance that among them was a rock maple. The pioneer knew the fine-grained maple so prized for gunstocks and chairbacks was not from a species entirely different from the sugar maple, but came only from trees in thin, dry soil where a slow growth made for small, fine, annual growth rings; but rock maple on the Cumberland was never so fine or abundant as in Pennsylvania and northward.

A "beech bottom" was good almost as a cornfield for the hogs in the fall, and a fine place for squirrel hunting at daylight on an October morn-

119 Williams, *Smith*, 25, dug ginseng in Stockton's Valley; Carey, *Museum*, II, 9, in writing of the "outrages of McGillivray" mentioned settlers on Holston killed while hunting ginseng, but I found no mention of it in Middle Tennessee where the soil was less suited, and the populace as a whole less inclined to used woods products.

ing. A good stand of chestnut was often kept, not only as a storehouse of fence rails and building material, but for the nuts, beloved by men and hogs. Even now a few of the very old can remember in the days before the blight came, the joy of standing on some high hill or crag up river and looking out and away across the woods where "in May the chestnut bloom was like a sea."

Young ones born in Middle Tennessee, even before the Louisiana Purchase, would have little memory of tall timber. Much of the land along the Cumberland in what is now Sumner and adjoining counties was not thickly forested in the first place, and the pioneer farmer used large quantities of timber for building and fence laying, but chiefly he used it for firewood. Prodigious quantities were needed on any farm; the weekly boiling of the family wash would soon make a hole in the limbs and debris of a fair-sized board tree; the cooking fires alone devoured whole trees; winter heating took more, but all these were little compared to the firewood needed in many farm activities—hog killing, lard rendering, soap making, dyeing, maple sugar making, not to mention the burning of a lime kiln or the whiskey run-off; all demanded firewood, while the blacksmith like the early iron manufacturer used it in the form of charcoal.

As early as 1801 in the rather remote world of Pulaski County, Kentucky, timber was so valued that a tenant in leasing land for cultivation agreed to "waste or cut no timber." [120] The editor of the Tennessee *Gazette* was by 1804 deploring the great waste of wood in Middle Tennessee caused by burning it wet; ". . . ask the distiller, the brick maker, the potter," he urged the farmer, for the farmer it was who had neglected to build proper woodhouses.

Bradford's concern for the scarcity of firewood came only thirty-five years since Kaspar Mansker and Isaac Bledsoe had seen the great herds of buffalo, only nine since the last Indian raid in Middle Tennessee, and even then in 1804, Creek, Chickasaw, and Cherokee still owned lands on three sides, but firewood had gone the way of the cane and the big game. Middle Tennessee was a farmer's world of fenced fields.

Scarce as firewood was in Middle Tennessee by 1804, and rich and valuable as was much of the land, not everybody cut his fence rows clean, or destroyed all the "groves of beautiful cedar," [121] and sold them for shingles, fence posts, and buckets. Many cleared steep land and rocky

[120] PD, I, 39.
[121] Williams, *Travels*, Schweinitz, "Report," 508.

glades that should never have been cleared, but this land to their eyes didn't look as rough as it does to us today, thinking in terms of farm machinery and the flat Corn Belt. The pioneers knew what they had and left trees for shade and by the creeks. They had learned much from seeing what had happened to the buffalo and the deer.

As early as 1784 the North Carolina Assembly had passed a bill "to prevent killing deer by firelight and at unseasonable times." [122] Some realized, even then, the old days were gone.

[122] NCR, XXIV, 595–596.

Chapter Ten

Industry

THERE WERE ten of the young Masons when they settled down on Richland Creek in late 1790,[1] and we can be certain that at least eight of them helped in the building of the new home—even a toddler could carry the chunks of heartwood that went between the hewed logs of the walls before plastering was put on. Yet, if one had remarked to any of the children, even Philip the oldest, and of an age to help in the hewing, that he was engaged in the building industry, he might have stared in wonder, thinking possibly the speaker meant to say, "He was showing great industry."

The word *industry* as commonly used today was not part of the average pioneer's vocabulary, for industry was not as a rule a separate way of

Headpiece: River scene showing flatboat and two keelboats. (Reproduced from *The Keelboat Age on Western Waters*, by Leland D. Baldwin, with the permission of the University of Pittsburgh Press.)

[1] A, III, 90.

life. Rooted for the most part in agriculture or readily available natural resources such as the trees that went into the Masons' home, industry of most kinds was ordinarily a part of family life, though building like other industries defies any classification. Centuries before the settlement of the Cumberland, other families had built whole villages of what must have been quite comfortable homes, made stone-lined graves, manufactured pottery, and many articles of shell, stone, wood, and bone. In time came the Chickasaw to build a temporary forted town near the old French Landing, and after these had come the hunters to build open-faced camps or small storage houses such as that put up by De Monbruen.

The building industry was thus old on the Cumberland when the white men settled, and as the Indian menace made building and fortification a necessity, it was also the first and most important industry of pioneer days.[2] Yet, because of the great increase in immigration, "two or three hundred a day in 1796,"[3] building continued important. Many settlers, once the fort pickets could come down, built elsewhere, or like James Robertson replaced the smaller home with a larger one, though Daniel Smith did not wait, for his stone home was finished around 1794.[4]

Daniel Smith's home, no more than Cragfont, also built of stone, was a typical pioneer home. Most were made of logs or somewhat later, framed, save in Nashville where by 1812, brick, because of the fire hazard, was mandatory; and few homes were built entirely by skilled workmen as was Daniel Smith's. As a rule the farmer and his help did much of the work themselves. However, one should avoid the other extreme—that picture too often painted of the pioneer family doing everything for itself. Dr. Doddridge, for example, grew up during the Revolution on a western Virginia frontier with much less wealth than Middle Tennessee. House raisings were common, but skilled help was called in for chimneys, windows, and other details.

I found no pioneer family a self-sufficient unit, either in services or in goods. The John Smith family in Stockton's Valley was one of the poorest; the only one found where deerskin trousers were made in the home. They may have done all the building themselves, yet when the corn crop was in, they went to mill, though it meant a trip of more than a hundred

[2] Arnow, *Seedtime*, Chap. X, 247–281, gives a somewhat detailed account of the pioneer's building activities.

[3] Smith, *Description*, 33.

[4] A, V, 293–294, a 1793 letter of Mrs. Smith describing to her husband the progress of the new home; she speaks of sawyers, stone cutters, carpenters, and other workmen.

miles. All family inventories yielded many items—books to spectacles—and of course kitchenware and dinnerware, produced elsewhere, sometimes in another country. Many of their possessions of materials native to the region—cherry press or loom—were made by skilled workmen.

Still, the pioneer family unit was much more self-sufficient than the Tidewater colonials who had imported even their woodenware, but never completely so. There is a tendency to identify the pioneers of the late eighteenth century with rural families in the Kentucky hills and other remote regions as seen by visitors in the latter half of the nineteenth and early twentieth centuries. Many families in out-of-the-way places supplied more of their own needs than did their ancestors on the same land a hundred years before. The main reason for this was poverty; no early traveler mentioned poverty in Wayne or Pulaski counties of Kentucky or in East Tennessee. The erosion of land and increase of population helped impoverish the region. Still more was caused by The War that in some counties such as Cumberland County, Tennessee, not only took all the livestock that could not be successfully hidden, but cut off many commodities such as sugar and rice brought up the Cumberland from earliest days.

The hill woman of a generation or so ago, carding wool and cotton and dyeing it from dyes made entirely of materials taken from the woods and fields—bark of black walnut, hickory, and maple, root of puccoon —often had great-grandmothers who had bought at the neighborhood store logwood, madder, indigo, and alum for the setting. Dyes were commonly stocked, and Andrew Jackson brought much logwood up the Mississippi. We associate the pioneer with latchstrings and ink of pokeberry juice, yet metal window latches and inkstands were being sold in Pulaski County, Kentucky, by 1800.[5]

True, the average family filled far more of its food, clothing, and furniture needs with home-grown produce and family labor than does any family today. Yet, never entirely. There were from earliest years skilled workmen. One of the first agreements recorded by Davidson County Court in early 1784 was that between an apprentice and a carpenter,[6] and by that date Haydon Wells was setting up as miller; between itinerant merchants, many of them French, and such early storekeepers as the Leneers, one could buy most anything from sugar to hanging-paper.

Any predominantly rural region of that day with fertile land was a

[5] PW, I, 3–4, estate of merchant John James.
[6] DW, I, 9.

haven for the workingman. More than forty trades, skills, and professions were represented in the Virginia size rolls of the French and Indian War. Court minutes, work agreements and later advertisements in the first newspapers reveal that by 1803 one could, without leaving Middle Tennessee, have almost anything made from a silver spoon to a flatboat, and by 1812 one could hire a scrivener or a sign painter.

Yet, one could not say that industry was in the hands of these skilled workmen; [7] most were wanderers, working on contract for a few months, or setting up shop for a season, then going elsewhere. More important to attempted classification, the hats, carriages, riding habits, boots, and shoes they made were for local consumption only; these articles did not enter into the commerce of the wider world of the Mississippi Valley. Rather they competed with it, for John Coffee like earlier merchants sold much —wool hats, all manner of materials, ready-made clothing such as silk hose —manufactured elsewhere, sometimes in France, England, and Russia.

The most important early industries on the Cumberland were those connected with the farm. Bacon, country cloth in the very early years, butter, whiskey were quite commonly exported. The average farmer was, in smoking bacon or distilling whiskey, not an industrialist, but a farmer processing a crop for sale. The land, whether forest to furnish barrel staves or in fields of corn for whiskey and fat hogs, was the mainstay of his livelihood, and it is impossible to say where farming ended and manufacturing began.

There were no rules. A large plantation owner like Jackson might sell nothing but cotton in the raw state; a small or part-time farmer might sell no crop unprocessed—flax as linen cloth, corn and hogs as bacon—but as a rule the larger the farm, the more apt it was to have some manufacturing devices.[8] The man with a cotton gin or slaughterhouse would also, taking toll instead of money, serve several of his neighbors, but his primary aim was to process his own crops for market.

One of the most common methods of processing a crop, both for use at home and for shipment, was the distillation of corn into whiskey. Whiskey was an old story in the United States by the time the Cumber-

---

[7] *Rights of Man or Nashville Intelligencer*, March 11, 1799, "wanted a Journeyman printer"; *ibid.*, July 17, 1799, a boot and shoe maker wants an apprentice; Tennessee *Gazette*, Feb. 25, 1800, a taylor and a watch maker advertise; *ibid.*, Oct. 28, 1801, E. Winchester wants a miller; *ibid.*, June 24, 1801, "—silversmith apprentice wanted"; *ibid.*, March 17, 1802, "Wanted one or two sober industrious well diggers."

[8] Tennessee *Gazette*, Jan. 13, 1802, "farm with mill seat." *Ibid.*, Feb. 16, 1803, Willie Barrow had a cotton gin, press, and still; Nashville *Clarion*, March 1, 1811, Richard Orton, a dairy and slaughterhouse.

land was settled. Governor Spotswood had, along with wines and other imported alcoholic beverages, carried "Esquebaugh" on his trek across the Shenandoah in 1716 with his Knights of the Golden Horseshoe.[9] We cannot, however, be certain the usquebaugh mentioned was whiskey; it may have been the cordial by that name. Yet, thirty years later, whiskey was so plentiful and common in Augusta County, Virginia, it was listed in tavern rates at only one dollar a gallon.[10] It had taken its place on the border as a substitute for rum, for at about this same time we also find it mentioned in connection with Indian trade on the Pennsylvania border.[11] Thirty years later, or during the Revolution, corn whiskey had become so plentiful that in the tavern rates of Augusta County it was only four shillings a gallon, as compared to eight shillings for rye.[12] American whiskey was on the way, for the word whiskey alone in earlier periods most probably denominated a drink made as in Scotland and Ireland—of malted small grains, preferably rye.

The making of whiskey is one of many things introduced by the Scotch and Scotch–Irish. It continued unfamiliar to many Englishmen as it was to young Keats who, traveling in 1818 to pay homage at the tomb of Burns, wrote, "We are now begun upon whiskey, called here 'whuskey' —very smart stuff it is. Mixed like our liquors with sugar and water, 'tis called toddy; very pretty drink." Peter Lockhart visiting Scotland at about the same time wrote, "I tasted for the first time the genuine Usquebaugh of Lochaber,"[13] but he, different from Keats, may have been referring to the cordial, for he did not use the word whiskey or speak of toddies.

Stills came with the first settlers to the Cumberland[14] Old Johnnie Boyd who came in the Donelson convoy is said to have been the first distiller;[15] Frederick Stump, another first settler, was not far behind; and by 1799 there were for the less than four thousand people in Davidson County, sixty-one stills.[16] All things on the Cumberland—the Scottish

[9] Summers, *Southwest Virginia*, "The Journal of Lynn Fontaine," 39.
[10] Waddell, *Annals*, 30.
[11] Thwaites, *Travels*, I, "The Journal of Conrad Weiser," 23, 30.
[12] Summers, *Southwest Virginia*, 260.
[13] Lockhart, *Letters*, 22.
[14] DW, I, 90; *ibid.*, II, 17; MW, I, 3.
[15] W, 6XX(50), 1.
[16] Materials used by permission of Dr. William T. Alderson, Tennessee State Librarian and Archivist, from the Jacob McGavock Dickinson Papers, Judge John Overton's Record of Distillers for the years 1795–1802 when he was Supervisor of Internal Revenue for the District of Tennessee (cited hereafter as Overton, Accounts), 9–11.

background of many of the settlers, the fine corn-growing soil, the abundance of firewood, plenty of white oak for barrels, and the ease with which whiskey could be stored or shipped as compared to many farm products—contributed to the manufacture of corn whiskey.

It was of especial importance to the small farmer up river. Here, the plenitude of firewood and white oak for barrels made it possible for him to show quite a profit on his corn crop if he turned it into whiskey, and particularly so if he and his neighbors built a flatboat and took it down river. They could stop in Nashville and get at least a dollar a gallon, and if they went on down to Natchez they could usually get double that price. Whiskey was the poor farmer's friend; unable to buy hogs or cattle to which to feed his corn, he could turn it into whiskey. Still, the Cumberlanders, law-abiding as they were, never revolted against the whiskey tax as did the farmers in Pennsylvania and North Carolina. But they did vote for Jefferson.

It is doubtful if any two owners of stills on the Cumberland made whiskey in exactly the same fashion, for the making of whiskey was, like the making of many pioneer products, a thing that "all depended." A man with nothing but new-ground fields and unable to grow small grains was inclined to make pure corn whiskey; "corn rum," [17] the French had called that which M. Bomer had for sale in 1776. This whiskey may have been a product of Illinois or it could have been made in the backwoods of Pennsylvania, though Old Monongahela, famous throughout the Mississippi Valley and advertised in early Nashville papers, was a rye whiskey.

Regardless of what grain was used, it had to be ground, and thus the larger distiller like Stump was usually a miller as well. The meal had neither to be very fine nor sifted, but good meal made good whiskey, and by tradition the maker of corn whiskey wanted yellow corn. Throughout the pioneer period the mash was set in tubs or barrels of between sixty and one hundred gallons capacity, or at least I found no inventory listing the larger vats commonly used at an early date in more northerly centers of brewing and distilling such as Cincinnati. The distiller first put into the mash barrel two bushels of corn meal with enough water to mix with a mash stirrer [18] until the whole was a lump-free mass of thin batter; he then poured in enough more water to make a total of fifty gallons of mash.

---

[17] I, V, 31, 32, 34, 36.

[18] Mash stirrers had to be made without iron. Mr. John C. Burton, Monticello, Ky., has a good example of a poplar mash stirrer—short cross pieces through holes bored into a heavy stick about four and one-half feet long.

He could stop there, and by adding nothing else, have in time a product that would yield around five gallons of 110-proof whiskey, for the distiller expected to get two to two and one-half gallons of liquor per bushel of corn.[19]

The same spontaneous fermentation from wild yeast that made salt-rising bread possible would in time bring alcohol to the mash tubs. If the farmer wanted to quicken matters he did as did his wife with her pot of emptins, throw into each barrel some sourdough made of wheaten or rye flour or whatever he happened to have. He could of course use the more orthodox yeast, but I never found anything to indicate the pioneer farmer ever did so. Nor did I find any mention of malt,[20] though some may have used it. Gradually the farmer had learned he could do with less and less malt, and soon he was doing without it entirely.

The very early distiller on the Cumberland would, when using malt at all, have used corn, and many are the tales told of how corn, lacking a proper place for sprouting such as a cellar, was sprouted by the small distiller. It could be tied loosely in a sack and left in the millpond or in winter put on nature's hot bed, a manure pile, preferably from the horse stalls. It was more commonly sprouted in a tub, but sprouting tubs were rare.

The main thing was that the corn be kept covered so that the "drake's tail," [21] or the corn-stalk shoot could not turn green, and growth must be stopped when the drake's tail was about a quarter of an inch long. The sprout was then knocked off, and the malt dried—that is usually, but there were no rules. Wet malt could be pounded up sprout and all, and put into the mash stands at about the rate of ten pounds of malt to one hundred gallons of mash.[22] The mash was then left to ferment. This, like the souring of cream for a churning, the rotting or bleaching or flax, all depended on the weather, though straight corn mash was slower than that containing small grains either in the malt or in the mash. The contents of the mash

---

[19] Anthony Boucherine, *The Art of Making Whiskey*, Philadelphia, 1819 (cited hereafter as Boucherine, *Whiskey*), 10. As in other matters pertaining to the early distilling of whiskey, there is no exact agreement. Old-timers who will admit to having made a run of corn whiskey think it was closer two gallons than two and one-half. The distiller's toll was sometimes as low as a bushel of corn for a gallon of whiskey, but in Kentucky of 1753, Toulmin, *Western Country*, 87, the distiller could get a bushel of wheat for a gallon, for Kentucky was not at this date producing enough to supply her needs, *ibid.*, 107.

[20] Boucherine, *Whiskey*, 32. Toulmin, *Western Country*, 62, found no malt for sale.

[21] This term was used by an old man who had made whiskey with nothing but corn.

[22] Boucherine, *Whiskey*, 10.

barrel varied from farmer to farmer and region to region; East Tennessee with upland fields and a shorter growing season was by 1785 producing enough rye whiskey that it was used in the payment of taxes at only two shillings, six pence per gallon.[23] Michaux, visiting Kentucky in 1802, remarked that most of the rye grown there was used in the manufacture of whiskey.

One of the most important ingredients of pioneer whiskey was proper water, not always easily had. Many of the springs on the edge of the Highland Rim carried traces of iron, and even a small amount of iron would turn the whiskey black; the sulphur found in others was equally bad; good limestone water had neither, but if too hard it left heavy encrustations in the boilers.

Fermentation completed, with the liquor fined as much as corn mash would ever fine, it was time for the distillation. All stills used at this time were a form of pot still. The largest commonly listed in Davidson County in 1795 held only around two hundred gallons,[24] the smallest around forty. Most distillers had at least two, a large still for the first distillation or the low wine; a much smaller, usually between forty-five and seventy gallons, for the second distillation or the high wine, but by no means all pioneer whiskey was double distilled, as indicated by ads offering "double-distilled" whiskey.

Stills were commonly of copper and consisted of the cooking part or boiler, really nothing more than a copper pot; the rounded covering was known as the bonnet, and leading out from it was the worm, not then a copper coil as used by later distillers, but a four-sided, pipelike affair, made of tin or wood, about five feet long and growing smaller toward the end. This was connected, sometimes to the cooling tub, and other times, if leading from the low wine still, directly to the small still or doubler, with the worm of this connected to the cooling tub.[25] The vapor was usually cooled in a spring or a small flume carried from a spring, though in East Tennessee the cooling "casks" were by 1799 being supplied with cold water by a system of bucket lifts powered by horses.[26]

Susan Overall and others had to work with only one small still, but such was their skill, they could turn out quite good first-run whiskey, and

---

[23] Ramsey, *Tennessee*, 297.

[24] Overton, Accounts, 7–9, list as do the inventories the varying sizes of the stills; these like everything else were custom made; they came in such sizes as 43, 59, 72, 91, 197, 204.

[25] Boucherine, *Whiskey*, 21, 30–31.

[26] Williams, *Travels*, Schweinitz, "Report," 449.

with no device for the testing of specific gravity save tallow. If the tallow sank quickly, hugging the bottom, Mrs. Overall could add a bit of water, for in order to satisfy the specifications set by the Sumner County Court for whiskey served in the local taverns, the tallow had only to sink,[27] but, alas, when it floated; too weak, she'd have to still again. A single or first distillation was hardest, for in order to get the whole of the alcohol from the mash, the distiller had to stir up the tub and distill meal and all with the consequent danger of scorching the meal in the bottom and so ruining a batch of whiskey.[28]

There was, also for the small distiller, during the first distillation much lifting and pouring to be done, for the contents of around twenty-five mash stands, each with about fifty gallons, had to be got into the boiler and out again in order to distill a hundred or so gallons of liquor, an amount that represented more than three days' work for the larger distiller with a two-storied building and equipment so arranged the mixing could be helped along by gravity. Such a one was the Croft Mill and Distillery, put up for sale with three hundred acres of land by General James Winchester in 1802. The stillhouse was of stone, two stories high, and 32 by 40 feet, equipped with "still and boilers of the best quality, sufficient to make one barrel or thirty gallons a day." [29]

Judging from sources such stills were rare, and for the small farmer up river the still continued for generations to be movable equipment, housed at best in a shed or not at all, with pouring of water and mash done by hand. In most of the pioneer stills, loose wooden connections caused a great loss of alcohol, and the smell of whiskey was so strong on all roads leading to distilleries [30] none needed any advertising. Distilling with the best of equipment took much skill, for the steam distillery affording low, even heat to keep "mash and all" from bubbling up with the whiskey was unknown on the Cumberland during pioneer years. [31]

The only thermostat or thermometer the pioneer had was in his hands, but he would manage. He could even make whiskey without a bit of cop-

[27] CS, I, 12, "—whiskey such as will sink tallow" or about 110 proof.
[28] Boucherine, *Whiskey*, 19.
[29] Tennessee *Gazette*, March 17, 1802. Such equipment appears to have been rare in the early years, for it was seldom advertised; among the few found was that on the plantation of Rees Porter, Nashville *Clarion*, July 17, 1811, "good still house with water supplied from overhead."
[30] Boucherine, *Whiskey*, 16.
[31] Neither travelers, Boucherine, nor Hamilton in his instructions for measuring, mention steam distilleries; but by 1823 there was at least one in Wayne County, Kentucky, see WD, III, 13.

per or any other metal for the matter of that. He could and often did make
a still, complete with connections, of wood. Blue poplar was preferred, but
since nobody could tell blue poplar until the tree was cut into, he often
used white. The boiler might be made of a hollowed length, but often it
was of two halves bolted together.[32] There are here and there a few old-
timers who remember wooden stills, and some hill men preferred whiskey
made in wood, declaring the other was less healthful and had a coppery
taste. Wooden stills were sometimes sold up river for as low as $3, quite
a saving compared to early copper stills that seldom brought less than
$100, with large ones going for twice that amount.[33]

It was not until after 1790 that the inventories of farm families contained whiskey, and then only in small quantities of twenty to fifty
gallons.[34] Much of the whiskey consumed in Middle Tennessee and further
south came down the river from the distillers in Wayne, Pulaski, and
nearby counties in southern Kentucky. Shut off from the world by hills
as were men on the Monongahela, with only the crooked Cumberland as
a highway, whiskey was by far the best way of marketing corn. The
Cumberland, the only highway, was a most imperfect one. A dry winter
meant the flatboats of tobacco, staves, saltpeter, bacon, lard and other
products could not go down river, but must wait for the next season.
The woods products would keep, and tobacco in hogsheads kept fairly
well, but whiskey in good barrels kept even better.

Typical of the distiller up river was John Hudson, who, though not
dying until 1821, made his whiskey as had the pioneer. He had three copper
stills, selling for $98.50, $127, and $135; his 45 mash stands brought $37.75,
and the 1,150 gallons of barreled whiskey on hand were evaluated at only
27½ cents a gallon.[35] Mr. Hudson had many other possessions including
a barrel of vinegar, a large family Bible and a small one, wheat stacks,
much corn, but the thing that showed him to be a canny man was his
107 head of hogs; much of their food came from the mast abundant in the
region, but they also were a by-product of his distilling, for pigs love and
thrive on cooked mash, and more than one revenue man of later years dis-

---

[32] I am indebted to Mr. Lant Wood, taster for the Jack Daniels' Distillery for
many years, for a penciled sketch and explanation of one type of wooden still used
with steam; in general principle it is the same as earlier ones used without steam, but
with rock or brick between them and the fire.

[33] DW, I, 90—a 72 gal. still and one of 91 sold for $400; *ibid.*, I, 253—"75 pounds,"
but by 1795 William Overall's 95 gal. copper still and 16 mash stands brought only
$95.

[34] DW, II, 4—4 gals., 1 qt; *ibid.*, II, 7—50 gallons; *ibid.*, II, 177—20 gallons.

[35] PW, II, 87.

covered a still by smelling a pig's breath and then following him. Mr. Hudson, with 1,150 gallons of whiskey, was, no different from a neighbor, Mr. John Sneed,[36] selling 1,200 gallons, still a farmer, merely processing his produce for market, and, different from the large distillers of Cincinnati who were by that date supplying much of the whiskey consumed in the Mississippi Valley, not an industrialist and nothing more.

The first whiskey tax, seven cents on each gallon distilled and fifty-four cents per gallon per year on total still capacity,[37] had, at Mr. Hudson's death, long since been repealed, but it had marked the beginning of the end of the farmer-manufacturer-businessman. Susan Overall in 1796 stilled 62 gallons of spirits on her small still and paid $4.25; over the river in Sumner County, Frederick Stump paid in the year 1795–96, $41.93, with 599 gallons produced from his four stills, two low wine stills of 197 gallons and two small doublers.[38] Much of Stump's whiskey was sold at a good price by the half-pint in his tavern, but the man up river who got less than thirty cents still paid the same rate of tax.

Thus, the moonshiner was born. He did not thrive until the second whiskey tax, but even then it was many years before his work was much frowned upon by any save the law—that is, as long as he made good whiskey.

Whiskey was to the pioneer what tranquilizers, stimulants, disinfectants, vitamins, rubbing alcohol, and anaesthetics are to us today. The newborn got weak toddy at birth, the mother had it stronger, the father straight, the old and cold bathed their limbs in it, and so on through life. William Faux, visiting the West of 1818 (Ohio and Indiana), termed the necessities of life bread, meat, and whiskey.[39] We find even the devout Reverend Asbury who hated "whiskey topers" and distillers writing: ". . . and the rain came on powerfully . . . took shoulders, elbows, and feet, for eight miles it was violent; I had not been so steeped for four years. I washed the wet parts with whiskey, and did not take the damage I feared." He would not however give praise to the hated whiskey, but to God, exhorting, "O, thou of little faith, wherefore didst thou doubt?"[40]

Joseph Brown was doctored by pouring whiskey into his green wound;[41] any soldier undergoing surgery such as a leg sawed off was

[36] *Ibid.*, II, 225.
[37] Overton, Accounts, 178.
[38] *Ibid.*, 8–9.
[39] Faux, *Travels, 1818–1819*, 177.
[40] Asbury, *Journal*, 252, Sept. 26, 1800.
[41] A, V, 203. The bone was splintered, but Brown, wounded during the summer, recovered enough to guide the Nickojack Expedition the following October.

given whiskey as was the sufferer from snake bite. It was drunk to break out the measles,[42] and rubbed on the pit of the stomach to cure cramps.[43] Whiskey was so important that all pledges of abstinence from "ardent spirits" I have seen contained the clause, "unless prescribed by a physician." Andrew Jackson in his old age advised his friend General Coffee, also growing old and rheumaticky, to bathe himself in whiskey,[44] and many were the infusions such as cucumber or pokeroot steeped in whiskey the pioneer used.[45] The most common smelling salts of the average farm family was made by dissolving camphor in whiskey, while good, strong hot toddy was ever the sovereign remedy for any ill or woe of life. And of all medicines, hot toddy with sugar was the least unpleasant to take; even children never minded it.

Whiskey as a drug represented only a small percentage of its importance. Strongly rooted in the Old World was the use of alcoholic beverages, not as in the United States today, heavily taxed luxuries, but as important splinters in the staff of life. The English sailor of the eighteenth century might have little but moldy ship's biscuit and pickled beef, but he expected his grog; likewise the half-starved Italian peasant had now and then a bit of sour wine. Whiskey on the Cumberland as elsewhere in the new West simply took the place of other alcoholic drinks as it had for the Highland Scot.

The soldier expected his half pint daily usually because he had known at least that much at home and sometimes more. A thirty-gallon barrel contained only 480 half pints, a minimum supply of an army private for 480 days; most things, including tradition, indicate the average farmer used more than a half-pint daily. Many men needed considerably more; one of my collateral relatives who died at the age of ninety-two about the time I was born always had to have a fog-lifter, sometimes called an eye-opener, a little drink from a jug kept by his bed, taken as he arose; tired at noon he had if convenient a little more; in the evening he needed some more to give him an appetite and always more on going to bed. His consumption for around seventy years averaged better than a pint daily; he was never in his life intoxicated, was a most respectable farmer and businessman, leaving a good estate for his children.

Different from many drinkers of today, he liked the taste of whiskey

[42] Michaux, *Travels 1802*, 62.
[43] Only one of many uses advised by Henry Wilkins, M.D., in his 1804 ed. *The Family Adviser*.
[44] Bassett, *Jackson Correspondence*, V, 73.
[45] Michaux, *Travels 1802*, 47.

just as he liked red pepper in his sausage, a little sharpness in his buttermilk, and biscuit too hot to handle slowly. Had he lived during pioneer days, instead of being born shortly after the War of 1812, the whiskey consumption of both himself and his family would have been greater. The average small farmer with a small family then would have been hard pressed to make out with less than two barrels or sixty gallons a year. The pioneer farmer with much company such as Andrew Jackson whose stillhouse burned in 1801 with loss of caps, worms, and three hundred gallons of whiskey,[46] needed several barrels a year. The plantation owner with a larger family, coupled with all the woes and joys to which man is heir—the birth of a child, snake bite, the death of an aged father, or an aging mother subject to chills, all needing whiskey—used still more.

The Meeces of Pulaski County, Kentucky, for example, have always been citizens of which the county can be proud, and always a people who take care of their own, never needing private or public charity; Thomas Meece, dying in 1817, directed his sons, George and Joseph, to care for his widow, and pay her yearly, "ten bushels of corn, five of wheat, one hundred pounds of bacon, fifty of pork, and five gallons of whiskey."[47] It was a slim enough ration, only twenty-five of today's fifths, less than a pint a week, but enough for a hot toddy of evenings when her bones ached and she was tired. More fortunate was the widow Mrs. Joel Madden. The court, while untangling the affairs of the estate, gave her and her family 300 pounds of flour, 550 barrels of corn, 18 fat hogs, also 25 pounds of brown sugar, 15 gallons of whiskey, and a pound of ginger.[48] She and her children could thus have at least a few of the very best toddies, for a little ginger root steeped in the water before adding the whiskey, sugar, and other spices, makes a drink good for colds, chills, fatigue, and fever.

During pioneer years practically all whiskey consumed on the Cumberland was drunk straight or as toddy, served in taverns by the pint and taken hot or cold. The Cumberland toddy seems to have been no descendant of the Virginia toddy made with rum and spiced, usually with nutmeg,[49] or of the "julap" of colonial days, but came from Scotland. It was 1809 before I found mention of a mint julep in Nashville, and it is more than doubtful if any Cumberland pioneer much cared for the drink; it was not indigenous, save among novelists, to the old Southwest, and of course

---

[46] Bassett, *Jackson Correspondence*, I, 57–58.
[47] PW, I, 251.
[48] Smith W, V, 140.
[49] Smyth, *Tour*, I, 41–42, and Carey, *Museum*, I, 245–246, each gave the English toddy using rum. Whiskey was not much used in the East until well past 1800.

any man in the hill country up river who preferred the taste of mint to whiskey would have been held to be a most curious person indeed.

A high whiskey consumption was one thing, drunkenness very much another, and there seems to have been little among the actual pioneers and Indian fighters. My own conclusion is that, though consumption of alcoholic beverages was heavy, there was among the Cumberland pioneers during the years 1780–1803 not only much less alcoholism than today, but even less than in most states during this same period. Much has been written of the hard drinking habits of the pioneer; drink heavily he did, and his wife was no teetotaler, but he did not glorify it; "dissipation" was a thing of which to be ashamed, neither a mirth-provoking nor pity-squeezing subject. There are a few early records of fines for drunkenness,[50] two physicians of the early 1800's were mentioned as alcoholics; biographers of Jackson sometimes paint a picture of a man drinking to excess in his wilder, younger days, and by 1804 Mr. Bradford was complaining of drunkenness and Sabbath breaking. On the other hand no early traveler to Middle Tennessee complained of drunkenness as Asbury often complained of Kentucky and later travelers commented on the excessive use of whiskey in the then Midwest—Kentucky, Ohio, and Indiana Territory.

Pioneer Middle Tennessee was no place for alcoholics; when we consider that for fifteen years most men were never more than a few feet from loaded guns, and working constantly at all manner of dangerous jobs from felling trees to making saltpeter and gunpowder, with no mention of any accident among the lot, we can only assume they were not much inclined to alcoholism. Life as a farmer, hunter, boatman, horseman, even uncomplicated by the constant need of avoiding Indians, was a more fertile breeding ground for accidents than is our own today. Many are killed in automobiles, but horses under the hands of the drunken or the unskillful could likewise be dangerous. The pioneer's psychological approach was entirely different from the modern one; whiskey was a right, not a luxury.

Whiskey, in addition to being an article of staple consumption as well as a most important drug, was a source of power, like a second motor hooked in when there was a hard and heavy job to do. Sally Buchanan, risking death to serve whiskey, saw it as a thing needed in time of stress, and this was the way the average pioneer saw it—a necessity of life. Jack-

[50] DC, I, 31, 37, 51, are accounts of fines for "drunkedness in a public place," that usually included swearing.

son was liberal in his whiskey rations for boatmen, and John Coffee's boatmen once drank a gallon in raising their sunken boat. Wine and the fashionable life went together. Whiskey during pioneer years had not the fashionable aura with which today's advertising surrounds it, a sad poor thing, the taste so objectionable men forever seek new ways to hide it, and if nothing else they so chill and weaken it with ice, they know not what they have.

There was no need to mask the taste of pioneer whiskeys, for in spite of being drug, source of power, necessity of life, and way of marketing corn, early Cumberland whiskeys were also good. No traveler ever complained of the quality of whiskey, not even from earliest years. The Bourbon princes visiting Tennessee in 1797 liked the whiskey they found in Nashville so well, the younger tied a container around his neck so as to have it on what promised to be a thirsty trip north across the Barrens into Kentucky.[51] The variety of the whiskey the princes so enjoyed has not come down to us, and it is doubtful if it had any brand name; even the term Bourbon of which so much is now made was not used until many years later, nor did Monongahela appear in advertising in Tennessee until around 1804. Most whiskey was listed simply as whiskey, which would seem to indicate it was made of corn, for John Coffee and others sometimes bought or sold rye whiskey; now and then such adjectives as prime, double-distilled, two years old, were also used, but not often.

The widespread manufacture and use of whiskey does not mean there was no feeling against it. Others besides the Reverend Francis Asbury thought distilling sinful, and there were from time to time attempts in the North Carolina legislature to prevent the manufacture of whiskey in Middle Tennessee, but judging from the results the laws were never enforced.

---

[51] Williams, *Travels,* "Tours of the Dukes," 440. It is possible the term Bourbon as applied to whiskey arose from this incident, but not probable. I found no use of the term in any source material, and nothing to indicate it was used as an adjective or simile for whiskey before the date 1851 as given by Mathews in *Americanisms.* Some whiskey historians credit Rev. Craig of the Kentucky Bluegrass with having made the first Bourbon in 1789; Rev. Craig undoubtedly made whiskey, chiefly of corn—it was by that date being made on the Cumberland and was plentiful in East Tennessee—but no authentication has so far been found to indicate that he or anyone else in the early years called the product Bourbon, or that the drink had much in common with the standardized Bourbon of today. My own feeling is that the term *Bourbon* arose not from a place name, Bourbon County, Kentucky, but from the ordinary use of the word Bourbon—a leader, a prince, a Southern Democrat—that was in time used to designate "a prince of whiskies" common in the South.

Whiskey was not the only alcoholic drink on the Cumberland, but it had a larger place in the lives of ordinary people than all others combined. Some rum continued to be sold and the wealthy consumed a good deal of wine as it often appears in store accounts, but there is no record that either wine or cider, also advertised and brought by wagon and boat from Pennsylvania, was made on the Cumberland. Quite large quantities of beer were, according to Toulmin, being brewed in Kentucky by 1793, but the Cumberlanders as a group had inherited no tradition of beer, and I found no early reference to it. Cherry bounce is now and then mentioned, but next to whiskey the most common alcoholic drink was peach brandy, being made in Tidewater by 1700.

Judging from accounts of travelers new to its peculiarities, peach brandy was one of the most palatable, but most deceptive, drinks known to man. A visiting Englishman found that of Virginia extremely pleasant, but even the fumes raised an "absolute delirium" and, though he had never been in a duel, he and his companions fought seven or eight after drinking it. The peaches for brandy were put, skins, seeds, and all, into large vats and left until "putrified"; they were then pressed and the liquid distilled; [52] the average yield about a gallon of brandy from seven bushels of fruit.[53] Peach brandy did not begin to appear in inventories until around 1795; after that date it grew increasingly plentiful, sometimes selling for as low as one shilling a gallon.[54]

Distilling continued for many years to be a legitimate part of farm life, but later federal license fees made whiskey manufacture on a small scale impossible, and the grinding of the grain for the man who wanted to make no more than a hundred gallons or so was ever a problem. Horse mills were cheap enough to build, but so slow and cumbersome that, though the taking of corn to mill and home again might mean a day's work and more for a half-grown boy with wagon and team, plus the toll, the small farmer did it.

Even after the Indian menace ended, good mills continued rare in Middle Tennessee,[55] largely because of lack of water power, for in that country of rainy winters and dry summers, along with numerous underground streams, mid-August often found even the biggest of millponds

---

[52] Anburey, *Travels*, II, 320, 411.

[53] A nameless Kentucky informer, now reformed, used to get this yield; it varied, I have heard, as high as a gallon to 4 bushels of crushed peaches.

[54] DW, II, 274—14 gal. peach brandy; *ibid.*, II, 303—92 gals. brandy. See also Michaux, *Travels 1802*, 229, 254.

[55] Williams, *Travels*, Schweinitz, "Report," 516.

empty. Still, there were some good ones before 1800. Most travelers commented on the Croft Mills of General James Winchester on Bledsoe Creek. Sold in 1802 with the adjoining distillery, the larger mill was of stone, two stories, 43 by 32 feet, with one "pair Goose Creek burrs in motion," two bolting clothes, and in "complete order for manufacturing flour, and pierced for other stones which may be put in at little expense." The other was a wooden mill with one pair of Laurel Hill stones, these last of local rock and used for grinding corn. There was also a storage house and, powered by the same stream of water, a sawmill.

Around any mill of that day one could have heard the terms still used during my childhood; we made biscuit of "flour," the cows ate "middlings," and some "ship-stuff" went into slop for hogs. These last two terms, though reminders of the old days, had, like so many words and phrases, gone through a change in meaning. General Winchester or his deputy inspector, sampling barrels of flour for export, had to obey the Tennessee law of 1801, and see to it that the word "Tennessee" was on every barrel, but it was only on those with first-class contents of a certain fineness and whiteness the word "flour" was stamped; next best or medium was middling grade, stamped "middlings"; the poorest was labeled "ship-stuff"—good enough for shipping but not fit for biscuit.

Hand in hand with the manufacturing and shipping of flour and most other produce, save hemp and cotton, was that of barrel- and stave-making, an industry long known in the Old World where the barrel, pipe, tun, hogshead, and keg had served for both packaging and storage. The New World history of the container made of staves was a long one, for never had the Old World known such a good supply of stave timber as was found in America, and staves were an important export from most of the colonies. In the colonies as in England, the container made of staves, its size, composition, and shape had ever been the subject of many controversies and regulatory laws, and many were the arguments. The backwoods colonial forced to bring his tobacco to a shipping point on a navigable river below the fall line wanted huge hogsheads as each must be rolled on wooden wheels, while the ships' captains preferred a more easily handled size.

Tennessee began where North Carolina ended.[56] Her 1801 law stipu-

---

[56] NCR, XXIV, 580–86, the law on which the Tennessee law of 1801 was based, is but one instance of much legislation on barrels; *ibid.*, XXV, 381, a colonial law of 1758, that stipulated among other things no barrel of meat should contain more than two heads; that staves should be ½-inch thick and seasoned three months after riving.

lated that beef or pork was to be shipped in "good and sufficient new white oak barrels, containing not more than 30 gallons wine measure, each half barrel 15 gallons—all barrels of timber well seasoned, staves not less than one-half inch thick when wrought, heading not less than three-fourth inch thick—the whole well doweled with 12 good and substantial hoops, each to be tight, fit to hold pickle." Meal and flour could travel in barrels with only ten hoops each, but each chime hoop must have four pins and each bilge hoop three, the flour-barrel stave must be 27 inches long, and the diameter of the head 17½ inches. Casks and kegs were smaller and of a corresponding shape, while the stave for the larger tobacco hogshead was 52 inches long, thicker and wider, and the head must be 36 inches in diameter. In addition to the barrels needed for produce, the Cumberlanders also did quite a business in barrel timbers and staves. Andrew Jackson, sending pipe staves down in 1806, was only one of many merchants who dealt in them.[57]

Cooper's tools came with the first settlers, but judging from the many agreements for the delivery of barrels and the many quotations on staves, barrel making or cooperage left the plantation at an early date. As timber grew scarce in Middle Tennessee, the industry moved up river where it flourished as long as there was a good supply of white oak or until the early decades of the present century; though later staves were sawed by small steam mills, known as stave mills.[58]

The early farmer up river with not too much rich level land but a good supply of white oak could alternate his farming with off-season work in making staves or getting out long straight saplings that when split would yield barrel ties. He, like the distiller, was a farmer processing a crop for market, though it happened to be from the woods and ready grown. Some made shingles, cedar staves for churns and other setware, and as the timber disappeared from Middle Tennessee, others could alternate farming with cutting timber for firewood and charcoal. Some men hewed logs for houses, and these known as "house patterns," grandfathers of the pre-fabricated homes of today, were rafted down the Big South Fork, into the Cumberland, and down to Middle Tennessee.

[57] Bassett, *Jackson Correspondence*, I, 141. These sold for $35 a thousand, and were by law 4 ft. 8 in. long, 4 in. "in the broad" and ¾ in. thick.
[58] FP, 28, Verhoeff, *Kentucky River*, 195–197, discusses the stave industry as carried on in the Kentucky hills a hundred years after the pioneer period; at that date the work was done largely by small steam sawmills; now and then one sees a small gasoline-powered stave mill, but most of the stave timber is now shipped unsawed.

Another part-time industry of the woods farmer up river, though but little developed during pioneer years, was the getting out of tanbark; small quantities were used on some farms, but most was shipped down river or taken to the local tanner. The tanning and curing of all the varieties of leather needed was an old industry using many crafts and skills. Most of the better goods made largely of leather continued after the Revolution to be imported from England.[59] The home manufacture of leather, like that of cloth, was in the Southern colonies quickened by the Revolution, but the average householder on the Cumberland was much less inclined to produce a large proportion of his needed leather than of his cloth.

The home tanning of deerskins for clothing was fairly common up river, as was that of small hides such as ground hog. There was no exact recipe; some used ashes to make the hair slip, but in tanning beef hides for shoes, lime water was preferred. When the hair would slip the hide was scraped and then put into the tan vat; for home use this might be nothing more than a large hollowed log of the same general shape and size as the meat trough, usually of poplar; into this was put a layer of tanbark, shredded by hand, a job for the children, and a layer of hides, and on for several layers with tanbark on top.[60] The whole was then filled with water and left until the tannin had soaked from tanbark into leather, a process that took several weeks, sometimes six months. Later steps in the treatment of the leather "all depended." The currier was one of the most skilled and highly regarded craftsmen in the Old World, able to finish leathers with various oils for a great variety of needs, but as most home-tanned leather on the frontier went into heavy work shoes, home-made harness or saddles, little dressing was done.

Many barks contain tannin, but that most commonly used was from the black oak; tanbark was taken in the early spring when all barks slip easily, stacked in ricks like cordwood, and left in the woods until dry.

[59] Michaux, *Travels 1802*, 156, declared that seven tenths of all manufactured goods used in the United States at the time of his visit was imported from England; this was opinion only, but judging from *Gazette* ads practically all of the more expensive clothes and furnishings were imported.

[60] Mereness, *Travels,* Fleming "Journal," 630, in describing the unsanitary conditions in Kentucky's crowded forts in 1779–1780 mentions, "steeping skins to dress." Kercheval, *Virginia*, Doddridge, "Notes," 276, gives a fairly detailed account of one method of tanning. W. A. Kinnie, *The Gum Tree Story*, 14, states that in the upper regions of the Big South Fork leather was tanned with chestnut-oak bark in a hollowed log vat as late as 1905.

The gathering of tanbark for sale was long a part-time industry of the up-river farmer or his help,[61] but the industry disappeared, partly for lack of oak, but largely because of a change in tanning methods.

The first notice of a Middle Tennessee tannery found was in 1804, though it may have been in use for some years as it was then going out of business.[62] Tanning was a slow and expensive process; a cord [63] of bark would tan only around ten hides [64] and as the process took from six months to a year, the tanner was by law permitted to ask a high toll, or one pound of leather for each two pounds of green hide brought.[65] It was not until around 1810 that tanneries became common in the neighborhood of Nashville.

Another industry centered in the woods was that of making tar. The pioneer had to have tar; burned into pitch and mixed with oakum or tow he used it to caulk his flatboat or keelboat; tar served as axle grease for his many turning wheels and was used on the many ropes needed in connection with harness and sails, and also formed an important ingredient in numerous medications for both humans and animals.

The need for tar almost cost Anthony Bledsoe, Jr., and his cousin David Ramsey their lives, for they were set upon by Indians when returning from a trip up White's Creek to get pine knots.[66] Pines were scarce in the limestone lands of the Middle Basin; here and there they could be found on the Highland Rim, but grew most plentifully on the Plateau and up the Cumberland.

It had taken the Southern colonial some little time to learn how to manufacture tar in the New World, though tar was so important England had offered bounties for its production, as she needed great quantities for her ever expanding navy, but during colonial days was largely dependent on Russia and the Balkans. Pines there were in abundance near the sea in the Carolinas, but when the early settlers had tried to make tar by girdling the trunk as was done in Russia with a different species of pine, the resins did not settle in the stump and roots as the tree died, but scattered throughout the tree, chiefly at the points where limbs joined

---

[61] Tanbark was so plentiful up river by 1817 it was used to cover the floors of tobacco warehouses, "so as to keep the tobacco from receiving damage from the dampness of the earth." PD, III, 370.

[62] Tennessee *Gazette*, July 11, 1804.

[63] A cord at this time was 8 ft. long, 4 high, and 4 broad, NCR, XXIV, 595.

[64] VS, I, 608. There were no absolute rules, much depended on the quality of the bark and weight of the hides.

[65] NCR, XIV, 384.

[66] W, 1S, 83.

trunks. Like true Southerners, the Carolinians in time learned to do much with little labor. Ready-waiting for them in the pine woods was the fat pine, usually in the form of pine knots from generations of rotted trees, for the hardened resins preserved the wood. It was but a pleasant and easy job to wander through the woods, gathering the knots of light-wood that had only to be split into pencil-size splinters to be ready for the tar kiln.

Young Anthony Bledsoe, bringing only what pine knots he could carry on horseback, would not have bothered with a proper kiln. Split, the fat pine was put on a flat and sloping rock, a drain or log pipe leading from the lower edge to the tar barrel; the family's biggest kettle was then turned over the pile, and a great fire built around and on top of the kettle; the splints would char and the tar run.

The man up river, making tar to send by flatboat to Nashville or New Orleans, and working with wagon loads of pine knots was more inclined to make a clay kiln around the knots as had been done in the Carolinas. A variation of this method, followed in the Rockcastle Country up the Cumberland, was to make first a clay floor, from ten to twenty feet in diameter, and with a central catch basin connected by the customary wooden pipes of the day to kegs outside the kiln. The splintered fat pine was then stacked in a thick circle on the clay floor around the catch basin, and the outside of the pile surrounded by a rail fence several inches from the splints. The space between pine splints and fence was then packed with damp clay and leaves mounded up and over the top. A small fire was started in the top of the pile, but "when in a good way of burning," it was partially smothered with wet clay or a sheet of tin. The fire had constantly to be regulated; if it flamed too much it had at once to be checked with the clay or tin, or tar would burn up along with pine splints; on the other hand, if it got too slow, clay had to be pulled back or tin lifted; and in "getting the most tar," one also got the most smoke and so the old saying, "as smoky as a tar kiln." [67]

The work was one of the most disagreeable jobs on earth, but it was quite well paying, for the tar brought fifty to seventy-five cents a gallon in Nashville.[68]

Such were the resources of the region up river and on the edge of the

[67] Reprinted by permission of the publisher, the late Russell Dyche, London, Ky., from the *Sentinel Echo*, Oct. 26, 1939, as told by Uncle Alex Arnold of Keevy, Ky.

[68] Tennessee *Gazette*, April 15, 1801 and *ibid.*, June 10, 1801.

Highland Rim, the farmer of Middle Tennessee could buy, and cheaply for he had them at his back door, most woods products that sold at high prices in England and sometimes in Philadelphia where even firewood was dear. Equally important, the farmer up river with only rough land could find a ready sale for his woods products. He could give most of the spring and fall to planting and reaping crops in creek and river valleys; midsummer or winter might find him in the pine woods, early spring in the tanbark, and most any off season in the stave woods. Rainy days often brought work in one of the many limestone caves that ringed most valleys up river and in Middle Tennessee. Though still a farmer he would at the moment be engaged in one of the most important industries on the Cumberland—that of digging saltpeter dirt, the first step in the making of gunpowder.

As early as 1775 at least one cave in the vicinity of what is now Mill Springs, Wayne County, Kentucky, was so well known the road leading to it was called the Salt Peter Cave Trace.[69] Many of the Long Hunters and first settlers such as Abraham Price, who in 1775 built a cabin, carried, instead of gunpowder, only brimstone or flowers of sulphur as it was known, and made their own powder. French powder could be had from wandering French and Spanish traders or in New Orleans, but homemade was cheaper, and because of this Joseph Bishop of Sumner County determined in 1793 to make a batch. In order to hasten the work he had a log-rolling; then burned the resulting pile of hickory from which he collected sixteen tubs of "fine ashes,"[70] and these he stored in a dry place. His next step was to get the "peter-beer," as it was called.

"Nitre dirt," one of the several names by which earth containing saltpeter was known, had long been scarce in England. France, on the other hand, had so much she could export powder; but as soon as the British colonials got into the limestone lands above the Fall Line, they, too, began to find saltpeter dirt in caves, and when they had crossed the mountains and got into the limestone valleys of the Highland Rim, they found more caves rich in peter dirt.

Saltpeter-digging in caves was slow and often heavy work. Once dug, the dirt was crushed by hand or ground in the pioneer's chief crushing machine, much like an oversize roller cotton gin made of ungrooved logs instead of rollers, turned by a crank at the end. The apparatus was slow and clumsy but capable of crushing earth, charcoal, or lime. Crushed,

[69] WD, I, 213, deposition of Nathaniel Buckhannon.
[70] Gray, *Bishop*, 81.

the peter dirt was put into a leaching vat. Most saltpeter leaching vats, though performing the same function as the ash hopper, were square, built of hewn timbers so carefully notched and fitted together they were watertight. The larger ones that made the imprints still to be seen in Mammoth Cave, once a center of the industry, were as much as ten feet long, half as wide, and ten feet deep, capable of holding many tons of peter dirt. The bottoms were cunningly contrived of two parallel layers of small "split white oak logs gouged out," the edges of the top layer meeting above the middles of the bottom layer, the whole made slightly slantwise so that the drippings from the ends of the bottom logs fell into another trough leading to a barrel, or in the larger works, connected by wooden pipes to some convenient storage vat outside the cave.[71] It took three men about a day to leach out peter-beer enough to make from fifty to one hundred pounds of saltpeter, for the yield depended on the richness of the dirt. Ordinary peter dirt yielded from three to five pounds per bushel.

The peter-beer or nitrate was then leached through ashes, the same process as leaching for lye water save peter-beer instead of water was used. One hundred pounds of finished saltpeter required about eighteen bushels of oak ashes for the leaching, though only ten of elm, or two bushels of ashes made by burning the dry wood of hollow trees.

The next step was boiling down the resulting watery potassium nitrate mixture. The farmer making a small quantity cooked near the mouth of the cave, if firewood were conveniently close, but in large operations such as that carried on in Short Mountain [72] in the Rockcastle Country as well as Mammoth Cave, the peter-beer was taken out of the cave, leached through ashes, and boiled at a location more convenient to firewood. The most dangerous part of saltpeter making was the last step; the liquid was treated roughly as was maple sugar water, the boiling continued with fresh additions of leachings; then the whole was cooked down into a thick, semiliquid mass; if left too long at the cooking and the fire got too

---

[71] Thor Borresen, Assistant Historical Technician, Mammoth Cave National Park, "Report on the Present Condition of the leaching vats, Salt Peter Works, Mammoth Cave, January 14, 1942," is one of the few studies made of early methods of saltpeter manufacture. The procedure is further explained by drawings; Plate 1, for example, shows the arrangement of the drains, and Plate 7 is a detail of the wooden pipes reconstructed from bits of the original. Typical of pioneer pipe, always of wood, these are not threaded, but one end of each length is tapered to fit into the next length. See also *Compressed Air Magazine*, June 1952, 156–160, George F. Jackson, "Nitre Caves."

[72] Short Mountain, mentioned by Dr. David Dale Owen in his *Kentucky Geological Survey*, 1855, 56, is now maintained as a tourist attraction by Mr. John Lair, Renfroe Valley, Ky.

hot the stuff could explode and several days' work be lost.[73] The salt-peter was taken from the kettle and dried slowly in shallow troughs; dried, it was crushed or ground on log rollers. The industry was a prof-itable one, particularly in Wayne County, Kentucky.[74] The cost for the man with wood, water, and peter dirt on his land was measured solely in time, and by 1801 he could exchange saltpeter at the James store near Somerset for nine pence per pound, though as in all up-river produce, Nashville prices were much higher.[75]

Gunpowder called for charcoal; dogwood was by tradition preferred, but for charcoal as for whiskey there was no one method; few if any would have made a kiln of rocks or clay, but simply stacked split lengths of wood and let it burn slowly from a fire lighted in the middle. The main thing was that the charcoal be finely powdered; this could be done first with the wooden roller, then in a pounder much like the corn pounder; the dry saltpeter was likewise ground and crushed; charcoal, saltpeter, and sulphur were then mixed in a proportion of around one-half saltpeter by volume and one-fourth each of sulphur and powdered charcoal.

Country stores commonly stocked brimstone or flowers of sulphur at a shilling a pound or less, and the only man found said to have made sulphur for his gunpowder was Daniel Boone, reported to have made it from a spring.[76]

The ease with which gunpowder could be produced explains why stations such as Buchanan's never ran low on powder. Lead for bullets was a different story; an old one remembering, "my mother had to melt her pewter basins, cups and spoons to shoot the Indians." [77] Others tell of breaking pots and using any metal in the blunderbusses when lead for bullets ran out, for lead was one of the few things neither produced in Middle Tennessee nor brought down the river. Some lead was mined,[78]

---

[73] As a child I heard many stories of the doings in the saltpeter caves; one con-cerned an explosion—the men had been using skulls found in the cave as dippers, and after an explosion a superstitious worker declined to use the dipper skulls any more; another concerned the first of the quakes of 1811 that found a group of men far back in a cave.

[74] Brown, *Gazetteer*, 96, declared that some Wayne County caves yielded 50 pounds of saltpeter per 100 pounds of dirt, an unbelievably high figure, though land with saltpeter caves was then selling for from ten to twenty dollars an acre.

[75] Coffee Papers, 1802, $50 for 240 pounds—up river at this date the shilling was commonly 8 to the dollar. MW, I, 12, is one of the few times saltpeter was found mentioned in Middle Tennessee, and later ads asking for it, Nashville *Clarion*, Jan. 4, 1811, would indicate scarcity.

[76] W, 31S, 348.

[77] *Ibid.*, 6XX, 980.

[78] Brown, *Gazetteer*, 96, described a lead rush in Wayne in 1815 after lead was

particularly in Wayne County, but on a very small scale. There had been by tradition a lead mine on our place on Little Indian Creek, said to have been first worked by the Cherokee about the time of the Revolution; however, though a neighbor found lead, we found no indications of mining operations. Some lead used in Middle Tennessee may have come from the Chiswell mines in western Virginia, an important source during the Revolution, but judging from John Coffee's many importations, most came from the lead mines in the Illinois.[79]

Searching for lead, salt, iron and other needed minerals was part of pioneering, for every farmer hoped to fill as many needs as possible from his own land.

The man up river with most of his crop land in narrow strips of creek bottom, but owning saltpeter caves, timbered hillsides, and piney woods, was, of course, much more inclined to turn to some industry centering about a mineral or woods product. Such a one was Samuel Kelly on Little Clifty Creek of Fishing Creek in Pulaski County. Though no pioneer for he never came until 1807, he had, in order to live well on his rocky farm, to turn his hand to many of the pioneering industries. Dressed in summer in a straw hat of his own weaving, "coarse home tanned shoes," made by a journeyman cobbler, homespun linen shirt and trousers, he at one time or another manufactured saltpeter, epsom salts, turpentine, linseed oil, and gunpowder; while his wife, in addition to being the local midwife, helped out by making cheese, and at sugar-making time most of the family, for there were nine children, turned to and helped make sugar. Such families who, with little fertile soil, had to process all crops possible were not necessarily penny-pinchers unable to think of anything but work and money. The Kellys were all lovers of books, and had books in the home that had also to serve as a Methodist church until one could be built in the community. Work was a habit; tired from heavy work they could always rest over some such thing as whittling buttons from bone, weaving a basket or a hat, knitting a stocking, or winding a skein of thread.[80]

Even the farmer in the fertile lands of Middle Tennessee took from his own holdings many needed things in addition to wood and timber, though he might have to buy tar, saltpeter, salt, and iron. One of the

discovered by a "water witch 1.2 miles from Monticello," but I find no record of lead shipments from the region.

[79] Bradbury, *Travels, 1811*, 248–250, described lead mining as carried on in the neighborhood of St. Genevieve, by that date in the United States.

[80] Kelly, *The Kelly Clan.*

most abundant was "lyme." Different from the work of Von Graffenried's settlers on the North Carolina coast, the making of lime was not the tedious operation of gathering oyster shells and burning them, nor did the Cumberlander waste time in making a kiln as did the New Englanders, for lime was often a by-product of cleaning land for crops. The farmer had only to snake half a dozen or so of tree trunks together and lay them in a row; on top of these he put a layer of limestone, much of which he would sooner or later pick up anyway, but taking care to select for lime pure rock, free of chert or streaks of iron. He topped the layer of rock with more tree trunks laid at right angles to the bottom layer, making as many layers of rock and tree trunks as feasible; big trees only a few, saplings, more layers with the rock layer thinner. He might leave it for six months or a year; when the trees were well seasoned and dry and the corn out of the way, he set the pile on fire; good wood, properly burned with good rock, left little but lime and a few ashes. If in a hurry he might slack what he needed with water, but he could as in other matters let air and rain do the work. One good-sized pile would yield mortar lime for many chimneys and cabin walls, lime for the tan vat, with some left over to trade, for lime sold down at Natchez for 25 to 37½ cents per bushel.[81]

The Cumberlander was less fortunate in salt, and it was with the exception of lead, the only prime necessity of which he could never produce enough. There were several salt licks—Neely's, Robertson's, Mansker's, and the French Lick—and salt making was one of the first industries attempted. William Neely was killed in the summer of 1780 while making salt, and numerous families around French Lick made small quantities. One of the best licks was on the holdings of James Robertson on Richland Creek,[82] and of this it was reported that eighty gallons of water would make one bushel of salt. Robertson, in accordance with his usual openhandedness, let any family who wished come and make salt, and many did so, using their biggest kettles and other cooking utensils for boiling. However, because of either impure brine or a scanty supply, the settlers in spite of the many licks were never able to supply themselves.

The Cumberlander, though he had to import most of what he used, from either Kentucky or the Salines, was still more advantageously located in regard to salt than he had been in western Virginia or North Carolina.

---

[81] Tennessee *Gazette*, Nov. 20, 1802. See also Coffee Papers, 1801–1805.
[82] W, 28S, 1 and *ibid.*, 29S, 72. See also Carolina *Gazette*, Feb. 22, 1798.

A salt works or furnace, as such was commonly known, was boiling twenty-five kettles on Salt River near Shepherdsville, Kentucky, by 1779,[83] and the Goose Creek works in what is now Clay County were in operation about five years later. One finds many notices of Mann's Lick and Goose Creek salt for sale at the upper ferry, for much salt manufactured at Mann's Lick and other sites east of Lexington was brought by wagon to the Cumberland and boated down. Still another source was the Salines of the Illinois, close enough to the lead mines so John Coffee often brought lead and salt in the same cargo.

The search for salt on the Cumberland continued; the two furnaces named, like Robertson's Lick, depended upon brine that rose in pits dug by hand, but men searching for salt, bored holes sometimes five hundred feet deep, the work done with no power save human muscle and hickory or maple saplings. The first step in drilling was the excavation of a pit about eight feet square down to solid rock; the loose earth was then walled away with logs. The walled pit, or crib, finished, the next thing was to find a likely hickory or maple for the spring pole, and set the larger end firmly in the ground above the pit. A rope was then fastened to the small end, and to the end of the rope a short length of pole, a shade smaller in diameter than that of the intended hole; into the lower end of the strung pole as it was known, an iron socket was screwed. The inside of the socket was also threaded and into this was screwed an oversize auger, made of steel with its bottom edge or bit facing the rock.

It took three men to work the spring-pole driller; one to turn the auger, one-half revolution each time the spring pole was brought down by the other two men. The spring in the pole jerked the bit away from the rock. As the hole deepened at the rate of about five feet a day, the length of rope between strung pole and spring pole had only to be lengthened; to keep the hole straight with the bit biting squarely into the rock, more strung poles were added.[84] The men drilling in 1802 for water in Nashville and mentioned by Michaux were no doubt using some such outfit. Hardly fifteen years after Michaux, men far up the river on the Big South Fork were drilling a well with the hope of finding salt water; deeper and deeper they went, past five hundred feet, but amid many

[83] Mereness, *Travels*, Fleming, "Journal," 620, gave quite a detailed description of the first works in Kentucky, and see Bradbury, *Travels 1811*, 276–278, for a description of salt warks at the Salines from which John Coffee brought much salt.
[84] John Haywood of the County of Davidson, *The Natural and Aboriginal History of Tennessee up to the First Settlements therein by the White People in the Year 1768*, Nashville, 1823, 381–382.

oaths growing ever blacker as the well got deeper, the driller swore he would find salt water if he had to drill clean to hell. Scarcely were the words spoken than bit and all flew out of the hole, and amid a mighty roaring there fell a shower of smelly, black and greasy stuff that soon ran in rivulets into the creek and down the river.

This, "Devil's Tar," was soon a problem in many salt wells. It got into creeks and river, and so ruined the feathers of flocks of geese from many farmyards that any driller unlucky enough to find it was soundly berated by housewives. Worse, the river once caught fire from a flood of this stuff, and many came to stand and watch the burning water. The more religious declaring, and doubtless with the satisfaction of those whose predictions are fulfilled, that Armageddon was at hand.

None of these early wells can exactly qualify as the first oil well, for in all cases the driller was hunting salt, though another salt well drilled in 1829 on Rennox Creek in Cumberland County, Kentucky, is often considered the region's first oil well. More prolific than most, it was described by one of its drillers as, ". . . running for the past three days throughing out large quantities of Rock Oil. It would spout out at least fifteen feet above the top of the ground as large as a man's Boddy—Cumberland River has been covered from Bank to Bank for three days. The River was set on fire—& I have no doubt it will be a good medison for man's complaints particularly the Rumatic pains—the hole atmospher is perfumed with it; it is a complete phenominon I could rite a hole shete and not say half." [85] The driller's prophecy was fulfilled; thousands of dollars worth of "medicine," used chiefly as a lotion for rheumatism, was sold from this well at a wholesale price of $60 per gross of pint bottles.[86] Years later the drilling for oil in this region became an industry.

All of the industries so far discussed were ordinarily undertaken by farmers; a good mill needed a fair amount of capital, but the miller was almost always farmer as well. Drilling for salt, like the making of tar, required little capital for a small outfit, but iron, one of the most expensive and badly needed commodities in the Cumberland Country, was a different story. The manufacture of iron, different from the other industries mentioned, could not be undertaken by a farmer in an off season. The

[85] Wells, *Cumberland County,* 172–174, quoting letter of Thomas Ellison, a driller, March 15, 1829. This well was 171 ft. deep, cased with hollowed poplar logs, soaked in linseed oil for preservation, and dug with an 80 ft. teeter pole, loose on both ends, and working in principle more like the walking beam in the old steam-powered Parkersburg drilling outfits than Haywood's spring pole.

[86] David Dale Owen, *Kentucky Geological Survey,* 1856, 151.

work called for numerous skills and materials not always readily available.

Iron manufacture began in East Tennessee at an early date, and Holston Iron is often advertised in early Nashville papers, but it was not until 1797 that the Cumberland Furnace of James Robertson on Barton's Creek, the first ironworks in Middle Tennessee, went into operation. Indians undoubtedly discouraged iron manufacture, for an Indian attack in the middle of a blast could mean the loss of a great deal of time and money, not to mention lives; but judging from Robertson's troubles as early as 1795 in raising the $10,000 capital [87] needed to get started, lack of capital was the chief holdback.

As late as 1799 Robertson's outfit on Barton's Creek was the only one in Middle Tennessee, but was so successful the price of iron had dropped by half,[88] but continued expensive. John Coffee, for example, paid in 1803 close to fifty cents a pound for steel, an extremely high price when measured in terms of other commodities. Robertson took as partners Adam Shepherd and John Jones; [89] but in 1803 the Cumberland Furnace, as the works were known, was sold to Montgomery Bell,[90] best known of early Tennessee iron masters and for him Montgomery Bell State Park is named.

Iron manufacture had by 1797 undergone little basic change since William Byrd described the blast and reheating furnaces used by Mr. Chiswell and Governor Spotswood of Virginia more than sixty years before.[91] Most blast furnaces were built of rough sandstone, sometimes of brick, and were usually between thirty and forty feet high, the smaller ones only eight or ten feet square in the boshes or bottom part, others as much as twenty-five feet square, but all growing smaller toward the top. When possible the blast furnace was built against the side of a hill to facilitate loading, or charging as it was known.

Details of Robertson's furnace are lacking, but all Tennessee iron ore was smelted with charcoal; limestone, mixed at the rate of about one ton to ten of ore, was used as a flux. The proportion of charcoal to ore was close to just the reverse; many times as much charcoal as ore was needed,

[87] A, IV, 75.

[88] Williams, *Travels,* Schweinitz, "Report," 517.

[89] Tennessee *Gazette,* June 15, 1803.

[90] *Ibid.,* February 29, 1804. Another early iron manufacturer was John Bosley who offered, *ibid.,* May 30, 1804, to sell or rent for ten years half the forge and iron works and mills on Barton's Creek.

[91] Byrd, *Writings,* "A Progress to the Mines," 333–386. See also John Leander Bishop, *A History of American Manufacturing from 1608 to 1860,* Philadelphia, 1864, I, 465–631.

though much depended on the quality of both the ore and the charcoal. The Highland Rim was rich in materials, but another basic need was water power to pump the great bellows, and sometimes two, that were a part of any furnace. A Pennsylvania blast furnace is described as having had a bellows twenty feet, seven inches long, and five feet, ten inches wide. The air from this was forced into the furnace through an opening around a foot square. The water wheels geared to do the pumping were large, that of Mr. Chiswell was twenty-six feet in diameter, fed by a flume 350 yards long. Once the furnace was charged, wheel gurgling, squeaking, and thumping, leather bellows hissing and wheezing, molten iron was usually from six to ten weeks away—if all went well, and the furnace did not blow out.

The molten iron, impure as it was, might be cast directly into molds— sand instead of clay was by the time of Robertson being quite commonly used—and the product whether giant salt-water kettle or fender was known as a casting, and sold by weight. However, as the early *Gazette* ads mention mills, there must have been at least one forging mill in operation before 1803; Robertson probably had one before 1800. Iron for forging was cast into pigs, "sow iron," Byrd had called it, then reheated in a furnace, also with a bellows and much like an oversize oven with a grate about six feet above the floor and a flue to carry off smoke and fumes.

Wrought iron was made by heating the pigs white hot, then withdrawing them, and pounding with giant hammers, powered by water. These hammers customarily weighed between five hundred and one thousand pounds, and by tradition could be heard for miles. Three or four heats were sometimes necessary before a pig could be shaped or wrought into a bloom, or piece of metal suitable for horseshoes, nails, and other articles demanding wrought iron. There were no rules, and the early forging mills did not automatically do away with the blacksmith who had for generations been able, if need be, to take a chunk of cast iron and with a foot-powered bellows and his own muscle make a piece of wrought iron suitable for most any need.

The amount of manpower required to produce a few tons of iron was prodigious; six men working three months could for example produce only sixteen thousand bushels [92] of charcoal or enough to make between eighty

---

[92] The amount needed depended on the wood from which the charcoal was made. Dr. Gerard Troost, *Fifth Report*, 41, was among the first to evaluate the heat potentials of the various woods as represented by their charcoals; white pine, for example,

and one hundred tons of iron. A wagon load was around eighty bushels, so that numerous teams of oxen with wagons and drovers were also required for the charcoal alone.

Iron manufacture, requiring as it did a very great deal of labor and much of it skilled, was one of the first industries in which management attempted to organize so as to regulate wages, for as early as 1733 Governor Spotswood was advocating that all owners of ironworks organize to hold down pay.[93]

There were under all industry on the Cumberland the same things that made most life possible; rich soil to make plenty of corn to furnish human and animal power—and plenty of timber.[94] The vast resources of coal on the upper Cumberland were for the most part above the white water of Smith Shoals, and though some coal did get down to Nashville in barges, the coal industry waited in the main for the coming of railroads. Wood continued important as a source of power, but the wood, whether used as charcoal in the iron furnace or as cordwood stacked by the steamboat landing, for all early steam engines were wood powered, still represented a good deal of human and animal labor, powered chiefly by corn.

The great timber resources of the Highland Rim and the Plateau in both Kentucky and Tennessee did not become centers of the lumbering industries until near the close of the nineteenth century, and as late as 1865 a visiting geologist saw the hardwood forests in the rougher and unsettled regions of Wayne and Pulaski counties, Kentucky, as potential sources of charcoal for the mining industry.[95] Cherry and walnut, like white oak for staves, were taken from the neighborhood of streams at a very early date as was some tanbark, but until the coming of the railroads to the upper Cumberland all timber had to go down stream.[96] The big trees went at pitifully low prices, ". . . 90¢ per thousand feet for first class logs—that is they are to be 30 inches and upward, straight, clear of

yielded only 455 pounds of charcoal per cord, that weighed only 15 lbs. per bushel; hickory yielded 1,172 pounds per cord, the bushel weighing 32.89.

[93] Byrd, *Writings*, 362. David Dale Owen, early geologist, estimated the cost of producing a ton of pig iron in 1865 as $18.

[94] Troost, *Fifth Report*, 35–36, lists among the needs of one furnace in the 1830's, 300,000 lbs. pork, and 7,000 bbls, of corn, for the ironmaster owned 235 slaves, used 200 head of mules and horses, and 35 yoke of oxen.

[95] J. M. Safford, *A Geological Report of the coal and oil lands in Pulaski, Whitney, and Wayne counties owned by the Cumberland River Coal Company of Kentucky.*

[96] Troost, *Fifth Report*, 37, estimated that in order to insure a perpetual charcoal supply the furnace owner should have 7 to 10 thousand acres of Tennessee forest or 5 up river.

knots, windshake, and all other defects." [97] This was the price for logs already in the river at Celina. The Cumberland had to compete with the Tennessee and other rivers with fine timber on their headwaters, and all of them together in demand only by builders down stream; hence, lumber in the Great Lakes region—Wisconsin and Michigan—was used before that on the Cumberland a few miles back from the streams.[98]

The forest, the first natural resource to which the pioneer turned, was the last to become a center of industry, unconnected with the plantation, for the pioneer working in timber took only wood for some specific purpose—boat timbers or charcoal, and men making and selling charcoal were like the woman selling linen cloth, skilled worker, capitalist, and retailer combined.

Flatboat building was another such industry, and by 1789 there was in Sumner County at least one builder of flatboats, Ellick Moone, able to bite a ten penny nail in two, for he "had monstrous big jaws and his foreteeth were pretty much in the shape of grinders." [99] Flatboat building, like the making of dugouts or perves, as they were sometimes known up river, went on all up and down the river for many years. Other types of craft were soon being built along the Cumberland, and by 1801 there was a boatyard at Neely's Bend.[100] The best known boatyard on the Cumberland was that of Matthew Lyon and Sons, which in the spring of 1805 built the sloop *Perseverance*, designed for the Philadelphia trade, and capable of taking a cargo of from four to five hundred barrels and thirty-five tons of cotton under the decks.[101] Another builder in the same year announced the brig *Industry*, designed for the Liverpool trade, was on stocks and would soon be ready for freight.[102] Boats continued to be built, but Middle Tennessee never became a great center of boat building, and many of the craft used came from Cincinnati or Pittsburgh.

Separation and segregation of employee and employer, labor and

[97] Clay County, Tennessee, Court Minutes, II, 1877–1889. Contracts mentioning sawmills, rafts, work oxen along with steamboat landings and ankle irons run through the minutes.

[98] *The Gum Tree Story* is a brief history of the Stearns Coal and Lumber Company that came from Ludington, Michigan, in 1902–1903 and bought some of the land that had belonged to the old Cumberland River Company; by 1905 the company owned 100,000 acres chiefly in Big South Fork drainage; in time the holdings were 40 miles across. All officials, even the teacher of the company school and the keeper of the company store, were brought from Michigan.

[99] W, 3XX(18), 6–7.

[100] Tennessee *Gazette*, April 15, 1801.

[101] *Ibid.*, March 20, 1805.

[102] *Ibid.*, Feb. 13, 1805.

capital, had already begun in New England when the Cumberland was settled. William Ruddle, small farmer of 1787, ginning his cotton on a homemade gin, would have been, had he lived, outdated less than a dozen years later; the more prosperous farmer had his own gin, with small farmers buying the service, and before 1802 a man could discharge his debts and never bother with bringing his cotton. He had only to bring to such a firm as Deadrick and Tatum his cotton ginning receipt.[103]

The small hand anvils on which farmers and their help had, at the settlement of the country, cut their nails fell gradually into disuse, and by 1801 the new cut nails were being retailed by King, Carson, and King at the upper ferry, and by 1812 Middle Tennessee had her own nail manufactory.[104] Old Johnnie Boyd, Frederick Stump, and Susan Overall, first settlers with stills, had to do the soldering and connecting themselves or depend upon a traveling tinker, but by 1802 Deadrick and Sittler were announcing the opening of a still manufactory.[105] There was by 1799, a powder mill, and soon another owned by Christopher Stump, versatile son of Frederick.[106] The mansion made of brick produced by slave labor on the plantation continued for many years to be a part of life, but by the early 1800's one could buy brick in Nashville or lumber ready dried in a kiln.[107]

There was by 1804 a rope walk to which farmers were urged to bring their hemp,[108] and the manufacturing of cotton thread and cloth had ceased to be a fireside industry. We cannot, however, be certain that Marsh and Bean, advertising their services in 1804, were the first cotton manufacturers on the Cumberland. Mention is made of a man being killed at his cotton manufactory before the Indian Wars were ended, and as early as 1801 notice was given in the *Gazette* of an attempt to start a cotton factory. There is nothing to indicate this was successful, or that another factory advertised even earlier in the Knoxville *Gazette* got past the planning stage. However, throughout this period there were homes in Kentucky in which the family made a business of spinning, weaving, or dyeing thread for others.[109]

[103] *Ibid.*, Dec. 18, 1802.
[104] *Ibid.*, June 17, 1801; Nashville *Clarion*, Aug. 11, 1812.
[105] Tennessee *Gazette*, Sept. 22, 1802.
[106] Williams, *Travels*, Schweinitz, "Report," 516; Tennessee *Gazette*, Nov. 28, 1804.
[107] Tennessee *Gazette*, March 7, 1804.
[108] *Ibid.*, Nov. 28, 1804.
[109] PW, II, 225. Mr. Ford had more than 50 dozen "cuts of spun cotton"—the length of a cut was about 300 yards, but varied. His several spinning wheels and lack of other appliances indicate he bought ginned cotton, and sold thread.

Marsh and Bean performed more services than could the little home "manufactory." The firm took unseeded cotton, ginned, carded, and spun it into medium coarse nine-hundred thread for three shillings, nine pence per pound, though the still coarser five hundred thread, suitable chiefly for work clothing, cost only two shillings, six pence per pound. There was an additional charge of four shillings, six pence per pound to dye the spun thread a deep blue; pale blue cost only three, while "tolerable blue" was halfway between, and the housewife could pay half the cost in cotton.[110]

Adam Maguire, the same year, offered a wider variety of services, dyeing wool as well as cotton in red, green, yellow, blue, and black; he also wove Draper carpets and summer counterpanes, spinning the thread, the warp, forty cuts to the pound, then doubled and twisted so that only six pounds would warp two counterpanes; the filler was coarse, only twenty cuts, or six thousand feet of thread to the pound.[111]

There was by 1812 a wool-carding factory where for ten cents per pound plus one pound of grease for each eight pounds of wool, the housewife might have her wool prepared for spinning.[112] Soon, even in Kentucky counties up river, there were carding factories, and many were the tales told by irate wives of the shady practices of the early carders and spinners; some were accused of saving the good clean hog's lard sent with the wool, and in its place substituting "half rotten bear or coon or dirty gut grease," that made the bats of wool "stink to high heaven."

Small manufactories flourished in now-forgotten places. The mouth of Buck Creek on the Cumberland is now a remote place, lost in dam waters, but the remains of the old ironworks can still be seen as can others in Wayne County, places now inaccessible by automobile. There were rope walks, tanneries, fulling mills, boatyards, and salt, saltpeter, tar, and iron works, with, sometime before 1819, at least one steam sawmill in what is now Smith County, with here and there a pottery. The first pottery firm I found was that of Schauss and Null, who in the winter of 1799 was doing a good business in the neighborhood of Nashville.[113] Equipment and methods would have been as primitive as those in Eastern Kentucky fifty years later; clay ground in a horse-powered hopper,

---

[110] Tennessee *Gazette*, Nov. 28, 1804.

[111] *Ibid.*, June 27, 1804, and *ibid.*, Aug. 15, 1804; see also Nashville *Clarion*, Oct. 26, 1810, *ibid.*, March 8, 1811.

[112] Nashville *Clarion*, Aug. 11, 1812.

[113] Williams, *Travels*, Schweinitz, "Report," 508.

turned on a wheel worked by a foot treadle, and glazed by handfuls of salt flung on while the pottery was still glowing.

Along with manufacturers there was an increase of appliances to speed the work at home; in 1803 the public was offered "a patented condensing tub" guaranteed capable of producing with a 110-gallon still and a 54-gallon doubler, from fifty to fifty-six gallons of liquor a day,[114] almost twice the production of Croft Distillery. There were soon on the market a patented washing machine, a corn-shelling machine, and an ever-increasing variety and abundance of clothing materials and ready-made clothing, as well as tools, furniture, and appliances that in the early years the pioneer farmer had made himself or ordered from a craftsman. The Industrial Revolution was being felt even in the agricultural South.

Most early industries discussed here were of a more or less temporary nature. The publishing industry was a different story. Nashville is today a center of publishing, and her many presses turn out a great variety of periodicals and books. The industry began in early 1799 with the publication by John McLaughlin of a weekly newspaper, the *Rights of Man* or *Nashville Intelligencer*.[115] The life of this periodical was short, but a few months later in early 1800, Benjamin J. Bradford, son of John Bradford, pioneer printer in Kentucky, began the Tennessee *Gazette*, published each Tuesday.[116] Middle Tennessee from this date was never without a newspaper, and as the years passed they multiplied.

The *Gazette*, no different from most weeklies of the day, was in content much like a magazine, publishing along with advertisements and the news, serialized novels such as *The Foundling*, much poetry, and many of the most popular works of the day including Thomas Paine's *The Rights of Man*. The cost in 1801 was $3 yearly or 12½ cents a copy, later reduced to $2 the year and 6¼ cents an issue, postage paid by the subscriber. The minimum cost for the first insertion of an ad was 75 cents, but only 25 cents for each succeeding insertion, provided the advertiser used at least two more.

Mr. Bradford in addition to managing and editing the paper, also supplied the county with blank deeds, an article always much in demand,

---

[114] Tennessee *Gazette*, May 18, 1803.
[115] A complete file of this paper has not been found; no. 5 of Vol. I is dated March 11, 1799.
[116] There is no complete file of the Tennessee *Gazette*. No. 7 of Vol. I is dated Feb. 25, 1800, but No. 1 of Vol. IV is dated Nov. 25, 1803; the extras may have been counted.

published handbills of all descriptions—sales, notices of runaway slaves, of horses at stud, a lottery, or a horse race. There was for 1801 and for several succeeding years a Tennessee *Almanac*,[117] and many other works known now only because they were advertised in the *Gazette* or mentioned by others: C. A. Smith's *Confessions of Pickering and Thornton*, murderers hanged July 3, 1811;[118] *Kaspar Mansker's Life Story*,[119] the two earliest works of Judge Haywood,[120] and several small things such as *A Primer Upon An Entirely New Plan*, and *A Wonderful Miracle*, this last advertised in the back of Haywood's works. Muster masters could by 1811 get *The Military Instructor*, published in Nashville,[121] though by this date there were several publishers and papers in Middle Tennessee.

The trials of any publisher in the old West were many. The news, and particularly that up from the South, was not only slow, but over the Natchez Trace, infested as it was by robbers, uncertain. There was, too, a shortage of paper in the whole of the United States; a paper mill was established in Middle Tennessee around 1811,[122] but was not too successful. In spite of Mr. Bradford's constant urging of the public to bring rags, there were never enough to keep the mill going. Nor could a book publisher be too zealous in soliciting manuscripts for possible publication. All postage was paid by the receiver, and the expense of accepting bulky manuscripts was so great that Mr. Bradford in the back of Haywood's early works, where he also advertised other publications, urged authors to send manuscripts, not by the mails, but by friends or neighbors. There was also the problem of keeping printers and printer's apprentices, and one wonders who made the woodcuts.

Manufacturing, diverse as it was on the Cumberland, was but a part of the bigger picture of manufacturing in the West. Kentucky outranked Tennessee and was at one time one of the most important of the industrial states, but Kentucky, situated as it was along the Ohio, got many more settlers from Pennsylvania and New York; men with more love of business and industry than had the farmers of Tennessee. Numerous as were its manufacturing establishments in 1803, the Cumberland Country was not destined to become a great industrial center.

[117] Tennessee *Gazette*, Feb. 8, 1801.
[118] Nashville *Clarion*, July 17, 1811.
[119] W, 6XX, 640; I found this mentioned only once; the work may have been written but never published.
[120] Nashville *Clarion*, Nov. 9, 1810. *Ibid.*, Oct. 19, 1810, Haywood's *Laws;* and *ibid.*, Dec. 7, 1810, Haywood's *Justices.*
[121] *Ibid.*, March 29, 1811.
[122] *Ibid.*, Jan. 25, 1811, and *ibid.*, Aug. 25, 1812.

The small farmer–manufacturer grew less and less able to compete with the mass-produced goods of New England and elsewhere. Middle Tennessee had little water power, but capital was the greater problem. As early as 1800 the populace was realizing that in order to keep any money at home manufacturing must be increased, and even the wealthy wore, as a patriotic gesture, summer linens and cotton of home manufacture. Still, they no more than the Virginia and North Carolina planters behind them could be entirely satisfied with homespun. Mrs. Thomas Butler was a thrifty housewife, sending much homemade linen and bacon to John Coffee's store, but she never saw money in their place. Instead, she bought bonnets, ribbons, muslins, calico for curtains. A thrifty New England family would have worn homespun, and used the money to buy spinning wheels and looms to be used at home or rented to the neighbors.

The average Cumberlander never showed much inclination to abide by Mr. Franklin's:

> Get what you can, and what you get hold;
> That is the stone which turns lead into gold.

He was more interested in a good and gracious life than gold, and this life would continue primarily agricultural with the plantation owner rather than the industrialist shaping the social, cultural, and political patterns.

Chapter Eleven

The Professions

THE TWO GREAT professions of the Old World and common in the United States today—the professional soldier and the professional religionist—had little appeal for the sons of first settlers on the Cumberland. The sword and the cross were in the early years not much in evidence. Swords in time became quite plentiful, but no first settler had one. Few of the Christian faiths on the Cumberland, in the first place, accepted the cross as a symbol; rather most looked upon it as a sign of "popery," and early church buildings of the old West, like those of New England, were built without crosses.

This may seem odd, particularly the lack of professional soldiers, when one remembers the multitude of military titles on the Cumberland. No group of families have, through the generations, supplied so many soldiers. Many individuals, like Colonel Daniel Ridley, served in both the

Headpiece: Townspeople as they appeared in the eighteenth and early nineteenth century.

French and Indian War and the Revolution; a very great many more such as Samuel Newell were in both Dunmore's War and the Revolution; still more—General James Winchester is an example—fought in the Revolution and again in the War of 1812; the younger generation represented by David Crockett and Sam Houston began with the War of 1812 and continued in Texas. Many of the first settlers, including James Robertson, never held officer rank in any major war, but struggled with Indian warfare on various borders for close to thirty years.

Yet, in spite of wars and the military titles the average Cumberlander like most Americans of that day who at one time or another served as soldiers considered himself a civilian. War at this time was never glorified; hatred for the Indian like hatred for the British was no part of the education of the pioneer young. Rather, their elders in the early years tried to explain the Indian atrocities in various ways. Daniel Smith whose courage was never questioned, but who at all times struggled for peace, blamed much of the Indians' butchery of whites on their poor education that glorified the shedding of blood. Governor Blount saw the Indian atrocities as the work not of a group, but of individuals. He felt most trouble came because the older systems of Indian government had been so broken down, the chiefs and the more responsible men of the tribe could no longer restrain the hot-headed younger men, often criminals and half-breeds, who committed most of the attacks. He, too, deplored the Indian way of life in which a man could distinguish himself only through war.[1]

Such thinking was not uncommon. Jackson and Sevier were, for example, mortal enemies yet each was opposed to large standing armies. This was part of British tradition; England preferred to muddle along with as small a standing army as possible, relying instead on her trained bands of citizens. There were, of course, Englishmen who did make careers of the army. Yet, such was the feeling of the day that a man was not trained as an officer by being sent to military school; rather, he bought his commission; money alone was not sufficient; he had, first of all, to be a gentleman acceptable to his future comrades, and if he had had an Oxford or Cambridge education so much the better. There were no Kiplings to glorify the military life; rather, "The Battle of Blenheim" was popular enough that in February of 1802 it appeared in the *Gazette*, authorless as was much of Mr. Bradford's poetry.

The tradition of the soldier-citizen and gentleman officer was brought

---

[1] TP, IV, 210, Gov. Blount to General Knox; see also *ibid.*, IV, 199, Daniel Smith to Governor Blount.

to the colonies, and flourished well in North Carolina that furnished so many men for border warfare. Fight they would when it was a matter of life and death, but the military life with all its trappings they cared for not at all. True, the trained bands of England were replaced by the militia in which all able-bodied men save Quakers and others morally opposed to war were potential soldiers. The militia turned out for training at the muster at stated intervals, but the muster in the South was never taken too seriously.

Actual war could not destroy the tradition of the gentleman officer and citizen soldier. Records of the North Carolina Line during the Revolution yield a record of citizens at war. Civilian rights were not sacrificed to military expediency, and men, when punished at all, were punished for offenses abhorrent to civilians. The only instance found of a death penalty carried out by a military court was that on a soldier executed for plundering;[2] the same court inflicted one of the few instances of whipping found, and that for one of the most hated civilian crimes—theft. Over and over the soldiers, no matter how tired and hungry they and their horses might be, were warned not to tear down fences for cooking fuel, or turn their mounts into farmers' meadows.[3]

In sharp contrast was the punishment for purely military offenses that today in the United States could bring long imprisonment or even death. A deserter, for example, pled guilty, but as he appeared to be "not abel in body and a stupid foolish person," he was only drummed out of the service.[4] This was more punishment than most deserters received; they were almost always pardoned as was the man who deserted his post and another who slept on duty—"as he appears to be a good soldier." Other cases were dismissed for lack of evidence, as was that of John Halfpenny, brought before a court-martial and charged with "getting drunk, causing a riot and abusing his officers."[5] Prussian militarism was not at that time admired.

Tennessee inherited the North Carolina pattern of militia and musters, but during the years of Indian warfare, most able-bodied men were called out so often for active service, regular musters were not ordinarily held. It was not until peace and more settlers came that the heyday of the muster in Middle Tennessee began.[6] Most men of the region had long since mas-

[2] NCR, XII, 489.
[3] *Ibid.*, XII, 476, 479.
[4] *Ibid.*, XII, 459.
[5] *Ibid.*, XII, 465, 489.
[6] TP, IV, 338–442, contains Blount's list of appointments for muster officers in the

tered the prime requisite of a soldier of that day—the ability to shoot; and the muster was more in the nature of a social gathering or, as described by Dr. Drake of Kentucky, "the learning was quite eclipsed by heterogeneous drama of foot racing, pony racing, wrestling, fighting, drunkenness, and general uproar."

The North Carolina attitude prevailed in the early years, and Tennessee, as did most other states, made provisions for the man morally opposed to war.[7] Yet, less than forty years after the officers of the North Carolina Line had pardoned men for sleeping on duty as well as desertion, General Jackson had a number of citizen soldiers executed for attempted mutiny. There was an almost universal gasp of horror and condemnation of the deed, but it was quickly forgotten as Jackson gained fame as a military man. Grandsons of Daniel Smith and John Donelson were soon attending the Military Academy at West Point. The world had changed. Visiting Englishmen deplored militarism as a separate way of life. "Military schools contain the seeds of death to American liberty,"[8] one exclaimed in 1818. Three years later another declared when viewing the rise of militarism in the United States, ". . . a standing army and disarmed population is the awful lever that with despotism and crooked policy have everywhere overturned the temple of liberty."[9] Each had apparently forgotten England's own Sandhurst, but the "Charge of the Light Brigade" was yet to be written.

There was also a great change in the attitude of the average man toward religion. This was particularly true of the Cumberland Country, that to begin with had inherited much of the North Carolina attitude that had so scandalized William Byrd when he ran the line in 1728. Byrd was of Virginia, a colony in which the clergy had almost as much influence in many matters as in England. Episcopal clergymen were not only supported by taxation, but served often as teachers, were among the social leaders of their respective communities, and had by the time of the Revolution succeeded in getting quite a number of better-than-average church buildings. All this in spite of the fact that on the Virginia borders

---

three countries then on the Cumberland. See also, *ibid.*, IV, 73 and Haywood, *Laws* 307–323, for the 1803 Tennessee muster laws based on those of North Carolina.

[7] Haywood, *Laws*, "Construction of the State of Tennessee," 1–13, sect. XXVIII, " . . . no citizen of the state to be compelled to bear arms provided he will pay an equivalent sum . . ." Throughout the United States any man could buy a substitute, and many did for the Union Army during The War, most commonly in the larger cities where immigrants, especially the Irish, could be cheaply had.

[8] Faux, *Travels, 1818–1819*, 106.

[9] Welby, *Travels*, 304.

Church of England communicants were much in the minority. Paying taxes for the upkeep of a church in which he did not believe, undoubtedly added to the zeal with which many of the Scotch-Irish fought the Revolution.

The war ended, the average pioneer seemed to feel the matter of church and state was also ended once and for all. No group showed any inclination to give the religion of its choice the same relative position in the United States as the Church of England had held in Virginia. Different from many constitutions of the day, that of Tennessee did not require the holder of public office to affirm a belief in God. The average pioneer belonged to no church. This did not necessarily mean he did not hold religious beliefs, but many felt that organized religion with paid ministers was not necessary to an individual's practice of religion. In general, however, morality, rather than religion, was stressed; many of the great political leaders of the day—Franklin, Jefferson, and soon Andrew Jackson—were not noted for their religious zeal. Deism and atheism were quite common, and it was many years before God got into American politics, entering chiefly on the abolition question in which each side claimed Him for its own.

God was, of course, not on any American money in the early years, and no early politician made ostentatious displays of religious zeal. This does not necessarily mean that men running for office were any less religious—or hypocritical—than those of today. Chiefly it was because, at least in Middle Tennessee, overmuch religious zeal might have cost more votes than it gained. Judging from tradition much of this feeling arose, not because of lack of feeling for God and Christ, but because as sacred beings they were not to be prostituted. Even to my childhood many of the older people were careful of the word Christian. It was never used on inanimate objects; "Christian patriotism," "Christian government" were never heard. Even when applied to people the old were mightily careful; obituaries in county papers seldom said of the deceased that he was a "Christian." This they felt was a matter to be decided only at The Last Judgment. If anything at all was said of religion, church affiliation only was given.

The Cumberland Country, with no minister of record for the first five years, had less organized religion than most communities. Even Thomas B. Craighead, the first, seems to have been more influential as an educator than as a minister. There were few early references to ministers or the church as an institution. In 1787 Christopher Lightholder of Davidson

County gave his goods to the Methodist Church,[10] influenced possibly by the Reverend Ogden, a Methodist minister who in that year "labored from Station to Station."[11] Three years later another itinerant minister, the Reverend August V. Pruegel,[12] preached for a time among the German families on White's Creek, and the Reverend John Kirkwell[13] went on the Nickojack campaign in 1794, but seemingly as a soldier rather than as chaplain. The Constitution of the State of Tennessee drawn up the following year stipulated that "no minister of the gospel or priest is to be eligible to a seat in either house." They literally wanted the religionist in no office of public trust, and I found no justice of the peace who was a minister; the populace feared the substitution of religion for morality.

Religious interest gradually grew. The Moravian missionaries,[14] arriving in the winter of 1799–1800, preached in private homes to overflow crowds as did the Reverend Asbury visiting Middle Tennessee for the first time a few months later. There was by this date a large stone church almost finished in Nashville, and possibly small Baptist church buildings of a more or less temporary nature in the Red River Country. The Baptist were, of all faiths, growing most rapidly; by 1796 there were five church bodies in Middle Tennessee, three on Sulphur Fork of Red River, one on the West Fork of Station Camp Creek, and one on White's Creek,[15] this last meeting monthly in the home of Frederick Stump. There were in 1800 only two Methodist circuits in all of Tennessee.[16] The Presbytery of Transylvania, organized in 1786, had included the Cumberland and the Presbyterians were quite active, but it was not until 1810 that the Presbytery of West Tennessee (then Middle Tennessee) was formed; it embraced a vast region from "the Ohio to the Gulf and the Cumberland Mountains to the Rockies," or most of the Mississippi Valley.[17] The American Episcopal Church, not organized in the United States until 1787,

---

[10] DW, I, 96.

[11] W, 6XX(50), 999.

[12] Williams, *Travels*, Schweinitz, "Report," 512.

[13] W, 32S, 257.

[14] Williams, *Travels*, Schweinitz, "Report," 510–517, is the only firsthand account of religion on the Cumberland. Made by men who went to a good bit of trouble to learn the state of religion, it reveals little evidence of organized religion twenty years after settlement; though not over the whole of Middle Tennessee, the Moravians found no completed church building, and not even the beginnings of one in East Tennessee.

[15] Sweet, *Religion, I, The Baptist, 1783–1830*, New York, 1931, 7.

[16] *Ibid., IV, The Methodist, 1783–1840*, Chicago, 1946, 53.

[17] *Ibid., II, The Presbyterians, 1783–1840*, New York, 1936, 32, 35.

had by 1799 one rector in Nashville, the Reverend Adam Boyd, lately come from Georgia.[18]

Mention of ministers and church bodies is not intended to give the impression of regular communicants organized enough to furnish buildings. Itinerant ministers continued in summer to wander "through the different countries, and preach in the woods where the people collect together."[19] Even when there was a church building, the Protestant Church was a center of religion only; the vast complex of social life, amusement, politics of which the modern church is often the center was unknown. There was not even Sunday School; the first in Middle Tennessee was organized by Mrs. Felix Grundy many years past the pioneer period.

The Great Revival came and went, but there is the question of how much religion was revived. Time and the modern attitude toward religion have softened many uglier aspects—break down of morals by the participants, "manifestations" helped along by the raw whiskey sold at every meeting,[20] and the generally disorderly and at times criminally inclined individuals who came as hangers-on.

The Great Revival, like other religious activity, went unnoticed in the Tennessee *Gazette*. Mr. Bradford's editorial policy was in the main much like that of most editors of the day; religion was a personal matter and hence had no news value. The only mention of matters religious in the early years were announcements in 1799 and 1804 of meetings called for the purpose of building churches.[21] The first intimation of what one might call propaganda making use of religion, though opposite to our own use today, came in 1811 when the old West, in contrast to New England, found more and more quarrel with England. There was thus quite an article detailing the evils of the English church–state system in which the church was supported by public funds.[22] Usually, there was nothing more than a mild anticlericalism that extended to all faiths. Jokes, the kind told of ministers for generations, were quite common. Typical was that of "an alehouse girl" who went to church. The Parson asked her name. "Lord,

[18] Williams, *Travels*, Schweinitz, "Report," 513.

[19] Michaux, *Travels 1802*, 304.

[20] Sweet, *Religion*, II, *The Presbyterians*, 88–89.

[21] *Nashville Intelligencer* Aug. 28, 1799—"a meeting called for plans for procuring of a house of worship." See also Tennessee *Gazette*, March 7, 1804.

[22] Nashville *Clarion*, April 16, 1811. The English Episcopal clergymen were called "among the most dissolute of all mankind—wallowing in all kinds of wickedness; 1800 clergymen supported by the public yet independent of the people."

Sir," said she, "how can you pretend not to know my name when you come to our house so often, and cry ten times in an evening, 'Nan, you whore, bring us another full pot.' " [23]

It is doubtful if any of Mr. Bradford's readers saw anything wrong with the joke. Religion without morality was frowned upon; the feeling then seems to have been that religion in itself was not necessarily a good thing; rather, they were, like Andrew Jackson, inclined to judge the tree by its fruit. Organized religion grew, not because of social or political pressures from outside, but like education, it developed from the activies of individuals. This was especially true of the early Baptist. Churches were organized, not by missions sent from some central organization, but each by a few individuals; sometimes no more than the members of one family holding services in the home.

In many ways the citizen-soldier and the minister like Craighead who had to farm, distill his own whiskey, teach in order to make a living were typical of other professional men on the Cumberland. Few could earn a living entirely from the proceeds of one profession. Dr. Roger B. Sappington, for example, did a great deal of farming, and also kept a medicine store in addition to his practice.

This was especially true of surveying, one of the most common professions on any Southern border. All the men who got the lucrative appointments in Middle Tennessee had other occupations as well. Most were political figures with various titles, both civil and military. Quite often a man with a surveying appointment hired someone else to do the work. Colonel Henry Rutherford, Edwin Hickman, and James Mulherrin, who was also a schoolteacher, made many of the early surveys.

Daniel Smith, who helped run the line in the hard winter, was possibly the only one able to draw a map with any degree of accuracy, or who had more than the most meager training. Most could read a compass, plot after a fashion, and with no knowledge of trigonometry get quite an accurate idea of the acreage of a given tract by reducing it to quadrangles and right-angled triangles.

Paid usually in land that through the years appreciated in value, surveying was, for the number of hours put in, possibly the best paying job in pioneer Middle Tennessee. Still, the lot of the early surveyor was no easy one; he was ever a target of Indians, and though he customarily received between a third and a fourth of the land he surveyed, he had to be, particularly in Kentucky, something of a gambler. If the title proved

[23] Tennessee *Gazette*, Aug. 5, 1801.

worthless as was so often the case, the surveyor lost along with his time the money gone to hire guards and chain carriers and pay for their food and other expenses.

The great days of surveying ended quickly. There were never again such lush appointments as those handed out by North Carolina to the Donelsons, Daniel Smith, and others. As land increased in value and the country grew safer from the Indians, the surveyor actually doing the work was more apt to be offered produce or even money instead of land. The County Surveyor of later years was only an employee paid by the day.

The surveyor, unprofessional as he was, was the only representative found on the Cumberland during pioneer years of all the modern professions in some way related to what is commonly referred to as engineering. There were by 1803 a good many examples of engineering and architectural skills in evidence in Middle Tennessee—mills of many varieties, at least one iron furnace, quite a number of good-sized stone buildings, sea-going ships, and a number of roads described as good. The names of these early shapers of water-to-wheels able to pump bellows or grind grain have not come down to us. They were lumped together as "skilled workmen," many undoubtedly like the Baltimore carpenters who shaped the roof timbers of Cragfont, living in the neighborhood only until their particular job was finished.

Law was a different story. It was the profession most commonly chosen by the son of the small farmer who wanted to rise in the world, and the son of the large landowner who with the overseer system had the promise of a life offering much free time. Travelers to the South of later years commented on the large number of lawyers in the county seat towns, and Captain John Donelson once complained of the many lawyers "gaping" about the courthouse in Nashville.

Law had long been a favorite profession of well-born but not-too-wealthy young men of Scotland, and it held the same appeal for the young Scotch-Irish and Scotch in the colonies and later the United States. Early colonial Virginia had had few lawyers and none at all in the county courts, or the court of quarter sessions as they were commonly known.[24] As time passed the law increased in importance, but it was not until the

[24] Robert Beverly, *The History and Present State of Virginia in Four Parts*, by a Native and Inhabitant of the Place, London, 1705 (pagination from the ed. of Charles Campbell, Richmond, 1855), Book IV, 30, "Every one that pleases may plead his own Cause, or else his Friends for him, there being no restraint in that case, nor any licensed Practitioners of the Law."

opening of the old West—Kentucky and Tennessee—that lawyers came into their own. New superior courts demanded at least prosecuting attorneys and judges with some knowledge of the law, but the pull of the West for young lawyers was the uncertain land titles. Lawsuits over land titles with the fees paid in land in the early years enriched generations of lawyers, Andrew Jackson among them.

Law, lucrative as it was for the lucky and skillful, quickly became in the young United States considerably more than a source of income. It was the steppingstone into politics. Andrew Jackson, John Overton, Henry Clay, Thomas Hart Benton, and later Abraham Lincoln and most other noted political figures began as lawyers. This was in sharp contrast to colonial and pioneering days immediately after the Revolution. None of the great border leaders so often mentioned—John Sevier, James Robertson, Daniel Smith, Dr. Thomas Walker—began life as a lawyer.

Richard Henderson was the first lawyer of record on the Cumberland; a judge and said to be the author of the Cumberland Compact, he certainly had more skill and training than most lawyers of his day, but his stay in Middle Tennessee was more in the nature of a land-business trip than a residence. I found no lawyer among the first settlers who actually stayed and fought the Indians, but by 1783 there was at least one in what was to be Middle Tennessee—George Neville.[25] They of course flocked to the young community as soon as a county court was established and continued to come. There was by 1784, Dr. James White and John Cole Mountflorence, but in keeping with other professionals of the day, both with many other irons in the fire. The well-dressed Mr. Gubbins was admitted to the Davidson County Bar[26] in 1785; close to three years later came Judge John McNairy and his prosecuting attorney Andrew Jackson.

In 1790 when what was to be Tennessee became a part of the Territory South of the Ohio River, lawyers licensed to practice in the North Carolina courts had to be relicensed to practice in the Territory. William Blount, governor, made a special trip to Nashville in December of that year and granted licenses to seven lawyers.[27] No one of these seven, ever gave his full time to law any more than did Andrew Jackson, one of the seven, though both John Overton and James White were also important in the history of Tennessee. They had acquired their training by "reading law" for around two years in the office of an established lawyer

[25] DW, I, 22–23, this a 1784 reference to 1783.
[26] DC, I, 62.
[27] TP, IV, 441.

to whom they paid tuition, the sum seldom less than $150 for the full course, several hundred in later years if in the office of a well known lawyer such as Felix Grundy under whom the future President Polk studied. Micah Taul, first county clerk of Wayne County, Kentucky, was granted a license with no examinations and no previous study of the law, save odds and ends picked up while serving as county clerk,[28] but a Tennessee law of 1798, based on an earlier North Carolina law, stipulated that a man in order to be a practicing lawyer must undergo an examination before two or more judges.[29]

The lawyer was the closest thing to a professional the pioneers knew. Any man able to read and write and with the means or credit of acquiring a suitable wardrobe, tools, and drugs, could set up as a physician. Many early surveyors such as Captain John and Stockley Donelson as well as James Robertson were given lucrative appointments with no more formal training in the work than what they had picked up from some book such as Love's *Surveying* or learned from a neighbor or relative. There was no law against neighbors with adjoining land borrowing a compass and running their own line.[30] Any man or woman with a fair degree of education and able to collect a sufficiency of paying pupils might start a school.

In contrast, law was the most respected of the professions, the most learned, and the most in demand. The seven lawyers licensed by Governor Blount in 1790, all working part time as they did, would have been no more than needed to defend and prosecute the citizens of Middle Tennessee in County Court. Davidson County with a population of scarcely four thousand, and less than half of these adults, had in the 1790 April term of County Court 192 cases on the docket; true, this was an unusually busy term, but for the whole of the four sessions of 1794 there were 397 cases.[31]

Criminal cases, like civil cases involving larger sums and suits over land, were held in the Superior Court, sitting twice yearly. It is doubtful if any lawyer licensed as was Joseph Sitgreaves to practice only in the lower courts made his expenses. Following a custom long observed in most of the colonies, the fees Tennessee lawyers were permitted to exact were set by law in 1796. A land suit, for example, was to cost the plaintiff

---

[28] RK, XXVII, Taul, "Memoirs," 4.

[29] Haywood, *Laws*, 239.

[30] Parton, *Jackson*, I, 158, gives the 1795 letter of Andrew Jackson to Daniel Smith, asking him to survey a boundary; if unable to do so would he please loan his compass.

[31] *Ibid.*, 135, quoting Putnam's summary.

no more than $6.25;[32] a suit in equity was $12.50, but this fee law seems to have been consistently broken and was almost impossible to enforce. Many lawsuits, particularly those involving land, were paid on a percentage basis, and usually based not on the price, but on a percentage of the land itself.

Crimes there were of many kinds, though as a rule those arising from what one might loosely call social decay—sex perversion, dope addiction, desertion of children, gang murders—appear to have been almost nonexistent. Yet there was, considering the smallness of the population, a good deal of mayhem, manslaughter, and considerable theft, particularly of horses, but civil cases comprised by far the larger share of the docket. Much less lucrative than trials involving land titles, but more common, were the many suits for the collection of debts. Justice during pioneer years was cheap enough; it was no uncommon thing to be sued for less than five dollars, and suffer the indignity of having the debt collected by the sheriff or his bailiff, the collector receiving a percentage. Suing and being sued were so common it was taken pretty much for granted that sooner or later all men and many women must go to law. Micah Taul, after a long eulogy on the goodness and uprightness of his father, summed him up as having been an unusually good man, and gave as proof the fact he had never been sued.[33]

The hope of every lawyer, of course, was a judgeship, though Judge McNairy, the first judge of the Superior Court for Middle Tennessee, got only $50 for each court session. In Kentucky, pay depended on the County Court and varied from county to county.[34] Jackson flourished as a prosecuting attorney, and at the same time built up quite a law business in the lower courts, although he knew little law. When on the bench of the Supreme Court of Tennessee, he earned a good salary for that day— $600 yearly. As a judge an early biographer wrote of him: ". . . tradition reports that he maintained the dignity and authority of the bench, while he was *on* the bench; and that his decisions were short, untechnical, unlearned, sometimes ungrammatical, and generally right. . . . When not blinded by passion, by prejudice, or by gratitude, Judge Jackson's sense of right was strong and clear."[35]

---

[32] Haywood, *Laws*, 214–217.

[33] RK, XXVII, Taul, "Memoirs," 4.

[34] PC, I, 41. The court in October of 1800 voted $100 as pay to Archibald Mills for his services as Commonwealth Attorney, and William Fox, clerk, was allowed $30 for "public service by him in erecting of his office."

[35] Parton, *Jackson*, I, 227.

Lawyers grew more and more plentiful. Soon anywhere from one to half a dozen could be found in any small Kentucky or Tennessee town. Somerset, Kentucky, for example, had only three hundred residents as late as 1840, but as a county seat town it had attracted six lawyers and five physicians.[36] Monticello, a few miles away, and with even fewer people had five lawyers and four physicians.[37]

Many businesses and professions such as medicine and teaching were carried on in the home, though the physician's office was much less important than today. The feeling then and for many years to come was that a person sick enough to pay good money for a doctor was too sick to travel, and so the physician visited the patient instead of the other way around. Thus, the most common and most-used office was that of the lawyer.

Followers of the law needed to be in the county seat town at least during court week, and even when he lived there, few men wanted to subject their wives and children to a constant procession of accusers and accused, and so the small log outbuilding serving as law office was built on many estates. The office of Spruce McKay in Salisbury, North Carolina, where Andrew Jackson studied law in 1785–86, was described as "a little box of a house, fifteen by sixteen feet, one story high."[38] Better than many, it was ceiled and covered with shingles instead of boards, had a proper fireplace, and shelves for books.

The log house John Coffee had put up when he needed a land office in 1809 is possibly quite typical of the early office building in Nashville. Built at a labor cost of $189.85, it was 22 by 25 feet, one story high, with a shingled roof, tongued and grooved floor, and the log walls covered with rived weather boarding planed smooth in front. One of its three rooms must have gone unheated as there were only two fireplaces, but three outside doors, and four windows.[39]

A society, William Byrd once observed when visiting the back parts of North Carolina, offering few of the advantages of civilization, particularly money, is seldom troubled with either priests or physicians. Pioneer Middle Tennessee was for some years a good example of such a community; physicians were no more plentiful than ministers, but the pioneer was more eager for physicians than ministers. More than once in accounts

[36] Collins, *Kentucky 1882*, II, 682.
[37] *Ibid.*, 753–754.
[38] Parton, *Jackson*, I, 103–104.
[39] Coffee Papers, 1809.

of Indian warfare, we find the old remembering and believing, "Could he have had a good surgeon he would have recovered." [40]

Most doctoring of all kinds from pegging a scalped head to curing the itch was done for many years by some woman or man such as Robertson with a knack for the business. Every household was both hospital and doctor's office, and homemade remedies as well as patent medicines had long been a part of life, particularly in the Southern colonies where even the wealthy might live many miles from a physician. William Byrd in 1728 and John Sevier seventy years later were well able to afford physicians, though Sevier appears to have trusted them more than Byrd, but both men wrote down many recipes for cures for all manner of diseases in both animals and men.

There was much less difference between home medication and that of physicians than today. The numerous teas, infusions, and poultices made from various plants, often wild ones,[41] used by laymen were also prescribed by the most learned physicians. The few midwives and "herb doctors" extant in the back hills a few years ago were only physicians somewhat behind the times. Research into the subject tends to indicate they made use of no herb or method not at one time prescribed by a physician, many from early colonial days. Home remedies, however, during pioneer days had changed in one notable respect since Byrd doctored ailing members of his surveying parties in the backwoods. Whiskey had taken the place of rum. Nor were the many beliefs concerning various foods and their effects for good or evil on the human body confined to the unsophisticated or the pioneer, but like moon lore varied with the nationality-background and region; some believed fevers came from eating cucumbers and melons. Many, Dr. Benjamin Rush, the most noted physician of the day, among them, thought overmuch drinking of cold spring water harmful; some believed meat was bad for children, and others gave the teething baby a crackled meat skin, but it is doubtful if anything was so universally believed in as the virtues of toddy.

[40] W, 32S, 314.

[41] Most early journalists wrote only of the healing properties of plants; early geologists now and then mentioned the healing powers of some springs; Red Boiling Springs in Tennessee, for example, was long a noted health resort; and the waters of Crab Orchard Springs in Kentucky were bottled and sold for medicinal purposes. Very few wrote of the healing effects of portions of animals as did Brickell. His *North Carolina*, "The Beasts," 107–132, gave some part of almost every mentioned animal as a cure: "the dung and Blood of the Wolf are excellent to expedite the Birth and after Birth," *ibid.*, 121; "the testicles of the possum given with Honey stir up Lust and cause Conception," *ibid.*, 126; "fat of the Squirrel good for pains in the Ears and the teeth," *ibid.*, 128; "bat gall good for dimness of sight," *ibid.*, 132.

The closest thing to a physician the Cumberlanders had in the very early years was "E. Winchester who had some knowledge of surgery learned in the army." He doctored all manner of ailments, even asthma, and was particularly useful in caring for the wounded, and "always without pay."[42] The writer did not go into details of E. Winchester's methods of treating wounds or asthma, but in general the pioneer period was in medicine as in many matters a time of transition. The faith in blood-letting as a universal cure was already on the wane before the death of Washington, but the use of powerful and poisonous drugs, especially arsenic, was increasing. Yet on the whole one might think of it as a rather temperate time in medicine when treatment was less drastic than usual. Some patients, of course, had more pleasant cures than others, though few were so lucky as the North Carolinian of whom it was reported in 1783, "Read has been ill with a putrid fever but Claypoole with a little bleeding, abundance of blisters, and a great quantity of porter, oysters, and beef steak has perfectly recovered him."[43] Few physicians of the day offered such pleasant cures. Dr. Rush, respected even in Europe, was something of an exception. His thinking in many matters was well in advance of his time. He preached cleanliness, fresh air—in the daytime only, for in common with the rest of the world, he held night air unhealthful—exercise, and was one of the first to attack alcoholism, not on the basis of immorality but because overmuch alcohol ruined the health. He, like most physicians of his day, prescribed wine or some form of alcoholic beverage even for children.

Medicine in the United States was as a rule more in the nature of a small business than a profession. Dr. Rush himself was one of its severest critics, declaring that "opulent physicians" specializing in the various branches of medicine, especially surgery, were a symptom of a country's decline.[44] At about the same time Matthew Carey deplored the fact that medicine in the United States was "being sacrificed to avaricious principles and pursued with a sordid desire of accumulating wealth." [45]

[42] W, 32S, 279.

[43] NCR, XVI, 963.

[44] Rush, *Observations, 1794*, 64–65. This was the second work by Dr. Rush with the same title; see his *Medical Enquiries and Observations*, Philadelphia, 1789. See also *Quarterly Publication of the Historical and Philosophical Society of Ohio*, III, no. 2, 29–60, a reprint of "Notices Concerning Cincinnati," by Dr. Daniel Drake, Cincinnati, 1812; and the Appendix of the *Quarterly*. Dr. Drake advocated the usual bleeding, blistering, and purging with much reliance on plants used by the pioneers, and these continued quite popular; see Robert T. Foster, *The North American Indian Doctor*, Canton, Ohio, 1838.

[45] Carey, *Museum*, IX, 68.

Close to thirty years later a visiting Italian commented in surprise, "the doctors themselves also act as apothecaries, so that it may well be imagined how much must be paid for medicines." [46] Most physicians in the United States of that day sold medicines as well as services, a custom unknown in Europe where the apothecary's shop was an important part of the pattern of medicine.

In spite of such complaints it is doubtful if any early physician on the Cumberland had earnings comparable with those of even the lowest paid doctor of today. First, the business of medicine, unorganized as it was, had no means of limiting the number of its followers; so that any neighborhood, once it was safe from the Indians and with a sprinkling of well-to-do prospective patients, became overrun with physicians. A modern major source of income, surgery, though long known, was resorted to only in the matter of amputations and the patching up of wounds. No appendix at that date had been removed. Worse, for the money-needing physician, there was no way of preventing the public from buying any drug or medicine. Laudanum, along with most other stand-bys of the day, was quite commonly owned by early settlers. Anybody could at least by 1799, and for how much earlier we do not know, buy most any drug at the shop of Hennen and Dickson.[47] Soon, several stores in Nashville sold along with "painter's colors," "dye stuffs," and spices, opium, camphor, laudanum, sugar of lead, borax, and a variety of patent medicines; [48] the most widely advertised of these was Bateman's Infallible Ague and Fever Drops. Beginning in 1810 the Medicine Store of J. R. Bradford in Nashville had, in addition to any drug available to the physician, a variety of books on surgery, anatomy, and midwifery.

Obstetrics, so lucrative for many modern physicians, was but a scanty source of income. All babies were, to begin with, delivered in the home, so that the work was time consuming compared to today when many obstetricians, the patient in the hospital, are in attendance only during the last few minutes of actual delivery.

Physicians learned in obstetrics were advertising in the Tennessee *Gazette* shortly after 1800, but the country woman, trained in midwifery, usually by her mother, continued to be a part of life in communities up the river for many years. Such a one was Nancy Kelly of Pulaski County,

---

[46] Handlin, *America*, Grassi, "Observations, 1819," 145.

[47] MW, I, 37. *Nashville Intelligencer*, March 11, 1799.

[48] Tennessee *Gazette*, Aug. 5, 12, 1801; *ibid.*, Jan. 13 (an extra), 1802. *Ibid.*, Aug. 4, 1802.

Kentucky.[49] Wife of a farmer and versed in all the home arts and crafts from cheese making to linen bleaching, she added still more to the family income through midwifery; her fee, one dollar or two days wages. Pay, like that of other professionals of the day, was taken in whatever she could get—two hundred fence rails or wool for her knitting needles. A few women, such as Rebecca Williams of Western Pennsylvania,[50] grew famous among the borderers for medical and surgical skills, especially with wounds.

There are from all borders numerous stories of men recovering from all manner of wounds with help from no physician. One of the best known is that of Hugh Rogan who, wounded down on the Tennessee during the Coldwater Campaign of 1787 and deserted with a few other men [51] by their commanding officer David Hay, had to walk all the way home with a hole in his breast. He ascribed his cure to the exercise and lack of food. More remarkable still is the story of Colonel William Fleming who at the Battle of Point Pleasant in 1774 received two bullets in his left arm, breaking two bones; a third bullet entered his chest "about three inches below my left nipple.[52] It lodged somewhere—when I came to be drest I found my lungs forced through the wound as long as my fingers." After several tries, in which he participated, and a good bit of pushing, the lungs were got back in; he survived Kentucky during the hard winter and lived, carrying the two bullets twenty-one years after the wound. Treatment of wounds varied; whiskey was a universal drug and most believed that a wound should bleed as much as possible; Joshua Thomas, for example, when wounded by Indians was held up by the heels so as to let the blood out.[53]

The first physician in Middle Tennessee was Dr. James White. He did not come until 1784, and lived for much of the time at Hickman's Station, several miles west of Nashville. It is doubtful if Dr. White earned much from medicine. He was also a lawyer and in 1786 was appointed Indian agent, only one of a long series of government posts he held. Seventeen eighty-six brought Dr. John Sappington, and only a few months later, his elegant brother Dr. Mark, who always wore his hair powdered and had a

[49] Kelly, *Kelly Clan*.
[50] Mrs. Elizabeth Fries (Lummies) Ellet, *Domestic History of the American Revolution*, New York, 1859, 298.
[51] W, 32S, 525.
[52] Thwaites-Kellogg, *Dunmore's War*, 255.
[53] W, 5S, 65.

weakness for massive silver knee- and shoe-buckles. Dr. Francis May came in 1790, but, different from today, there was then no complete agreement between these members of the medical fraternity, for Dr. May killed Dr. Francis Sappington in a duel.

How much these men and others such as Dr. Hays who came about 1801 added to the health of Middle Tennessee is a question, but they certainly increased the topics of conversation. Dr. James White, though a "learned and talented gentleman," was addicted to drink and buckskins; and all seemed somewhat fond of the wild life, for Dr. Hays also fought a duel, but his death came from an attack of delirium tremens, catching him in "indigent circumstances." [54]

As the community grew safer from the Indians and increased in size and wealth, physicians became even more numerous, and early *Gazettes* have many of their ads; in 1801 John Collins offered to cure rupture on any person, forty-five years old or less, "no cure, no pay"; [55] the following year John Rhodes advertised a cure for consumption; [56] and by 1804 Cornelius Baldwin had set up as a country physician, practicing general medicine, midwifery, and surgery near Haysborough.[57] He would also clean, extract, transplant or put in artificial teeth. In the same year James L. Armstrong of Lexington advertised from Drake's Creek.

Medical services in proportion to wages, food, and most commodities were even higher than today. A visit of three miles or less was the equivalent of one hundred pounds of beef or six days labor for an unskilled workman—three dollars, with a shilling added for each mile over three; once in attendance medical costs mounted rapidly; one powder was nine pence and other drugs in proportion.[58] Charges on the Cumberland were no greater than those in the rest of the country; John Coffee, for example, paid five dollars for a "kine pox" vaccination in Philadelphia in 1803. High as were the fees on the Cumberland, earnings were still not enough to support the many practitioners.

The physicians tried to form an organization in which each promised to charge no less than the fees agreed upon. The plan failed. There were charges that one doctor was treating patients at reduced rates in order to

[54] Felix Robertson, *The Nashville Journal of Medicine and Surgery*, VIII, 449–453.

[55] Tennessee *Gazette*, May 6, 13, 1801.

[56] *Ibid.*, Dec. 4, 1802.

[57] *Ibid.*, May 23, 1804.

[58] *Ibid.*, April, 14, 21, 28, 1802.

get all the business. The *Gazettes* through April of 1802 were filled with the charges and counter charges. Growing ever more heated, they ended at last in duels that decreased the number of doctors.

Dr. Nathaniel Smith, dying in Cumberland County, Kentucky, in 1819, was an early settler, owed at his death by most of the countryside. His effects were probably fairly typical of the average pioneer physician. His medical library included: "Cullen's *Practice*, Thomas's *Dictionary*, Darwin's *Testimonials*, Medical and Surgical Journals, Bell's *Operative Surgery*, *A System of Midwifery*, Bree, *On the Anatomy*, Burson's *Inflammatory and Treatments Thereof*, *Anatomical Examination*, Jackson's *Fevers*, a *Medical Dictionary*, Abernathy's *Observations*, Sesfield's *Cowpox*, a *Medical Lexicon*, and *Purgatives*, by Hamilton."

He had a marble mortar and a case of surgical instruments that most likely included forceps for the pulling of teeth, as physicians usually served as dentists. His chief stock in trade was twenty-five bottles of wine. There were smaller quantities of the most commonly used drugs of the day—white vitriol, opium, sugar of lead, gum myrrh, magnesia, manna, aloes, blue vitriol or copperas, calomel, castor, tartar potash, gum arabic, spermaceti, borax, digitalis, and two herbs used from early colonial days and still gathered on the Cumberland, Seneca snakeroot and Black snakeroot.[59] There were also five pewter syringes and three six-ounce bottles of Spanish flies, but nothing was said of leeches, still stocked by most country doctors of that day.

Such a physician attended the more difficult of the maternity cases, took care of injuries resulting from accidents, though in the very early years these seem to have been uncommon, struggled with the dreaded "milk-sick," not understood until a hundred years later, applied plasters to patients dying of tuberculosis, bled for all manner of ailments, and though childhood diseases such as whooping cough and measles were usually treated with divers home remedies from hot toddies to chicken manure, the physician was often sent for when a severe complication, usually referred to as "a fever," arose.

Journals, guardians' accounts listing numerous expenses for medicines and doctors' fees, tombstone records,[60] and the great proportion of second

---

[59] CW, II, 114.

[60] RK, XXVII, No. 79, 39–43; William Simpson, "Wayne County Vital Statistics," prepared during the 1850's reveals that many individuals born during and before pioneer days did live to advanced ages, and also sheds some light on matrimonial habits of the day—many died unmarried at rather late ages. See also *ibid.*, XXVII, No. 79, 49–58, "Kentucky Tombstone Inscriptions."

marriages as well as orphans being bound out, all indicate that the Cumberlanders, though healthier than much of the rest of the population of the United States,[61] still had a rather short average life span.

If the letters and journals of Andrew Jackson, Sevier, and James Robertson are indicative of the health of the population, it was a sickly one. Jackson seemed particularly inclined to colds while diarrhea and rheumatism plagued him most of his adult life. In general, diseases appear not to have been radically different from those of today, though heart diseases as evidenced by young or middle-aged men dropping dead was not common, and the average businessman of that day, such as Martin Armstrong, was certainly a tougher individual than today's carefully coddled executive. Most other diseases were present; cancer was fairly common, and many were the cures advertised. The populace then as now wrestled with colds, influenzas of various kinds, pneumonias, though not known by that name, and rheumatism. One of the most hated diseases, but now pretty well banished, was the itch. Andrew Jackson had it as a boy, and it continued common over much of the United States for generations.

Yet in spite of rather low average longevity, large numbers of individuals did reach rather advanced ages; Frederick Stump, Colonel Daniel Ridley, Naomi Sevier,[62] wife of Valentine, all died when well past ninety; Hugh F. Bell, Mary Purnell Donelson, Edward Swanson, Mrs. James Winchester, Timothe De Monbruen were only a few of those who lived beyond eighty. Dr. Draper, for example, collected much material on early Middle Tennessee in the 1840's, but even then, sixty years after first settlement, many first and early settlers were yet living; some like Colonel Samuel Newell up river, wounded in the Revolution; even puny Jackson reached seventy-seven.

Many ills that plague the population today, and that taken as a whole are possibly symptomatic of a bigger illness, were in pioneer days almost nonexistent. I found in the early years, except in the few cases of "woods-fever," nothing indicative of mental illness. I found no mention of suicide; drug addiction seems to have been unknown in the pioneer world, and

---

[61] Thwaites, *Travels*, III, Michaux "Journal," 92–93; Williams, *Travels*, Schweinitz "Report," 210–211, found the populace of Middle Tennessee subject to many ailments, especially "fevers," while the younger Michaux, *Travels 1802*, 291, thought Middle Tennessee "less salubrious" than either Kentucky or the Holston Country. On the other hand Brown, *Gazetteer*, 96, declared Wayne County, Ky., of 1815 to be the most healthful part of the state with diseases and physicians almost unknown, and the land between the Cumberland and Tennessee rivers on the Plateau, the most healthful in the United States.

[62] W, 31S, 64; W, 30S, 273.

the only cases of alcoholism were the physicians named. Gallie La Mar, dying of a fall from a tree, was the only accidental death found among grownups during the days of Indian warfare, though in 1801 the *Gazette* carried notice of the death of a workman in a boat-building accident in Neely's Bend. Accidents there no doubt were that went unmentioned, but it seems safe to say the pioneer was much less accident-prone than are we today.

Modern medicine like other aspects of the Industrial Revolution was on the way when the Cumberland was settled. One of mankind's greatest enemies—smallpox—was being conquered. The Cumberlander who wanted vaccination from a doctor had for several years to travel either to Philadelphia or later to Lexington, but by 1805 Dr. Wheatan of Nashville was advertising the "Genuine Vaccine or cow pox." [63] Quinine, still known as Jesuit Bark, was in rather wide use, and surgery was increasing. There was as yet no knowledge of germs, but people were at least getting suspicious, and by 1810 some citizens of Cincinnati were declaring that Ohio River water, filled as it was with human excrement, the refuses of tanneries and meat-packing plants, was unhealthful, though Dr. Daniel Drake, leading physician of the town, assured them it was not.

The many professions now in some way allied with communication by means of language, and usually denominated by such terms as writer, newspaperman, dramatist, etc., were in one sense lacking in early Middle Tennessee. The very word "writer" was not then used in modern meaning; to those of Scots descent the term meant a certain stage in the career of a lawyer—one accredited to write up cases but not permitted to practice before the bar.

Yet, considering the smallness of the population, much writing was done by Cumberland settlers, even from earliest years, though seldom, if ever, was the work considered as a profession, separate from the rest of life. The Draper Manuscripts, taken as a whole, are the largest and most representative body of writings of the pioneer. Many are purely factual such as muster rolls and verbatim accounts of what was said at Indian treaties, but a large portion consists of little narratives, usually memories written at the request of Dr. Draper, of battles, journeys, life histories, surveying activities, hunting expeditions, even remembered songs. Dr. Draper was trying to recreate a world, vanished even then, a hundred and twenty years ago, almost as completely as the elk. He also rescued from possible oblivion a large body of correspondence before or during the

[63] Tennessee *Gazette*, March 6, 1805.

pioneer period and three journals of the hard winter in the West. How much material vanished we shall never know.

Most prolific writer of early Middle Tennessee was Daniel Smith, well represented in all pioneer source materials. Even before the Revolution he was mapping East Tennessee and writing letters in connection with Dunmore's War. In addition to all this he kept a journal of his surveying activities during 1779–1780, and in 1796 published the first known work on Tennessee.

Benjamin Bradford, who in 1800 put the newspaper business on a permanent footing in Nashville, has already been mentioned in connection with the publishing industry. His many other activities as editor, writer, even printer when shorthanded, as, judging from his ads for printers and apprentice boys was often the case, well illustrate the difficulties of separating the writer from the businessman, the editor, or for the matter of that the rest of life.

We cannot be certain, but it is probable that Mr. Bradford authored the almanacs and many other small things he published, and though much of his newspaper was written by others, he did do a very great deal of writing not to mention editing. His profession of editor-writer-owner-publisher was soon a common one and continues to be, for practically every county on the Cumberland, no matter how small, has at least one weekly paper; many have two. These county newspapers, no different from those of Bradford, give the author a chance to get published, and thus one continues to find not only the community news written by housewives, but little travelogues, much verse, and long letters on a variety of subjects, all written by subscribers.

Many books were produced in much the same fashion. Tennessee's best-known early writer and "Father of Tennessee History," Judge John Haywood, whose early works were published by Bradford, was throughout his life a busy lawyer and judge. Though coming past the pioneer period, his publications in their great diversity of interests—from the duties of justices of the peace to the geological formations of Middle Tennessee—link him intellectually with the many-sided men of pioneer days. Haywood fathered a tradition; much of the history of Tennessee has been written by judges—Ramsey, Guild, Williams, and lately Douglas.

Contemporaneous or coming just after Haywood was a torrent of Tennessee writers, with many like Davie Crockett remembering pioneer days. Still, during the early years, writing, much in evidence as it was, were better thought of as but one of many activities of a busy, many-handed, and often highly articulate people, who, though on the frontier, were still a part of the eighteenth century, golden age of correspondence and private journals.

Wayne County, Kentucky, for example, is a small county on the edge of the hill country and even today with less than fifteen thousand people. Yet one of its early settlers, Micah Taul, wrote an autobiography in addition to all the other writing done in the course of his clerkships; Rhodes Garth, an early teacher in the county, kept a journal of his doings in the War of 1812. Another early journalist was William Wait, little of whose work is as yet published. He in 1818 emigrated from Chester, Massachusetts, to Somerset, Kentucky, by wagon and kept a journal of his travels.

There is no bibliography of the many publications, usually privately printed and never written with an eye to mass circulation, that have come out of the Cumberland Country. They range all the way from the poetry of Judge J. W. Wells, who also wrote a county history, to the work of S. A. Morey and Russell Dyche of London, Kentucky, who in preserving the early history of the region, told the little known story of early coal mining. There are cookbooks, family and county histories, autobiographies, and works such as *The Handbook of Smith County* that reminds us of the now forgotten pearl-fishing industry on the Cumberland. There are, too, a multitude of scholarly works by Cumberlanders, often on some aspects of life in Middle Tennessee such as the writings of W. E. Myer, nationally known anthropologist.

The scientist was another professional man also lacking in pioneer days, but if science be thought of as a search for the truth concerning the phenomena of the natural world, scientific thinking was more widespread than today. Daniel Smith experimenting in chemistry, M. J. J. DuFours trying to grow wine grapes, Haywood measuring a sinkhole, and soon Dr. Gerard Troost calculating the heating capacities of charcoals were parts of the scientific thinking in the United States of their day. Some like Haywood and Dr. Troost—collecting things in which there could never be any money—had genuine intellectual curiosity, but most American scientific thought like most today was a handmaiden of the profit motive. Most scientific interest in the early years was agricultural, directed toward bettering crop production, improving breeding stock, or learning the know-how of some new product such as silk. These interests along with many others of a scientific nature are all reflected in the earliest *Gazettes.*

Regardless of a man's profession—saving a neighbor from Judge Jackson or curing him of the shingles—there was the ever present problem, lack of a circulating medium. The teacher paid in pork, like the lawyer paid in land, had usually to go into business, as did Andrew Jackson, solely with the hope of translating earnings, if not into cash, into something that could in turn be exchanged for cash.

The professional man with some business and industry on the side and more income from plantations, but living in Nashville, was often hard put to make ends meet. Even the good log house with tongue-and-grooved floor was expensive when measured in terms of the produce a lawyer or teacher received in payment. True, he could rent; there was, for example, on Water Street in Nashville of 1811, a brick house, "well calculated for the accommodation of a genteel family"; it commanded a "beautiful view of Cumberland River," had a good kitchen, stables, coachhouse, poultry houses, and other conveniences.[64]

How many bales of cotton, pounds of beef and pork, barrels of whiskey and white oak staves, received and sold, required to rent the house and keep it in the style of one's neighbors with carriage, good horses, coachman in livery, sufficient servants, giving now and then "an elegant dining" featuring plenty of imported wines and small trifles such an anchovies brought by keelboat from New Orleans, is a problem in higher mathematics.

Much has been written of the Southern sharecropper perpetually in debt to the storekeeper; the sharecropper was but the bottom layer of a vast pile, with the owner of the broad acres and the "big house" not always on top, not even if he were lawyer-plantation-owner-storekeeper as was Jackson who once went broke.

Numerous as were the members of the various professions even in the early years it would not be truthful to speak of a professional class. Members were too closely integrated with the rest of life, which was in turn like that of Virginia and the Carolinas—primarily agricultural.

Yet, of all groups, it was from the hard-pressed professionals, who could seldom afford to give all their time to the one calling, that most of the men remembered by history came. Among them were famous judges, lawyers who became presidents, and others who remained lawyers but like Felix Grundy noted for their skill. There were teachers, historians, statesmen, scientists, novelists, and poets. There would in time be many ministers and generals, but Tennessee's most widely remembered soldier, Sam Davis, was no general.

[64] Nashville *Clarion*, June 4, 1811.

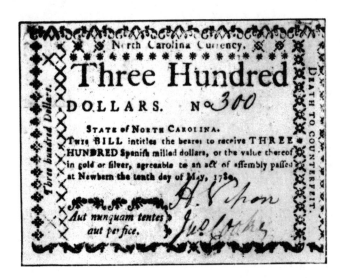

Chapter Twelve

The Business World

THERE WAS among the first and early settlers in the old West no man today remembered primarily because he amassed a large fortune or was a great businessman. Yet, most settlers on the Cumberland from Daniel Smith in the land business to Martha Turner advertising "18 or 20 barrels prime whiskey" [1] for sale were in some kind of business. In preparation for this work around two hundred lives were gone into quite deeply. There were a good many published autobiographies and biographies; others wrote short life histories for Mr. Draper, and many more were well enough represented in source materials one could piece out the patterns of their lives.

No one was a career man in the sense his whole life was bound up in the one thing. Practically all studied were landowners, usually farmers,

Headpiece: North Carolina paper currency of 1780.

[1] Nashville *Clarion*, Aug. 13, 1811.

but all were at one time or another store- or tavern-keeper, ferryman, land speculator, trader, hunter, and no fairly large farmer, in the process of changing crops into some salable commodity, could escape the ramifications of business. Many were active in political, governmental, and social life, though relatively few were prominent at State and Federal levels as was John Overton or James Winchester. Most served on juries, supervised road workings, laid out towns, planned schools, took part in military campaigns, and were active in some form of business.

The effects of the first settlers are those of men who planned to buy and sell—scales, measures, steelyards, and business agreements were plentiful. Death and burial were conducted on a businesslike basis; Thomas McCain, for example, was buried in 1789 at a cost of ten pounds with the administrator getting the usual 2½ per cent.[2] Even up the river where life was a good deal less sophisticated, the cost of whiskey required to sell his goods were,[3] like the paling of the grave,[4] charged against the dead man's estate.

Much has been written of pioneer openhandedness, but travelers seldom found it. The difficulties of James Smith and Jamie in the Yadkin Country of 1766, jailed on suspicion of character, are fairly typical of the fate of any poorly dressed stranger, unable to give a proper account of his situation.[5] More than thirty years later Francis Baily in the rough dress of a workingman and mounted on a cheap pack horse, found no latchstrings out in the Cumberland Country. He stopped at several prosperous plantations, but he at last concluded, "the idea of their being hospitable and doing a kindness to strangers for nothing is false. This hospitality is only shown to neighbors and kin where they expect it will be repaid by the same return and arises from a want of inns on the road. . . ." His feelings were colored by the dollar he had had to pay a Tennessee farmer for one night's keep for his two horses, and food for himself which had consisted of only "Indian bread, butter, and milk."[6]

The Dukes of Orleans, coming the same year as Baily, found little between Southwest Point and Dixon's Springs but bear meat and corn

[2] DW, I, 107.

[3] PW, I, 125. This item showed considerable variation. Whiskey to sell the goods of Benjamin Barnes mentioned here cost little for only 3 gallons were needed; but the sale of the estate of Andrew Cowan, *ibid.*, I, 151, required $5.20 worth or around 25 gallons.

[4] *Ibid.*, I, 106.

[5] Up in Pulaski County, PC, I, 78, a man was haled before the court for being "a vagrant and leading a lazy life without visible means of support or using any industry —for himself or his family."

[6] Baily, *Tour 1796–97*, 416.

bread, and the fact of their being dukes neither increased the service nor lowered the rate. Bishop Asbury, one of the most highly esteemed ministers of his day, was almost always charged in taverns and quite often in private homes. John Sevier, the best-known and loved man in all the West, paid for his lodging when traveling except when he visited an old friend like James Robertson.

During the Revolution such was the feeling against Tories, particularly in East Tennessee, that travelers in order to avoid suspicion carried letters known as Whig chits, attesting to their patriotism and signed by several prominent men of their neighborhoods.

The Cumberlanders were more interested in character chits. In the spring of 1784 Davidson County Court deliberated and cogitated upon the papers brought by Mr. Jacob Shivley from "Sundry Gentlemen in the State of Virginia." Happily for Mr. Shivley, the court decided that "nothing ought to operate against his character." [7] Years later up in Kentucky, Samuel Forrest removing from Mercer and Lincoln counties, brought before the court, sitting at Somerset, his character certificates to which nine signatures and one mark were affixed, all testifying to the fact the signers had known the bearer for seven years.[8] Justices of the county court and other prominent men of any western neighborhood not only had to evaluate character certificates, but in return to give them to their neighbors. The young hunter Joseph Bishop, leaving Middle Tennessee for a trip back east in 1794, was mightily pleased when, without having asked for it, he was presented with a fine character certificate signed by a number of the leading men of the community.[9]

Sometimes the most promising of chits was regarded with suspicion. There was always the chance that even when the signatures were those of men known to members of the court, they were forgeries. There was also the question as to how good a judge of character the signer of the chit was; the most celebrated case of doubt arose when Andrew Jackson refused to accept the challenge of young Mr. Swann who came well recommended by notable men, among them Edward Randolph of Richmond, Virginia. The many signatures failed to convince Jackson the young lawyer was a gentleman, and as gentlemen dueled only with other ·gentlemen, Jackson could never bring himself to fight Mr. Swann, but killed Dickinson instead.[10]

The average businessman on the Cumberland didn't fight duels, but he

[7] DC, I, 9.
[8] PD, I, 153.
[9] Gray, *Bishop*, 29.
[10] Parton, *Jackson*, I, 265–285.

did need to know, much more so than today, the character of the man
or woman with whom he did business. First, practically everything was
done on credit of at least one year's time, and usually more; even small
store accounts as revealed in the John Coffee papers frequently covered
a period of three or four years of purchases with no interim payments.
This custom, no different from other features of pioneer business, had
been inherited from England where the large landowner collected rents
yearly and yearly paid his London bills.

English sea captains trading with planters of the Southern colonies attempted to draw up accounts yearly, balancing the commodities furnished
against the tobacco, rice or indigo received, and often the planter like the
Englishman of good family and credit lived perpetually in debt. Everybody was in debt; Daniel Boone like many other hunters got a yearly
stake of supplies, the debt to be paid with the proceeds of his hunting; the
Indian trader got goods on time in Charles Town, and paid for them with
skins on his next yearly visit, and most laborers in the South, even those
not connected with a plantation, were paid with keep on a yearly or
seasonal basis. Clothing and other supplies needed were furnished by the
employer and charged against the man's wages.

The first settlers to the Cumberland planted this pattern of debt, and
seemingly enlarged upon it, for it is hard to believe that the proportion of
indebtedness was as high in the whole of the young United States as in
the small world of the Cumberland. Men owed, not only storekeepers,
tavern keepers, ferrymen, teachers, physicians, and other men doing business with the public, but usually a large circle of friends and neighbors;
the inventories of most farmers yield accounts both payable and receiv-
able.[11] Business ethics in the young United States, particularly in the
East,[12] was low, and even honest men were often slow pay. Andrew

[11] No inventory was entirely free of debts and debtors, but see in particular DW,
I, 36, James Shaw, merchant; *ibid.*, I, 47, James Moore, merchant; *ibid.*, I, 247, J. Sitgreaves, teacher; *ibid.*, I, 255–259, John Rice merchant; *ibid.*, I, 75–76, is a list of
98 men from whom De Monbruen's agent was trying to collect.

[12] Several early travelers to the Cumberland complained of high prices, but I
found no complaints comparable to those of tourists to the central and eastern
coastal regions. See Handlin, *America*, Moreau "Travels, 1793–1798," "The American
has no dignity when it comes to money.—Love of gold often goes so far as to over-
whelm delicacy. There is no security in business.—They [farmers in the neighborhood of Philadelphia] hardly feed themselves and treat their slaves badly. It is impossible to push stinginess any further," 94, 95. Also *ibid.*, *America*, Grassi, "Observations, 1819," 140–141. "Among the inhabitants of the United States, those from New
England called the Yankees, are regarded as the most knavish and capable of the most
ingenious impositions. . . . It is certain that to deal with such people one needs much
sagacity and an exact knowledge of their laws of trade. But it seems to me unfair to
extend this reputation—to all the inhabitants of those states."

Jackson, proverbial for his personal honesty, let bills run for years; his Natchez wine bill went on for twenty-two, and always at six per cent interest.

A further hazard to any businessman in a new settlement, and one he could eliminate only by being a good judge of character or character certificates, was the wandering nature of a large percentage of borderers. There were no means whereby the Nashville merchant could collect debts from a man gone off to Natchez or Texas or into the Illinois. It is not surprising to see ads in the early *Gazettes* offering as much as a twenty per cent discount for cash, or anything else to be had on the spot—"likely Negro fellow"—"first rate cow with calf"—"the worth in horsestock." This scarcity of currency was an old, old story to most of the United States, but most particularly in the South where even the wealthiest of colonial planters had seen little cash from one year's end to the next—produce went to England and goods came in its stead.

Conditions were often no better after the Revolution, particularly in the primarily agricultural West. Daniel Drake wrote how when a boy in Kentucky he retailed whiskey from a barrel in the family home—and his parents, different from most of their neighbors, hated whiskey. The whiskey sales came about because Daniel's father had had to take most of the price he got from the sale of a horse in whiskey. Much business on the Cumberland arose simply because the farmer and the professional man, unable to get money for goods and services, had to go through several exchanges before they could even get produce each could use.

Lack of a circulating medium was not the only aspect of business the average Cumberlander inherited from the colonial South. None of his business ventures were to begin with exactly new, though they were often different; even the land business that west of the Appalachians took on a peculiarly American flavor had been a source of income to many wealthy Virginia colonials. This was the only business in the South liberalized by the Revolution; the many colonial restrictions on land ownership by large holders were forgotten, and for the first time in the history of America an individual or a group could buy and sell lands that by title still belonged to Indians. This dual ownership was a great advantage to the white holder because he had to pay no taxes until the land was free of Indian title.

In no other business did the settlers of Middle Tennessee show any wish to do away with the old regulatory laws of colonial days. We can never know why the average Whig soldier of the Southern Colonies fought the British; certainly some for one reason, some for another, and many, no different from soldiers in every war before and since, fought because they had to fight, never knowing exactly why. In any case the establishment of a free enterprise system in the South was not one of them. If one gives the term "business" the somewhat restricted meaning of commercial enterprise or simply the buying and selling of goods and services with no inclusion of manufacturing, one can truthfully say that business after the Revolution continued as before.

The many laws of the Southern Colonies regulating business remained unchanged. The North Carolina meat packer, for example, was not only told how he should package his beef and pork for shipment, but laws dictated the size of the barrel, the woods of which it must be made, thickness of the staves, number of ties, and a great many other matters, even how much salt should go on the meat. Other colonial products such as tar and flour were also regulated and subjected to inspection, the fee paid by the seller. The tavern keeper had his prices set by county court as did the ferryman, who under North Carolina law had also to keep a tavern. The North Carolina miller, like the millers of the other colonies, must first get permission to build a mill, if water power were planned; he must by law take customers in their proper turn and his grinding fee or toll was also regulated by law.[13]

Most of the laws regulating business were retained when North Carolina became a state, and were in turn applied to the pioneer business of Tennessee just as the business laws of Virginia were in force in Kentucky. The justices of Davidson and Sumner, like those of counties on the other side of the mountains fifty years before, gave much time and attention to the regulation of tavern and ferry rates, and permissions to erect water-powered mills. When Tennessee became a state in 1796, she soon adopted with slight modifications most of the old colonial laws regulating business.[14] Judging from the many fines meted out for retailing liquor without a license, taking customers out of turn at the mill, selling liquor and other commodities above the legal rates, these laws were enforced.[15]

Hand in hand with the popular conception of the government as a regulator of business was the feeling that a government, either local or Federal, could, if it wished, go into business. Thus, states did many things which would today be considered, if not subversive, at least socialistic—

[13] NCR, XXIV, 131–133, 580–586, 658–661, are examples of North Carolina laws regulating shipments, tolls, and other business matters.

[14] Haywood, *Laws*, 180, 264–272.

[15] DC, I, 75; included among the offenders was Timothe De Monbruen.

built tobacco warehouses,[16] leased salt licks,[17] bought patents which were in turn sold to farmers,[18] and later chartered banks, and invested in various enterprises such as railroads. They also through laws relative to slavery and the bound boy or girl, produced quite a body of labor legislation. Such laws were accepted as a matter of course; save for those pertaining to slaves, they were not only a heritage from Britain, but commonly found in all of Europe. Practically all early laws relative to business were made for the protection of the consumer. The Southerner seems to have seen business as he saw government—a servant of the people, instead of a master. Thus, in spite of the need for keeping money at home by the manufacture of necessities, no attempt was made through favorable taxation patterns to encourage industry or business. Instead, it was the farmer who continued to get preferential treatment; he paid only on his acreage, not improvements. The law requiring owners to pay twenty-five cents tax on each "saw" of a cotton gin seems never to have been enforced, but it is fairly typical of the attitude toward most forms of business and manufacturing; inspection fees were by the laws already mentioned exacted of most packaged produce that entered into commerce.[19]

The Constitution of Tennessee permitted the justices to levy special taxes of several varieties; these almost always fell heaviest on the businessman and the industrialist. Smith County Court, for example, in 1809 levied a special tax of only $6\frac{1}{4}$ cents on each hundred acres of land, regardless of improvements or quality, but each town lot was taxed four times as much, and any retail store, no matter how small, must pay $5—the equivalent of the tax on 8,000 acres.[20]

In spite of being rooted in the traditions and laws of England, business on the Cumberland had a flavor all its own. Once any settler had crossed the Appalachian Mountains, he became part of the old French trade pattern. At the settlement of the Cumberland it was almost a hundred years since La Salle had come down the Mississippi in 1684. His dreams of a great trading empire had never completely materialized. French influ-

---

[16] NCR, XVII, 352–362, a 1785 bill for the establishment of a number of tobacco warehouses, including one at Nashville.

[17] *Ibid.*, XXIV, 915. See also Mereness, *Travels*, Fleming, "Journal," 620, for a description of the largest salt licks in Kentucky of 1779, owned and operated by Virginia.

[18] NCR, XX, 132. The State was in 1787 to buy from John Fitch his patent for a steamboat. See also the Tennessee *Gazette*, Aug. 27, 1804, for a discussion of Tennessee's purchase of "Whitney's" cotton gin patent.

[19] Haywood, *Laws*, 264–272, law of 1801.

[20] Smith C, II, 260.

ence and traders though at times reaching high up the Tennessee to the Cherokee towns, had never been strong east of the Mississippi, save among the southern tribes adjacent to its banks; in spite of Fort Duquesne, site of future Pittsburgh, seldom had the French trader done much business on the Ohio above the mouth of the Cumberland. The Indians were dangerous, but the greatest deterrent was the English. British feeling against the French trader in English territory, strong even before the French and Indian War, grew stronger during the Revolution, and before the coming of George Rogers Clark, the French trader, if caught dealing with the Americans, was apt to be charged with treason.

It is because of this that M. Bomer [21] got, apart from the dozens of other traders plying the rivers, a little nook all his own in history, for instead of finding customers in English or French territory, he went up the Ohio "hunting Virginia." He was, according to one witness, met on the River Ohio about a league above the mouth of the Chaouan, as the French still called the Cumberland, but another said he was on the Chaouan. There is no record that any one in future Kentucky or Tennessee in 1776 bought any of M. Bomer's wares. These included orange juice, a thousand pounds of gunpowder in jars, the usual taffia, coffee, cloth, guns, wine, salt, lead, bed clothes, and also "corn rum," better known as whiskey, the whole valued at around 30,000 livres.

The French trader on the order of M. Bomer persisted. Venturesome, energetic, a wanderer, his canoe or batteau, home, storehouse, and transportation all in one, he was an exchanger of coffee and other goods for deerskins and beaver. Practically all stories dealing with Long Hunters and explorers mention traders along the Cumberland and in the Illinois. He was not, however, an unmixed blessing, for the French trader also supplied ammunition to the Chickamauga and other Indian tribes who made life hazardous for families emigrating by way of the Tennessee.

Soldiers returned from the Coldwater Campaign of 1787 with several boatloads of goods confiscated from French traders on their way up the Tennessee to the Cherokee towns near present day Chattanooga. The wine, coffee, ammunition, striped silk shirts, silver trinkets and other goods were auctioned off at Eaton's and used to pay the soldiers who had been on the expedition.[22] The confiscated merchandise like M. Bomer's assorted cargo had reached the Cumberland by various routes from many countries. A good deal came as in the days of La Salle, up the

[21] I, V, 31, 32, 34, 36.
[22] W, 30S, 487; see also for entire campaign, *ibid.*, 1S, 91–95.

Saint Lawrence and into the Great Lakes. The trader, from present day Toledo could portage to the Wabash, the route of goods for Vincennes, or he could go north, past Detroit, through the Straits of Michilli-Macki-nac, and once in Lake Michigan go on to Green Bay, and then by dint of upstream travel and portage reach the Illinois, the oldest route of all, and used by many including De Monbruen. A trader could also reach the Illinois by coming to the southern end of Lake Michigan, going up the Chicago River, and then portaging into the Mississippi system.[23] Still other goods came up river from New Orleans as in the days of M. Charle-ville who many years before had traded with a band of Shawnee, tempo-rarily settled near the French Lick.

England's victory in the French and Indian War had broadened this already far-flung trade pattern. The first English trading firm west of the Mississippi in the Illinois—Baynton, Wharton, and Morgan, estab-lished in 1766—had taken the old towns and routes of the French traders, and to them added Philadelphia; this meant wagons up and over the mountains to Pittsburgh, or Fort Pitt as it was then known, batteaux down the Ohio, then up the Mississippi to Fort Chartres.[24]

The Cumberland merchant inherited the whole of this giant pattern—Montreal to New Orleans, Philadelphia to Kaskaskia. He did not himself go into British territory, but he did business with French traders whose goods had come by way of Montreal and Detroit. He also inherited that institution unknown in the Old World—the store, dealing in many com-modities. Baynton, Wharton, and Morgan had represented an early ver-sion of what we would today call a department store, but the development of this institution was not confined to the British colonies. It began before colonization; the first sea captains trading with the Indians had a form of floating department store—trinkets, rum or brandy, kettles, and brightly colored cloth had represented many shops.

Generations later, sometimes among the Indians, but more often among the ever-thickening colonials, the trader settled down and became a per-manent institution with a store of goods always at hand. English visiting the American colonies commented in wonder on the lack of shops and in their stead that institution strange to them—the store.

[23] Mereness, *Travels*, "Minutes from the Journal of Mr. Hamburgh's Travels in the Michigan and Illinois Country, 1763," 360–364, is an account of a trip to the Illinois by this route.

[24] I, XVI (III British Series), indexed, is devoted chiefly to the correspondence, accounts, inventories, and relations with the French and Indians of the British merchants in the Illinois.

The tradition of one man or firm dealing in many articles, the vast geographical framework, all overlaid with English laws and traditions were only some of the complications with which the Cumberland trader had to deal. Few merchants ever had to wrestle with so many forms of currency, plus the Mississippi with Spain at the lower end.

Not every trader had all these worries. Trade was often a casual affair, travelers or settlers merely disposing of unneeded articles for food or something they could use—hard money if it could be had. Dr. Thomas Walker and Daniel Smith may be thought of as the first American traders on record in Middle Tennessee, for on April 5, 1780, they sold "four horses, 3 kettles some tents etc. . . ."[25] John Montgomery seems to have been the first Cumberland settler to bring a boatload of goods up from New Orleans.[26] Finished with this bit of trading, done in 1780, there is no record of his having done any more. He was no more full-time merchant than was Samuel Cole Mountflorence—teacher, lawyer, investor in Nashville lots—who in 1790 sent a load of swan skins, much in demand for hats, down river by Andrew Jackson.[27] It is doubtful if Jackson had on this trip much mind for trading; he was on his bridal journey with Rachel and Colonel Stark, who was a frequent visitor to the Cumberland Country in his attempts to recruit settlers for Spanish holdings. One of the earliest full-time traders and possibly the first to use the path that came to be known as the Natchez Trace was John Turnbull.[28] He was chiefly a trader to the Chickasaw, and when white settlers came to Middle Tennessee he added them to his rounds, and was soon dealing heavily in slaves much in demand by the Spanish settlers.

The settler or traveler selling surplus food or wares, the traveling trader doing business from a pack horse, or the itinerant French or Spanish trader who continued to visit the Cumberland for many years were, at least by 1783, getting competition from Cumberland settlers who had established more or less permanent trading posts or stores. These first stores were small affairs as indicated by the inventories of James Moore or the Leneer brothers, but they did supply many of the needs of the first settlers, offering such diverse wares as salt, fish hooks, chairs, "hanging" paper,

[25] THM, I, Smith, "Journal," 62.

[26] W, 32S, 357. There was also Maxwell, and *ibid.*, "a Frenchman named Skean who came prior to 1784 with a few Indian goods and taffy (taffia)." *Ibid.*, 6XX (50), 19–20, also mentioned a French trader coming in 1781.

[27] Parton, *Jackson*, I, 241.

[28] Turnbull is mentioned by most historians, and was one of the most active of the early traders in slaves, see DW, I, 13, 14.

and hat linings.[29] No one of their owners was a full-time merchant, but also farmed, speculated in land,[30] or like Jackson followed a profession.

Regardless of how much trading he did or whether from a boat or building, the Cumberland trader had one of the most complex currency problems with which any mortal ever tried to wrestle. The story of a lack of currency in the primarily agricultural South is long and well known. It was old when the Revolution began, and continued for generations. However, lack of currency was not the chief problem of the first Cumberland settlers. The Revolution had along with British troops brought gold for the supplying of them. A good deal of this by roundabout methods got into the hands of even such a good Whig as William Blount whose correspondence concerning land in the 1780's often mentions largish sums of hard cash.

More hard money reached the Cumberland by way of New Orleans and Natchez where among the Spanish and the French sound money was plentiful. Spanish laws in regard to duties and the amount of hard money that could be taken out of the country changed often, but sources are quite well agreed that such was the Spaniard's eagerness for slaves, he would even advance traders like Turnbull cash for well trained ones.

When one considers the smallness of the population, scarcely a thousand by 1784, a sale involving 5,156 Spanish milled dollars and another of 1,300 means a relatively large amount of gold and silver.[31] Such transactions were larger than most, but not unusual; gold and silver coins are mentioned in the earliest court records of 1783, and in 1785 a transaction involving "900 pounds Virginia money, gold or silver," [32] was not uncommon. Many were dead, but others prospered; Frederick Stump in that year had 400 Spanish milled dollars with which to buy a Negro man.[33]

The problems of the businessman lucky enough to get hard money down were by no means ended. He had to know a sound dollar when

[29] DW, I, 47, James Moore; *ibid.*, I, 63, James Leneer (Lenear) carried a great variety including a bag of paint, coat buttons, snuffers, and fish hooks, *ibid.*, I, 255–50, John Rice whose stock included "framed pictures"; *ibid.*, I, 274, Jonathan Gee with "30 pair of cotton cards"; *ibid.*, II, 133, Henry Wiggin—velet to cupboard locks. Up river inventories were equally various, PW, I, 3–5, John James—16 bolts of tape—32 horse mill bolts.
[30] DW, I, 255–259, John Rice, and John Deadrick, *ibid.*, II, 105–106.
[31] *Ibid.*, I, 13, 14.
[32] *Ibid.*, I, 5, 55, 56, 76, 156.
[33] *Ibid.*, I, 161.

he saw one, just as he had to know a prime beaver hide. Counterfeiting was common, but worse for the ferryman, tavern keeper or any other businessman dealing in small sums was the custom, universal in the United States, of dividing coins.[34] The quarter of a Spanish dollar was more apt to be a fifth than not, and even a half or a whole was often nicked or filed; arguments could and often did lead to fights.

Any early merchant such as James Shaw,[35] in business in Middle Tennessee by 1784, had still a deal of reckoning to do, once he had a solid Spanish dollar. James Shaw, like most of those about him, had been bred a British colonial; his business methods were unchanged by the Revolution, and he still thought in terms of colonial law and pounds and pence. The trouble was that to Martin Armstrong, come out from North Carolina in 1784, the pound meant 966¾ grains of fine silver, while to Captain John Donelson, lately of Virginia and Kentucky, it meant 1,289 grains, and, hence, each a different number of shillings.

Figuring out the shillings was only the beginning, for the shilling was unstandardized. Using the Spanish dollar as a unit of measurement, the settler from Georgia reckoned its worth at five shillings; the man from Virginia, seven shillings six pence; while by North Carolina law the Spanish dollar was worth eight shillings.[36]

Such was the confusion that court entries stipulated the value of the coins in which a debt was to be paid; for example, in 1786 a debt of twenty pounds if paid in Spanish milled dollars was to have the dollars reckoned at six shillings the dollar; if paid in half Johannes, each coin was to be reckoned at two pounds, eight shillings.[37]

It was natural that the United States should adopt the dollar as a money unit, for the Spanish dollar had long been used in localities so diverse as the Moravian store in North Carolina and Morgan's firm in the Illinois, but, once adopted, the American dollar contained less silver than the Spanish dollar, and was in Middle Tennessee in 1796 generally reckoned at six shillings.[38] The Tennessee law of 1798 decreeing that dollars and cents must be used in all monetary matters of court record [39] did not

[34] Ashe, *Travels*, 169–170, gave the most detailed description, but practically all other early travelers to the west mention it; see Toulmin, *Western Country*, 126; and Michaux, *Travels 1802*, 159, who commented on the amount of cheating.

[35] DC, I, 36.

[36] ASP, I, *Finance*, 91–107, contains brief discussions by Thomas Jefferson, Robert Morris, and Alexander Hamilton on the money situation, 1782–1791; see in particular, *ibid.*, 106–107, for varying colonial evaluations of the pound and shilling.

[37] DW, I, 56.

[38] Thwaites, *Travels*, III, Michaux, "Journal," 86.

greatly clarify the matter. The populace took readily enough to dollars, but one often finds such a court entry as that of Leah Lucas, $2.3 s, meaning $2.50. Ten years later Jackson had to remind a correspondent that the shilling was by that date the eighth part of a dollar.[40] So great was the confusion that gradually the fractions of a dollar were used— though accounts were kept and goods reckoned in pounds and pence for many years past the pioneer period.

Such a businessman as John Turnbull, riding up from Natchez and doing business on the Cumberland, had to be able to reckon, not only in pounds and pence, guineas, and crowns, shillings, and soon two varieties of dollar, livres, piasters, "joes and half-joes," tobacco, cotton, milk, cows, ginseng, slave children, green hides, tar, and pipe staves, but he also had at times to wrestle with the paper money of the day.

The hazards of doing business with Continental currency are familiar, but troubles arising from its continued depreciation were, on the Cumberland, slight compared to those of other regions. Different from Kentucky, legal rates for taverns, ferries, and taxes were not in Tennessee set up in inflated currency. Lacking money, skins, cloth, and whiskey were established as the basis of legal tender in the State of Franklin in East Tennessee, while on the Cumberland, as already stated, taxes could be paid in provender, this in turn evaluated on North Carolina hard money.

Some of the first settlers had one or more forms of Continental money; James Freeland,[41] for example, had at his death in 1781 one bond of 200 pounds in Virginia currency, a bond of 15 pounds in Pennsylvania currency, along with a note for 6 French crowns and 16 Spanish dollars. A few like John Sevier had North Carolina currency or "forty to one," as he called it.[42]

Better suited for any business transaction and much more commonly used were the several forms of "paper" in circulation. One of the most important was the land warrant. Some had been in circulation since troops were paid with land after the French and Indian War. The opening of the North Carolina land office in 1784 was in the matter of land warrants the undamming of a millrace, for they flooded the country; most were good but some were uncollectible on land that could not be located and others were outright forgeries. The warrant often became a form of currency without being located and entered in the clerk's office;

[39] Haywood, *Laws*, 240.
[40] Bassett, *Jackson Correspondence*, I, 66.
[41] DW, I, 16.
[42] THM, VI, Sevier "Journal," 159.

this avoided not only the fee, but sometimes taxes, and was, particularly in Kentucky, the cause of endless lawsuits and overlapping claims. But absentee owners were much inclined to trade in land in just such fashion.

More commonly used for money than the land warrant or land was the promissory note, for any man of good character could always buy on time through the giving of a note; the note might specify money, deerskins, barrels of corn, or anything else except a wife and children. These notes earned never less than six per cent interest and were transferable. Many specified a given amount of some commodity: "debt of three cows," [43] "debt in 24 lbs bear fur," [44] "debt in skins," [45] while a few such as the "2,000 pounds security on James Shaw," dead, held by Lawyer Gubbins when he died, did not specify the commodity or the kind of money to be used in payment. Such arrangements were not satisfactory to either debtor or creditor; some commodities such as slaves increased in price, but as most farm products decreased, more and more agreements as time passed specified first the fixed amount, then the commodity in which it was to be paid, as "debt of 900 pounds or 9 likely Negroes." [46] Practically all early *Gazette* ads offered to take payment in any kind of produce, but the sum of money, rather than the amount of goods to be given was usually specified.

There were mortgages, not greatly different from today's mortgages, save they were given by individuals as there were no local banks. These were even more diverse than the currency, for anything might be mortgaged from the clothing worn by one's wife and children [47] to the brandy to be made from peaches still green on the tree, or a boatload of pine knots, split, and ready to be made into tar.[48] Anything to which a man had affixed his signature, either in the original or as an endorsement, was known as his "paper," and a man's paper could become worthless if he died insolvent or had endorsed the notes of other men unable to pay.[49]

Such paper, both mortgages and promises to pay for goods received,

---

[43] DC, I, 63.
[44] *Ibid.*, I, 36.
[45] *Ibid.*, I, 32.
[46] DW, I, 56.
[47] PD, II, 36.
[48] *Ibid.*, II, 96.
[49] Parton, *Jackson*, I, 242–244, gives a detailed account of Jackson's near disaster when the notes given him by David Allison for land became worthless when Allison failed; Jackson had used the notes to buy goods for his store, but had to take produce instead of cash for the goods he sold. Jackson sold land and home, paid the notes, and forever after had a reputation for honesty, and also very strong ideas about sound money.

was bought and sold, traded, and in general used much like money, though a man hard up might sell a note, not yet due, at a heavy discount. Typical of the pocketbook of the more affluent citizen was the red morocco one of William Barrow, lost in 1804.[50] It had contained: one bond for the conveyance of lots, two deeds of conveyance for other land, an order from William McCoy in favor of William Wray, and notes of sixteen other men, each promising to pay different sums to various people, only a few to be paid directly to Mr. Barrow. Most, he had bought, or taken in payment for goods or farm produce.

Later, merchants also used sight drafts. These were drawn up to avoid the dangers of carrying hard money and to facilitate commerce in cases where there was no money, but credit in a distant place; a man might take cotton to a broker in New Orleans; the broker instead of giving him money or goods gave instead a draft on a Nashville or Philadelphia merchant who owed the broker. All this came somewhat later for little produce was shipped south until close to 1790; as late as 1793 a Kentucky visitor remarked there were only two merchants in that state doing business with New Orleans.[51] There was at this date in the Cumberland settlements even less trade with the South. The population was not only small, but so harassed by Indians there was little surplus farm produce, and hunting the few deer and beaver left was too hazardous. There was in the first years of settlement, thus, little to send down river. In spite of all this now and then a Cumberlander did venture down with a small cargo.

Such a one was Martin Armstrong who took the 900-mile boat trip down to Natchez in the winter of 1788–1789. He got a write-up in a Philadelphia magazine, but solely because of some not entirely unexpected adventure connected with his trip.[52] There is nothing to indicate the trip was in itself unusual; General Martin Armstrong was no more, nor was he any less, pure businessman than many others engaged in river commerce. Like everybody else he was in debt; Edwin Hickman's inventory, listed after he was killed the following year while surveying, named among his many debtors, Martin Armstrong for twenty-five pounds.[53]

He had, judging from his spelling, more formal education than Andrew Jackson, for example, and was far more experienced in most matters. He had been in the Battle of Alamance as a Tryon Man, then served as an officer in the Revolution, been active in North Carolina politics, and

[50] Tennessee *Gazette*, March 28, 1804.
[51] Toulmin, *Western Country*, 124.
[52] Carey, *Museum*, V, 417. See also W, 33S, 59–60, and The Kentucky *Gazette*, June 6, 1789.
[53] DW, I, 287–290.

had received the not inconsiderable plum of appointment as surveyor in charge of military warrants in Middle Tennessee.

He had come out on this business in 1784 and remained as a settler, and as he was a surveyor he was the professional-farmer-businessman-politician common on the Cumberland. Like James Robertson and other leading citizens, including Andrew Jackson, he was a Mason, but different from many men of his day, he was deeply religious with a great distaste for the deism then quite prevalent on the Cumberland. He was on the whole a respectable as well as beloved figure, familiarly known as "Chunky-Pipe." [54]

Details of his trip are lacking, but since he had six boats and thirty men, he must have gone in rather small batteaux, each carrying a cargo of from twelve to fifteen tons; keelboats required more hands, and we can be certain they were not flatboats as the company returned by water. His whole convoy probably carried less than two sixty-ton freight cars of today, but the business of getting cargo, hands and boats all together would have had almost endless ramifications. The chances are at least some of the six were made to order. In that case a contract was drawn up with the builder specifying not only size, but species of wood, dimensions of timbers, date of delivery, and who should supply the tar and oakum for calking, with the builder paying a penalty for later delivery.[55]

This was only one of many contracts Colonel Armstrong had to sign in preparation for his trip down river. The code of honor much in vogue between gentlemen stopped at agreements of any description; two gentlemen pledged to refrain from ardent spirits unless ordered to drink by a doctor put the matter in writing. Even gambling debts, the most binding of all, were, if cash and goods were lacking, not left to the word of a gentleman, but paid in personal notes of indebtedness or the notes of other men owned by the loser.

Colonel Armstrong would thus have drawn up contracts with his boatwrights, and other contracts with those who were to furnish supplies, or barrels and kegs for the cargo, each contract specifying amount, price, date of delivery, method of packaging, time, and manner of payment.[56] Meat, meal, and whiskey were the prime necessities for any crew of

[54] See NCR, XVI, 524; Bassett, *Jackson Correspondence*, I, 69, 168; Williams, *Travels*, 248, 513.

[55] FP, 28, Verhoeff, *Kentucky River*, 61, a 1790 boat-building contract.

[56] Coffee Papers, 1803, "Articles of agreement between Puroy Bell and Reuben Payne," July 9. Payne was to deliver 250 pork barrels for $1 each—provided all the specifications of the contract were met.

workmen, though John Coffee, a generous, easy-going man, bought chickens, eggs, milk, butter, buttermilk, and flour for himself and hands several years later on trips to the Illinois.[57] Colonel Armstrong could depend on buying little between Nashville and Natchez for there were few settlements and ever present danger from Indians.

Some men were more liberal with their hands than others, but taking a cargo down the Cumberland in December when Armstrong's trip was made, was hard, cold, and dangerous; a man had not only to be well fed, but the whiskey ration for boatmen was always more liberal than for army privates who were lucky to get their half-pints daily. Andrew Jackson, for example, never noted for generosity in business dealings, used twenty gallons to get two boats with thirteen hands from Nashville to the mouth of the Cumberland and home again [58]—average time around sixteen days—considerably more than half a pint per day per man. Such a ration was liberal enough unless some misfortune on the order of a boat stove-in or sunk overtook the crew.

Cargo and supplies had to be got from source of supply to the river. Pack horses were employed for longish overland transportation of goods, usually manufactured articles fairly light in proportion to worth. Short distances and heavier goods—lime, saltpeter, corn, barreled pork—called for carts or wagons. The waggoner or drayman, or teamster as he came to be known, was usually an independent businessman, owning his outfit, and sometimes farming enough to make feed for his horses. His was one of the most numerous of the many small businesses of the day, and up river he continued to be the connecting link between source of supply and shipping point by water for close to one hundred and fifty years, changing little in general characteristics from those of pioneer days as described by Parton, ". . . an important, peculiar, and reckless class of men, with something of the Indian, and a little of the highwayman in their composition." [59] The waggoner, love him or no, was still a man with whom every merchant and shipper had sooner or later to deal, paying him sometimes by the day—$2.50 was about standard by 1801 [60]—or on long trips such as that between East Tennessee and the Cumberland or Philadelphia and Pittsburgh, by the hundredweight.[61]

[57] Coffee Papers, 1800–1804, have shipping-cost accounts, and food and drink are listed with other needs.
[58] Bassett, *Jackson Correspondence*, I, 94–95.
[59] Parton, *Jackson*, I, 340.
[60] Coffee Papers, 1801.
[61] Cost varied, depending on the season—roads were worse and time slower in spring and winter. The lowest rate found for cartage between Philadelphia and

More important to Colonel Armstrong than any other men he hired were his boatmen. Small boats often traveled without captains or mates, but each had a man in charge, sometimes merely a neighbor with an interest in the cargo, who would receive the equivalent of $1.50 per day. On the other hand the captain in complete charge of the cargo of even a rather small craft was quite a personage, earning eight or nine dollars a day, and even a master sometimes got three. One of the most important men on any boat was the steersman whose main job when going down was to keep in a current that would take him places, but at the same time avoid planters, sawyers, floating logs, caving banks and all the other hazards of the Mississippi. He had to stay out of the slow backwater, yet avoid the eddies that could in flood time swing him into the treetops; for all this he got between $1 and $1.75 and keep per day.

The wages of the ordinary boatman who rowed, poled, pulled, and pushed the craft were higher than those of the unskilled laborer who could be had for as low as $50 with keep by the year, or fifty cents a day. The boatman sometimes got $50 for the few weeks required to work a craft down to New Orleans; there he could hire on as a keelboat hand or walk back, but he was often paid by the day, never less than fifty cents with keep, and usually sixty-six to seventy-five, and sometimes more than a dollar a day.[62] The job of taking cargo down and up the rivers was not only one of the hardest with exposure to all the hazards of weather, swift water, and Indians, known in that day, but along with strength and hardihood, the work called for unswerving honesty and fidelity. A good boatman was always ready to risk his life for cargo, often did, and sometimes lost it.

Much has been written of the boatmen on the Western waters, but as a group they were probably closer akin to the skilled marksman, Dieverbaugh, in the Illinois, a "most excellent fellow," who could be trusted with a small craft from Kaskaskia to Pittsburgh, than today's popular conception. Some were undoubtedly dishonest, drunken bullies, but taken as a group they seem never to have matched the legends that had grown up about them even by 1818. Estwick Evans, a traveler in that year, observed: "The numerous stories, which have so often been

Pittsburgh was $5 CWT, Coffee Papers, 1803; see also Bassett, *Jackson Correspondence*, I, 15—two rates in the 1795 account, $6⅔ CWT and $8.

[62] Coffee Papers, 1800–1804, have many boatmen contracts and wage accounts. Common hands of the *Industry* captained by Mr. Cook in 1801, each got $13.50 and keep for an 18-day period; a year earlier other hands as listed in the "Bill sent to Madam Pequod" earned $1 per day, plus 50¢ for their board. See also Bassett, *Jackson Correspondence*, I, 15, 94–95.

circulated and believed, respecting the cruel modes of fighting prevalent among the boatmen of the west, are, generally speaking, untrue. During the whole of my tour, I did not witness one engagement, or see a single person, who bore these marks of violence which proceed from the inhuman mode of fighting, said to exist in the west, particularly Kentucky and Tennessee." [63] Evans, a religious New Englander, was deeply shocked by many things on the Mississippi, especially the profanity of the boatmen, but he like several other travelers saw less of the bloody, brutal, and generally dissolute life of the then wild West than he had expected. He found drunkenness less prevalent than he had been led to believe, and there seems no question that the wild side of life on the Mississippi was exaggerated as was life on the frontiers. Thirty years before Evans, Toulmin had commented on the falsities of the "old tales," such as the prevalence of gouging, circulated first about the Virginians. In spite of the many who like Toulmin found that "no country was ever settled by such respectable people as the western country," the tales persist to color the modern picture. In later years Judge Guild characterized the boatmen as having been "as generous and noble hearted set of men as ever trod the face of the earth." [64]

It must be remembered early boatmen, in common with early businessmen, were not members of a definable group. Some of Colonel Armstrong's boatmen may have been small farmers owning part of the cargo, thrifty men earning a penny and seeing the world, good enough rivermen from long acquaintance with the Cumberland to manage an oar or sail on the Mississippi,[65] and in any convoy there were always some adventurous souls on the order of David Crockett, ignorant and unskilled, but at least learning after a ducking that boating was not the life for them.

The Mississippi, like a forted station, was no place for the drunken, the lazy, or the loud-mouthed bully with no concern for his companions. Reams have been written of the hazards of travel on the river, though it is doubtful if, in proportion to their numbers, as many employees and passengers on the early craft lost their lives in accidents as later during the era of steamboat disasters. We know only of Armstrong's adventure that none of his men was lost, but it is doubtful if the six boats in the Armstrong fleet got down to Natchez without at least one upset; some-

---

[63] Evans, *Tour*, 157–158.

[64] Guild, *Old Times*, 325.

[65] William Martin's remark of his flatboat trip down to New Orleans some months later, "All unacquainted with the business," W, 3XX (18), 6, would indicate that none of the men in the convoy was a riverman; certainly he and the Winchesters were not.

times the cargo was lost, but usually the boat was raised, cargo fished out, dried off, and taken on.[66]

Convoys customarily went into camp each night, and round the fire the campers talked, played cards, sang songs, and did all the chores of housewifery lone men ever had to do, from mending leather breeches to sewing on buttons. Horses, fat cattle, and hogs were often among the cargoes, and these had to be watered and fed, sometimes grazed by night.

A most pleasant topic of conversation would have been the reckoning of profits. Whiskey, for example, that could be had up river for as low as 25 cents a gallon seldom sold in Natchez for less than a dollar, and often two, and so it was with most other produce. Goods bought in Natchez and sold up river showed an even higher return; coffee could be had sometimes for as low as 3½ cents and sold in most stores for around fifty cents a pound; brown sugar could be sold usually for only around three times its original price of eleven cents, but wine like most alcoholic drinks, going or coming, yielded a high profit.[67]

Still, it didn't do to reckon profits too closely. There were the hazards of the river and the Indians, but these were minor compared to the risks of trading with Spain. Spanish officialdom could forbid their trading at all and seize the cargo. Spanish laws on import and export duties were constantly changing; sometimes each was as high as twenty-five per cent; other times only five, or none at all for slaves. A man might be permitted to sell his cargo but forbidden to take hard money out of Spanish territory, though normally a captain could take $200, each ordinary seaman, $100. However, as Colonel Armstrong went down prospects were good. A fire in New Orleans a short time before had made provisions of all kinds scarce. Dire need of goods might cause the Spanish authorities to overlook the import duties.[68]

There were ways to avoid such troubles, though all ways led to the one—keep on the good side of Spanish officialdom. This was usually best done through James Wilkinson of Kentucky, trading ambassador without portfolio from the pioneer West to Spain. Colonel Armstrong

---

[66] Coffee Papers, 1801, list the expenses in raising the *Howard*, though most of the cargo was lost. Three years later, Hutchings, partner of Jackson, raised a boat and dried off and saved the cargo, see Bassett, *Jackson Correspondence*, I, 86.

[67] *Ibid.*, I, has numerous references to New Orleans prices, particularly of slaves; for commodities, see 84–85, 141. Coffee Papers, 1801–1804, with their many retail store accounts and records of wholesale prices in the Illinois are revealing.

[68] FP, 28, Verhoeff, *Kentucky River, Appendix*, 224–225, letter of Charles Wilkins to Judge Harry Innes; Wilkins made trips from Kentucky to New Orleans in 1789, 1790.

probably carried a pass and certificate of character from Wilkinson just as did William Martin on his flatboat trip the following spring.[69] Armstrong also undoubtedly had the benefit of Wilkinson's advice; second-hand maybe but much like that written to the leader of a similar trading expedition in 1791: "When you come within six leagues of Lance a la Grace get with a canoe and two hands, push down to the command and order the boats to go on without waiting—you will show the invoice of your Cargoe and the list of your hands to the Commandant, make him a present, beg him to pardon your hurry and push the boat— never stop anywhere after this before you reach Natchez, unless at night. When you get to that place put on your best Bib & Tucker and wait upon the Governor—make him a present—beg his passport for New Orleans—Say to the Governor, that having formed a determination to make settlement in Louisiana, you have invested some of your property in tobacco. . . ." [70]

Proof of a man's determination to settle was an oath of allegiance. Colonel Armstrong and several of the men with him may have calmly contemplated the taking of the oath; if so they would have been among only several good Masons and citizens of the West who took oaths of allegiance to His Catholic Majesty the King of Spain. Such oaths were only a part of business; [71] nobody gasped with horror at the thought. Colonel Armstrong as he whirled down the bends of the muddy Mississippi did not record his thoughts for posterity, but such words as treason and traitor, merely because he hoped to be allowed to take the oath of allegiance to Spain, should not be laid upon him. It was not a nationalistic age. It was, on the other hand, a well dressed one, and we can be certain Colonel Armstrong put on, if not his best, at least a good "bib and tucker," that is if he had ever worn anything but such, for he as head of the fleet would not have worn the buckskin or linsey overalls, buckskin jerkins, woolen hats or silk handkerchiefs, and coarse shoes of the "common hands." He was a self-respecting man, satisfied he was committing no sin, as he prepared to go through the rigamarole of conducting business with the Spanish at Natchez.

[69] W, 32S, 525.

[70] FP, 28, Verhoeff, *Kentucky River*, Appendix, 226–229, letter of James Wilkinson to Hugh M'Ilvain, Frankfort on Kentucky, March 17, 1791. See also Toulmin, *Western Country*, 117–127, who of all early travelers gave the most detailed account of the problems of dealing with Spain.

[71] One of the few extant permits given by the Spanish authorities during this period is that to William Martin, on display by the William Martin Youngs in the Tilman Dixon Home.

It may have been his best bib and tucker were not good enough, his presents, if any, not big enough, his oath of allegiance, if any, not convincing enough. He was refused a passport; and though the Spanish garrison at Lance a la Grace above Natchez was in need of supplies, the commandant refused to do business with him on the grounds his prices were too high.

Armstrong knew supplies were needed; he wasted no time in dickering, but hurried on down to Natchez. Passportless though he was, he there sold his goods to some American settlers. He lost no time in starting home, and doubtless pulled an oar himself, for only twenty-five of the men went back up the Mississippi with him.

They couldn't row fast enough to lose the Spanish officer and fifty soldiers sent in pursuit by the fort commandant. Armstrong had just managed to get far enough up the Mississippi he could declare himself within the boundaries of the United States when the Spaniards overtook him. They told him he and his men were under arrest and must return to Natchez for trial. Old "Chunky Pipe" roared back that he was "subject to no control of any power on the face of the earth, except that of the laws of his country." [72]

Accounts of Martin Armstrong indicate he was a kindhearted man, almost conciliatory, not caring for quarrels or bloodshed. Now, following his nature, he begged the Spanish officer to let him and his convoy go quietly on their way. The officer continued to insist, and while he insisted one of his men, "imprudently presented his musket at Colonel Armstrong's breast."

The ending of diplomatic relations, the declaration of war, and war itself were all on an instant. Armstrong's men waiting with rifles at the ready killed five Spaniards and wounded twelve so severely they could not run away with the rest. Some of the wounds may have come from hatchets, for the Spaniards claimed the Cumberlanders handled their tomahawks "pretty freely." They even called them Blanco Savago, though there is no record the boatmen took Spanish scalps.

Such encounters, sometimes with Indians, sometimes with Frenchmen, were not uncommon in the lives of pioneer businessmen, but did not always have such triumphant endings. Colonel Benjamin Logan of Kentucky who went down by keelboat with a load of horsestock had to spend time in a Spanish jail.[73] Some years later, John Coffee, too much a

[72] Carey, *Museum*, V, 417.
[73] W, 29S, 103.

gentleman to rush the guard of a female, was held at the Salines by Madame Pequod for several days, and forced to stand the expense of feeding himself and crew during the delay.[74]

It is doubtful if Coffee fretted overmuch; he was a big easy-going man who for most of his life helped his father-in-law, John Donelson, keep their mutual in-law, Andrew Jackson, soothed, comforted, and at times reined in. He was by 1800 quite well seasoned after three years of business in Middle Tennessee that had taken him over most of the businessman's world—Philadelphia, Baltimore, New Orleans, and the Illinois. His boats, usually costing only around $120 complete with cordage and oars, were small batteaux of around twelve to fifteen tons, manned most of the time by only a master, steersman, and two hands. Quite often he hired smaller boats for a dollar a day, but paid as much as five for larger ones.

He carried cargo both ways, sometimes to New Orleans or all the way to the Salines for salt. Other times he would send a boat only to Shawneetown on the Ohio, near the mouth of the Cumberland, a spot that served as freight depot for the Illinois, just as Smithland at the mouth of the Cumberland was a depot where goods bound from Pittsburgh to Nashville were often unloaded and sent up the Cumberland on smaller craft. At Shawneetown, the Coffee boats took on cargoes of salt and lead, and were back at Haysborough in about eighteen days, while the trip to the Salines took around six weeks.

There were no rules; in 1801, for example, the *Howard* carried a cargo of corn, bacon, whiskey, "lyme," saltpeter, and tobacco all the way to New Orleans. In the same year the *Child* went down with pork, tobacco, 240 pounds of saltpeter, one slave, and a small amount of cotton, while the *Resolution*, going down to New Orleans in 1803 carried nothing but 111 bales of cotton, weighing between 210 and 338 pounds each. In the same year still another Coffee boat delivered 25,261 pounds of cotton to New Orleans.[75]

The Coffee Papers list no import or export duties paid to Spain, but for most merchants the uncertainties and expenses continued until 1803; now and then a traveler visiting New Orleans found the harbor, usually so

[74] Coffee Papers, 1800.
[75] *Ibid.*, 1800–1804. Date, cargo, cost of boat, port of delivery were usually specified, along with the many contracts necessary, such as that of John Doak, Master, who agreed "to deliver in like good order & condition (dangers of the Rivers excepted) and at the proper Risque & Charge of the Said John Coffee & Co."

crowded, empty because the port was closed to all foreign ships. The merchant with no speedy or even certain means of communication could never know the state of affairs until he was actually there. The announcement of the port's closing coming late in November of 1802,[76] for example, would have found many traders, taking advantage of the fall rains that flooded the Cumberland, already on their way.

It was not until 1799 that John Coffee and other importers had to wrestle with United States customs. On March 2 of this year Palmyra at the mouth of Deason's Creek was designated as the port of entry and delivery for the District of Tennessee. Here, all cargo must stop for inspection by Morgan Brown, United States Customs Collector.[77] In 1800, for example, Mr. Coffee's accounts reveal that when he stopped with his cargo from the "Salines in Louisiana," he paid $1.50 entrance fee, 20¢ for a permit to land, and $1.19 duty on 41 casks of salt and 1,550 pounds of lead. He had no cash and had to make bond for the amount, and this cost 40¢. In 1802 his duty entries and office fees amounted to 54 pounds, 9 shillings, and 3 pence, enough that smuggling over the Natchez Trace must have been quite profitable for those who knew somebody on the order of La Fitte.[78]

Yet in spite of customs and the hazards and hardships of transportation there seems always to have been plenty of goods to supply the many stores that flourished as soon as the end of Indian warfare hastened settlement. Beginning with the first extant copies of the *Nashville Intelligencer* of 1799, newspapers carried the many and diverse offerings of such early merchants as James Hennan; King, Carson & King; Anderson & Weir, advertising goods from Philadelphia; Bustard and Fasin; Black and Williams; Thomas Deadrick. Among them almost anything was to be had from grindstones to tamarinds, camomile flowers, hair powder, sugared almonds, gold ear bobs, French brandy.[79] Thomas E.

[76] Tennessee *Gazette*, November 20, 1802.

[77] National Archives, "An Account of the Receipts and Expenditures of the United States for the years 1799–1807." Report No. 12652 of Sept. 24, 1801, shows that Mr. Brown was credited with $230, the cost of a lot he bought and the building put up for "a public store for the use of the customs." The office was in 1802 moved down to Massac. Correspondence, Lyle J. Holverstoll of the Records Service.

[78] Guild, *Old Times*, 198–199, insinuates that some Nashville businessmen grew wealthy from selling La Fitte goods.

[79] All newspapers studied carried many ads; James Hennan in *Rights of Man or The Nashville Intelligencer*, March 11, 1799, offered most any small thing; Tennessee *Gazette*, June 24, 1801, and *ibid.*, July 8, 1801, carried ads of the other merchants named.

Waggman's grand opening in 1804 offered about everything from bridles
to chip bonnets, artificial flowers, and "most fashionable lace cloaks." [80]
     Not all goods were sold from buildings. There were all up and down
the Cumberland traveling traders who like M. Bomer and Joshua Mounts,
pot merchant of the mid-nineties, sold directly from their boats. Such a
firm, though larger than most and coming past the pioneer period, was
that of Sump and Rapier who sold directly from their keelboat, the *Mary
Ann.* Her cargo of 1811 included Jamaica "spirits," port, sherry, claret,
and Madeira wine, brown and loaf sugar, coffee, Hyson and Imperial tea,
pepper, spice and cloves, cinnamon and nutmegs, almonds, fresh orange
juice, smoked herrings, salmon, codfish and mackerel, molasses, pineapple,
cheese, brown soap, gunpowder, assorted shot, tanner's oil and lampblack,
Spanish Segars, window glass, logwood, cordage, and nails. [81]
     The following year Stump had much the same goods for sale, except
the variety of seafood was greater—pickled oysters, shad, anchovies,
mackerel and codfish; there were also sweetmeats, oranges, mustard, sweet
oil, and spermaceti candles. [82] Stump's food offerings were in keeping
with other goods being offered by Nashville merchants even before that
date. Hard-muscled boatmen made it possible for the Cumberland family
to buy Russian sheetings, French cambrics, India muslins, French silks
and satins, Cossack boots, English and German steels, "real" or "mock"
Madras handkerchiefs, "Old Monongahela by the barrel," or figs from
Turkey. Materials for clothing could be chosen from tow cloth to
mourning crepe or the iridescent lute strings that shimmered and winked
like peacock feathers. Kirkman's, "in the new brick building fronting
on the Nashville square," offered most anything in the line of dry
goods and hardware from coffee mills to silk-worked hose, and just
across the street one could buy Euclid, or Pope's *Essay on Man.*
     John Coffee's store held in partnership with Mr. Harney at Hays-
borough was nothing to compare with some of the Nashville stores,
but was fairly typical of the country store of 1802. [83] It was housed in a
two-storied log house, 32 by 20, with a shingled roof of twenty-foot
pitch; the outside walls were covered with clapboards, rived and planed
smooth, though seemingly never painted. When Mrs. Thomas Butler who

[80] Tennessee *Gazette*, Sept. 12, 1804.
[81] Nashville *Clarion*, May 14, 1811.
[82] *Ibid.*, May 19, 1812.
[83] Coffee Papers, 1801–1803; list labor—total cost $247.95—and materials, but the cost
of these, most no doubt had in exchange for produce, is not given.

did much trading there rode up to a hitching block, she could have told, blindfolded, that she was by the store. Rising from the thirteen drawers, eighty-six pigeon holes, four nail boxes; seven hat racks, 307 feet of shelves, and the barrels, hogsheads, kegs, and pipes that held merchandise was a heady mixture of odors. The faint smell of dye and paste in the dressed chip bonnets was all but smothered under the leathery, oily smell of new saddles and bridles; this in turn competing with the odors of New England cheese, vinegar, freshly broached keg of port or Madeira, and barrel of whiskey. Other powerful smells came from the chewing tobacco, ginger, nutmeg, mace, and cloves. Stored outside or under a shade were all the products waiting for shipment—oozing tar barrels, green hides, white oak staves, new woolen cloth, country cloth, butter, smoked bacon, pork in brine, barrels of lard, kegs of saltpeter; [84] and under and over everything the smells that ran through all life on the Cumberland—horse manure, horse sweat, and new wood.

The life of this store, no different from the several kept by Jackson, was brief. The partnership was officially dissolved in 1804,[85] but Coffee continued doing a little of this and that, farming, trading, planning a venture with Jackson in salt making that never materialized, and working for a time in the land office. Coffee's business career, bounded in all directions by debts he could never collect, and hence those he could not pay, was like that of most merchants of his day.[86]

Hard money, quite plentiful immediately after the Revolution, grew scarcer and scarcer; a storekeeper's life was a merry-go-round; he took farm produce for manufactured goods, and unable to get money for farm produce in New Orleans, took more goods, which he could never sell for cash. And, too, the United States, then as now, was so geared to the rest of the world that events in far off places touched even the backwoods storekeeper; the suspension of Britain's specie payments in 1797 brought panic and depression to the Eastern merchants. This was followed soon by the booming times of the Napoleonic wars. The War of

---

[84] The John Coffee boat cargoes list goods received; commodities bought may be found in such items as "Account of Thomas Butler, per Lady," and "John Brownlee's Account" each with Coffee & Harnett; also John Coffee's purchases from Jackson and Hutchings, Robert Barnet of Lebanon, and in Baltimore and Philadelphia for 1803.

[85] Tennessee *Gazette*, June 13, 1804.

[86] Coffee Papers, 1802–1807, record many judgements obtained against Coffee; some for as low as $3; it was not until 1807 that John Doak, mentioned as boat master, was able to collect anything, and then only $10.29 ¾ "by order of the court."

1812 in turn checked foreign trade, but like all wars of the United States it was followed by a great boom, followed by depression, felt less in agricultural Tennessee than in the more industrialized East; there was no hunger, but many of the businesses, including the many of old Frederick Stump and his sons, went under.

Few early businessmen prospered so well or so long as the Stumps. The most lucrative business, that of land speculation, laid the basis for family fortunes in Middle Tennessee that survive until now, but it also destroyed a good many. Judging from the increasingly long lists of lands sold by order of the sheriff for taxes, a very great many men, if they did not lose all, at least lost much.

The merchant continued for many years to be the most important business man in most communities. His relationship to his country customers was never so simple as is the role of the average merchant today—a mere seller of goods. Southern storekeepers for generations continued to be bankers, carrying families on credit until the crop was in, brokers selling the crop, and advisers in general on all matters from the best patent medicine to the kind of cloth for the coffin.[87]

There were, in addition to merchandising, all the forms of trade that had flourished in the Southern colonies; the peddler of small wares, the trader who would take anything on four feet and gradually build up a herd of hogs or cattle, the horse trader—a good one able to start a circuit with one old sway-backed mare and a yoe-necked foal, and in three months time get home with several head of "likely horsestock." The traveling tinker recasting the old pewter to make it like new was, like the man selling gingerbread at the muster, but the New World version of a little business long familiar in Europe.

Many small businesses were carried on by women, and women were met quite often in the course of business; Leah Perkins trying to collect the debts of her late husband; Sarah Shaw suing for divorce; Nancy Paxton warning trespassers off her property; and others like Olive Shaw going to court and winning a judgement [88] were examples of the many women in the business world.

One of the most common small businesses of the day and often handled by women was that of taking in travelers and keeping boarders.

[87] One of the best works detailing the role of the southern storekeeper, many years past the pioneer period, but still in the era of "trading" is *Pills, Petticoats, and Plows*, by Thomas D. Clark, Indianapolis, 1944.
[88] Tennessee *Gazette*, June 10, 1801; *ibid.*, Sept. 26, 1802; *ibid.*, Nov. 13, 1802; and DC, I, 140, in the order of their naming.

Travel was slow and many were the stopping places needed, but in the early years the greatest need was living accommodations for the numbers of men who came out for a time on business as did Daniel Smith, or single men like Andrew Jackson. Kaspar Mansker can be put down as Middle Tennessee's first tavern keeper, for Dr. Thomas Walker and Daniel Smith lodged there for almost a week in the spring of 1780. Better known and sanctioned by official permission was the tavern kept by the Frederick Stumps, but most forted stations had some family such as that of Edwin Hickman or a widow willing to sell board and lodging.

One of the best places for well recommended, professional men was that of Rachel Stockley Donelson, widow of Flotilla John. Such was its attractions that Andrew Jackson stayed there, though across the Cumberland and several miles from Nashville and his work as prosecuting attorney. Less fortunate women such as the Widow Martin in 1796 took any chance traveler and kept what amounted to a public inn.[89] Many had never planned to be tavern keepers, and were not officially so with permission from County Court, but only took advantage of circumstances as did Granma Bull. She, before the country was safe from Indians, found herself living on the Kentucky Road, not far from the Hazel Patch in the Rockcastle Country, some miles north of present day London, Kentucky. "She told them the travel was so great that she kept cooking from before daylight till after dark. Bear meat and corn bread was the fare, and so great was the press that she got whatever price she asked for something to eat. She said she would have to empty the gold and silver from her pockets before night would come because the bulk was uncomfortably heavy. The men would broil bear meat on the coals while she would bake the bread; they would pay her the money and go on." [90]

The weight of gold and silver for bear meat and bread may seem like the exaggerated memories of the old, but hungry travelers took what they could get when no choice was offered. In general the private homes and out-of-the-way taverns in the Cumberland Country were not much different from those in the thinly populated western districts of Virginia, where the traveler was shown into a room furnished with little but benches, "a miserable bed, and a pine chest with lock and key. Breakfast, dinner, and supper were all the same—corn bread, bacon, and eggs. The

[89] Thwaites, *Travels*, III, Michaux, "Journal," 85.
[90] *The Mountain Echo*, London, September 4, 1896, a reprint of her story told to the Rev. J. J. Dickey who had toured the upper Cumberland country in 1813.

house dog of the large wolf breed comes and sits down by you and looks directly up into your face as you eat." Eating was further interrupted by children and poultry wandering in and out, and there were the usual complaints of poor horse accommodations.[91]

Nashville, in contrast, soon became famous for her taverns. Francis Baily stopping by in 1797 found three, but even Major Lewis, owner of the best, was not exactly in the business of winning friends, though he did influence people. The food must have been excellent and the horse fare good, for critical Baily did not complain of these, but he did find, "Very poor accommodations for lodgings; three or four beds of the roughest construction in one room, which was open at all hours of the night for the reception of any rude rabble that had a mind to put up at the house; and if the other beds happened to be occupied, you might be surprised when you awoke in the morning to find a bedfellow by your side whom you had never seen before, and perhaps might never see again. All complaint is unnecessary, for you are immediately silenced by that all-powerful argument—the custom of the country and an inability to remedy it; or perhaps your landlord may tell you that if you do not like it you are liberty to depart as soon as you please."[92]

Baily on his way to Knoxville stopped in several private homes for "dry entertainment," that is, board and lodging, but without any spirituous liquors. For this entertainment "they generally take care to charge enough," Baily complained, though as an Englishman much of his quarrel was at having to eat cornbread. Yet, he so enjoyed the fare of Major George Blackamore, who lived about twenty miles west of present day Carthage, he stopped with him several days. There was in 1797 when Baily crossed the Plateau no stopping place between Walton's Tavern at Carthage, kept in connection with the ferry, and Southwest Point near the junction of the Clinch and the Holston where there was also a ferry.

The Moravian missionaries coming two years later had heard of the excellent tavern there and planned to stop, but so many were the tricks to the trade that the traveler was often purposely misdirected. He then found himself in the bedless hovel described by the Moravians, where brawling card players monopolized the fire, and kept up a racket most of the night. Once these were quiet, and the shivering traveler with at best a bench around the wall for a bed, and if a late-comer the floor, and no bedding save what bear or buffalo skin he could find, tried to warm

[91] Carey, *Museum*, VIII, 278.
[92] Baily, *Tour*, 416.

himself, he still had to contend with a parcel of dogs, also eager to take advantage of the fire in the absence of the card players.[93]

There were by this date, 1799, two other stopping places east of the Cumberland; if the traveler took the newer road that crossed at the mouth of the Caney Fork, he could before reaching Carthage stop at Mr. Shaw's place where everything was in "the first beginnings," or if he took the Fort Blount road he could spend the night with Mr. Blackburn "who lived by the chase."

Travelers across the Plateau managed as did Baily and the missionaries; they camped out between taverns; one of the favorite camping grounds was the beautiful bowl-shaped valley east of present day Crossville. Known as the Crab Orchard, it offered plenty of cold spring water, and lower in the valley, a meadow where the cattle and horsestock could graze. Here in 1800 was begun a tavern, finished enough by October of that year that Reverend Asbury riding from Nashville to Knoxville could be refreshed with "a dish of tea."

The ending of the Indian Wars with settlers flocking in at the rate of two or three hundred a day increased the need for taverns; as settlement thickened so did river commerce and, hence, the use of the Natchez Trace. Nashville marked the end of this road and was thus not only a stopping place for travelers bound west for Clarksville and the Illinois, but also those going north, with a few southbound by land. The inns multiplied. Many taverns became splendid establishments famous throughout the South and West. None of the early ones could, of course, rival the Maxwell House of later days, but they were far removed from the accommodations of a Granny Bull.

There was in addition to that of William T. Lewis, already mentioned, a tavern begun around 1800 by Timothe De Monbruen. "A commodious dwelling house with three fireplaces, a brick kitchen, stone meat house, and a two-story stable with a good floor and 24 stalls," it stood on the public square opposite the general store of Bustard and Fasin, and in the early years was also something of a store advertising items so diverse as window glass and paper.[94] Thomas Talbot's Tavern with "14 chambers, most of which have a fireplace";[95] William Roper's Tavern in front of the court house;[96] and another at the Sign of the Square and Compass, op-

---

[93] Williams, *Travels*, Schweinitz, "Report," 517.
[94] Tennessee *Gazette*, Feb. 11, 1801; Nashville *Clarion*, Feb. 18, 1811.
[95] Nashville *Clarion*, Feb. 1, 1811.
[96] *Ibid.*, Nov. 30, 1810.

posite the Nashville Bank,[97] were only a few of the taverns advertising by 1810, though Nashville was still a small place with only a few hundred people. By that date all of the better traveled roads offered taverns; as early as 1801, travelers could stop at the "Sign of the Indian Queen,"[98] kept by Micajah Roach near Bairdstown, Kentucky, and soon there was a wide variety in any direction, "the brick house under the sign of the Square and Compass," large enough to accommodate "ten genteel gentlemen"; Richard Cross's "House of Entertainment for Gentlemen," and another under the sign of the "Morning Star."

The North Carolina law forcing the owner of a ferry to keep also a tavern was repealed before Davidson County was created, and soon ferrying was one of the most numerous small businesses. The first court of Davidson County established a ferry below where[99] Nashville was to be laid out, and as was the custom set the rates. There was soon another ferry further down the river below Eaton's Station at the Old French Landing; there was also the Upper Ferry, and still another, owned by Davidson Academy, at the foot of Broad Street.

The ending of the Indian wars multiplied the roads and hence the ferries; a road could be cheaply and quickly built for early ones were little more than slashes through the timber with stumps cut low enough to permit the passage of wagons. Dozens of ferries were established across the Cumberland between the crossing of the Kentucky Road below Cumberland Gap and Smithland at the mouth. In time other ferries were established at strategic points on all of the larger streams that had to be crossed on the way to Nashville. One of the most lucrative was that at Southwest Point earning more than $20 a day by 1799. Colbert's Ferry established somewhat later where the Natchez Trace crossed the Tennessee probably took in more than this during the heyday of keelboatmen and travelers over the trace.

The larger, busier ferries were usually operated by hired hands who rowed the boats, sometimes more than forty feet long, though, judging from ads, always narrow, usually no more than eight feet. Later ones were like those described by travelers in the more settled older East, powered by horses, but none required any great investment. Most ferrymen on out-of-the-way roads had outfits as simple as that of Joseph Bishop who "in 1798 took a lease on both sides of the Cumberland,

[97] *Ibid.*, Sept. 30, 1812.
[98] Tennessee *Gazette*, January 14, 1801.
[99] DC, I, 26.

erected a small cabin, built a flat boat, and began to keep ferry." County court in setting rates made no distinction between the small ferry, for which the owner sometimes had to be hunted or hailed from the other side of the river, and the busy ferries with two boats. In fact, rates on out-of-the-way roads were often higher. Edmund Jennings, Indian scout and Long Hunter, who tried his hand at ferrying, as did Michael Stoner up the Cumberland, was permitted in 1800 to charge $1.25 or the equivalent of more than forty pounds of beef for a wagon and one team; a single horse or lone man, 18 1/3 cents; a man on horseback, double, with everything else in proportion.[100]

At even these high rates, the ferryman on an out-of-the-way road with few travelers made little money. Joseph Bishop found the life a hard and poorly-paying one. He was haled out by travelers at all times of the day and night; often they could only pay by singing him songs; other times the call at three o'clock in the morning in weather "cold enough to freeze off the horns of a bull" was a practical joke from his competitor.[101]

Bishop quit the business without too much worry for his future. There were other things a man could do, but there is no line one can draw and say when Bishop was in business and when not. Most on the Cumberland present much the same problem.

Some like General James Winchester had several businesses; one of his was what must have been during the early years of the United States, the most miserable, time-consuming, poorly paid, and generally nerve-racking business in which a man could find himself—that of keeping post office. Nashville's first postmaster, John Gordon,[102] began his duties April 1, 1796, but no record was found of any building set aside especially for the mails until 1804 and then only a notice in the paper of plans for the building of one.[103] No building was needed in the early years with only fortnightly mail and the whole of that to the West, including Kentucky, weighing in 1795 only forty pounds. Early postmasters managed as their successors in out-of-the-way-places with only bi-weekly mail managed for generations; a nook with scales, window, and other necessities was set aside in a corner of a store, owned usually by the postmaster. No one was in attendance save during certain hours on mail days, but

[100] Smith C, I, 3.
[101] Gray, *Bishop*, 155–161.
[102] TP, IV, 396–397.
[103] Tennessee *Gazette*, May 23, 1804.

as somebody was always dropping around at odd hours to mail a letter
or see if he had mail, there was much running back and forth; this done
usually by the postmaster's wife, for the government mails could not be
entrusted either to children or to the help.

The problem was complicated in the early years by the first cumbersome system under which, as in Europe, postage was paid by the receiver,
the amount depending on distance and weight. This gave the postmaster
a deal of reckoning to do, but worse was the job of collecting the postage.
There was, to begin with, a constant stream of new settlers whose ad-
dresses were unknown; emigrating families often changed their minds
in the middle of a journey. What may have been a worse problem were
those who either did not want their mail enough to pay the postage, or
else could not get the cash—and cash was scarce—to pay it. In any case,
most newspapers, beginning with the Nashville *Intelligencer* in 1799,[104]
carried long lists of unclaimed letters and continued through the years;
soon such small places as Cragfont where General Winchester kept the
post office in connection with his store were also advertising.[105]

Side by side with the lists of unclaimed letters were the long lists of
unpaid taxes, especially lengthy in 1801.[106] These with notices of strayed
horsestock and lost pocketbooks indicate a somewhat unbusinesslike
people. This was not entirely true. There were on the Cumberland many
individuals who like Frederick Stump and his sons amassed large fortunes through a mixture of business and industry. General James Wilkinson of Kentucky went so far as to call the early Cumberlanders a "set of
sharpers," [107] and the old song, "They chew their tobacco thin in Nashville," indicates, as do inventories, court minutes, and the remarks of
travelers, that the Cumberland pioneer was no simple-minded, open-
handed, forever-trusting soul.

The successful pioneer was by his very nature peculiarly fitted for
the tedious bargaining coupled with the ability to venture, not only
money and goods, but life itself, business in that day demanded. A man
who could stand motionless hour after hour behind a porthole waiting
for the Indians he knew were there, yet never yield to the impulse to
rush out and get the business over with, had the coolness and patience
for the lengthy dickering required in a good horse swap, when, like

[104] Nashville *Intelligencer*, Aug. 28, 1799.
[105] Tennessee *Gazette*, May 13, 1801.
[106] *Ibid.*, Jan. 7, 1801.
[107] FQ, I, 172–173, "James Wilkinson to Nathaniel Massie, 1786."

Andrew Jackson, he discovered his horse had at the beginning of a long journey come down with the scratches, and had to be got rid of and a sound one had in his stead.[108] Yet Jackson was like most other men of his time and place, never wholly businessman or politician; a part of himself he always kept for Andrew Jackson. He was, for example, a follower of Jefferson, but when he risked his military future by a harangue in support of the innocence of Aaron Burr, whom Jefferson wanted out of the political picture, he was Jackson's man.[109]

It is doubtful if Jackson ever lost sleep of nights thinking he had ruined his career because he couldn't keep his mouth shut. He was not part of a community that believed career came first and the individual's life as a human being second. There seems to have been in the South little feeling that a man's success could be entirely measured in terms of money. True, all wanted, if not money, at least the fine things it would buy, but there was no business, not even the land business, important enough to dominate completely the social, cultural, and political life of any man.

Most settlers on the Cumberland had in some measure been shaped by the old South where, different from New England, business was not a sacred ritual with success a token that God had smiled. Rather, there were men on the Cumberland who felt as did Captain John Donelson that "business and the things of the world," [110] were not compatible with religion. Respecting religion too much to try to prostitute it, hating hypocrisy, but unable to live without business, they joined no church at all, or like Jackson waited until the need for the dirtier businesses of life was ended, and then joined a church.

The code of all from the "noble hunter" who refused an offer of work from a visiting Frenchman to ambition-driven Jackson spending time and money on the unfashionable sport of cockfighting was that life was for living. One sees this feeling still in the wideness of the fence rows of the wealthy, the big yards of the poor where most grow flowers, and studies of the food habits of Tennessee farmers that indicate "good living" still. The old story of the thrifty woman who watched her potatoes and always for eating selected those beginning to rot and so from fall to spring had always to eat half-rotten potatoes is remembered still.

---

[108] Bassett, *Jackson Correspondence*, I, 90.
[109] Parton, *Jackson*, I, 333–335.
[110] Burke, *Emily Donelson*, I, 199, John Donelson to his daughter, Emily, June 26, 1829.

Over and over their lives seem to say, "A man mustn't try too hard." Few were ever too poor to pass up the wrong kind of bargain. Saddles, for example, usually sold for between fifteen and twenty-five dollars, but now and again when thumbing through will books one is stopped by the entry, "Woman's saddle 25¢"—not a worthless saddle, but a forced sale in which the neighbors refused to buy articles that rightfully belonged to the widow; in some sales the widow bid in just about everything at low prices. Joseph Bishop had a run of bad luck that left him in debt so that all his goods had to be sold; the auctioneer "cried long and loud," but none of the assembled company would bid.[111] Up in Pulaski County we find Martha Jasper returning "for love and good will" to Polly Long "all the whole amount of goods which I bought at the sale of John Long, which was sold to satisfy a judgement which I obtained against him for $35.50 and costs." [112]

Money was important and, no different from life before and since, the good life was hard to live without it, yet money was not everything. Men appeared to fear financial ruin far less than today; failures there were, but I found no record of a suicide because of a business failure—or anything else for the matter of that.

The "rotten-potato woman" had for husband the "meanest man," and he, of course, the stingiest man; in order to save food he gave each of his children a penny not to eat any supper; during the night he stole their pennies; next morning when the children could not find their pennies they cried so they ate no breakfast; after breakfast he whipped them for having "lost" their pennies; they then cried so they ate no dinner.

---

[111] Gray, *Bishop*, 207.
[112] PD, III, 300.

Chapter Thirteen

River, Road,
and Town

WINDING THROUGH most life already discussed—agriculture, business, industry, exploration, settlement—was the Cumberland River. A soldier rushing in 1813 with Jackson and his troops by flatboat down the river could in spite of freezing rain and scanty food exclaim, "The Cumberland should be the pride of Tennessee—consider what would be the condition of the country if this river had not flowed through it." [1] There were by that date along its banks many small towns plus busy, handsome Nashville, ferries, landings, boatyards, with most of the rich bottom lands, not too swampy for cultivation, cleared and in crops. Streams of the Cumberland were grinding grain, pounding pig iron, sawing lumber, but

Headpiece: A helmsman on a flatboat.

[1] Nashville *Clarion*, Feb. 9, 16, 1813, the anonymous "Journal of a Voyage from Nashville to Orleans by the Tennessee Volunteers," is one of the best accounts of the rigors of winter travel on the Cumberland.

chiefly the Cumberland was a burden-bearer carrying all things out into the mainstream of commerce, bringing much in return. Steamboats were on the Mississippi, but the great days of steamboats on the Cumberland had not yet come. Still, the Cumberland carrying troops for the revenge of the Fort Mims Massacre did, as the soldier said, make most life in Tennessee possible.

Pack horses had ever been important as bringers of settlers and goods, but well before 1813 the Cumberland had a long history of up-river travel. The river had known the craft of the stone-grave people, the birch bark canoes of Martin Chartier and his wandering band of Shawnee, the hollowed log "wherries" of the Cherokee who now and then made the long roundabout trip down the Tennessee to take scalps of the French hunters collecting deerskins, bears' oil, and buffalo tongues for the New Orleans trade. These had traveled by batteaux as had the first Englishmen up the river, come in 1768 to hunt, harry the French, and chart the course of the river. There had been the temporary skin-boats of the Long Hunters, and in the cold, wet spring of 1780 the flatboats and hollowed log pirogues of John Donelson and other settling families, always traders of many kinds, and now and then more settlers come by keelboat or batteaux.

The Cumberland, though described as the quietest of all the western waters and more suited to navigation than any other tributary of the Mississippi, was still so swift upstream travel was a miserable job. A traveler of 1785 remembered, ". . . we commenced ascending the stream with the aid of eight oarsmen, but found the current much stronger than we expected; and thus was passed 15 days, laboring harder than galley slaves, before arriving at Nashville." [2] Michaux, the elder, going up the Cumberland ten years later was one of a party that spent five days rowing up the short stretch of river between the Kentucky–Tennessee line and Clarksville; here, he gave up and bought a horse.[3]

The river, particularly for the poor man, had many advantages over travel by horseback. A hunter or traveler could make his own hollowed-out log pirogue, or even travel on a log raft. Any small craft was not only cheaper than a horse, but such problems as horse feed and strayed horses never troubled the traveler on the river; he could, as did the Indians, sink his canoe and take a wander through the woods. Travel by water, though far from carefree, was during the Indian-troubled years less hazardous

[2] Williams, *Travels*, "The Journal of Lewis Brantz," 284.
[3] Thwaites, *Travels*, III, Michaux, "Journal," 85.

than that along the roads where men almost always went in companies and quite often with guards.

Early tree-trunk canoes or pirogues, designed for only one or two men, were usually from eighteen to twenty feet long, but seldom more than eighteen inches wide, and in time every family along the river had one, used for short trips by water, for crossing, or fishing. They continued to be used for generations; Cordell Hull had one as a boy, and not many years ago I found an ancient one, bleached, sun-cracked, and split, carried by a long-ago tide down to a spit of land on Barnett's Bend some miles above Smith Shoals. Paddling a log canoe with a rounded bottom without upsetting was another one of those seemingly simple skills used by the pioneer that looked easier than it actually was.[4]

Requiring even greater skill was the birch bark canoe, and as late as 1796 Michaux met *coureurs de bois*, near Nashville. These, like the Northern Indians, often used this fragile craft, and one may now and then have appeared on the Cumberland, but as the greatest advantage of the birch bark canoe to white men, able to saw or hew lumber, was the ease of its portage, traders traveling only on the Mississippi and her tributaries had little need of it. Those from the Illinois had preferred the sturdier batteaux of sawed or hewed lumber. Rowed instead of paddled, square-sterned, varying in size, but usually little more than open boats, their cargoes covered with canvas, the batteaux brought most of the goods the Cumberland pioneer got by way of the river.[5]

Better adapted to swift water was the boat that we now refer to as the keelboat, a most unfortunate title, as most boats including the birch bark canoe and some of the batteaux had keels. Worse, the pioneer seldom called it that, but referred to it usually as a "barge," and as late as 1813 one of the most elegant and better known was listed in the paper as the "barge *Mary Ann*." [6]

The first mention I found of a keelboat up the Ohio was in 1778 when

---

[4] Michaux, *Travels 1802*, 100, 102, 136, not only described the small dugout, but took a long ride in one; the difficulty was not only one of traveling with no upsetting, but after some hours the strain of the unaccustomed position of the legs became almost unbearable.

[5] James Hall, *The West, Its Commerce and Navigation*, Cincinnati, 1848 (cited hereafter as Hall, *The West*), 108–118, discusses and describes the batteaux and other types of craft used before the steamboat age. See also, Micheau, *Travels 1802*, 70–88, for descriptions and prices of boats built at Pittsburgh.

[6] Nashville *Clarion*, May 14, 1811; *ibid.*, May 21, 1812. Thomas, *Nashville*, 18, remembered one of the Stump barges, "two keel boats lashed together." Baily, *Tour 1796–1797*, 270, "Here we saw a barge coming up the river. These barges are a kind of keel-boat, which are rowed by fifteen or twenty men."

George Rogers Clark had a load of rum and sugar brought from Kaskaskia to The Falls,[7] but all during pioneer years such boats could be found on the Cumberland with now and then a family coming up by keelboat. The Masons, already mentioned as settling on Richland Creek in 1790, came down the Ohio, and at The Falls stopped and had a "large keel-bottomed boat" made. In general the keelboats' greatest service was in bringing goods up the rivers. They were speedier than any other craft of the day; in 1811 the *Mary Ann* made the more than 1,200-mile trip up from New Orleans in only seventy-one days;[8] a time that would have seemed incredibly short to the French batteaux-men of seventy years before. The *Mary Ann*, though not put into service until around 1808, was in principle the same as the pioneer barge; eighty-seven feet long, but only fifteen wide, she had been built in Cincinnati at a cost of eleven hundred dollars,[9] and like most boats of any size was completely equipped with masts, spars, rigging, and was described as an "excellent sailer."

Sailing was only one method of working the *Mary Ann* or any other boat up the rivers; in a hard stretch of going, men in a canoe would paddle ahead with a rope, and with the aid of a convenient tree, sometimes with pulleys and sometimes without, and sometimes without tree, they would literally pull her up the river, really a form of towing and done in various ways. Considerable ingenuity was required when the bank offered instead of trees foot-deep mud. In some stretches there was nothing to do but use oars, and most of these boats carried oars as did the batteaux.[10]

More suited for use in shallow-watered, rock-bottomed streams such as the Cumberland was poling. This was done with long, usually at least eight foot, iron-tipped poles, variously known as setting-poles, poles, or staffs, made of some stout wood such as oak or ash. These, in common use well before 1790, were not always used with a keelboat.[11] Most any craft could be poled, but the distinguishing feature of the *Mary Ann* and

[7] W, 32S, 413.

[8] Nashville *Clarion*, May 14, 1811.

[9] S. A. Weakley, Cumberland River Floods Since the Settlement of the Basin with Special Reference to Nashville, Tennessee, submitted to the Faculty of Vanderbilt University in fulfillment of the requirements for the degree of Civil Engineer, 1935, quoting the Knoxville *Gazette*, June 24, 1809.

[10] Nashville *Clarion*, May 14, 1811, "17 ton keel boat, light roof, poles and oars included." *Ibid.*, May 7, 1811, "a keel boat, nearly new about 20 tons Burthen with poles and oars."

[11] FP, 28, Verhoeff, *Kentucky River*, 129; the photograph on the opposite page is undated, but as the boat, shown with the crew, poles lifted, had carried goods from a railroad down river in Eastern Kentucky, the time would have been late nineteenth or early twentieth century. This boat was called a push boat.

other keelboats were the narrow runways, set with cleats, especially adapted for the feet of strong-backed men with poles in hand, and it took twenty-two to "work up" the *Mary Ann* with fifty tons of cargo from New Orleans.[12] Down river, keelboats might carry most anything, but because of their speed were better suited to live cargo; Benjamin Logan around 1790 went down with two keelboats loaded with beef cattle.[13]

As speed was the only thing the keelboat had to offer, she disappeared with the coming of the steamboat, but the flatboat, familiar on western waters when the Cumberland was settled, continued to flourish, and even in the present century could be found on smaller streams.

Useful as the Cumberland was as highway for incoming people and goods, it was as a carrier of produce into the Mississippi Valley and down to New Orleans and so into the mainstream of world commerce that the river was most important. It was more important still to those up in Kentucky. Middle Tennessee had no barrier of mountains to shut her off from the rest of the world. Once the Indian menace was removed, she, wealthy and populous, was building roads and wagons were coming from all directions.

The up-river counties in Kentucky had only the Cumberland as a highway for the tar, feathers, tobacco, grindstones, saltpeter, staves, bacon, whiskey, and other produce. Much of this stopped in Nashville and often in the early years was sold at the upper ferry,[14] but a good deal, especially tobacco, went on to New Orleans and from there to Europe. Smith Shoals where the Jacksboro Road crossed above Point Isabel ordinarily marked the end of navigation of the main river, but high water made it possible for coal barges and flatboats to get down. The shoals and rapids and shallows of the Big South Fork were less formidable, and any fairly large tide made of it a highway from deep into Tennessee or up the Little South Fork and other creeks. Most Cumberland tributaries in Middle Tennessee were also navigable, at least in high water, but Stone's River, the Harpeth, and others could never mean so much to any settler in Tennessee as the Cumberland meant to the family in the roadless world up river.

Much of this down-river travel was by flatboat. Built as it was without nails, and requiring no tools, skills, or materials unavailable to the

---

[12] Nashville *Clarion*, May 14, 1811.

[13] W, 29S, 103.

[14] Tennessee *Gazette*, June 9, 1802, one of many issues listing items for sale at the upper ferry.

average pioneer farmer, the flatboat was within the means of any family able to get timber and a three-foot-deep stream together. It could be built to a large size, afforded some protection from weather and Indians, and though most river travelers tied up at night, this was not in moonlight weather absolutely essential to the flatboat traveler, for flatboats were sometimes built with living, and often barnyard,[15] quarters. Sturdily constructed and of slow motion, all the hazards of the rivers from rocks to floating logs that time and again ruined speedier craft seldom harmed it.

Flatboats were built all up and down the Cumberland; even far up the Big South Fork at the mouth of the Little South Fork, the Moodys in time had a boatyard.[16] Now and then a family from those upper regions would make one flatboat or a fleet and take off; the Moodys to Texas, and the Lees with slaves, household goods, and livestock to Missouri. Different from other craft, there was for the flatboat no returning. The Donelsons and others who early in 1780 brought flatboats almost two hundred miles up the Cumberland were, in all the history of the West, among the very few even to try such a thing. This was the big disadvantage of the flatboat, but as hewed timber was always in demand, the flatboat owner wherever he happened to end his journey, Nashville or New Orleans, could sell his boat, or if a settler, he could dismantle her, carry the timbers overland, and use them in his house.

Most flatboats, once on the Mississippi, almost always went at least as far as Natchez, and quotations of prices in the early Nashville papers more commonly came from Natchez than New Orleans. Natchez also marked the beginning of the Natchez Trace, for even when the boatmen went to New Orleans, he ordinarily came by water across Lake Pontchartrain as did Baily and other travelers, and at Natchez took to "shank's mare" or a horse.

When Martin Armstrong sold his produce there in 1789 the whole district contained only around three thousand people, and the town itself was no more than a village, but even then it had a long and turbulent history. Established by the French around 1716 as Fort Rosalie on the high bluffs above the Mississippi, and named in time for the scattered Natchez Indians, it had like the Illinois known British rule, but during the Revolution changed hands again, falling to the Spaniards. No different

---

[15] Michaux, *Travels 1802*, 87–88, 114–115. See also FP, 28, Verhoeff, *Kentucky River*, 61, a 1787 contract for a flatboat. They were in later years sometimes advertised—Nashville *Clarion*, Feb. 22, 1811, "a flatboat 14 × 50"—but most were built to order.

[16] WD, V, 389.

from most towns of the day it was, at least to modern eyes, greater than the sum of its parts. Like New Orleans and Nashville to a lesser extent, the place was a mixture of many peoples—Spanish, French, Creole, Indians, Mulattoes, Negroes, with a goodly seasoning of Scotch-Irish Baptists who had, many as Regulators, fled the English colonies before the Revolution. Other English colonials in search of wide and fertile fields with some land speculation on the side had also settled because Natchez was the only place the King's Proclamation of 1763 had left open for settlement west of the mountains.

There was as in any town more than one Natchez, depending upon the pocketbook and social status of the visitor. There was for the boatman the notorious Natchez Under the Hill, of which Joseph Bishop wrote, "It is my candid belief it has never been slandered enough even by the most vulgar narrator," [17] but for the man with money to spend there was the Natchez above where by 1807 Mickie's Tavern was a favorite of Tennessee gentlemen. All over, under the hill and above, were wicked men, waiting, sometimes with daggers in the dark, to steal a flatboat of produce, and others waiting only with marked cards.

The district grew rapidly under American rule, and by 1806 the town had around three hundred houses with more than two thousand inhabitants.[18] Many of these were as wealthy as any to be found in the South, for it was said that some of the nearby cotton plantations earned five to twenty thousand dollars a year, but the wealth above, like the gambling, drunkenness, and general depravity of that "sink of iniquity" below the bluffs by the river, was probably exaggerated.

Around three hundred miles below Natchez was New Orleans, a city beloved by most Europeans because "the morose habits of the sad Americans" had not inflicted upon it either Blue Laws or Sunday closings. Deplored by most New Englanders, it was described by Estwick Evans as a place of unlimited vice where "broad indeed is the road to ruin; and an insulated spectator sees the multitude passing down the stream of pleasure to the gulf of remorse. Here men may be vicious without incurring the ill opinion of those around them; for all go one way." [19]

The old New Orleans, small as she was with only around fifteen thousand people as late as 1806, offered drinking, gambling, and wenching

---

[17] Gray, *Bishop*, 186; Baily, *Tour 1796–1797*, 283–291, also had rather unpleasant experiences in Natchez ten years earlier.
[18] Ashe, *Travels*, 287–288.
[19] Evans, *Tour*, 234.

at a price to suit anyone's purse from the flatboatman down from the Little South Fork and smelling of the white oak staves he had slept among for days to the wealthy plantation owner, enjoying for the moment the feel of ready cash from the sale of cotton and slaves.

New Orleans was, however, to most of the many travelers who wrote of her, considerably more than a place where a man might satisfy any appetite—provided he had the cost. Even scientifically minded Baily loved the levee planted with orange trees, and along its broad top the mall on which in the cool of the evening the belles and beaux would promenade, usually by carriage. All wrote of the beautiful New Orleans women, the wealthier much given to driving out in their cabriolets, never alone but always with a Negro boy or girl standing behind. Beyond the levee lay the harbor where sometimes as many as four hundred ships from all nations of the world waited three deep to unload cargoes of many varieties and take on the products of the South and West.[20]

On the town side of the levee were many little shops, kept by Spaniards and "persons of color," offering goods from all the world. The town had all things lacking in New England—gaiety, music, dancing, especially on Sunday, a day kept by the French as a holiday rather than a holy day. No man need feel a stranger in New Orleans, for, "Perhaps no place in the world, excepting Vienna, contains a greater variety of the human race than New Orleans. Besides foreigners of all nations, there . . . is every shade of complexion. Creoles, quadroons, mulattoes, Samboes, Mustizoes, Indians, and Negroes." There were boatmen and brokers from up the Mississippi; Scotch, English, and Irish traders; the ever officious Spanish officials—until 1803—with the whole overlaid with the basic life of the city, French, and many of these intelligent, cultivated, and wealthy.

Travelers seldom found New Orleans a tedious place in which to wait either to sell a cargo or to find some means of going home. Few men of that day traveled alone, even after the world east of the Mississippi was safe from Indians. Depending on his purse and inclination, the returning Cumberlander might wait for a keelboat, or round up a party to go by the Natchez Trace. In either case, card-sharpers, thieves, Indians in the early years, lewd women, miry road or turbulent river were usually the least of his dangers. A trip up the Mississippi often took as much as six

---

[20] Baily, *Tour 1796–1797*, 298–319, and ten years later Ashe, *Travels*, 302–313, represent only a small fraction of the very great deal written of New Orleans by early travelers.

months with around seventy days the shortest possible, and even a man on horseback as was Baily might be several weeks on the Trace. This meant the traveler leaving home on the fall tides that sometimes did not come until close to Christmas [21] was on his return trip liable to be caught in the marshy lands along the Mississippi when the malaria season came on. The ague and fevers killed many boatmen, and early the banks of the Mississippi were strewn with their graves.

Such a great deal has been written of the Natchez Trace and the trials of up-river travel one is inclined to forget that many early travelers went home by ship from New Orleans. Most of the British merchants in the Illinois, including George Morgan, had gone home by sailing vessel from New Orleans, and as late as 1802 Michaux commented that many boatmen returned by sea.[22] At a time when much coastal trade and travel were carried on by sailing vessel all up and down the Atlantic coast, the wait for a ship was not often a long one. Waiting in New Orleans was no hardship; Americans and English, who had to pass for Americans as did Baily, usually stayed at Madame Charbout's House, that made an especial business of catering to them.

Most of these disembarked at Philadelphia, which had been sending men and goods west since the French and Indian War. At the time the Cumberland was settled and for several years to come, Philadelphia was the most important city in the young United States, more important than any city we have today. It was New York and present day Philadelphia all in one with a good deal of Chicago and Detroit, for in and around it much manufacturing was done, everything from Conestoga wagons to stockings knitted by machine. It was, too, for most of the time during the early years the political center of the United States.

During colonial days Philadelphia had been praised by all kinds of travelers.[23] Different from other cities of the day, its streets were wide, clean, free of wandering animals, and with brick foot pavements. The town was an almost perfect combination of agriculture, commerce, and manufacturing; stores and shops had all imported wares from books to saddles, and its daily markets offered along with a great variety of seafood, imported drinks and other delicacies, produce from the fine farm lands that surrounded the town.

[21] Stump's keelboats left usually in December; Nashville *Clarion*, Nov. 5, 1811—"*Mary Ann* to sail Dec. 20," was one of several such announcements for various boats through the years.

[22] Michaux, *Travels 1802*, 224–225.

[23] One of the most enthusiastic was Burnaby, *Travels*, 88–101.

Early, there was a night watch and police by day, and on the whole
an atmosphere of peace, prosperity, and cleanliness, but what earned more
praise than Philadelphia's material comforts was the high level of her intellectual and social life. There were many schools, including a college,
a library where anyone might read, a museum, and an asylum for the
insane. The town had something of the ease and graciousness of the South
along with the love of industry and order of New England, but none of
the complete freedom of New Orleans. As late as 1796 when a city of
around seventy thousand, Baily found many of the citizens believing a
recent scourge of yellow fever had been sent because of the wickedness of
the authorities in permitting a theatre.[24]

The ending of the Revolution bringing rapid settlement in Kentucky
increased the importance of Philadelphia and the route to it from the west.
Most Cumberland businessmen sooner or later, and sometimes yearly,
visited Philadelphia. The city not only offered most merchandise to be
had anywhere in the world, but, equally important, Philadelphia businessmen would exchange goods for land or drafts on New Orleans cotton
brokers who made a business of shipping cotton to Philadelphia.

Andrew Jackson, exchanging land warrants for goods, ever fretted
and fumed at delays in Philadelphia and never liked the place either as
man of business or as politician, but John Coffee as a well-set-up young
bachelor had a gay time, riding in a hack to a ball with other gentlemen,
visiting Peale's Museum, the circus, a ventriloquist, and a "learned pig,"
buying a locket, "telliscope," and guitar strings, and getting fitted by a
Baltimore tailor.[25]

Most Cumberland travelers, Philadelphia bound, were by this time,
1803, using the overland routes both ways. The road west from Philadelphia was one of the oldest in the United States; it had been followed long
before the Revolution by the Moravians and other settlers emigrating to
the Southern borders—New River or the Yadkin Country. The sixty-six-
mile stretch from Philadelphia to Lancaster was by 1794 a paved turn-
pike, the only one in the United States. Both west- and south-bound
travelers continued together until Carlisle and sometimes Shippensburg
was reached. Here, the man on the way to the upper Cumberland or East
Tennessee and sometimes Middle Tennessee would continue south, up the
Valley of the Shenandoah, gradually working his way into and through

[24] Baily, *Tour 1796–1797*, 114.
[25] Coffee Papers, 1803.

the Appalachians. Following at last the old Hunters' Trail, he passed Abingdon, Virginia, Jonesboro in what is now East Tennessee; and after many jogs and turnings, creek crossings, and steep hills, went through Cumberland Gap, across the Cumberland, and by way of the Kentucky Trace reached Central Kentucky. Mail into the West followed this route until 1794, as did most of the early travelers to and from Middle Tennessee.[26]

This old, completely overland route grew less important while that by way of Pittsburgh grew more so but neither was used exclusively. One of my great grandmothers, Permelia Jane Dick, born in Wayne County, Kentucky, in 1819, remembered the trips her father made during her childhood, the same he and his father had been making for years before she was born. Yearly he would go with pack-horse loads of home manufactured goods, chiefly linen cloth, knitted gloves, and stockings to Philadelphia, and weeks later get back with books and other goods, and loaded down with news and family gossip gleaned from the relatives scattered along the way from East Tennessee down the Great Valley. Others traveled by two-wheeled, ox-drawn carts, "three months, three sets of hickory withe tires," or so the stories went. Farmers on the upper Cumberland like those in Central Kentucky continued to drive hogs, horses, and cattle over the Cumberland Gap Road, some bound east to Baltimore or Philadelphia, others south; before the March of Tears a good bit of stock was sold to the Cherokee.

However, most Cumberland businessmen, politicians, returning boatmen along with emigrating families, Conestoga wagons bearing goods, and now and then a tourist on the order of a Baily or a Michaux took the Pittsburgh route. Most crossed the Appalachians as did Michaux by way of Bedford, this last hundred of the 318-mile trip one of the hardest and roughest in the whole of the United States, the hills so steep travelers often dismounted and walked.[27] In spite of improvements on the eastern end, it still took a driver and wagon drawn by four and sometimes five horses around three weeks to get 2,500 weight of goods from Philadelphia to Pittsburgh. As a rule it cost more, sometimes as much as $8 a hundredweight, to get goods from Philadelphia to Pittsburgh, than to bring them the more than twelve hundred miles by water from New Orleans to

[26] TP, IV, 396–397, 402–403, 416–417, is an exchange of letters concerning routes, costs, and time intervals of the U.S. mails, 1792–1795. ·

[27] Michaux, *Travels 1802*, 28–70, is one of the most detailed accounts of this trip; there was by this date stagecoach service between Philadelphia and Lancaster.

Nashville.[28] The high price of the overland carriage is not unreasonable when one remembers that out of this the driver and horses had to be fed for almost twice the length of time taken to bring the goods, as the wagons, Philadelphia-bound, were almost always empty in the earlier stage of the journey. There was in the whole West no product, save possibly ginseng or cleaned cotton, that would pay its way to market when carried up river and across the mountains.[29]

Fort Pitt had grown during the Revolution, for with seaports closed by the British, it was the only way for many to get goods to market, and the chances are that the "corn rum" M. Bomer had for sale in 1776 was made in the backwoods of Pennsylvania and shipped out by way of Pittsburgh. There had been, too, some traffic up the rivers; in 1776 Whigs had managed to get 136 kegs of powder from New Orleans to Pittsburgh.[30]

The rapid settlement of Kentucky increased the importance of the town and by 1790 it had become Pittsburgh, the funnel through which goods, settlers, soldiers, farm products, and manufactured goods poured into the old West and deeper South by way of the Ohio and the Mississippi. Michaux in 1802 found it a bustling place with around four hundred houses, mostly of brick, and practically everybody in some form of manufacturing or trade. Boat building in particular flourished, for here goods and travelers had to buy some form of river craft; most has been written of the flatboats or broadhorns that floated down from Pittsburgh, but all other kinds of craft were produced from the batteaux made there since the days of the Illinois merchants to sea-going ships, not to mention the first steamboat on the Mississippi. Pittsburgh, all trade and business as she was, had none of the glamour surrounding Natchez.

The water route from Pittsburgh to Nashville was around 1,200 miles, or about the same as that from New Orleans to Nashville, but as all of this was down stream save for the 180 miles up the Cumberland, the carriage of this part of the trip cost only around $2.50 per hundredweight, but this, added to the cost by land from Philadelphia, plus drayage from the Cumberland, sometimes storage at Smithland, plus insurance, sometimes made the cost of goods from Philadelphia store to Cumberland store as much as $12 per hundredweight, with the time seldom less than two months and usually more. The route was made more attractive when in

[28] Coffee Papers, 1801–1804, have many bills for carriage of goods from these places as well as references to horse keep at Limestone. See also Bassett, *Jackson Correspondence*, I, 15, 84–86, 94–95.
[29] Michaux, *Travels 1802*, 158.
[30] Hall, *The West*, 112.

early 1794 a packet service was put into operation between Cincinnati and Pittsburgh; the four keelboats used were armed and equipped with passenger cabins.[31] They also served as carriers of the mail, and in this year the old mail service by horseback through Cumberland Gap was discontinued.

Most bound for the Cumberland save those who had to travel with the boats left the river at Limestone, now Maysville, 426 miles from Pittsburgh, and from there came overland. Many Cumberland travelers made it a practice to ride up from Nashville to Limestone, and there leave their horses on pasture until needed again for the return trip. A traveler, however, could usually get a wagon ride, for goods bound for Lexington came overland from Limestone, and most Cumberland travelers followed this route, with everybody stopping in Lexington, for years the most important city in the old West.

Visitors praised it almost as much as they praised Philadelphia. Josiah Espy, visiting the place in 1805, declared its main street had "all the appearance of Market Street in Philadelphia on a busy day." [32] Three years earlier Michaux had been impressed by the town with, at that early date, around three thousand people, its buildings mostly of brick, and merchants offering practically everything to be had in Philadelphia save fresh seafood. Surrounded by fertile farm lands, and centrally located, Lexington was an inland shipping and shopping center for most of Kentucky and Tennessee. Much manufacturing was also done; there were rope walks, tanneries, paper mills and powder mills, and large numbers of skilled workmen making all things from stills to silver teapots. Lexington, like Philadelphia and Nashville, too, also had a rich intellectual life with its two printing presses, schools, and a college.

Few businessmen as yet visited Louisville or The Falls as some still called the place; as late as 1805 the town consisted of only two hundred dwellings, chiefly of wood.[33] Regardless of the Kentucky town from which the Nashville-bound traveler started home—Lexington, Danville, or Louisville—the road lay across the Barrens where settlement was slow; in 1796 the elder Michaux rode thirty-seven miles without seeing a farm;[34] six years later his son coming from Lexington found, while hunt-

[31] *Ibid.*, 116, quoting an ad in the *Sentinel of the Northwestern Territory*, June 11, 1794.
[32] *Ohio Valley Historical Series*, No. 7, Cincinnati, 1871, Josiah Espy, "A Tour in Ohio, Kentucky, and Indiana Territory in 1805," 8.
[33] *Ibid.*, 15.
[34] Thwaites, *Travels*, III, Michaux, "Journal," 92.

ing a strayed horse, a farm wife who had seen no one save her own family for eighteen months.[35]

The fertile lands of Middle Tennessee north of the Cumberland were by 1802 dotted with plantations and cut by numerous roads, most leading to Kentucky. The first road ordered cut by Davidson County Court in 1784 went eighteen miles north to Kaspar Mansker's place; others, some connecting with this one, came in from Louisville by way of the Red River Country, and the first road ordered cut by newly created Sumner County in 1787 was from Bledsoe's Lick or Castalian Springs to the Blue Spring.[36] Shown on Filson's 1784 map, this spring was a stopping place for most travelers and emigrants to the Cumberland Settlements, for even those from no further way than East Tennessee were still forced to take the long, rough, and dangerous route through Cumberland Gap and across Kentucky.

There was of course a much shorter route, that of Tollunteeskee's Trail across the Plateau, parts of it used by the Long Hunters, and followed back in 1766 by James Smith when he went home after his exploratory trip into Middle Tennessee. The trouble was that a strip of country around 150 miles wide continued to be owned by the Cherokee, and the old trail was almost too dangerous for white man's use. In spite of plans laid in the North Carolina Assembly as early as 1784, and a very great deal of correspondence and more legislation, nothing was accomplished.[37]

Meanwhile the strip of unsettled land was narrowed; Tilman Dixon and others spread the Cumberland settlements eastward. Settlements in East Tennessee took a big jump south and west when in 1786 Captain James White built the first cabin near where the Tennessee River is formed by the junction of the Holston and French Broad. The following year James Robertson and a handful of other men spent seventeen days clearing a pack-horse trail across the Plateau from the Cumberland Settlements to White's Station.[38] This road, little more than the old Indian trail cut to pack-horse width, was a few months later widened and improved by the Winchesters and Bledsoes.[39]

Rough as it was and dangerous, this route formed the basis of future roads across the Plateau that tied the two parts of Tennessee together.

[35] Michaux, *Travels 1802*, 178–179.

[36] SC, I, 1.

[37] NCR, XIX, 576, was only the beginning of the voluminous correspondence carried on for years, much of it by Anthony Bledsoe, eager for a road. See *ibid.*, XX, 654, 714, 758, 759, 771, 772, 773.

[38] W, 32S, 501.

[39] *Ibid.*, 32S, 525.

The first party of around a hundred people protected by Colonel Kaspar Mansker and other guards came over it in late 1787,[40] more than a year before the official opening, September 25, 1788. The following November there came another large group of emigrants that included Judge John McNairy, Prosecutor Andrew Jackson, and the widow of General William Davidson, for whom Davidson County had been named.[41]

There was at this time no ferry over the Clinch, but once the traveler had got over it by makeshift raft or fording, near present day Kingston, his trials were only beginning. Twelve miles beyond the crossing, the climb up and onto Walden's Ridge was so steep that seven horses were needed to pull up an empty wagon; goods and sometimes the dismantled wagons were taken up in many trips by horseback. But once on top, the traveler could draw no breath of relief. He had to go down again by way of Spencer's Hill where good Thomas Sharpe Spencer was killed in 1794, on roads so steeply falling that whole trees had to be tied to the wagon tails to keep the vehicles from over-running the horses.[42] Down the worst part, the traveler was rewarded with the noted camping place, the Crab Orchard, but soon it was climb again until the comparatively level Plateau was reached. This was a varied land of pine, oak, and seas of high grass, with here and there stretches of bare rock, affording neither water nor food for cattle. Francis Baily traveled the whole of a hot day in 1797 without even drinking water for himself and horses.

Dreaded by travelers more than summer's drouth were rainy times that overflowed the creeks; for the Plateau cut as it is by large tributaries of both Cumberland and Tennessee rivers had many creeks, and before reaching it there were Mammy's Creek and Daddy's Creek.

The original road swung north of present day Crossville and west to the headwaters of Flinn's Creek; it followed the creek down with many jogs and turnings across the Highland Rim to the mouth. Here, it forded the Cumberland and the traveler was in Middle Tennessee in a flat but miry stretch of land that in wet weather made harder going than a steep hill. This was the Big Lick where Big Lick Garrison,[43] later known as Fort Blount was built.

[40] *Ibid.*, 32S, 526.
[41] Parton, *Jackson*, I, 121, quoting the North Carolina *State Gazette*, No. 28, 1788, gives the opening as Sept. 25.
[42] Williams, *Travels*, Schweinitz, "Report," 439, 501, is one of the most detailed accounts of travel over the road as it is described both going and coming, but by that date it had already been described by Bishop, Baily, and the elder Michaux.
[43] Smith, *Description*, 14, as late as 1796 referred to the garrison by that name, though the first reference found to a Fort Blount was that of Michaux, "Journal," 94-95.

Here the traveler turned north and went thirty-two miles to Bledsoe's Lick, which in the first years marked the beginnings of civilization, but not of safety, for until 1795 Bledsoe's Lick and the surrounding region were especial targets of the Indians. At Bledsoe's Station he turned west, passing Winchester's Station and mills, shown on early maps as Cragfont, and in the neighborhood of present day Gallatin. He had by the time the road across the Plateau was cut quite a choice of roads in Middle Tennessee though the most important one continued to be the old road from Kaspar Mansker's place to Nashville. This in time became part of the Gallatin Pike and continued to carry the major traffic to Nashville from both central Kentucky and East Tennessee.

White's Station, little more than a fort surrounded by wilderness when the road was cut, increased rapidly in size and importance after William Blount as governor of the territory made his headquarters there, and he it was who named the place "Knox—Ville," in honor of General Knox. The road became somewhat safer when Fort Southwest Point was built on a small amount of land leased from the Cherokee in 1792. There was also on this same plot of ground near present day Kingston a tavern and a ferry over the Clinch. The place was soon for the traveler one of the most important points in the old West, for leading north from Southwest Point was a heavily traveled road into Kentucky.[44] In spite of the fact that the Road Through the Wilderness as this route was long known cut the mileage from Knoxville to Nashville almost in half, many travelers went by way of Kentucky for the road continued dangerous. During the times of great Indian alarm as after the siege of Buchanan's Station, Robertson had to pay fifty dollars to get a message taken by the shorter, quicker route to Blount in Knoxville.[45] It was not until after the ending of the Indian Wars in 1795 that the road was used for most travel between the two parts of Tennessee. In 1796, some 28,000 persons paid ferry tolls over the Clinch at Southwest Point.[46] Not all these were emigrants bound for Middle Tennessee; many came to Southwest Point and then turned north and followed the Jacksboro Road into Kentucky. There was, too, by this

[44] Abraham Bradley, Jr., "Map of the United States Exhibiting the Post-Roads, the Situations, connections, and distances of the Post Offices," 1804, though not exactly accurate shows Southwest Point and most places mentioned by travelers. A better idea of the very early roads may be had from *42nd Annual Report of the Bureau of American Ethnology,* Plate 14, 746, W. E. Myer, "Archaeological Map of the State of Tennessee," and *ibid.,* Plate 15, 748, "The Trail System of the Southeastern United States."

[45] TP, IV, 359, Robertson to Blount, October 8, 1794.

[46] Williams, *Travels,* Schweinitz, "Report," 439, 501.

date much travel between the two parts of Tennessee for the capital was at Knoxville.

The road cut by Robertson had before this date undergone many changes; travelers made many; it was easier to cut a new way around a miry stretch or a big mudhole than pull through it; Spencer's Hill was so formidable three routes for going down were made, but always the road went through the Crab Orchard, and until 1795, crossed the Cumberland at the mouth of Flinn's Creek. In this year, beginning on "the last mountain" a little south of present day Monterey on the Plateau, a new road branched off in a southwestward direction to cross the Cumberland at the mouth of the Caney Fork, future site of Carthage. Usually the traveler stopped at Walton's Tavern on the northern side, but by this date plantations were scattered along most roads in Middle Tennessee north of the Cumberland.[47]

Settlement south of the Cumberland was another story; as late as 1797 there were no plantations more than twelve miles south of Nashville, not even on the most important north-south highway, the old Middle Chickasaw Path, by that date known as the Natchez Trace. The old trail, already undergoing change by the white man, had crossed the Cumberland at the mouth of the Lick Branch; on the other side below Eaton's first station it had intersected with a network of other trails that with those on its southern end tied the Great Lakes to the Gulf of Mexico. Though used by some such as John Turnbull, said to have brought New Orleans goods over it as early as 1780, Robertson had for the Coldwater Campaign to get Chickasaw to serve as guides to the towns on the Tennessee not far from where the trace crossed the river.

The first known account of Cumberland boatmen over the route was in 1789 when the Winchester brothers, William Martin, and others took a few flatboats of produce down to New Orleans. They walked back, "800 miles, and more than half through Indian country,"[48] following much the same route later known to thousands of home-coming boatmen. Francis Baily described the road as he found it in 1797, but even at that date, two years after the end of the Indian Wars and considerable travel, the Natchez Trace was little more than a path, most of it through Indian country, and with neither tavern nor ferry along the way.

Baily's lengthy description of the trials of the road gives a picture

[47] Baily, *Tour 1796–1797*, 423–424, was the first to give an account of travel over this by way of Walton's Ferry, future site of Carthage.

[48] W, 3XX (18), 6.

somewhat out of focus. He saw it as an inexperienced woodsman, too ignorant of the distance to start with a food supply, and, unskilled in hunting, he almost starved. He spent several pages describing his heroism in crossing the Tennessee on a raft he had much trouble in making.[49] A Cumberlander in one short paragraph told how Edmund Jennings and others in the Nickojack Campaign of 1794 made rafts of cane and pawpaw strings, loaded them with guns, ammunition, and clothing, and with a string between their teeth, swam over towing, Jennings five times in the one night. William Martin, who like the Winchesters was "unacquainted with the business," wrote only of 1789, "rafted the Tennessee and all that."

The Winchester party was gone six months, but even in later years when there was no danger from the Indians, a few taverns by the road, and the Colberts kept a ferry on the Tennessee, the trip down and back again seldom took less than four months. The flatboatmen who walked home over the trace, strong men able with no deep breath to do forty miles a day on dry road, found the muddy, miry, mosquito-infested Natchez Trace hard going.[50] Even when they rode the scrawny New Mexico horses or mules bought in Natchez, the mud, heat, mosquitoes, flies, constant danger from robbers and the "ague" made of the trip a terror.

The old Chisca trail that went southeast from Nashville to cross the Tennessee near present day Chattanooga was as late as 1794 still so little known to the settlers that leaders of the Nickojack Expedition in the fall of that year had to have young Joseph Brown, former Indian captive at Nickojack, as a guide.[51]

The trip to Nickojack by paths that might be waylaid by Indians with troops and ammunition to be got over the swift river too deep for fording was a dangerous one, but even ferries and peace with the Indians did not automatically make the roads and river safe. The white robber, ever in wait for men who in bankless days carried gold and silver, especially those homeward bound over the Natchez Trace, accounted for a great many deaths, some of which were no doubt blamed on Indians. The Trace was unusually dangerous in 1803; in May, Mr. Reuben White was killed and the mailman fired upon, "and this the third attack in the past three weeks."

[49] Baily, *Tour 1796–1797*, 384–394.
[50] Jonathan Daniels, *The Devil's Backbone, The Story of the Natchez Trace*, New York, 1962, tells with much interesting detail the story of this road.
[51] W, 32S, 257–271, is one of the best of several accounts of this campaign by a participant.

The following July one man was killed and twenty-six robbed by a gang said to contain fifteen, and in August a traveler was found dead on the road.[52]

The Harpes and Philip Mason, who lived for a time near the Cumberland Ford of the Kentucky Road, had been all over the Cumberland Country as well as the Natchez Trace. A horrified young boy on the Plateau could only hide behind a tree and watch as they tied up his brother, tipped his head back, and cut his throat from ear to ear.[53] Many stories are told of how old Frederick Stump who had lost his oldest son Jacob to the Indians, lost a second son to the Harpes. But Mr. Stump had his revenge in 1803 when he went to Natchez as captain of a company in Colonel George Doherty's regiment, called out at the threat of trouble with Spain. Stump there had the pleasure of recognizing the man with Mason's head and trying to claim the bounty as Little Harpe, the worst of the lot.[54]

There had by this date been many improvements on most of the main roads north of the Cumberland, and those south in the immediate vicinity of Nashville. The Moravian missionaries found them in late 1799 nicely worked and covered with limestone. By 1802 the road by the Caney Fork to Knoxville, then known as Walton's Road, was set every three miles with markers, and Michaux going over it declared it was "broad and commodious as those in the environs of Philadelphia," and better than much of the road to Pittsburgh.[55]

In general the main roads of Tennessee, like those in Central Kentucky, were better than most in the United States of that day. The freest of free enterprise was coming to the fore, and the old dream of government-built roads embodied in the Constitution was practically abandoned for toll roads, privately owned canals, and soon railroads. Some idea of what constituted road building can be had from the letters and papers of James Robertson who in 1807 offered to "open and clear the road commonly called the Natchez Road 12 feet wide at 6 and 7 dollars per mile," depending on the terrain. He was to receive somewhat more where in the miry lands south of the Tennessee he had to build

---

[52] Tennessee *Gazette*, May 18, 1803; *ibid.*, July 13, 1803; *ibid.*, Aug. 24, 1803.

[53] W, 29S, 132–137. Much has been written of the Harpes, but lovers of gore will find much more among Mr. Draper's correspondents; for a disembowling episode see above.

[54] W, 31S, 55; but it should be remembered that several others also claimed this honor.

[55] Michaux, *Travels 1802*, 265.

causeways. The powers felt this was too high, so, needing money, Robertson lowered his bid to $4 a mile. He was later criticized for his poor results, as he was for $4 a mile supposed to build a stretch of Federal highway suitable for the carrying of the mails.[56]

Possibly one of the most remarkable feats in all her history was Middle Tennessee's success at keeping silk hats on her coachmen and anchovies in the cupboard, though for the first thirty years of her life surrounded by wilderness in all directions. Yet, she did it; her merchants traded with and traveled to the major seaports of the day—1,100 miles by land to Philadelphia, more than 1,500 by rivers and land; more than 1,200 to New Orleans by water, around 800 by land, with the two closest towns, Lexington and Knoxville, each around 180 miles away.[57] Knoxville, though no trading center as was Lexington, was the center of the political life of early Tennessee. Such men as Andrew Jackson, especially when he became judge, had yearly to make many trips back and forth across the still uninhabited plateau, and as the Road Through the Wilderness grew safer, many more travelers, Philadelphia, Baltimore, or Charleston bound, used it. This route continued as the main route for immigration into Middle Tennessee, the Kentucky Barrens, and in time what is now West Tennessee.

Mail also traveled these roads, though at this date daily mail was undreamed of; that up from New Orleans came only monthly for years, and the northern mail by way of Danville every three weeks. Judging from the many requests for carriers in the Nashville papers, carrying the government mails was not the glamorous job it came further west in the days of the Pony Express.[58] The pay was extremely low and the work dangerous, not only from Indians and robbers, but from the road itself. In January of 1802 the mail carrier was drowned in Duck River,[59] and many are the old stories of struggles "to get through" with the mail.

Center of all this—mail service, travel, transportation—was Nashville, the most important town in the old Southwest, even after the boundary

[56] A, V, 253, 185–189.

[57] Roads were constantly changing, and few travelers down the Mississippi traveled exactly the same number of miles; most travelers gave mileage, but they agreed neither among themselves nor with Daniel Smith in his *Description*. All of these are usually different from those given by Jedidiah Morse, *American Gazetteer*, Boston, 1797, and *ibid.*, Boston, 1804; in general most early roads were less straight than the roads of today.

[58] Rates varied, that proposed in 1794 for carrying the mail from Abingdon to Knoxville—a new route as Knoxville as yet had no mail service—was $2.50 the mile by the year for a trip every two weeks; see TP, IV, 343–345.

[59] Tennessee *Gazette*, January 27, 1802.

was run and Natchez became part of the United States. The site of Nashville was to begin with a strategic one—near the ford of Cumberland where the old Chickasaw Trail had crossed and where other Indian trails came in from all directions. Nashville really began in the winter of 1779–1780 when the Buchanans and others started French Lick Station "in the upper part of what came to be Nashville." As Indians destroyed other stations one by one, French Lick in which Robertson and other noted men lived gained in importance. After Nashville began to be laid out in 1784 and first settlers moved to their own forts, French Lick declined in importance, but as late as 1787 it was a busy, crowded place with two rows of cabins set at right angles to form a cross, with more cabins built into the stockade walls that enclosed about an acre and a half.[60] Most of the land about was in corn, some with watermelons like the patch of Old Johnny Boyd.

The cornfields around the fort walls gradually gave place to Nashville that, in spite of starting life with a building code and two hundred one-acre lots, was little more than a name during the times of Indian trouble, and any one of several forted farms was larger than it. Lewis Brantz coming in the fall of 1785 found Nashville had only two houses "that merit the name; the rest are only huts. . . ."[61] Six years later, Joseph Bishop, a hunter from the backwoods and not a critical observer, found Nashville but a collection of log shanties, scarcely deserving the name of village.[62] There were, however, by this date a courthouse and jail of sorts and the establishments of several merchants.

The fall of 1792 found Nashville with no buildings well enough made to be held against the Indians, though two were being built and the place was beginning to grow. Baily stopping by five years later went "round to view the town," and found it "pleasantly situated on the southwest bank of Cumberland River," with about sixty or eighty families; the houses were chiefly of logs and frame and so scattered over a wide area the town seemed larger than it actually was. He remarked the large number of stores and the three taverns. Nashville had by this date, 1797, become the stopping place for travelers up the river or down, or like Baily coming overland. The three taverns all did such a thriving business that the Dukes of Orleans, coming the same year as Baily, had to sleep three to a bed.

Two years later the Moravian missionaries in spite of fine plantations

[60] W, 30S, 252–253, 273.
[61] Williams, *Travels*, 285.
[62] Gray, *Bishop*, 61.

seen along the way found Nashville "the most attractive place in Cumberland"; though with only around three hundred inhabitants, it was "a regularly laid out city with a number of fine buildings." [63] These travelers as did others commented on the wide variety of European goods to be had in the town at low prices.

Michaux found in 1802 about 120 houses, though all except seven or eight were of logs or frame.[64] He saw the town as chiefly a stopping place for travelers, but Nashville, though the food and drink of her taverns were ever famous and still with less than four hundred people, was a good deal more than a place to go through. There were, in addition to the printing office and two churches, a courthouse, possibly the new brick one for which bids were offered in 1800,[65] and with this all the other accessories of justice—jail, whipping post, and stray pen. There were fifteen or twenty mercantile houses, offering goods from the far corners of the world, and taking in exchange anything from beeswax to slaves. There were grammar schools, at least one academy, and the beginnings of a college. Early, the town was a center of services; tailors, cabinetmakers, physicians, boot and shoemakers, saddlers, tinsmiths, silversmiths, and a host of others to serve the farmer and his lady. Long before it was incorporated as a town, Nashville was the object of a good deal of legislation; in 1787 Davidson County Court appointed John Hay keeper of the Standard of Weights for Nashville,[66] and in 1803 rules and regulations were set up for the town market.[67]

Much of the town life revolved about the public square; here were the courthouse, in time a post office, stores, taverns, and a multitude of lawyers' offices.[68] An 1812 act regulated the foot pavements around the square and stipulated that doorsteps and cellar doors were not to extend more than four feet into the street.[69] A great fire in 1811 made brick buildings mandatory, and the unknown soldier hurrying down river in 1813 contrasted "rich and populous Nashville, presenting a number of

[63] Williams, *Travels,* Schweinitz, "Report," 508.

[64] Michaux, *Travels 1802,* 245–246; 250–251.

[65] Tennessee *Gazette,* Feb. 25, 1800.

[66] DC, I, 158.

[67] Tennessee *Gazette,* April 13, 1803.

[68] Parton, *Jackson,* I, 390–394, in describing the fight between Jackson and the Bentons sketched and explained the square as it was in 1813. The Tennessee *Gazette* and the Nashville *Clarion* advertising through the years give quite a good idea of the buildings about the square—"Wm Roper's Tavern in front of court house," "Kirkman in the new brick building on the South Side of the public square."

[69] Nashville *Clarion,* Sept. 30, 1812.

beautiful brick edifices," with the "sorrowful looking towns of Eddyville, Palmyra, and Clarksville."

There was no doubt about it; Nashville was The Town, serving early as travel and trade center for an area of several thousand square miles, though as late as 1813 it had only around twelve hundred people. The place was in a way even more important to the Kentuckians up river than to the settlers in Middle Tennessee; Nashville was not only buyer or trans-shipper for much produce from woods and farm, but source of practically all manufactured goods for those within a reasonable distance of the river. Even those not on the river, but south of the Cumberland in Kentucky, found it more convenient to come to Nashville. "Away back before The War," one of my great-grandfathers had a tavern near Powersburg, once a stopping place in Wayne County on a long-since-forgotten road to Nashville, and thither by wagon would he go to get supplies for his tavern. One can only imagine how impressed and delighted he and others from up river must have been by the sight of Nashville of which well traveled Robert Baird wrote in 1833, "I have never seen a town of the same size which contains as few mean houses and as little that offends the eye. It is a remarkably beautiful place. It contains more elegant mansions and pleasant seats in and around it, than any other town of equal size in the United States."

Yet, it should never be forgotten that Nashville was not the only town. The Cumberland settlers were not townspeople by inheritance as were many immigrants to America; the home was too important and beyond it the farm community to permit the town to be a center of religious, educational, or social life in the early years, and the New England town with its town meetings was unheard of on the Cumberland. Nor was a town needed for trade; much trading for many years was done in neighborhood stores; neither was any town a center of manufacturing save for such skilled workmen as supplied consumer needs. The most important products of commerce were manufactured either on the plantation or at the source of supply or demand or both—iron out on Barton's Creek where water power and iron ore were convenient, boatyards all up and down the river, staves in the woods.

There were by 1803 dozens of towns in Middle Tennessee, most established by the Tennessee legislature, for, following the custom of the day, a lawmaking body at the state level could establish a town in the woods where there was not even a house. Many towns mentioned as inspection

points and even appearing on maps—Heatonsburg, Haysborough, Parm-
leysville—never completely materialized, but remained little more than a
thickening of rural settlement. Others, particularly those in Middle Tennessee—Gallatin, Murfreesboro, Lebanon—were wealthy and large enough
to maintain lives of their own and become centers, not only of county
justice, but of trade and to a large extent social and educational life. Still,
most early towns, even those in time to be important were much as
Michaux found the average town of the West—"A group of seven or
eight houses—the half and frequently the whole built of wood."

Yet, no matter how small and unimposing the county seat town, even a
new one with court meeting in a private home, it was, if for no other
reason, important as a center of justice. A visitor during court week or
even on a pleasant Saturday would find the place crowded with horses
hitched in the shade, buggies, wagons, carts, men, many with their wives
and children. The greatest attraction of course was court, meeting as a
usual thing four times yearly at the local level; Superior Court, twice,
with judge and lawyers as a rule traveling from county to county. In the
small populations of the early counties a large percentage of the citizens
was directly involved, if nothing else, as possible jurors. It was, too, a
time when the populace as a whole enjoyed trials and many were the
books of trials published and advertised in early papers. The spectacle was
even more interesting when the observer, though he had not even a minor
part, knew everybody from judge to defendant. Long distances and bad
roads seldom kept a man from knowing most families in his county.

In addition to court, musters were frequently held near the county
seat towns, and in the early years up river all men had to go to the county
seat town to vote—by voice with the booth open for three days; most
stayed the full three days and some longer.

Any farmer, too, had need of a crowd for his business; in town the
man with some white oak suitable for barrels might find a cooper hunting
somebody with staves or stave timber to sell, or better a shipper who
needed barrels; the man who wanted pork to ship and the farmer with
pork on the hoof could get together. There was always a good deal of
business that could be done only at the courthouse—taxes to pay, a mortgage to record, a strayed horse to study, daughter's cattle markings to
record, or some business to set before the court—request for a mill dam,
petition for a road or ferry. There was, too, much to enjoy at little or no
cost—impromptu quarter races, horse swappings to watch, extemporaneous sermons, fights in the cockpits, drinking and talk in the taverns.

Monticello, Kentucky, for example has today only a few thousand people, but its history as a county seat town goes back more than 160 years. In 1815 the place consisted of "fifty inelegant hewn log dwelling houses, a rude courthouse, a place of public worship, four stores, three taverns, and three blacksmith shops." [70] There were also several doctors and lawyers, at least one school, and a sprinkling of skilled workmen. Small as the place was, the Saturday's trip to Town was by that date a must for many. Few men stayed home on court days, and in good weather whole families would go, though it might mean a round trip of more than forty miles.

In more fortunate places with better roads, the wealthy might travel by carriage, the middle-class farmer by wagon, but for the largely road-less world up river most travel in the early years was by horseback. The husband would ride the best horse, usually with the third child from the bottom on behind. Side by side or sometimes in front, setting the pace, was the mistress of the household, her sidesaddle no less good than her husband's and she no less expert as a horsewoman. Cradled on one arm would be the baby, clinging behind was the second child from the bottom, and as she usually rode a gentle brood mare, frolicking around and about would be a foal. The rest of the children would be of the company, two to the horse for the less affluent and the younger, but by tradition most households were able to afford a horse with some kind of saddle for each teen-aged child. The family dogs, save the feist forced to stay home, would also come along, and in the small household in which the slaves were allowed a good deal of freedom, they too would come and usually by horseback, and so they would go to church, to visit a neighbor or a relative, and to Town.

In spite of numerous road-workings ordered by county courts where each man and his polls were made to contribute one day's work, a custom that persisted in some counties until World War II, most roads not used by mail or stagecoach continued rough for generations. Toll roads were soon a common part of life, but as these were never profitable in sparsely settled districts, many farmers endured worse roads than those known to the first settlers. This was particularly true in the part of Kentucky drained by the Cumberland, for state funds in Kentucky were seldom spent on anything east or south of the Bluegrass. The Jacksboro Road [71]

[70] Brown, *Gazetteer*, 96.
[71] The Jacksboro Road roughly followed the route of the Southern Railway, though it forded the Cumberland at Smith Shoals, after passing through present day Pine Knot, and was in general much like the Southern Wilderness Road that in

was during times of high water on the Cumberland useless, and in any season almost impassable.

Still, it was the only highway many knew, and most south of the river had none but the Cumberland. Students from Cumberland County, Kentucky, attending the University of Kentucky had to come to Burnside and there wait for a steamboat, for it was not until 1928 that Burkesville, county seat of Cumberland, was connected with the outside world by any means save the river. Wayne County had a toll road; Pulaski County had a railroad after 1878; but a free highway suitable for cars with a bridge, toll, over the Cumberland, did not come until 1936. The Cumberland had served for more than 160 years. It made life possible, and throughout that period Nashville was for most, south of the Cumberland, more easily reached than Lexington, Kentucky.

The back of the Cumberland was not broken until Wolf Creek Dam was finished. Never again can a boat go from the upper river to Nashville. The upper river like most of the lower has, with its lakes and its hydroelectric plants, become a tourist attraction; yearly several million people come to boat and swim and fish on some reach of the cold and silent Cumberland, still now, for most of its length until one is near Cumberland Falls, another tourist attraction.

No one of those enjoying the dead river can ever know what it was when the creeks were dry half the year and flooded the other half, and farmers, with wheat stacked by the riverbank and hungry chickens cooped, listened for steamboats slow in the coming because of low water. The life of the Cumberland, its importance to the people not only on the main river but high up the tributaries, can never be measured by the amount of work it did.

It works still; tonnage on the lower river is high and yearly Wolf Creek Dam, not to mention others lower down, makes a vast amount of electricity. Yet, the old Cumberland was so many things other than work horse. It was for most of us a beloved but completely unpredictable neighbor of whom we never tired of talking and whose house we never tired of watching and of visiting.

---

turn grew out of the Great Lakes Trail. In contrast to most roads of the region it has received little attention from historians, though it was an important highway.

Chapter Fourteen

Social Life
and Diversions

MOST LIFE in the Cumberland Country during pioneer days was somewhat like the river—unpredictable, often cruel, eternally changing, filled with upsets, surprises, disappointments, now and then an unexpected pleasure, yet loved as many loved the contrary river, and like the river always interesting and often diverting. The hardships and dangers of pioneer travel by boat can scarcely be over-exaggerated—fogs, hidden snags, rocks, sandbars, planters, sawyers, unexpected freshets, close and uncomfortable quarters for the lucky on a craft with some kind of shelter. All this for the boatmen overlaid with hard work or the uncertainty of traveling

Headpiece: Group of travelers smoking and telling stories on a flatboat.

down when "our course was where the stream carried us." Yet, many travelers wrote of the music on the Mississippi, the songs and dances of the boatmen, of card playing and shooting matches. Those who traveled the southern rivers belong as a group to a people who did not take "Work while you work and play while you play" for a maxim.

Travel overland by any means was even worse. Constant danger first from Indians and then robbers; the eternal struggle with axle-deep mud or choking dust on roads so bad horses went lame, wagons broke down, and travelers walked. The ever-changing weather from sudden thunderstorms that made a dry creek belly deep on a horse to blizzardous snows were endured without shelter by all horseback travelers. Still, the Reverend Asbury and Andrew Jackson were among the very few who saw travel as we see it today—nothing but a means of reaching a given destination as quickly as possible.

Travel for most was just another part of living. John Lipscomb, riding in 1784 through dangerous Indian country, was on a business trip to see about land in Middle Tennessee, but there was time on the way for hunting, horse swapping, helping fellow travelers, and writing down the words of a hunter's song.[1] Nothing to John Lipscomb was quite so important as living, not even business.

The abilities that made the physical survival of a Daniel Boone or Michael Stoner possible when alone in the woods were almost always matched with equal abilities at mental and social survival. James Smith in the Middle Tennessee woods of 1766 did not merely sit and wait for his wounded foot to heal; he amused himself by reading the two books he had, singing songs, and composing one of his own.

The forted life was in a sense but a waiting for better days; nobody expected to spend the whole of his life in a little cabin in the miserable crowding behind picketed walls. Certainly it was an uncomfortable, insecure, ugly life, but those who wrote of the old days were always, in accounts of the battles and historical events on which Mr. Draper had questioned them, straying off with their memories into the fun they had had—dances, jokes, exciting hunts, music, and other diversions.

Few had before settling on the Cumberland ever known security and a life so patterned that certain things could be done at certain hours or even dates—the farm boy went to mill and waited for his grinding turn; families waited for bread until their corn crop was hard enough to grind,

[1] Williams, *Travels*, Lipscomb "Journal," 276–279.

and the religious put off the funeral sermon until a minister visited the community.[2]

There are from earliest years mention of somewhat formalized and planned events—balls, wedding suppers, Christmas dances, and other occasions on which social life has ever revolved. There was, too, behind most of the well-to-do of English origin, a tradition of holidays, trips to watering places such as Bath, travel for pleasure, some spectator sports, especially horse racing, the theatre, parades of many kinds, and in general quite a variety of planned diversions and amusements. Most of these were planted in Tidewater that had during colonial days many amusements in contrast to New England that had almost none. The well-to-do of Middle Tennessee were in time to have much the same pattern, trips to watering places sometimes no further away than the Plateau or Red Boiling Springs, but often to the Blue Ridge, long a favorite with Tidewater planters, and much travel for pleasure that sometimes included Europe. There were in time most of the formal amusements known to the rest of the civilized world.

First settlers had few of these diversions. Indian warfare knew no vacation, but it is doubtful if many pioneers suffered from boredom. A family that could from day to day and year to year see the results of each day's work—the sight and smell of just-put-up pickets in 1780, then out from these the widening fields, the loss, the moving, the beginning again, and at long last the great day when the pickets came down, a milestone, like the first apple from the planted tree—had much less time or need for a diverting change than has the average person of today.

Life was at all levels constructive. More important, maybe, was the knowing the creation—child or another panel of fence—was needed. Even the old slave able to do little but split shoe pegs or burr wool could know he was needed and feel part of a world busy planting civilization in the woods. Tradition indicates that many slaves took much pride in their work. True, there was dreary work for all; stirring a kettle of ugly-looking, evil-smelling soap on a cold day was no fun, but there was always the joy, regardless of whether the stirring hands were black or white, of the anticipation of fine soap—and soap was a needed thing. Lives were not geared to machines; everybody had to be to some extent his own executive; nobody was much inclined to tell the slave-coachman how to handle the high-spirited team—when he was the only person on the place able to do so.

[2] This custom was followed in some back-hill communities until the 1940's.

The team was alive, and, though not always pleasant, work with living things is seldom dull. The pioneer not only had animals but he had people. So much has been made of Daniel Boone's singing to himself in the woods, we forget that practically all other Long Hunters and explorers traveled in groups. The lone man, even when hunting or traveling, seems to have been such a rarity he was commented upon. Most early settlers though they wanted elbowroom and privacy were on the whole a most sociable people.

Many necessary activities were social in nature. It was in a way a grievesome thing for any busy, middle-aged woman to have to drop her work when sent for to help at a borning. Still, it was a social occasion with other neighbor women and male relatives gathered, crowned usually with the joy of a new baby that everybody would come to see. Sitting up with the dead, burials, nursing the sick, like attending court or going to mill, these last two reserved usually for males, were all things that had to be done. Time consuming they were, and not always pleasant, but they gave what the Cumberlander ever loved, and what was undoubtedly his greatest diversion—an opportunity for conversation.

Another favorite meeting place was the tavern, but for some the livery stable with blacksmith shop had a still greater appeal. Women quarreled for generations, but it was at such places the young male often learned the facts of life. The "rough anecdotes" of loose-tongued men who had been around—Natchez, New Orleans, the Illinois—were often more edifying than today's marriage manuals, save that the raconteur did not equate sexual adroitness with love.

There was always in the conversation of any chance gathering something to discuss—news, weather, politics, business, and farming—and all had their diverting side. They never, for example, seem to have wearied of court. It was not enough to attend the whole of every session, but between times the doings there must be discussed, and in and out through sober conversation ran the stories. Many like that of the damage suit for the hearing of Sharp, the slow-track hound, told and retold, as was the tale of James Hannah, who, when hauled into court, addressed the worshipful justices, "I am Saul, the son of Kish, sent out to hunt asses and lo, now I have found them." [3]

People took their fun where they found it. Funerals, religious gatherings, road-workings, musters, or simply while waiting for the ferry boat or the creek to go down, all offered an opportunity for conversation

[3] W, 6XX, 999.

seasoned with jokes and fun. Seldom was the pioneer a respecter of persons and occasions simply because he was supposed to respect them. More than once a gigglesome young thing, gone a-visiting, may have sat down to some unexpectedly scanty table and whispered a grace famous throughout the West:

> "Oh Thou who blest the loaves and fishes:
> Look down upon these empty dishes." [4]

Many of their jokes would today be considered in poor taste. Others were cruel. Andrew Jackson's cruelty in inviting the local whores to a Christmas dance would, at least to the unsuspecting women he invited, seem cruel in any age as well as crude. Still, the pioneer might have questioned the good taste of our most common joke, that, found in the comic cartoon and pseudo-intellectual magazine and most everything else in between, in which over and over women are portrayed as symbols of some foible held up for ridicule. The many forces tending to make woman the symbol of all the fears and hatreds of the whole of a frightened society were, outside of New England, not yet much in evidence. Woman was in the South still the yoke-fellow. Hence, the stupid-wife joke like the mean-mother-in-law joke, along with male self-pity over mommism, would, in a world that believed a man deserved no better than he got, have been a joke on the males involved. There were plenty of jokes about women, the old American stand-bys—the young girl joke and the dialect joke involving an immigrant were not yet in evidence—but usually most jokes were about all kinds of men.

Many read a great deal on a wide variety of subjects. Much diversion, if not exactly amusement, came also from correspondence, and, considering the smallness of the population and the number of journals that have survived, many kept journals for their own private entertainment.

More widely enjoyed than the keeping of journals, and possibly second only to conversation as a pastime was music, especially singing. Everybody sang: the boatman sang to the river, the teamster to his team, the baby tender to the baby, and even the hunter, rejoicing in his kill, might sing:

> "Oh you little deer who made you breeches
> Mammy cut them out
> And daddy sewed the sitches
> Sewed the stitches." [5]

---

[4] Townsend, *Tom Johnson*, 13.
[5] Williams, *Travels*, Lipscomb, "Journal," 277.

The hog drover coming back from Georgia sang on his way to the Gap:

> "Tazewell County and Tazewell Town
> Lord have mercy and do look down
> Pore and rocky and hilly, too.
> Lord have mercy, what will these pore people do."

This "traveling" song like the cry of "school butter" could be the challenge for a pioneer version of gang warfare, and like many ditties had the advantage of versatility; any county or town could be named, and the song is undoubtedly much older than Tazewell County.

Work songs, play songs, traveling and other special occasion songs formed only a small part of the musical heritage of the pioneer, and like the rest of his music was not exclusive property. There was a great variety of ballads, many old when Scotland was young, most probably of Scandinavian origin as the well known "Barbara Allen" may be.[6] Regardless of their history, most were sad tales of unrequited love and death and war. A few continued to live on in the back hills where there was less intercourse with the outside world, but just because of these, one should not envisage all pioneers as singing the old ballads. Even during colonial days most any fashionable young buck or lady would have held "Barbara Allen" downright backwoodsy. The revival of the old Scotch ballads that came to England around the third quarter of the eighteenth century seems not to have taken place in America.

There was a lively intercourse with Philadelphia, and any songbook there or music sheet would, though belatedly maybe, reach the Cumberland. The average well-to-do family of early Middle Tennessee owned not only sheet music for both voice and instrument, but also a book or so of popular songs.[7]

There were on the Cumberland other ballads, not of warriors and lovers across the ocean, but of doings in America. Some may have circulated on broadsheets, but many were never printed. The most commonly

---

[6] There were of course many versions of "Barbara Allen." That in our family began, "It was in the month of May/ The green buds they were swellin'/ Young Jimmy Grove on his death bed lay/ For the love of Barbara Allen."

[7] DW, II, 177. Tennessee *Gazette*, Dec. 25, 1802—*Patriotic Songs* for sale; *ibid.*, Sept. 12, 1804, *Sailor's Medley of Songs*. Coffee Papers also list a good many musical items bought and sold; see in particular Coffee's purchases in Philadelphia for 1803— guitar strings, "1 set musick strings," "4 musick sheets."

sung around Nashville were possibly those that grew out of the Battle of Point Pleasant, since such a large proportion of the early settlers had taken part. More than sixty years after the event William Martin remembered hearing the old men sing:

> "There was good Captain Buford and old Captain Ward,
>   They were both in the battle and fought very hard,
>   They fought like two heroes, and like heroes did die,
>   And in a short time on the ground there did lie.
> There was Goldman and Allen and a great many more.
> Had the honor of dying on the Ohio shore." [8]

Most of these sorrowful doggerels were sung in a wailing minor key, though no one really knows the tune today in which they sang of dead Charles Lewis:

> "Farewell, Colonel Lewis, till pity's sweet fountains
>   Are dried in the hearts of the fair and the Brave
> Virginia shall weep for her chief of the Mountains
>   And mourn for the heroes who sleep by his grave." [9]

Sadder still was the dirge for the ill-fated Crawford who was burned at the stake, a song of thirty-two verses by William McCoule who saw him die:

> "When he crossed the Ohio as I understand
>   Colonel Williams wanted two hundred men at his command
> If they had been granted and make no doubt about
>   We soon should have put the proud Indians to rout." [10]

There were numerous songs of the Revolution, many published, and citizens continued for years to whip up odes and songs for special occasions. In commemoration of the Battle of King's Mountain there was in 1810 a celebration with an especial ode. In Nashville after the Battle of New Orleans every window held a lighted candle, and many songs of victory

---

[8] Thwaites-Kellogg, *Dunmore's War*, 435, quoting from W, 3XX(18), 51.
[9] *Ibid.*, 437, quoting W, 8ZZ(18), 54.
[10] W, 2S, 36.

were sung, among them, "The Hunters of Kentucky," honoring the valor
of the Kentuckians.[11]

Old-timers like Colonel Ridley who had fought at Braddock's defeat
may now and then have forgotten themselves and burst into a British
fighting song with a rousing tune.[12] I found no fighting songs among
the pioneers, only mention of battle shouts.

Hymns, too, were widely sung; the works of Watts and Wesley were
ever favorites, appearing in many inventories. They were for the religious
a form of devotion, but even the unbeliever could join in the simple tunes
and words of "How firm a foundation, ye saints of the Lord; have faith,
oh have faith in his excellent word," or "Amazing grace how sweet the
sound that saved a wretch like me." They were sung to put the baby to
sleep, "lined out" in the poorer churches where hymnbooks were few,
taught in singing school, but mostly one suspects sung in the home and
at work for no reason at all save they satisfied the singer.

Many, particularly the Psalms as arranged by Watts, had much of the
simplicity and beauty of language characteristic of the King James Version. Their music, simple but tuneful, lent itself to learning by rote as
well as to all voices. They, too, followed the Bible in that the singular
pronoun was almost always used. The singer could always feel that he or
she was the particular one who was believing, suffering, or on the way to
Paradise. The soul was never merged in the mass; the old-time religion
was for "me"; the singer was untroubled as to how Christian his nation
might be, but his concern was: "Was it for crimes that I had done, He
groaned upon the tree."

Hymns, too, both enriched and softened their religion. As the Indian
menace decreased, God in many of the sermons became a terrible God,

---

[11] Thomas, *Nashville*, 29, 52. Scattered in source materials are the names of
numerous songs and tunes of the day: Draper, *King's Mountain*, 228, 591, 593, mentions many such as "Barney Linn, a favorite jolly tune of the times," sung by a spy.
Bassett, *Jackson Correspondence*, I, 261, "Logan Water," the soldier's dirge; Tennessee *Gazette*, Aug. 19, 1801, a "popular fiddle song, Bobbin Joan." The Kenneth
Rose Music Collection, Reference Department, Tennessee State Library and Archives,
contains many books of popular songs and much sheet music that John Coffee and
others may have bought in Philadelphia: Scott's *Musical Museum* of 1788; *Seven
Songs for the Harpsichord*, Francis Hopkinson, Philadelphia, 1788; *The Vocal Companion and Masonic Register in 2 parts*, Boston, 1802; and the well known *Federal
Harmony*. Popular songs included "Jem of Aberdeen" and "The Unfortunate
Sailor." Also being published by this date and for sale in Philadelphia was a fair
amount of what is by now known as "classical music."

[12] Thwaites-Kellogg, *Dunmore's War*, quoting from "Newell's Journal," 361–362,
gives the words of "Here's health to King George." Less than a year later most of
the singing men had taken the American side.

His hands tight on the doors of salvation, His infinite justice able to embrace the eternal agony of souls in fiery hell, but the hymn was there to give a more comforting picture:

"Oh, bless the Lord my soul; His mercies bear in mind:
Forget not all his benefits; the Lord to thee is kind."

Even the doubting could take comfort from the hymn. There was no hairsplitting theology in a religion that was "tried in the fiery furnace." Such tormenting questions as faith versus works, foreordination and predestination were not about when "Jesus is a rock in the weary land," or when the singer reminded himself, "Must I be carried to the skies on flowery beds of ease?" This hymn like many others was rich in similes, metaphors, and situations that encompassed the world and the whole lot of man. The pioneer sang of "Canaan's fair and happy land"—onyx stone"—"death like a narrow sea"—"streams of living water"—"pomegranates"—"honey and milk"—"cinnamon, saffron, all incense trees"—aloes and myrrh, rings of gold, beautiful city of gold, and of joy and sorrow and pain and death. Over and over he comforted himself, "Then I would smile at Satan's rage/And face a frowning world."

Life with heaven above, hell beneath, and all the aspects of the world from fountains to deserts and rivers and seas were gathered in his songs; so that a man singing in a small and lonely fort was carried by his hymn into a wide rich world, but no matter how big or crowded the world, the lone singer was important:

"Since I can read my title clear
To mansions in the skies
I'll bid farewell to every fear
And wipe my weeping eyes."

Many in going about their work sang and hardly knew they sang. Important as the hymn was during pioneer years, with the hymnbook the most commonly owned book of songs, it undoubtedly comprised a smaller segment of the total singing than in later years. Calvinism was soon to take on a sterner aspect, and as the fiddle, the dance tune, and in some homes even the ballad, were all barred, the hymn became for many their only form of music.

Much older than any work of Watts and Wesley were other devotional songs that were undoubtedly sung by some Cumberland pioneers as they can still be heard in out-of-the-way places. The few that survived might roughly be denominated varieties of *Twelve Songs* as they were sung long ago during the Twelve Days of Christmas, for during pioneer days Christmas was in much of the South as in England a season, the twelve days between Christmas and Twelfth Night, kept with good will and jollity rather than ostentatious religious devotions.[13]

One of the songs celebrating the season was destined for at least two singers or preferably two groups. The first would announce, "I'll sing you a song." The second sang the question, "And what will be your song?" The other answered singing, "I'll sing you a song and one, oh one, is all alone, and never no more shall be so." The asking was repeated twelve times, and each time the answer added one, until, "I'll sing you a song—'Twelve of the twelve apostles, eleven of the eleven that went to heaven, ten of the ten commandments, nine oh nine, how bright they shine, and eight of the Gabriel angels, seven of the seven stars all fixed in the sky, and six of the small bell waiters, five of the bamboo over the bow, and four of the gospel makers, and three of them was drivers, and two of them was little old babes all dressed in darlen green oh, and one oh one is all alone, and never no more shall be so.' " [14] Then the subtraction began until there was left only the one all alone.

This version was only one of several; another still heard at times with the refrain, "Green grow the rushes, oh," is much like the first, though the one may have reached the Cumberland by way of Scotland, the other from England. The best known of these songs is that now called "The Twelve Days of Christmas," though the version on the Cumberland differs somewhat from that commonly found in print.[15]

Much of what the pioneer sang is now completely lost, or at best the tunes forgotten with only scraps of words. There were religious chants twisted into nonsense rhymes, old before America was settled, local

---

[13] Thomas, *Nashville,* 101–102, 104, spoke as did Dr. Johnson of "all through Christmas," and "Christmas week."

[14] I am indebted to Mrs. Grover Foster, Burnside, Ky., for this version, brought by the Frogge family by way of Virginia and Tennessee. The song gains added interest when compared with other versions; I am inclined to think for example that "five of the bamboo over the bow" is a corruption and should yield to something like "Fives' the hymnlers o'er my bower," but that the "six of the small bell waiters" is more apt than the more common, "six of the echoing waters."

[15] Nelly Leander Brooks, *Rugby Sketches,* Rugby, Tenn., 1941, gives, 26, a version of this song as sung in Tennessee that seems to me a much better one than many now found in print; newspapers are inclined to transform the "collie birds" into "calling birds," and out of these it is very hard to get blackbirds.

ballads that lived, died, and left no trace. The average child learned all manner of rhymes, riddles, and tongue twisters, just as he learned the lore of the sky, the woods, and fields—so unconsciously most seemed part of his language instead of amusement or education. Most Cumberland babies like generations of British babies behind them learned their fingers—Thumbkin, Lick Pot, Long Man, Ring Band, Little Peter Playman—and more rhymes and stories for the toes; we children inherited the little pig who cried because he couldn't go. There were scraps of *Mother Goose*, and chuckling games for the eyes and the mouth and the nose, all these with old backbones, but changing and twisting through the generations as did the counting-out rhymes. "Wire Briar Limberlock, three geese in a flock," and all the rest, including the cuckoo, we still chanted in my childhood though the only cuckoo we knew was in a neighbor's clock.

There were innumerable rhyming problems, some learned from books, but many never printed at all, for all mankind has ever loved a good puzzle. There were many that did not rhyme such as that of the man who had to get safely across a river with his geese uneaten by foxes; he, like the boy sent to the spring for a certain amount of water but without a proper unit of measurement, had to use his wits. Most of these, like stories and riddles, were best for winter evenings by the fire when all hands were busied with some routine job—shelling a turn of bread corn on one side while on the other wool cards and knitting needles flew.

Whole families, babies included, went to the house-raisings, log-rollings,[16] and other forms of community workings; many took as did Sevier the slaves with the rest of the family. Such gatherings, or the home when company came to bring enough participants, gave an opportunity for play. Young and old might join in such games as Pussy Wants a Corner, Hide and Seek, Blind Man's Buff, Rotten Egg, Tag, Prisoner's Base, Romps,[17] or divided into two groups and amid much running, laughter, and shouting of cries of "Anthony Over" have tossed and caught a ball thrown over the roof. Bad weather brought out the checkerboard or a slate made into one, while others sat over a game of Fox and Geese played with grains of corn.

Always popular were the many singing games inherited by the pioneer

[16] Gray, *Bishop*, 81, had a logrolling for the purpose of getting ashes for gunpowder, and Anthony Bledsoe was killed just after he had had a logrolling, see W, 31S, 194.
[17] Ellet, *American Revolution*, I, 87, 105, mentions in connection with stories of family life, this and a number of other amusements and games.

—Needle's Eye; [18] London Bridge; The Miller; Cobbler, Cobbler—usually from Scotland and England. Now and then one was Americanized as was "The Old Woman from Germany," though many of its couplets are out of Mother Goose. It was, like Sugar Loaf Town, long remembered in out-of-the-way places, and some children may play it still, the first of two groups singing, "Here comes the old woman from Germany, from Germany, from Germany. Here comes the old woman from Germany with all her children around her." The second group consisting of the old woman and her children had a solo part by the mother, "Won't you please take one of my children, oh; one can knit, the other can sew; one can make fine clothes to show; please take one of my children for the Nancy Tancy Tee." The first group replied, "They're all too black and dirty, dirty, dirty, dirty; they're all too black and dirty for the Nancy Tancy Tee." And they again repeated, "Here comes the old woman. . . ." The Old Woman tried again, beginning, "Won't you please . . ." and ending, "They're just as clean as you are, for the Nancy Tancy Tee." She then repeats the merits of her children. The first group, after repeating the refrain of "Here comes the old woman . . ." relents, and decides, "The finest one that I can see, that I can see; [chooses one] the finest one that I can see may come and work with me." [19]

Long a favorite with young people, and one of the few with a chant American in origin though the action was old was Buffalo. This game may have developed during pioneer years, but it was not until religious faiths became sterner, forbidding all dancing, even Skip-to-my-Lou, that Buffalo became popular. Young boys and girls could then, with no music save the chant, act out, "Come to me, my dear, and give to me your hand / And let us take a social ramble to some far and distant land / Where the hawk shot the buzzard and the buzzard shot the crow / And we all ride around the canebrake and shoot the buffalo." Parents could not object, and boys and girls would join hands and go stepping around the circle, happy in the knowing they were committing no sin.

In many places religion soon forbade not only dancing but all instruments—the guitar, violin, and banjo—commonly used for dance music. The one instrument that continued to be tolerated was the jew's-harp, [20] also the most commonly owned instrument of pioneer days. Small, cheap, handily carried in a coat pocket, it was ideal for the lone man who wanted

[18] Parton, *Jackson*, I, 42, quoting McSkimin's *History of Carrickfergus.*
[19] I am indebted to Mrs. Hulon Dobbs, Keno, Ky., for the words of this game.
[20] DW, I, 7; see also Coffee Papers, 1803, 6¼¢.

to while away some weary watching job, such as boiling tar into pitch, that left his hands free for several minutes at a time. The music was also good for a trudging ride, like going home from mill, or when walking. They were stocked by the dozen by the English merchants in the Illinois of 1768; one of the first settlers on the Cumberland, James Biswell, had one, and they could be had at many general stores.

Years ago I had the privilege of sometimes riding, sometimes walking to church in a back-hill community, where some one of the men or boys in the company would play the jew's-harp while others sang as we traveled along. Playing the harp looked remarkably easy. I tried it; after whanging my teeth and bruising my tongue, I realized that, like the gritting of bread, it was one of those "simple things," not to be lightly undertaken.

Livelier, more suited to the crowd, and also quite commonly owned and stocked in stores was the French harp.[21] However, the favorite of the crowd that wanted to dance was the fiddle, as the pioneer almost always called the violin. At least two violins came with the first settlers, and they continued to come.[22] Most forted farms had a fiddler; sometimes he was black and sometimes he was white, and mostly, we suspect, he played by ear, but whatever his qualifications, he supplied the need for a lively dance tune.

The dulcimer of which so much has been written in connection with our "pure-blooded Anglo-Saxon ancestors," I found not at all during pioneer years, up the river or down. I did in time find two in Pulaski County, Kentucky,[23] but these not until past 1820 after several violins. I hoped for a bagpipe but found none, though Estwick Evans heard in 1815, along with violins and fifes, a bagpipe on the Mississippi. Many of the Cumberlanders were of Scotch descent, and though never found or mentioned, it is not going beyond reason to imagine that some Buchanan, Douglas, McGregor, or Rankin played the bagpipe. On the other hand, one of the occupations listed in the Virginia Size Rolls was that of piper, a fairly

---

[21] Coffee Papers, 1802–1804, commonly list harps at $1 each.

[22] DW, I, 107, 296; *ibid.*, II, 177. Gray, *Bishop*, 127, mentions James Gamble, "fiddler" at Morgan's Station in Sumner County; and now and then notice of a runaway slave speaks of his music-making abilities as Tennessee *Gazette*, Feb. 18, 1801, Judge McNairy's "Negro fellow—plays well upon the violin."

[23] PW, II, 261. Listed with a trumpet, $1.12½, this dulcimer sold for $4.25 in 1825. Several years later, *ibid.*, III, A, 626, a dulcimer brought only 50¢ as compared to "1 school harp and case $3.00." Guitars were often homemade; Mr. Grover Foster, Burnside, Ky., described for me the traditional method; violins were less commonly made, though Mr. Lee Keeney of Colo, Ky., many years ago owned one he had made.

common skill during colonial days, as the British army even when deep in the backwoods almost always marched to a drum and fife, this last the instrument commonly played by the piper. Francis Baily heard drums and fife in the vicinity of Knoxville, but no traveler through Middle Tennessee mentioned either.

There were, of course, in the wealthier homes, harpsichords and soon pianos, but their music comprised little of the spontaneous, widely enjoyed amusement afforded by the violins and harps. The learning to play the piano with a teacher and music sheets from Philadelphia might better be considered a part of the educations of many young ladies than a community pastime. There were other forms of music, though little in evidence. The German settlers on White's Creek would be expected to own winds, woodwinds, tympani, and strings, but we know of only one, a flute, played by Frederic Kapp in a religious service.[24] It seems safe to say that as the population increased, instrumental music was, at least for some years, less commonly heard. There appear to have been no community or military bands, for during the War of 1812, Thomas Hart Benton advertised in a local paper for a "band of martial music." [25]

The Cumberlander supplied most of his musical needs with his tongue. The biggest exception was the dance tune, and the pioneer's love of dancing doubtless explains why fiddles were brought by pack horse through the hard cold of 1779-1780. The first settlers brought with them a variety of dances handed down through many generations of dancing Scots and English. Dancing had long been a favorite amusement in the Southern colonies, especially among the gaiety-loving descendants of Tidewater,[26] though of course not all of Tidewater was gay, any more than all Scotch–Irish were thin-lipped and dour.

There were dances of all descriptions, ranging from the stately quadrilles and reels in the many-servanted mansion after a dining, to the "squatting dance" of the boatman, done in a ring of watchers on some hard-packed riverside with no music save handclappings and cries. One could a few years ago still find an occasional "squatting-dancer" in the hills, usually a soloist or at most a couple, their Cossacklike leapings learned from their fathers. I never knew if what I saw was the remnant of the Sailor's Hornpipe, steps from an ancient Scottish sword dance, something

[24] Williams, *Travels*, Schweinitz, "Report," 515.

[25] Nashville *Clarion*, Dec. 15, 1812.

[26] Fithian and many others gave firsthand accounts of dancing and balls in Virginia; one of the most exact descriptions is that of Burnaby, *Travels*, 57–58; he in late colonial days found the Virginians "inordinately fond of dancing."

learned from a wandering Cossack generations before, or picked up in Russia by a Huguenot taking temporary refuge there and in time brought to America.

Life in the old West was never too rugged to prevent the enjoyment of a dance. A soldier writing of a ball George Rogers Clark gave at The Falls in the winter of 1778 remembered, "the ladies did look very different when they were dressed in their ball clothes—and the General lead off with a jig." [27] Clark had just got a boatload of rum and sugar up from Kaskaskia, and this was reason enough to invite his neighbors for several days' dancing and feasting. Christmas, as at Eaton's in 1781, was more commonly than not celebrated by a dance, as was any other eventful day or special occasion—marriage, Twelfth Night, the Fourth of July, the visit of a noted man, and for the less sophisticated the finish of a logrolling or a house-raising. Indians, few neighbors, and rough puncheon floors when in winter they could not use the hard-packed earth in the fort enclosure never prevented a dance, and early, one could in Nashville buy a book of country dances.[28]

Judge Guild wrote in his old age of the dances to violin music on the hard-packed earth of the fort yard: the Virginia reel in which "twenty couples faced and eyed each other"—"Jenny, put the kettle on; Molly, blow the bellows strong; we'll all take tea"—"Leather Britches full of stitches"—"Billy in the wild woods"—and "Nappycot and petticoat and the linsey gown, if you want to keep your credit up pay your money down." [29] Miss Jane Thomas who came to Nashville in 1804 when she was four years old remembered the country dances near Nashville where they danced until midnight, and then had tea cakes, biscuit and butter, coffee, nuts, and apples. She remembered, too, a wedding of the leading colored citizens of Nashville; General and Mrs. Jackson attended as did Judge McNairy who danced a reel with the bride.[30]

Many in their social lives were somewhat like John Sevier. There were for him and his family house-raisings, corn huskings, last days of school, celebrations of Saint Patrick's Day, and all manner of affairs that were in a sense community gatherings, but Sevier also, sometimes with his wife and sometimes without, attended teas, dinings, and balls with the Blounts and other first families, not open to the general public. Beginning often

[27] W, 32S, 413.
[28] Tennessee *Gazette*, Dec. 25, 1802; *ibid.*, April 13, 1803.
[29] Guild, *Old Times*, 43.
[30] Thomas, *Nashville*, 22.

with an "elegant dining," the grand ball, informal on the surface, yet exclusive—kin and friends instead of all the neighbors—soon had an important place in the social life of Middle Tennessee.

Sevier's short visit in 1797 was a quick whirl of social affairs. He had of his dinings and balls in East Tennessee usually written "nice ball," or "grand ball," but of the ball Judge McNairy, then living just west of Nashville across the Lick Branch, gave for him he wrote,[31] "a handsome and elegant ball." And elegant it no doubt was, for Judge McNairy, though a sober, straight-laced man, continued to give great affairs, and twenty-five years later Captain John Donelson wrote of one he had just attended: "I did suppose there was upwards of two hundred persons, everything that was grand and splendid was displayed in the brightest color—cost two or three hundred dollars." [32] Measured in pork and days' wages, the hundreds would be thousands today. Judge Guild wrote much of the balls and dinings in Middle Tennessee of later days. One of the grandest was that given by Red DuBarry in 1804 to celebrate the winning of his race horse Gray Medley. It opened with General Jackson and Mrs. Hall, sister of the hostess, leading the grand march.[33] This ball, like many others, was given on short notice, and in the large household with a well stocked pantry and plenty of help, little or no notice was needed.

Miss Jane Thomas recalled how the ladies kept nice things in the house so "they might prepare for company at a moment's notice . . . for the ladies used to try to surpass each other in the elegance of their dinings." There would be one table for meats, another for candy, cakes, and fruit with sillibub and boiled custard in the center. Another table held tea, coffee, and chocolate plus a bowl of toddy with baked apples in it. Everybody sat down and "at each place there was a small pie, made in patty pans. The first course was always soup, rich and highly seasoned, then came a large boiled fish, elegantly cooked and served with Irish potatoes, then followed boiled ham and turkeys dressed with oysters, roast beef and all kinds of vegetables." There were, in addition to the sillibubs and custards, "rich desserts of boiled puddings with rich sauce," and the "ladies

[31] Sevier's brief account of this trip to Middle Tennessee, THM, V, 235–236, gives a lively picture of social life in 1797—"dined and tarried one night at James Robertson's"; there was the Judge's ball, and dinings at the Maclains, the Joel Lewises, the Tates, and he also stopped with Robert Hays of Haysboro who the previous year had entertained Michaux.
[32] Burke, *Emily Donelson*, I, 99.
[33] Guild, *Old Times*, 245.

always kept calf-heel jelly on hand and dried beef and cakes of every description." [34]

Good, but nothing to compare with later banquets such as that Mrs. Jacob McGovack gave for Felix Grundy, the food prepared by caterers brought up from New Orleans, that when it came to banquets surpassed anything known in the rest of the country. Still, Rachel Jackson in her unasked for role as wife of the conquering hero found the many through which she sat, including one that featured among many other elegancies a gilded ham, but little to her liking.[35]

Less elegant and more of an American development was the "big dinner" for men only. Democratic in that it drew from all strata of society from Daniel Smith down to the small farmer or workingman able to afford the price—usually a dollar—it almost always had political overtones. Politics colored in one way or another much of life, but the Cumberlander's politics is not easily defined; a good deal of it had little to do with the art and science of government and none could be reduced to a simple theory acceptable to any two men. The pattern, if there were a pattern, changed from point to point and year to year; the Cumberland was, for example, after the election of Jefferson more inclined to view the Federal Government, if not with love, at least with less distaste.

The barrels of whiskey and pounds of ham consumed in the cause of Jefferson and Burr in Tennessee between the electioneering in 1799 and the loud, wet dinners of celebration in the spring of 1801 were never toted up. One also wonders how any man was able to do more than lie on his back and whisper after such a dinner as that held at Sommerville's Tavern in Knoxville in the summer of 1799. All the great of Tennessee came, and as usual drank, along with and after the dinner, sixteen toasts, with mighty cheers after each. In May of 1801 much the same group gathered for the still louder and wetter dinner celebrating victory. The first of these was held at Henderson's Springs in Sumner County. Daniel Smith was President of the day, and Andrew Jackson, Vice-President; John Overton and other important men were there along with "three or four hundred farmers." Dinner was served at four o'clock and in addition to the sixteen planned toasts there were four extra, with the usual cheers. Men of the old West were by this date growing fonder of their Federal Constitution, and thus the toast to it brought sixteen cheers as did Thomas

[34] Thomas, *Nashville*, 39.
[35] Bassett, *Jackson Correspondence*, VI, 450.

Jefferson and the "Fair of Tennessee." There were, however, only nine for Burr; Freedom of Speech, Press, and Religion; and past these the company was undoubtedly weary, for each of the remaining toasts brought less than nine cheers each. Wearier still many such as Jackson must have been when, after a long horseback ride through the wilderness, the whole celebration had to be gone through again only a week later in Knoxville.[36]

Politics in Kentucky was much more all embracing, entering into most of life, the diverting side included. One of the more prolific areas for tall tales was the old Green River District that embraced most of the Kentucky counties drained by the Cumberland. One of its most colorful as well as versatile characters was Matthew Lyon, "by the bulls that bought me Lyon," who had a boatyard, printing office, and store down at Eddyville, which activities he often advertised in the early Nashville newspapers. "Colonel Lyon," Micah Taul, then clerk of Wayne County, wrote, "was a man of Herculean frame and constitution—could drink grog all day long without getting drunk; tell pretty good rough anecdotes, and take him altogether was a good 'electioneer.' His having been a victim of the Sedition Law, however, did more for him than everything else. His opponent was an accomplished Virginia gentleman—a man of respectable talents and attainments—a good speaker; but old Lyon generally got him drunk before dinner time and in that way triumphed over him.

"I think it was possibly in 1803, they were drinking in a Whiskey Tavern, at Somerset in Pulaski County, at the July Court; the day was very warm and Maj. David Walker fell early in the action. Lyon got him on a bed in the room, called for a fan and sat by him and fanned him, requesting the people, as the day was very warm, to give him as much air as possible, saying that the Major was an excellent man, but unfortunately he sometimes drank too much. The good people of Pulaski who witnessed the attention of the 'old sinner' to his competitor were completely imposed upon by the trick—sounded his praises and voted for him because they believed he was a kind-hearted, good old man." [37]

Matthew Lyon's ability to drink his opponents under the table was matched with an equal ability at eating; other stories concerned his mammoth appetite, especially for strawberries. Whatever Lyon or any other politician did was only the beginning; stories of their activities like those told by Judge Guild of later days and hundreds of others in some

[36] Nashville *Intelligencer*, Aug. 28, 1799; Tennessee *Gazette*, May 20, 1801; *ibid.*, May 27, 1801, are detailed accounts of these banquets.
[37] RK, XXVII, Taul, "Memoirs," 18–19.

way concerned with politics would be told and retold, each growing a bit in the telling.

Most such stories were heard by the tavern crowd. Unimposing as the taverns in the small towns were they drew farmers from the whole of a county, particularly during the three days of election. Micah Taul told many stories of election campaigns, the tavern the background, the great joke it was when a man down from the back hills ate heartily of one campaigner's free dinner, drank heartily of his free whiskey, and in a loud voice voted for his opponent.

The tavern, too, was often the scene of a Fourth of July celebration, and in 1799 Sommerville's tavern in Knoxville drew men from all over Tennessee to a great patriotic dinner with the usual toasts and cheers, though this dinner like most Fourth of July dinners and celebrations held throughout the United States, was larded with politics for the Jefferson campaign was on.

As a rule, however, the Fourth of July dinner overflowed any tavern and like many great dinners and soon barbecues was held outdoors. Such a one was that in Nashville of 1801. The day began early with the firing of artillery; next, came the parade around the town square, led by members of the Mechanics Society. The parade finished and the crowd assembled in front of the courthouse; thirteen-year-old Joel Lewis delivered an oration. It was then time to sit down to dinner served up to five hundred men, and all in all much like the victory dinner at Henderson's Springs two months before, save that it was noisier with gunfire added to the cheers after each toast that included such sentiments as "The alien and sedition laws, oblivion to their principles and eternal disgrace to their advocates," and ". . . perpetual itching without benefit of scratching to the enemies of America." The only cloud on the day was that Jackson was ill at Hunter's Hill, but a letter from him was read to the assembled company.[38] The Fourth of July celebration of 1803 featured a liberty pole on the public square, the usual procession with seven discharges of artillery, an "elegant dinner" with seventeen planned toasts, and after all this "the ladies assembled and all partook of a hop and supper."[39]

Big dinners were given for a variety of reasons. "Shipp's famous elk dinner" of 1806 was held because hunters had killed the by-then rare elk and they wanted everybody to at least taste elk meat.[40] Horse racing also

[38] Tennessee *Gazette*, July 8, 1801.
[39] *Ibid.*, July 13, 1803.
[40] W, 28S, 8.

gave, in addition to an opportunity for gambling, a chance for those who had most of the day to spare to dine together. There were by the end of the pioneer period several race courses within riding distance of most farmers of Middle Tennessee. In July, races were run over the Nashville Course; August brought sweepstake racing at Gallatin; while Clover Bottom down near the mouth of Stone's River was the scene of spring and fall meets.[41]

Women as a rule came only for the races while the men, particularly owners, took dinner together at a long outdoor table, food served by borrowed help in borrowed dishes.[42] The organization of racing clubs and horse-breeding associations gave still more opportunities for men to wine and dine together; best known was the Nashville Jockey Club,[43] though it was not organized until past the pioneer period.

Still, colorful as these public festivities were and common as balls and dinings came to be, the two groups together seem never to have been so important in the overall picture of social life on the Cumberland as the sometimes spontaneous and usually informal visits and dinners and dances enjoyed by a wider circle. The middle-class farmer and his wife never knew dinings with champagne, but company dinners and wedding suppers were ever a part of their lives. Most had no table wines, instead a barrel of whiskey handy for all comers. A country wedding after the end of Indian troubles might call for the slaughter of fifteen to twenty turkeys and half as many fattening pigs with corresponding quantities of vegetables and pastries, enough to serve two or three hundred kith and kin.[44]

In spite of the large number of guests, the buffet seems never to have been resorted to in the early years. If temporary tables, borrowed dishes, chairs, and help were insufficient to feed everybody at one time, there were successive tables. The older and more important guests would eat at the first table, a mark of respect. Joseph Bishop remembered in his old age how he, then only a penniless hunter, had in 1793 eaten at the first table with a visiting preacher.[45] First table finished, dishes were washed, fresh servings of food dished up, and a second table begun. The guests at the wedding of one of Sevier's daughters spent the night; but the need for a second table or even a third or fourth table did not necessarily signify a special occasion such as a wedding or a burial. Sevier's notations in his

[41] Tennessee *Gazette*, Aug. 22, 1804; *ibid.*, March 27, 1805.
[42] Parton, *Jackson*, I, 341, described one in which Jackson had a fight.
[43] Nashville *Clarion*, April 30, 1811.
[44] Guild, *Old Times*, 351–356.
[45] Gray, *Bishop*, 48–49.

journal of whole families come home with him from church for Sunday dinner,[46] could have been made by thousands of farmers before and since. It hasn't been too many years since my neighbor, a prosperous hill farmer, had thirty-two people for breakfast; this, during a revival—services had continued late and the farmer and his wife had prevailed upon others further from the church to spend the night.

"Spend the night" in a Southern home did not necessarily mean, save for the very young, much sleeping, any more than waiting at the mill meant sitting still. The whole pattern of life as we know it today with its numerous long and often silent waits—sitting in a car or plane or train, standing in line at the self-service store, or sitting hour after hour in a doctor's office—were unknown to most people of that day. Even the very old man was seldom content to sit in complete idleness; if nothing else he could whittle. There was no form of travel save that by carriage over a good road, and that a rarity, that left the body completely idle; most women never sat in idleness but carried with them sewing or fancy work, and save at the grand ball or the formal dinner, sewing or knitting while carrying on a conversation was not considered bad manners.

Unaccustomed to inactivity from birth, the young overflowed with energy. Hunting in dangerous Indian territory still left John Lewallen, for instance, so much energy that after putting up his open-faced camp he must go jumping back and forth over the ridge poles, but when attacked by Indians he still had plenty of strength for the fighting.[47] Depending on the season and the make-up of the crowd, the tedium of waiting for the second table or the coming of the mail was relieved by several pastimes, almost never peculiar to the pioneer, but enjoyed at one time or another by most of America and the British Isles. Whittling, horse-swapping, knife-throwing, extemporaneous contests of physical agility such as jumping high enough to crack the heels together three times, wrestling, chinning, weight lifting, throwing the long bullet, or a game of horseshoes were all amusements common for generations in much of the rural United States.[48] Troops waiting to march to Nickojack in 1794 amused themselves with foot races; Sandy Donelson as usual won, for he was long the champion runner of pioneer Middle Tennessee.[49]

[46] THM, V, Sevier, "Journal," 168, 183, 184; the journal contains almost constant references to visits and visitors.

[47] W, 30S, 243.

[48] Most travelers and those who wrote of childhoods on the borders mention a variety of sports; see in particular, RK, XXVII, Taul, "Memoirs," 13.

[49] A, V, 201, quoting Joseph Brown from the Draper Manuscripts.

More formalized, and much more common on the Southern frontier and the old Southwest than other regions, was the shooting match. This often took the form of a turkey shoot to which tickets were sold with the marksmen allowed to take the birds killed; others had only marks and in these prizes were given. However, in a world where the carrying of firearms was the rule rather than the exception, much shooting was done just for the fun of learning who in the crowd was the best shot, and with no thought of a prize. Equally spontaneous and unformalized was most hunting during the early years, that is, it should be remembered, after the end of Indian warfare. Any hunting done before 1795 in Middle Tennessee might better be classed as a dangerous occupation done for food or peltry, but after the country was safe from Indians, the woods were an endless source of amusement for young and old—through them men, women, children, parties of boys and girls hunted all manner of things from squirrels for scalp bounties to chestnuts, pawpaws, and wild grapes. Most such hunting was like most pastimes—a mixture of work and play. The squirrel "scalps" were acceptable for taxes just as wolf heads had been on the Virginia frontier fifty years before or in Wales at a much earlier date. Everybody wanted plenty of chestnuts for winter use, but the gathering of them was fun. The river also offered many amusements; boating, swimming for boys, pearl hunting, picnic parties, but most of all fishing, that often included all the others. In the early days, Easter Monday was always set aside for a fishing party enjoyed by both boys and girls.[50]

Few amusements had such an especial day. Most hunting, for many years to come, was done in the spontaneous, unformalized fashion in which the Cumberlander liked to do things. Fox hunting as carried on in Tidewater after the English fashion in red coats, and with not a little ceremony, in time reached Middle Tennessee, but even now a man needs neither red coat nor horse to have a good fox hunt, though he does need a good hound. There are still men on the Cumberland who will spend time and money on foxhounds just for the love of a good fox chase. Usually the hunter never sees fox or even hounds once the race has begun, and seldom does he ever catch a good strong-legged, sharp-witted fox. At the end of a race he has nothing more than a memory of sound, but this memory plus the knowing he has a fine hound is to him more than many silver cups or wreaths of roses. As long as there were deer to hunt they were often chased with hounds, and many a hunter like Joseph Bishop

50 Thomas, *Nashville*, 105.

had the usual mingling of fun and work in listening to the hounds and hoping to overtake the deer.[51]

The children, like the women, might never go on a fox hunt but they could share in some of the hound-dog music and never leave the porch. Many amusements of children were just such casual sharings, and in spite of a lack of spectator sports and organized recreation, many had a more diverting and interesting childhood than have most children today. Compared to today's child, the lot of the average farm boy or girl was not easy. Children were economic assets in a world where everybody's work was needed. Added to this were long walks to a school in which education was often rigorous and usually uncomfortable—rough benches in a poor building, cold in winter; the heat of summer intensified by seed ticks and chigger bites. Still, there was fun on the way to and from school; long recesses gave an opportunity for playing with other children of one's own sex and age, enjoyable but not then considered important as today. Church might mean long and tedious sermons, but the picnic dinner afterward was something to look forward to, for the more religious families who went quite a distance to church as did the Drakes took their dinners.

The most constant playmate for many pioneer children was the world itself. There were dragons in the thunder "heads" and chariot wheels in the rain on the clapboards, and races down the pasture hill against the shadows of flying clouds. What with indirect lighting our children can never know the joy of shadow pictures on the wall, awesome and witchlike in bright flickering firelight, or merely funny little donkeys or rabbits by grease-lamp or candlelight. There were witches, elves, and goblins in the fireplace flames, castles in the sunset, and real flutter wheels in the millrace. Little girls, who never saw a dollhouse, built, as did later generations, playhouses in the woods with acorn cups for dishes and carpets of moss wondrously thick and soft, and like their brothers created worlds of make-believe; even their games such as Sugar Loaf Town and Needle's Eye called for imagination. There were baptizings and burials in the autumn leaves, and over them shouts of salvation or funeral sermons; there were make-believe weddings, balls, and long trips on a limestone boat in a river of leaves.

Boys enjoyed many of these things with the girls and as always played at war, but with no toy soldiers. Joseph Bishop in the back parts of Virginia had a corn-stalk navy on his father's tan vat, and hunted deer with a cane-stalk gun. Dr. Daniel Drake on the Kentucky border where

[51] Gray, *Bishop*, 29–30.

life was uncomplicated by Indians grew up in a home stricter than most and with no help for much of the time save the family, but childhood fun and pastimes were a daily part of life. When a little boy he enjoyed, as did country people everywhere, watching the big road, conveyances, horses and people, going slowly enough a child could see the dress, study the faces, and wonder on the strangers. Older, he learned the fun and wonder of the woods while bee hunting, sugar making, or cow hunting; these, like the rest of life, work at the bottom, but never all work; sharing the woods with him was his dog, "Old Lion."

Children lived without the Easter Bunny, but Easter was in many homes celebrated in various ways, chiefly with colored eggs given as love tokens or used in egg rollings as in Scotland.[52] The Christmas season was marked by firecrackers, general jollity, and above all feasting—turkeys dressed with oysters, baked hams, plum puddings with rich wine sauce, and sillibub.[53] Country people seldom had the last two or even oysters, but there were roasted geese and hams, plates of high stack-pies, with cakes of all description, and shotgun and anvil blasts added to the firecrackers.

We can be certain there were hilarious times when on New Year's Eve of 1792 a group in Sumner County held an American version of the Court of Fools. Robert Hays was "Lord Chief Joker and General Humbugger of North America West of the Appalachian Mountains," but his brother-in-law, Andrew Jackson, acted for him and appointed wealthy bachelor George Winchester, "Lieutenant Colonel Commandant of the Regiment of the Cyprian Goddess."[54]

Many amusements such as horse racing were seasonal in nature, but cards like dancing knew no season, and the various card games were popular on the frontier as they had been in the Southern colonies and Europe. Sevier mentions many a game of whist, now and then winning or losing small sums, though a most devout and religious man, for during early years no religion frowned upon card playing any more than dancing. Ideas of good and evil changed quickly, and soon John Smith in stricter Stockton's Valley was, in order to escape the anger of his stern father, sneaking off to the woods with companions to enjoy a game.[55]

[52] Parton, *Jackson*, I, 42, quoting McSkimin, described the egg rollings of Scotland; Anburey, *Travels*, I, 500–501, traveling in western Virginia during the Revolution, mentioned the custom of exchanging colored eggs at Easter, seemingly new to him, an Englishman.

[53] Thomas, *Nashville*, 101–102, 104.

[54] W, 6XX, 117.

[55] Williams, *Smith*, 29.

Micah Taul in nearby Monticello blamed cards and the consequent gambling for the loss of a fair start in life. It was hard to stay away from the card table, for cards, like strong drink and the offer to swap horses, were met at all gatherings from the muster to the group sitting up with the dead.

Sevier also played billiards [56] and, though not found mentioned in the very early years, billiard tables were fairly common in Middle Tennessee tax lists by 1803. Both Kentucky and Tennessee had laws forbidding "excessive gambling," but little attempt was made to enforce these among the really heavy gamblers—the gentry. There was, too, little popular feeling against gambling of any kind.[57] The Cumberland merchant, following an old and common custom, often sold his goods by lottery; the buyer of a ticket was assured of getting some little something for his money, and there was always the chance he might get gold ear bobs, a locket for his lady, or a set of saws for a cotton gin.[58]

Another old sport that gave ample opportunity for gambling was cockfighting, but, different from horse racing, it was frowned upon by the more conservative element and was not commonly attended by females. On the Cumberland even the most religious, such as Rachel Jackson, went to the races, with or without a husband, but I found no woman at a cockfight. A widely advertised match could draw champion cocks and high-betting spectators from an area of several hundred square miles. Such a series of fights was held on Christmas Day of 1798 at Winchester, Kentucky. The public square of the town was given up to the event. A pit was dug in the center, an amphitheatre built around it, with admissions of twenty-five and fifty cents, depending on the nature of the seats. The opposing cocks came from Lexington and the Slate Furnace about thirty miles to the east, and "for days before," a boy who was there remembered in his old age, "nothing was to be seen but the preparation for this cock fight. Nothing else was heard or talked about. . . . They were

[56] THM, V, Sevier, "Journal," has numerous references to all manner of games including billiards in 1794, but he said nothing of having won or lost, 171; he more commonly played cards, usually whist, and often mentioned the result, 162, "won one guinea at whist," or 177, "won at whist."

[57] "Minutes of Fishing Creek (Ky.) Baptist Church," typescript furnished by Mrs. A. S. Frye, reveal that as late as 1814 a member asked, 12, "Is it right to purchase a ticket in a lottery?" Answer, "Not Right." There is no record that tenets of other Protestant faiths at this time forbade it.

[58] Announcements of lotteries appear in the earliest newspapers and continue through the years: *Rights of Man*, July 17, 1799, John Nelson announces a lottery; Tennessee *Gazette*, Sept. 21, 1803—a lottery of 200 tickets at $3. each with "an elegant gold watch" as first prize; *ibid.*, Feb. 1, 1804—1200 tickets at $2. each—prizes here were land, cows, a cotton gin, etc.

to fight the best six out of eleven . . . at least the winner had to come off
conqueror six times to win, and my recollection is that they fought 11
battles. . . . There was an immense crowd. . . . I never witnessed more
betting on any occasion, not even a race track." [59]

Well attended as were cockfights and horse races, spectator sports
formed a much smaller percentage of the total amusement of the people
than they do today, but any spectacle, especially a branding or a hanging,
was certain of a large crowd. The last day of school like the public
examinations of academy pupils drew overflow audiences, for all were
eager to see the young act their farces and speak their pieces and the older
pupils sweat through the questionings of the examiners. In East Tennessee
hundreds gathered yearly to watch the ball play of the Cherokee.[60] In the
later part of the period, camp meetings also drew great crowds; some
came in the name of religion, others for amusement only, and others hoping for a little of both.

Many of the more distasteful jobs of life held some element of amusement or at least sociability. Working a road on a hot July day and earning
not one penny was no fun, but everybody had to do it. The road-working
like the muster gave a man a good excuse to get away from home and
out of work, or so the women, left to wrestle with work and children,
sometimes complained. Men of the Cumberland, no different from men
elsewhere, had at the direction of the county court to furnish a road hand
for each poll. These gathered at the appointed time and place, this in the
immediate neighborhood, so that, different from the trip to the county
seat to vote which sometimes kept a man three days, the road-working
did not customarily keep him overnight, but it was still a good way to
meet the other men of the neighborhood for an exchange of news and
gossip. It was a little like the house-raising; work got done, but along with
the work there was fun, whiskey, and rich working side by side with
poor, though so quickly did the world change that by 1804 the man able
to send three polls did not have to go.

The muster to which all free men between eighteen and forty-five had
to go was a different story, for I never found anything to indicate that
anybody did anything save have a good time. Women for generations
quarreled about the muster, nothing but an excuse to take a man away
from home and let him run wild and drink and gamble and sometimes

---

[59] RK, XXVII, Taul, "Memoirs," 12–13.

[60] The Bourbon Princes were so pleased by the ball play of the Cherokee in 1797,
they gave the winners six gallons of rum, see Williams, *Travels*, "Tour of the Dukes,"
437.

fight, they always said. One should add that the men also sang songs and ate gingerbread.

Tennessee like other states passed acts for musters, stipulating dates, arms and ammunition, even the size of the muster-master's horse. He was supposed to be at least fourteen hands high, but it is doubtful if any muster-master rode such a small animal, for he was a very grand person indeed, the muster-master. Farragut remembered how fine his father looked in his muster-master's uniform with a cockade of white horsehair; Miss Jane Thomas remembered that her father as a muster-master near Nash-ville in the early 1800's had worn white pants and vest, a red and blue cloth coat trimmed with brass buttons, sword and belt, ruffled shirt, high boots, with the whole surmounted by a crescent-shaped hat trimmed with a cockade and a silver eagle. How much influence the muster-master had in teaching military discipline and drill is a question. Young John Smith from Stockton's Valley spoke of the "merriement and dissipation" [61] of the muster where he would sing his best songs, but nobody mentioned anything that pertained to the art of war.

It was in this atmosphere of gingerbread and songs, the man on the Cumberland exercised his one right to vote for office at the local level—in this case the lower ranking of the officers of the muster. Feeling between contenders and their backers for a captaincy could run high, ending sometimes in fights, "fist and skull—biting, gouging, etc." At such times the onlooker had the not-too-unusual mingling of amusement, politics, and the military life—and something to tell when he got home.

Women as a group had fewer formalized amusements than men, though they shared more completely in the overall lives of their menfolks than do women today, a thing true of most farm families whether pioneers or no. Women got as do women today much pleasure from many forms of needlework, some of it like many other things in life, part work, part amusement. The family might get along without fancy stitching on each square of the silk and velvet crazy quilt, another braided rug, or knitted lace on the pillow slips, but such things were nice to have and fun to make.[62]

I found no mention of any woman's organization, but the average

[61] Williams, *Smith*, 44.
[62] The Tennessee State Museum has many interesting examples of early needlework and much can be found in private homes. What must have been an outstanding example was that Mrs. Blount and other leading ladies of East Tennessee lavished upon a standard presented to General Jackson in token of his victory at New Orleans. Parton, *Jackson*, I, 383, wrote with enthusiastic detail of its stars, sprigs of laurel, balls, pontoons, swords, etc.

middle-class man on the Cumberland had, from earliest days, to attend many meetings of every description. In a world where everything had to be created from fort to county, there was a deal of talking to be done; early groups were often informal, met by chance, and took advantage of the meeting to discuss a hunting trip or the need for hiring another scout. Later, definitely organized bodies of men such as the trustees of Davidson Academy and soon Cumberland College gave much time and mind to organizing and running schools, banks, and soon a library in Nashville.

In addition to these bodies and the churches that were just getting organized and into buildings by the end of the pioneer period, there was a Philosophical Society, the Mechanics Society already mentioned, various racing and horse-breeding associations, but oldest, largest, and most in evidence was that of Masonry, well established in the United States by the time of the Revolution. The organization flourished and by early 1800 there was in Nashville a Masonic Hall and a membership large and rich enough to pay elaborate funeral honors to George Washington.[63]

The fair in some form had been important for centuries in many countries of the world before the Cumberland was settled. Tennessee laws were passed at an early date creating county fairs, or at least the time and the grounds for race course and exhibit halls, but none became an actuality during pioneer years; in time most counties on the Cumberland had one, though in some sections "Mule Day" was a greater event than the fair. However, Nashville with neither fair nor Mule Day ever had something to offer. Early, the town was visited by many traveling shows; in 1805 Duff and Arnold offered for only fifty cents admission to entertain with slack-wire dancing along with the great-grandfather of the moving picture—"magical deceptions" formed by a "new Philosophical apparatus which will exhibit 100 figures as large as life in brilliant colors." Also around was a "patent physiogonist," who would for only fifty cents make "four correct likenesses in profile."[64] There was for a time even a waxworks with "life-like figures" and a great organ to furnish music for the viewers.[65] Middle Tennessee ever had money enough to pay for enter-

---

[63] Tennessee *Gazette*, Feb. 25, 1800, gave much space to this ceremony in which half of Nashville must have taken part; there were young ladies dressed in black satin that included black turbans; young ladies all in white satin, a vast array of pennants, banners, emblems, gold wands, etc.

[64] Tennessee *Gazette*, April 17, 1805.

[65] Nashville *Clarion*, Sept. 16, 1812.

tainment—a ball for Lafayette, a seat for Jenny Lind, or, earlier, a man ascending and descending by balloon.

There was a constant effort to increase the number of diversions, as in 1811 the Thespian Society put on both *Speed the Plough* and *The Way to Get Married*,[66] but even without any special attraction Nashville had much to offer. The backwoods boy might gape at fine gentlemen with blooded horses, elegant ladies, top-hatted coachmen, non-English speaking visitors from far places, while the visitor himself might be amazed at what he found. And always the visitor, a Michaux or a Featherstonhaugh or a flatboatman from our world up river, come down on a falling tide, each got what everybody on the Cumberland loved—something to tell when he got home.

The entertainments, the organizations, the games, and all the rest can in the end give but a meager idea of the pastimes of a people who enjoyed living, and found themselves in a world so abundant, so varied as that of the Cumberland. I like to think of some nameless boy riding near twilight down the old road that led past General Daniel Smith's Rock Castle to the river and the ferry there. The boat is on the other side and the boy must wait, maybe until the ferryman has finished his supper. Though supperless still, the boy does not fume or fret, but rather misses the barn chores, as he had wanted another look at the new colt. Nobody will quarrel at him; for he has been at work, leaving home not much past daylight with cold biscuit, gingerbread, and bacon in his wallet, a turn of wheat behind. There were closer mills, but Winchester's ground the finest flour, and there his mother sent him, for his older sister is getting married come three weeks next Saturday.

While waiting his turn at the mill, he had for a time watched the water wheel and the machinery; as the early September Saturday grew hotter, he had sneaked a swim up the creek, fed and watered his horse, then hungry himself and thirsty, he had washed down his lunch with a mug of toddy from the tavern; next, he had visited General Winchester's store, bought writing paper and a Morse's *Geography* just in from Philadelphia, and caught a glimpse of one of the beautiful Winchester daughters. He had then sat awhile in the shade, thinking to read in Morse, but a knot of men whittling on the store porch had been more attractive, for they talked of two Frenchmen come by water from St. Genevieve, and met on the way up river to buy a load of tar.

His turn had come at last, and now he sat his horse and listened to the

[66] *Ibid..* Oct. 15, 1811.

whip-poor-wills and katydids, and as twilight deepened watched the Big Dipper come into the sky. Then as he waited, listening for the clank of chain on wood to say the ferryboat had started, he saw a rush of whiteness like a cloud, and wished he could have seen the flustered swan rise out of the water; they were so few now. A moment later he heard clearly from up river, the Frenchmen; they had found their tar, and dark though it was, were traveling still, their oars keeping time to the song:

"Derrière Chez nous, il y a un stang
　　ye, ye ment
　Trois Canards s'en vont baigans
　　Tous du long de la rivière . . ." [67]

He wished he could see the men, but more than anything he wished he could sing their song. The words would not come and so he whistled the tune, and somewhere out in the half dark the ferryman answered whistling.

[67] There must have been hundreds of versions of this song, sung over most of Canada and the Mississippi Valley; Bradbury, *Travels 1811*, 39, heard it in the neighborhood of St. Louis and translated it thusly: "Behind our house there is a pond, Fal, lal, de ra / There came three ducks to swim there on—." As in other versions the ducks were killed by the prince with the silver gun.

Epilogue

Now, AFTER the long searching, the miles traveled, the manuscripts read, the librarians bothered, the authentications of handed-down tales searched out, I should have a bundle of gleanings, some pattern of life for the old dead on the Cumberland; something I can wrap in adjectives and label truth. The trouble is that many facts do not make a truth. And what is truth? Finding it I might not know it. I cannot say of even one first settler he was exactly thus and so at all times in his life. The nameless boy riding home from mill would laugh at me for trying, as would his sister milking in the twilight. Even new milk from the same cow and fresh-ground flour from the one crop of wheat were not always the same, and among the people who used them there was even less sameness.

There are many fitting words of quality—courage, generosity, hardihood, concern for others in the face of danger, tenacity. Yet, no one of these was the sole property of the pioneers. Nor did such attributes guarantee a success in pioneering. Nothing guaranteed success, and if untimely death or loss of land and goods be failure, then most were failures. Many failed in spite of having the two prime requirements for any pioneer—complete mastery of the long learning needed to live in the woods as a civilized human being in spite of enemy Indians, and confidence in the ability to do so. The pioneer also needed a wife; the old Southwest was not won by armies, but crept westward forted farm by forted farm. Still, all knew that the strongest of forts and the bravest of wives did not insure success.

This was a prime asset of the pioneer. He could live without the promise of security, or even help from any institution save his family. Shaped largely by the South, he had seldom known the protecting walls of strong institutions. He had been taught no single-guiding principle of life that put business, patriotism, or religion above humanity. Unfettered by any rigid pattern, he was able to develop the self-reliance needed to take and hold the border.

He had to do the best he could, and while doing it life was not always beautiful. The pioneers have been portrayed as stupid, drunken, lazy, dirty beings in a variety of animal skins, featuring raccoon for a head covering. There were on all borders a few of the no-good, but survival in Middle Tennessee, as on most borders, required a high degree of intelligence, not a little industry, some executive sense, and above all an ability to get along with other people.

Men who kill wild things only for fun, have shown the pioneers as violent and lawless. True, hard as it is today to understand, the borderers were in the main descended of a people who had less fear of lawlessness than of overmuch law. Yet, judging from their petitions, their eagerness for counties, their inclination to take a vote on even minor matters, few people, so circumstanced, have ever shown a greater eagerness for law and order than did the pioneering communities of Kentucky and Tennessee.

Cruelty to and hatred of the Indian has also been held up as part of the pioneer pattern of life. Cruelty there undoubtedly was, but it is doubtful if all the Indian wars of Kentucky and Tennessee combined caused as much suffering and as great a loss of life as did the March of Tears. This came past the pioneer period. Most borderers had grown up under British colonial policy—exploitation of a subjected people, maybe, but not extermination. There had been for the colonists no "The Indian," but enemies and allies; thanks to diplomacy this was after the first few years true on the Cumberland. It can even be said with much truth that many borderers who lost their land, suffered from the same source as did the Indian—the land speculator wanting more land.

Early settlers, particularly those in what came to be Tennessee, have also been accused of a lack of patriotism. More than one devout patriot of later years has, for example, looked askance at those who named the Middle Cumberland Settlements Mero in honor of Governor Estevan Miro, official of Spain. Much has been written, often in a hinting, tongue-in-cheek fashion of the flirtations of many men in the old West with Spain along with the disinclination of the majority of Middle Tennessee voters for the Constitution of the United States and later statehood. One might remember that it was not to begin with a nationalistic age, and also that a very great many Americans did not approve the Constitution.

I don't know, but after reading much, though by no means all of even that part of the correspondence translated into English, my feeling is that neither McGillivray of the Creeks nor any leader on the Cumberland had any thought of permanent alliance with Spain. There was in the early years, little hatred of England. Had Middle Tennessee been inclined to make any alliance with any power other than the United States, England would have been chosen over Spain. The wonder to me is that she did not at least try during the dark years when Jay's Treaty choked her commerce, and there came no help against the Indians; instead only the Whiskey Tax to let the settlers know they had a Federal Government.

What-ifing history is a waste of time, and patriotism means different things to different people. One cannot help but wonder, however, what would have been the size of our country without these "unpatriotic" borderers, and those before them with the land hunger. Governor Spotswood exploring the then far Shenandoah; Byrd running the line and buying Western lands, followed in 1750 by Dr. Thomas Walker hunting land in Kentucky west of the mountains were not pushed forward by King and Country, but in acquiring land for themselves they sent the border westward.

Dr. Thomas Walker, guardian of Thomas Jefferson, friend and business associate of Daniel Smith, was also active in furthering the plans of George Rogers Clark to win the Northwest Territory—which the East at this time scarcely knew existed. The same western parts of Virginia and North Carolina that furnished settlers for Kentucky and Tennessee, also furnished soldiers—and often borderer and soldier were one—for Clark. The same regions furnished more men for the Battle of King's Mountain. This battle, compared to many others in the Revolution, has been given little place in our history, yet, had the outcome been different, the southern boundary of the United States might have stopped considerably north of Byrd's line of 1728; and certain it is the southern back parts would have been lost.

Whatever the reason, the anti-Federalist pioneers anchored the West, and more than twenty years later were behind Jefferson and the Louisiana Purchase. Tennessee was no longer the frontier West. It was a time of transition in attitudes and ideals as well as in the physical aspects of life. Attitudes toward England were almost reversed. Eastern leaders wanted no War of 1812; no more territory, and were even suggesting secession as a means of ridding themselves of the belligerent Southwest. Middle Tennessee pushed the war, and though she changed in many ways was ever consistent in her land hunger. In time came Texas and the rest, and one wonders if without Sam Houston, his thinking shaped in Tennessee, and without the eagerness and the push of Jackson, Texas would ever have come into the Union.

One could go on with a long list of what-ifs. The pioneers, patriotic or no, seem to have given us a good bit of land. They also gave us many other things including contradictions. Not the least of these was Andrew Jackson. He more than any one man demonstrates the change in the thinking of Middle Tennessee. His young manhood was spent among men who rather feared a strong Federal Government—Jackson much more so than most presidents added power to the office. The planters among whom he had lived were not greatly concerned with the growth of capitalism; Jackson with his money policies, his Indian policy, and in divers other ways hastened the flowering of free enterprise. Pioneer Middle Tennessee showed little love of the military life, though ever ready to fight when she had it to do. Jackson showed at times a great respect for the military life, not as a temporary state of civilian life, but as a thing in itself. Jackson as a young man lived in a community opposed to statehood for Tennessee, yet Jackson preserved the Union—and without a war.

One could go on with a long list of other contradictions and ponderings on the roots of this and that. It is much easier and pleasanter merely to look at the life in the Cumberland Country after the ending of the Indian Wars, for it was not enough to take the land and hold it, first and early settling families shaped the pattern of a world, much of which still endures.

Seen through modern efficiency experts, Nashville and environs as revealed in early Tennessee *Gazettes* is a falling-apart world, inhabited but not run by anybody. Notices of strayed horses vie for place with long lists of unclaimed letters, unpaid taxes, runaway bound boys and a few slaves, with, during early 1803 when soldiers were called out at the threat of trouble with Spain, many notices of deserting soldiers. There were long lists of unpaid debts, forced sales, lost pocketbooks, strayed horses and wandering cows, plainly a world of poor fence, and of book borrowers who did not return their books. There is nothing of religion and patriotism, not even editorials urging the citizenry to fly more flags and to go to church on Sunday.

It was by all standards the most imperfect world, a place with neither security nor efficiency. The strange thing is that this seemingly aimless, leisurely, extravagant world not only was a beautiful place, praised by all early travelers, but it was a world not to be destroyed. It was in itself to become a center of political, cultural and religious life, influencing the whole of the Southwest. The religions that did not even have buildings twenty years after settlement would be the most numerous in the deeper South and the Southwest. Much of this spreading was done by emigrating families, for the Cumberland Country like the rest of Tennessee and most of Kentucky sent a steady stream of settlers into the deeper South, Texas, and soon the further West.

Possibly the greatest single attribute of pioneer society, was its ability to survive, if need be, as a family unit, but almost always with an awareness of the wider world beyond the fort picketing. Lack of institutions of learning did not mean lack of education, religion could live without ministers, and the populace could be reasonably law-abiding without, in the first years, even a county court.

To most of us today, a pioneer couple moving west into a world that offered neither security nor any kind of certainty, might seem lacking in common sense. Many lived, saw children start other families, and died with the loose ends of their lives—a land title in doubt, threat of an Indian raid—never tied into secure knots. We can also wonder how we would seem to Sally Buchanan and all her kin and neighbors.

Index